INTERNET AND SUICIDE

INTERNET AND SUICIDE

LEO SHER AND ALEXANDER VILENS
EDITORS

Nova Science Publishers, Inc.
New York

LIBRARY OF CONGRESS CATALOGING-IN-PUBLICATION DATA

Internet and suicide / editors, Leo Sher and Alexander Vilens.
p. cm.
Includes index.
ISBN 978-1-60741-077-5 (hardcover)
1. Internet--Psychological aspects. 2. Suicide--Prevention. I. Sher, Leo. II. Vilens, Alexander.
BF637.C45I63 2009
362.2802854678--dc22

2009002421

Published by Nova Science Publishers, Inc. ✢ New York

Contents

PREFACE

Internet has become an integral part of the life of millions of people in the Western countries and in the developing world. Millions of people search for mental health information on the Internet, and there is a lot. Multiple web sites offer a plethora of information on different topics.

Recent research suggests that Internet may play a role in suicide prevention. At the same time, there is an increasing concern that Internet may promote suicidal behavior. Some authors call Internet a double-edge tool. Internet providers try to seek a balance between preventing Internet-arranged suicides and safeguarding freedom of expression. Internet addiction may be associated with depression and suicidal behavior. The relationship between Internet and suicide is perplex. Understanding the impact of Internet on suicidal behavior is an important challenge for future research. We hope that this book will contribute to this goal.

The contributors to this book are the leading international experts in the field of suicidal behavior. We would like to acknowledge and thank all the contributors. Our task as the editors was greatly facilitated by their swift and positive response to our initial inquiry, and thereafter by producing their manuscripts diligently. We believe that this book will be of interest to clinicians, researchers, and the general public.

We welcome comments from readers. Please, submit your comments via the website at www.internetandpsychiatry.com.

Leo Sher, M.D.
Alexander Vilens, M.S.
November 2008

In: Internet and Suicide
Editors: L. Sher and A. Vilens

ISBN 978-1-60741-077-5

Chapter 1

THE INTERNET IN SUICIDE PREVENTION AND PROMOTION

Jess G. Fiedorowicz and Raveendra B. Chigurupati
The University of Iowa Hospitals and Clinics, Iowa City, Iowa, USA

ABSTRACT

There has been considerable debate as to whether the Internet predominantly prevents or promotes suicide. With recent unfettered growth and the broad-reaching popularity of this technology, the study of the role of the Internet in suicide prevention and promotion is assuming greater relevance. This topic defies systematic study and subsequently the debate over its role in suicide will undoubtedly persist. Further, efforts to address concerns about the potential of the Internet to promote suicide face several barriers and challenge freedom of expression. Internet content may indeed assist in suicide prevention efforts or influence the expression of suicidal behaviors in vulnerable individuals. Those treating such vulnerable individuals should be wary of potential risk and assume appropriate monitoring strategies. Those interested in preventing suicide should consider utilizing this valuable resource. Despite the aforementioned inherent limitations to research, further study is warranted on this important topic for which debate is likely to persist.

INTRODUCTION

The Internet contains diverse and voluminous material related to suicide. More than a million sites about suicide now appear on the world wide web [1]. When writing this chapter, the search engine Google yielded more than 98 million results on "suicide" and more than 980,000 results for "suicide internet." Given this large volume of material and its potential influence on vulnerable individuals, often when isolated, the role of the Internet in influencing suicide has been arguably under-studied. The influence of the Internet, in general, is large and growing. In North America, 74% of the population uses the Internet with 130%

growth in the past eight years. Worldwide, 22% of the population uses the Internet with more than a tripling in growth over the past eight years [2].

Systematic study of the role of the Internet in suicide is hindered by several unmistakable barriers. Suicidology, in general, is hampered by the relative infrequency and irregularity of the event. With the exception of very large, prospective cohort studies, this limits the ability to study the outcome of suicide completions with adequate statistical power [3], often necessitating the use of surrogate outcomes such as suicide attempts or the study of aggregate data. Adding to the complexity, Internet use may be a difficult predictor variable to operationalize and measure. Should Internet use in general be employed as a predictor, ignoring the type or content of the web-sites? How can one know whether the Internet was involved in facilitating a suicide? These barriers to study invariably limit the available data to expert opinion, case reports, and a few observational studies. Nonetheless, the study of how the Internet may influence suicide remains meaningful.

The Internet may influence suicide through means as diverse as the medium itself. Broadly, Internet content on suicide can be separated into sites aspiring to prevent suicide and sites that may intentionally or unintentionally promote or encourage suicide. While numerous sites are dedicated to both causes, the proportion of web-sites that may promote suicide is thought to exceed that of those attempting to prevent suicide [4] though this remains a subject of some debate [5, 6] and may depend on the search strategies applied.

Further, for vulnerable individuals, sites that promote suicide may be more readily accessible through commonly applied search strategies [4], particularly those likely to be employed by an individual contemplating suicide. These web-sites may be directly accessible to such vulnerable individuals. Sites targeting prevention and intervention may benefit vulnerable individuals directly or indirectly by providing relevant resources to providers and other supports. Much of the more broadly-defined prevention content may benefit vulnerable individuals only indirectly.

Vulnerable Populations

Certain groups may be more vulnerable to the undue influence of the Internet and thus more likely to attempt or commit suicide. Examples of vulnerable individuals include adolescents, young adults, those with mental illness and perhaps already suicidal, and men. According to the United States Department of Health and Human Services, suicide is the third leading cause of death among adolescents and young adults, the very ages most likely to use the Internet. Adolescents and young adults represent a vulnerable population largely because of their greater likelihood of encountering interactive or non-interactive web-sites with suicide content. Individuals with mental illness represent a higher risk group for suicide and may be more likely to initiate use of the Internet for the purposes of facilitating suicide. Cross-sectional and correlational studies discussed later in this chapter have identified men as an additional group potentially vulnerable to suicide-promoting influences on the Internet.

THE INTERNET IN THE PROMOTION OF SUICIDE

There are numerous web-sites that indirectly or directly may be viewed as potentially suicide promoting. One study has suggested that these sites can be divided into two general groups: general pro-suicide web-sites and physician-assisted suicide web-sites [5]. This chapter will focus on the former category of general pro-suicide web-sites, encouraging suicide or the freedom to commit suicide for individuals, irrespective of medical status. The latter category is discussed in the chapter entitled "Internet communication about assisted or "Rational" suicide: Legal and ethical considerations for practice." Other studies have presented a more refined classification of suicide-promoting web-sites. A variety of sites may promote suicide and include, though are not limited to: sites dedicated to encouraging suicide, sites describing methods for suicide, sites glamorizing suicide, chat rooms discussing suicide methods, or chat rooms facilitating suicide by means ranging from providing other information to fostering suicide pacts.

Research has previously established a relationship between media reporting on suicide and subsequent mortality by suicide. Despite a panoply of reports of the Internet facilitating suicide, there has been limited study of Internet use as a predictor of suicide. One such study, utilizing aggregate data from Japan between 1987 and 2005, found that Internet use was a significant predictor of suicide completions in men [7]. This correlational or ecological study utilized aggregate data for monthly household Internet use in Japan. Thus, this data might not extrapolate to the individual level. While further study is desperately needed in this area, there remains compelling evidence that the Internet may influence suicidal behavior. Our discussion of how the Internet may promote suicidal behavior will divide web content into two types: interactive and non-interactive.

Non-Interactive Web-Sites as a Means Of Promoting Suicide

A large volume of Internet content consists of non-interactive web-sites, which may contribute to suicide. Non-interactive sites may promote suicide through description of methods, glamorizing suicidal behavior, or discouraging psychiatric treatment for mental illness. Non-interactive content places the viewer in an active role in accessing and reading the information.

Web-Sites Describing Methods

There exist a variety of web-sites variably dedicated to providing information on available methods for the completion of suicide. When encountered by vulnerable individuals, this information may be deadly. Estimates of the proportion of actual suicides which involve Internet "education" are difficult since this information may perhaps only be available should the person live. The methods reported on the Internet vary widely and include uncommon methods. A case series of two patients who attempted suicide, survived, and revealed the Internet as their source for the methods demonstrates this [8]. A 16 year-old male of low intelligence ingested a nearly fatal dose of two castor oil beans, the seed coat of which contains ricin. He reported getting the idea to commit suicide and the method from the Internet. He fortunately recovered from the episode. In the same report, a 34 year-old female with a diagnosis of borderline personality disorder and chronic suicidality attempted suicide by water intoxication. These cases illustrate the diversity of potentially lethal methods that may be propagated to vulnerable individuals online.

A variety of methods for completing suicide may be detailed online including hanging, overdose, carbon monoxide poisoning, overdose, electric shock, and use of firearms. One web-site details the 10 most common methods employed for suicide completions, followed by some resources for help [9]. For vulnerable individuals, descriptions of the methods alone may help formulate a final plan. Other web-sites detailing methods attempt to do so humorously, often in questionable taste with titles such as "How to kill yourself like a man" [10], which was the first result on a Google search of "how to kill yourself." For those seeking information on methods by which to kill themselves, little effort is required to find potentially lethal means. On a recent clinical encounter, a patient of the author who had recently developed suicidality in the setting of worsening depression spontaneously commented that she was going to be getting Internet access soon and couldn't stop thinking about using the Internet to find a potentially lethal combination of medications. She made mention of the death by presumed accidental overdose of Heath Ledger, an actor from *Batman "The Dark Knight"* and *Brokeback Mountain*. While officially ruled an accidental overdose in the case of Heath Ledger, suicides of celebrities may exert an insidious public impact.

Web-Sites that Glamorize Suicide

In addition to providing information on methods to commit suicide, a number of web-sites provide information that glamorizes suicide. This information can take many forms. One example includes media reporting on celebrity suicides, which has been suggested as potentially promoting suicide, particularly among adolescents [7]. Adolescents or other vulnerable individuals may imitate in attempt to emulate the celebrity. Other sites may glamorize suicide by romanticizing the behavior. This can include the portrayal of suicide as an intellectual, heroic, or romantic act. A classic and commonly cited example of this includes the literary description of the suicide of an unrequited lover in Goethe's *The Sorrows of Young Werther*. Since then, suicides resulting from media contagion have sometimes been referred to as resulting from the "Werther" effect. These include examples of purported media contagion in which carbon monoxide poisoning by charcoal burning was "romanticized as an easy, effective, and comfortable" method of suicide in Asia [11].

Web-Sites that Oppose Established Treatments for Mental Illness

While writing this chapter, an inpatient at high risk of suicide under the author's care declined electroconvulsive therapy (ECT) after searching for information about the treatment from the Internet. An Internet search for ECT indeed revealed several prominently displayed web-sites categorically opposing the use of ECT, describing ECT as a "crime against humanity" [12] or presenting unilateral information in opposition to ECT [13]. The patient ultimately elected to forgo treatment with ECT.

Sites opposing established treatments for mental illness extend beyond mere opposition to ECT. These web-sites may be affiliated with the Church of Scientology, more general anti-psychiatry movements, or individuals working in isolation. Anti-psychiatry sites may go as far as to deny the existence of psychiatric illness and describe psychiatry unconditionally as "quackery." Related sites may frame suicide as a civil right or even encourage suicide on an ethical basis. Many of these sites deal with physician-assisted suicide. This topic extends beyond the scope of this chapter and is discussed in greater detail in the chapter entitled "Internet communication about assisted or "Rational" suicide: Legal and ethical considerations for practice."

Regardless of the source, web-sites opposed to treatment of mental illness have the potential to steer vulnerable individuals away from established, evidence-based treatments. These web-sites may further foster isolation. In so doing, the vulnerable individual may be less likely to be referred for evaluation, receive a professional suicide risk assessment, and receive treatment for potentially modifiable clinical risk factors such as the presence of a depressive syndrome.

Interactive Web-sites as a Means of Promoting Suicide

A variety of interactive web-content may contribute to suicide, including but not limited to chat rooms, formation of suicide pacts, and joke forums. Given the nature of the content of study, much inference comes in the form of anecdotal data with case reports and case series.

Chat Rooms

Chat rooms are Internet locations where people can interact with others while also online. Individuals are identified in most chat rooms by a screen name, providing a certain degree of anonymity. Chat rooms are frequented by individuals of a variety of ages, especially adolescents. Individuals may share an array of information though rooms that often have a specific focus, whether it be romance, social networking, or a topic of debate. Currently popular platforms for such social networking include Google Talk, MySpace, and Facebook. Chat rooms may be private or public. In the setting of chat rooms, suicide can be encouraged or stressors that precipitate suicide encountered. The communications in this setting may be problematic to vulnerable individuals because of anonymity or failure to accurately gauge the other individual's response to the communication, which can more readily be done in person.

In one highly publicized case of a chat room suicide, Megan Meier, a 13 year-old girl, committed suicide after the termination of an online, romantic relationship with a fictitious boy [14]. Lori Drew, the mother of Megan's former friend and classmate, allegedly had an employee create fictitious profile to find out what Megan was saying about her daughter on the social networking site, MySpace. The fictitious online boyfriend later sent her numerous hurtful messages, presumably precipitating her suicide. Many suggested this suicide was a consequence of "cyber-bullying," highlighting the potential impact of interactive sites on vulnerable individuals.

Suicide Pacts

A suicide pact represents an agreement between two or more individuals to commit suicide at a given time. Suicide pacts account for less than 1% of all suicides overall [15]. Suicide pacts are discussed in more detail in the chapter entitled "Internet and suicide pacts" and can be initiated in the setting of chat rooms. By allowing people to contact each other from literally across the globe, the Internet may more readily facilitate the formation of suicide pacts than other forms of communication. Prior to the Internet, suicide pacts were primarily seen between closely related people, such as friends, family members, or lovers. The Internet may extend traditional social boundaries and more readily facilitate the formation of suicide pacts. A variant of suicide pacts sometimes referred to as a suicide-homicide pacts occur when in a planned fashion an individual kills others followed by his or herself.

In 2004, Japan witnessed seven suicides in one Internet pact and two in another [16]. This drew significant attention to the role of the Internet in facilitating suicide pacts. The group of seven consisted of three female and four male adolescents and young adults. The group of two consisted of two women. All died by carbon monoxide poisoning as a result of using charcoal burners in a vehicle, an increasingly common means attributed to Internet propagation of the method [17] previously discussed in this chapter under the section "web-sites that glamorize suicide." Unlike traditional suicide pacts involving individuals in close relationships, these pacts arranged over the Internet may be more readily involve strangers [18].

Message Boards, Weblogs, and Joke Forums

Joke forums and message boards or blogs typically require individuals to register to obtain a user name and password before being able to post content. A variety of material can be presented including advice, experiences, and questions to be shared by those who access the sites. The content of these sites may also be used encourage or share information about how to commit suicide. One survey of blogs created by depressed individuals revealed that men were more likely than women to discuss suicide or self-harm online, with 37.5% versus 7% discussing self-harm [19]. It was further suggested that female bloggers were more likely to discuss deliberately harming themselves through cutting rather than actual attempts at suicide. Nonetheless, a survey of 164 individuals using one Internet purpose board focused on suicide suggested the majority had constructive rather than destructive intentions, leading the authors to conclude that these sources may foster suicide prevention as well [20]

Acquisition of Dangerous Substances

Vulnerable individuals may utilize the Internet as a tool to acquire otherwise unobtainable and potentially lethal items or substances, such as medications. Lisa, a 17 year-old German adolescent female with a history of prior suicide attempts developed a depressive syndrome in the setting of a break-up with her boyfriend. She encountered an anonymous individual on the Internet who supplied her with a blue liquid containing diazepam, which she self-administered with alcohol in a suicide attempt. She was found unconscious on the floor by her mother and fortunately survived with medical intervention [21].

The Internet may facilitate the acquisition of items or substances, which may be used in suicide, as above. Further, the Internet may be employed to acquire items or substances not obtainable within a given country or other political boundary. Law and enforcement regarding the sale of pharmaceuticals over the Internet vary considerably. There are numerous "rogue" pharmacies offering the sale of substances controlled by the United States Drug Enforcement Agency. Many of these pharmaceutical-clearing houses market aggressively through use of spam mailings and other techniques. The United States Food and Drug Administration has warned consumers against purchasing medications online given the potential for these pharmaceuticals to be inadequately labeled, sold illegally, counterfeited, or contaminated [22]. In the case illustrated above, such acquisition may bypass potential safeguards such as physician-prescribing with its potential to assess risk and appropriately intervene.

Table 1. Groups of individuals with greater vulnerability to impact of Internet on suicide

Vulnerable Group	Level of Evidence		
	Observational Study	Case Series	Expert Opinion
Adolescents		X	X
Young Adults		X	X
Mentally Ill		X	X
Men	X		X

For the purpose of this chapter, vulnerable individuals may be defined as those at risk of being influenced by Internet content to attempt suicide. The level of published evidence for each potentially vulnerable group of individuals is highlighted with the understanding that controlled study is not feasible. While case series involving men exist, these do not appear with greater frequency than those involving women.

THE INTERNET IN THE PREVENTION OF SUICIDE

While attention and academic discussion have focused on potentially suicide-promoting Internet content, many assess the majority of information regarding suicide on the Internet as neutral or assisting in the prevention of suicide [5, 6]. It has been further suggested that time trends in suicide rates for the age groups most likely to use the Internet in England suggest a decreasing rate of suicide in the setting of increasing popularity of the Internet [4], however, numerous other social variables are temporally associated with these changes as well [23].

The broad and pervasive reach of the Internet supports its potential to be a powerful tool in directing those at risk of suicide toward support and treatment. Some have suggested the Internet is under-utilized in suicide prevention efforts:

> "It is time for preventative strategies to adapt, evolve and keep pace with technological advances and cultural changes in the use of communications technology by society at large and by individuals seeking to commit suicide. To rely mainly on telephone, television and print media without investing in internet-based strategies today would be akin to a musician

recording only on vinyl records, cassette tapes and compact discs in a market dominated by internet downloads of digital music [24]."

Table 2. Selected web-sites focused on suicide prevention

Address	Organization	Description
http://www.hopkinsmedicine.org/Psychiatry/moods/outreach_adap/index.html	Adolescent Depression Awareness Program	Outlines school-based program with the goal of reducing risk of suicide through education and reducing stigma for mood disorders.
http://www.suicidology.org/	American Association of Suicidology	Targets clinical education and research with listings of local support groups and community resources.
http://www.afsp.org/	American Foundation for Suicide Prevention	Contains educational resources, information on grants to support research, and information on advocacy and support.
http://www.befrienders.org/	Befrienders Worldwide	Provides emotional support to individuals in distress with the stated purpose of reducing suicide. Recently affiliated with Samaritans.
http://metanoia.org/suicide/	Metanoia	Provides some advice and resources for those with suicidal ideation.
http://www.ncspt.org/	National Center for Suicide Prevention Training	Outlines educational resources for coalitions, providers, and public officials to develop effective suicide prevention programs.
http://www.suicidepreventionlifeline.org/	National Suicide Prevention Lifeline	Web interface for national suicide prevention lifeline. Integrates services for United States Veterans.
http://www.preventingsuicide.com/	Preventing Suicide Network	Developed with support from the National Institute of Mental Health to assist individuals in preventing suicide. Provides education, professional resources, and treatment resources.
http://www.save.org/	Suicide Awareness Voices of Education	Emphasizes education about mental illness, stigma reduction, and networking with community resources.
http://www.spanusa.org/	The Suicide Prevention Action Network	Focuses on advocacy, public policy, and community suicide prevention training.

This list highlights some readily accessible Internet content with an explicit focus on suicide prevention. This listing is not intended to be comprehensive, rather to provide a survey of available content with a focus on English-language web-sites. Resources were selected considering distinctiveness of content and the profile of the site.

The Internet may play an important role in suicide prevention through a variety of means. It is important to recognize that suicide prevention efforts need not rely exclusively on an explicit focus on suicide [25]. Web-sites educating consumers with mental illness, encouraging treatment, and facilitating connection with general community resources may also be of benefit. Early recognition and treatment of depression and other mental illnesses is critical to any suicide prevention effort. These resources may be too numerous to mention and may further shift the balance of Internet resources in favor of those attempting to prevent suicide. For the purpose of this discussion, we will focus largely on Internet resources exclusively dedicated to the prevention of suicide. Table 2 presents a number of selected, predominantly high-profile web-sites explicitly dedicated to the prevention of suicide. This brief listing illustrates some of the diversity such sites.

The content of web-sites dedicated to preventing suicide varies widely. Some sites may focus on education, dispensing advice, directing individuals to resources for treatment, listening, or networking with support. With this variance in available content, some inconsistencies in content are not surprising. It has been suggested that postings of warning signs of suicide vary widely, however, no clear consensus exists for such information [26]. It could be argued that the diversity of suicide prevention material may assist patients in finding individually compelling resources, albeit through a potentially time-consuming exercise. Many argue that Internet resources should be better regulated to mitigate the impact of potentially suicide-promoting content and maximize the availability of resources intending to prevent suicide. This poses inherent difficulty.

Difficulty in Regulating Internet Content

The Internet faces less regulation and may be less impacted by market forces than other forms of media. If a newspaper publishes or radio station broadcasts material of questionable content, they may face scrutiny from regulators or lose ratings, depending on the setting and circumstance. Additionally, the identity of a responsible party for content may not be transparent on the World Wide Web. The global nature of the Internet may also complicate any external attempts to modify or constrain content. Some have suggested that the Internet differs from other media sources as a "pull" rather than a "push" technology, wherein users have to actively seek out specific content [27]. While this argument holds for situations where vulnerable individuals actively seek out content, it neglects aforementioned examples where individuals may inadvertently encounter or interactively engage with others online. In the case of interactive formats, the Internet may serve as a "pull" and "push" technology, blurring this distinction.

To protect freedom of expression and liberty, methods to protect the public from potentially suicide-promoting sites largely rely on voluntary use of filtering software. Australia has outlawed the use of the Internet to promote suicide and Internet service providers in Japan and Korea have attempted to block specific sites [4]. Search engines can also preferentially list sites targeting suicide prevention. The global accessibility of the Internet may impede any practical enforcement of regulations and lend itself to questions about jurisdiction.

Freedom of expression has been upheld in cases attempting to block specific Internet content in the United States with exception perhaps of child pornography [27]. Some have suggested suicide-related Internet materials should not be regulated in the absence of epidemiological evidence to support a causal connection between Internet content and suicide, given the importance of freedom of expression and the difficulties inherent to filtering content. Any attempts to regulate content certainly must be thoughtfully applied and may only partially succeed in mitigating the effects of suicide-promoting content and maximizing the accessibility of content committed to suicide prevention.

The Prevention/Promotion Debate

As highlighted in this chapter, there has been considerable debate about whether the Internet leans toward preventing or promoting suicide. With an enormous diversity of material, attempts to catalogue data may ultimately be biased by the search strategies employed. Regardless of whether a majority of Internet content promotes or prevents suicide, there clearly exist large volumes of readily-accessible content that may promote, prevent, be indifferent to, or unpredictably influence suicide. Available information that may promote suicide can be only partially regulated at best and at the cost of personal liberty and freedom of expression. A more fruitful focus of discussion, therefore, rests on how clinicians and the public can appropriately direct those at risk of suicide who utilize this medium to appropriate resources. The public and clinicians further must recognize the complex and idiosyncratic influence this medium may pose for consumers and patients.

Conclusion

Mirroring the influence of the Internet in everyday life, the Internet is playing an ever-growing role in the promotion and prevention of suicide. Web-sites may play a nefarious role in contributing to suicide in vulnerable individuals. For some cases, this role may be obvious. For many cases, this role may go unrecognized and occur in isolation, preventing the influence of protective factors. While there have been several efforts to provide greater accessibility to sites focusing on prevention and to reduce accessibility to sites which may promote suicide, rights of free expression and the global nature of the Internet will likely make web-sites promoting suicide an indefinite clinical reality. The burden of responsibility will continue to rest on those caring for vulnerable individuals. Professionals interested in suicide prevention should be encouraged to take an active role in the shaping of online content by providing education about available resources to vulnerable individuals and the public. With increasing recognition, hopefully more mental health professionals will regularly assess Internet use with patients, encourage use of supportive resources, and assess the access of suicide-promoting web-sites as a potential risk factor for suicide, in some circumstances a modifiable risk factor. From a community perspective, continued work is necessary to classify the risk of the Internet and improve the accessibility of supportive materials.

References

[1] Dobson R: Internet sites may encourage suicide. *Bmj* 1999; 319: 337.

[2] Miniwatts Marketing Group; "World Internet Usage and Population Statistics." *Internet World Stats: Usage and Population Statistics Retrieved 8/22/2008,* from http://www.internetworldstats.com/stats.htm.

[3] Fiedorowicz JG, Leon AC, Keller MB, Solomon DA, Rice JP and Coryell WH: Do risk factors for suicidal behavior differ by affective disorder polarity? *Psychol Med* 2008: 1-9.

[4] Biddle L, Donovan J, Hawton K, Kapur N and Gunnell D: Suicide and the internet. *Bmj* 2008; 336: 800-802.

[5] Recupero PR, Harms SE and Noble JM: Googling suicide: surfing for suicide information on the Internet. *J Clin Psychiatry* 2008; 69: 878-888.

[6] Grohol JM: Suicide and the internet: Study misses internet's greater collection of support websites. *Bmj* 2008; 336: 905-906.

[7] Hagihara A, Tarumi K and Abe T: Media suicide-reports, Internet use and the occurrence of suicides between 1987 and 2005 in Japan. *BMC Public Health* 2007; 7: 321.

[8] Alao AO, Yolles JC and Armenta W: Cybersuicide: the Internet and suicide. *Am J Psychiatry* 1999; 156: 1836-1837.

[9] The List Universe; "*Top 10 Common Methods of Suicide.*" Retrieved 8/24/2008, from http://listverse.com/health/top-10-ways-to-commit-suicide.

[10] Unknown; "*How to kill yourself like a man.*" Retrieved 8/24/2008, from http://www.thebestpageintheuniverse.net/c.cgi?u=manly_suicide]/.

[11] Lee DT, Chan KP, Lee S and Yip PS: Burning charcoal: a novel and contagious method of suicide in Asia. *Arch Gen Psychiatry* 2002; 59: 293-294.

[12] Stevens L; "*Psychiatry's Electroconvulsive Shock Treatment: A Crime against Humanity.*" Retrieved 8/24/2008, from http://www.antipsychiatry.org/ect.htm.

[13] Lawrence J; "*ect.org Position Statement.*" Retrieved 8/24/2008, from http://www.ect.org/.

[14] ABC News; "*Parents: Cyber Bullying Led to Teen's Suicide.*" Retrieved 8/25/2008, from http://abcnews.go.com/GMA/Story?id=3882520.

[15] Brown M and Barraclough B: Epidemiology of suicide pacts in England and Wales, 1988-92. *Bmj* 1997; 315: 286-287.

[16] BBC News; "*Nine die in Japan 'suicide pacts'.*" Retrieved 8/24/2008, from http://news.bbc.co.uk/1/hi/world/asia-pacific/3735372.stm.

[17] Patel F: Carbon copy deaths: carbon monoxide gas chamber. *J Forensic Leg Med* 2008; 15: 398-401.

[18] Rajagopal S: Suicide pacts and the internet. *Bmj* 2004; 329: 1298-1299.

[19] Clarke J and van Amerom G: A comparison of blogs by depressed men and women. *Issues Ment Health Nurs* 2008; 29: 243-264.

[20] Eichenberg C: Internet message boards for suicidal people: a typology of users. *Cyberpsychol Behav* 2008; 11: 107-113.

[21] Becker K, Mayer M, Nagenborg M, El-Faddagh M and Schmidt MH: Parasuicide online: Can suicide websites trigger suicidal behaviour in predisposed adolescents? *Nord J Psychiatry* 2004; 58: 111-114.

[22] US FDA; "*FDA Finds Consumers Continue to Buy Potentially Risky Drugs over the Internet.*" Retrieved 8/25/2008, from http://www.fda.gov/bbs/topics/NEWS/2007/NEW01663.html.

[23] Biddle L, Brock A, Brookes ST and Gunnell D: Suicide rates in young men in England and Wales in the 21st century: time trend study. *Bmj* 2008; 336: 539-542.

[24] Tam J, Tang WS and Fernando DJ: The internet and suicide: A double-edged tool. Eur *J Intern Med* 2007; 18: 453-455.

[25] Swartz KL, Kastelic EA, Hess SG, Cox TS, Gonzales LC, Mink SP and Depaulo JR, Jr.: The Effectiveness of a School-Based Adolescent Depression Education Program. *Health Educ Behav* In Press.

[26] Mandrusiak M, Rudd MD, Joiner TE, Jr., Berman AL, Van Orden KA and Witte T: Warning signs for suicide on the Internet: a descriptive study. *Suicide Life Threat Behav* 2006; 36: 263-271.

[27] Mishara BL and Weisstub DN: Ethical, legal, and practical issues in the control and regulation of suicide promotion and assistance over the Internet. *Suicide Life Threat Behav* 2007; 37: 58-65.

In: Internet and Suicide
Editors: L. Sher and A. Vilens
ISBN 978-1-60741-077-5

Chapter 2

THE INTERNET: ITS ROLE IN THE OCCURRENCE AND PREVENTION OF SUICIDE

Puneet Narang and Steven B. Lippmann
Hennepin County Medical Center, Minneapolis, Minnesota, USA; University of Louisville, Louisville, Kentucky, USA

ABSTRACT

As advances are made towards the understanding of suicide, new risk factors keep cropping up with the passage of time and the advent of new technology. One of the features of new technology which can play its role in either direction is "Internet". Internet is the new form of mass media and communication which connect people from geographically distinct locations instantly.

The sharing of ideas, beliefs and practices on internet has extended to issues like suicide with both negative and positive impact. Internet use is highest among teens and adolescents, the group with a disturbing trend of rise in suicide rates by 8% in the last ten years.

Many authors have tried to evaluate the role of internet in suicide, they observed the noticeable impact internet had on selecting the choice of suicide method with descriptive and elaborate instructions made easily available on web. Besides the information on the methods of suicide, various forums and chat rooms can also be found which influence vulnerable people with suicidal tendencies to overcome their doubts, in a way instigate them to commit suicide.

However, there are support forums and help lines available on internet which can be accessed by vulnerable population for their benefit. Lack of strict guidelines about the content to be advertised on internet and suicide being considered personal choice, it becomes difficult to counter the pro-suicide force on internet.

Introduction

Understanding the phenomenology and complex risk factors associated with suicide is important to prevention. Although the rate of suicide in America is highest among people over age 65, the most disturbing trend is the rise by 8% in suicide rates for young people aged 10-24 [1,2]. Although various factors could have resulted in this increase, mood disorders and substance abuse remain the two most common presentations observed in victims of suicide [3]. Concern focuses on the strong influence of the media, which provides wide exposure to stories about completed suicides. Among the sources of mass media, one that has dramatically gained in its popularity is the internet. Younger people who commit suicide are less likely to be clinically depressed or mentally ill, as compared to adults where these disorders are common risk factors [4,5]. Associations between suicide and internet access are of current concern.

The Influence Of Media

The effect of print media and television on suicide has been evaluated extensively, and reportedly it can influence people to engage in suicidal behavior. The portrayal of such cases by the media is known to influence suicidal planning, particularly the choice of method selected. This is especially true following publicized suicidal deaths in celebrities. Clustering of suicides follows media coverage of a such an event or personal contact with a victim [6,7].When suicide is publicly discussed, some vulnerable individuals may be more readily influenced to accept this as a problem solving strategy.

Suicide "contagion," is a term used to describe the phenomenon when exposure to the suicidal behavior influences others to commit or attempt suicide [8]. The effect of contagion is not limited by geographic barriers. The role of newspaper and/or television coverage of suicide has been associated with a statistically significant increase in suicides [6]. This type of contagion is more predominant among younger people, who seemed to have greater vulnerability to such news [9-12]. Suicides that occur in clusters account for up to 5% of youth suicides, and this demands extraordinary community effort at prevention. [11]. One famous suicide cluster involved four teenagers from New Jersey who committed suicide by carbon monoxide poisoning in a parking garage. One of them had previously been suicidal and they had a friend who recently died in an accident that they witnessed. Despite vigorous preventive follow up after this incident, two other adolescents made a suicide attempt in the same garage, one week later [11].Clustering was also documented in New Zealand among younger age groups, especially in 15–24 year olds.[13] Age specificity of time or space clusters had a similar pattern in the US [9]. In Taiwan it was observed that extensive media reporting of celebrity suicide was followed by an increase in suicides with a modeling effect. This supports the need for more conservative reporting of suicides as part of a prevention strategy [14].

Although suicides are themselves not caused by media attention itself, people who have psychiatric disorders or poor coping skills may find in these reports a model for resolving their problems. This group of vulnerable individuals may desire the attention given to victims of suicide. This is particularly true when the profile of the victim is similar to them in age, ethnicity, race, or gender. Teenagers and the elderly persons are more susceptible to this type of pattern [15, 16].

The Internet

The internet is a worldwide system that provides services like electronic mail, online chatting, file transfers, etc. via the World Wide Web. It is an interactive medium which connects millions of users to facilitate exchange of ideas and information, without the constraints of distances or supervision. It is a service that is accessible to everyone, with either potentially productive or destructive aspects that are not easily subject to regulation. Recently various academic institutions, governmental agencies, and business networks have tried to confine access for positive outlets only, and parents, too, try to track and/or control their children's internet exposures.

Internet use is highest among teens and adolescents, especially in areas where access is easy. In September, 2001, 174 million people (66% of the population) in the United States used computers. Ninety percent of children between the ages of 5-17 use computers, and 65-75% of 10-17 year olds use the internet [17]. Recent data reveals that 97% of high school students utilized computers and 80% access the internet [18]. Some have heightened suicide rates and little peer support. Thus, psychiatrists are becoming aware of internet exposure as a risk factor for suicide and are following the internet applications of their vulnerable patients. It is suggested that people who access the net regularly are qualitatively different than those who indulge in other hobbies; reportedly they were psychologically more vulnerable, with higher risk taking, substance abuse, and depression as compared to controls [19].

Internet and Health

Among internet users in United States, 35 % of them are searching for health care education [17]. Today, in this era of informed medical consumers, who wish to be knowledgeable on treatment options and alternatives available, the internet is a valuable source of data about various health related issues. Unfortunately, there is no control over the accuracy of the information. Mental health problems are prominent among the issues about which they consult the internet rather than their physicians to minimize social stigma. It remains to be seen whether this public information is positive or negative in effect.

One of the most alarming trends for physicians has been the use of the internet to facilitate suicidal behaviors. The influence of media on the suicide has been studied in television, newspapers, and movies, while the internet has gained popularity only in recent years. A dramatic portrayal of suicide in any form leads to increased risk to those predisposed, especially adolescents. Individuals who are socially isolated, going through an embarrassing issue, or mentally ill may find solace in the anonymity they get from computers in isolation from other people.

Another danger of health related internet issue is the pharmaceutical availability. In United States, drugs have been divided into prescription medicines and over the counter drugs. Prescription medications can only be obtained through a doctor, whereas over the counter drugs are readily available without physician consultation required. The safety and effectiveness of prescription drugs in the US is regulated by the federal government. The Food and Drug Administration is responsible for implementing this law. However, on the internet there are many pharmaceutics available without prescription or supervision, even for controlled substances. This exposes people to dangerous consequences, especially in an emotionally unstable person with suicidal tendencies.

Internet as a Pro-Suicide Tool

Suicide Methods

The accessibility of computers has led to increased use of internet as a source of general information. There is a large amount of data available there on methods of how to commit suicide. In a review of sites providing information on means of committing suicide, it was found that several common search engines revealed numerous instruction sites describing "how to kill your self" and most were somewhat encouraging of such behaviors. The pros and cons of suicide were enumerated in both emotional and factual terms and included chat room discussion sites. The study reveals that among the top search results which appeared in internet search for the suicide related terms majority were pro- suicide with details on methods of suicide [20].

Another recent study documented that many internet sites were suicide neutral and anti-suicide intent with only 11 % being encouraging of suicide. When search terms used the wording "suicide methods" most of the sites were pro suicide with information on methodology. Using the term "suicide" resulted in more information for anti-suicide, crisis interventions or suicide prevention resources. The "Church of euthanasia.org" and the "Alt.suicide.holiday newsgroup" were the main ones associated with pro-suicide information [21]. The heavy influence of these two pro-suicide sites was also noted by another author [22]. Some of the websites provided links to online pharmacies where even controlled drugs can be ordered in lethal quantities without prescription

Influence of internet on choosing a method of suicide cannot be doubted, although there is only a small body of evidence available. Many case reports have cited the use of unique methods for suicide not commonly utilized and learned via the internet. One vignette described an attempted suicide by ingesting wolfsbane, a poisonous plant, and injecting lighter fluid [23]. Another person used asphyxiation by homemade mask and forced helium breathing learned on the internet [24]. Other cases tried ingestion of castor oil beans and large quantities of water [25]. More conventional methods, like hanging, are also described and are frequently searched on internet.

Newsgroups or Discussion Forums / Chat Rooms

Almost every kind of issue now has an online discussion forum where people can share there views about a particular topic. Similarly, there are such forums on suicide, with a wide variety of advice favoring or discouraging suicide. The AOL suicide bulletin board, for example, contains all kinds of postings from supporting to discouraging suicide. Whereas, some like alt.suicide.holiday are dedicated pro-suicide forums, where anti-suicide views are not entertained[22].

There are known cases of suicidal individuals whose postings announced their intent of committing suicide [26]. All had sought advice on methods of suicide and its reliability and all of them received responses. Reportedly ambivalence about suicide was overcome and resolve for successful completion of suicide strengthened. There was evidence for feeling pressurized by others to go ahead with committing suicide.

Suicide Pacts

Internet suicide pact or a cybersuicide pact refers to an arrangement made between strangers who meet on the internet and agree to commit suicide simultaneously, often sharing similar methods. This phenomenon, first reported in Asia, represents a new trend which can influence the epidemiology of suicide especially in younger people.[27]

Suicide pacts provide the psychologically vulnerable or socially isolated person to find like minded people who give strength and reason to their plans. This is especially true for adolescents and elderly individuals who find themselves lacking the social support to overcome crisis. There was a news report about arrest of a man planning a mass suicide pact involving several people over the internet [21].

Online Disinhibition Effect and Cybersuicide

An “online disinhibition effect” has been described by John Suler as "The term refers to what people say in the anonymity of cyberspace that they would not say in public." [28] People feel freer to express themselves more honestly when not face-to- face with others.

An example of this effect can be seen in chatrooms or discussion forums where people encourage others to go ahead with their suicide plans and even provide information on methods. It tends to remove ambiguous feelings people might have had about ending their life. There is a case report of a person who took an overdose in front of his chat room audience who encouraged him to do so [21]. Such individuals may not have done so under more normal circumstances.

Internet as an Anti-Suicide Tool

Support Groups/Help Line

Professional mental health organization and other suicide prevention websites are not well represented among many internet websites. Among the popular ones used for suicide prevention in North America are the American Association of Suicidiology, the Canadian Association for Suicide Prevention, the Suicide Information Center, and the National Suicide

Prevention Lifeline, the latter of which now has a customized profile with "MySpace", a social networking website popular among the younger population.

In European countries, the Samaritans have a popular site which provides support by email.. Infact, one study reportedly quotes that email is better at detecting suicidal ideation than is telephoned contacts [21]. The Samaritans revealed that number of telephone conversations decreased, while there was a 25% increase in email contacts last year [29]. Obviously the internet is growing in popularity and its resources could be harnessed by mental health organizations to provide help to vulnerable individuals. In England, the rates of suicide among young persons (15-34 years old) have been declining this past decade, coinciding with the time since use of internet grew so dramatically [30]. Many individuals with suicidal ideations were identified on the internet and their intentions provided to rescue services to help obtain timely crisis intervention [31]. The Samaritans now took over the work of maintaining the network of international suicide prevention centers that makes up Befrienders Worldwide. This is a network of more than 400 volunteer centers in 39 countries across the world, providing help to those in need of emotional support. The Befrienders website lists 1,000 help lines for assistance in 21 languages.

Online counseling, or e-therapy, involves a professional counselor or psychotherapist consultation with a patient over the internet, to provide emotional support, mental health advice, or related other professional services. Contacts might be brief or longer term. The website Metonia is one of the few online resources where one can get information on e-therapy and contact a professional mental health therapist, listed through the website.

CONCLUSION

From a psychiatrist's perspective new technologies will obviously create new risk scenarios. But scope for prevention will also be presented. Internet has created a realm which raises many ethical and legal issues about whether this medium could or should be monitored in some way. Although, Internet could potentially be used to intervene when a vulnerable individual contemplating suicide is traced through chat room/discussion forum or simply by content of surfing. This again poses the risk of invading the privacy and the freedom of speech, as suicide is considered personal choice and there is no law proclaiming otherwise in most countries. However, in some countries like United Kingdom, the Suicide Act of 1951 prohibits others from encouraging suicide ; there could be legal grounds for attempting to do so at internet. It could be argued that interventions are justified for public health reasons as reducing suicide rate is national issue.

The Internet seems to assist self-disclosure of suicidal ideation rather easily, this could prove to be advantageous in identifying and communicating with those contemplating suicide. Strategies aiming at introducing professional help via websites that provide support and educational information on suicide should be introduced. As evidenced by the exponential growth of this medium, it seems that further research in this area is required to establish a causal relationship between internet activities and suicide. Without which effective interventional strategies to control various internet suicide promotional activities cannot be achieved.

REFERENCES

[1] Homicides and Suicides – National Violent Death Reporting System, United States,2003-2004. *CDC:Morbidity and Mortality Weekly Report* (MMWR). July 7, 2006 / 55(26);721-724.

[2] Suicide Trends Among Youths and Young Adults Aged 10--24 Years – United States, 1990—2004. *CDC:Morbidity and Mortality Weekly Report* (MMWR). September 7, 2007 / 56(35);905 908.

[3] Shaffer D,Gould M S,Fisher P, et.al.: Psychiatric diagnosis in child and adolescent suicide. *Arch Gen Psychiatry.* 1996 Apr; 53 (4):339-348.

[4] Shaffer D, Garland A, Gould M, et.al.: Preventing teenage suicide: a critical review. *J Am Acad Child Adolesc Psychiatry* 1988;27:675-87.

[5] O'Carroll PW. Suicide. In: Last JM, Wallace RB, eds. Maxcy-Rosenau-Last public health and preventive medicine. 13th ed. Norwalk, *CT: Appleton & Lange,* 1992:1054-62.

[6] Gould MS, Davidson L. Suicide contagion among adolescents. In: Stiffman AR, Felman RA, eds. Advances in adolescent mental health. Vol III. Depression and suicide. *Greenwich*, CT: JAI Press, 1988.

[7] Schmidtke A, Hafner H. The werther effect after television films: New evidence for old hypothesis. *Psychological Medicine* 1988; 18:665-676.

[8] Davidson LE, Gould MS. Contagion as a risk factor for youth suicide. In: Alcohol, Drug Abuse, and Mental Health Administration. Report of the Secretary's Task Force on Youth Suicide. Vol 2. Risk factors for youth suicide. Washington, DC: *US Department of Health and Human Services, Public Health Service,* 1989:88-109; DHHS publication no. (ADM)89-1622.

[9] Gould MS, Wallenstein S, Kleinman MH, O'Carroll PW, Mercy JA. Suicide clusters: an examination of age-specific effects. *Am J Public Health* 1990;80:211-2.

[10] Phillips DP, Carstensen LL. The effect of suicide stories on various demographic groups, 1968-1985. *Suicide Life Threat Behav* 1988;18:100-14.

[11] CDC. Cluster of suicides and suicide attempts -- New Jersey. MMWR 1988;37:213-6.

[12] Davidson LE, Rosenberg ML, Mercy JA, Franklin J, Simmons JT. An epidemi- ologic study of risk factors in two teenage suicide clusters. *JAMA* 1989;262:2687-92.

[13] Madelyn S Gould, Keith Petrie, Marjorie H Kleinmanand Sylvan Wallenstein: Clustering of Attempted Suicide: New Zealand National Data. *Int. J. Epidemiol.* 1994;23(6): 1185-1189.

[14] A. Cheng, K. Hawton, T. Chen, A. Yen, J. Chang, M. Chong, C. Liu, Y. Lee, P. Teng, L. Chen The influence of media reporting of a celebrity suicide on suicidal behavior in patients with a history of depressive disorder. *Journal of Affective Disorders,* Volume 103, Issue 1 - 3, Pages 69 – 75.

[15] Stack, S. (1991). Social correlates of suicide by age: Media impacts. In A. Leenaars (Ed.), *Life span perspectives of suicide: Timelines in the suicide process* (pp. 187- 213). New York: Plenum Press.

[16] Schmidtke, A., & Schaller, S. (2000). The role of mass media in suicide prevention. In *International handbook of suicide and attempted suicide.* (pp. 675-697). Chichester, UK: John Wiley and Sons.

[17] U.S. Department of Commerce (2002). *A Nation Online: How Americans are Expanding their Use of the Internet.* Washington, DC: Author.

[18] Kleiner, A., and Lewis, L. (2003). *Internet Access in U.S. Public Schools and Classrooms: 1994-2002* (NCES 2004–011). U.S. Department of Education. Washington, DC: National Center for Education Statistics.

[19] MARTIN.G. (1996) The influence of television suicide in a normal adolescent population. *Archines of Suicide Research,* 2. 103-117.

[20] Lucy Biddle., Jenny Donovan, Keith Hawton, Navneet Kapur, David GunnellSuicide and the internet. *BMJ* 2008;336:800-802.

[21] Patricia R. Recupero, J.D., M.D.; Samara E. Harms, B.A.; and Jeffrey M. Noble, A.B Googling Suicide: Surfing for Suicide Information on the Internet. *J Clin Psychiatry.* 2008 Jun;69(6):878-88.

[22] Susan Thompson: Internet and its potential influence on suicide. *Psychiatric Bulletin* (1999), 23: 449-451.

[23] Haut,F. & Morrison,A. (1998) The Internet and the future of psychiatry. *Psychiatric Bulletin,* 22. 641-642.

[24] Gallagher KE, Smith DM, Mellen PF. Suicidal asphyxiation by using pure helium gas: case report, review, and discussion of the influence of the internet. *Am J Forensic Med Pathol.* 2003 Dec;24(4):361-3.

[25] Adekola O. Alao, M.D., Jennifer C. Yolles, M.D., and Wendy Armenta, M.D. Cybersuicide: The Internet and Suicide(Letter). *Am J Psychiatry* 156:1836-1837, November 1999.

[26] Baume P, Cantor CH, Rolfe A.Cybersuicide: the role of interactive suicide notes on the Internet. *Crisis.* 1997;18(2):73-9.

[27] Akihito Hagihara; Kimio Tarumi; Takeru Abe.: Media suicide-reports, Internet use and the occurrence of suicides between 1987 and 2005 in Japan. *BMC Public health.* 2007 Nov 11;7(147):321.

[28] Suler, J. (2004). *CyberPsychology and Behavior*, 7, 321-32.

[29] *Samaritans: Annual Report & Accounts* (2007/08). Available at http://www. samaritans.org/media_centre/annual_report.aspx.

[30] Biddle L, Brock A, Brookes S, Gunnell D. Suicides rates in young men in England and Wales in the 21st century: time trend study. *BMJ* 2008;336:539-42.

[31] Janson MP, Alessandrini ES, Strunjas SS, Shahab H, El-Mallakh R, Lippmann SB. Internet-observed suicide attempts. *J Clin Psychiatry.* 2001 Jun;62(6):478.

In: Internet and Suicide
Editors: L. Sher and A. Vilens
ISBN 978-1-60741-077-5

Chapter 3

THE ADVANTAGES AND THE DISADVANTAGES OF THE INTERNET IN PREVENTING SUICIDE

Kalmár Sándor
County Hospital, Kecskemét, Hungary

ABSTRACT

The author examines the contents and applicability of results of Internet searches by using the keywords 'öngyilkosság' (suicide) and 'öngyilkosság megelőzése' (suicide prevention) in Hungary. In spite of some difficulties and many controversial problems, such as fearful, harmful and faked messages posted on many websites, the Internet can be a useful tool in combating suicide. It is a legitimate and efficiant mean of providing psychological help and it can be exploited to provide significant assistance to people in severe distress who contemplate suicide, and the complex system usually functions quite efficiently. The evaluation of the Internet in the causes and prevention of suicide is quite controversial similarly to that of many other means of the media. But most of this disadvantages reside in the inapposite usage, similarly to all new scientific discoveries. The discovery of the stone axe was not only useful in the fight against the beasts in the prehistoric age, but was a weapon against other people. The discovery of the first knife was suitable onto the facilitation of daily work but onto the extinction of the man's own life. The discovery of steam engine was not only useful for the traffic but it was a new mean of comitting suicide. The discovery of nuclear energy led to creation not only nuclear power plant but nuclear weapon as well. We may not say that the discovery of knife, the discovery of steam engine or the discovery of nuclear power are harmful for the humanity after all.

The professional revision and social control of contents of the internet is still unresolved. Ariadne's thread is missing from the labyrinth of the enormous vast and chaotic mass which can be hit on the internet. It is not possible to establish order of importance between the different web sites. Its largest benefit is its largest disadvantage since there is too much information in one. Some web sites contain misleading information, there is not supervision, which would call the attention for these mistakes, and would correct the mistakes. Among the examined web sites, there were none where the motive system of a reasonable life would be found, although this would be very important in prevention. There was neither national program nor a county program, nor the national or county commissions' web sites, dealing with the prevention, nor workgroups' sites, psychiatric Professional Colleges and Societies' opinion in connection with prevention. We could not find material supporting high risk groups.

From among the advantages the free and fast spread of immeasurable amount of information increase the body of knowledge of users and may be exceptionally useful for them. 50% (suicide prevention) or 27% (suicide) of the examined web sites concerned were useful in terms of the prevention. 11% (suicide prevention) or 25% (suicide) of sites contained information without scientific basis or harmful, dangerous information. Those Forums, Suicide-sites, Encyclopaedias and other sites, which do not only imply useful information, but unscientific false information are dangerous and harmful ones.

We consider reports and results of prevention programs based on individual initiations especially valuable that can be the basis of national and the regional programs to decrease the number of suicide – the small monsters of our civilization.

INTRODUCTION

There is no other social phenomenon and general public health problem, so much unexplained, meaning such an individual fate, so tragic, painful, and unreasonable, so difficult, contradictory and mystified like suicide. [1] It does not simply mean the loss of life, but causes a serious pain among the family members, friends, with a shocking effect for the environment and imposes a huge economic burden on all of the society. In 2002 cca. 877,000 people died as a result of a suicide in the world which is more than 20 million disabilities-adjusted life years (DALY). [2] The global suicide rate will be increasing and in the 2020 year there will be estimated 1,53 million deaths. [3] The highest rates among suicidal indicators can be found in East Europe, the lowest ones in Muslim countries. We do not know the real reason, but we can not know it because suicidal behavior is multi-causal, which can never be traced back to one single cause, but always a large number of biological, psychological-psychiatric, historical, social and cultural factors play essential roles in its development.

It proved however, that more than 90 percent of those died in suicide and those attempting one suffer from a psychiatric illness in the time of event, which is in most cases major depression (56-87 %), alcohol concerned or drug related illness (26-55 %) or schizophrenia (6-13%). In the United States the most common psychiatric diagnostic class associated with suicide is mood disorders, accounting for about 60% of all suicides. [4] If the major depression is connected with alcohol or drug illness, the risk of suicide is especially high. [5] [6][7] On the other hand, the vast majority of the depressed or schizophrenic patients and addicts never commit suicides, and more than 50 percent of them never attempt one, so beside the psychiatric illness, psycho-social factors play essential roles in the formation of the self-destructive behavior as well. [8] Beside the current psychiatric disorders several undesirable psycho-social phenomenon, concerned event (unemployment, isolation, easy accessibility to lethal devices, chronic or acute psycho-social stressors) also play role in the development of suicidal behavior. The above factors exceptionally rarely lead to suicide in themselves, but quite often among psychiatric patients. So the psycho-socially underprivileged people are endangered in the concern of a suicide, especially if they suffer from a psychiatric illness. It has been known for a long time, that relevant family support, real (not formal) piety, and the large number of children count as protective factors in suicide. Since approximately one third of those died in suicide had at least one antecedent suicidal attempt, it must be considered a serious risk in the anamnesis. An attempted suicide is the strongest predictor of a finished suicide, especially when it goes together with major depression. [9]

Although the immeasurable development which can be experienced in the last few years, which was able to significantly reduce the suicidal mortality being linked to psychiatric abnormalities with modern antidepressants and antipsychotic medicines in several countries - and improved significantly the quality of life in a number patients - the illness of the depressed patients' majority does not get to recognition even today in the primary care system and so the suitable treatment is not obtained. The lack of recognition of depression and proper treatment is obvious in depressed patients who commit suicide. Most individuals who commit suicide were not receiving adequate antidepressant treatment at the time of their death. About only 15-20% of such depressed patients are being adequately treated at the time of death and the vast majority (85-90%) are not being adequately treated or treated at all. [10]

In the mid 1980's a study of Gotland island in Sweden was the first, which showed that the short, intensive depression recognition program for the primary care physician (PCPs) reduces the suicidal mortality of a given area, primarily as a result of the decrease of the depressed suicides' number. [11] [12] That fact, that 83% of those who attempted or committed suicide visited their primary care physician during their last year, and half of them visited their primary care physician in the last 3 months of their life underlines the family doctors' role in the recognition of the suicidal danger and the prevention of suicide. This proportion is higher in developed countries. Results of the Gotland study were confirmed in Nürnberg, Germany, Jamtland, Sweden and Hungary too. (Kiskunhalas-region) [13] [14] [15] [16]

Considering the above facts, we must conclude, that preventing suicide is a complex phenomena. The crucial part of prevention programs lay in the screening and effective treatment of depressed patients in the primary care at family doctors. Recognizing the depressed patients' syndromes at the primary care system is not only in Hungary but in other parts of the world; consequently their diagnoses and treatment are inadequate, insufficient as well. Stoppe and his research group revealed that only 3% of the primary care physicians ask their aged depressed patients about suicidal thoughts. [17]

Since male patiens rarely visit psychiatrists with their depressed complaints the only solution for them are aware primary care physicians, who can diagnose their depression, who can provide proper treatment or forward them to specialists when they visit them with other complaints. [18] The most of male patients find it more difficult to express themselves. (maybe they have alexithymia?) The Internet could be an easier way by which they could actually express how they feel. [19]

It does not seem to be enough to be aware of the proper treatments of depression, it is also necessary to organize the way of patients to specialists where they can get the proper treatment. The health organization and the health policy is not developed enough to provide the available treatment for every patient who need it. Preventing suicide is a primarily social responsibility, partly the problem of the emergency health care and only partly psychiatric problem. The big part of this task falls to the primary care physician's system as the psychiatrists does not fit for the treatment of all depressed patients.

Based on WHO's 1991 examination: 12.5% of family doctors' patients are depressed. The family doctors diagnose only 15% of depression, and only 6.5% of depressed patients were provided proper treatment. [20] This proportion made progress in the latter years. Berardi found it in their research including 191 primary care physicians (PCPs) in Italy in 1996, that the proportion of the depressed patients recognized by the PCPs was 79,4% (127 out of 160 patients)

They examined 361 patients in this study. According to ICD-10 criteria, 160 out of 361 patients were affected by depression. (44,3%) 127 out of 361 patients were true-positive cases (35,2%), 104 out of 361 patients were false-positive cases (28,8%), 33 out of 361 patients were false-negative cases (9,1%) and 97 out of 361 patients were true-nagative cases (26,9%)

According to the primary care physicians' evaluation, 231 patients suffered from depression. Out of these 231 patients, 127 were true-positive cases (79,4%), The proportion of unrecognized cases of depression was 20,6% (33 out of 160 patients) PCPs prescribed antidepressants to 40,9% of true-positive patients, 26,9% of false-positive, 1% of true-negative and 3% of false-negative cases. Among the patients to whom PCPs prescribed antidepressants for 'depression' 52 patients satisfied ICD criteria for current depression while the remaining 28 paients were not depressed according to research criteria.In sum: 53 out of 160 depressed patients (31,1%) were treated with AD medication, and 28 out of 104 patients (26,9%), who were not really depressed according to BNO-10 criteria were treated with AD medicines. Bellantuono concluded that the proportion of the depression recognized by the PCP is 61.7%, among whom 32.7% is given AD treatment. German researches report better results, here 85% is the proportion of recognition and 44,3% is the proportion of the treated patients. [21] This is important not only because 16-20% of suicide victims visit their PCP the week preceding their suicide and 34-38% of them visit in the preceding four-week-period, but because the depressive symptoms mean the risk in other sicknesses with national health significance. Isometsa found it in 1995, that 18% of the victims met their PCPs on their last day, but merely 21% of them talked about suicide. We face data in the literature differing from this, particularly if an interview is made with the survivors after the suicide attempt. According to a Pécs study 18.4% of men and 17.4% of women attempting suicide contacted their doctor the week preceding their act, and 36.8% of men and 47.6% of women contacted their doctor the month preceding the attempt. The 55.3% of men and 65.1% of women came in for an ambulant psychiatric treatment, and 47.4% and 47.6% of them respectively came in for a psychiatric class treatment earlier. It is generally acceptable, that roughly half of the victims visit their doctors in the preceding weeks, and 20-25% of them is provided a psychiatric treatment. [22] These patients visit their PCPs not primarily for the direct communication of their suicidal intention, but with some kind of other problem, minor laboratory results, increased urge to complain, usually only indirectly indicating their hopelessness, the hopelessness of their situation and the opportunity of the potential suicide.

WHO in 1980 marked three areas of successful suicide prevention agendas in the program 'Health for all in Europe by the year 2000'. [23]

First, making improvements with regard to the underlying societal factors that seem to put a strain on the individual, such as unemployment, the social isolation of elderly people living on their own, and failure at school, would be important means of intervention. Although our present knowledge of the sophisticated web of contributory factors involved in insufficient and greater research in this field is necessary, it has already been known enoughto warrant positive action as from now.

Secondly, ways of strengthening the individual's general ability to cope with the events of life must be a key concern.

Thirdly, since most people who commit or attempt suicide are seen shortly before by general practitioners or other health professionals, there is an opportunity for preventive action.

There is evidence, however that owing to a lack of training in diagnostic and treatment methods and of necessary skills, health professionals are often not adequately equipped to deal with suicidal patients. The same applies to the staff of emergency and intensive care wards od general hospitals to which attempted suicide cases are referred. Finally, public knowledge of suicide risk is still relatively sparse. [1]

There is also need for the education of the public, and especially young people through schools, on the causes and means of preventing suicidal behaviour and the mismanagement of life events that often lead to it.

At this time the use of the Internet or similar means of communications were not considered. WHO started the program SUPRE in 1999, which set the prevention of the suicides as an aim worldwide. The media is mentioned in this program in general, the Internet is not.

An efficient complex suicide prevention program in which the Internet will be useful to the highest degree has to include the following areas:

I. In general:
- The development and realization of a National (and Regional) Suicide Prevention Program. [24] [25] [26]
- Providing resources for the realization of the National and Regional Suicide Prevention Programs.
- The analysis of effects of political and economic decisions in regards of mental health development, depression recognition and suicide prevention, and a widespread announcing of the results.
- Paying more attention to doctors coping with alcohol problems or using psycho-active substances, and/or suffering depression, and provide them the optimal treatment to make them to be suitable for their profesison.
- Paying special attention to elderly people. It is necessary to prevent the de-socialization of elderly people and to enhance their social self-organization processes.
- Paying emphasized attention to the realization of the prevention of the drinking problem and the alcohol illnesses and its treatment strategies. (It is one of the most important problem in Hungary)
- The development of mental aid telephone lines and providing the necessary financial conditions of their function.
- Efficient acting against misinformation on the treatment of depression on the basis of medical science.
- National co-ordination of research on suicide.

- Re-evaluating opportunities of the youth and child psychiatry services. Child and puberty psychic disturbances lay the foundations for the adulthood mental disorders. Currently the child psychiatry services are not functional; the national development of the network of the medical attendance is not feasible. It is necessary to lay a bigger emphasis onto primary prevention.

II. Education and Awareness Programs

- Public Education
  - The increase of knowledge connected to the psychiatric illnesses among the population, primarily in health professionals and social workers, and among the teachers. Coping refusal of such illnesses and the acceptance of suicide. [27]
- Primary Care Physicians [20]
  - Paying emphasized attention to primary care physicians onto the recognition of the depression and distressful disturbances by using the available self-report probability scales.
  - Building up tighter cooperation between (community-) psychiatric supplying service and primary care physicians.
  - It is necessary to pay emphasized attention to the population above 50. In 2000 in Bács-Kiskun county 48.9% of the victims of the suicides were above 50. This proportion reached 64.7% by 2006. The suicide rate over 75 years is up to seven times higher than adolescent suicide rate in most of countries except Bács-Kiskun county, Hungary. In all continents, despite the huge/tremendous cultural variability, older people present higher suicide rates than adolescent people. [28] The proportion of 70 years or older suicides was 30,4% and this was 18,7 times higher the 19 years at younger victims.
  - Complement the obligatory primary care physician's screening protocols with the screening of the distressful disturbances and depression. (Beck scale, ZUNG scale, Hopelessness scale etc.)
  - Taking notice of the fact that the depression screening is a basic examination just like measurement of temperature of the taking of blood pressure. Every doctor has to be aware of that.
  - It is necessary to further the social integration of those who attempt suicide, and to do everything in the interest of the prevention of the social branding.
- Other Physicians
  - Laying a bigger emphasis on the distressful and depressive disorders and the prevention opportunities of the suicide in the medical training.
  - Ensuring that any specialist doctor with a degree of MD would be prepared for the diagnosis of depression and the pre-suicidal syndrome and its primary care.
  - Providing the knowledge to all doctors that depression screening is part of routine examinations (like any other medical examinations just like measurement of temperature or the taking of blood pressure. [29]
  - In medical professional training and continuing professional education, especially at primary care physicians, internists, surgeons, at obstetricians

and gynecologists a special emphasis to be taken to the diagnosis of pre-suicidal syndrome and its emergency psychiatric treatment. [24]
    - Eliminating deficiencies which can be found at all doctors with intensive psychiatric and addictology professional trainings resulting from the inadequate training.
    - Laying special emphasis on doctors with refusing attitudes towards depression and accepting suicide.
- Health and social workers, health visitors, pharmacists.
    - Developing the syllabus of hygienic training colleges' and technical colleges' onto the recognition of the depression and the suicidal danger and its treatment to a specialized nurse level.
    - Developing positive problem solving skills of students of hygienic and social areas in the course of their training.
    - Regular training and development of employees of social area in order to fill the possible gaps in their education concerning the identification of depression and the risk of suicide.
- Community and Organizational Gatekeepers
    - Developing positive mental health in schools.
    - Laying emphasis in the education of teacher to the recognition of childhood and juvenile depression and the suicidal danger.
    - Supporting the development of positive problem solving skills in students of teacher training schools and universities.
    - Teaching positive problem-solving skills, the development of the social conflict solution skills and efficient stress treatment for students of the primary schoo's upper classes and the high schools classes for both teachers and children.

III. Screening aims to identify individuals and groups at risk and direct them to treatment.

- endangered counties' and micro-regions' inhabitants,
- those coping with serious psychosocial problems,
- men,
- elderly people,
- widows and the lonely,
- family members of those committed suicide,
- Those who suffer in a psychiatric illness especially: Psychiatric disorders are present in at least 90% of suicides and more than 80% are untreated at time of death. Depressive Disorders, (Male-Depression, Masked-Depression, Bipolar Disorders, Schizophrenia and Other Psychotic Disorders, Alcohol-Related-Disorders, Anxiety Disorders, Eating Disorders, Borderline Personality Disorder.
- Those who suffer from a serious bodily illness, especially: malicious tumors, primarily those of the breast and the genitals. HIV infection and AIDS, states after a stroke, cardiovascular sicknesses, endocrinology sicknesses. Neurological sicknesses (epilepsy, Parkinson illness, traumatic brain and spinal cord injury), chronic pain syndromes, low cholesterol level. [30]

IV. Treatment intervention
- Pharmacotherapy
- Psychotherapy
- Follow-up Care After Suicide Attempts
  - Compulsory support and treatment for the families of suicide victims. It is a proven fact that in those families where a suicide appeared the risk of suicide is 26 times higher. [31] Attempted suicide is the strongest and probably the most universal of all known predictors of suicide. [9]
- Follow-up Care the Family of Victims
  - Compulsory support and treatment for those who attempted suicide and their families. Ten percent of those who attempted suicide will die of suicide within 10 year after the first attempt. [8]

V. Means restriction
- Limiting acces to lethal devices is very important, but in Hungary its significance is lower, since the most often used method is hanging. The limitations to the availability of firearms, the detoxification of insecticide implements and domestic gas, limitations of barbiturates and the blister packaging of medicines, the support hybrid cars and those with catalytic converter, the placement of safe bars at high places, the development and distribution of antidepressants with little toxicity proved to be an efficient prevention method in other countries.

VI. Media.
- The media and the internet can both help or hinder suicide prevention efforts. [32][2][33] [34]
- Paying higher attention to the distressful and depressive disorders meaning serious national health trouble, and their consequences, primarily onto suicide and its prevention in the media and on the internet. Suicide websites on the Internet have often been reported as suicide-facilitating stimuli and many studies focus on the authors pointed out but the Internet may have a lot of beneficial effects on suicide as well. [35]
- Shaping of a responsible media activity, safe representation of the suicides in the media.
- Increasing knowledge of psychiatric illnesses and suicide in the population.
- Surveying the population's attitude and the alteration of the acceptor attitude related to suicide. [36] [37] [38]

In almost all of these areas the internet can provide help to the endangered groups' members or specialist. Despite several of its controversial problems the Internet may be a useful device in coping suicide. The overall evaluation of the Internet in the development and prevention of suicides is highly controversial, but most of his disadvantages reside in the inapposite usage, similarly to all new scientific discoveries during the history. The discovery of the stone axe was not only useful in the fight against the beasts in the prehistoric age, but was a weapon against other people. The discovery of the first knife was suitable onto the facilitation of daily work but also useful to commit suicide with one. The discovery of steam engine was not only useful for the development of traffic but it was a tool to suicide as well.

The discovery of nuclear energy has led not only nuclear power plant but to nuclear weapons as well. After all we may not say that the discovery of knife, steam engine or the discovery of nuclear power are harmful for humanity.[34]

On the one hand several helping, useful information which are connected to suicide and its prevention can be found on the internet, on the other hand there are several suicide support pages can be found, encouraging those preparing for the suicide are providing means for the realization of their intention. In connection with the prevention the situation is better, but the applicability of the pages found, their reliability is quite dubious most of them announce anonymous, unsubstantiated, information implying commonplaces many times partly, presupposes medical knowledge which is not suitable for the majority of citizens using the internet with no medical education.

The specialists of United States dealing with the prevention of a suicide are in a lucky situation because several web sites help in their work, e.g. (www.afsp.org, www.psych.org, www.nimh.nih.gov/research/suicide.htm, www.suicidology.org, www.depression.com etc.) Unfortunatelly the lack of a good command of English language of the Hungarian health professionals is a huge obstacle, because they are not able to use these valuable web sites.

PURPOSE

To examine the representation of suicide in Hungarian web pages in terms of the prevention of a suicide by using the search phrases 'suicide prevention'(öngyilkosság-megelőzés) and analyzing the first 100 pages. Also to examine the first 100 resulting pages for the search 'suicide' on the basis of the situation of suicide in Hungary. A second purpose is to evaluate the resulting pages in terms of their applicability according to the following criteria:

- Useful pages:
  1. Pages implying suitable information with scientific foundations for ones dealing with the prevention of the suicide, (physicians, health professionals, teachers)
  2. Pages implying theoretical communications in general.
  3. Pages providing suitable information and help for members of high risk groups.
  4. Pages implying suitable information with scientific foundations for laymen (health education).
  5. Suicide prevention book reviews, pages recommending books that are connected to suicide prevention.
  6. Pages presenting suicide cases with intention preceding a suicidal case (case-reviews, diaries, farewell letters etc.)
  7. For survival pages.
  8. Churches' information.
- Harmful pages:
  9. Directly or indirectly encouraging information for ones with suicide intentions
  10. Information dealing with suicidal methods, but actually does not encourage to commit a suicide.
  11. Information without scientific background.

12. Anti-psychiatry pages
- Indifferent sides in terms of prevention:
13. News informing on suicide
14. Indifferent news in terms of prevention, in which the term 'suicide prevention' appears.
15. Reviews and advertisements of civil organizations dealing with suicide.
16. Universities', colleges' guides for students, who learn about suicide prevention. (Timetables, item rows, exam schedules, theses.)

METHODS

Questions Applied at the Analysis of the Sites

I. General questions.

At the time of the examination of the information we looked for the answers for the following questions:

- Does it imply a national program?
- Does the commission coordinating prevention affecting the country have a website?
- Does it contain mental care organizations and/or associations and a helpline with availability (phone number)?
- Does it imply fair information about depression, as the number one cause of suicide and as a successfully treatable disorder?
- Does it contain the review of the signs of a crisis?
- Does it contain causes of a reasonable life, which may help with overcoming suicidal thoughts?
- Does it contain methods that help in coping conflicts?
- Does it imply medical misinformation?

II. Is the given pages beneficial for those working in suicide prevention.

- Primary care physicians
- other specialists
- health professionals
- employees on a social area
- teachers
- employees of special areas
- church persons, priests, clergymen
- politicians
- media workers

III. Is the given page beneficial for the high risk or endangered groups?

- men
- elder age, particularly women
- bigger children and adolescents/juveniles
- the family members of the victims

- the suicide attempt perpetrators and their family members
- depressed patients
- sufferers of other psychiatric sickness: schizophrenics, sufferers of borderline personality disorder, addicts of psychoactive drugs, primarily alcoholics
- those experiencing serious negative life event
- with an endangered occupation (physicians, medical university students) [39] [40]
- serious somatic patients
- widows or widowers
- prison inhabitants
- the inhabitants of endangered areas
- other groups: homosexuals etc.

RESULTS

In the last years, the Internet increased considerably. Statistics show that the Internet represents an increasingly important medium, especially among adolescents and young adults who use it as a source of information and communication.

In the year of 2006 there were 1 329 625 Internet subscription in Hungary. (The number of Population, 1 January 2007: 10 066 000)

In spite of this on Hungary, compared to some other countries the internet penetration was low. At the end of 2005 the incidence of the internet was 30,3% in Hungary according to the data of Internet World States (http://www.internetworldstats.com). This is a low number, if we compare it to 68,1% in the USA and 49,8 in the EU. But the number of internet users in Hungary was growing 326,6% between 2000-2005 while this number was 113,8% in the United States and 147% in the EU.

At the time of the examination of the web sites we found the following results:

- the examined web sites did not imply a national preventive program
- there was no web site of the National Preventive Committee
- the web sites contained mental care organizations and associations and some available hotline (phone number)
- the web sites did not imply enough fair information about depression which could be treated successfully and the number one cause for suicide
- the web sites did not contain the signs of a crisis
- the web sites did not contain causes of a reasonable life, which might help with overcoming suicidal thoughts
- the web sites did not contain enough information of methods that help in coping conflicts
- there were some web sites which implied medical misinformation.

The following three figures contain the detailed results of the analysis of the wed sites.

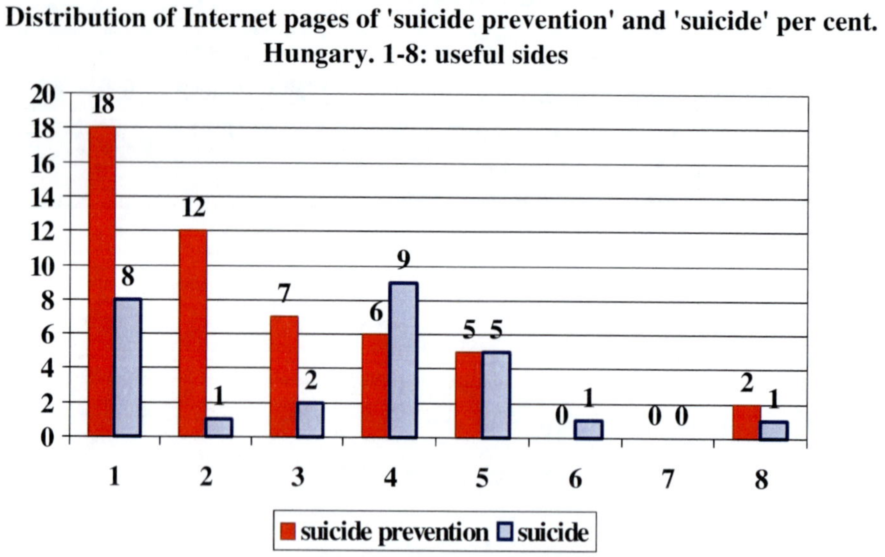

1. Pages implying suitable information with scientific foundations for ones dealing with the prevention of the suicide, (doctors, hygienic employees, educators). 2.Pages implying theoretical communications in generality. 3. Pages providing suitable information and help for members of high risk groups. 4. Pages implying suitable information with scientific foundations for laymen (health education). 5. Suicide prevention book reviews, pages recommending books that are connected to suicide prevention. 6. Pages presenting suicide cases with intention preceding a suicidal case (case reviews, diaries, farewell letters) 7. For survival pages. 8.Churches' information.

Figure 1. Useful WEB sites: 1 - 8.

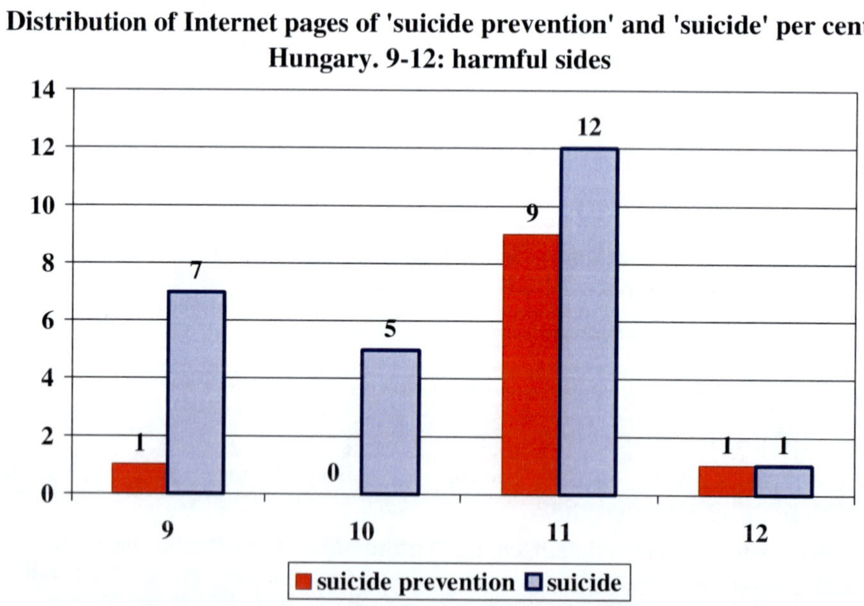

9. Directly or indirectly encouraging information for ones with suicide intentions. 10. Information dealing with suicidal methods, but actually does not encourage to a suicide. 11. Information without scientific background. 12. Anti-psychiatry pages.

Figure 2. Harmful WEB sites: 9 – 12.

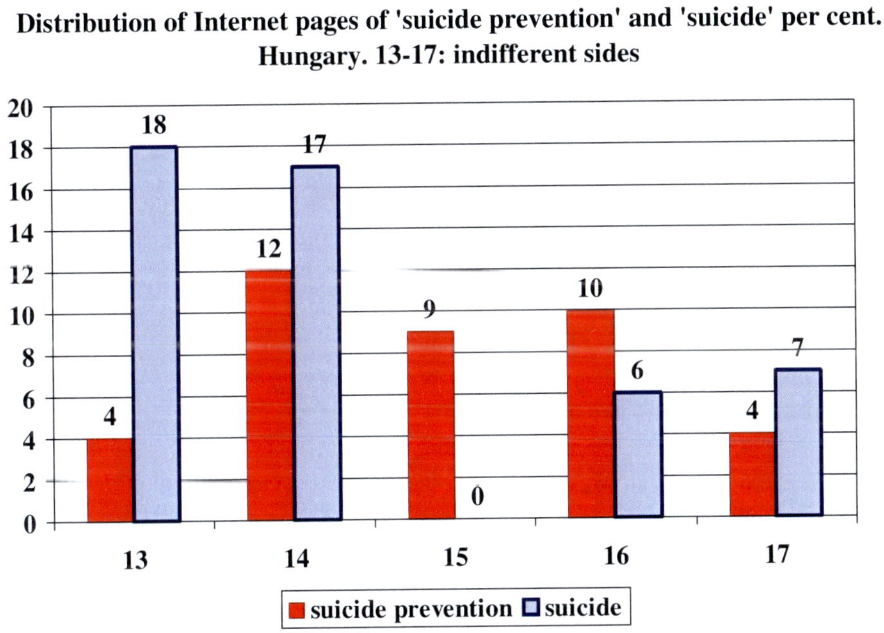

13. News informing suicide 14. Indifferent news in terms of prevention, in which the term 'suicide prevention' appears. 15. Reviews and advertisements of civil organizations dealing with suicide. 16. Universities', colleges' guides for students, who learn about suicide prevention. (Timetables, item rows, exam schedules, theses.)

Figure 3. Indifferent sites: 13 – 17.

DISCUSSION AND CONCLUSION

For the search phrase 'suicide prevention' there were 60,400 resulting page, one hundred of these were examined. While examining these pages, we found that 18% of the pages contained proper information with a scientific basis for those who professionally deal with suicide prevention. There are useful information for family doctors and specialists as well. There are useful pages for those working in health care and social support systems and teachers. On these pages, there are lots of useful information for those interested in suicide on a non professional basis. To gain information, there are lots of pages containing unimportant information to be reviewed. 12% of thepages contained theoretical communication, political opinion in general. 7% of the pages provide information and help for those in crisis or with a high suicide risk, in most cases telephone numbers for help lines, 6% of pages provide proper information with scientific background in laymen's term. Of course the first group of pages can be useful for non-professionals as well. 5% of the pages contained reviews of books on suicide some of them are duplicated.

11% of the pages contained harmful or misleading information or that of without scientific basis, mostly questioning treatment methods and medications of modern medicine. There was only one page that contained covert encouragement for suicide.

12% of the resulting pages presented news containing the phrase suicide prevention. These pages are not useful in suicide prevention with unpredictable effect on an average internet user. 9% of pages contained information of religious origin, but none of these contained detailed suicide prevention program and pages were those of non-governmental organizations dealing with social problems like suicide, most of them were advertisements for donations. 10% of pages dealt with the exam questions and information of different, universities and colleges dealing with social work training, without actual preventive proposals.

Unfortunately, the examined pages did not contain proposals for improving basic social factors, nor national homepage, nor a national suicide prevention program. The pages examined contained hidden information on crisis and depression. There were some misinformation on depression and the treatment of depression and wrong statistical data. There was no page supporting the reasons of a meaningful life that can be quite useful in coping with suicidal thoughts. There was no page found dealing with conflict solving methods or improving coping system. There was no information available dedicated for high risk groups. Single pages formulated general governing principles generally. Neither of the pages examined provided a detailed prevention program for groups taking a part in prevention of suicide. From among the examined groups we did not find information prepared for (fulfilling the information needs of) priests, a clergyman, young persons, politicians or journalists.

From among the endangered groups we did not find pages that even tangentially aimed for the support of family members of suicide victims or for the ones attempted suicide. From among the high risk groups the doctors figured on the news sides, but we did not find help regarding the prevention. We did not find information in connection with the endangered counties' and regions' prevention, although in Hungary in 2007 there was a county with a 38.9 suicide rate. (man: 61.4; woman: 18.3)

For the search phrase 'suicide' there were 353,000 resulting page, one hundred of these were examined. While examining these pages, we found that 8% of the pages contained proper information with a scientific basis for those who professionally deal with suicide prevention. There are useful information for family doctors and specialists as well. There are useful pages for those working in health care and social support systems and teachers. On these pages, there are lots of useful information for those interested in suicide on a non professional basis. To gain information, there are lots of pages containing unimportant information to be reviewed. 1% of the pages contained theoretical communication, political opinion in general. 2% of the pages provide information and help for those in crisis or with a high suicide risk, in most cases telephone numbers for help lines, 9% of thepages provide proper information with scientific background in laymen's term. Of course the first group of pages can be useful for non-professionals as well. 5% of the pages contained reviews of books on suicide some of them are duplicated.

25% of the pages contained harmful or misleading information or that of without scientific basis, mostly questioning treatment methods and medications of modern medicine. There were seven pages (7%) that contained covert encouragement for suicide. 18% is only news.

17% of resulting pages presented news containing the phrase suicide prevention. These pages are not useful in suicide prevention with unpredictable effect on an average internet user. 6% of the pages dealt with the exam questions and information of different, universities and colleges dealing with social work training, without actual preventive proposals.

Those Forums, Suicide-sites, Encyclopaedias and other sites, which do not only imply useful information, but unscientific false information are dangerous and harmful ones. Many sites like that can be found, where laymen make a statement as an expert, with misinformation. It would be necessary that the Ministry of Public Health, State Public Health Office, the Hungarian Psychiatric Association check these sites and value the single sites from a professional point of view.

Despite the Internet controversial evaluation it is more useful, than harmful in terms of the suicide prevention. Experts of suicide prevention can find useful information through a variety of the Internet including websites which implying suitable information with scientific foundations, suicide prevention book reviews, and books that are connected to suicide prevention.

The Advantages of the Internet

The Internet is a treasury of information which can be attained easily for interested one today already. Every school, health service, hospital and outpatient clinic has Internet-availability.

Its immeasurable benefit is the free and fast spread of information, that infinitely widen one's knowledge and scope. 50% of the examined pages useful in terms of prevention. Vulnerable and risk-groups, and individuals accessing the Internet can find useful information and support through a variety of Internet services including informative web sites, suitable information and help, lists of support organizations, various telefon hotlines and emergency services. We consider pages based on individual initiations, reporting depression recognition and suicide prevention results especially valuable, which can provide basis for national and regional programs. The Internet is a device, which is possible to use well and badly. This can be the base of participant doctors', healthworkers, socialworkers, teachers, gatekeepers training in the suicide preventive programs and postgraduated education. This could replace the PCP's and other physicians, healthworkers, socialworkers, teachers, gatekeepers absent knowledge in a contact of depression and suicide. It can provide with reliable, fair statistical data, correct the misinformations which can be found among the population in connection with suicide. It can offer the population help in the development of their problem-solving skills, it can help the policymakers to make the correct decisions and can help the people who struggle against suicide.

The Internet would be useful especially the young people. According to a spokesman for the Samaritans in 1998 they received more than 15,000 e-mails from people who were feeling suicidal at the time of the contact and of those whose age they knew, over half were under 25. [19]

Onto a separate reference worthly the www.sahar.org.il, which is a good initiative. In Hebrew, the word SAHAR means a banana-shaped moon, a metaphor used on the website to stress the idea that darkness might only be a temporary condition and that lighteness will eventually prevail.

Though the www.sahar.org.il site has operated only in the Hebrew language,- because it is intended for Hebrew-speaking people - we consider it a very good initiation. It is a content-rich website with several sections. SAHAR contains several informative articles about various areas of distres, psychological treatments, myths concerning suicide, how to help a suicidal friend etc. This website publishes a comprehensive, well-organized, user-friendly, well informed, continuously updated list of support organizations, various telefon hotlines and emergency services for people who need immediate emergency assistance. At the end SAHAR contains numerous links to relevant sites and to online articles on the other websites, and a list of recommended books and other readings for those who are interested in expanding their knowledge. SAHAR proved that as an online service has several advantages over telefon hotlines: * it allows better anonymity, * allows the provision of relevant, updated, rich, continuously available, easily accessed information relating to any area of distress, without human mediation. * allows working with groups, * allows both syncronous and asyncronous support as requested, * allows multi-conversing, * easily saves the communication.

In spite of some difficulties and many controversial problems, such as the fearful, harmful and faked messages posted on many websites, the Internet is a legitimate and efficiant means of providing psychological help and it can be exploited to provide significant assistance to people in severe distress who contemplate suicide, and the complex system usually functions quite efficiently. [32] SAHAR can be a good example for other countries.

It is necessary to call the population's attention to the useful web sites in the mediaover and over again. Summary, we may say that the Internet did not provide even his fraction for opportunities today we take advantage of it, though the internet availability today already in all of the country assured.

The Disadvantages of the Internet

Its largest disadvantage is, that we do not take advantage of the opportunities of the Internet. The fair sites checked technically, which would provide useful information and help to the endangered target groups' members, the members of the groups dealing with prevention are missing. We do not take advantage of that the internet got it opportunities in the health education, neither the changing the dismissive attitude in connection with the depressive disorders and the acceptive attitude which is in connection with the suicides.

Ariadne's thread is missing the labyrinth of the enormous vast and chaotic mass which can be hit on the Internet. It is not possible to establish order of importance between the different web pages. Some web pages contain misinformation, there is not supervision, which would call the attention for these mistakes, and would correct the mistakes. Among the examined web pages, there were none where the motive system of a reasonable life would be found, although this would be very important in prevention but there were some anti-psychiatry pages and on more sites, particularly in the methodological chapters, they encouraged a suicide openly or impliedly.

There was neither national program nor a regional or county program, nor the national or county commissions' web pages, dealing with the prevention nor workgroups' pages, psychiatric professional colleges and societies' opinion in connection with prevention. The available sub-programs are too general.

The health policy did not cover it altogether yet up the huge benefits residing in the Internet and because of this they do not use ita lot. There is also a lack of the fair explanation on the Forums, and the participants send very obscure and harmful councils to each other many times. We could not find material supporting endangered groups. The professional revision and social control of contents of the internet is still unresolved.

Proposals

It would be quite useful to utilize the possibilities of the internet with the elimination of known disadvantages. The exact regulation the obligations of the internet service providers would be important.

It is necessary to draw up the proposals that would be obligatory the website makers and that proposals would imply the undermentioned items/ones at least:

- it is forbidden and dangerous to make a sensational report about suicide
- it is forbidden and dangerous to report suicide as a mysterious act of healthy person
- it is forbidden to present suicide as a reasonable way of problem solving
- it is forbidden and dangerous to present suicide as a heroic or romantic act.
- it is forbidden to report misconclusion or misinformation.
- It is forbidden, unethical and dangerous to misinterpret any medical news. In both the United States and the Netherlands, SSRI prescriptions for children and adolescents decreased after U.S. and European regulatory agencies issued warnings about possible suicide risk with antidepressant use in pediatric practice, and these decreases were associated with increases in suicide rates in children and adolescents. [4]
- it is forbidden and dangerous to present detailed description of method of suicide
- it is compulsory to indicate that suicide is most often fatal complication of different types of mental disorders, especially depression, and many of these disorders are treatable.

With first-rate importance a technically fair, suicide prevention program based on consensus the formation of schools dealing with prevention, starting of a national website dealing with suicide prevention that contain complex national, county and regional programs, and can be a guideline for suicide prevention would be of primary importance. The detailed presentation of these pages exceeds the limitations of this article, but they must contain information on the use of the internet in preventing suicide. These pages must accept all positive initiatives concerning suicide prevention; they must organize them and guarantee their scientific reliability. It must be clear for the users, that this information is controlled and reliable. [41] The National Suicide Prevention Board and the Professional College has to supervise and comment information on suicide prevention on scientific basis.

The prevention program has to deal with every field of suicide prevention; it has to contain training materials for the suicide prevention groups. It has to pay a special attention to the training of family doctors and the education of the employees of Primary Care and education systems. We have to make contact with the churches and ask them to join the prevention activities more efficiently, to deal with psychiatric problems and disorders that can lead to suicide and their treatment. We have to prepare health education materials for the whole population, and especially for the endangered high risk groups that can increase the population's knowledge about suicide. Information with scientific supervision can only guarantee the professional content of these materials. We have to look for possibilities of the medical supervision of information available on the internet in order to block materials supporting suicide or encouraging information for ones with suicide intentions with no professional explanation. These pages have to support politicians, form proposals towards them and demand information their activities on preventing suicide. National programs must include smaller regions' and counies' prevention programs too, and have to be linked to community programs from what the WHO can build a pyramid of unified system.

In the immediate future it will be necessery to analyze the instrumental using and the social using of the Internet. The first is useful for ones dealing with the prevention of the suicide, (doctors, health workers, social workers, teachers etc. and the second is useful for the vulnerable and risk-groups, and individuals, the tolls of suicides. This can lead to the elimination of disadvantages and to the multiplication of advantages. The Internet for the purpose of suicide prevention seems not only possible but higly desirable, and it is too wasting not to use this almost boundless possibilities of the Internet. We hope that in the near future the number of suicide will decrease; 'the darkness might only be a temporary condition and that lighteness will evantually prevail' with help of Internet all over the world. [32]

References

[1] Kalmár S. Reversing the rising trends in suicides in Bács Kiskun County. Moscow International WHO Training Course for Public Health Administrators. 1990. *Course paper.*

[2] Mann J.J, Apter A, Bertolote J, Beautrais A, Currier D, Haas A, Hegerl U, Lonquist J, Malone K, Marusic A, Mehlum L, Patton G, Philips M, Rutz W, Rihmer Z, Schmidtke A, Schaffer D, Silverman M, Takahashi Yoshitomo, Varnik A, Wasserman D, Yip P, Hendin H. Suicide Prevention Strategies. A Systematic Review, *JAMA,* 2005; 294: 2064-2074.

[3] Bertolote J.M. Suicide in the world: an epidemiological overview. 1959-2000. Edited by Wasserman D: Suicide - An unnecessary death. *Martin Dunitz London,* 2001. pp 3-10.

[4] Gibbons R.D,Brown H, Hur Kwan, Marcus S.M, Bhaumik D, Erkens J.A, Herings R.M.C, Mann J.J. Early Evidence on the Effects of Regulators' Suicidality Warnings on SSRI Prescriptions and Suicide in Children and Adolescents. *Am J Psychiatry* 2007; 164:1356-1363.

[5] Kalmár S. (2003) Depressziós páciensek öngyilkossági veszélyeztetettsége. *Háziorvosi Továbbképző Szemle* 8:520-525.

[6] Makara P. szerk. *Mentális egészségfejlesztési stratégia – pozitív egészség-fejlesztés és primér prevencia.* OEI, Budapest. 2007

[7] Rihmer Z. Suicide risk in mood disorders. C*urr Opin Psychiatry*, 2007; 20: 17-22.

[8] Kaplan HI, Sadock BJ. *Synopsis of Psychiatry.* Williams & Wilkins Baltimore 1991. 555.o.

[9] Retterstol N, Mehlum L. Attempted suicide as a risk factor for suicide: treatment and follow up. Edited by Wasserman D: *Suicide - An unnecessary death.* Martin Dunitz London, 2001. pp 125-132.

[10] Hendin H., Mann J.J. *The clinical Science of Suicide Prevention.* The New York Academy of Sciences, New York, 2001. Introduction.

[11] Rihmer Z, Rutz W, Pihlgren H. Depression and suicide on Gotland. An intensive study of all suicides before and after a depression-training programme for general practitioners. *J. Affect Disord,* 1995; 35: 147-152.

[12] Rutz W, Walinder J, von Knorring L, Rihmer Z, Pihlgren H. Lessons from the Gotland study on depression, suicide and education: effects, shortcomings and challenges. *Int J Methods Psychiatr Res.* 1996; 6:S9-S14.

[13] Henriksson S, Isacsson G. Increased antidepressant use and fewer suicides in Jamtland county, Sweden, after a primary care educational programme on the treatment of depression. *Acta Psychiat Scand,* 2006; 114: 159-167.

[14] Isacsson G, Holmgren P, Wasserman D, Bergman U. (1994) Use of antidepressants among people committing suicide in Sweden. *BMJ,* 308:506-9.

[15] Kalmár S, Szanto K, Rihmer Z, Sati Mazumdar, Harrison K, Mann J.J. Antidepressant prescription and suicide rates: Effect of age and gender. *Suicide and Life-Threatening Behaviour*. 2008; 38(4) August 363-374.

[16] Szántó K, Kalmár S, Hendin H, Rihmer Z, Mann J.J. A Suicide Prevention Program in a Region With a Very High Suicide Rate. *Arc Gen Psychiatry,* 2007; 64(8): 914-920.

[17] Stoppe G, Sandholzer H, Huppert C, Duwe H, Staedt J. Family physicians and the risk of suicide in the depressed elderly. J*ournal Affective Disorders* 1999; 54: 193-198.

[18] Rutz W, Knorring L, Pihlgren H,Rihmer Z, Walinder J. Prevention of male suicides: lessons from Gotland studdy. *Lancet,* 1995; 345: 524.

[19] Dobson R. Internet sites may encourage suicide. *BMJ Volume* 319. 7 August 1999; 337.

[20] Rihmer Z, Kalmár S. (szerk.) A depresszió felismerése és az öngyilkosság megelőzése a háziorvosi gyakorlatban. *Országos Pszichiátriai és Neurológiai Intézet,* Budapest. 2000 ISBN: 963 00 4376 9

[21] Berardi D, Menchetti M, Cevenini N, Scaini S, Versari M, De Ronchi D. (2005) Increased Recognition of Depression in Primary Care. *Psychother Psychosom,* 2005; 74: 225-230.

[22] Osváth P, Fekete S, Boncz I, Varga G, George D. Szuicidiummal kapcsolatos attitűdök összehasonlító vizsgálata – *Regionális különbségek Psychiat Hung,* 2001; 16 (2):166-172.

[23] *Targets for health for all 2000.* WHO Regional Office for Europe, Copenhagen, 1985.

[24] Hendin H. The Surgeon General's Call to Action to Prevent Suicide: American Foundation for Suicide Prevention Responds. *TEN* (The Economics of Neoroscience) 2000; 2 (3) : 54-56.

[25] Wilson J.F. Finland Pioneers International Suicide Prevention. 2004. *Annals of Internal Medicine.* Volume 140. No. 10. 853-853

[26] Zöld Könyv. A lakosság mentális egészségének javítása. Az Európai Unió mentális egészségügyi stratégiájának kialakítása. Brüsszel, 2005. október 14. (magyar változat: 2006) I*mproving the mental health of the population. Towards a strategy on mental health for the European Union.* (COM) 484, October 2005. Bruxelles.

[27] *Preventing suicide: a resource series.* Geneve:WHO: 2000.

a. A resource for general physicians.
b. A resource for media professionals.
c. A resource for teachers and other school staff.

d. A resource for primary health care workers.
e. A resource for prison officiers.
f. How to start a survivors' group?

[28] De Leo D, Meneghel G. The elderly and suicide. Edited by Wasserman D: *Suicide - An unnecessary death.* Martin Dunitz London, 2001. pp 195-208.

[29] Akiskal H. Targeting suicide prevention to modifiable risk factors: has bipolar II been overlooked? *Acta Psychiatr Scand.* 2007; 116: 395-402.

[30] Lönnqvist J. Physical illness and suicide. Edited by Wasserman D: *Suicide - An unnecessary death.* Martin Dunitz London, 2001. pp 93-98.

[31] Kopp M, Skrabsky Á, Magyar I. Neurotic at risk and suicidal behaviour in the Hungarian population. *Acta Psychiatr Scand.* 1987; 76: 406-413.

[32] Barak A. Emotional support and suicide prevention through the Internet: A field project report. *Computers in Human Behaviour* 23 (2007) 971-984

[33] Németh E. A média szerepe az egészség-kommunikációban és a megelőzésben. Edited by Csépe A: Összefogás a depresszió ellen. Budapest. *Semmelweis Kiadó.* 2007. pp 70-87.

[34] Sher L. 'The Internet,Suicide, and Human Mental Function. *Can J Psychiatry* 2000. Apr; 45(3) 297.

[35] Biddle L, Donovan J, Hawton K, Kapur N, Gunnel D. Suicide and the Internet. *BMJ* 2008; 336; 800-802.

[36] Fekete S, Osváth P, Jegesy A. Attitudes of Hungarian students and nurses to physician assisted suicide. *J Med Ethics* 2002; 28:126.

[37] Gould M.S. Suicide and the Media. Edited by Hendin H, Mann J.J: *The Clinical Science of Suicide Prevention.* The New York Academy of Sciences, New York, 2001. pp 215-216.

[38] Moksony F. (2003) Születési régió és öngyilkosság: létezik-e az önpusztítás területi szubkultúrája? *Demográfia.* 46. No. 2-3. 2005; 203-225.

[39] Gönczi A, Márton H. Depresszióra gyanús hangulatzavar előfordulása orvostanhallgatók körében a pályára való felkészülés különböző időszakaiban. CSAKOSZ VII. Kongresszus. Budapest, 2008.02.29-03.01.

[40] Hendin H, Maltsberger J.T, Pollinger Haas A. (2003) A Physician's suicide. *Am J Psyciatry* 160:12, December. 2094-2097.

[41] http://www.webbeteg.hu

In: Internet and Suicide
Editors: L. Sher and A. Vilens

ISBN 978-1-60741-077-5

Chapter 4

WEB-BASED SUICIDE PREVENTION EDUCATION: INNOVATIONS IN RESEARCH, TRAINING, AND PRACTICE

Paul Quinnett and Aaron Baker
QPR Institute, Spokane, Washington, USA

ABSTRACT

Suicide remains a significant public health problem in the United States, and across the world. Suicide prevention gatekeeper training in the recognition and referral of potentially suicidal persons has been found to be a promising and effective public health intervention. Traditionally, gatekeeper training has been taught in classroom-based venues. This chapter explores the advantages of utilizing e-learning technologies to train more gatekeepers at lower cost and with greater learner convenience by leveraging the power of web-delivered education. Further, it reports the results of the first randomized, controlled evaluation of one gatekeeper training program. Future directions in online suicide prevention education are then discussed.

INTRODUCTION

Suicide remains a leading cause of death in the United States and in nations around the world. According the World Health Organization, of the 1.6 million deaths each year from violence, 54% are from self-inflicted injuries, far surpassing the combined deaths by homicide or collective violence (1). In the US alone, 32,637 individuals died by suicide in 2005, which is 14,513 more deaths than those individuals who died by homicide (n=18,124) that same year (2). Further, the actual rates of suicide are likely to be higher than the official statistics report (3, 4).

To stem this worldwide loss of life and to reduce medically serious self-injury, suicide prevention strategies are being researched and employed. While the number of scientifically-rigorous evaluations of potentially life-saving interventions remains small, the emerging strategy of gatekeeper training has begun to receive significant support as a safe and effective intervention. Gatekeeper training has been identified as one of a small number of promising prevention strategies (5, 6, 7, 8, 9).

A selective suicide prevention strategy, gatekeeper training is designed to improve early identification of individuals at high risk for suicide within a community and to facilitate timely referrals for mental health services (6). The premise underlying gatekeeper training is that suicidal persons often go undetected in their communities and, as a result, do not access professional assessment and potentially life-saving care. The role of the gatekeeper is to recognize suicide warning signs and to intervene to achieve a positive outcome (e.g., avert a suicide attempt by taking the person to a professional).

Those targeted for gatekeeper training include: healthcare professionals, mental health workers, school counselors, police officers, as well as those already filling natural helper roles in their communities, such as case managers, emergency services professionals, coaches, clergy, crisis line and other volunteers. Several gatekeeper training programs have emerged, and most include common elements: information on myths and misconceptions about suicide, statistical data, examples of suicide warning signs, and what referral or assessment steps to take in the event a suicidal community member is identified (7). In general, studies of gatekeeper programs have reported positive effects on attitudes and knowledge about suicide and on referral skills (10, 11, 12, 13, 14, 15).

Among these emergent gatekeeper training programs, QPR Gatekeeper Training for Suicide Prevention (16) has received several recent positive evaluations (17, 18, 19). The QPR (Question, Persuade, and Refer) Gatekeeper training program is widely-taught throughout the United States and is designed to train ordinary citizens, as well as professionals, in how to recognize suicide warning signs and to provide an immediate, bold intervention to produce a pre-determined result. The working premise of the QPR intervention is that the presence of suicide warning signs are a sufficient reason for referral to a professional able to determine suicide risk and initiate care if needed. Properly carried out, mass public health training in QPR should accomplish three interlocking goals: 1) increased awareness about suicide, its causes and its preventability, combined with the inspiration of public and political will to address suicide prevention, 2) the establishment of effective community gatekeepers available for intervention with at-risk persons, and c) a reduction in suicide attempts and completions.

The majority of suicides are completed by persons suffering from Axis I psychiatric disorders (20, 21, 22). If gatekeeper training increased the detection of untreated major depressive disorder in developed countries from below the current estimated high of 45% to just 50% (23, 24), and if these new cases were successfully treated 52% of the time (25), then the suicide rate among depressed persons in defined communities now being treated would see a reduction of 7.8% (26). On a global basis this would result in a reduction of suicide rates among clinically depressed persons from the current 15.1 per 100,000 to 13.9 per 100,000, which translates into 72,000 lives saved. However, this outcome depends on the "identification of psychiatric disorders in the general population."

To the degree suicide warning signs appear to be reliable markers for the presence of serious psychiatric disorders, their early recognition provides a unique opportunity to detect untreated cases for which symptoms may be otherwise masked, disguised, and minimized by the sufferer. Thus, brief gatekeeper training represents a potential public health case-detection method capable of identifying potentially fatal illnesses before it is "too late," (i.e., the person attempts suicide). Finally, given that suicide warning signs may be the most telling, observable, and teachable markers that a serious undetected psychiatric disorder is present and entering its final, life-threatening phase, only trained gatekeepers *already living in the general population* in close proximity to the suicidal person are in a position to recognize warning signs, act on them, and make referrals. If, in the nature of human relationships we are "our brother's keeper," then it follows that the person most likely to save us from suicide is somebody we already know.

The Challenge

Gatekeeper training, specifically QPR Gatekeeper Training, has been heavily tested in traditional classroom settings and enjoys a registered "best practice" designation in the United States (27). Evaluations of learner acquisition of knowledge gain and retention of the QPR steps are uniformly positive, and several studies support increased learner perceptions of self-efficacy and self-confidence in making an actual QPR intervention across a variety of adult learner populations and professional groups (17, 18, 19).

Despite these positive findings and the broad acceptance of gatekeeper training, availability and affordability of training remains a challenge. While the training is increasingly accessible in the United States, it is less so in other countries. Nevertheless, the efforts of more than 4,000 instructors trained and certified in the QPR train-the-trainer model since program inception in 1995, had produced approximately 650,000 gatekeepers by mid-year in 2008. Currently, approximately 10,000 gatekeepers per month are trained in the US, Canada, Australia, Korea and New Zealand. While these numbers may sound impressive, suicide remains a rare event and rare events are not only difficult to predict, but difficult to prevent. For example, it is not known how many trained gatekeepers are required for a defined community of 100,000 persons to prevent a single suicide. Moreover, exactly what warning signs gatekeepers should be taught to recognize and respond to when exhibited by suicidal community members remains poorly understood (28). While the number of gatekeepers trained each month by all gatekeeper training programs may be growing, it is unknown how many gatekeepers will be needed to intervene before some 25 million people worldwide attempt suicide over the next 12 months (1).

In this chapter we will define a "suicide event" as either a non-fatal or fatal suicide attempt (29). Not all suicide attempts lead to death but, all suicide completions involve an attempt. Collectively, then, people who experience a suicide event represent a more at-risk group for medical injury and death than do those who only think about suicide and communicate suicide desire or intent without having demonstrated a capacity for self-injury (30). Moreover, suicide attempt behavior is often a precursor to eventual death by suicide, and risk increases with age (29). From the perspective of cost-benefit analysis, preventing a non-fatal suicide attempt may not result in the same community benefit and cost-savings as preventing a suicide completion. However, there is merit in the argument that the gatekeeper's mission is broader than preventing completed suicides, and includes not only reducing self-inflicted non-fatal injuries, but also suicide completions and some homicides, including those for which a murder-suicide may have been planned.

How Many Suicide Prevention Gatekeepers do we Need?

The authors are unaware of any available formula or study that might answer the question of how many gatekeepers a given community might need to lower its rates of suicide attempts and completions. If it is true that gatekeepers play a preexisting role in the suicidal person's life then, from a public health perspective, many millions of gatekeepers need to be trained. Since we can calculate the cost to treat self-inflicted medical injuries, the cost of disability due to such injuries, and the loss to the economy of an age-adjusted life lost, perhaps a more useful question might be, "How many gatekeepers need to be trained to prevent a single suicide event? This question could be reduced to a formula, as follows:

- What is the ratio of NGNT to prevent 1 SuiE?
- Where number of gatekeepers needed to train = NGNT
- Where one suicide event (non-fatal or fatal outcome) = 1 SuiE

Whatever this number might be, it is presumed at present that the more gatekeepers who are trained in any community, the more probable it is that one of them will be in a position to recognize suicide warning signs in someone he or she knows and to initiate a helpful response. Clearly, some gatekeepers are in greater strategic positions to recognize and refer suicidal persons relative to high risk populations with whom they interact on a frequent basis. The return on investment for training these key persons should be calculable. However, as a broad public health initiative, if the cost to train gatekeepers can be made sufficiently affordable, then large numbers of gatekeepers could be trained to "saturate" both high and relatively low risk populations, thus creating more "eyes on the problem" for what, fortunately, remains a rare event.

Leveraging the Power of the Web

Given the cost of traditional classroom delivery of gatekeeper training, perhaps the only conceivable way to carry out such a massive public health educational project would be to harness the power of the digital age and deliver gatekeeper training over the internet using developing educational technology. The problem of suicide is clearly global, and only the internet can provide a global solution.

Contemporary distance learning has been defined in several ways. Greenberg (31) defines distance learning as "a planned teaching/learning experience that uses a wide spectrum of technologies to reach learners at a distance and is designed to encourage learner interaction and certification of learning." Teaster and Blieszner (32) describe distance learning by the relationship of teacher to learner, in that they are "separate in space and possibly time," while

Keegan (33) defines distance education and training by the technological separation of teacher and learner which frees the student from the necessity of traveling to "a fixed place, at a fixed time, to meet a fixed person, in order to be trained."

Distance learning is growing globally as country after country comes to the same realization: the cost of brick and mortar buildings, transportation, and the availability of expert instructors to train tens of thousands of people, some living in remote areas, is fundamentally impossible. As bandwidth and connectivity grow, developing countries are turning to state run distance learning educational programs to leapfrog infrastructure costs and to reach what have historically been unreachable students (34).

To explore the possibility of training thousands of suicide prevention gatekeepers a day around the globe instead of thousands a month, a review of the outcome literature was undertaken to examine the potential value of what has variously been called e-learning, distance learning, online learning, or Web-based education.

Time Savings

In a comprehensive review of more than 40 studies, Fletcher (35), found a reduction in time spent by e-learning students to master the same material as traditional classroom-based students, ranged from 20-80 percent, with most savings between 40-60 percent. These findings have been confirmed by a number of other researchers as well (36, 37, 38, 39, 40). It is also important to note that none of the investigators found a decrease in training effectiveness in terms of retention and transfer of learning.

Convenience

As the importance of suicide prevention education and gatekeeper training grows, service organizations with 24/7 staff, multiple locations, or rural and remote sites may be unable to deliver classroom-based gatekeeper training in a cost-effective fashion. Using high-speed connections, standardized gatekeeper training content can be delivered digitally to anyone, in any place, at any time, and even on demand when needed. Some rural and remote areas can only be accessed using asynchronous delivery of training across time zones. Finally, interactive programs can be built to provide self-paced learning, and links to emergency and crisis response services can be programmed into the training.

Cost and Return on Investment

Cost alone for traditional classroom based gatekeeper training may prohibit what many feel should be mandatory training to prevent suicide. Delivery of the same training online could reduce these costs to an acceptable level, relative to the level of perceived risk of preventing an adverse event. As the acceptability of e-learning grows, and as the cost of delivery goes down, leaders should find a greater potential return on investment for suicide prevention education. This perceived return could be further increased if preventing suicide can be reframed as a community or consumer health and safety issue.

Acceptance of e-learning has also shown reductions in associated travel and entertainment costs associated with traditional training, in the range of at least 50 percent, and as high as 80 percent (40, 41, 42, 43) - no small savings for budget-minded leaders responsible for public health education. Given these savings, continued justification for traditional classroom gatekeeper training is increasingly difficult to defend.

Also, because e-learning can be asynchronous, flexible, self-paced, customized for specific populations, and taken anywhere at anytime, it is perfectly suited for training large numbers of employees or students in multi-site organizations, those with 24/7 employee shifts, and those with staff working in their homes, and at an acceptable price point. With suicide rates highest in rural and frontier America (2), once sufficient bandwidth becomes available in these remote areas, perhaps the only practical, cost-effective approach to gatekeeper training will be through the Web, as all other options are far too costly, inconvenient, and impractical.

Standardized Training Delivered in a Standardized Fashion

In the litigious environment in which many public safety, educational, service and treatment provider organizations now find themselves, makes it especially important that suicide prevention gatekeeper training be: a) evidence-based, b) standardized from presentation to presentation, and c) able to produce measurable and reportable relevant outcomes.

There is high potential for variations among "live" performances in on-site training. Adams (37) found that classroom instructor delivery variance averaged as much as 59% from one presentation to another. For a subject matter as critical to saving lives as gatekeeper training, it is important to minimize any errors in content delivery in terms of what, exactly, learners learned.

A summary of the research comparing e-learning verses traditional instruction found that e-learning students:

- Demonstrated a 50% higher content retention
- Demonstrated 56% greater gains in learning
- Enjoyed a 60% faster learning curve
- Experienced consistency in learning (60% improvement)
- Experienced consistency of presentation (40% improvement)
- Enjoyed a more efficient delivery of information (up to 70% faster for e-learning)

Overall, e-learning achieves consistently better results when compared to traditional classroom settings. It also provides considerable savings in time, training delivery, direct transportation costs, money, and "hassle-factors" (e.g., parking, congested city travel, baby-sitting, etc.). Similar to effective medical services, public health education to prevent suicide must be accessible, available, affordable, and adequate to the meet the educational goal. Only internet based gatekeeper training seems able to meet these four requirements.

Online QPR Gatekeeper Training: A Standard Core Program with Customization

The QPR Gatekeeper Training for Suicide Prevention program has been entirely digitized and programmed for delivery online over the internet to individual participants. The training is delivered in a media-rich blend of video, text, interactive components, and voice-over lecture. Pre-post survey, quiz, and evaluation components require learner participation to complete and earn a printable certificate of course completion. Available over any high-speed internet connection, or assisted by a video rich web-enabled CD-ROM for dial up learners, the program is delivered with perfect fidelity each time. Host organizations can tailor and customize elements of the program with regard to referral and resource information (e.g., local crisis telephone numbers, maps to counseling centers, and other key instructions to gatekeepers regarding organizational policy and procedures). These elements are included in the online program to enhance participant perceptions of self-confidence and self-efficacy in carrying out the QPR intervention.

Each gatekeeper who is trained also has the option of exploring areas of special interest, if desired - text files on high risk groups, Web links to resources, and free telephone consultation with certified crisis response hotlines. To accommodate individual learning, participants may enter and leave the program as necessary or convenient and return to it at any time (i.e., the computer "remembers" where the learner left off and returns the participant to the "next module" to be completed).

Once a learning account is activated using a unique user ID and password, review and retraining is available for three years. A certificate and a wallet card highlighting the three QPR steps are printable. Upon completion of the 12 modules, learners receive an immediate email asking if they would like to conduct an "enriched review" of the training program. This 12-page text file reviews, reinforces, and expands upon the training experience and includes frequently asked questions. Upon completion of the enriched program, learners receive a courtesy email to review its content at six weeks, 46 weeks, and three years after opening the learning account. The learner's access codes are included in the courtesy email to make retraining or review accessible.

Blending Face-to-Face Support with Online Training

To bolster the QPR online learning experience, qualified professionals (including Certified QPR Instructors) may conduct follow up face-to-face training sessions in order to facilitate question and answer periods, role-plays practice sessions, and to review organizational policies and procedures regarding referral resources and mechanisms.

Cultural Adaptation and Customization

Suicide events occur in cultural, social, religious, ethic and racial contexts. Therefore, customization of the "look and feel" of QPR training is critical to its wide acceptance and its potential to break down the fear, stigma, and taboos surrounding suicidal behavior. Like any consumer product, the acceptance of gatekeeper training depends, in large part, on individual receptivity to the intended public health message.

To assist with stakeholder acceptance of QPR training, and with the help of the Aberdeen Area Indian Health Service, the QPR video was re-shot with all Native American people, symbols, stories and music. This nine minute review of QPR and its purpose precedes the standard 21-slide core curriculum required in the standard delivery program. Once programmed into the online e-learning format, American Indians and First Nations people from all over North America are now able to take QPR training online anytime and anywhere that a high-speed internet connection is accessible. Upon viewing the video content, as well as the visual images, learners see the faces and hear the names of other Indian peoples telling their stories and expressing their views about suicide and the need for prevention education. Strong "brand recognition" with the option to customize non core elements of the evidence-based content is seen as a pathway to greater acceptance of the QPR training and intervention.

The Australian Experiment

To date there have been no reported evaluations of an online delivery of suicide prevention gatekeeper training. In the summer of 2007, the Salvation Army in Australia and the QPR Institute in the United States formed a partnership to customize and test the *QPR Gatekeeper Training for Suicide Prevention* program with participants throughout Australia, entirely over the internet. The U.S. version of the online QPR training program was customized for the Australian participants, as the Salvation Army-Australia videotaped new visual material, inserted relevant facts, web sites, voice-over sections, and added national hotlines and other Australian suicide prevention resources to the program in order to customize the program for cultural appropriateness and relevance.

For this evaluation, a total of 158 Salvation Army employees/volunteers were recruited by Salvation Army-Australia to participate in the Australian-customized online QPR Gatekeeper Training evaluation. All 158 participants were randomly assigned to one of two groups; a training (experimental) group or a control group. Of the initial 158 participants, 107 completed the first phase of the evaluation process, 56 in the training group, and 51 in the control group.

The evaluation was completed entirely by e-communications, through which the evaluation team sent out introductory information to participants. At an agreed upon start time, all 158 participants were simultaneously sent instructions, as well as hyperlinks to the online pre-training surveys. The online survey consisted of a 15-item multiple choice knowledge-based quiz, seven self-efficacy items designed to assess participant perceived efficacy related to intervening with suicidal people, and three suicide-related behavioral self-report items inquiring about how many times the participant had interacted with a suicidal person in the past six months. Upon completion of the pre-training survey, the training group participants were emailed a hyperlink to the customized QPR Australia online gatekeeper training program. After completing the QPR Gatekeeper Training, the training group participants again completed the training survey (knowledge quiz, and self-efficacy items).

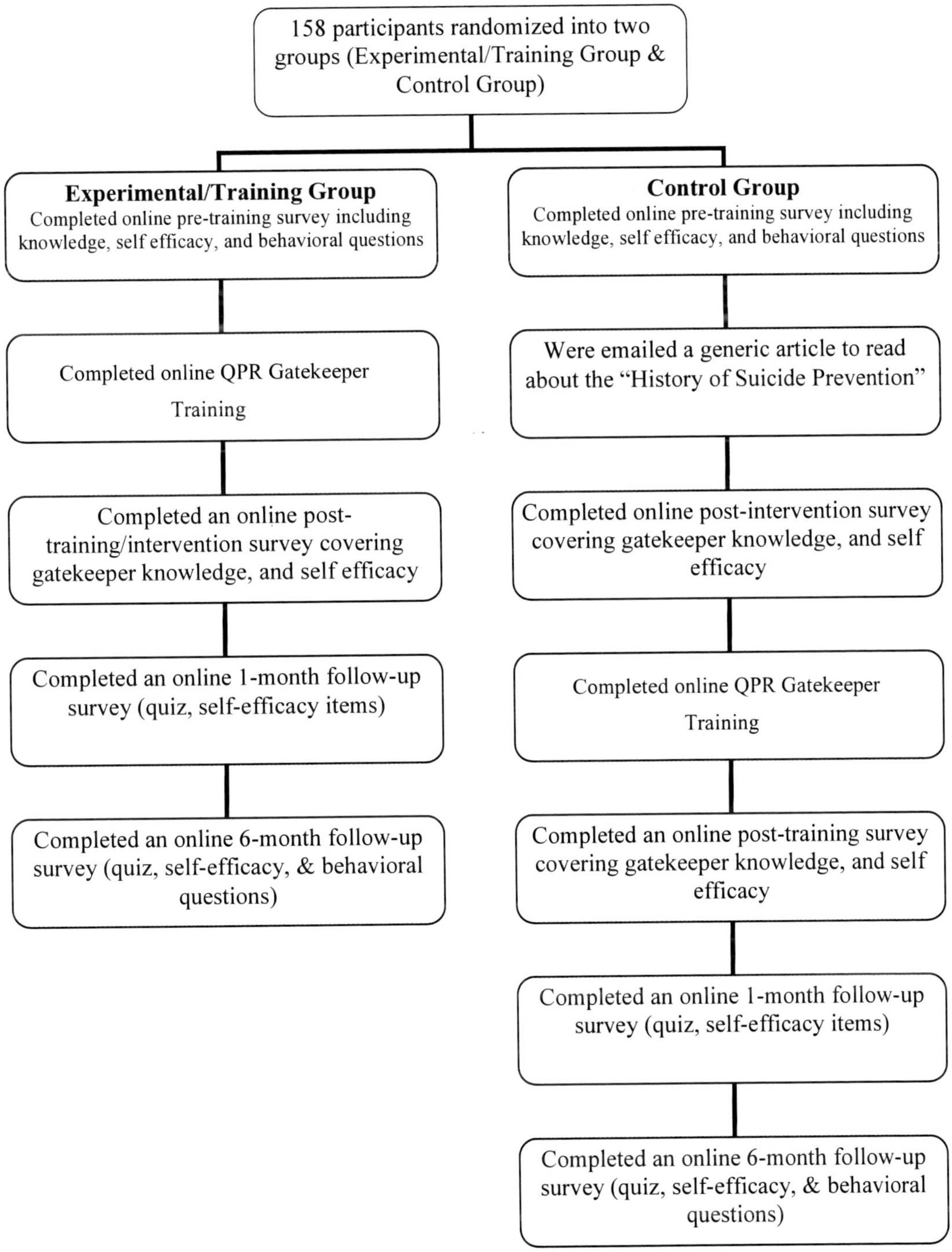

Figure 1. Flowchart of the On-line QPR Gatekeeper Training Evaluation.

Upon completion of the pre-training survey, participants in the control group were emailed a 10-page article about the "History of Suicide Prevention" with the request that they read it before they would be supplied with a hyperlink to the online QPR Australia Gatekeeper Training. The 10-page article contained generic information about the history of suicide prevention and did not contain information that would influence the survey measures used in the study. Once the control group participants had competed both reading the article and responding to the online post-intervention survey (which again contained the same knowledge quiz and self-efficacy items), they were emailed a hyperlink to the QPR Gatekeeper Training. Since the control group received the QPR Gatekeeper Training (the experimental intervention) after they completed the control intervention, the two groups were then combined into one large experimental group for the 1-month and 6-month follow-up evaluation intervals. In the follow-up stages, all participants were emailed a hyperlink to the same survey they had completed at each stage of the evaluation. Figure 1 provides a flowchart for the experimental design and procedures.

RESULTS OF THE EVALUATION

Analysis of the results of this evaluation found that both groups produced equal scores at baseline on the knowledge quiz and self-efficacy items (See Table 1), suggesting that they were of equal knowledge and self-efficacy prior to receiving their respective interventions. Analysis of the training and control group differences after the initial intervention (online QPR Gatekeeper Training vs. reading a 10-page history of suicide prevention article) found statistically significant pre- to post-intervention mean differences on the 15-item knowledge-based quiz for the training group, but not for the control group. Participants who completed the online QPR Gatekeeper Training program (training group) had a mean score on the 15-item knowledge quiz that was 1.96 points greater than the control group's knowledge quiz mean score. The Cohen's *d* effect size for this difference was 1.13, indicating a "very large" effect size (44). Table 1 presents the between-group differences on the knowledge quiz.

Table 2 presents the differences on the knowledge quiz from pre-training to post-intervention within each group for the training and control groups. The training group exhibited a statistically significant improvement in knowledge quiz scores from pre-training to post training (an increase of 2.14 points), whereas the control group exhibited non-significant improvement on the knowledge quiz (an increase of 0.24). Again, a "very large" effect size (*d*= 1.22) was found for the training group's increase in knowledge from the pre-training interval to the post-training interval.

Table 1. Training Group vs. Control Group on Knowledge Quiz Performance Pre- and Post-Intervention, Post-Training (all), 1 month & 6 month follow up

	Training Group	Control Group	Mean Difference	F-score	p	Effect size Cohen's *d*
Pre-Training Quiz	11.00	10.90	0.10	0.092	.762	--------
Post-Intervention Quiz	13.14	11.18	1.96	32.88	.000	1.13

Note: n=106 (Training Group n=56, Control Group n=50).

Table 2. Pre- to Post-Intervention Knowledge Quiz Results

	Pre-Training Quiz	Post-Intervention Quiz	Mean Change	t-score	p	Effect size Cohen's *d*
Training Group	11.00	13.14	2.14	-9.68	.000	1.22
Control Group	10.94	11.18	0.24	-1.23	.224	-------

Table 3 displays the quiz scores for *all* participants at each stage of the evaluation and compares those scores to the mean scores at the previous stage. There is a statistically significant improvement in the suicide prevention quiz scores from the pre-training stage to after both groups completed the QPR Gatekeeper Training, which is a "very large" effect size. From these results, one can observe a significant decrease in the quiz scores as the participants reach the follow-up stages of the evaluation. Thus, as would be expected, there is evidence of a decrease in knowledge after the initial training effects. Yet, when the differences are examined between the participants' pre-training quiz scores and 6-month follow-up quiz scores (calculated for the 52 participants who completed both stages), a statistically significant, "medium" effect size, increase in quiz scores is still observable. This finding suggests a noticeable and enduring increase in suicide prevention knowledge over time.

Based on the finding that the training group exhibited greater knowledge of suicide and suicide prevention (both relative to their pre-training scores and those of a control group) after receiving the online QPR Gatekeeper Training, the evaluators concluded there is clear evidence that the online QPR Gatekeeper Training increases an individual's knowledge and awareness about suicide in Australia: its prevalence, possible contributing risk factors, and potentially helpful preventative interventions.

Table 3. All Participant Quiz Scores at the Four Stages of the Evaluation

Pre-Training Quiz	Post-Training Quiz	Mean Change	t-score	p	Effect size Cohen's *d*
10.95	13.28	2.33	-14.50	.000	1.44
Post-Training Quiz	1 Month Follow Up	Mean Change	t-score	p	Effect size Cohen's *d*
13.50	12.45	-1.05	4.473	.000	0.64
1 Month Follow Up	6 Month Follow Up	Mean Change	t-score	p	Effect size Cohen's *d*
12.64	12.08	-0.56	1.938	.060	------
Post-Training Quiz	6 Month Follow Up	Mean Change	t-score	p	Effect size Cohen's *d*
13.70	11.92	-17.78	6.044	.000	1.03
Pre-Training Quiz	6 Month Follow Up	Mean Change	t-score	p	Effect size Cohen's *d*
11.15	11.92	0.77	-2.260	.028	0.41

PERCEIVED SELF-EFFICACY

As previously mentioned, participants were also asked to answer seven self-efficacy items related to their self-perceptions about intervening with a suicidal individual. Statistically significant differences were found between the two groups (training and control) for six of the seven items after the initial intervention. Effect sizes ranged from "large" to "very large" on these items, with one exception. A "medium" effect size was found for the sixth self-efficacy item, "*I don't think I can prevent someone from suicide.*" (See Table 4).

Table 4. Training vs. Control group differences Post-Intervention for the 7 Self-Efficacy Items

Self-Efficacy Items	Training Group	Control Group	Mean Change	F	p	Effect Size (Cohen's *d*)
Item 1: *If someone I knew was showing signs of suicide, I would directly raise the question of suicide with them.*	4.86	4.14	0.72	23.997	.000	0.96
Item 2: *If a person's words and/or behavior suggest the possibility of suicide, I would ask the person directly if he/she is thinking about suicide*	4.75	4.04	0.71	22.92	.000	0.94
Item 3: *If someone told me they were thinking of suicide, I would intervene*	4.95	4.34	0.61	45.799	.000	1.33
Item 4: *If I became aware that somebody had suicidal thoughts and feelings over the next few months, I would try to find help for this person*	4.82	4.66	0.16	1.648	.202	--------
Item 5: *I feel confident in my ability to help a suicidal person*	4.54	3.70	0.84	36.596	.000	1.19
Items 6: *I don't think I can prevent someone from suicide* [1]	4.34	3.68	0.66	11.482	.000	0.73
Item 7: *I don't feel competent to help a person at risk of suicide* [1]	4.46	3.66	0.80	25.699	.000	1.00

Note: All 7 items were scored on a 1-5 Likert scale, where 1=Strongly Disagree, 2=Disagree, 3=Neutral, 4=Agree, and 5=Strongly Agree.

[1] Items 6 and 7 are reverse scored.

Table 5. Pre-Training to Post-Training Changes on the Self-Efficacy Items for the Training Group

Self-Efficacy Items	Pre-Mean	Post-Mean	Mean Change	t-score	p	Effect Size (Cohen's *d*)
Item 1: *If someone I knew was showing signs of suicide, I would directly raise the question of suicide with them.*	4.00	4.86	0.86	-7.266	.000	1.05
Item 2: *If a person's words and/or behavior suggest the possibility of suicide, I would ask the person directly if he/she is thinking about suicide*	4.05	4.75	0.70	-6.123	.000	0.92
Item 3: *If someone told me they were thinking of suicide, I would intervene*	4.32	4.95	0.63	-6.660	.000	1.24
Item 4: *If I became aware that somebody had suicidal thoughts and feelings over the next few months, I would try to find help for this person*	4.50	4.82	0.32	-2.192	.033	0.40
Item 5: *I feel confident in my ability to help a suicidal person*	3.38	4.54	1.16	-8.803	.000	1.48
Items 6: *I don't think I can prevent someone from suicide* [1]	3.34	4.34	1.00	-6.831	.000	1.05
Item 7: *I don't feel competent to help a person at risk of suicide* [1]	3.43	4.46	1.03	-6.874	.000	1.25

Note: All 7 items were scored on a 1-5 Likert scale, where 1=Strongly Disagree, 2=Disagree, 3=Neutral, 4=Agree, and 5=Strongly Agree.

[1] Items 6 and 7 are reverse scored.

Increases in self-efficacy ratings for the training group were seen from the pre-training to post-training period for all seven of the self-efficacy items. Effect sizes ranged from "medium" for item 4; to "large" for items 1, 2, and 6; to "very large" for items 3, 5, and 7, (See Table 5).

Table 6. Pre-Training to Post-Intervention Changes on Self-Efficacy Items for the Control Group

Self-Efficacy Items	Pre-Mean	Post-Mean	Mean Change	t-score	p	Effect Size (Cohen's *d*)
Item 1: *If someone I knew was showing signs of suicide, I would directly raise the question of suicide with them.*	4.04	4.14	0.10	-1.043	.302	------
Item 2: *If a person's words and/or behavior suggest the possibility of suicide, I would ask the person directly if he/she is thinking about suicide*	4.06	4.04	-0.02	0.159	.875	------
Item 3: *If someone told me they were thinking of suicide, I would intervene*	4.40	4.34	-0.06	0.829	.411	------
Item 4: *If I became aware that somebody had suicidal thoughts and feelings over the next few months, I would try to find help for this person*	4.68	4.66	-0.02	0.256	.799	------
Item 5: *I feel confident in my ability to help a suicidal person*	3.36	3.70	0.34	-3.226	.002	0.37
Items 6: *I don't think I can prevent someone from suicide* [1]	3.44	3.68	0.24	-1.950	.057	------
Item 7: *I don't feel competent to help a person at risk of suicide* [1]	3.46	3.66	0.20	-1.698	.096	------

Note: All 7 items were scored on a 1-5 Likert scale, where 1=Strongly Disagree, 2=Disagree, 3=Neutral, 4=Agree, and 5=Strongly Agree.

[1] Items 6 and 7 are reverse scored.

The control group exhibited a statistically significant increase in self-efficacy ratings on Item 5, "I feel confident in my ability to help a suicidal person," yet there were no significant changes in ratings across any other self-efficacy items. It is interesting to note that on Items 2, 3 and 4, the control group's mean rating decreased after reading the presumably neutral 10-page "History of Suicide Prevention" (See Table 6).

Analysis across all participants at each stage of the evaluation found a statistically significant increase in self-efficacy from pre-training to post training, with item 4 exhibiting a "small" effect size; item 1 exhibiting a "medium" effect size; items 2, 3, and 6 exhibiting "large" effect sizes; and items 5 and 7 exhibiting a "very large" effect size. Self-Efficacy items 3, 5, and 6 exhibited significant decreases from the post training stage to the 1-month follow-up stage, with the largest effect size for this decrease being "medium," for item 3. There were no further significant decreases in perceived self-efficacy by the participants from the 1-month follow-up to the 6-month follow-up.

Likely the most important comparison between stages of the evaluation concerns examination of the differences between participants' perceived self-efficacy at pre-training and their perceptions at the 6-month follow-up. As this is the longest-term assessment interval, it likely demonstrates any lasting impact of the training on participants' self-efficacy in intervening with suicidal individuals. Six of the seven self-efficacy items maintained statistically significant increases from pre-training to the 6-month follow-up. Only self-efficacy item 4 did not exhibit any significant increases. "Medium" effect sizes were found for item 1, 2, 3, and 6, while item 7 exhibited a "large" effect size, and item 5 exhibited a "very large" effect size from pre-training to 6-month follow-up.

Overall, training group participants exhibited improved self-efficacy ratings on all seven items related to their perceived ability to intervene with a suicidal individual after completing the online QPR Gatekeeper Training. By contrast, Control Group participants only exhibited a "small" effect size improvement on item 5. Thus, there is evidence that the online QPR Gatekeeper Training program increases individuals' perceived self-efficacy in intervening with a suicidal individual.

CHANGES IN BEHAVIOR BY PARTICIPANTS

In the pre-training survey, participants were asked three questions about their personal experience with suicidal individuals in the previous six months. These same three questions were asked again at the 6-month follow-up survey. The three questions were:

(1) How many times in the past 6 months have you thought a person's behavior might indicate he/she was considering suicide?
(2) How many times in the past 6 months have you asked a person whether he/she was considering suicide?
(3) In the past 6 months, how many people did you personally refer to appropriate professional services because you were concerned that they might be suicidal?

Analysis of the means on these three items found that for items 2 and 3 there were statistically significant increases. The effect size for the increase mean score on these two items was "small." (See Table 7).

At the 6-month follow-up participants were asked questions about their application of the QPR Gatekeeper Training since they had completed the training six months earlier. Of particular note is an item related to the participant raising others' awareness and knowledge about suicide. Of the 53 participants who answered the question, 44 (83%) stated they "Agree" or "Strongly Agree" that they had increased others' awareness and knowledge. (See Table 8) Participants reported talking to a mean number of 5.42 people about the QPR Gatekeeper Training. By taking the 53 participants who reported they talked to others about the QPR Gatekeeper Training and multiplying that number by the mean 5.42 people they reported talking to, we can estimate that 287 have been exposed, to some degree, to gatekeeper interventions.

Table 7. Pre-Training vs. 6-Month Follow-up for the 3 Behavioral Intervention Questions

	Pre-Training	6-Month Follow-Up	t	p	Effect Size (Cohen's *d*)
How many times in the past 6 months have you thought a person's behavior might indicate he/she was considering suicide?[1]	1.90	1.94	-0.146	.884	--------
How many times in the past 6 months have you asked a person whether he/she was considering suicide?[2]	1.35	1.98	-3.444	.001	0.28
In the past 6 months, how many people did you personally refer to appropriate professional services because you were concerned that they might be suicidal?[1]	1.08	1.61	-2.588	.013	0.30

Note: [1] n=51, [2] n=52

Table 8. 6-month follow-up question: "Over the last 6 months I have increased others' general awareness and knowledge of suicide"

	N	Percentage
Disagree	4	7.5%
Neutral	5	9.4%
Agree	40	75.5%
Strongly Agree	4	7.5%

Discussion of Results of this Study

Overall, this initial evaluation of a suicide prevention gatekeeper training program delivered entirely via e-learning technologies can be considered successful. Statistically significant increases in knowledge of suicide prevention, as well as perceived self-efficacy in intervening with a suicidal individual, were found for those participants who received the online QPR Gatekeeper Training when compared to those participants who received the control intervention. One self-efficacy item did not exhibit any significant differences between the training and control groups at the post intervention interval; item 4 (*"If I became aware that somebody had suicidal thoughts and feelings over the next few months, I would try to find help for this person"*). It is hypothesized that the wording of this question, given its Good Samaritan implications, was such that most participants would endorse it positively (given that individuals who tend to be associated with an organization such as the Salvation

Army are likely to be caring individuals). Thus, it is not surprising that no significant differences were found between the two groups on this item. Perhaps this question would discriminate between groups in some audiences, but not in others.

The finding that participants reported they more frequently asked someone about suicide and referred him or her to professional services after receiving the gatekeeper training is a very significant result from this evaluation. It suggests that, not only do people trained in QPR online learn something, but they apply the acquired intervention in real life situations. Of particular interest is the fact that, on average, each participant discussed the QPR Gatekeeper Training with 5.42 people. In this study, this finding equates to 287 additional people being exposed to the concept of gatekeeper training and at least some of its inherent educational content. This is a significant impact on population awareness, from just 53 individuals who completed the training. If this finding were replicated for the 650,000 people trained in QPR as of summer 2008, it would translate into approximately 3.5 million lives having been touched by the suicide prevention message as delivered by trained gatekeepers.

PROBLEMS ENCOUNTERED

While the results of this single evaluation are promising, there were some problems encountered during its implementation. These problems included:

- Slow internet connection speeds, leading to a failure of large video files to load quickly for some participants
- Inadequate computer power to handle the rich multimedia format, leading to failure in delivery of any of the training content
- Email communications failures, e.g., some correspondences with evaluators, or notifications to begin training were lost in cyberspace between the United States and Australia

Overall, however, the delivery of the program proceeded smoothly. While some technical problems were significant and frustrating (for example some participants had set aside personal and professional time to complete the training and yet could not do so), the evaluation team's computer expert, working with his counterpart in Australia in real-time, made adjustments to the program and fixed some of the problems encountered. With practice and more experience in online training, and perhaps with better instructions and greater computer literacy among learners, it is anticipated that the complications and problems encountered in this first test can be avoided in the future.

Another significant lesson learned was the importance of participant knowledge and experience with computers and internet technologies. The evaluation team found that the participants who were well versed in email applications and had sufficient skills to negotiate the internet and hyperlinked files, had few complaints or problems with the program. Conversely, those participants with less computer and internet technology experience encountered more difficulties in accessing the online surveys and the online training program. However, the evaluation team was, in many cases, able to assist with program entry, adjustment, and exit points during training completion.

CONCLUSION

Clear evidence now exists that rates for suicide and other forms of violence can be significantly reduced through an educational systems approach to suicide risk reduction (45). Gatekeeper training appears to be one of the more promising strategies to prevent premature death or injury by suicidal behaviors, especially when integrated into a medically-competent system of emergency response and ongoing care, as has been demonstrated with CPR training (46). In order to further advance the underlying goal and mission of gatekeeper training, new avenues need to be pursued in order to further facilitate the education of the general public about suicide. The authors posit that e-learning technologies are one such avenue since they allow large audiences to access training at acceptable costs anywhere broadband connections are available.

The Australian QPR evaluation reported here provides initial support for the use of such e-learning technologies in suicide prevention education. Results found significant increases in suicide prevention knowledge, perceived self-efficacy in helping a suicidal individual, as well as increases in actual suicide prevention behaviors (asking others about suicide and referring for professional services). With approximately 2,700 people dying each day by suicide around the world, and representing 54% of all violent deaths (1), harnessing the educational power of e-learning technologies to train suicide prevention gatekeepers has never been more timely, relevant or important.

Given that a variety of distance learning studies have shown as much as a 60% savings for online training, greater convenience in learning, and no significant loss in educational benefit, the authors conclude that the Australian QPR Gatekeeper Training evaluation represents a promising and positive breakthrough in suicide prevention education. Specifically, it represents effective gatekeeper training for those people who fill critical roles in the social matrix and fabric of a defined community. The program might be especially beneficial if delivered to all gatekeeper groups identified in national strategies (e.g., clergy, police officers, school teachers, child welfare workers, geriatric case managers, youth counselors), and dozens of other groups who fill positions of frequent contact with potentially at-risk persons.

It is of note that, to date, evaluation of advanced online suicide prevention training for first responders and healthcare professionals (who are in need of suicide risk detection, assessment, and management knowledge and skills) has not been attempted. However, beginning in the fall of 2008, the QPR Institute, in partnership with Essential Learning Inc., (a national provider of online behavioral healthcare training), will launch a series of continuing education-approved suicide prevention courses targeted at a wide variety of community mental health stakeholders and professional level gatekeepers. Included in this targeted training effort are child welfare workers, emergency response professionals, elder service case managers, mental health and substance abuse counselors, nurses, psychologists, and social workers.

Future studies of online gatekeeper training, as well as advanced suicide prevention educational programs, should compare the online delivery of such programs with traditional classroom-based training. Such a comparison is needed to ascertain whether the advantages of increased learning, time savings, and cost savings that have been found in other e-learning trainings, hold up for suicide prevention education. Blended training, combining some online learning with face-to-face practice and interactive skill training, also needs to be tested and evaluated. There may be an ideal combination of knowledge acquisition and skill-based training that produces the desired outcome: demonstrable behavioral competencies in suicide prevention, intervention, assessment and treatment of suicidal consumers. The current online QPR Gatekeeper Training program does include a downloadable role-play option and instructions in how to practice the intervention with a colleague, friend or family member. However, no research has been conducted on the possible benefit of such rehearsal behaviors.

Finally, the authors assert that suicide prevention is too important to be left to traditional, slow-evolving, monolithic, institutionalized classroom models of education and training. Absent an aggressive research and technology-transfer agenda to evaluate the merits of e-learning technologies in the prevention of suicide, lives may be unnecessarily lost.

Acknowledgment

The authors are extremely grateful to Alan Staines and Wilma Gallet from the Australian Salvation Army for their assistance in the coordination the QPR Australia evaluation. Without their assistance and leadership the evaluation could never have happened. The authors would also like to acknowledge the essential work of Brian Quinnett and Matt Brown in the implementation of the QPR Australia evaluation. The authors wish to thank Monica Matthieu and Julianna Machell for their assistance in the editing and shaping of this chapter.

References

[1] Institute of Medicine: Violence Prevention in Low- and Middle-income Countries: Finding a Place on the Global Agenda. Washington, DC: The National Academies Press. 2008.

[2] Center for Disease Control: *Deaths: final data for 2005. National Vital Statistics Reports 2008;* 56: Retrieved on July 25, 2008 from http://www.cdc.gov/nchs/data/nvsr/nvsr56/nvsr56_10.pdf

[3] O'Carroll PW: Validity and reliability of suicide mortality data. *Suicide Life Threat Behav* 1989; 19:1-16.

[4] O'Donnell, I, & Farmer, R: The limitations of official suicide statistics. *Br J Psychiatry* 1995; 166:458-461.

[5] White J, Jodoin N: *Before-the-fact interventions: A manual of best practices in youth suicide prevention.* Vancouver, BC: Suicide Prevention Information and Resource Centre of British Columbia 1998.

[6] Centers for Disease Control. (1992). *Youth suicide and prevention programs: A resource guide.* Atlanta: Centers for Disease Control.

[7] Gould MS, Kramer RA: Youth suicide prevention. *Suicide Life Threat Behav* 2001; 31(suppl):6–31.

[8] Guo B, Harstall C: *Efficacy of suicide prevention programs for children and youth.* Edmonton, AB: Alberta Heritage Foundation for Medical Research 2002.

[9] U.S. Department of Health and Human Services, Public Health Service: *National strategy for suicide prevention: Goals and objectives for action.* Rockville, MD: Author, 2001.

[10] Eggert, LL, Randell BR, Thompson EA, & Johnson CL: *Washington State Youth Suicide Prevention Program: Report of activities.* Seattle, WA: University of Washington, 1997

[11] Garland AF, Zigler E: Adolescent suicide prevention: current research and social policy implications. *Am Psychol* 1993; 48:169-182.

[12] King KA, Smith J: Project SOAR: A training program to increase school counselors' knowledge and confidence regarding suicide prevention and intervention. *J Sch Health* 2000; 70:402-407.

[13] Ramsey R, Tanney B, Tierney R, Lang W: *Suicide intervention handbook.* Calgary, Alberta Canada: Living Works Education, 1994.

[14] Shaffer D, Garland A, Gould M, Fisher P, Trautman P: Preventing teenage suicide: a critical review. *J Am Acad Child Adolesc Psychiatry* 1988; 27: 675-687.

[15] Tierney RJ: Suicide intervention training evaluation: a preliminary report. *Crisis* 1994; 15:69-76.

[16] Quinnett P: QPR: *Certified QPT Gatekeeper instructors training manual.* Spokane, WA: QPR Institute, 1995.

[17] Cross W, Matthieu MM, Cerel J, Knox KL: Proximate outcomes of gatekeeper training for suicide prevention in the workplace. *Suicide Life Threat Behav* 2007; 37:659-670.

[18] Wyman PA, Brown CH, Inman J, Cross W, Schmeelk-Cone K, Jing G, Pena J: Randomized trial of a gatekeeper program for youth suicide prevention: Impact on knowledge, attitudes and referral behaviors of school staff. *J Consult Clin Psychol* 2008; 76:104-115.

[19] Matthieu MM, Cross W, Batres AR, Flora CM, Knox KL: Evaluation of gatekeeper training for suicide prevention in veterans'. *Archives of Suicide Research* 2008; 12:148-154.

[20] Moscicki EK. Epidemiology of completed and attempted suicide: toward a framework for prevention. *Clinical Neuroscience Research* 2001; 1:310-323.

[21] Beautrais AL, Joyce PR, Mulder RT, Fergusson DM, Deavoll BJ, Nightingale SK: Prevalence and comorbidity of mental disorders in persons making serious suicide attempts: a case-control study. *Am J Psychiatry* 1996; 153:1009-1014.

[22] Harris EC, Barraclough B: Excess mortality of mental disorder. *Br J Psychiatry* 1998; 173: 11-53.

[23] Spijker J, Bijl RV, de Graaf R, Nolen WA: Determinants of poor 1-year outcome of DSM-III-R major depression in the general population: results of the Netherlands Mental Health Survey and Incidence Study (NEMESIS). *Acta Psychiatr Scand* 2001; 103:122-130.

[24] Suominen KH, Isometsa ET, Henriksson MM, Ostamo AI, Lonnqvist JK: Inadequate treatment for Major Depression both before and after attempted suicide. *Am J Psychiatry* 1998; 155:1778–1780.

[25] World Health Organization: *The World Health Report 2001 Mental Health: New Understanding,* New Hope. Geneva, Switzerland: World Health Organziation, 2001.

[26] Bertolote JM, Fleischmann A, De Leo D, Wolk-Wasserman D: Psychiatric diagnosis and suicide: Revisiting the evidence. *Crisis* 2004; 25:147-155.

[27] Suicide Prevention Resource Center: Best practices registry section III: *Adherence to standards 2007:* Retrieved August 5, 2008 from: http://www.sprc.org/featured_ resources /bpr/PDF/QPR_FactSheet.pdf

[28] Berman, AL: AAS to host conference on warning signs. *American Association of Suicidology's NEWSlink* 2003; 29:4.

[29] Friedmann H, Kohn R: Mortality, or probability of death, from a suicidal act in the United States. *Suicide Life Threat Behav* 2008; 38:287-301.

[30] Joiner TE: *Why people die by suicide.* Cambridge: Harvard University Press, 2005.

[31] Greenberg G: Distance education technologies: Best practices for K-12 settings. *IEEE Technology and Society Magazine 1998;* Winter:36-40.

[32] Teaster PB, Blieszner R: Promises and pitfalls of the interactive television approach to teaching adult development and aging. *Educational Gerontology* 1999; 25:741-753.

[33] Keegan D: *Distance education technology for the new millennium: compressed video teaching.* ZIFF Papiere. Hagen, Germany: Institute for Research into Distance Education, 1995.

[34] Bollag B, Overland MA: Developing countries turn to distance education. *Chronicle of Higher Education* 2001; 47:29-31.

[35] Fletcher JD: Effectiveness and cost of interactive videodisc instruction in defense training and education. Washington DC: Institute for Defense Analyses, 1990.

[36] Kulik CC, Kulik JA: Effectiveness of computer-based instruction: An updated analysis. *Computers in Human Behaviors* 1991; 7:75-94.

[37] Adams GL: *"Why interactive?" Multimedia & Videodisc Monitor* 1992; March: 20-25.

[38] Janniro MJ: Effects of computer-based instruction on student learning of psychophysiological detection of deception test question formulation. *Journal of Computer-Based Instruction* 1993; 20:58-62.

[39] Hofstetter FT: "Is multimedia the next literacy?" *Educator's Tech Exchange* 1994; Winter: 6-12

[40] Hall B: *Web-based training cookbook.* New York: John Wiley and Sons, 1997.

[41] Phelps RH, Rosalie AW, Ashworth RL, Hahn HA: Effectiveness and costs of distance education using computer-mediated communication. *American Journal of Distance Education* 1991; 5:7-19.

[42] Whalen T, Wright D: *The business case for web-based training.* Norwood, MA: Artech House, 2000.

[43] Wisher R, Priest AN: Cost-effectiveness of audio teletraining for the U.S. Army National Guard. *American Journal of Distance Education* 1998; 12:38-51.

[44] Cohen J: *Statistical power analysis for the behavioral sciences* (2nd ed.). Hillsdale, NJ: Erlbaum, 1988.

[45] Knox KL, Litts DA, Talcott WG, Feig JC, Cain ED: Risk of suicide and other adverse outcomes after exposure to a suicide prevention programme in the U.S. Air Force: cohort study, *BMJ* 2003; 327:1376-1381.

[46] Sanddal ND, Sanddal TL, Berman A, Silverman MM: A general systems approach to suicide prevention: Lessons from cardiac prevention and control. *Suicide Life Threat Behav* 2003; 33:341-352.

In: Internet and Suicide
Editors: L. Sher and A. Vilens
ISBN 978-1-60741-077-5

Chapter 5

IMPROVING PUBLIC HEALTH PRACTICE IN SUICIDE PREVENTION THROUGH ONLINE TRAINING: A CASE EXAMPLE

Deborah M. Stone[1], Catherine W. Barber[1] and Marc Posner[2]
[1]Harvard School of Public Health, Harvard Injury Control Research Center, Boston, Massachusetts, USA and
[2] Education Development Center, Inc. Newton, Massachusetts, USA

ABSTRACT

Suicide is a serious public health problem and training in suicide prevention has lagged behind the recent growth in the field. Using the National Center for Suicide Prevention Training (NCSPT), a federally-funded project developed in collaboration between the Harvard Injury Control Research Center and Education Development Center, Inc., as a case example, this article describes how the Internet has assisted in bringing training in suicide prevention up to speed. Using a public health framework of prevention, NCSPT offers an online workshop series for professionals, individuals, and community groups interested in suicide prevention. To date, more than 4,000 users from across the country and from many countries outside the U.S. have accessed the online courses. The broad context underlying NCSPT's development along with particular aspects of the project's evolution is included. Evaluation results gathered from January 2007 to August 2008 highlight the knowledge gains resulting from the online workshops and provide information about who is accessing the online series and for what purpose or reason. Concluding remarks about the benefits of online training, the future development of NCSPT, and ideas for research to better optimize the Internet in suicide prevention are offered.

INTRODUCTION

The widespread use of the Internet has revolutionized the ability of people in the field of suicide prevention to access data, information, and training and to communicate with one another in real time across great distances. The field of public health has always been in the forefront of applying new technologies to distance education both for the purpose of delivering information to resource-poor areas –such as combating infectious disease in developing areas—and for the purpose of keeping even the most highly trained and skilled public health workers up to date in a world of rapidly evolving research findings and practice guidelines. Online courses, webinars, podcasts, and other innovative educational modalities have rapidly become part of every public health practitioners' professional life (and vocabulary).

This expansion of the public health training repertoire to include web-based modalities occurred during the same period in which the re-framing of suicide as a public health problem gained traction. Before the 1990s, suicide prevention activities largely consisted of hotlines, crisis intervention programs, and individual mental health treatment. Spurred by suicide survivor groups in the 1990s and by the expansion of the field of public health beyond disease to injury and violence, federal and state governments began outlining public policy strategies for tackling suicide. The publication of *The Surgeon General's Call to Action to Prevent Suicide* (1) in 1999 and the *National Strategy for Suicide Prevention* (2) in 2001 called for more comprehensive, population-based approaches. By 2007, all but two states had published state suicide prevention plans or were in the process of doing so. (3) Most of these plans called for greater training of practitioners and the general public in suicide prevention.

Training can be divided broadly into two categories: clinical skills (to improve providers' ability to screen for, protect, treat, and refer suicidal individuals) and public health skills (to better understand the characteristics and incidence of suicide and to develop and evaluate population-based interventions and policies). Training in both areas has lagged. For example, Feldman and Freedenthal (2006) found that 70% of master's level social workers reported having fewer than three hours of class time devoted to suicide. (4) Among directors of training in internal medicine and pediatrics who responded to a survey by Sudak et al (2007), less than half reported that training about suicide was adequate. (5) In their 2002-2003 survey, the Association of Schools of Public Health and the Centers for Disease Control and Prevention (CDC) found that no school of public health offered a graduate level course focused on suicide. (6) (The Harvard School of Public Health has since added one such course, "Principle of Suicide Prevention.")

The *Garrett Lee Smith Memorial Act* (2004) (7) was the first major federal legislation to address suicide (youth suicide in particular), and it provided millions of dollars in prevention and training funds – at the same time that increasing workloads and decreasing funds for public employee travel made it more difficult for practitioners to attend conferences and training events. Like other public health specialties, the field of suicide prevention has turned to distance learning and the Internet to fill the training gap.

Table 1. Examples of Internet-based Suicide Prevention Training Initiatives

Course name	**EndingSuicide.com**	**Holding the Lifeline: A Guide to Suicide Prevention**	**Attitudes and Approaches for Clinicians Working with Clients At-Risk for Suicide**	**Making Educators Partners in Suicide Prevention**
Developer	Clinical Tools Inc (CTI)	SAMHSA, Center for Substance Abuse Prevention	AAS	Society for the Prevention of Teen Suicide
URL	http://www1.endingsuicide.com	http://pathwayscourses.samhsa.gov/suicide/suicide_intro_pg1.htm	http://aas.selfip.org/sptraining/	http://spts.pldm.com/
Funding	National Institute of Mental Health	Substance Abuse and Mental Health Services Administration	Non-profit professional association	Non-profit
Audience	Physicians, social workers, counselors and professionals in substance abuse and related fields	Professionals in prevention, addictions, mental health, and related fields	Mental health clinicians	Educators, open to anyone
Cost	$15/credit	none	none	none
Credits available	ACCME, ACPE, CAADAC, NASW, NBCC, and NYS OASAS	NASW, NCHEC, NBCC, CAADAC, CME,	contact AAS	2 hours professional development credit to NJ educators

Table 1. Continued

Title of courses/contents	More than 15 courses are available including: Introduction to Suicide Facts, Figures, and Theories; Understanding Therapeutic Interventions for Patients with Suicidality; Postvention: Dealing with the Consequences of Suicide; Aging and Suicide; and Immigrants, Refugees, and Suicide.	Several courses are available including: The Nature and Scope of Suicide; Recognizing the Progressive Development of Suicide; Substance Abuse as a Major Contributor to Suicide; Suicide Across the Life Span; and Special Populations and Suicide Risk;	Two courses: Manage your reactions to suicide and Working with clients at-risk for suicide. Note: These modules can be taken as an independent online learning experience, but also are part of Recognizing and Responding to Suicide Risk: Essential Skills for Clinicians.	Several courses are available including: Understanding the Role of the School; Dealing With At-Risk Students; Required Reading & Resources; Addressing Myths & Misinformation; and Outlining Risk, Warning, and Protective Factors

Course name	**Question, Persuade, Refer (QPR)**	**Prevention Researcher Continuing Education**	**National Ctr for Suicide Prevention Training**	**Teen Suicide: The Preventable Tragedy**
Developer	QPR Institute	Prevention Researcher	Harvard School of Public Health and EDC's Suicide Prevention Resource Center	Zur Institute
URL	www.qprinstitute.com	http://www.tpronline.org/courses.cfm	http://training.sprc.org	http://www.zurinstitute.com/teensuicidecourse.html
Funding	Private	Private	HRSA Maternal and Child Health Bureau	Private
Audience	Individuals, organizations, college students at Eastern Washington University, primary healthcare professionals, mental health professionals	Social workers, counselors, therapists	Members of suicide prevention coalitions, public health and mental health practitioners	Psychologists, social workers, family therapists, counselors, nurses

Cost	From $9.95 for a certificate of completion to $229/university credit	From $10	None	$39
Credits available	College credit and CEUs offered through Eastern Washington University	APA, ASWB, NBCC	CECH, NASW	APA, BBS, ASWB, NBCC, BRN
Title of courses/contents	Several courses are available including: Gatekeeper Suicide Prevention Training; Suicide Triage Course; Suicide Risk Assessment and Training Course	Two courses are available: Practical Strategies for Preventing Adolescent Suicide; and Youth Suicide Prevention Program	A series of four available courses and three in progress, addressing public health approaches to suicide prevention.	This course consists of four sets of articles including information on suicide statistics, commonly held attitudes, beliefs and assumptions about teen suicide; assessment and management of suicide risk, and postvention strategies.

Course name	Student Suicide: Law and Policy Issues	University Lifeline: Issues Surrounding Student Suicide for College Campuses	PREVENT
Developer	StudentAffairs.com	Reslife.net	University of North Carolina
URL	http://www.studentaffairs.com/ONLINECOURSES/summer2004course3.html	http://www.thehousinguniversity.com/selfdirectedlearning/2007course3.html	http://www.prevent.unc.edu/education/distance_learning/mod2/part1/mod2p1_intro.htm

Table 1. Continued

Funding	Private	Private	CDC and Doris Duke Charitable Fund
Audience	Student affairs professionals	College and university residence professionals	Staff and employees of organizations working in the field of violence prevention.
Cost	Unknown	$90	None
Credits available	1 CEU	Unknown	None
Title of courses/contents	This course examines the law and policy issues related to student suicide with attention paid to causes and prevention of suicide, legal developments and liability issues; the scope and limits of confidentiality; and issues pertaining to the Americans with Disabilities Act.	This course includes information on: Students at risk for suicide; the costs of suicide; legal issues and university respondes; prevention information and how to develop a recovery plan on campus.	A 20 minute audio lecture accompanied by a PowerPoint presentation. Competencies addressed include being able to describe and explain suicide as a major social and health problem, explain how suicide is preventable, and the inter-relationship of suicide with other forms of violence.

Table 1 presents a number of distance learning opportunities in suicide prevention that utilize the Internet. This summary is restricted to structured, substantial, learning programs and excludes the wealth of fact sheets, publications, checklists, webinars, e-newsletters, and other information on suicide prevention available on the Internet. Many of these can be accessed by visiting the website of the Suicide Prevention Resource Center (SPRC), a national information clearinghouse established with Garrett Lee Smith Memorial Act funds http://www.sprc.org.

The remainder of this chapter presents a case study of one of the earlier efforts to bring suicide prevention training through use of the internet and demonstrate the versatility of this new medium to bring a wide range of content and programmatic information to suicide prevention practitioners.

History

In 2000, the Harvard Injury Control Research Center (HICRC) and the Northeast Injury Prevention Network (NEIPN) initiated a research and training partnership to assist recently established state suicide prevention coalitions. Network members expressed a need not only for in-person training but for internet-based training that could be accessed at any time to meet the demands of a rapidly expanding field. HICRC and Education Development Center, Inc., (EDC) received funding from the Maternal and Child Health Bureau (MCHB) of the Health Resources Services Administration (HRSA) to develop a distance education program for maternal and child health professionals and others on youth suicide prevention. Decreased youth suicide is one of 18 performance measures for states receiving Title V funds under the Social Security Act block grants. (8)

The three partners in this effort were especially well-placed to undertake this effort. The Harvard Injury Control Research Center, part of the Harvard School of Public Health, is one of the nation's leading academic centers in the field of injury prevention. NEIPN is a coalition of state injury prevention practitioners from the Northeastern region of the United States, most of whom had taken a key role in initiating state policy initiatives on suicide prevention in their respective states. EDC is a nonprofit educational organization that houses the Children's Safety Network (CSN), which is funded by Federal MCHB to provide technical assistance to state MCH agencies in injury, violence, and suicide prevention. Professionals from all three organizations participated in the creation and evaluation of these distance education programs under the banner of the National Center for Suicide Prevention Training (NCSPT), whose mission is *to provide educational resources to help public officials, service providers, and community-based coalitions develop effective suicide prevention programs and policies.*

From 2001 to 2004, NCSPT designed, tested, implemented, and evaluated three suicide prevention training workshops (available online and free of charge at http://training.sprc.org). In 2004, SPRC took over administration of the workshop series, while HICRC continues to develop new workshops for the series.

Workshop Content

The topics and content of the online workshops were based on a needs assessment of NEIPN members. Two versions of each workshop were created: a facilitated 6-week learning experience and a non-facilitated self-paced version that would be used independently, or as a follow-up and refresher to the facilitated version. The facilitated workshops include a series of self-paced modules, a series of real-time teleconferences presented by invited experts in the field, and an online discussion board available to both workshop teachers and learners. The self-paced workshops lack the teleconferences and discussion board. The recommended timeline for both modalities is typically between four and six weeks with 2 to 4 hours of work each week. Currently, only the self-paced workshops are available. See Appendix 1 for a list of workshop objectives.

Each workshop includes three modules. Each module includes didactic information, pre- and post-tests, self assessment quizzes, case studies, slide shows, audio files, links to internet resources, and worksheets that can be downloaded and used in the field.

Workshop 1, *Locating, Understanding, and Presenting Youth Suicide Data* focuses on the first step in the public health model of prevention: defining and understanding the problem by examining available data. The first module of this workshop introduces national and statewide data sources on suicide and self-harm injury. Users learn how to access these data and learn the strengths and limitations of each data sources. Module 2 explores data interpretation and analysis. Module 3 discusses effectively presenting data to various target audiences including policymakers and the public.

Workshop 2, *Planning and Evaluation for Youth Suicide Prevention*, focuses on public health prevention planning for suicide prevention. Module 1 explores several strategic planning models and the use of community planning groups. Module 2 discusses assessing a state suicide problem, the resources available to address the problem, and how to write measurable goals and objectives based on these needs and resources. Module 3 presents information on public health prevention strategies used to prevent suicide, how to choose appropriately among them, and how to create a logic model to plan, implement, and evaluate the implementation of these strategies.

Workshop 3, *Youth Suicide Prevention: An Introduction to Gatekeeping* is based on the State of Maine's *Preventing Youth Suicide through Gatekeeper Training: A Resource Book for Gatekeepers.* (9) Module 1 discusses common misperceptions about suicide, provides the rationale for gatekeeper training—a suicide prevention strategy which involves training adults who routinely work with youth to recognize and respond to youth displaying indications that they may be at risk of suicide. Module 2 discusses the link between mental illness and suicide and how to identify warning signs that a young person may be at risk of suicide. Module 3 provides information and resources on self-care—that is, ways that gatekeepers can cope with the often emotional process of helping a young person at risk of suicide. Workshop participants are encouraged to sign up for an in-person gatekeeper training program, complete with role playing opportunities and feedback, to become certified gatekeepers.

Workshop 4, *The Research Evidence for Suicide as a Preventable Public Health Problem*, examines the research evidence underpinning the claim that suicide is a preventable public health problem. Module 1introduces the public health approach to prevention. Module

2 examines the evidence for a "lethal means reduction" approach to preventing youth suicide. Module 3 provides an overview of comprehensive community prevention strategies.

A fifth workshop, “What Works? Results of Evaluations of Suicide Prevention Programs and Policies,” will be added in 2009. Two additional workshops are planned—Workshop 6, *Counseling on Reducing High-Risk Youth’s Access to Lethal Means* and Workshop 7, *Emergency Department Policies for Pediatric Self-Harm Patients.*

MARKETING

The NCSPT workshops were marketed using e-mail listservs, including those hosted by SPRC and American Association of Suicidology (AAS); via links to NCSPT on partnering web sites (e.g. SPRC, AAS, CDC, National Center for Mental Health Promotion and Violence Prevention, Preventing Suicide Network), and through announcements placed in professional journals and newsletters. The power of the internet and the demand for training were demonstrated when the first email was sent to the AAS and SPRC announcing the first facilitated workshop; within hours, the class was filled.

CONTINUING EDUCATION UNITS

All courses award continuing education credits to participants in selected professions. To receive these credits, participants must complete both a pre- and post-test and achieve a passing grade of 70% on the post-test. For a limited time, credits were made available for physicians, psychologists, certified counselors, health educators, and social workers through the American Association of Suicidology. However, due to administrative costs, credits are currently only available for health educators and social workers via the National Commission for Health Education Credentialing (NCHEC) and the National Association of Social Workers (NASW), respectively.

HUMAN RESOURCES AND INFRASTRUCTURE

NCSPT was initially funded from June 2001 to June 2004 by a HRSA grant of approximately $178,000 per year for establishing the website and developing the first three workshops; subsequent funding has been at the level of between $65,000 and $98,000 a year to add a new course approximately every 18 months. The initial grant covered approximately 1.75 FTEs (full-time equivalent positions), including a full-time project director and portions of a writer, senior scientist, technology specialist, and administrative support. In addition, there were costs for server access, software purchases, and web site development. The major costs of the project included designing and creating the course management system (i.e. the web site that would house the workshop and its affiliated events), writing the workshops, establishing the technical infrastructure for course registration, preparing the pre- and post-tests and the evaluation survey, developing and implementing the evaluation, and applying for the ability to provide continuing education units. Compared with development, the actual implementation of the courses is relatively inexpensive. Costs of implementing each workshop includes, the moderators' time, periodically updating the workshops, fielding students' technical problems, maintaining the website, and reporting to the professional organizations that confer continuing education credits. NCSPT provides workshops and continuing education units free of charge.

HICRC partnered with EDC because of EDC's technical expertise in online training and the expertise of CSN division in youth suicide prevention. With the establishment of EDC's Suicide Prevention Resource Center, administration and maintenance of the courses has transferred from CSN to SPRC, a mutually beneficial relationship for both SPRC and the Harvard Injury Control Research Center because SPRC can have input on course content and offer these workshops to its constituency without incurring development costs, while HICRC can be assured of ongoing sustainability for the courses it creates and dissemination through a resource center that is widely respected and has high visibility in the suicide prevention field.

The first three workshops were created using software called Trellix Site Builder. (10) Registration, pre and post-tests were created with Perseus Survey Solutions (11) and the discussion board was created using WebBoard. (12) It became evident over time that this was not an optimal setup. In 2007, all workshops were migrated to Moodle, (13) open source content management system that provided all the functionality needed for the workshops (e.g. registration, interactive assessments and quizzes, and participant communications).

Evaluation

The workshop content was reviewed by suicide prevention experts, including staff from both HICRC and SPRC. Each workshop underwent a formative evaluation involving learners from NEIPN, HICRC, and SPRC to test and refine the functionality of the workshops. In addition, each workshop was pilot tested by a group of volunteer learners from across the country. Workshops were then revised in response to pilot feedback. Process evaluation included monitoring participation in the workshops by tracking the number of hits to the NCSPT web site, the number of registrations received, the type of registrants, the number of pre-tests, posttests, and evaluations completed, and open-ended comments posted on the discussion board.

To measure outcomes, all participants were asked to complete both a pre- and post-test to assess the change in knowledge after they completed the workshop. Post-test scores of 70% or higher were considered passing. Participants who failed were given the option to retake the test. Certificates of completion were sent via e-mail to all successful students. At the same time that participants completed the post-test, they were asked to evaluate the course along several dimensions:

- Satisfaction with workshop content and format
- Whether they would recommend the workshop to others
- Their satisfaction with the time required by the workshop
- How they thought the workshop material would assist their suicide prevention work.

In the first funding period, a limited number of follow-up surveys were sent to participants after approximately 6 to 8 months to assess knowledge retention and to document ways in which participants were applying what they learned to their work. With budget cuts in the second funding period, this impact evaluation was no longer possible.

EVALUATION RESULTS

Over 4,000 students have registered for NCSPT workshops from 2002 – 2008. The following results are based on workshop participation after the migration to Moodle when workshop usability and evaluation data were improved. In total 1,708 people accessed the NCSPT workshops between January 1, 2007 and August 5, 2008. Of these people, 610 signed up for workshop 1, 156 for workshop 2, 774 for workshop 3, and 168 for workshop 4. Most people (approximately 85%) have taken one workshop in the time period reported here with 15% taking two, three, or four courses. Participants' affiliations were most often mental health professionals except for workshop 3 where the affiliation most often cited was state/local government. Most people were new to suicide prevention within the past year. Registrants most frequently reported finding out about the workshop series through work and via the National Commission for Health Education Credentialing web site which maintains a listing of courses available for continuing education contact hours. In this most recent evaluation, participants have come from 48 states, Washington DC, two U.S. territories, and 19 countries on six continents. (See Table 2)

Ninety-four percent of those who completed the post-test reported that they would definitely or probably recommend the workshop to others. Only 1% would not (See Table 3 below). Mean post-test scores improved over pre-test scores by between 18 points in workshop 3 and 40 points in workshop 4 (See Table 5 below). These positive outcomes are among course completers. Many participants appeared not to complete the courses (i.e. they did not complete the post-test and evaluation).

In an evaluation of the first three years of the project (14), we could not determine what proportion of non-completers might be casual "window shoppers," – people who may have been interested in only a portion of a given workshop or who wanted a "taste" of the content or technology, but never had an intention of actually completing the workshop. The inability to differentiate window shoppers from committed learners who did not complete the workshop because of dissatisfaction with the content or the technology made it difficult to interpret the high attrition rates characteristic of free online courses. The most recent iteration of the course registration forms asked participants about their main motive for taking the course (e.g. to receive continuing education credits, to fulfill a job requirement, or solely due to interest in the topic area).

We hypothesized that users requesting CEUs or who were required by their employer to take the courses would have greater rates of course completion (as proxied by completion of the post-test) compared with users who had a general interest in the material. This was indeed the case though completion of the post-test among the former groups was, in some cases, still low (as shown in Table 4).

Table 2. About NCSPT online participants, January 1, 2007-August 5, 2008

Workshop number	1	2	3	4	Total
# of people registered	610	156	774	168	1,708
Affiliations (Most common in bold):					
State/local health department employee	5%	5%	4%	8%	5%
State/local maternal & child health department	1	0	1	1	1
Other state/local government employee	15	9	**41**	11	26
Student	15	13	12	7	13
Teacher/school staff (primary or secondary)	9	11	5	8	7
Teacher/school staff (college/university)	7	8	2	7	5
Survivor of own attempt	5	4	2	1	3
Survivor of other's attempt(s)	9	4	2	6	5
Member of statewide suicide prevention group	8	5	4	14*	6
Mental health professional/provider	**25**	**29**	17	**43**	**23**
Primary care provider	1	1	<1	0	<1
Nurse	8	8	4	9	6
Other health professional	12	11	4	5	8
Law enforcement	3	3	1	4	2
Parent/guardian/caregiver	6	4	2	3	4
Other	23	20	17	20	20
Time in suicide prevention					
New in past year	53%	59%	51%	42%	51%
1-2 years	14	11	13	14	13
3-5 years	12	11	13	17	13
6-10 years	8	6	10	11	9
Greater than 10 years	13	13	13	16	13
Total (%)	100	100	100	100	100
Why are you taking this course?*					
Required	27%	30%	67%	26%	38%
Credits	19	23	7	23	18
Interested, other	54	47	26	51	44
Total (%)	100	100	100	100	100
# States participating	47	38	45	41	48
# Countries participating (not including the U.S.)	19	9	7	7	19

* recruited in part from listserv of state coalitions.

In workshop 1, the completion rate by people requesting CEUs and those required to take the course was similar at 55 and 50% respectively. In Workshops 2 through 4, the completion rate by these two groups was different. People taking the courses for CEUs had a lower completion rate than those required to take the courses (e.g. 78% vs. 98% respectively, in Workshop 3 and 50% vs. 86%, respectively, in workshop 4).

Table 3. Evaluation results by workshop

Workshop number	1 (n=294)	2 (n=76)	3 (n=637)	4 (n=132)	Total (n=1139)
I would take another NCSPT online workshop…					
Definitely	55%	71%	49%	75%	53%
Probably	31	23	38	18	33
Not sure	9	3	11	5	9
No	5	3	2	2	3
Total	100	100	100	100	98*
How satisfied were you with the workshop overall?					
Very/Somewhat dissatisfied	5%	13%	3%	1%	4%
Neutral	15	14	10	6	11
Very/Somewhat satisfied	80	72	87	93	85
Total	100	99*	100	100	100
Would you recommend this course to others?					
Yes, definitely	53%	44%	49%	75%	53%
Yes, probably	39	48	45	19	41
Not sure	7	7	5	5	6
No	1	1	1	1	1
Total	100	100	100	100	101*
How satisfied were you with the online learning environment?					
Very/Somewhat dissatisfied	11%	4%	11%	4%	10%
Neutral	15	7	19	14	17
Very/Somewhat satisfied	74	89	70	82	74
Total	100	100	100	100	100*
How much new information did you learn in this workshop?					
A lot	52%	68%	31%	53%	41%
Fair amount	42	28	51	43	46
A little	5	3	17	3	11
None	1	1	1	1	1
Total	100	100	100	100	99*

*Does not equal 100 due to rounding

Table 4. Percent completing post-test by reason for course initiation

Workshop Number	1	2	3	4	Total
Required by employer	50%	72%	98%	86%	77%
CEUs	55	61	78	50	61
Interested (non CEU/not required)	21	41	73	43	45

Table 5. Average pre- and post-test scores by reason for course initiation

	Workshop Number											
	1			2			3			4		
Reason for initiation	Pre	Post	Point increase	Pre	Post	Point increase	Pre	Post	Point increase	Pre	Post	Point increase
Required	48	86	38	69	92	23	76	93	17	53	88	35
CEUs	47	87	40	68	91	23	77	94	17	34	89	55
Interested	44	82	38	62	89	27	76	94	18	58	86	28

Pre-test scores were similar across groups within workshops except for in workshop 4 where the pre-test score for CEU participants was significantly lower (34%) compared to the other two groups (53 and 58%, respectively). Post-test were also similar across groups within each workshop (See Table 5 above). Of people eligible for CEUs in workshop 1, post-test scores averaged 87% compared to 86% among participants required to take the workshop and 82% among interested participants. The average percentage point increase in workshop 1 was 39 points. In workshop 3, all groups attained a similar average post-test score with both the interested and CEU-eligible group averaging 94% and the required group receiving an average of 93%. The average increase from pre-test to post-test in workshop 3 was 18 points. Workshop 4 participants attained average post-test scores of 88, 89, and 86% among the required, CEU, and interested groups, respectively. The average increase from pre to post-test was 40 points. Workshop 2 results fell between those of workshops 3 and 4. Overall, it appears the greatest gains were made in workshop 4 and the least gain in workshop 3.

The proportion of Workshop 3 students who took the course because it was required by their employers (67%) was far higher than for the other three workshops. Unlike the other three, which emphasize public health leadership skills, Workshop 3 emphasizes hands-on skills in recognizing and responding to people at risk for suicide. While the other three workshops assist those who *plan* interventions, Gatekeeper Training is itself an intervention that has been embraced by many statewide suicide prevention planning groups and figures prominently in the workplans of Garrett Lee Smith Memorial Act grantees. Gatekeeper training is aimed very broadly at anyone who may come into contact with suicidal youth – coaches, teachers, clergy, police officers, etc. – and is being incorporated as standard institutional practice in many organizations. For example, Workshop 3 is used by a foster care agency to train its foster families in recognizing signs of suicide and responding appropriately.

CONCLUSION

The online workshops provided by NCSPT have reached thousands of individuals – both in the United States and in other countries. Our evaluation has shown that participants who complete the workshop show increases in suicide prevention knowledge. The workshops are to some extent drawing people who cannot attend more expensive and time-consuming face-to-face trainings according to feedback from participants. The ability of a free, online, course to attract casual users, while complicating evaluation efforts, would seem to offer added value in educating both practitioners and the lay public about suicide and suicide prevention.

The very limited evaluation did not allow us to understand how effective the workshops were in promoting or improving suicide prevention practices and, more importantly, how effective the online modality is compared to more traditional face-to-face learning experiences. There are a number of important questions that need to be answered in this respect. We need to understand the relative effectiveness and, importantly, the relative cost-effectiveness of face-to-face workshops, facilitated online workshops, and non-facilitated online workshops, ideally using a rigorous random assignment outcome evaluation. We also need to understand how the workshops that seek to teach public health leadership skills that emphasize informational content compare in effectiveness to those that teach clinical skills.

It would be useful to explore the use of a mixed modality model, in which a "class" of learners might come together at (for example) a professional meeting or conference and then continue learning together using web-based distance technologies. Lessons often seem far clearer in the classroom than when applied in the field, and internet-based technologies can supply forums in which learners can compare notes, ask questions, and receive "booster" sessions. Similarly, a mixed model in which, for example, informational content would be taught on line and skills content taught in a subsequent face-to-face session may prove effective. It would also be interesting to learn whether emerging web technologies including avatars, instant chat, and videoconferencing could be used to effectively teach the type of role-playing and personal interaction skills formally thought to be effectively taught only in a face-to-face situation.

And finally, it would be worthwhile to explore how web-based training and culture intersect and whether, for example, web-based learning modalities are more effective with younger people who have come of age in the world of the Web, SmartPhones, and social networking than they are with older people, who still might find these technologies alien, difficult to master, and intrusive.

Appendix 1. Workshop Learning Objectives

Workshop 1. Locating, understanding, and presenting youth suicide data

- After completing Workshop 1, participants will be able to:
- Describe the role of data in suicide prevention
- Describe internationally-accepted coding schemes for suicides and suicide attempts
- Identify suicide-related data sources at the national, state, and local levels
- Understand the strengths and limitations of these data sources
- Describe the distribution of suicides/attempts in populations
- Understand considerations in data interpretation
- Describe how to effectively report youth suicide data to decision makers

Workshop 2. Planning and Evaluation for Youth Suicide Prevention

- After completing Workshop 2, participants will be able to:
- Describe why state planning is needed for suicide prevention
- Identify partners for creating a comprehensive suicide prevention plan
- Understand the community assessment process
- Select appropriate prevention strategies
- Describe levels of prevention
- Describe three suicide prevention interventions
- Write goals with SMART objectives (specific, measurable, achievable, relevant, time-based objectives)
- Develop a logic model
- Identify five ways to find resources for plan implementation
- Describe different types of evaluation
- Outline an evaluation plan
- Outline an evaluation report

Workshop 3. Youth suicide prevention: An introduction to gatekeeping

- After completing Workshop 3, participants will be able to:
- Understand the rationale for gatekeeper training
- Define standard suicide prevention terms
- Identify the risk and protective factors for suicide
- Understand the link between mental health and suicide
- Identify warning signs and clues of suicide
- Understand, in theory, how to ask about and respond to suicidal behavior
- Identify appropriate local suicide prevention support resources
- Understand the link between postvention and prevention of suicide
- Describe self-care techniques for gatekeepers

Workshop 4. The Research Evidence for Suicide as a Preventable Public Health Issue

- Describe the public health approach to suicide prevention
- Describe the general epidemiology of suicide in the U.S.
- Summarize risk and protective factors for suicide as identified by psychological autopsy studies
- Describe a new data source for suicide: the National Violent Death Reporting System.
- Present a conceptual models for suicide prevention.
- Describe the research evidence for means reduction as a suicide prevention strategy.
- Describe the impact of firearm availability on suicide in the U.S.
- Outline an integrated approach to suicide prevention and control.

REFERENCES

[1] U.S. Public Health Service. *The Surgeon General's Call to Action to Prevent Suicide.* Washington, D.C: 1999.

[2] U.S. Department of Health and Human Services. National *Strategy for Suicide Prevention: Goals and Objectives for Action.* 2001. Rockville, MD.

[3] Harvard Injury Control Research Center. *Summary of Key Findings from the Means Matter Survey.* 2007. Boston, MA. Accessed online September 15, 2008 at: http://www.hsph.harvard.edu/means-matter/files/Survey_results.pdf

[4] Feldman, BN and Freedenthal, S. Social Work Education in Suicide Intervention and Prevention: An Unmet Need? *Suicide & Life Threatening Behavior*, 2006; 36 (4):467-80.

[5] Sudak D, Roy A, Sudak H, Lipschitz A, Maltsberger J, Hendin H. Deficiencies in suicide training in primary care specialties: a survey of training directors. *Acad Psychiatry*;2007; 31(5):345-9.

[6] Centers for Disease Control and Association of Schools of Public Health. Injury prevention and control in accredited schools of public health: 2002-2003 summary of research, faculty expertise, curricula, and traning. 2004. Atlanta, GA.

[7] Public Law 108-355. *Garrett Lee Smith Memorial Act.* October 21, 2004. Accessed online September 15, 2008 at: http://www.jedfoundation.org/articles/GarrettLee SmithS2634.pdf.

[8] U.S. Department of Health and Human Services. *Maternal and Child Health Services Title V Block Grant.* Accessed online September 15, 2008 at: http://mchb. hrsa.gov/programs/blockgrant/overview.htm

[9] O'Halloran S. and Coleman, L. *Preventing Youth Suicide through Gatekeeper Training.* 6th ed. 2003. Augusta, ME: Medical Care Development, Inc.

[10] Web.Com. *Trellix Site Builder.* 2008. Jacksonville, FL.

[11] Perseus Development Corporation. *Perseus Survey Solutions.* 2008. Braintree, MA.

[12] Akiva Corporation. *WebBoard.* 2008. Vista, CA.

[13] Moodle version 1.7. http://moodle.org accessed 2004.

[14] Stone DM, Barber CW, and Potter L. Public Health Training Online: The National Center for Suicide Prevention Training. Am J Prev Med; 2005;29(5S2):247-251.

In: Internet and Suicide
Editors: L. Sher and A. Vilens

ISBN 978-1-60741-077-5

Chapter 6

INTERNET RESOURCES FOR PREVENTING SUICIDE

Maurizio Pompili[1,2], David Lester[3], Marco Innamorati[4], Alberto Forte[1], Giulia Iacorossi[1], Giovanni Dominici[1], Laura Sapienza[1] and Roberto Tatarelli[1]

[1]Sant'Andrea Hospital, Sapienza University of Rome, Italy;
[2]McLean Hospital - Harvard Medical School, USA;
[3]The Richard Stockton College of New Jersey, USA;
[4]Università Europea di Roma, Italy

ABSTRACT

Internet usage has grown exponentially in the last decade and seeking health information has become one of the most common reasons for using the Internet. There are resources on the Internet for those contemplating suicide and who are seeking help either for themselves or for loved ones. The aim of the present paper is to address Internet usage related to suicide and suicide prevention. The present article will also discuss some of the issues (advantages and drawbacks) of counseling suicidal individuals using these methods. In general, the Internet is unregulated, and there is no guarantee about the quality and safety of information provided from web sites and search engines page-ranks.

INTRODUCTION

Internet usage has grown exponentially in the last decade. It is estimated that the number of web users worldwide is almost 1 billion, including more than 578 million users in Asia (15.3% of the population), 384 million users in Europe (48.1% of the population), and 248 million users in North America (73.6% of the population) [1]. The number of USA users rose from 124 million in 2000 (44.1% of the population) to almost 220 million in 2008 (72.5% of the population) [2]. The number of UK users rose from almost 15 million in 2000 (26.2% of the population) to 38 million in 2007 (63.8% of the population) [3]. In Italy, the number of

Internet users rose from almost 13 million in 2000 (22.8% of the Italian population) to over 32 million in 2007 (54.1% of the Italian population) [4].

The Internet has emerged as a social arena in which people interact and build social networks via e-mail, chat rooms, instant messaging, newsgroups, forums, and support groups, to which can now be added blogs and Internet-based networks such as MySpace and Facebook [5]. The Internet is also a useful tool seeking health information, which has become one of the most common reasons for using the Internet [6]. At the beginning of the 21st Century, there were about 100,000 websites dedicated to health information [7]. Internet surfers use the Internet not only to seek health information but also to seek counseling and therapy by mental health specialists [5,8]. The aim of the present paper is not to address the multitude of uses of e-therapy but to focus on Internet sites related to suicide and suicide prevention.

There are pros and cons for the use of internet-mediated therapy and counseling [9]. The advantages include greater access to remote and rural areas, reduced cost, and ease of communication for patients dissatisfied with traditional intervention methods [10]. The disadvantages include and absence of training programs, lack of developed standards, lack of evidence of effectiveness, and the inadequate pace at which professional organizations are responding to online therapy.

There are resources on the Internet for those contemplating suicide and who are seeking help either for themselves or for loved ones (www.suicidology.org; www.befrienders.org).[1] Befrienders, an international organization devoted to suicide prevention (whose centers are typically called Samaritans) introduced crisis intervention for suicidal individuals by e-mail in 1994. In recent years, informal counseling of suicidal individuals has also utilized Instant Messaging (IM). The present article will discuss some of the issues (advantages and drawbacks) of counseling suicidal individuals using these methods.

The Internet as a Facilitator of Suicide

The Internet has become of great significance for suicide [12-13], including the facilitation of suicide, with websites concerned with the right to die (www. compassionandchoices.org; www.finalexit.org), helping individuals choose a method for suicide (ash.spaink.net/nazgmethods.html) [14 -19] and obtaining lethal medications [20].

Biddle and colleagues [15] searched the internet in 2007 for sites providing instructions and information about methods of suicide using the four most popular search engines (Google, Yahoo, MSN, and Ask) and 12 simple search terms likely to be used by distressed individuals (suicide, suicide methods, suicide sure methods, most effective methods of suicide, methods of suicide, ways to commit suicide, how to commit suicide, how to kill yourself, easy suicide methods, best suicide methods, pain-free suicide, and quick suicide). The authors limited the search to the first 10 web pages for each search (for a total of 480 web pages) and categorized web sites into one of 14 categories: dedicated suicide sites encouraging or facilitating suicide; web sites describing methods but not encouraging suicide; web sites portraying suicide in fashionable terms; information sites providing factual information about suicide methods; information sites partly joking or tongue in cheek information but suggestive of real methods; information sites with completely joking information; suicide sites against suicide; prevention or support sites; academic or policy sites; pages not found or not relevant to the search terms; news reports of individual suicides; chat rooms focused on suicide methods; chat rooms discussing various general issues relating to suicide; and miscellaneous sites reporting on topical issues relating to suicide. The results identified 240 web sites giving information about suicide; 90 web pages were for dedicated suicide sites, half of which were judged to be promoting or facilitating suicide; another 44 web pages provided factual information about suicide; and 121 hits accounted for sites offering support and discouraging suicide. Furthermore, sites providing factual information and pro-suicide sites occurred frequently in the first ranks of the searches.

The study of Biddle and colleagues shows that it is very easy to obtain detailed technical information about suicidal methods, and the danger of such sites is not merely hypothetical. For example, Alao et al. [21] reported two cases of people researching methods for suicide online and utilizing that information. Becker, et al. [22,23] reported the case of a young 17 year-old girl who contacted web forums in order to research methods for suicide and who purchased medications from an anonymous user to ingest for her suicide. They also reported the case of a 15 year-old girl who said that the Internet inspired her to commit suicide. Haut and Morrison [24] reported the case of a woman who obtained data from the web on using wolfbane (a poisonous plant) and lighter fluid for her suicide attempts. Beatson et al. [25] reported the case of a 34 year-old man who killed himself using clomipramine which he obtained over the Internet from an overseas pharmacy. The Internet can also provide publicity for the suicidal individual by committing suicide on live video-cam.

The Internet has also made it easy to find strangers with whom to commit suicide in suicide pacts [26,27]. In 2000, the first use of the Internet to form suicide pacts was reported in Japan. This is now a common form for suicide in Japan [28], increasing from 34 suicides in 2003 to 91 suicides in 2005 [29]. In South Korea, this arrangement may account for a third of all suicides [30]. In Hong Kong, the use of charcoal burning for suicide, a method that was disseminated over the Internet, has become popular for these suicide pacts [31]. An earlier case was reported by Mehlum [32] in which a man in his 20s in Norway made contact via an Internet discussion group with a 17-year old Austrian girl who traveled to Norway to commit suicide with him by jumping off a cliff. In Japan, Internet providers now provide the police with information on suicidal people attempting to link up via the Internet, and 14 suicides were prevented by police from October to December 2005 [29]

It is well-documented that suicidal behavior can be provoked by newspaper and television publicity of suicide, especially by celebrities [33] and by the suicides of friends and family members, and now media reporting on the Internet can play a similar role [34]. A famous suicide (such as that of Kurt Cobain) provokes an enormous number of Internet references that are easily accessible to those interested. There are suicide jokes sites, suicide game sites, and suicide music sites [35]. Baume et al. [35] documented suicide newsgroups, mailing lists (listservs) and suicide notes on the Internet [36]. In one case noted by Baume et al. [35], a young man informed the alt.suicide.holiday newsgroup of his intention to commit suicide on November 12, 1996, using drugs and car exhaust. The next day, he sought information on overdosing with sleeping pills and received helpful messages on their use. On November 14, he posted his last message, indicating that he would kill himself at 1.00 am

[1] Local programs have also incorporated websites into their suicide prevention programs (11).

using sleeping pills, vitamins, allergy medication and vodka and then using car exhaust. The Heaven's Gate cult, which resulted in a mass suicide of its members, maintained an online website (www.heavensgate.com) and tried to recruit more members for the cult [38,39]. Whitlock, et al. [40] studied message boards on self-injurious behavior and found that they normalize and encourage self-injurious and potentially lethal behaviors. However, Eichenberg [41] studied postings on a German web site (www.selbstmordforum.de) and found many constructive postings as well as destructive postings.

Mishara and Weisstub [42] discussed the feasibility of legally banning or restricting suicide-promoting websites using filtering techniques and blocking access to the sites. Laws passed to block Internet content have been passed in several countries but overturned by courts in most cases (such as the United Kingdom) because of constitutional guarantees of freedom of expression. Only Australia currently has a law making suicide-promoting Internet activity a crime.

The Internet and Suicide Prevention

As well as proving encouragement for those who are suicidal, the Internet can help prevent suicide. Suresh and Lynch [43] reported a case in which a woman who had overdosed posted a suicide note online. A computer hacker traced her whereabouts and alerted the local police who broke into her apartment and took her to the hospital. Janson et al. [44] reported a similar case where an AOL representative notified the police after a subscriber reported a woman making suicidal threats in a chat room. In another case reported by Janson et al., a friend of a potential suicide saw a video that the suicidal man placed online and called the police who intervened. Neimark et al. [45] reported a case of a therapy client who denied suicidal motivation, but a Google search of his name found a recent suicide attempt in which he jumped from a bridge.

The use of the Internet for providing psychological help began in the mid-1990s [46,47], and has grown in recent years, sometimes focusing on particular groups such as adolescents [48]. The services have grown to include psychological advice, support groups, testing and assessment, and counseling and therapy. This may especially useful for some segments of the population, such as adolescents, who may not turn to other media for their information [49]. The Internet can provide information about mental health issues, including suicide but, as Mandrusiak et al. [50] have documented in their study of warning signs for suicide posted on various websites, there is great disparity on the information presented and, furthermore, there is little validity for many of the warning signs listed. Internet sites often provide incorrect information.

The Internet has been used to screen incoming undergraduate students for suicidal risk and other mental health problems at some universities [51], provide on-line training in crisis intervention and suicide assessment [52,53], and provide information, education and support for suicide prevention workers [54], especially those in remote areas [55].

Two published examples of using the Internet for counseling suicidal clients have appeared (SAHAR and the Befrienders), and these are described in the following sections.

SAHAR

SAHAR is the Hebrew acronym for Support and Listening on the Net which was designed to attract people in crisis and provide listeners, who were trained paraprofessionals, online [56]. SAHAR uses Hebrew but, being online, is accessible to Hebrew-speakers anywhere in the world. Barak [56] noted that an online service provides easy accessibility and greater anonymity since tracing is not possible and because age, sex and ethnicity are more easily hidden than when speaking (rather than typing) is required. An online service also provides access to information of a variety of topics immediately by clicking on links. Online services make working with groups easier. In addition, there are advantages such as saving the dialogue for future reference, permitting a counselor to handle several clients at the same time, and allowing both immediate feedback (Instant Messaging) and delayed feedback (e-mails).

SAHAR was established in mid-2000 and began operation in February, 2001, after training the first group of counselors and after formalities (such as getting insurance coverage and organizing as a non-profit organization). SAHAR is managed by one paid person, supported by volunteers, including counselors and programmers. The website (www.sahar.org.il) has several sections: (1) informative articles on various aspects of distress, such as psychiatric disorders, helping a suicidal friend, and myths about suicide; (2) a list of community support services with addresses, telephone numbers, e-mail addresses and links where available; (3) information on telephone hotlines and emergency services for those needing immediate help, (4) an extensive list of recommended books and other readings, (5) links to other relevant sites for people in distress; and (6) a page about SAHAR and information about volunteering and donating.

For counseling, SAHAR offers (1) individual, personal communication via personal chat software or Instant Messaging; and (2) counseling via e-mail for those who prefer this medium. In the latter case, clients can use their own e-mail address or use an online forum at the site in order to preserve their anonymity. In addition, SAHAR offers group communication by online forums and (in the future) chat rooms (protected by passwords and monitored by paraprofessional helpers). At the time of writing, there were four forums: youngsters, adults, enlisted soldiers, and creative support (using poetry, stories and painting). The counselors all remain anonymous to prevent relationships developing between clients and helpers.

At the time of writing, SAHAR operated only three hours each day. Conversations last on the average 45 to 60 minutes, and the website is accessed more than 10,000 times each month (350 times each day). The data indicated more than 300,000 visits by 120,000 unique users. About 1,000 personal conversations take place each month, with about 50 percent from clearly suicidal clients. SAHAR has also intervened using community services such as the police in roughly 100 cases where people were in the process of committing suicide.

Barak noted problems, similar to those reported by telephone counseling services [57]: imposters presenting as suicides, fake messages in the forums which distress the other participants, emotional stress and burnout in the counselors, maintaining discipline in the volunteers (so that they act professionally), and software glitches that interrupt the service. The fact that all e-therapy sessions are saved makes supervising the volunteers easier than in telephone hotlines, the majority of which do not automatically record all calls. However,

Barak noted that many distressed individuals do not find writing easy, and so this type of service is not for them.

Gilat and Shahar [58] compared clients using a service which provided a telephone hotline, personal chat over the Internet and an asynchronous online support group. They found that high risk suicidal communications were much more common in the asynchronous online support group than in the two others modes (15.3% versus 1.4% and 0.3%).

Support Groups

There are many support groups on the Internet [59]. Some are for those who are suicidal or self-injurers [60], others for those who have had a significant other complete suicide [61]. Hollander [62] explored the resources on the Internet for survivors of suicide (that is, those who have lost a significant other to suicide). She subscribed to online suicide support services and listserves for survivors and, in nine weeks, she received and read roughly 10,000 e-mail messages. She quoted one survivor "Without the Web.....I know I would have bought a gun and followed him [her son] to the next world" (p. 141). Hoffman [63] described a web-based program that he developed for adolescent suicide survivors.

The Befrienders: Suicide Prevention By E-Mail

Although suicide intervention involving the Internet has been reported in situations where an individual reports on the Internet having attempted suicide and someone elsewhere on the Internet responds immediately by calling emergency services in the attempter's neighborhood, the focus here is with sustained counseling using e-mail communications as offered by the Befrienders (also known as the Samaritans). In these situations, a client contacts the suicide prevention center by sending an e-mail communication. Within twenty-four hours, a counselor reads the communication and writes and sends a response. This exchange may continue for a period of time.

For the Samaritans, there is a central "address" for e-mail messages from clients [64-68]. The central computer then assigns the message to a center. Encryption (scrambling) of the letters is possible if clients desire this.[2] In 1998, this service had 15,309 contacts of which 51% involved suicidal ideation [66]; in 2001, 61 branches online had received 64,000 e-mails, with 50% suicidal in nature [67].

The Client

Suicide prevention centers using the telephone as the mode for communication have noted that their typical caller is a young female; males are much less likely to use these services even though they have the higher suicide rate. Men are less likely to seek assistance,

[2] Access is limited to a Web site (http://www.compulink.co.uk/-careware/samaritans/) and Internet e-mail. This is always answered by real volunteers; there are no "automatic" response. Other Internet techniques, such as Telnet or anonymous ftp will not work.

and they rarely telephone or walk into suicide prevention centers. Computers and the Internet are used extensively by men and especially by men in their twenties and thirties, a group which suicide prevention centers would like to target. However, Howlett and Langdon [67] noted the percentages of male and female users are similar for the Internet and the telephone. It has not been possible to ascertain whether the disabled (especially those with hearing and speech deficits) and those in remote regions with poor telephone access use the service to any great extent. A higher proportion of the contacts made by e-mail than by the telephone seem to be suicidal in nature, 53% versus 26% in one survey [65].

As in counseling by letter, e-mail offers advantages to the hearing-impaired and speech-impaired clients, clients who would find telephone communication difficult. E-mail provides ease of access in general and to the disabled in particular (as does the telephone).[3] E-mail provides privacy as to the identity of the client, even more so than the telephone, since with e-mail the gender of the caller can be disguised if desired. Students often have their telephone use monitored by their parents, which inhibits their use of telephone crisis services, but parents are less likely to monitor their children's use of the Internet. Furthermore, whereas caller ID (unless blocked by the caller) identifies from where the client is calling, e-mail can be sent via a service which removes the Internet address of the client.

E-mail also appeals to clients who have a lack of trust and who fear loss of face in calling a suicide prevention center. As with telephone counseling, clients find safety in their increased control over the process, and they are working with a medium with which they are familiar.

The Process

Suicide prevention by e-mail permits a time lapse between each communication. This time lapse is not as long (twenty-four hours or less) as that required for mail sent by postal services (several days to more than a week). This time allows a period for the client and the counselor to consider what is happening in the client's life. There is time for the counselor to consult with peers and supervisors before sending the reply. There is an opportunity for the client to study the counselor's response.

Suicide prevention bye-mail elicits more comments from the counselor, since a simple "hmm-hmm" no longer suffices. Counselors have to show that they are listening carefully in other ways. Just as telephone counseling can degenerate into conversation, counselors using e-mail can easily forget that they are engaged in crisis intervention and suicide prevention. It is also easy for the counselor to make errors such as diagnosing and advising.

In contrast to counseling by e-mail, telephone counseling is immediate, feedback is obtained from the client quickly, and there is opportunity to correct mistakes. Counselors can hear the client's voice and realize if they have touched an area which is sensitive for the client. There are many cues, such as the tone of voice, silence and crying, and these cues can guide counselor responses.

When using e-mail, it is harder to avoid direct questions from the client. Whereas, in telephone counseling, client-centered responses often by-pass answering questions, e-mail

[3] Crisis intervention over the Internet also permits the use of a broader range of volunteer counselors, such as the hearing impaired.

exerts a stronger demand on counselors to answer. A question such as "Am I being selfish?" requires that the counselor answer "Yes" or "No." However, it is possible to acknowledge the question without directly answering - for example, "You ask if you are being selfish? As you have asked, that seems to indicate that it has crossed your mind as a possibility, but only you can really answer. The fact of it crossing your mind tells me that you are willing to consider other views and this says a lot of good things about you."

E-mail counselors sometimes find it hard to zero in and, for example, directly ask about "suicide" - typing it seems harsher than asking about suicidal thoughts during telephone counseling, and so a gentler, more caring lead-in is required. Furthermore, since the counselor cannot be sure about the client's age, and since children use the Internet quite easily, counselors must be a little more cautious about inquiring about suicidal inclinations, with this one proviso. The Samaritans feel that they fail their clients if the opportunity to acknowledge and discuss suicidal thoughts and feelings is not actively sought and encouraged.

The language used in e-mail counseling is another area in which the counselor can have difficulties. In telephone counseling, it is easier to assess the nuances of meaning by the tone of the voice. E-mail requires simpler more straightforward language in order to avoid any confusion. Using the word "we" for example can be interpreted as you (the client) and me, suggesting togetherness and support; or it can mean me and my associates in the counseling center. Similarly, "they", an important word, which, if used without care, as in "You'd think they would do something about......," might encourage the client to blame the group of people referred to as "they" rather than face his or her own problems and situation. A simulated example of a typical exchange using this system can be found in Wilson and Lester [69].

Discussion

In 15 months, the Hong Kong Samaritan branch had 467 total e-mail contacts, including repeat contacts. Worldwide in the first three months of 1997, there were 1157 contacts, of which 35 percent have been new contacts. At the Hong Kong Samaritan branch, the length of contact has varied from once daily for two or three weeks, all the way to intermittent contacts over a period of months.

A greater proportion of the writers appear to be suicidal than those contacting centers by telephone or by visiting. Many e-mail writers have a local telephone crisis counseling nearby, but they prefer the medium of the Internet.

For example, one writer could not bring himself to contact his local crisis intervention center, writing of his loneliness and his feelings of despair, partly because of his homosexuality and partly because of his low self-esteem [70]. The counselor and he discussed options and how he might go out and meet people and make friends. When asked what stopped him from doing this, he wrote "I can't because I'm B-()))) and I want to X-(." (He meant that he was ugly and very fat and that he wanted to kill himself.) Thus, even writing does not always make it easy to express oneself directly.

It is evident from this discussion that many of the skills and styles of telephone crisis intervention do transfer to e-mail crisis intervention, but that modifications are necessary because of type of communication. It is also clear that the use of this medium for crisis intervention may provide crisis counseling for those who might not otherwise use face-to-face or telephone counseling. Furthermore, other possibilities exist for crisis intervention via e-mail, including informational messages on improving social skills, assertive behavior and relaxation techniques.

There are disadvantages to the service. E-mails from one individual do not always go to the same branch or to the same counselor in any branch. This prevents attachments of client to counselor, but it also results in less consistency in the counseling approach. However, whereas telephone calls to one center may have a brief synopsis of the previous calls on file, the e-mail system keeps a complete record of all previous e-mails attached to the current e-mail according to Howlett and Langdon [67].[4]

Howlett and Langdon reported that e-mails are more direct, raw and intense than telephone conversations, perhaps because e-mails are less personal than telephone calls so that it is easier to share emotions when there is no one to witness the emotional reaction (such as crying), because the "distance" is greater, and because the privacy more protected. However, this makes the counseling more stressful for the counselors, many of whom report that the e-mails can be a "big shock." In addition, whereas in telephone counseling, the counselor gets a sense of the client's emotional state by the end of the call, in e-mail counseling there is long wait before the client e-mails back, and then it may go to a different counselor at a different branch.

Counselor anxiety is also increased by the public nature of their response (it is saved on subsequent e-mails) and the inability to correct unforeseen nuances in their replies. All replies are checked by a second counselor before sending, and so this diffuses the responsibility. One advantage for the client is the permanent record of the e-mails, so that they can be read and re-read by the client, whereas telephone calls are fleeting.

This form of crisis intervention appears to be viable and useful. It stands on its own as an accepted service alongside telephone and face-to-face contacts, and it can also serve as a stepping-stone to telephone contacts. E-mail clients frequently tell the centers that they have been helped by their interaction with the counselor.

E-Therapy

In recent years, e-therapy, as it has come to be known, has broadened to include Instant Messaging (IM). In recent years, web companies have introduced services that link clients with therapists (MyTherapyNet.com and HelpHorizons.com, for example) where counseling can be conducted using IM, and some therapists are offering IM as a supplement to office-based counseling [71].

Interestingly, LaVallee [71] noted that online providers generally agree that IM is not appropriate for suicidal clients. The e-therapy sites typically urge suicidal people to call 911 and ask them to indicate that they have read this warning before a chat session can begin. However, there is no guarantee that suicidal clients will actually read such a warning or heed it.

The growth of e-therapy has led professional organizations to devise ethical standards, such as the American Psychological Association and the American Psychiatric Association.

[4] The system uses special software to prevent clients deleting all previous communications and replies (Robert Langdon, personal communication, August 3, 2007).

This is important especially since some e-therapy websites appear to be of questionable therapeutic value [72]. The American Psychiatric Association [73] listed the following advantages of e-therapy:

(1) It can be synchronous (IM) or asynchronous (e-mails)
(2) It allows access 24/7
(3) It can provide services in areas that have little or no service such as islands and rural areas
(4) It is accessible for people with disabilities (paralysis, agoraphobia, chronic disease, deafness, etc)
(5) It can alleviate clients' fears of confidentiality and stigma since they remain unseen and can remain anonymous
(6) Some clients prefer e-therapy
(7) Clients who have to travel can maintain counseling with the same therapist
(8) Using e-mail, clients and therapists can organize their responses and think them over before transmitting them
(9) Clients do not have to wait until the next appointment in order to communicate
(10)Schedules can be more flexible.

These advantages are similar to those proposed for telephone therapy in the past.

The American Psychiatric Association [73] also listed the risks and limitations of e-therapy:

(1) There are no non-verbal cues which can, therefore, limit the assessment of the client
(2) The medium seems to be unsuited for suicidal clients and those with thought disorders such as paranoia and schizophrenia [74]
(3) It is not secure from breaches of confidentiality [74]
(4) Clients can easily deceive the therapist
(5) Clients must be literate, have computer literacy, and the financial means to purchase the hardware and software necessary

Again, these disadvantages were noted many years ago when counseling by telephone was explored.

Caveats From Experiences with Telephone Therapy

There are issues that arise with e-therapy simply as a result of the medium involved in the communication. For these issues, much can be learned from the experiences of psychotherapists using the telephone as a medium of communication with clients. Lester [57] discussed three problems that can arise in conducting counseling by telephone, and he subsequently noted that these same problems can arise in e-therapy [75].

(1) Conversation or Therapy?

When psychotherapists see clients in their offices, the setting is formal. There may be a waiting room, a receptionist, a desk behind which the therapist sits, etc. Counseling by telephone or the Internet can occur with the therapist and client both in their own homes, and it uses a medium which is used for conversation with friends, relatives, and lovers. It is, therefore, easy for the therapist to slip from a therapeutic mode into a conversational mode, thereby minimizing, distorting, and even eliminating the therapeutic process. In telephone crisis intervention centers, this error was not common in acute crisis calls from first-time callers, but it was a potential problem with chronic callers, that is, those who called regularly [76]. E-therapy clients can become long-term ("chronic") clients, and so slipping into conversational mode may be a real danger for both therapist and client.

(2) Transference and Countertransference

In psychoanalysis, transference (from client to therapist) is facilitated by the psychoanalyst sitting out of sight of the client and, initially, by saying very little. Telephone therapy removes visual contact between client and therapist, thereby increasing the potential of strong transference and countertransference. E-therapy goes further and removes the quality of the voice of both agents, increasing the potential even further.

Transference in psychoanalysis is part of the process of therapy, but the psychoanalyst has three to five years to resolve the transference. Conventional therapy is less intensive, and the transference can be more disruptive to the therapeutic process. This relative anonymity may be advantageous for some clients who can then imagine their therapist to be whatever they need the therapist to be - positive transference [57]. On the other hand, the transference can become destructive if the relationship between the therapist and client becomes nontherapeutic. The relationship can easily become one of friendship on both sides and even romantic.

In telephone counseling services which also have walk-in clinics, this transference and countertransference can be dealt with by having the client visit the center to meet the telephone counselors so that the fantasies of each can be confronted by reality [57]. E-therapy can occur between therapists and clients in different regions of a country and even in different countries. Such face-to-face confrontations are not possible when client and counselor are separated in this way. Although the use of video instant messaging may overcome this to some extent, this addition to instant messaging may discourage some clients from using the service.

(3) Client Control, Anonymity and Immediacy

As in telephone therapy, clients using the Internet for counseling can more easily remain anonymous, and the medium gives them more control. It is easier to disconnect from the Internet (as it is by hanging up the telephone in telephone counseling) than it is to get up and walk out of a therapist's office. This gives the client more power (which may be useful for the client), but this also tends to make the therapist more anxious. Such anxiety may interfere with the therapist providing effective counseling.

Immediacy is also possible in Internet counseling. Therapists can be contacted at any time and, if they log on to check on clients (or if they remain permanently online), then they can see that a client has sent an e-mail or an Instant Message. They may be tempted to respond immediately. In contrast, office visits are scheduled, and the prospect of a visit to the therapist's office several days hence can be useful in helping clients learn how to cope with today and tomorrow by themselves.

In addition, the immediacy of e-therapy communications from clients can result in irritation and annoyance on the part of the therapists who may come to resent such continual "demands" (in contrast to the scheduled sessions of face-to-face therapy sessions), thereby creating further problems of countertransference.

The possibility of hoaxes is greater with online communications, and Ball [77] reported receiving a suicidal communication by e-mail to which he responded. When he sent the police to the person's home, the person was safe and well and denied sending the e-mail.

Conclusion

The Internet is unregulated, and there is no guarantee about the quality and safety of information provided from web sites and search engines page-ranks, a measure of site inter-connectiveness and popularity. Content-related problems have been recognized by the European Commission since October 1996 [78,79]. They categorized problematic material as illegal versus harmful and stated that these categories of content are different, pose radically different issues of principle, and call for very different legal and technological responses. The difference between illegal and harmful content is that the former is criminalized by national laws, while the latter is considered as offensive or disgusting by some people but certainly not criminalized by national laws [80]. This latter is the case for sites and material considered to be pro-suicide. Possible approaches for reducing the risk from harmful material are based on self regulation by Internet service providers and regulation by concerned parents. However, attempts to regulate information delivered on Internet and to enhance public protection are opposed by groups who supporting freedom of expression. Since suicide is considered by some individual to be a matter of personal choice, it should be protected by freedom of expression laws. Furthermore, "pro-suicide" sites are viewed only as "pro-choice" sites [81].

The methods used to rate sites and the currently available filtering software are not without limitations and criticisms [80]. In the latter case, the evidence is that parents are frequently less informed and skilled in information technologies than their children are. Thus, there will most likely always be accessible websites, even for children, that encourage suicidal behavior alongside websites whose aim is to prevent suicide and help those who are suicidal. For these latter websites, there will never be a feasible way to assess their quality and make clear to users whether the information on the website is correct or whether those presenting themselves as helpers and counselors are trained and qualified to help.

In discussing how professionals should react to suicidal communications that they encounter via the Internet, Richard et al. [82] suggested that the response should focus on information-sharing and references to useful sources of information. Professionals should avoid establishing a relationship that resembles a psychotherapeutic contact, and they should specifically disclaim any psychotherapeutic role. However, many professionals will ignore such advice.

In addition to the risks and problems associated with e-therapy discussed above, there are other issues that impact on e-therapy simply from the nature of the Internet. The Internet, for many reasons, such as the easy access to all kinds of materials, results in many users engaging in disinhibited behavior [83]. Aside from behaviors such as flaming, there is often a reduction in concerns for self-presentation and the judgment of others, as is evidenced in Facebook and MySpace.

Second, Internet addiction is a common phenomenon, and e-therapy permits clients to spend enormous amounts of time writing. A similar phenomenon has been observed by telephone counseling services. Brockopp, Lester and Blum [84], in a discussion of the management of chronic callers to telephone counseling services, documented one client who spent 35 hours a week talking to counselors at the center and another client who called up to five times each evening. Such "addictive" behaviors are not psychologically healthy.

On the other hand, the Internet may be attractive as a medium for people with particular life-styles and personality traits. Some of these styles and traits may be useful for e-therapy, while others may pose problems. For example, Weisskirch and Murphy [85] found that college students who reported using the Internet for instant messaging scored significantly higher on a measure of sensation-seeking. Since sensation-seeking is associated with higher levels of self-disclosure [86], those using the Internet for therapeutic purposes (via e-mail or instant messaging) might find it easier to self-disclose. Some segments of the population, such as adolescents [49], may also find the Internet attractive as a source of information and help. On the other hand, Mathy and Cooper [87] found a positive association between the number of hours spent online and suicidal ideation and attempts in a community sample, while Mihajlovic et al. [88] found evidence that excessive Internet use is associated with depression. Kim et al. [89] found that Korean adolescents who were addicted to the Internet were more depressed and had more suicidal ideation than non-addicted adolescents. Although correlational studies do not provide evidence for cause-and-effect conclusions, these types of association are troubling and illustrate the need for further in-depth research on these issues.

References

[1] Internet usage statistics - the internet big picture world internet users and population stats. http://www.internetworldstats.com/stats.htm. Accessed September 6 2008.

[2] *United States of America internet usage and broadband usage report.* http://www.internetworldstats.com/am/us.htm. Accessed September 6 2008.

[3] *United Kingdom internet usage stats and market report.* http://www.internetworldstats.com/eu/uk.htm. Accessed September 6 2008.

[4] *Italia internet usage stats and telecom reports.* http://www.internetworldstats.com/eu/it.htm. Accessed September 6 2008.

[5] Amichai-Hamburger Y: Internet and well-being. *Comput Human Behav* 2007; 23:893-897.

[6] Powell J, Clarke A: The www of the world wide web: who, what, and why? *J Med Internet Res* 2002; 4:E4.

[7] Dearness KL, Tomlin A: Development of the national electronic library for mental health: providing evidence-based information for all. *Health Info Libr J* 2001; 18:167-174.

[8] Bell V: Online information, extreme communities and Internet therapy. *Journal of Mental Health* 2007; 16:445-457.

[9] Christensen H, Griffiths K: The internet and mental health practice. *Evid Based Ment Health* 2003; 6:66-69.
[10] Kurioka S, Muto T, Tarumi K: Characteristics of health counselling in the workplace via e-mail. *Occup Med* 2001; 51:427-432.
[11] Omar HH: A model program for youth suicide prevention. *Int J Adolesc Med Health* 2005; 17:275-278.
[12] Prasad V, Owens S: Using the Internet as a source of self-help for people who self-harm. *Psychiatr Bull R Coll Psychiatr* 2001; 25:222-225.
[13] Sher L: The Internet, suicide, and human mental functions. *Can J Psychiatry* 2000; 45:297.
[14] Alao A, Soderberg M, Pohl EL, Alao AL: Cybersuicide. *Cyberpsychol Behav* 2006; 9:489-493.
[15] Biddle L, Donovan J, Hawton K, Kapur N, Gunnell D: Suicide and the Internet. *BMJ* 2008; 336:800-802.
[16] Dobson R: Internet sites may encourage suicide. *BMJ* 1999; 319:337.
[17] Nordt SP, Kelly K, Williams SR, Clark RF: "Black plaque" on the Internet. *J Emerg Med* 1998; 16:223-224.
[18] Prior T: Suicide methods from the Internet. *Am J Psychiatry* 2004; 161:1500-1501.
[19] Thompson S: Suicide and the Internet. *Psychiatr Bull R Coll Psychiatr* 2001; 25:400.
[20] Banberry J: The Internet and its actual influence on suicide. *Psychiatr Bull R Coll Psychiatr* 1999; 23:747-751.
[21] Alao AO, Yolles JC, Armenta W: Cybersuicide. *Am J Psychiatry* 1999; 156:1836-1837.
[22] Becker K, Mayer M, Nagenborg M, El-Faddagh M, Schmidt MH: Parasuicide online. *Nord J Psychiatry* 2004; 58:111-114.
[23] Becker K, Schmidt MH: Internet chat rooms and suicide. *J Am Acad Child Adolesc Psychiatry* 2004; 43:246-247.
[24] Haut F, Morrison A: The Internet and the future of psychiatry. *Psychiatr Bull R Coll Psychiatr* 1998; 22:641-642.
[25] Beatson S, Hosty GS, Smith S: Suicide and the Internet. *Psychiatr Bull R Coll Psychiatr* 2000; 24:434.
[26] Rajagopal S: Suicide pacts and the Internet. *BMJ* 2004; 329:1298-1299.
[27] Samuels D: Let's die together. *Atl Mon* 2007; 299(4):92-98.
[28] Naito A: Internet suicide in Japan. *Clin Child Psychol Psychiatry* 2007; 12:583-597.
[29] Hitosugi M, Nagai T, Tokudome S: A voluntary effort to save the youth suicide via the Internet in Japan. *Int J Nurs Stud* 2007; 44:157.
[30] Anon: Elusive, but not always unstoppable. *The Economist* 2007; 383(8534, June 23):66-67.
[31] Lee DTS, Chan KPM., Yip PSF: Charcoal burning is also popular for suicide pacts made on the Internet. *BMJ* 2005; 330:602.
[32] Mehlum L: The Internet, suicide, and suicide prevention. *Crisis* 2000; 21:186-188.
[33] Stack S: Celebrities and suicide. *Am Sociol Rev* 1992; 52:401-412.
[34] Sisask M, Varnik A, Wasserman D: Internet comments on media reporting of two adolescents' collective suicide attempt. *Arch Suicide Res* 2005; 9:87-98.
[35] Baume P, Cantor CH, Rolfe A: Cybersuicide. *Crisis* 1997; 18:73-79.

[36] Stoney G: Suicide prevention on the Internet. In RJ Koskey, HS Eshkevari, RD Goldney, R Hassan (Eds.). *Suicide prevention:* The global context. New York, Plenum, 1998, pp 237-244.
[37] Baume P, Rolfe A, Clinton M: Suicide on the Internet. *Aust N Z J Ment Health Nurs* 1998; 7:134-141.
[38] Quittner J: Life and death on the web. *Time* 1997 April 7th; 47.
[39] Robinson WG: Heaven's Gate. *Journal of Computer-Mediated Communication* 1997; 3(3): no pagination specified.
[40] Whitlock JL, Powers JL, Eckenrode J: The virtual cutting edge. *Dev Psychol* 2006; 42:407-417.
[41] Eichenberg C: Internet message boards for suicidal people. *Cyberpsychol Behav* 2008; 11:107-113.
[42] Mishara BL, Weisstub DN: Ethical, legal, and practical issues in the control and regulation of suicide promotion and assistance over the Internet. *Suicide Life Threat Behav* 2007; 37:58-65.
[43] Suresh K, Lynch S: Psychiatry and the www. *Psychiatr Bull R Coll Psychiatr* 1998; 22:256-257.
[44] Janson MP, Alessandrini ES, Strunjas SS, Shahab H, El-Mallakh R, Lippmann SB: Internet-observed suicide attempts. *J Clin Psychiatry* 2001; 62:478.
[45] Neimark G, Hurford MO, DiGiacomo J: The Internet as collateral informat. *Am J Psychiatry* 2006; 163:1842.
[46] Huang MP, Alessi NE: The Internet and the future of psychiatry. *Am J Psychiatry* 1996; 153:861-869.
[47] Murphy LJ, Mitchell DL: When writing helps to heal: e-mail as therapy. *Br J Guid Counc* 1998; 26:21032.
[48] Swanton R, Collin P, Burns J, Sorensen I: Engaging, understanding and including young people in the provision of mental health services. *Int J Adolesc Med Health* 2007; 19:325-332.
[49] Gould MS, Munfakh JLH, Lubell K, Kleinman M, Parker S: Seeking help from the Internet during adolescence. *J Am Acad Child Adolesc Psychiatry* 2002; 41:1182-1189.
[50] Mandrusiak M, Rudd MD, Joiner TE, Berman AL, Van Orden KA, Witte T: Warning signs for suicide in the Internet. *Suicide Life Threat Behav* 2006; 36:263-271.
[51] Ellen EF: Identifying and treating suicidal college students. *Psychiatric Times* 2002; 19(8):1,4,6-7.
[52] Seabury BA: An evaluation of on-line interactive tutorials designed to teach practice concepts. *Journal of Teaching in Social Work* 2005; 25(1/2):103-115.
[53] Stone DM, Barber CW, Potter L: Public health training online: The National Center for Suicide Prevention Training. *Am J Prev Med* 2005; 29(5S2):247-251.
[54] Cohen D, Putney R: Suicide website resources for professionals and consumers. *Journal of Mental Health & Aging* 2003; 9(2):67-72.
[55] Penn DL, Simpson L, Edie G, Leggett S, Wood L, Hagwood J, Krysinska K, Yellowlees P, De Leo D: Development of ACROSSnet. *Health Informatics J* 2005; 11:275-293.
[56] Barak A: Emotional support and suicide prevention through the Internet. *Comput Human Behav* 2007; 23:971-984.
[57] Lester D: Crisis intervention and counseling by telephone. Springfield, Thomas, 2002.

[58] Gilat I, Shahar G: Emotional first aid for a suicide crisis. *Psychiatry* 2007; 70:12-18.
[59] Murero M, Rice RE (Eds.): *The Internet and health care.* Mahwah, Lawrence Erlbaum, 2006.
[60] Rodham K, Gavin J, Miles M: I hear, I listen and I care. *Suicide Life Threat Behav* 2007; 37:422-430.
[61] Lukas C: *Silent grief* (revised edition). London, Jessica Kingsley, 2007.
[62] Hollander EM: Cyber community in the valley of the shadow of death. *Journal of Loss & Trauma* 2001; 6:135-146.
[63] Hoffman WA: Telematic technologies in mental health caring. *Issues Ment Health Nurs* 2006; 27:461-474.
[64] Armson S: Suicide and cyberspace. *Crisis* 1997; 18:103-105.
[65] Bale C: Befriending in cyberspace. *Crisis* 2001; 22:10-11.
[66] Baughan R: E-listening. *Counselling* 2000; 11:292-293.
[67] Howlett S, Langdon R: Messages to Jo. In G Bolton, S Howlett, C Lago, JK Wright (Eds.). *Writing cures.* New York, Brunner-Routledge, 2004, pp 160-169.
[68] Morgan C: Befriending by e-mail. Befriending Worldwide 1996; issue 49:11.
[69] Wilson G, Lester D: Crisis intervention by e-mail. *Crisis Intervention & Time-Limited Treatment* 1998; 4:81-87.
[70] Scott V: Listening to the silence. *Paper presented at the Befrienders International Conference,* Kuala Lumpur, Malaysia, July 1996.
[71] LaVallee A: Chat therapy. *Wall St J* 2006; March 28:D1,D3.
[72] Gray A: Cybertherapy. *Psychiatr Bull R Coll Psychiatr* 1999; 23:690-691.
[73] American Psychiatric Association: Frequently asked questions e-therapy/ www.psych.org/psych_pract/clin_issues/etherapyfaqs.cfm. Accessed March 29, 2006.
[74] Luo J: Instant messaging. *Psychiatr News* 2005; 40(8):56-60.
[75] Lester D: E-therapy. *Psychol Rep* 2006; 99:894-896.
[76] Brockopp GW: The telephone call; conversation or therapy. In D Lester (Ed.). *Crisis intervention and counseling by telephone.* Springfield, Charles Thomas, 2002, pp 88-91.
[77] Ball D: A virtual cry for help? *Br J Psychiatry* 2000; 177:568.
[78] European Commission: Illegal and harmful content on the internet. *Com* (96) 487, Brussels, 16 October 1996.
[79] European Commission: Green paper on the protection of minors and human dignity in audovisual and information services. Brussels, 16 October 2006.
[80] Akdeniz A: Controlling illegal and harmful content on the internet. In Wall DS (Ed.). *Crime and the Internet.* London, Routledge, 2001, pp 113-140.
[81] *Pro suicide sites.* http://www.mentalnurse.org.uk/2008/04/13/pro-suicide-sites/. Accessed September 8 2008.
[82] Richard J, Werth JL, Rogers JR: Rational and assisted suicidal communication on the Internet. *Ethics Behav* 2000; 10:215-238.
[83] Joinson A: Causes and implications of disinhibited behavior on the Internet. In *J Gackenbach* (Ed.). Psychology and the Internet. San Diego, Academic, 1998, pp 43-60.
[84] Brockopp GW, Lester D, Blum D: The chronic caller. In D Lester (Ed.). *Crisis intervention and counseling by telephone.* Springfield, Charles Thomas, 2002, pp 154-170.
[85] Weisskirch RS, Murphy LC: Friends, porn, and punk. *Adolescence* 2004; 39:189-201.

[86] Zuckerman M: *Behavioral expression and biosocial bases of sensation seeking.* New York, Cambridge University Press, 1994.
[87] Mathy RM, Cooper A: The duration and frequency of Internet use in a nonclinical sample. *Psychotherapy* 2003; 40:125-135.
[88] Mihajlovic G, Hinic D, Damjanovic A, Gajic T, Dukic-Dejanovic S: Excessive Internet use and depressive disorders. *Psychiatr Danub* 2008; 20(1):6-15.
[89] Kim K, Ryu E, Chon MY, Yeun EJ, Choi SY, Seo JS, Nam BW: Internet addiction in Korean adolescents and its relation to depression and suicidal ideation. *Int J Nurs Stud* 2006; 43:185-192.

In: Internet and Suicide
Editors: L. Sher and A. Vilens
ISBN 978-1-60741-077-5

Chapter 7

PREVENTING SUICIDE THROUGH THE INTERNET

Marco Sarchiapone [1]***, Sanja Temnik*** [2] ***and Vladimir Carli*** [1]
[1] University of Molise, Campobasso, Italy
[2] University of Primorska, Koper, Slovenia

ABSTRACT

In this chapter, we direct our focus to the possibilities for suicide prevention, as well as the dangers for suicide promotion, through the Internet. Internet is a virtual representation of our real world, which adds new modalities to the latter. One could therefore argue, that the various pro-suicide content on the World Wide Web might foster the individual`s advancement through the stages of the suicidal process, putting the suicidal peson at even greater risk of behavioral expressions of suicidality. On the other hand, Internet provides new possibilities for the release of emotional distress, the broadening of the individual`s social network and getting information on different ways to get help in case of a mental disorder or the absence of psychological well-being. As such, it might encourage the person in need to seek help or even professonal treatment, before committing suicide. Different strategies for maximizing effective suicide prevention while minimizing suicide promotion on the Internet are discussed.

INTRODUCTION

Internet is not an independent world by itself; instead, it is a virtual representation of our `real world`. It is produced, as well as used, by people with various bio-psycho-social backgrounds. As such, issues of our `real` lives are represented on the Internet, albeit with more or less new modalities. One of the key peculiarities of this instrument is certainly the breaking of borders and distances. Nowadays, the access to unlimited amounts of information is available to anybody, and so is the opportunity to share ones thoughts, feelings and experiences with others. Greater anonymity makes self-disclosure easier for a lot of people; Internet might therefore represent the most honest of all media.

The impact of Internet on the individual becomes clear if we remember, that it is possible, through imagination, to reach any information stored in our memory in the shortest time, and forge it – like a blacksmith - through fantasy (a function in which thought is involved), according to our actual needs. Internet renders this phenomenon in a very similar way, multiplying its dimensions thousand-fold and more. So, the same result is multiplied – and, furthermore, the range of its consequences. Internet could therefore very well foster the growth of a passive suicidal thought into an active one, and make it easier for the individual at risk to advance through the stages of the suicidal process.

Whereas the memorial functions always localize an experience in the rememberer`s past, imagination does not [1]. It may create the same kind of experience over and over again, but it may also give it a different setting each time. Its setting is more varied than that of memory. While there is only one personal past, there are several directions in which the objects and events of the imagination may be referred [1]. Enormous amounts of data, available online, can therefore, in our minds, take numerous possible imaginary pathways. The outcome is always a question of absorbed information, the individual`s biography (life history and experiences), dispositional background (genetic makeup, personality characteristics) and living environment (socio-economical situation, social network, activities and involvement in everyday life). Additionally, there are some interesting phenomena, associated with imagination, such as the `imagination inflation`, for example. The term relates to people's considering as real those events from their past which were only imagined [2]. Imagination of contrary-to-the truth, but possible events, may lead people to believe that this event really took place in their life. This happens in 25-30% of cases, when people imagine a certain experience. Also, when people imagine that other people experienced something, they might begin to believe that this event happened to them, as well [2]. The psychological mechanisms of these phenomena could be based on a misinformation effect, a specific mechanism of reconstruction of autobiographical memories (specific events information may be built into narratives concerning personal past; this information is of fragmentary nature and an individual is not aware of the fact that it refers to a counterfactual event). Internet and imagination go hand in hand; one feeds of another, and they push each other to new dimensions, creating a new reality in a similar way.

The majority of Internet users are adolescents or young adults, that, as an age group, represent the population sample, that is, apart from the various benefits of their tender age, exposed to a high risk of life-endangering behaviour patterns and experiences, suicide being one of them. In the age group 15 – 34, suicide is one of the most important causes of death, and ranks as the second cause of death, after traffic accidents and other injuries, in the ages 15-19. In Europe each year, approximately 13,500 young men and women, aged 15-24 years, die by suicide. Serious health and safety issues such as motor vehicle crashes, violence, substance abuse, and promiscuous sexual behaviors adversely affect adolescents and young adults. Various forms of violent behavior among youth, i.e. dating violence, peer violence and suicidal behaviors, substantially overlap and intensify the consequences of individual violence forms [3]. Significant positive correlations have been identified among Internet addiction, depression and suicidal ideation in adolescents [4].

In the so-called *cyber-era,* it is very easy to contact people from all over the world who share the same interest with you – suicide being one of them. And if you want a comprehensive *how-to* guide, you simply find yourself an Internet suicide manual, which is easier than you might imagine. With all these concerns in mind, one could easily forget about the numerous opportunities, that the Internet provides for positive (mental) health promotion and negative (mental) health prevention. It can, for example, foster the exchange of useful information, enable an efficient collection of valuable data and even provide additional options for treatment of suicidal individuals. If used appropriately, the power of Internet as a communication tool can be turned into a positive direction and benefit mental health patients, including suicidal ones.

INTERNET: E-MERGENCY ROOM

On the Internet, the information is organized in different ways. The basic forms of information exchange are websites, e-mail, chat, forums and blogs. Every method of information organization has its specific features, i.e. in terms of interactivity, number and kind of users that can be reached, as well as accessibility to the public.

Basically, interactions on the Internet occur in 2 types of groups:

a. Groups, in which professional figures are present
b. Groups, consisting of peers (however, leaders exist in this case, too)

In the first group, the interaction is usually directed `contra` suicide, whereas in the second group, either `pro` or `contra` may be the case. Somehow, Internet can be considered as an `e-mergency room`, where people seek - and receive - information and support either in one direction or another.

There are three major categories of suicide-related information on the Internet. The first category covers pro-suicide information, information on how to commit suicide, or sites that encourage suicide. Then there are news that describe suicide and suicide-related events. Finally, there are sites about suicide prevention that may be aimed at professionals, involved in the field of Suicidology, or suicidal patients themselves.

Recently, Internet websites, chat rooms and forums, that may encourage people to commit suicide by providing detailed information about different ways on how to take your own life, received a lot of attention. This issue has been specifically raised in England, in the framework of the England Country Questionnaire. Together with other government departments, England is working on non-legislative action that might discourage sites like this. The actions include:

a. Raising awareness amongst parents and the general public about the possible harmful implications of such websites/chat rooms, that might be accessed by vulnerable people at risk of suicide
b. Assurance of a greater prominence of more responsible sites in results, returned by web search engines. This can be achieved with the help of service providers of such search engines
c. Encouragement of a proactive role of Internet service providers when it comes to the observation and evaluation of the websites` content.

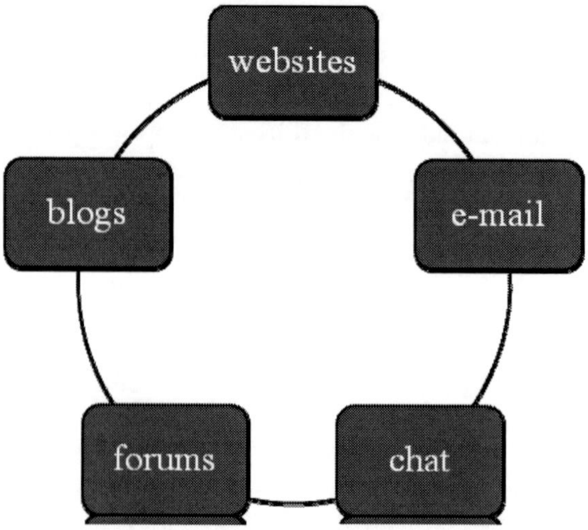

Picture 1. Different forms of information exchange via the Internet.

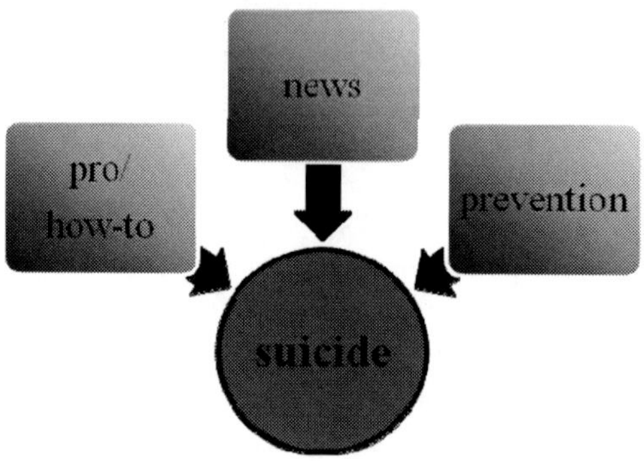

Picture 2. Suicide-related information on the Internet.

Nowadays, the majority of newspapers and news agencies additionally disseminate information via the Internet. The issues raised may be the same as in other types of media. However, the dissemination of information on the Internet has some specific characteristics that make it a unique media in many ways. For example, while providing immediate and easy access to various news sources, Internet also enables us to easily search for a specific topic and browse through news archives. One could say that something like a `historical archive `is accessible to everybody. I.e. sensationalistic news about suicide, that is the topic of discussion on the TV or in the newspapers for a few days, might stay on the Internet forever. An intrinsic problem of the Internet is the lack of editorial supervision, which would define minimal required standards for published material.

Information on suicide prevention on the Internet covers, for example, websites of numerous associations, dealing with suicide research (i.e. AAS, IASP, IASR), websites of suicide prevention centers and websites, based on suicide-related research projects. The World Health Organization devoted some pages of their website to suicide prevention as well. These sites are mainly aimed at researchers and health care professionals. They enable an efficient exchange of information between researchers as well as the transmission of information from investigative environment into clinical practice. However, there is no doubt that the latter could be improved and expanded even further, since the Internet is still quite underutilitized in terms of active suicide prevention. Especially the interactive nature of such pages should be emphasized.

`The Blueprints for Violence` webpage is one example of positive information exchange on the Internet [5]. It is a site that recommends interventions, promoting social and interpersonal skills as well as reducing or preventing violence and drug and alcohol abuse. The Web site provides information on eleven programs that meet the standards established by the CSPV Advisory Committee. One of the strengths of this Web site is the rigorous criteria they claim to use for support of their recommendations for practice. The addition of cost-benefit for success of Blueprint program arms in diverse settings is valuable information for health care providers' decisions about whether or not implement such programs in their setting with their specific populations.

The second group of suicide prevention websites are those aiming to reach suicidal patients. Contrary to the `*how to die*`- content of pro-suicide websites, these websites provide support and information on `*how to survive*`. They usually contain emergency telephone numbers and addresses in different areas, where a suicidal individual can receive proper help and care. Additionally, they often include information and advice from suicide survivors and educate their visitors about the nature of suicidality and mental disorders in general.

Numerous studies show an almost surprisingly high rate of suicide-related material that can be found on the Internet. E.g. Biddle et al. [6] performed a search on popular Internet search engines (Google, Yahoo, MSN and ASK), using the following terms:

a. Suicide
b. Suicide methods
c. Suicide sure methods
d. Most effective methods of suicide
e. Methods of suicide
f. Ways to commit suicide
g. Ways to commit suicide
h. How to commit suicide
i. How to kill yourself
j. Easy suicide methods
k. Best suicide methods
l. Pain free suicide
m. Quick suicide.

They retrieved, visited and viewed a total of 480 web addresses (first ten from each search) and 240 unique sites. 20% of the sites were based on suicide as the primary focus, and about half of these pages encouraged, promoted or facilitated it. 13% of sites focused on suicide prevention or offered support, while 12% sites forbade or discouraged it. Almost all the sites, dedicated to suicide and those including factual information, offered information about suicidal methods. Google and Yahoo returned the most sites dedicated to suicide, while MSN search results were more likely to focus on prevention, support, academics and policy. Three most common sites, occurring in the search, promoted suicide, and Wikipedia's informational article on suicide was fourth. These top four sites all contained detailed information on suicidal methodology, specifically addressing method speed, certainty, and potential amount of pain. The authors note, that an attempt to remove web pages, containing potentially most risky information, would practically not be possible. They concluded that the best strategy in order to make Internet more pro than contra in the battle against suicide, would be the pursuit of website optimization strategies in order to maximize the likelihood that suicidal people access helpful rather than potentially harmful sites in times of crisis.

The promotion of suicide and detailed description of suicide methods on the Internet have led to widespread concern that legal control is mandated. Apart from value concerns pertaining to attitudes about suicide, the guarantee of freedom of expression presents a serious challenge to the introduction of restrictive laws, and will undoubtedly become one of the crucial subjects of discussion in future [7].

There is a general consensus between experts, that mental health professionals should ask patients about their Internet use. Psychiatric exploration should include questions of manner and frequency of media use [8]. Depressed, suicidal and potentially suicidal patients who use the Internet, may be especially at risk [9]. Clinicians could assist frequent Internet users in locating helpful, supportive online resources, so that their Internet use would be more therapeutic than harmful.

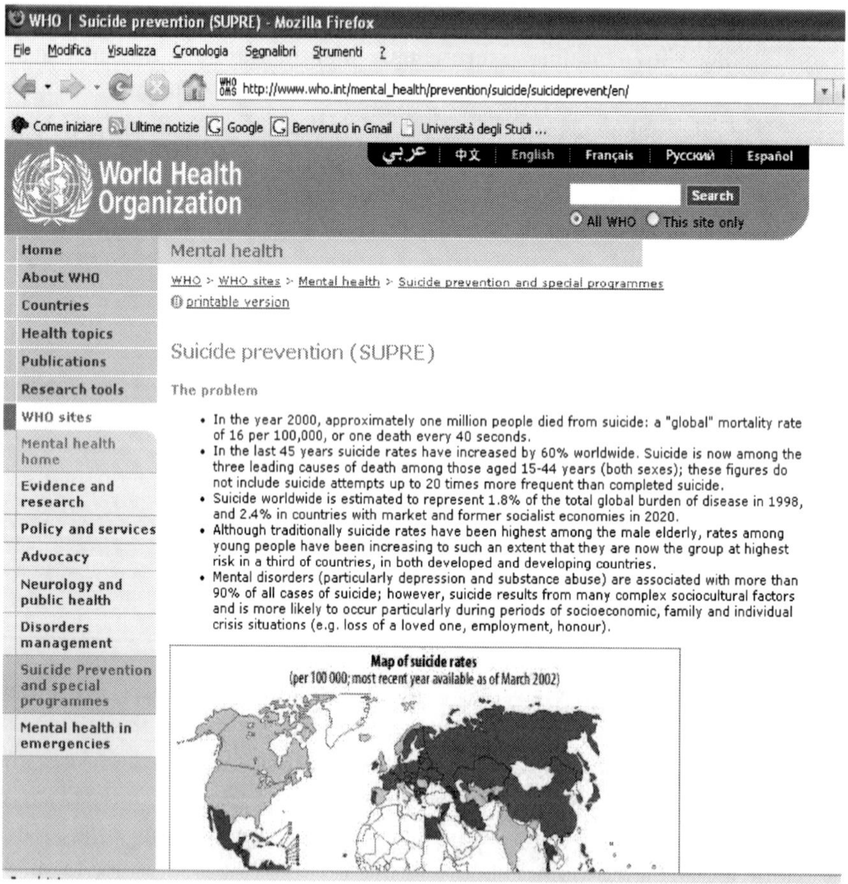

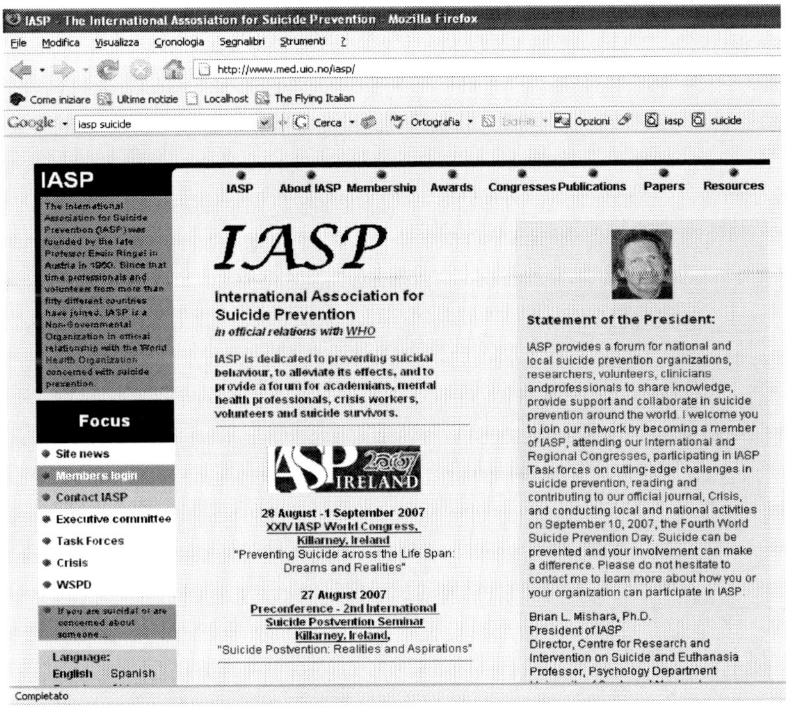

Picture 3. (Continued)

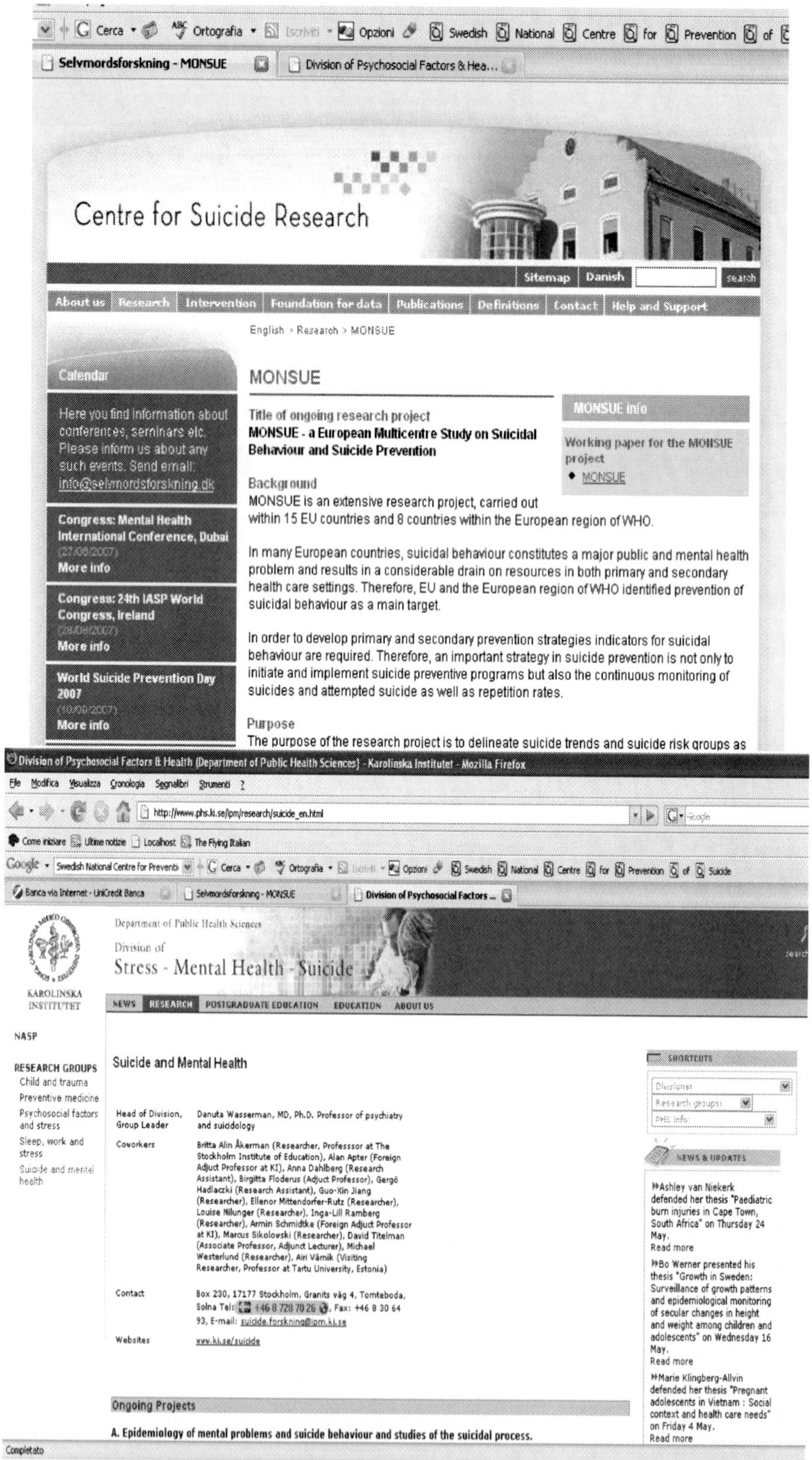

Picture 3. Some webpages on suicide prevention.

SUICID-E-PREVENTION

If we take a closer look at suicide-related resources on the Internet, it becomes clear that it is everything but easy to differentiate between websites, aimed at mental health professionals, and those aimed at suicidal individuals, when looking for information on suicide help or prevention via an Internet search engine. You get a very heterogenous mixture of websites and someone, looking for help, could very easily get lost in a jungle of suicide-related statistics and, instead of finding an emergency phone number, find information about the upcoming Suicide Symposium instead. The latter probably wouldn`t have been of much help for the individual in question.

As Alao et al. [10] have pointed out, Internet has great potential in psychiatric education, clinical care, and research. It has expanded into the domain of psychiatry and psychotherapy, and is used by psychiatric patients for information, communication and therapeutic purposes [11]. But not only Psychiatry, other medical fields as well have discovered the potential of Internet in terms of improving the efficiency of information and knowledge exchange. E.g. The Neuropsych Questionnaire (NPQ), an Internet-based symptom questionnaire that is reliable, valid and available to psychiatrists, psychologists and neurologists [12], is probably a good example of where the interconnection between Internet and the field of health is going to be heading in the future.

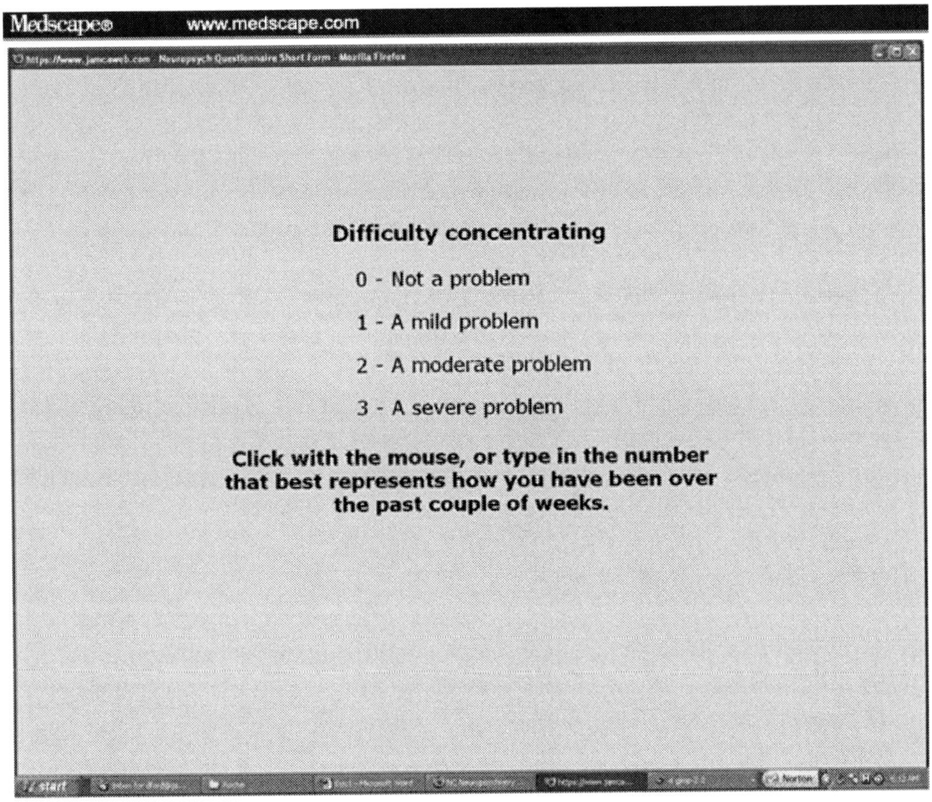

Picture 4. 'On-screen' item presentation in the NPQ.

Internet can be of great help when trying to help people in severe emotional distress, including those, contemplating suicide. In can offer emotional support, act as a source of helpful – sometimes even life-saving – information, enable a broadening of the individual`s social network, and much more. In Israel, for example, a project named SAHAR was launched in 2005, that was based on the idea to initiate an anonymous, confidential online environment, which woud attract people going through a crisis and offer them a listening ear and a shoulder to lean on. The help would be provided by anonymous, skilled helpers. The core of this exclusively online service is a content-rich website, that provides information for people in need, as well as personal communication with users through synchronous and asynchronous support. Group communication is enabled via online forums and a chatroom. Barak [13] found out that their website was accessed more than 10,000 times a month, or 350 times a day, which is not a low number, especially considering Israel`s small population. Approx. 1000 personal contacts per month get initiated; more than a third of those are clearly suicidal. Over 200 new messages are posted on the forum each day. In Australia, a unique Internet-based mental health service Reach Out! was launched in 1998 [14]. Since then, it has been accessed by over four million users and 332 young people have been directly involved in the development and delivery of the service. This data clearly suggest, that people in need benefit profoundly by applications and web portals like the ones mentioned.

Technological progress brought us Internet, and Internet brought us e-health. *E-health* is a term for healthcare practice, which is supported by electronic processes and communication. Eysenbach [15] defines it as an emerging field in the intersection of medical informatics, public health and business, referring to health services and information delivered or enhanced through the Internet and related technologies. In a broader sense, the term characterizes not only a technical development, but also a state-of-mind, a way of thinking, an attitude, and a commitment for networked, global thinking, to improve health care locally, regionally, and worldwide by using information and communication technology. It can encompass a range of services that are at the crossroads of medicine/healthcare and information technology:

a. *Electronic Medical Records* enable easy communication of patient data between different healthcare professionals (GPs, specialists, care team, pharmacy).
b. *Telemedicine* includes all types of physical and psychological measurements that do not require a patient to travel to a specialist. When this service works, patients need to travel less to a specialist or conversely the specialist has a larger catchment area.
c. *Evidence-Based Medicine* entails a system that provides information on appropriate treatment under certain patient conditions. The healthcare professional can look up whether his/her diagnosis is in line with scientific research. A big advantage is that the data can be kept up-to-date.
d. *Consumer Health Informatics* (or citizen-oriented information provision): both healthy individuals and patients want to be informed on medical topics.
e. *Health Knowledge Management* (or specialist-oriented information provision): e.g. in an overview of latest medical journals, best practice guidelines or epidemiological tracking.
f. *Virtual Healthcare Teams* consist of healthcare professionals who collaborate and share information on patients through digital equipment.
g. *M-Health* includes the use of mobile devices in collecting aggregate and patient level health data, providing healthcare information to practitioners, researchers and

patients, real-time monitoring of patient vitals, and direct provision of care (via mobile telemedicine).

h. *E-health Grids* are being used in medical research to provide powerful computing and data manegement capabilities to handle large amounts of heterogenous data.

E-therapy can be understood as one of the numerous dimensions of e-health. It is getting more and more popular. It covers different forms of counselling from the part of a mental health professional. The expert can offer emotional support, mental health advice, or other professional guidance. It can be the answer to one question or an ongoing conversation; it can be done by e-mail, chat, video or over an Internet-phone [16]. It is a viable alternative source of help when traditional psychotherapy is not accessible, or a suitable source of additional support to the regular psychiatric and/or psychotherapeutic treatment. In this sense, it is in no way a substitute for traditional mental health care, but rather a complementary tool that might efficiently improve the outcome of the individual`s treatment. It has many positive sides, i.e. it is effective, private, easily accessible and conducted by skilled and qualified professionals. For some people, it might provide the only opportunity to receive help from a professional therapist. E-therapy could also prove to profoundly lower the so-called `treatment gap` (referring to the number of people in need of treatment but not receiving any), which is especially high in the case of mental disorders.

Some of the benefits of e-therapy are listed below:

a. Clients can access services at any time, any day of the week.
b. Clients in remote and under-served regions can access these services. Clients from various areas are given the access to highly specialized practitioners, that might otherwise not be available in an acceptable geographical distance.
c. Clients who are physically unable to leave their homes can access these services.
d. Clients in small communities get provided confidentiality.
e. E-counselling may encourage those, who find it particularly hard to be relaxed in interpersonal contacts, to talk more openly about their problems and painful experiences.
f. Even individuals who are (be it for one reason or another) unwilling to seek help `face to face` may be reached therapeutically.
g. Nowadays, a lot of people are travelling often. E-therapy makes services available from anywhere in the world.
h. A higher degree of reflection on the issues discussed may be possible by the use of e-mail and other asynchronic forms.
i. It makes it possible for practitioners to develop more specialized practices.
j. It is evidently efficient when it comes to time economy: It reduces the time needed for the client and practitioner to develop rapport. It allows practitioners more flexibility in their work schedules.
k. Perhaps the most crucial benefit of e-therapy is that it makes help available to the client in time of greatest need.

At this stage, where e-therapy is still fighting to earn itself recognition and a secure place in mental health care, there are still many weak points, in which Internet counseling needs to improve. As Recupero and Rainey [17] have found, these websites often encounter the following problems:

a. They contain confusing information about the nature of the service offered, and do not always specify qualifications of providers.
b. Some providers do not appear qualified to provide the services the Web sites advertise.
c. Some Web sites exclude individuals with specific diagnoses, others render prospective clients ineligible to receive services (e.g. suicidality).
d. Web sites are not generally proactive about providing resources for visitors in crisis.
e. Only a minority of these Web sites disclose limits to client data security and confidentiality.

Since experiences with e-therapy might influence a patient`s attitude towards traditional psychotherapy, as well as the individual`s (mental) health, it certainly is our duty and responsibility to keep the quality of Internet-based counselling as high as possible.

Another example of how the experts might benefit with the use of Internet, comes in the form of online workshops and training. E.g. in the US, the National Center for Suicide Prevention Training (NCSPT) has been launched [18]. It offers an online professional development workshop series for public officials, service providers, and community-based coalitions involved in suicide prevention. Using a public health framework of prevention, the three workshops implemented to date have drawn over 1200 participants nationally and internationally over the past 3 years. Workshop participants, completing the post-test and evaluation, show consistent improvement in their knowledge of suicide, rate their online training experience positively, and report that they would take additional online courses, if offered. Online training is a valuable option to help meet suicide prevention training needs employing flexible, easy-to-use, and inexpensive Internet technology.

Computer-assisted instruction is able to bridge the gap between classroom learning and bedside competence of health workers. I.e. Fleetwood et al. [19] reported confirmed efficiency of MedEthEx Online, a computer-based online program for an ethical decision-making course for students. The process of education can also take place in the form of discussion groups, either on the national or international level, using list-servers on the Internet [20].

Let us not forget, that writing, which is like oxygen of the Internet, can provide the most honest and truthful information about an individual. Analyzing and investigating the writing characteristics of suicidal people on the Internet could be the pathway to understanding them better than it would ever be possible otherwise. Barak and Miron [21] performed one such analysis and found out, that: a. Suicidal persons have significantly more stable and global attributions than people, who are either emotionally distressed, non-suicidal or non-distressed, b. Suicidal people are distinctively self-focused in their writing and c. Suicidal individuals express significantly more unbearable psychological pain and cognitive constriction than emotionally highly distressed, but non-suicidal persons.

PRO-SUICID-E-LIMINATION

There are many risks, associated with Internet, when it comes to suicide as well. Perhaps the most dramatic example of facilitating suicide via the World Wide Web may be in the form of *suicide pacts*. These are pacts that are prearranged between strangers who meet over the Internet. Two or more people come to the agreement to commit suicide together at a given place and time [22]. A *suicide cluster* is a group of suicides that occur closer together in time and space than would normally be expected in a given community, with suicides occurring later in the cluster being motivated by earlier suicides. In *mass suicide*, several people commit suicide usually influenced by charismatic leadership, strong loyalties, or religious beliefs. A common term for such actions, when occurring on the Internet, is `*net suicide*` [23].

This phenomenon is not, as one might believe, limited to our Western culture, but becoming more and more common in the Eastern world, too; e.g. in Japan, which already has one of the highest suicide rates in the world, approx. 60 people a year might die on the basis of a suicide pact. In an international comparison of suicide pacts, pacts between spouses were found to predominate in the United States and England, between lovers in Japan, and between friends in India [22].

Authors like Mehlum [24] talk about a new form of the so-called `*suicide contagion*`, first described by Phillips (1974) in the case of sensationalistic newspaper stories on suicide. Later, Phillips and Carstensen (1986) confirmed the same effect in the case of real television studies on suicide, while Schmidtke and Häfner (1989) did it in the frame of fictitious television stories on suicide. However, these contagious effects may be counteracted through collaboration between responsible people in the media and experts in suicidology.

Not only do numerous websites, be it `pro` or `contra` suicide, provide detailed description on various suicide methods - which are, being just a few mouse clicks away, now closer to everyone than ever before - one can even learn about new, inventive and previously less known ways on taking the own life, such as the more recent cases of `charcoal burning` [25] or suicidal asphyxia by using helium [26].

Suicide clusters in the young are a well-known problem. As we know, the young are the most susceptible to various influences of mass media. In the case of Internet, there are many possible ways, in which a suicide contagion might be provoked. Pro-suicide websites that present suicide as a solution rather than a problem are one of the basic examples. Some of these websites are highly graphic, with copies of suicide notes, death certificates, and color photographs. There are also electronic bulletin boards, where suicide notes or suicidal intentions are posted. Many news groups and bulletin boards on the net positively advocate suicide and discourage individuals from seeking psychiatric help, dismissing it as worse than useless. Dobson [27] even mentions a site that aimed to set up the world's first suicide assistance telephone hotline, which would include touch key access to an A-Z of suicide techniques. The callers would even be offered the opportunity of making a final recorded message!

It seems rather impossible to find all websites with such content and remove them from the World Wide Web. Unlimited possibilities of the latter allow no traditional boundaries. Neither is it possible to avoid the exposure of children and the young to unsuitable content, although parents should certainly aim to involve themselves in their children's lives, including Internet use. The youngest members of our society should certainly learn how to use Internet for the best, and avoid destructive influences.

Certain forms of control, however, are possible. E.g. the use of keywords, on the basis of which one accesses specific websites, can be regulated. One can reach practically every corner of the Internet using a few powerful search engines, such as Google or Yahoo, which react to keywords, inserted by the users. One possibility for such intervention would be to encourage major companies, which run these search engines, to shift the traffic, resulting from specific keywords (such as `suicide`), to anti-suicide and pro-help websites, rather than sites with pro-suicide content.

Interactive forums on the Internet seem to be particularly attractive to youth, including suicidal adolescents. The controversial debate about whether the participation in these forums might be dangerous because of imitation and contagion, or whether it should be considered as helpful, since it is providing a chance to talk openly with others, seems never ending. Compared to telephone and personal chat, threats of suicide have found to be much more frequent among participants in asynchronous support groups [28].

Mutual social support seems to be an important factor [29]. Winkel et al. (2005) carried out an online survey in German online forums and a content analysis of forum postings. They found that social support in suicide forums is rated as high as support from friends and higher than support from family. Social support is higher in those forums where discussion of suicide methods does not occur. It correlates with participant`s ratings of reduction of suicidality.

Eichenberg [30] defined the possible endangering as well as suicide-preventative effects of Internet forums as follows:

Endangering Effects	Suicide-Preventive Effects
Further emotional labilization in particular of youth and persons with mental disorder	Removing or reducing the taboos associated with this strongly stigmatized issue in society
Spreading of suicide methods Contagion and Imitation (`Werther Effect`)	Release of the tension to commit suicide through discussion about suicide methods Anonymous and uncensored exchange with other affected people, which provides social support
Lowering the threshold in the sense of peer or group pressure possibly removing any ambivalence a person might have	Enabling professionals to contact suicidal people who otherwise would not have been reached
Change in attitudes toward suicide	Easier access to professional crisis counseling
Conclusion: Official government measures to censor relevant Internet material and to close forums	*Conclusion: Encouragement of the self-help activities of suicidal Internet users*

Discussion groups are quite similar to forums in terms of interactive exchange of information. Some of them have been established by mental-health-related agencies with positive motives and are frequently used as meeting places for people with severe depressive or other mental illness. Primarily young people use these discussion groups, and among the common discussion topics are suicidal feelings and the question of whether or not one should commit suicide [24]. For suicidal individuals who lack support in their social network, this may serve as an opportunity to ventilate and share emotional distress. Internet may give them the social support they do not have in life. In this sense, Internet discussion groups may lower suicide risk. They may, however, work in the exact opposite direction, since a lot of the suicidal youngsters are given the opportunity to rapidly and directly interact with others who share the same tendencies. Geographical and social boundaries are practically non-existent in cyber-space. Suicidal messages can thus be spread across the globe, lead to self-destructive acts and even suicide pacts.

So, while social support undoubtedly plays an important role in terms of suicide protection, monitoring of the forums` and discussion groups` content from the part of an administrator, as well as a clear `pro-life` statement within the content of the webpage, seem to be necessary, if we aim to lower the suicide risk of visitors.

CONCLUSION

As suicidologists, we certainly carry the responsibility to help optimizing the Internet for effective suicide prevention. A close collaboration with the mass media as well as the extension of our efforts into the new highly flexible and interactive media is one of the key steps. There are already numerous examples of improvement of quality and safety of media productions through an effective cooperation between suicidologists and representatives from traditional mass media. This may even lead to favorable changes in public attitudes toward suicide. Suicidologists should also aim to create their own Internet sites in order to strategically use this medium as a pathway to target groups that are everything but easy to contact otherwise. Fortunately, the number of attractive suicidological Internet websites seems to be on the rise.

As Tam et al. [31] have stated, the challenge to physicians of the 21st century is to harvest the Internet in a beneficial manner. We wholeheartedly believe, that the possibilities for this are more than numerous, and should not be overlooked or underestimated in contemporary (mental) health care.

REFERENCES

[1] Bentley M: The modes of apprehension: III. Imagination. In Bentley M. *The field of psychology: A survey of experience: Individual, social, and genetic.* New York, NY, US: D Appleton & Company 1924.

[2] Maruszewski T: *Imagination inflation as a source of autobiographical memory Psychologiczne* 2002; 40 (1): 5-29.

[3] Swahn MH, Simon TR, Hertz MF, Arias I, Bossarte RM, Ross JG, Gross LA, Iachan R, Hamburger ME: Linking dating violence, peer violence, and suicidal behaviors among high-risk youth. *Am J Prev Med* 2008; 34(1): 30-38.

[4] Ryu EJ, Choi KS, Seo JS, Nam BW: The relationships of Internet addiction, depression and suicidal ideation in adolescents. *Taehan Kanho Hakhoe Chi* 2004; 34 (1): 102-10.

[5] Frederickson K, Levis RF: Evidence-based practice: A reliable source to access interventions for youth risk behaviors. *Research and Theory for Nursing Practice: An International Journal* 2007; 21(3): 149-52.
[6] Biddle L, Donovan J, Hawton K, Kapur N, Gunnell D: Suicide and the Internet. *BMJ* 2008; 336, p 880.
[7] Mishara BL, Weisstub DN: Ethical, legal, and practical issues in the control and regulation of suicide promotion and assistance over the Internet. *Suicide Life Threat Behav* 2007; 37(1): 58-65.
[8] Becker K, Mayer M, Nagenborg M, El-Faddagh M, Schmidt MH: Parasuicide online: Can suicide websites trigger suicidal behaviour in predisposed adolescents? *Nord J Psychiatry* 2004; 58 (2): 111-4.
[9] Recupero PR, Harms SE, Noble JM: Googling Suicide: Surfing for Suicide Information on the Internet. *J Clin Psychiatry* 2008, ahead of print.
[10] Alao AO, Soderberg M, Pohl EL, Alao AL: Cybersuicide: Review of the Role of the Internet on Suicide. *CyberPsychology & Behavior* 2006; 9(4): 489-93.
[11] Pfeiffer-Gerschel T, Seidscheck I, Niedermeier N, Hegerl U. Suicide and Internet. *Verhaltenstherapie* 2005; 15(1): 20-26.
[12] Gualtieri CT: An Internet-based symptom questionnaire that is reliable, valid and available to psychiatrists, neurologists, and psychologists. *MedGenMed* 2007; 9(4): 3. Review.
[13] Barak A. Emotional support and suicide prevention through the Internet: A field project report. *Computers in Human Behaviour* 2007; 23 (2): 971-84.
[14] Swanton R, Collin P, Burns J, Sorensen I. Engaging, understanding and including young people in the provision of mental health services. *Int J Adolesc Med Health* 2007; 19(3): 325-32.
[15] Eysenbach G. What is e-health? *J Med Internet Res* 2001; 3(2): e20.
[16] Santhiveeran J, Grant B. Use of Communication Tools and Fee-Setting in E-Therapy: A Web Site Survey. *Social Work in Mental Health* 2005; 4(2): 31-45.
[17] Recupero, P R; Rainey, S E. Characteristics of E-Therapy Web Sites. *J Clin Psychiatry* 2006; 67 (9): 1435-40.
[18] Stone DM, Barber CW, Potter L: Public health training online: the National Center for Suicide Prevention Training. *Am J Prev Med* 2005; 29 (5 Suppl 2): 247-51.
[19] Fleetwood J, Vaught W, Feldman D, Gracely E, Kassutto Z, Novack D: MedEthEx Online: a computer-based learning program in medical ethics and communication skills. *Teach Learn Med* 2000; 12 (2): 96-104.
[20] Jones RB, Ostbye T, Clarke A: Comparative health systems: International collaborative education using the Internet. *Med Educ* 2000; 34 (1): 72-4.
[21] Barak A, Miron O: Writing characteristics of suicidal people on the Internet: A psychological investigation of emerging social environments. *Suicide Life Threat Behav* 2005; 35 (5): 507-24.
[22] Rajagopal S: Suicide pacts and the Internet. *BMJ* 2004; 320 (7478): 1298-9.
[23] Naito A: Internet suicide in Japan: Implications for child and adolescent mental health. *Clinical Child Psychology and Psychiatry* 2007; 12(4): 583-97.
[24] Mehlum L: The Internet, Suicide and Suicide Prevention. *Crisis* 2000; 21 (4): 186-88.
[25] Lee DT, Chan KP, Yip PS: Charcoal burning is also popular for suicide pacts made on the Internet. *BMJ* 2005; 330 (7491): 1298-9.

[26] Gallagher KE, Smith DM, Mellen PF: Suicidal aspyxiation by using pure helium gas: case report, review, and discussion of the influence of the Internet. *Am J Forensic Med Pathol* 2003; 24 (4): 361-3.

[27] Dobson R: Internet sites may encourage suicide. *BMJ* 1999; 319 (7206): 337.

[28] Gilat I, Shahar G: Emotional first aid for a suicide crisis: Comparison between telephonic hotline and internet. *Psychiatry: Interpersonal and Biological Processes* 2007; 70(1): 12-18.

[29] Winkel S, Groen G, Petermann F: Social support in suicide forums. *Prax Kinderpsychol Kinderpsychiatr.* 2005; 54 (9): 714 – 27.

[30] Eichenberg C: Internet message boards for suicidal people: A typology of users. *Cyberpsychol Behav* 2008; 11 (1): 107-13.

[31] Tam J, Tang WS, Fernando DJ: The Internet and suicide: A double-edged tool. *Eur J Intern Med* 2007; 18(6): 453-5.

In: Internet and Suicide
Editors: L. Sher and A. Vilens

ISBN 978-1-60741-077-5

Chapter 8

WARNING SIGNS FOR SUICIDE: SAFE AND EFFECTIVE INFORMATION DELIVERY ONLINE

Michael Mandrusiak
Adler School of Professional Psychology, Vancouver, British Columbia, Canada

ABSTRACT

The goal of this chapter is to encourage the delivery of safe and effective information about suicide prevention. The current quality of information being provided online is reviewed, along with a discussion of the existing literature on how internet users access and use online information and the potentially harmful effects of misinformation. Warning signs and risk factors are then distinguished and the current expert consensus on elements of an effective public message for online suicide prevention information is outlined. The chapter will conclude with case examples of innovative online efforts to spread awareness about early recognition and response to warning signs for suicide.

INTRODUCTION: WHY FOCUS ON WARNING SIGNS?

Warning signs are a source of information typically included in awareness raising efforts for health campaigns targeting a variety of important health concerns, including heart disease [1,2], because they are intended to facilitate early recognition and response. However, up until recently considerable confusion has existed about the concept of warning signs in the field of suicide prevention [3]. For the above reasons, warning signs are a key piece of mental health information that can be communicated to the public via the internet and will therefore receive special attention in this chapter. Warning signs for suicide identified by a working group of the American Association for Suicidology are presented. These signs of imminent risk for suicide are accompanied by clear and effective response steps and offer a useful online tool for suicide prevention efforts.

PUBLIC AWARENESS AND EDUCATION

How do we get effective information about warning signs for suicide to the people that need this information? This key question was asked by a working group on warning signs for suicide initiated by the American Association of Suicidology [3] and is not without precedent. In 1999, the Surgeon General recognized suicide as a serious health problem and called for efforts to enhance awareness about suicide as a preventable public health problem [4]. In the 2001 National Suicide Prevention Strategy, the Surgeon General called upon the health community to "appropriately broaden public awareness of suicide and its risk factors" – as discussed later, the current authors would argue that this statement likely refers to both risk factors and warnings signs, two separate but often confused concepts - and to increase state participation in "public information campaigns" designed to educate the public about suicide prevention [5]. Similarly, a Canadian national suicide prevention strategy also calls for each province to establish "coordinated public awareness campaigns" [6, p.9]. At the foundation of these awareness efforts is a belief that increased public knowledge about suicide will serve to reduce stigma, enhance recognition, increase involvement in prevention efforts and ultimately increase "… realistic opportunities to save lives…" [6, p.9].

Several public health educational campaigns for suicide prevention have been implemented. While empirical support for suicide awareness campaigns have tended to lag behind the implementation of these programs [7], there is some emerging evidence for their ability to increase public usage of mental health crisis services [8]. There is also a quickly growing body of support for the ability of gatekeeper training to increase self-reported knowledge about suicide and ability to recognize and respond to imminent risk (e.g. 9, 10). Unlike traditional public health campaigns that target the whole community through a variety of media modalities, gatekeeper training involves providing instructional training to key "gatekeepers", or individuals who as a result of their community roles come in contact with many people from that community.

In an article on promoting effective public messages related to suicide prevention, Chambers and colleagues describe several mediums for public advertising, including "television, radio, bus stops, subway cars, roadside billboards, newspapers, and magazines…" [7]. The internet is an obvious omission to this list, given its accessibility and ubiquitous nature in today's world. Suicide awareness efforts have already begun to adapt themselves to this technology, consistent with the mandate set forth by the Surgeon General to "use information technology appropriately to make facts about suicide and its risk factors and prevention approaches available to the public and to health care providers" [4]. Some innovative online programs include MTVu's "Half of Us" and the Substance Abuse and Mental Health Services Administration [SAMHSA]'s Myspace page [11,12]. Similarly, online applications of gatekeeper training have been explored and appear to hold tremendous potential for distributing information about warning signs for suicide [13]. These programs will be reviewed later in the chapter. For the moment, we will turn our attention to use of the internet in providing mental health information.

The Internet and Mental Health Information

Over the past decade, the internet has quickly become a primary medium for accessing health information for both the general public and for clinical providers [14,15,16]. Recent surveys show that 113 million adults in the US in 2006 and 35% of Canadian adults in 2005 were reported to have accessed health information online [15,16]. The popularity of the internet as a medium for accessing health information has been attributed to increases in available content on health-related websites, consumer self-reliance for management of personal health care, consumer comfort and sophistication with internet use and industry marketing of online products [17]. In the past decade, the proportion of US adults who have ever sought out health information online has increased markedly, from 27% in 1998 to 71% in 2007 [14]. Whatever the reasons, it is becoming clear from the literature that the internet has become a common reference for health information for professionals and the public alike.

Far from being the exception, online search for health information appears to be especially prevalent in the area of mental health. One early poll of internet health information seeking found that depression was the most frequently searched medical condition, with 19% of responding online searchers looking for information about this mental illness [18]. Bipolar disorder was ranked fourth, accounting for 14% of health users. More recent data shows that 22% of internet health users searched for information related to mental health issues [15]. Given recent findings that 90% of suicide attempters display depressive symptoms and that individuals with mixed manic and depressive symptoms may be at particularly high risk for suicide [19], the internet appears to offer substantial promise for delivering the right information about recognition and prevention of suicide to those who need it most.

Within the field of mental health, the internet is now being used in a variety of ways, including to provide online therapy and self-help services and to promote online support communities [20, 21, 22]. The internet has also been described as a "double-edged tool" for suicide prevention because of the existence of easily accessible websites offering information about suicide methods as well as "extreme communities" involving chat groups or online suicide-pacts that explicitly encourage suicidal behavior [23, 24, 20]. The present chapter focuses on neither of these phenomena but instead on helping organizations dedicated to suicide prevention to deliver safe and effective information to facilitate early recognition of warning signs for suicide as well as to promote effective prevention responses. Rather than viewing the internet as a "double-edged tool", we echo a previous description of the internet as a medium for information that in itself is neither good nor bad [20]. By promoting empirically supported education and information, we seek to maximize the utility of this medium for suicide prevention.

Online Information, Misinformation and its Impact

Quality of Information Online

While online applications hold great potential, questions about the quality of information found on the internet have been raised as a major challenge for online awareness efforts. Studies have shown that although health providers believe that online resources can improve their own access to information, they are often sceptical about the quality of information provided online for public consumers [25, 26]. In fact, the few studies that do exist about the quality of online information suggest that quality varies considerably and that information available online is often highly inconsistent [27, 28].

Two recent studies of the quality of information found online about depression are particularly informative. Lissman and Boehnlein [29] surveyed the top 20 sites related to treatment of depression generated by each of ten major search engines. The purpose of the study was to determine how accurately these sites described clinical symptoms of depression and treatment recommendations. The study is revealing in that only half of the sites were found to mention DSM-IV diagnostic information and almost half failed to make any mention of basic treatment options, including medication, psychotherapy or another form of professional consultation. The study also found that two thirds of the web pages examined were for-profit in nature and that for-profit sites tended to have lower quality information than not-for-profit websites, such as those maintained by scientific organizations and health-focused foundations.

In a study of Japanese websites, Nemoto and colleagues [30] echoed these earlier findings. Their study evaluated 17 Japanese websites devoted exclusively to information on mental health disorders. Depression was found to be the most commonly covered disorder, being mentioned on 78% of the websites. These authors utilized the DISCERN instrument, which examines the reliability, clarity and comprehensive nature of the health information in order to evaluate overall quality of information. The study concluded that over half of the websites were for-profit and that, apart from a few exceptions, the quality of information on these websites tended to receive a poorer rating.

One study specifically examined the consistency of information about warning signs for suicide found online [28]. A Google search for "warning signs" AND "suicide" produced approximately 183,000 hits and a random sample of 200 websites was taken from the 500 most relevant hits. A review of the first 50 websites in this sample was used to identify 138 distinct supposed "warning signs". Eighteen of these warning signs were found to be displayed on at least 30% of the 200 websites sampled and were included as the most frequent warning signs (See Table 1). It is promising that 9 of the 12 warning signs for suicide agreed upon by the AAS task force (to be discussed in a later section) were among the most frequently displayed warning signs. However, a high degree of inconsistency in information was also revealed, with 63 of the distinct warning signs being unique – those displayed on only one site.

Internet User Behavior and the Impact of Health Information

Thus, it appears that quality information does exist online but that it is embedded amid 183,000+ web-pages of questionable quality. An important concern that emerges is the ability of internet users to locate high quality information, to discriminate between high and low quality information and to use this information appropriately. Research examining how the public searches for, accesses and uses health information is limited but expanding rapidly. This section will provide a review of the literature to answer five key concerns related to internet user behavior.

Table 1. The Most Frequently Mentioned Warning Signs for Suicide on the Internet

Warning Signs	Percent of Web sites	On AAS consensus list?
Giving away prized possessions	86%	N
Isolation or withdrawal	**78%**	**Y**
Use or increased use of alcohol or drugs	**68%**	**Y**
Changes in sleeping patterns	**64%**	**Y**
Indirect verbal statements (talking about dying/not being around)	**62%**	**Y**
Changes in eating patterns or weight	56%	N
Risk-taking or reckless behavior (death wish)	**54%**	**Y**
Loss of interest in previously enjoyed activities (hobbies, school, work)	54%	N
Putting affairs in order		
Feelings of sadness or indications of depression	48%	N
Recent loss (death/divorce/break-up)	48%	N
Feelings of hopelessness	48%	N
Previous suicide attempt	**46%**	**Y**
Sudden change in behavior	44%	N
Direct suicidal threat (talking about killing oneself)	44%	N
Talking about suicide or death	**42%**	**Y**
Sudden change in mood, particularly mood elevations following	**40%**	**Y**
depression	**38%**	**Y**
Decreased performance or loss of interest in school	38%	N

Note. Random sample of 50 sites drawn from 200. AAS = American Association of Suicidology. Bold print indicates the warning signs that were included on the AAS consensus list. From "Warning Signs for Suicide on the Internet: A Descriptive Study" by Mandrusiak et al., 2006, *Suicide and Life-Threatening Behavior, 36*(3), p. 266. Copyright 2006 The American Association of Suicidology. Used with permission from Guilford Press.

A first key concern is whether or not people who need information related to suicide prevention will actually search for it online. We have already seen that health consumers are increasingly turning to the internet for mental health information [18] but have not explored whether these findings apply to individuals at risk for suicide or to concerned others. In a study of high school students aged 13 to 19 from six New York State high schools, Gould and colleagues found that 18% of students reported seeking help for emotional difficulties on the internet [31]. Of these help-seekers, 11.7% reported that suicidal thoughts were a reason for seeking help. While it is difficult to make generalizations to other demographics, this study offers some evidence that individuals experiencing thoughts of suicide do seek help online. At the same time, there are reports that male gender, older age, rural location and lower socioeconomic status are associated with decreased internet health information seeking [32, 16], which limits the universal accessibility of this information and underscores the continued need for information about suicide prevention to be delivered via multiple mediums.

A second concern is the ability of users to locate quality information for which they are searching. Data suggests that most internet users can obtain some form of information related to what they are seeking for within an average of 5 minutes and 42 seconds [33] and that 88%

of searchers report being at least somewhat successful [14]. However, findings from the Pew Internet and American Life Project suggest that some internet health users may have difficulty finding the precise information for which they are searching [15]. Twenty-five percent of respondents described feeling overwhelmed by the volume of information online whereas 22% reported feeling frustrated by an inability to locate sought after information. The finding that popular search engines often include pro-suicide websites among the top 10 displayed sites also provides challenges for at-risk individuals seeking support [24]. Levels of perceived self-efficacy and proficiency with internet applications have also been linked to satisfaction with results of searches for health information [34], suggesting that some users may be better than others at locating quality health information. Biddle and colleagues suggest that "website optimization strategies", designed to increase the relevance of a site so that it appears near the top of the search results may be an effective way to promote accessibility to helpful information [24].

Since certain online sources are likely provide safer and more effective information than others, a third key concern relates to which sources individuals turn to in order to access information. Unfortunately, research findings in this area specific to suicide are limited. In one study, English language internet users experiencing chronic illness looked primarily to scientific websites for information, possibly because they are perceived as more credible [17]. General web-sites were also used frequently, though commercial websites and discussion groups were not as widely utilized for information. This data is echoed by a Harris Poll of health information indicating that 40 percent of users reported visiting medical society websites, while 32% reported going to patient-advocacy or support group websites [18]. However, this predominant use of scientific websites for information may not be universal across cultural, linguistic and age demographics [31, 35]. Gould and colleagues indicated that chat rooms were the most utilized internet resource among their sample of adolescents seeking support for emotional difficulties [31]. The authors highlight some of the dangers associated with misinformation received in these informal online communities.

A fourth concern is whether internet users evaluate the quality of health information that they find online. The evidence here is mixed. There is some evidence that consumers assess the credibility of information by examining the source, professional design of the site, ease of use and language [33]. Other findings suggest that the source of information impacts the users intention to act on the information [36]. Specifically, information from websites seems to influence behavioral intentions more than information from blogs, homepages or other internet sources. Perhaps not surprising, information from websites was perceived as most credible when coming from doctors [15]. Alternatively, information found on personal home-pages was perceived as more credible when coming from lay persons. Survey data found that 75 percent of users of online health information do not consistently check the source of information [15]; however, 67% of consumers believed that the health information that they found online is reliable [32]. Clearly, these findings suggest some limitations to the extent that consumer evaluate the quality of online information they receive online. The impact of distress or suicidality on ability to evaluate quality of information online deserves attention but has yet to be explored.

A fifth key concern is the impact that the information has on consumer behavior and mental health. It is our hope that this information will help a suicidal individual to feel supported and understood, to provide hope and to encourage the individual to seek out professional help. Alternatively, it would also be desirable for this information to empower an individual to recognize and appropriately respond to warning signs that they notice in others by referring them to professional help. There are some research findings suggesting a positive impact of health information.

Findings suggest that consumers tend to use the information for diagnostic and treatment related purposes and that this information can help them to feel more prepared and better able to be active participants in their own treatment decisions [37, 38]. Fifty-six percent of adult health users in one survey reported feeling relieved or comforted by online information, while 53% reported that the information had an impact on how they care for themselves or others [15]. There is also evidence that adolescents who seek help online are more likely to seek help from other sources, such as mental health professionals or family members, which suggests that internet resources may potentially augment use of other resources such as crisis hotlines or mental health professionals [31].

Further, access to quality online mental health information can be therapeutically beneficial. In a randomized clinical trial, two treatment groups, an online CBT intervention and access to an informational website, were compared with each other and with a placebo group [21]. Using symptoms of depression as the outcome measure, only the CBT intervention was statistically significant at the 6-month follow-up. However, reduction in depressive symptoms for both the CBT and informational website interventions were statistically significant at 12 month follow-up. The above studies, combined with the wealth of data supporting the therapeutic benefits of psycho-educational initiatives [e.g. 39] suggest that quality mental health information can have a positive and potentially therapeutic impact on health consumers of online information. However, the specifc impact of exposure to suicide-related information deserves closer attention.

Effects of Exposure to Information about Suicide

Is exposure to information about warning signs and other suicide-related information safe? This important question was asked by the AAS working group on warning signs for suicide [3]. Although health professionals might intuitively believe that more information is better, there are indications that exposure to some forms of information about suicide can increase risk for suicide. While an in-depth review of these iatrogenic effects or harmful effects can be found elsewhere [40], a brief review will serve to underscore the importance of delivering carefully considered, safe and effective information.

First, there is a history of concern that some forms of information about suicide may in fact lead to harmful emotional consequences or heighten suicidality. For example, Phillips offered one of the first studies to suggest a possible imitation or contagion effect, in which incidents of suicide were thought to increase following media coverage of a suicide [41]. Some studies have also suggested negative or iatrogenic effects of suicide awareness programs targeting high school students [42, 43].

While a fear of iatrogenic effects need not exclude suicide prevention efforts, it highlights the necessity of carefully considering the information that professionals want to include in suicide prevention materials. As an example of research initiatives designed to safeguard prevention efforts, preliminary evidence failed to find any negative emotional effects of exposure to the AAS consensus list of warning signs for suicide [44]. In addition, excellent media guidelines are available to assist the media and professionals working with the media

[45]. Guidelines provided by Chambers and colleagues [7] contribute to the emerging consensus on creating a safe and effective public message for suicide prevention.

The impact of suicide related information on public attitudes about mental health and individuals experiencing thoughts of suicide is another area of interest. For example, public perceptions that serve to blame suicide completers and their families for failing to cope with emotional difficulties [46] may heighten stigma related to suicidal ideation and lower the likelihood that individuals experiencing suicidal ideation will reach out for help. Alternatively, public attitudes promoting the perception that suicide is the result of treatable mental health difficulties [47] and that suicide is preventable [48] may encourage suicidal individuals to seek help and the public to become involved in community prevention efforts.

For these reasons, it is important to know the effect of suicide prevention information on public attitude. Material leading to negative and unhelpful public perceptions would not only be counter-productive but also stigmatizing and dangerous. Fortunately, there is some evidence that exposure to information about the AAS consensus list of warning signs for suicide led to increased self-efficacy for identifying at risk individuals without increasing stigmatizing beliefs [49]. This evidence offers preliminary support for previous endorsements of openness and public involvement and education in suicide prevention efforts [48].

All together, there appear to be ample reasons why it is important to carefully shape the content of messages sent to the public about suicide prevention. While high quality information is available, this information is embedded within 183,000+ other user hits [28]. User sophistication and ability to locate quality suicide prevention information and to discriminate high and low quality information will also likely vary. We next turn out attention to building a consistent public message.

Warning Signs for Suicide: AAS Consensus

Warning signs are an important piece of health information that have been effectively integrated into public health campaigns in a variety of health fields. However, the field of suicide prevention has lagged significantly behind other health fields in establishing agreed upon warning signs. The development of a consensus list of warning signs for suicide will now be discussed.

Warning Signs vs. Risk Factors

It was not until a working group was established by the AAS in 2003, that an agreed upon definition for warning signs was introduced to the field of suicide prevention [3]. Prior to the formation of this working group, the terms “warning signs” and “risk factors” were frequently used interchangeably, with risk factors frequently being cited as warning signs. Previous sections of this chapter have already covered some of the consequences of disseminating poorly organized information about suicide. Thus, the American Association of Suicidology (AAS) working group represented an important step for the field in shaping a safe and effective message about warning signs for suicide.

As outlined elsewhere [3], the AAS working group came to an agreement on the definition of warning signs for suicide and specifically outlined how warning signs differ from risk factors The working group offered the following definition for warning signs for suicide:

> A suicide warning sign is the earliest detectable signs that indicates heightened risk for suicide in the near-term (i.e., within minutes, hours or days). A warning sign refers to some feature of the developing outcome of interest (suicide) rather than to a distinct construct (e.g., risk factor) that predicts or may be casually related to suicide [3, p. 258].

Thus, a primary distinguishing feature of warning signs is their predictive power for identifying a near-term time frame (within minutes, hours or days) for a specific outcome (a suicide attempt). A complete listing of other identified differences between warning signs and risk factors can be found in Table 2.

To illustrate, consider the risk factors of gender and age, neither of which are included on the AAS list of warning signs for good reason. For example, among the elder population, males are at increased risk for suicide because significantly more males than females of this age demographic complete suicide [50]. While this data might be instrumental in guiding health professionals to identify appropriate groups to target for preventative interventions, it is of limited value for helping to identify when a specific person might attempt suicide. Many more older males are not going to attempt suicide in the next hours or days than those who will and this information simply lacks any real predictive power on a case by case basis. Thus, being male and an elder are known risk factors but simply do not qualify as warning signs because they offer neither predictive power, nor a time-frame to assist intervention efforts. Many supposed warning signs found online, such as "physical illness" or "chronic fatigue" similarly lack any predictive power or time frame and do not represent effective warning signs [28]. This does not preclude the sensitive clinician from considering the constellation of warning signs and risk factors (eg. Elder male with chronic fatigue and verbal statements about suicide) when assessing the risk of a near term suicide attempt.

AAS Consensus Warning Signs

In constructing their consensus list, AAS working group examined existing literature related signs associated with an identified time frame. Although research involving a time frame is highly limited, a handful of findings do exist. The following is a brief summary of warning signs with some limited empirical support for association with near term risk (i.e. with an associated time frame):

- Within one week to months of an intense emotional state in addition to depression [51, 52]. One well-designed study demonstrated that severe anxiety or agitation was associated with increased near term risk for a suicide attempt within the following week [52].
- Within the following 24 hours [53] to months [51] of speech or actions that are suggestive of suicide or other direct or indirect communication of suicidal intent.
- Within 24 hours [53] to months [51] of increased use of substances

- Within months of deterioration of social and/or occupational functioning [51].

Table 2. Differentiating Warnings Signs and Risk Factors for Suicide

Characteristic Feature	Risk Factor	Warning Sign
Nature of Relationship to Suicide	Distal	Proximal
Definitional Specifity	Defined Constructs (eg. DSM-IV diagnosis)	Poorly defined constructs (eg. Behaviors such as buying a weapon)
Empirical Foundation	Empirically derived	Clinically identified/derived
Population	Population dependent (i.e. clinical samples)	Individually applied
Timeframe	Implies enduring or longer-term risk	Implies imminent risk
Nature of Occurrence	Static nature (e.g. age, sex, abuse history)	Episodic or transient in nature (i.e., warning sign resolves)
Application Context	Can be individually explored and applied	Likely useful only within a constellation
Experiential Character	Objective	Subjective
Intended Target Group	Experts and clinicians	Lay public and clinicians

From "Warning Signs for Suicide: Theory, Research and Clinical Applications" by M.D. Rudd et al., 2006, *Suicide and Life-Threatening Behavior, 36*(3), p. 257. Copyright 2006 The American Association of Suicidology. Used with permission from Guilford Press.

Although not included in the AAS consensus list, a small body of findings also show "situational warning signs" that are associated with a time frame for near term risk:

- Within months of a precipitating event (e.g. bereavement, loss of job or relationship) [51].
- Within three months of discharge from hospitalization for elderly patients [54].
- Within one week after discharge for hospitalization due to a previous suicide attempt [55].
- Within seven to thirty days of initial confinement, within three days of a court appearance or within 28 days of release for inmates [56, 57, 58].

The brevity of these lists highlight the limited nature of empirical findings related to warning signs for suicide. In addition, many of the studies experience methodological limitations and caution must be exercised in interpreting the findings. As a result, the working group also needed to utilize expert consensus in constructing an agreed upon list of warning signs, which is shown in Table 3. The working group also decided that in order to be effective, warning signs needed to be presented to the public along with other critical information about how to respond when they are identified [3]. The warning signs were therefore presented in a hierarchical format, with each level accompanied by clear directions for responding either by immediately contacting 911 or a mental health provider in some instances or by contacting a mental health provider or dialing 1-800-TALK in the U.S. (1-

800-SUICIDE in U.S. or Canada) for a referral in other instances. In order to allow for easier recall and user-friendly dissemination, the acronym IS PATH WARM was also adopted to display the warning signs (see Figure 1).

Table 3. Consensus Warning Signs for Suicide

Are you or someone you love at risk for suicide? Get the facts and take action.

Call 9-1-1 or seek immediate help from a mental health provider when you hear, say or see any one of these behaviors:

- Someone threatening to hurt or kill themselves
- Someone looking for ways to kill themselves: seeking access to pills, weapons, or other means
- Someone talking or writing about death, dying, or suicide

Seek help by contacting a mental health professional or calling 1-800-273-TALK for a referral should you witness, hear, or see anyone exhibiting any one or more of these behaviors:

- Hopelessness
- Rage, anger, seeking revenge
- Acting reckless or engaging in risky activities, seemingly without thinking
- Feeling trapped—like there's no way out
- Increasing alcohol or drug use
- Withdrawing from friends, family, or society
- Anxiety, agitation, unable to sleep, or sleeping all the time
- Dramatic changes in mood
- No reason for living; no sense of purpose in life

From "Warning Signs for Suicide on the Internet: A Descriptive Study" by Mandrusiak et al., 2006, *Suicide and Life-Threatening Behavior, 36*(3), p. 259. Copyright 2006 The American Association of Suicidology. Used with permission from Guilford Press.

How do you Remember the Warning Signs of Suicide?
Here's an Easy-to-Remember Mnemonic:

IS PATH WARM?

I Ideation
S Substance Abuse
P Purposelessness
A Anxiety
T Trapped
H Hopelessness
W Withdrawal
A Anger
R Recklessness
M Mood Change

From American Association for Suicidology, n.d., Retrieved July 23, 2008 from: http://www.suicidology.org. Used with permission from the American Association of Suicidology.

Figure 1. Is Path Warm?

This consensus list represents an important step forward in the field of suicide prevention, as well as an important tool for websites seeking to promote suicide prevention. Keeping in mind that some limited evidence already suggests that exposure to this list of warning signs does not lead to negative emotional effects [44], nor to negative public attitudes [49], this list appears to offer a safe and effective way of communicating suicide prevention information to the public and is already being integrated as a key part of online prevention efforts that will be discussed in the next section.

Informational Resources on the Internet

Having explored the best practice information about warning signs for suicide, we will now turn our attention to examining a selected list of online resources that provide information about warning signs for suicide on the internet. Presentation of these resources will be grouped into those that target individuals at risk for suicide and their supportive caregivers and those that target professional helpers, though many provide useful information for both groups. Please note that this is not intended to be an exhaustive list and that there are likely to be many excellent resources that are not included here. Rather, this list is intended to highlight a few examples of innovative and potentially effective ways that information about warning signs for suicide is being distributed via the internet.

Resources for at Risk Individuals and Concerned Others

MTVu: Half of Us (www.halfofus.com)

MTVu is an MTV network targeting college students that is delivered entirely via a 24 hour broadband stream accessed online. In collaboration with the JED Foundation, MTVu, features a mental health awareness campaign entitled "Half of Us", which is designed to de-stigmatize and promote and accurate understanding about mental illness [11]. Accessed directly or via a link on the MTVu home page (www.mtvu.com), "Half of Us" offers accurate information about several mental illnesses, AAS consensus list warning signs for suicide and video clips of celebrities and regular citizens discussing their experiences with suicidal ideation, suicide attempts and mental illness. It also contains information about national telephone hotlines and other helpful resources. One unique feature is that college students in the U.S. can use the built in locator to find the counseling centre at their school.

Ulifeline (www.ulifeline.org)

Ulifeline is a JED Foundation program developed to provide information and resources about suicide prevention and mental health to college students and college professionals [59]. In addition to providing supportive information about suicide, its warning signs and helpful resources, the website also links students to www.halfofus.com if they wish to connect with a mental health professionals at their college or university.

From mtvU, 2008, Half of Us, Retrieved July 23, 2008 from www.halfofus.com. Half of Us is a joint venture of mtvU and The JED Foundation. Used with permission from The JED Foundation.

Figure 2. Half of Us.

Lifeline 1-800-273-TALK MySpace Page (www.myspace.com/suicidepreventionlifeline)

The National Suicide Prevention Lifeline (www.suicidepreventionlifeline.org; 60), part of SAMSAH's National Suicide Prevention Initiative, is a toll free 24 hour suicide prevention telephone service. The service connect callers to over 120 crisis centers in the U.S. An article in the *SAMHSA News*, reported that Lifeline staff noticed that Myspace had become the top referrer to the Lifeline website and decided to set up their own MySpace page [61, 12]. It went on to report that the Lifeline Website received approximately 150,000 visitors referred through Myspace in 2006. The Myspace page offers information about what first time callers to the lifeline service can expect, information about the AAS consensus list of warning signs for suicide and how to help someone who is experiencing suicidal ideation. In addition, the Lifeline telephone number (1-800-273-TALK) is prominently displayed.

Centre for Suicide Prevention (www.suicideinfo.ca)

This site provides information targeting both individuals at risk, concerned others and helping professionals, with the site organized into the following three sections: information, suicide prevention training and research [62]. This site does not list the AAS consensus list of warning signs for suicide, though useful suggestions for how to respond to help someone once warning signs are recognized can be printed out on a wallet sized card. Users can also search for crisis call centres located in the U.S., Canada and internationally.

Befrienders Worldwide (www.befrienders.org)

Operated by Samaritans UK, this site is available in multiple languages and provides information and support for people who are feeling suicidal and for concerned others [63]. It also helps individuals to seek out local crisis centres and provides an email support service for suicidal or distressed individuals. While the site does provide valuable information as well as information on warning signs for suicide, it does not currently provide information about the AAS consensus list of warning signs for suicide.

Resources for Helping Professionals

American Association of Suicidology (www.suicidology.org)

This site provides information on the current status of suicide prevention, including information about suicide and the IS PATH WARM acronym for warning signs, as well as information about crisis centre, conferences and research and clinical resources [64].

Suicide Prevention Resource Centre (www.sprc.org)

A wealth of useful information for suicide prevention professionals is offered on this site [45]. A "best practices registry" describes the up to date status of information related to treatment, prevention and warning signs for suicide. Links to free online training resources are also provided.

The JED Foundation (www.jedfoundation.org)

This organization is dedicated to promoting suicide awareness and prevention on college campuses and offers information about suicide prevention tailored to college campuses [65]. Resources for college administrators is provided to help in establishing suicide prevention programs.

Chooselife (www.chooselife.net)

Chooselife is Scotland's national suicide prevention campaign, which was implemented in 2002 as a ten-year plan to reduce suicide's in that country [66]. The comprehensive website includes local suicide statistics, information about warning signs for suicide and how to respond, suicide bereavement resources, an information resource database and other useful information. The Information from the Chooselife campaign can also be found via the SeeMe website, Scotland's national public health campaign targeting stigma and discrimination related to mental health (www.seemescotland.org).

The National Centre for Suicide Prevention Training (www.ncspt.org)

While gatekeeper training shows great promise, its instructional format is cost and resource intensive compared to other awareness and informational interventions. Flexibility, cost-effectiveness and ease of use have made the internet an attractive alternative to explore [13]. The NCSPT provides an online suicide prevention workshop that has shown to be effective in increasing knowledge about suicide and provides some tentative, preliminary support for the effectiveness of such online interventions [13; 67]. An online training workshop entitled "Youth suicide prevention: An introduction to gatekeeping" can be found on their site. However, the site advises that this online training is not intended to replace intensive face-to-face instructional training.

QPR Institute (www.qprinstitute.com)

An online version of QPR (Question Persuade Refer) Gatekeeper Training, designed and offered by The QPR Institute, can be purchased at their website [68]. Consumers are provided with three years of 24 hour access to the online training, which includes instructional video streams and informational modules about the prevalence of suicide, warning signs for suicide and how to refer someone at imminent risk for suicide to a mental health professional. The authors of this chapter are also aware that The QPR Institute is currently involved in studies to evaluate the effectiveness of online QPR Gatekeeper Training.

Conclusion

Reaching individuals who need it most with the right information in a safe, timely and effective way will continue to be a challenge in the field of suicide prevention. The internet is a promising tool to aid in this effort and has already demonstrated its promise and potential, along with potential risks. Efforts to develop an consensus list of warning signs for suicide, along with clearly specified intervention steps, represent an important tool that can be effectively distributed via the internet. At the same time, it is clear further research efforts are required for developing effective online suicide prevention efforts.

References

[1] Carter, A: *Warning signs of heart disease 2004.* Retrieved June 27, 2005, from University of Michigan Health System Web site: http://www.med.umich.edu/1libr/aha/aha_warning_sha.htm

[2] Lee, TH: Planning pays off if heart attack strikes. *Harvard Heart Letter* 2004; 14(5), 1-3.

[3] Rudd, MD, Berman, AL, Joiner, TE, Nock, MK, Silverman, MM, Mandrusiak, M, Van Orden, KV & Witte, T: Warning signs for suicide: Theory, research and clinical applications. *Suicide and Life Threatening Behavior* 2006; 36(3), 255-262.

[4] U.S. Public Health Service: *The Surgeon General's Call to Action to Prevent Suicide 1999.* Retrieved July 24, 2008, from http:// www.surgeongeneral.gov/library/calltoaction.

[5] U.S. Department of Health and Human Services: National strategy for suicide prevention: Goals and objectives for action 2001. Retrieved July 24, 2008, from http://mentalhealth.samhsa.gov/publications/allpubs/SMA01-3518/default.asp

[6] *Canadian Association of Suicide Prevention:* The CASP Blueprint for a Canadian National Suicide Prevention Strategy 2004; Retrieved July 24, 2008, from http://www.casp-acps.ca/Publications/BlueprintFINAL.pdf

[7] Chambers, D, Pearson, JL, Lubell, H, Brandon, W, O'Brien, K, Zinn, J: The science of public messages for suicide prevention: A workshop summary. *Suicide and Life-Threatening Behavior* 2005; 35(2), 134-145.

[8] Oliver, RJ, Spilbury, JC, Osiecki, SS, Denihan, WM, Zureick, JL, Friedman, S: Brief report: Preliminary results of a suicide awareness mass media campaign in Cuyahoga County, Ohio. *Suicide and Life-Threatening Behavior* 2008; 38(2), 245-249.

[9] Cross, W, Matthieu, MM, Cerel, J, Knox, K.L: Proximate outcomes for gatekeeper training for suicide prevention in the workplace. *Suicide and Life-Threatening Behavior* (2007); 37(6), 659-670.

[10] Wyman, PA, Brown, CH, Inman, J, Cross, W, Schmeelk-Cone, K, Gou, J, Pena, J: Randomized trial of a gatekeeper program for suicide prevention: 1-year impact on

secondary school staff. *Journal of Consulting and Clinical Psychology* 2008; 76(1), 104-115.

[11] MTV-U: *Half of Us 2008*. Retrieved July 23, 2008, from the World Wide Web: http://www.halfofus.com

[12] *Substance Abuse and Mental Health Services Administration*. National Suicide Prevention Lifeline 1-800-273-TALK Myspace Page No date. Retrieved July 23 from the World Wide Web: http://www.myspace.com/800273talk

[13] Stone, D, Barber, C, Potter, L: Public health training online. *American Journal of Preventive Medicine* 2005; 29(5S2), 247-251.

[14] Harris Poll No. 76: Harris Poll Shows Number of "Cyberchondriacs" – Adults Who Have Ever Gone Online for Health Information– Increases to an Estimated 160 Million Nationwide 2007. Retrieved July 24, 2008, from http://www.harrisinteractive.com/harris_poll/index.asp?PID=792

[15] Fox, S: *Online health search 2006*. Washington, DC: Pew Internet and American Life Project.

[16] Statistics Canada. *Canadian Internet Use Survey 2006*. Retrieved July 24, 2008, from http://www.statcan.ca/cgi-bin/imdb/p2SV.pl?Function=getSurvey&SDDS=4432&lang=en&db=IMDB&dbg=f&adm=8&dis=2

[17] Kechine, H, Pascot, D, Premont, P: Use of health-related information from the internet by English-speaking patients. *Health Informatics Journal* 2008; 14(1), 17-28.

[18] Bennet, AH: Surveys find more physicians online. *Family Practice Management* 1999; 6(6), 50-51.

[19] Balazs, J, Benazzi, F, Rihmer, Z, Rihmer, A, Akiskal, KK, Akiskal, HS: The close link between suicide attempts and mixed (bipolar) depression: Implications for suicide prevention. *Journal of Affective Disorders* 2006; 91(2/3). 133-138.

[20] Bell, V: Online information, extreme communities and internet therapy: Is the internet good for our mental health? *Journal of Mental Health* 2007. 16(4), 445-457.

[21] Mackinnon, A, Griffiths, K & Christensen, H: Comparative randomized trial of online cognitive-behavioural therapy and an information website for depression: 12 month outcomes. *The British Journal of Psychiatry* 2008; 192, 130-134.

[22] Ybarra, ML, Eaton, WW: Internet-based mental health interventions. *Mental Health Services Research* 2005; 7, 75-87.

[23] Tam, J, Tang, WS, Fernando, DJS: The intern, et and suicide: A double-edged tool. *European Journal of Internal Medicine* 2007;18, 453-455.

[24] Biddle, L, Donovan, J, Hawton, K, Kapur, N, Gunnell, D: Suicide and the internet. *British Medical Journal* 2008; 336, 800-802.

[25] Gilmour, JA, Scott, S, Huntington, N: Nurses and internet health information: A questionnaire survey. *Journal of Advanced Nursing* 2008; 61(1), 19-28.

[26] Huang, GJ, Penson, DF: Internet health resources and the cancer patient. *Cancer Investigation* 2008; 26, 202-207.

[27] Eysenbach, G, Powell, J, Kuss, O, Sa, ER: Empirical studies assessing the quality of health information for consumers on the World Wide Web: A systematic review. *Journal of the American Medical Association* 2002; 287, 2691-2700.

[28] Mandrusiak, M, Rudd, MD, Joiner, TE, Berman, AL, Van Orden, KA, Witte, T: Warning signs for suicide on the internet: A descriptive study. *Suicide and Life-Threatening Behavior* 2006; 36(3), 263-271.

[29] Lissman, TL, Boehnlein, JK: A critical review of internet information about depression. *Psychiatric Services* 2001; 52(8), 1046-1050.

[30] Nemoto, K, Tachikawa, H, Sodeyama, N, Endo, G, Hashimoto, K, Mizukami, K, Sasada, T: Quality of internet information referring to mental health and mental disorders in Japan. *Psychiatry and Clinical Neurosciences* 2007; *61*, 243-248.

[31] Gould, MS, Munfakh, JL, Lubell, K, Kleinman, M, Parker, S: Seeking help from the internet during adolescence. *Journal of the American Academy of Child and Adolescent Psychiatry* 2002; 41, 1182-1189.

[32] Al-Shammary, N, Awan, S, Butt, K, Yoo, J: Internet use before consultation with a health professional. *Primary Health Care* 2007; 17(10), 18-21.

[33] Eysenbach, G, Kohler, C: How do consumers search for and appraise health information on the World Wide Web? *British Medical Journal* 2002; 324(7337), 573-577.

[34] Rains, SA: Seeking health information in the information age: The role of internet self-efficacy. *Western Journal of Communication* 2008; 72(1), 1-18.

[35] Khechine, H, Pascot, D, Premon, P: Information from the internet and health. *International Journal of Computers, Systems and Signals* 2004; 5(1), 58-66.

[36] Hu, Y: Health information on the internet: Influence of online sources on credibility and behavioral intentions. *Dissertation Abstracts International* 2008. Section A, *68*, 10A.

[37] Bazzoli, F: Gateways to the internet. *Internet Health Care Magazine 2000; 1*, 70-77.

[38] Dolan, G, Iredale, R Williams, R, Ameen, J: Consumer use of the Internet for health information: A survey of primary care patients. I*nternational Journal of Consumer Studies* 2004; 28(2), 147-153.

[39] Roth, A, Fonagy, P: What Works for Whom?: A Critical Review of Psychotherapy Research. New York: Guilford, 2005.

[40] Gould, MS, Marrocco, FA, Kleinman, M, Thomas, JG, Mostkoff, K, Cote, J, Davies, M: Evaluating iatrogenic risk of youth suicide screening programs.: A randomized controlled trial. *JAMA* 2005; 293(13), 1635-1643.

[41] Phillips, DP: The influence of suggestion on suicide: Substantive and theoretical implications of the Werther effect. *America Sociological Review* 1974; 39(3), 340-354.

[42] 42. Shaffer, D, Vieland, V, Garland, A, Rojas, M, Underwood, M., Busner, G: Adolescent suicide attempters: Response to suicide prevention programs. *JAMA* 1990; 164, 3151-3155.

[43] 43. Overholser, JC, Hemstreet, AH, Spirito, A, Vyse, S: Suicide awareness programs in schools: Effects of gender and personal experience. *Journal of the American Academy of Child and Adolescent Psychiatry* 1989; 28, 925-930.

[44] Rudd, MD, Mandrusiak, M, Joiner, TE, Berman, AL, Van Orden, KA, Hollar, D: The emotional impact and ease of recall of warning signs for suicide: A controlled study. *Suicide and Life-Threatening Behavior* 2006; 36(3), 288- 295.

[45] Educational Development Centre: Suicide Prevention Resource Centre 2005. Retrieved July 23, 2008, from the World Wide Web: http://www.sprc.org

[46] Cvinar, JG: Do suicide survivors suffer social stigma? *A review of the literature.* Perspectives in Psychiatric Care 2005; 41, 14-21.

[47] Wallin, U, Runeson, B: Attitudes towards suicide and suicidal patients among medical students. *European Psychiatry* 2003; 18, 329-333.

[48] Hjelmeland, H, Knizel, BL: The general public's views on suicide and suicide prevention and their perception of participating in a study on attitudes towards suicide. *Archives of Suicide Research* 2004; 345-359.

[49] Van Orden, KA, Joiner, TE, Hollar, D, Rudd, MD, Mandrusiak, M, Silverman, MM: A test of the effectiveness of a list of suicide warning signs for the public. *Suicide and Life Threatening Behavior* 2006; 36, 272-287.

[50] World Health Organization: *Distribution of suicide rates (per 100 000) by gender and age,* 2000. Retrieved September 1, 2008 from http://www.who.int/mental_health/ prevention/suicide/suicide_rates_chart/en/index.html

[51] Hendin, H, Maltsberger, JT, Lipschitz, A, Haas, AP, Hyle, J: Recognizing and responding to a suicide crisis. *Suicide and Life Threatening Behavior* 2001; 31, 115-128.

[52] Busch, KA, Fawcett, J, Jacobs, DG: Clinical correlates of inpatient suicide. *Journal of Clinical Psychiatry* 2003; 64, 14-19.

[53] Chiles, JA, Strosahl, J, Cowden, L, Graham, R: The 24 hours before hospitalization: Factors related to suicide attempting. *Suicide and Life Threatening Behavior* 1986; 16, 335-342.

[54] Karvonen, K, Rasanen, P, Hakko, H, Timonen, M, Meyer-Rochow, VB, Sarkioja, T, Koponen, HJ: Suicide after hospitalization in the elderly: A population based study of suicides in Northern Finland between 1988-2003. *International Journal of Geriatric Psychiatry* 2008; 23(2), 135-141.

[55] Deisenhammer, EA, Huber, M, Kemmler, G, Weiss, EM, Hinterhuber, H: Psychiatric hospitalization during the last 12 months before suicide. *General Hospital Psychiatry* 2007; 29(1), 63-65.

[56] Jenny, S, Baker, D, Hunt, IM, Moloney, A, Appleby, L: Suicide by prisoners: A national clinical survey. *British Journal of Psychiatry* 2004; 184(3), 263-267.

[57] Marcus, P, Alcabes, P: Characteristics of suicides by inmates in an urban jail. *Hospital and Community Psychiatry* 1993; 44(3), 256-261.

[58] Pratt, D, Piper, M, Appleby, L, Webb, R, Shaw, J: Suicide in recently released prisoners: A population-based cohort study. *Lancet* 2006; 388, 119-123.

[59] *The Jed Foundation: Ulifeline 2004*. Retreived July 23, 2008, from the World Wide Web: http://www.ulifeline.org

[60] *Substance Abuse and Mental Health Services Administration: National Suicide.* Prevention Lifeline 1-800-273-TALK n.d. Retrieved July 23, 2008, from the World Wide Web: http://suicidepreventionlifeline.org

[61] Quander, Woolridge, L: *Suicide prevention through Myspace.com.* SAMHSA News, 15(4). Retrieved August 25, 2008 from the World Wide Web: http://www.samhsa.gov/ SAMHSA_NEWS/VolumeXV_4/article7.htm

[62] *Center for Suicide Prevention: Centre for Suicide Prevention 2004.* Retrieved July 23, 2008, from the World Wide Web: http://suicideinfo.ca

[63] Samaritans UK.: *Befrienders Worldwide 2003.* Retrieved July 23, 2008, from the World Wide Web: http://www.befrienders.org

[64] *American Association of Suicidology: American Association of Suicidology* n.d. Retrieved July 23, 2008, from the World Wide Web: http://www.suicidology.org

[65] *The Jed Foundation:* The Jed Foundation 2005. Retrived July 23, 2008, from the World Wide Web: http://www.jedfoundation.org

[66] *NHS Health Scotland: Chooselife 2005.* Retrieved July 23, 2008, from the World Wide Web: http://www.chooselife.net

[67] *Education Development Centre: National Suicide for Suicide Prevention Training 2003.* Retrieved July 23, 2008, from the World Wide Web: http://www.ncspt.org

[68] *QPR Institute: QPR Institute 1999.* Retrieved July 23, 2008, from the World Wide Web: http://www.qprinstitute.com

In: Internet and Suicide
Editors: L. Sher and A. Vilens

ISBN 978-1-60741-077-5

Chapter 9

A POTENTIAL SOURCE OF DATA IN UNDERSTANDING YOUTH SUICIDE — INSTANT MESSAGES

Paul W. C. Wong, King-Wa Fu and Paul S. F. Yip
Centre for Suicide Research and Prevention, The University of Hong Kong, Pokfulam, Hong Kong SAR, China

ABSTRACT

Psychological autopsy study has been used in yielding detailed and complete information on suicides. Studying the suicide notes of suicide decedents as part of a psychological autopsy enhances the quality of the information. However, one limitation of the psychological autopsy study approach is that it may easily lead to recall or other information bias because most of the information is collected from interviews of informants. Studying suicide notes also has its limitation because only a minority of suicide decedents leave notes and most of the notes are typically brief. This chapter will illustrate the practicability of using the instant messages of people who die by suicide as a source of information to enhance the reliability and validity of the information collected from a psychological autopsy, and its added value to overcome some of the limitations of suicide notes and psychological autopsies. We will first summarize the findings gathered from the coroner's file and the interview with a young girl's mother, and then present some of her instant messages in which we have found this extra information has enhanced our understanding of the her suicide and helped us to reconstruct the psychological state of the young girl.

INTRODUCTION

The number of suicides among 15–24 year olds has increased dramatically over the last four decades in many European and Western countries [1]. Youth suicide is one of the leading causes of death in many countries [2]. Various research approaches to the understanding of youth suicide have been utilized. Broadly speaking, there are two approaches to studying the reasons for youth suicide. First, epidemiological investigations are done to find out possible risk factors of suicide at a population level [e.g., 3, 4-6], and second, the detailed study of a series of individual cases, preferably using the psychological autopsy approach, at an individual level [e.g., 7, 8, 9].

Psychological autopsy study has been suggested as by far the most extensive research approach in the study of suicide. The phrase 'psychological autopsy study' refers to a procedure for reconstructing an individual's psychological life after the fact, particularly the person's lifestyle and those thoughts, feelings, and behaviors manifested during the weeks preceding death, in order to achieve a better understanding if the psychological circumstances contributed to a death [10]. Psychological autopsy studies have been conducted in a number of countries in Europe, North and South America, Australia, and Asia [11-22]. Although these psychological autopsy studies vary in regard to their measure of psychiatric disorders and life events, interview procedures, selection of control groups, they generally include (i) face-to-face interviews with knowledgeable informants, and (ii) reviews of records and archival information related to the deceased (e.g., medical, autopsy, school, and police records, personal letters, diaries, and suicide notes). The major finding of these studies is that they have demonstrated consistently across countries with different cultures that 80–90% of suicides had psychiatric disorders, particularly depression and substance abuse [23]; but with a lower percentage in the Chinese population [14, 19, 22].

The psychological autopsy research approach has its advantages in yielding more detailed and complete information on various domains linked to suicide that are not available from epidemiological studies [24]. However, it associates with numerous methodological issues that may affect the reliability and validity of the data derived from it. One major limitation is that it may easily lead to recall bias or other information bias because informants may have differential awareness of the problems among suicide deceased and controls, or may not recall detailed information after a certain period following the incident, or may have limited knowledge about the deceased [25-29]. In particular on studying youth suicide, parents and teachers may not be aware of some of the problematic behaviors, e.g., substance and alcohol use, sexual orientation, of the younger individuals [30]. Recent psychological autopsy studies have used different methods to enhance the quality of the information. These studies involve simultaneous interviewing of more than one investigator [19] and informants [11], and extracting information from other sources, i.e. medical records, personal documents, and suicide notes, to supplement the data collected from interviews [14].

Suicide notes and personal documents have been widely used to understand the reasons for suicide [31]. However, after a few decades of well-intended attempts, several limitations in the study of suicide notes have been identified. First, suicide notes are typically brief. Many are simply sets of instructions as last wills or testaments [32]. Second, suicide notes were often left by a minority of suicide decedents ranging from 4% to 43% [33-37], which implicates that findings from suicide note studies may not be applicable to the general suicide population. Thus, it is generally agreed that without detailed background information about the note-leavers, their suicide notes would be difficult to interpret [38].

All in all, given the methodological concerns and limitations of the psychological autopsy process and the studying of suicide notes, we wonder if the recent emergence of information technology and the Internet would provide alternative and adjunct sources of information for the study of suicide. The Internet has been used for both formal and recreational purposes. Using technologies such as instant messaging (IM) and text messaging (TM) as a means of communication has been one of the major recreational reasons for computer usage among adolescents. Instant messaging is a form of computer "chat" that allows one to have a real-time, typed "conversation" with one or more individuals while connected to the Internet. IM allows efficient and effective communication, featuring immediate receipt of acknowledgement or reply. It is also possible to save a conversation for later reference. If instant messaging is accustomed to translating young people's thoughts and feelings into words, we wonder if instant messages would become a useful document for the study of suicide. Would instant messages provide additional information that their parents may not be aware of? Would instant messages review the cognitions of the suicidals? Would they provide information about the interactional dynamics between personal, interpersonal, socio-cultural, and psychological factors related to suicide? Or would they also give indication of the sequence of events leading to a suicidal act?

In this chapter, we will make use of a student's instant messages as part of a psychological autopsy process to illustrate how we can gain a better understanding of a suicide based on the various sources of information. There were three broad categories of information about the student. First, a coroner's report that compiled 26 witnesses' statements (including classmates, school social worker, class teacher, school head master, parents, siblings, and other witnesses), an autopsy report, a toxicology report, and school reports. Second, a semi-structured interview with the mother conducted about six months after the death. Third, archival information related to the subject that included two-years of ICQ (the first Internet-wide instant messaging service, with the name as an initialism on the phrase "I seek you") records retrieved from her computer. We will first summarize the findings gathered from the coroner's file and the interview with her mother, and then present some of her instant messaging records in which we found this additional information had deepened our understanding of the student's suicide and helped us to portray the development of her suicidal process.

Ann's Death

Ann (a pseudonym) was a 15-year-old Hong Kong Chinese female secondary school student. At around 0130 on 11 November (the specific year is omitted to avoid personal identification), she put on her slippers and crept out of the family flat, climbed up the stairs to the 20th floor, squeezed through a window on to a ledge outside, jumped to a concrete beam where she left her slippers, and jumped to her death. She landed on the 1st floor podium at about 0200. At 1100, her body was found lying on the podium by a resident.

Information from the Coroner's Report

Ann was a new immigrant from Mainland China to Hong Kong in 1999. She lived in a stable family environment with her mother, father, elder sister, and younger brother in a public housing flat. Her father was a construction worker and her mother was a homemaker. Ann was a Form 3 (equivalent to year 9 in the US) student at a government secondary school at the time of death. She was an exemplary student who was academically bright, hard working, reasonably popular, coupled with a perfect attendance and conduct records. Ann's school report card indicated that she was one of the top students in Form 2 (equivalent to Year 8). Her overall position in Form 2 was 23 out of 235 students and progressed to a class in Form 3 that comprised the top 20 percent of the students. She was nominated as a "Leader of the Students" at the school. In other words, nothing unusual was apparent until Ann became a Form 3 student in September (the general starting month of a school calendar).

During the first month of her school life in Form 3, Ann had been trying hard to adapt to this new environment. Because this new class composed of the top students in her form, Ann found the new classmates competitive and she felt that they were not as friendly as the ex-classmates. On 18 October, a former classmate of Ann completed suicide by jumping from a height. Ann was upset on hearing about this tragic death but the impact on Ann was unclear. However, according to the reflective letter, which Ann was asked to write as one of the postvention activities organized by the school, she wrote "*I am upset about her leaving. I remember we used to hang out, cook, and have tea. When I think about all these, tears started to roll down my cheeks …… but I have also learned to cherish more in life, especially the people around me*."

A week prior to her death (3-6 November), Ann took a school test which had no bearing on her end of year result. On 4 November, a classmate received a note from Ann in the classroom telling her to prepare condolence money as she was going to kill herself by jumping that night, because she felt that she had failed on the tests. Her classmate believed that it was a joke and she ignored it.

On 6 November, Ann's class teacher spotted that Ann was crying at a corridor. On seeing him, Ann rushed into a female toilet and locked the door. The class teacher requested the head prefect to check up on Ann. Ann refused to open the door of the cubicle, but agreed to talk to the head prefect between the door. Ann told the prefect that she had done badly in the mathematic test that morning. The prefect comforted Ann and then left her alone in the toilet. The prefect later saw Ann undertaking prefect duties in the canteen and appeared to have calmed. A few hours later, however, the class teacher saw Ann was again crying in the classroom and her classmates were comforting her. The class teacher did not want to embarrass Ann and left Ann and the other students alone in the classroom.

On 9 November, the class teacher met up with Ann and one of her classmates for a lunch. The teacher felt that it would be a good opportunity to discuss Ann's problems outside the school environment. However, the class teacher found Ann appeared to be very happy and thus, her concerns were not discussed over the lunch.

On 10 November, Ann gave photo stickers of herself to her classmates, saying that this would be the last day they would see her and she hoped that they would not miss her too much. Though this was not the first time Ann had expressed her suicidal wish, her classmates once again thought it was a joke and did not follow up on this issue. On the evening of the same day, Ann went on-line to chat with the class teacher through ICQ. The class teacher recalled that much of the conversation was inconsequential but Ann did make some references to "leaving" (a word that is often used interchangeably with the word 'death' in Cantonese). The class teacher asked Ann to elaborate on this issue but she refused. At the end of the conversation, they had a little dispute about when to actually go offline. Ann appeared to have been upset by the class teacher saying "*If you want to go, just go!*" and felt pressured of doing so.

About 20 minutes later when they were both offline, the class teacher sent a text message from his cell phone to Ann's and stating "*I am not telling you to go.*" At 0142 hours, the class teacher received a reply text message from Ann and it read "*I am really going, I hope you can remember me for the rest of your life,Goodbye.*" Although the class teacher was very concerned because he knew that the word "going" in the text message meant "completing suicide", without knowing Ann's home telephone number and address, he could not contact Ann's family.

At 0700 hours on 11 November, Ann's mother woke up and was panicked on not finding Ann at home. This was unusual because it was the first time that this had happened. She then checked Ann's last call on her cell phone and finding that it was to her class teacher. She called him and he urged Ann's mother to report to the police whilst he would go to school to check and see if Ann was there. However, Ann's mother did not call the police until 1100 hours because she thought that reporting to the police would attract public reactions. At around 1130 hours, the police arrived and found Ann's shoes at the 20th floor of the building and established the jumping off point. They also found a note (date unknown, but believed to have written shortly before her death, thus a possible suicide note) in Ann's room that read "*Why did everyone do better than me in the exams? Why? Was it that I hadn't done enough revisions? Even though I havebeen spending so much effort in revisions, the results were still poor. I have tried to analyze my learning attitude to see what has gone wrong. However, I don't see any faults. Why? I don't know – I cannot come up with a solution. I am very anguished. HELP ME!*"

Ann's body was examined at a nearby hospital with massive injuries found consistent with falling from a height. She was found to be dead before arrival to the hospital. The autopsy report indicated that the cause of Ann's death was multiple injuries. The toxicology report found nothing of interest.

Information from the Interview with Ann's Mother

After obtaining a written informed consent, Ann's mother was interviewed six months after Ann's death. The interview lasted for three-and-a-half hours. In the semi-structured interview, we examined her socio-demographics characteristics, psychiatric and family history factors, psychological factors, and social and life events variables. Psychiatric factors investigated including history and current presence of psychiatric disorders and psychiatric treatment, previous suicide attempt, presence of chronic illnesses and physical disability, were assessed by the SCID-I-DSM-IV (Structured Clinical Interview for Diagnostic and Statistical Manual of Mental Disorders – Fourth Edition, American Psychiatric Association, 2000), the Child Depression Inventory [39], and the Child Behaviour Checklist for Ages 6-18 [40]. Psychological conditions investigated including impulsivity and problem-solving ability were assessed by the Impulsivity Rating Scale [41], and the Social Problem-Solving Inventory [42].

Below is the information collected from the interview:

1. Socio-demographics Characteristics

Ann migrated from Mainland China when she was 11-year-old. She had good relationships with the extended family members in Mainland China. Ann was an optimistic girl, loved challenges, and was liked by her classmates and teachers in primary school in China. She enjoyed reading Chinese literature and her idol was a Chinese poet. She welcomed the idea of migrating to Hong Kong and seemed to have well adapted to the lifestyle of Hong Kong. There were no family history of psychiatric illness, suicidal behavior, and no physical or psychological abuse within her family. After all, Ann adopted well in the new environment in Hong Kong.

2. Psychiatric Conditions

Ann had no history of suicide attempt and she had not been suffering from any psychiatric disorder. According to the SCID, Ann experienced a number of depressive symptoms within a month prior to her death. The depressive symptoms included depressed mood, markedly diminished interest or pleasure in almost all activities, sudden increased appetite, insomnia, fatigue, worthlessness, diminished ability to think, and recurrent thought of suicide. Ann did not show any psychotic symptoms, no indication of alcohol use, substance use, or gambling habits. She did not seem to be suffering from anxiety disorders, somatoform disorders, eating disorders, or adjustment disorder due to the possible difficulties for adjusting to live in Hong Kong at the time of death. According to the Child Depression Inventory, during the last two weeks prior to death, Ann was sad all the time, felt nothing would ever work out for her, felt nothing was fun at all, felt like crying most of the time, things bothered her all the time, could not make up her mind about things, had to push herself all the time to finish the school work, had trouble sleeping every night, felt tired most of the days, and did badly in subjects that she used to be good at. According to the Child Behavior Checklist (DSM-Oriented Scale, parent version), the results again showed that Ann seemed to be suffering from affective problems and ranged in the borderline clinical range. Again, results for the anxiety, somatic, attention deficit/hyperactivity, oppositional defiant and conduct problems were all within the normal range.

3. Psychological Factors

Ann did not show any abnormal impulsive behaviors in the last week prior to her death. She was a romantic, cheerful, creative, and loving person. Ann's mother also thought that Ann was a decent problem-solver. Ann was a perfectionist, and tended to have a tendency of experiencing symptoms of anxiety and self-doubt and related responses upon life stressors, especially on academic-related issues. She appeared to have a low self-esteem as she always thought that her elder sister and other students were academically brighter than she was.

4. Recent Life Events Variables

A number of recent life events happened to Ann in the last month prior to her death, and her mother suspected that those events might have contributed to her death. About a month prior to Ann's death, a female ex-classmate of Ann died by suicide by jumping from height. Her mother believed that Ann was upset about it, but she did not think that the impact lasted long. Besides this incident, Ann's mother reviewed two other life events that were not mentioned in the coroner's report. About two weeks before (24 Oct) Ann's death, Ann was being accused of lying to her classmates and she told her mother that she had been feeling very upset about that. The incident was that Ann told her classmate that the class teacher had hit her after class. Her classmate took this seriously and asked the class teacher to give them an explanation. It was later found that, for unknown reasons, Ann made up this story. However, Ann's mother did not know much about the incident and the coroner's files had no record of it. Then about 10 days prior (31 Oct) the death, Ann joined a barbeque party with her classmates and class teacher. During the party, the class teacher suggested that he would like the students to change their seats in the classroom so that they could get to know more about other students. Ann was very upset about his suggestion, she bursted into tears and ran away from the group.

INFORMATION FROM ANN'S INSTANT MESSAGES AND WRITINGS RETRIEVED FROM HER COMPUTER

Ann's mother brought to us some personal letters written by Ann to her friends (but the dates were unknown), and a soft copy of her two-year instant messages from ICQ. We studied these personal documents and found some information that had not been mentioned in the coroner's file and the interview with her mother. In most of her instant messages a few months prior to death, Ann would gossip with her friends about others' romantic relationships, and talked about school work, music, movie, and shopping etc. However, since late October (about 20 days prior), one of the major topics in her instant messages with friends was mainly about the concerns for Ann's "unhappiness". Her classmates or friends probably had noticed that Ann was feeling sad or unease at school, and thus, most of them expressed their concerns and tried to encourage her via instant messaging. We will quote some of these messages below that relate to how Ann had perceived the aforementioned life events. All messages are in Chinese and were translated by the first author.

About the suicide of her ex-classmate (8 Oct at 1516):
A(nn): So unhappy.
A: XXX is dead.
F(riend): ????
A: XXX killed herself.
A: If I die, will you cry for me?
F: Yes.
F: For sure.
A: That's great.

A: I have learned to cherish what I have.

After this conversation, the incident was not discussed again in the instant messaging.

About the joke that she made up (24 Oct at 2201):

Ann blamed her friend for accusing the class teacher of hitting Ann after class. This incident seemed to have a greater impact on Ann than anticipated. There were two instant messaging entries that Ann had talked about this with two of her friends.

F(riend): Hi.

A(nn): What's up?

F: Feeling down?

A: How do you know?

F: I read your on-line diary everyday.

F: Needless to say, not getting along well with people… …

A: NO, being accused of doing something wrong.

F: Yeah?

A: Anyway, OK now. Don't worry.

F: Why? What happened???????

A: Difficult to say

F: ???

A: Just feeling really down about it.

Another entry about this incident:

A(nn): Did you scold the class teacher yesterday?

F(riend): No.

F: I just asked him why did he hit you.

A: Why did you do that ><

F: …sorry…

A: Anyway… …, what happened had happened… …

A: I dare not to pass his office anymore.

A: Don't want to feel embarrassed.

F: haha ~ you have to walk pass it after school no matter what.

A: True. But, if I have a choice, I will not…

Because of this incident, Ann had probably started to contemplate suicide. One day after the previous two entries, a friend urged Ann not to kill herself in the instant messages (*25 Oct at 2231*).

F(riend): Don't die!!

F: Don't die!!

F: Please, really, don't die … … … … … … … … …

A(nn): WHAT?! Who said so?

F: Please just don't. You are such a smart person.

F: Why don't you study in another school instead?

A: I am fine now.

F: If you are being accused of doing something wrong, just change school and start a new life.

A: OK

About the barbeque incident (happened on 31 Oct):

Ann's classmates asked her why she became so emotional at the party, they chatted on-line for hours about this incident (from about 1315 to 1530, then 1922 to 2358 on *1 November*). Most conversations were initiated by the classmates of showing concerns for Ann. They then exchanged ideas about the proposal of changing seats in the classroom, and finished by asking Ann not to worry about it.

F(riend): What happened to you last night?

A(nn): Nothing.

A: Hate the idea of changing seats.

F: Let's talk to him again next week!

A: No need. Don't want to make a big fuss about it. Otherwise, he (the class teacher) *may think that the whole class is doing something for me.*

F: No. We all don't like his idea anyway.

A: True, but not as opposing as I am.

F: well, we all have our ways to express ourselves.

A: last night... so unhappy...won't join this kind of party again.

F: No...... please... ><

Another suicidal communication (on 6 Nov 2236)

Ann had expressed her suicidal ideation to her friend again and he tried to comfort her.

F(riend): Don't die!

A(nn): What?

A: Who said so?

F: Just don't die!

A: How did you know about it?

F: From your on-line diary.

A: oic~~

F: Please don't die...

A: ok~~thx

F: Please Please don't die

A: OK

A: Things can't leave behind

A: That suicidal thought was horrible.

F: Please don't die................ Please don't die............. Please don't die..................... Please don't die

A: I am not thinking about it now

F: Let me know when you are down.

F: Cry... BABY... CRY

A: I have been crying for the whole day

F: Cry out loud

A: Never tried

F: Why are you down?

A: don't want to tell

F: You have to tell people about it to feel better

A: When I tell, I will cry

F: Cry out loud.

A: I am tired~ don't want to think.
F: Please don't die
A: :-D
F: Feeling better now?
A: Yes.
F: Don't think about killing yourself please?
A: OK.
F: You know what?! Sometimes your friends know more about you than yourself.
A; How?
F: Your heart.
F: Really.
F: I know you will do it.
F: So, I am hoping that you will change your mind.
A: Then.
F: Don't think about it.
A: I am ok.
F: Don't say that you are ok.
A: I REALLY am OK.
F: I know you have a thorn in your heart...
A: hum hum
F: Hope you may grow out of it.
A: I am not thinking about it now.
F: Just concern about you.
A: Thank you. :-D

The last hour of Ann's life

On 11 November at 0105, her class teacher (CT) had the following ICQ conversation with Ann that clearly indicated that Ann (A) was contemplating of killing herself:

A: If you don't see me at school tomorrow, how will you feel?
CT: Yes, especially you wrote "I really want to go... Goodbye".
CT: If you go, are you sure you can leave me behind?
A: I am serious.
CT: Can "Go" really solve your problems? Is that the sole solution to you? Others will have to solve more problems after you "go".
A: When time comes, I just have to let go/leave everything behind me.
CT: If you must go, Just GO! :'(

DISCUSSION

The psychological autopsy of Ann's death yielded both significant methodological and clinical implications for the study and prevention of suicide. The three sets of data sources combined offer valuable information of Ann's suicide. Specifically, the instant messaging records have provided us the opportunity to look into Ann's suicidal mind in greater detail.

In the original psychological autopsy study, the purpose of it was to clarify whether a death was due to accident or suicide [10]. In Ann's case, however, the mode of death was not under scrutiny. Ann had died by suicide and she clearly intended to end her life by jumping from a height from the building she lived in. Instead, the questions asked in this psychological autopsy study were to answer whether her friend's suicide and her perception of failing an exam were significant contributory factors in her suicide, and whether Ann was suffering from any diagnosable psychiatric illness at the time of death. The information collected from the coroner's file and the interview with her mother seems to suggest that the suicide death of her classmate had a lesser impact on Ann than the latter events. We come to this conclusion basing on the facts that the potential suicide note that was found from her room was about her feelings of hopelessness and powerlessness to excel in studying, and the note that she asked a classmate to prepare for her death was written out of her fear in failing the mathematic test. On the other hand, Ann did not mention much about her friend's suicide. Nonetheless, the copycat aspect among the youth population could not be emphasized more and the impact of a peer suicide should never be underestimated. More, from a diagnostic perspective, Ann would probably have suffered from an undetected diagnosable depressive episode that started about two weeks prior to her death.

Hence, based on the information collected from the Coroner's court file and the interview with Ann's mother, we would have concluded that had it not been for this young girl's friend completed suicide and fear in failing a test and thus feeling depressed, powerless, and hopeless, Ann would not have died by suicide at the particular time she did. Also, if Ann's teacher and fellow students responded adequately to Ann's "crying out for help", her death would be prevented. Consequently, one would suggest suicide prevention interventions for youth at risks should include better recognition and treatment of youth depression, enhancing postvention efforts in better screening of at-risk adolescents, strengthening referral system for youth who have exhibited suicidal ideation and related behavior, and limiting access to suicide means [43]. These conclusions and recommendations would be justifiable if Ann was part of a large-scale community-based psychological autopsy that was used to establish that psychopathology or psychiatric diagnosis as a major contributory cause of suicide.

However, if we are eager to understand the suicidal process of this young girl or even to address the issue of causation about her death, there are still many questions have left to be answered. The extra information gathered from the instant messages has helped us to fill in some of the missing links between the diverse circumstances that Ann had experienced.

After studying her instant messaging records and comparing her pre- and peri- suicidal periods, we speculate that Ann's suicidal process probably started on 24 Oct (18 days prior to death), when she explicitly told her friend that she was thinking of suicide and it was precipitated by the embarrassment to have started a joke about being hit by the class teacher (rather than the friend's suicide or the feeling of failing a test). This incident created such a negative impact on Ann probably because it had affected the relationship with her class teacher. Although the bonding between the class teacher and Ann was relatively brief, in terms of time, this class teacher might probably be the first caring, mature, and peer-liked authoritative attachment figure for Ann. Ann seemed to care a lot about how the class teacher perceived her and the class teacher seemed to be one of a significant personswithin her support system. When this suicidal wish had established, suicide became *a* or even *the* option for relieving her from emotional pain. This cognitive rigidity about pursuing suicide as the only problem-solving solution have also been observed in other suicidal adolescents [44]. As days went by, the emotional outburst at the barbeque party and the fear of failing a mathematic test had reinforced Ann's feelings of hopelessness and powerlessness to control her emotions. Ann expressed her suicidal wish repeatedly over the Internet to her friends probably as a cry of pain, a cry for help, and as a way to assist her in anticipating the effect of her suicide on others while ignoring its finality [45]. In the final hour, Ann was crying for help and testing out how her class teacher would react to her suicidal tendency. Unfortunately, the last typed conversation statement by the class teacher "just go" was probably perceived by Ann as a rejection and this unintended but uncaring attitude had motivated her from wishing to die to acting on it. Ann's last entry on her computer had detailed the finale of her suicidal mind:

Title: "Goodbye"

Don't say that I am fragile
I am afraid of physical pain... but I am more afraid of facing adversities...
Don't be sad...
Time will be the best cure...
I will always love you ... all of you...
I hope you will remember me forever

To:
Class teacher Wishing you a happy day forever*
Queeny Learn how to look after yourself, I will no longer be there for you*
Mandy give opportunities to those around you*
Cheuy Don't be so grumpy, I am afraid of you.. Don't be sad, and don't cry for me. Good girl*
Yin Don't cry for me... Be strong...*
SumSum Keep smiling... and bring happiness to everyone*

Dad Take care of yourself*
Mom Though you have been healthier than before, still, look after your health*
Sister I have never called you "sister", study harder and be a usual person*
Little brother My most worrisome person, don't give so many excuses to your poor academic results. Being good at sport is great, but still, you have to be good in studying.*

Today is 11-11

CONCLUSION

Advancement of information technology has indeed changed our lives. There is a paucity of study on Internet and suicide, and those studies tend to focus on the negative impact of the Internet [46-49]. Very little has been said about the positive side of utilizing the Internet in the study of suicide and to enhance its prevention. In this chapter, we have illustrated the added value of analyzing a young girl's instant messaging records as part of a psychological autopsy process not only to elucidate significant contributory factors, but also to reconstruct the psychological state and the suicidal process of a suicidal young girl. While instant messaging has become a significant communication means among the youth population, if their peers are more equipped to respond constructively to their friend's suicidal communication, they may have a potential and viable means of intervening effectively (as a gatekeeper) with their suicidal friends and achieving suicide deterrence or prevention among those at risk. In addition, while the use of the psychological autopsies has received its share of controversy, we believe that with the emergence of information technology, the validity and reliability of this study methodology can be improved and will continue to assist our understanding of suicide. However, while there are additional values that instant messaging may bring to the study of suicide, we should also acknowledge its limitations. Particularly, unlike traditional writings or letters, people who communicate using instant messaging may not know the real identities of each other, their typed conversations may not truly reveal their actual cognitions and emotions.

ACKNOWLEDGEMENT

We are indebted to Ann's mother who lent her heart to this study. We thank Prof. Arthur Kleinman for his helpful comments and criticisms. We are grateful to Ms. Fiona Yau for her editorial effort and Ms. Wincy Chan for her assistance in the interview with Ann's mother.

REFERENCES

[1] Varnik, A., Kolves, K., Allik, J., Arensman, E., Aromaa, E., Van Audenhove, C., Bouleau, J. H., Van Der Feltz-Cornelis, C. M., Giupponi, G., Gusmao, R., Kopp, M., Marusic, A., Maxwell, M., Oskarsson, H., Palmer, A., Pull, C., Realo, A., Reisch, T., Schmidtke, A., Sola, V. P., Wittenburg, L. & Hegerl, U. Gender issues in suicide rates, trends and methods among youths aged 15-24 in 15 european countries. *J Affect Disord* 2008 [Epub ahead of print].

[2] Gould, M. S., Greenberg, T., Velting, D. & Shaffer, D. Youth suicide risk and preventive interventions: A review of the past 10 years. *J Am Acad Child Adolesc Psychiatry* 2003; 42: 386-405.

[3] Macneil, M. S. An epidemiologic study of aboriginal adolescent risk in Canada: The meaning of suicide. *J Child Adolesc Psychiatr Nurs* 2008; 21: 3-12.

[4] Cantor, C. & Neulinger, K. The epidemiology of suicide and attempted suicide among young Australians. *Aust N Z J Psychiatry* 2000; 34: 370-87.

[5] Shaffer, D. Epidemiological aspects of some problems in child and adolescent psychiatry. *Epidemiol Psichiatr Soc* 1998; 7: 151-5.

[6] Juon, H. S., Nam, J. J. & Ensminger, M. E. Epidemiology of suicidal behavior among Korean adolescents. *J Child Psychol Psychiatry* 1994; 35: 663-76.

[7] Brent, D. A. The psychological autopsy: Methodological considerations for the study of adolescent suicide. *Suicide Life Threat Behav* 1989; 19: 43-57.

[8] Fortune, S., Stewart, A., Yadav, V. & Hawton, K. Suicide in adolescents: Using life charts to understand the suicidal process. *J Affect Disord* 2007; 100: 199-210.

[9] Houston, K., Hawton, K. & Shepperd, R. Suicide in young people aged 15-24: A psychological autopsy study. *J Affect Disord* 2001; 63: 159-70.

[10] Shneidman, E. S. Suicide, lethality, and the psychological autopsy. *Int Psychiatry Clin* 1969; 6: 225-50.

[11] Appleby, L., Cooper, J., Amos, T. & Faragher, B. Psychological autopsy study of suicides by people aged under 35. *Br J Psychiatry* 1999; 175: 168-74.

[12] Arieli, A., Gilat, I. & Aycheh, S. Suicide among ethiopian jews: A survey conducted by means of a psychological autopsy. *J Nerv Ment Dis* 1996; 184: 317-9.

[13] Beautrais, A. L. Gender issues in youth suicidal behaviour. *Emerg Med* 2002; 14: 35-42.

[14] Chen, E. Y. H., Chan, W. S. C., Wong, P. W. C., Chan, S. S. M., Chan, C. L. W., Law, Y. W., Beh, P. S. L., Chan, K. K., Cheng, J. W. Y., Liu, K. Y. & Yip, P. S. F. Suicide in Hong Kong: A case-control psychological autopsy study. *Psych Med* 2006; 36: 815-825.

[15] Cheng, A. T., Chen, T. H., Chen, C. C. & Jenkins, R. Psychosocial and psychiatric risk factors for suicide. Case-control psychological autopsy study. *Br J Psychiatry* 2000; 177: 360-5.

[16] Chiu, H. F. K., Yip, P. S. F., Chi, J., Chan, S., Tsoh, J., Kwan, C. W., Li, S. F., Conwell, Y. & Caine, E. Elderly suicide in hong kong - a case-controlled psychological autopsy study. *Acta Psychiatr Scand* 2004; 109: 299-305.

[17] Hawton, K., Malmberg, A. & Simkin, S. Suicide in doctors. A psychological autopsy study. *J Psychosom Res* 2004; 57: 1-4.

[18] Heila, H., Isometsa, E. T., Henriksson, M. M., Heikkinen, M. E., Marttunen, M. J. & Lonnqvist, J. K. Suicide and schizophrenia: A nationwide psychological autopsy study on age- and sex-specific clinical characteristics of 92 suicide victims with schizophrenia. *Am J Psychiatry* 1997; 154: 1235-1242.

[19] Phillips, M. R., Yang, G., Zhang, Y., Wang, L., Ji, H. & Zhou, M. Risk factors for suicide in china: A national case-control psychological autopsy study. *Lancet* 2002; 360: 1728-1736.

[20] Vijayakumar, L. & Rajkumar, S. Are risk factors for suicide universal? A case-control study in india. *Acta Psychiatr Scand* 1999; 99: 407-411.

[21] Chynoweth, R., Tonge, J. I. & Armstrong, J. Suicide in Brisbane - a retrospective psychosocial study. *Aust N Z J Psychiatry* 1980; 14: 37-45.

[22] Wong, P. W., Chan, W. S., Chen, E. Y., Chan, S. S., Law, Y. W. & Yip, P. S. Suicide among adults aged 30-49: A psychological autopsy study in Hong Kong. *BMC Public Health* 2008; 8: 147.

[23] Arsenault-Lapierre, G., Kim, C. & Turecki, G. Psychiatric diagnoses in 3275 suicides: A meta-analysis. *BMC Psychiatry* 2004; 4: 37.

[24] Brent, D. A., Perper, J. A., Moritz, G., Allman, C., Friend, A., Roth, C., Schweers, J., Balach, L. & Baugher, M. Psychiatric risk factors for adolescent suicide: A case-control study. *J Am Acad Child Adolesc Psychiatry* 1993; 32: 521-9.

[25] Ebert, B. (1991) Guide to conducting a psychological autopsy, in: Anchor, K. N. (Ed.) *The handbook of medical psychotherapy: Cost effective strategies in mental health*, pp. 249-256 (Ashland, OH, US, Hogrefe & Huber).

[26] Isometsa, E. T. Psychological autopsy studies--a review. *European Psychiatry: the Journal of the Association of European Psychiatrists* 2001; 16: 379-385.

[27] Pouliot, L. & De Leo, D. Critical issues in psychological autopsy studies. *Suicide Life Threat Behav* 2006; 36: 491-510.

[28] Zhang, J., Conwell, Y., Wieczorek, W. F., Jiang, C., Jia, S. & Zhou, L. Studying chinese suicide with proxy-based data: Reliability and validity of the methodology and instruments in china. *J Nerv Ment Dis* 2003; 191: 450-457.

[29] Beskow, J., Runeson, B. & Asgård, U. Psychological autopsies: Methods and ethics. *Suicide Life Threat Behav* 1990; 20: 307-323.

[30] Brent, D. A., Perper, J. A., Kolko, D. J. & Zelenak, J. P. The psychological autopsy: Methodological considerations for the study of adolescent suicide. *J Am Acad Child Adolesc Psychiatry* 1988; 27: 362-366.

[31] Shneidman, E. S. & Farberow, N. L. Some comparisons between genuine and simulated suicide notes in terms of mowrer's concepts of discomfort and relief. *J Gen Psychiatry* 1957; 56: 251-256.

[32] Lester, D. & Linn, M. The content of suicide notes written by those using different methods for suicide. *Percept Mot Skills* 1998; 87: 722.

[33] Asgard, U. A psychiatric study of suicide among urban swedish women. *Acta Psychiatr Scand* 1990; 82: 115-124.

[34] Beck, A., Morris, J. & Lester, D. Suicide notes and risk of future suicide. *JAMA* 1974; 228: 495-496.

[35] Canetto, S. & Lester, D. Love and achievement motives in women's and men's suicide notes. *J Psychol* 2002; 126: 573-576.

[36] Capstick, A. Recognition of emotional disturbance and the prevention of suicide. *BMJ* 1960; 1: 1129-1182.

[37] Chynoweth, R. The significance of suicide notes. *Aust N Z J Psychiatry* 1977; 11: 197-200.

[38] Wong, P. W. C., Yeung, A., Chan, W. S. C., Yip, P. S. F. & Tang, A. K. H. The characteristics of suicide note-leavers and non-note leavers. *Death Stud* In press

[39] Helsel, W. J. & Matson, J. L. The assessment of depression in children: The internal structure of the child depression inventory (cdi). *Behav Res Therapy* 1984; 22: 289-928.

[40] Achenbach, T. M. & Rescorla, L. A. (2001) *Manual for the aseba school-age forms & profiles.* (Burlington, VT, University of Vermont, Research Centre for Children, Youth, & Families.).

[41] Lecrubier, Y., Braconnier, A., Said, S. & Payan, C. The impulsivity rating scale (IRS): Preliminary results. *European Psychiatry* 1995; 10: 331-338.

[42] D'Zurilla, T. J. & Nezu, A. M. Development and preliminary evaluation of the social problem-solving inventory (SPSI). *Psyc Assess*1990; 2: 156-163.

[43] Bridge, J. A., Goldstein, T. R. & Brent, D. A. Adolescent suicide and suicidal behavior. *J Child Psychol Psychiatry* 2006; 47: 372-394.

[44] Cross, T. L., Gust-Brey, K. & Ball, P. B. A psychological autopsy of the suicide of an academically gifted student: Researchers' and parents' perspectives. *Gifted child quarterly* 2002; 46: 247-264.

[45] Parrish, M. & Tunkle, M. Clinical challenges following an adolescent's death by suicide: Bereavement issues faced by family, friends, schools, and clinicians. *Clinical Social Work Journal* 2005; 33: 81-102.

[46] Biddle, L., Donovan, J., Hawton, K., Kapur, N. & Gunnell, D. Suicide and the internet. *BMJ* 2008; 336: 800-802.

[47] Krysinska, K. E. & De Leo, D. Telecommunication and suicide prevention: Hopes and challenges for the new century. *Omega* 2007; 55: 237-253.
[48] Naito, A. Internet suicide in japan: Implications for child and adolescent mental health. *Clin Child Psychol Psychiatry* 2007; 12: 583-597.
[49] Recupero, P. R., Harms, S. E. & Noble, J. M. Googling suicide: Surfing for suicide information on the internet. *J Clin Psychiatry* 2008: 1-11.

In: Internet and Suicide
Editors: L. Sher and A. Vilens
ISBN 978-1-60741-077-5

Chapter 10

INTERNET AND EMERGING SUICIDE METHOD: A CASE STUDY OF CONTAGION OF CHARCOAL BURNING SUICIDES VIA THE INTERNET

King-Wa Fu
Journalism and Media Studies Centre & Centre for Suicide Research and Prevention, The University of Hong Kong, Pokfulam, Hong Kong SAR, China

Paul W. C. Wong, Paul S. F. Yip
Centre for Suicide Research and Prevention, The University of Hong Kong, Pokfulam, Hong Kong SAR, China

ABSTRACT

This chapter aims to address the role of contagion of the Internet in the adoption of specific way of dying of suicidal people. It first reviews the current literatures and case reports indicating some suicidal people's choices of suicide method(s) are associated with their prior exposure to the web contents of one or more than one specific method(s). Second, this chapter reports a case of contagion of a novel method of self-killing, charcoal burning suicide, which was originated in Hong Kong and then spread across several Asian countries. This case study demonstrates the potential contagious effects of the Internet on the emergence of charcoal burning suicides. Finally, the theoretical explanations and the preventive measures are discussed. Future research directions are also suggested.

INTRODUCTION

A growing amount of research has been demonstrating a positive linkage between human exposure to suicide stories in the media and subsequent suicidal behaviors [1-4]. Concerns over such adverse media effects have arisen in Asia where suicide rates of several countries in the region have been increasing in the past few years. In particular, there has been evidence showing that the extensive media coverage of famous Asian pop star suicide deaths led to the increased suicide rates in Taiwan, Hong Kong and South Korea [5-7]. These studies collectively find that there were gender-specific and method-specific increases following the celebrity suicides; and such sub-group effect has provided strong evidence to suggest that it is resulted from modeling effect of celebrity suicide [6].

A classic example of positive linkage between media depiction of suicide and increased suicide rate is about a ripple effect of an instructional manual on suicide. *Final Exit,* a suicide manual written by a right-to-die advocate, was published in the United States in 1991. In the year after its release, the number of suicides by plastic bag asphyxial deaths, an uncommon way of dying but was recommended by the *Final Exit*, surged by four times in the New York City. But neither changes in the overall suicide rate nor the rates of other suicide methods were detected [8]. A similar pattern of elevated suicides by this method also appeared soon after the release of its second edition in 2000 [9]. This ripple effect has also been observed in South Australia [10].

In the past, mass media was generally referring to radio, television and newspaper. Since the emergence of the Internet in the late 1980s, this electronic media has become a powerful communication channel. Unlike the traditional means of communication, the Internet is characterized by its interactivity, user-centric architecture, and always-on nature and it has currently become one of the dominating communication mediums. The Internet allows users to acquire information on demand at any time and place as long as the communication device is accessible, and users are no longer being the passive receivers of news stories from traditional media.

Nevertheless, this interactive medium is often known as "a double edged tool" [11, 12]. On one hand, the Internet is a convenient medium for acquiring broad range of knowledge. Some studies demonstrate its beneficial effects on preventing suicide, which the approaches included discouraging people from self-harm or suicidal behaviors [13-15], saving life by picking up "electronic suicide note" [16], searching patient's suicidal history for emergency use [17, 18], rescuing suicidal people who express their intentions on the web [19], as well as educating people's understanding on the warning signs of suicide [20].

But on the other hand, it also provides a platform for broadcasting or publishing unfiltered and undesirable information, e.g., child pornography, violence, racist opinions, and pro-suicide materials. To contain the possible adverse effects of online suicide messages, a paediatrician recommends to take legal actions against the websites carrying messages of pro-suicide [21]. Furthermore, Sher [22] suggests that the undesirable effect of Internet is attributable to an uneven pace of development between technology and human mental function.

Although evidence of positive linkage between exposure to traditional media and subsequent suicidal behavior is now available, there is very limited research that looks into the influence of the Internet on subsequent suicidal behavior [1]. Some anecdotal evidence, nevertheless, have suggested a positive association. An early account of the controversy over the open discussions about euthanasia on the Internet was found in 1995 [23]. A later study reported three suicide cases of teenagers who posted their suicide notes on the web to express their suicidal plans and requested other web users for suggestions on the suicide methods [24]. A more recent review on nine cases of completed and attempted suicides reported that these suicide victims had been exposed to information of some rare suicide means obtained from the Internet prior to their suicidal acts [25]. Reports from Japan documented that following the extensive and replicated mass media coverage on unusual incidents of cyber-suicide pacts [26] – a way of suicide that strangers are linked up by websites or online forums and then kill themselves together at a specific time or place, or even by the same suicide method - a total of 120 people in 2003 and 2004 (or nearly 40 episodes) took their own lives in cyber-suicide pacts [27]. In 2008, Japanese media reported that at least six people killed themselves by using homemade gas poisoning or mixing cleaning liquid and bath salts, over a single weekend [28]. More worryingly, this cyber-suicide pact phenomenon has also been observed in the United Kingdom [27].

Besides the anecdotal evidence, two studies using content analysis were conducted to examine the suicide related contents on the web pages. These two studies revealed interesting, but not surprising, findings that pro-suicide websites are common and can be easily located by a number of generic search engine keywords like "suicide", "suicide methods" or "how to commit suicide" [29, 30]. However, both studies failed to consider the user-initiated web search for specific ways of dying by using keywords of suicide methods, like "charcoal burning" or "homemade gas", through which some vulnerable web-users may look for the details about a specific suicide method that they have in mind, along with some technical descriptions on how to carry them out. Besides World Wide Web, the Internet users may also find information about suicide methods from chat rooms [31] or websites with specific domain name [32].

Rapid emergence of suicide method across countries has been witnessed since the end of 20th century and it is suggested to be attributable to the contagion via the Internet [33]. Carbon monoxide poisoning by burning charcoal (or charcoal burning suicide in short) has been portrayed by mass media since 1998 in Hong Kong as an easy, painless and effective means of ending one's life [34]. It appeared to have been widely spread from Hong Kong to some other places through the media, including the Internet [34, 35].

In order to provide a systematic and comprehensive review of the Internet and its role in the widespread adoption of some specific ways of dying among the suicide deaths, this chapter aims to report a review of the existing case reports that document the suicides which were associated with the exposure to information about specific suicide method via the Internet. More, an "Asian pandemic" of cross-border propagation of a novel way of self-killing, charcoal burning suicide, which was originated in Hong Kong and its contagious effect across several Asian countries, will be reported in this chapter to provide a show case of the ripple effect of the Internet on subsequent suicidal behavior. At the end of the chapter, we will provide two theoretical explanations for this human modeling behavior and suggest future preventive measures and research directions on this topic.

Review of Case Reports

In this section, we conduct a narrative review to summarize the published case reports that identify the connections between the choice of suicide method and the exposure to suicide related information from the Internet. We identified such information through electronic databases, i.e. PubMed, Medline, PsyINFO, and Google Scholar by using keywords "Internet" and "suicide". Our initial inspection found majority of these suicides killed themselves by using rare suicide methods or ways of dying with technical details, like poisoning by uncommon chemical. We therefore further strengthened the quality of search by using additional keywords "poisoning" and "rare method". To be included in this review, the articles have to meet the following three criteria: 1) if at least one real (non-fictional) incident of suicide death or attempted suicide has been reported; 2) if the report has presented sufficient evidence, but not speculation, supporting that the suicide victim or suicide attempter had been exposed to information about suicide method from the Internet before the suicidal act; and 3) if the main body of the report or its abstract is written in English. Finally, fifteen case reports were found to meet all three inclusive criteria.

Table 1 summarizes the 15 cases, which spanned across six different countries including Australia, United Kingdom, United States of America, Greece, Germany, and Canada. There were 19 suicide victims among the 15 cases, of which 14 (74%) were male and 5 (26%) were female. About 70% (13 victims) aged between 15 and 39, whereas only one victim aged less than 15 and two aged between 40 and 59. The age of the remaining three victims was not identified in the reports. All cases are categorized by suicide methods as follows: poisoning by inhalation of gas (Case 1,10), taking poisonous substance or fluid (Case 1-4,6,9,12-15), asphyxiation by plastic bag and inhalation of gas (Case 5,7,8), and firearm or hanging (Case 1,11).

The majority of the victims was reported to have learnt the suicide methods from the web via search engine or dedicated websites. Some victims had made use of the website information to reconfirm their prior knowledge about a specific suicide method (Case 2, 8), and some had even involved into direct discussions with other web users on specific approaches of self-killing via the chat room or discussion board (Case 1, 9). Six victims (Case 8, 9, 12, 14, 15) were found to mail-order the required poisons for their suicidal acts, through either websites of drug companies or online auction sites. These mail-order cases appear to have happened in more recent years, i.e. between 2004 and 2007.

Despite the limitation that the above review is unable to obtain a representative sample from a huge amount of unreported cases, the result sheds some light on the characteristics of the cases that the choice of suicide method may link with Internet exposure. We have the following observations that are worthy to be discussed further.

Age and Gender

More male suicide victims are found to obtain web information about suicide methods than their female counterparts. Since a US study finds no marked discrepancy in Internet penetration between genders but males have more intensive web usage [36], it appears to suggest that heavy Internet usage may be an associated factor to explain the gender differences. Moreover, people at younger age have a relatively higher Internet penetration than older people [36], and therefore more younger age suicide victims are observed to pick up their ways of dying based on web information.

Rare Suicide Methods Requiring Know-how

Majority of these suicide victims chose rare suicide methods by which the suicidal people are required to learn the knowledge about certain technical details, such as poisoning [37] or plastic bag asphyxiation by inhalation of gas [38-41]. Such information on rare suicide methods is typically not available in public domains, like printed publications or television channels. Internet therefore provides the suicidal people an easy access to searching for information about rare suicide methods on the web.

Ways to Locate the Information Sources

Many case reports indicated that the suicide victims had sought the information about suicide methods intentionally through search engines, or participated actively in discussions about the choice of suicide method with some other strangers on the web forum. One victim was even able to type in the domain name (URL) directly with keywords in relation to a specific suicide method.

Motivations

Most of the victims appear to have strong motivation to seek information about one or more specific suicide methods that they have probably already known, maybe through other mass media channels. They may try different keywords via search engines and may "shop" for the websites or chat rooms that are able to address their concerns. This shows that these suicide victims are active, rather than passive, Internet users of seeking suicide related information.

Case Study: Charcoal Burning Suicides across Asian Countries

In this section of the chapter, we report a case study to illustrate the widespread of method-specific suicides across some Asian countries through the Internet. Before 1998, suicide by carbon-monoxide (CO) poisoning (excluding the suicides by domestic gas) was rare in Asia. In 1997, there were less than 1% of suicide deaths by using gas poisoning in Hong Kong, Taiwan, and South Korea, and around 5% of these suicide deaths in Japan (Figure 1). Since 1998, the number of suicides by CO poisoning in Hong Kong and Taiwan has considerably increased. In Japan, this type of suicides has surged from 5% of the overall suicide deaths in 2002 to 15% in 2005. Suicides by gas poisoning in South Korea, however, do not show similar increasing pattern and has remained at a very low level until 2005.

What happened in 1998? According to Lee, Chan, Lee & Yip [55], the source of the "epidemic" started in a top circulation newspaper in Hong Kong, namely *the Oriental Daily*, which published a suicide case in November 1998. This story reported the suicide death of a mid-aged lady, who burnt charcoal using a barbeque grill in a confined and sealed bedroom.

Table 1. Reviewed Case Reports of Suicides in this study (Chronological Order)

Case.	Suicide method	Country	Year	Summary
1	Firearm/poisoning by sleep gels/Carbon monoxide poisoning in car	Australia	1997	Reports of three cases (Male, 26; Male, unknown age; Male, unknown age) in which their specific ways of dying and suicidal intention were discussed in an online newsgroup [24].
2	Poisoning by wolfsbane	UK	1998	A woman (unknown age) attempted suicide by ingestion of roots of wolfsbane, which was a suicide method found online and was recommended by the web as being "certain" and relatively quick [42].
3	Propoxyphene and acetaminophen poisoning	USA	1998	A 24-year-old man collected the information about poisons from the Internet and then attempted suicide. An 11-page document was found to report the detail procedures of his suicide attempt [43].
4	Poisoning by castor oil beans/Drinking excessive water	USA	1999	Reports of two suicide attempters (Male, 16; Female, 34) who learned the ideas of suicide methods from the Internet and killed themselves by using some rare ways of dying [44].
5	Plastic bag suffocation and diethyl ether Inhalation	Greece	2002	A 49-year-old male was found by his wife sitting on his desk with a plastic garbage bag, securely fastened around his neck and contained with diethyl ether. His wife confirmed he had actively searched online for suicide method before his death [45].
6	Yew poisoning	Germany	2003	A 14-year-old boy learned the poisonous plants as a suicide method on various websites. He then cut leaves from a yew tree and ingested them. He died soon afterwards [46].
7	Helium asphyxiation	USA	2003	A female, aged 19, researched on suicide online and found an advocated method of suicide by using helium [47].
8	Helium asphyxiation	Canada	2004	A male, aged 20, with multiple suicide attempts history purchased necessary equipments for dying by

				helium asphyxiation. He learned this idea of suicide method from the Internet [48].
9	Poisoning by diazepam and an unknown substance	Germany	2004	A 17-year-old female visited many suicide web forums, where she researched for suicide method, and then she purchased diazepam and an unknown substance for suicide [32].
10	Poisoning by homemade carbon monoxide	USA	2005	A male killed himself by using homemade carbon monoxide (CO) poisoning. Evidence showed that he discovered the method of CO production by searching various Internet sites dedicated to suicide [49].
11	Hanging amid watching download video	Germany	2006	A 30-year-old man hanged himself in his apartment. He wore a headphone connected to a computer which was playing a video movie showing a naked and allegedly hanged lady. This video file was downloaded from the Internet [50].
12	Poisoning by barbiturates	Germany	2006	An 18-year-old female learned about the method of suicide from the Internet and then she ordered the barbiturates for poisoning [51].
13	Poisoning by radiator fluid	USA	2006	A15-year-old boy attempted suicide by drinking radiator fluid. He learned about the suicide method by searching through the Internet [52].
14	Yellow oleander poisoning	UK	2007	Report of a 41-year-old male who used the Internet to obtain suicide information and then purchased the poison from a tropical plant for suicidal use [53].
15	Heavy metal poisoning	USA	2007	Two cases (Male, 30; Male, 22) of self-killing by using significant heavy metal poisonings (arsenic trioxide and mercuric chloride). Both chemicals in pure powder form were ordered by the victims through the Internet [54].

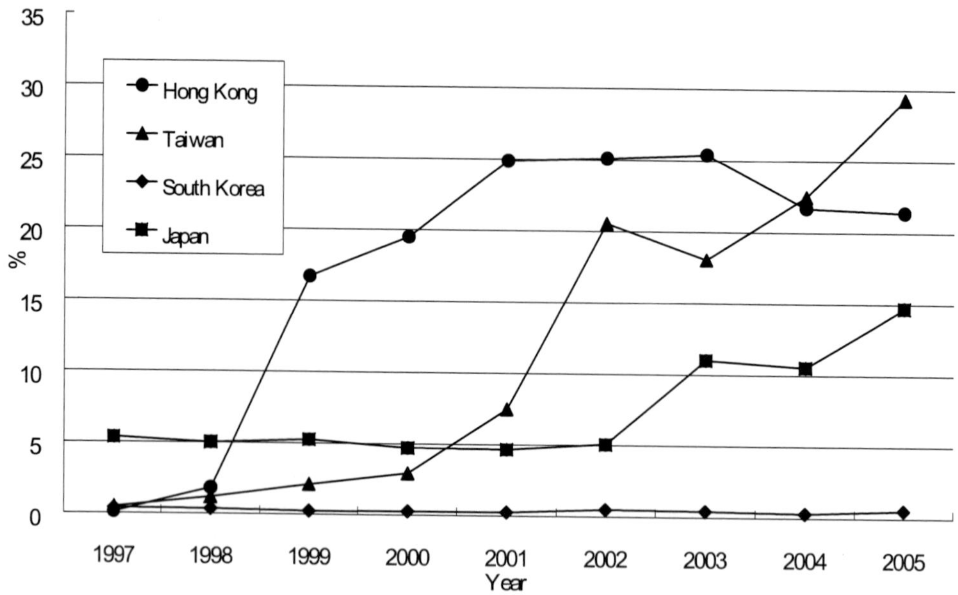

Note: Suicides by gas poisoning (excluding the suicides by domestic gas) is defined by the ICD-9 code E952 in Hong Kong and Taiwan, or the ICD-10 code X67 in South Korea and Japan.

Sources: World Health Organization Mortality Data Base and HKJC Centre for Suicide Research and Prevention.

Figure 1. The proportion of suicides by gas poisoning in Hong Kong, Taiwan, South Korea, and Japan (1997-2005).

She killed herself by the inhalation of generated carbon monoxide from burning charcoal. Such news story entitled "*A woman died by suicide in a novel poisoning gas chamber*" (English translation, original in Chinese) was accompanied with two color pictures which one showed her body lying in bed and the other one showing the burning charcoal on the barbeque grill. A small column located next to the article presented the FAQ-like information about the chemical reaction of burning charcoal and the lethal characteristics of carbon monoxide inhalation.

Since then, this novel way of self-killing has gained its momentum in Hong Kong. Nine more cases of burning charcoal suicides were reported in the ensuing month [55]. Suicide deaths by charcoal burning and other gas poisoning accounted for 16.7% of the overall Hong Kong suicide deaths in 1999. Between 2001 and 2003, it became the second most prevalent suicide method in Hong Kong, representing one out of four suicides died by this method. It killed more than 320 people in 2003 [56]. A number of studies have identified that the reporting of suicide stories in local media is among the contributing factors underscoring such drastic growth of suicides by using charcoal burning [34, 55, 57]. Unfortunately, this epidemic not only had spread within Hong Kong, but had also spread to other nearby Asian countries, and elsewhere. Charcoal burning suicide has been known as an "Asian pandemic" [57] or even a "global plague".

To better understand the extent of its effect, we conducted a thorough search for the first reports (or at least one of the first batch of released reports) on charcoal burning suicides in different countries occurred between 1998 and 2005 from academic literature databases

(PubMed, Medline, PsyINFO) and a global newspaper archive Lexis Nexis database. Table 2 shows these reports of suicides by burning charcoal in the countries ranging from Asia to Europe and North America, the United Kingdom, and the United States.

As shown in Table 2, the first case of charcoal burning suicide in Taiwan was reportedly occurred in June 2000 [64]. A female suicide victim had obtained information about charcoal burning from the web and killed herself by this method afterward. Starting from year 2000 (Figure 1), suicides by gas poisoning (mainly charcoal-burning) skyrocketed from 2.9% of all suicide deaths in 2000 to 29.3% in 2005, and it becomes the second most prevalent suicide method in Taiwan in 2006 [58, 59]. Taiwan suicide has increased from 6 per 100,000 in 1993 to nearly 20.0 per 100,000 in 2005 which is its historical high.

From Table 2, a suicide pact of three Japanese strangers, which occurred in February 2003, is known as the first "net suicide" in Japan. This incident seems to have boosted the charcoal burning suicides in Japan since 2003. The proportion of charcoal burning suicides and other gas poisoning increased from 5.1% of all suicide deaths in 2002 to 14.7% in 2005, as shown in Figure 1. Charcoal burning is often associated with the Internet suicides and the suicide pacts in Japan [60].

Table 2. Reports of burning charcoal suicides in the countries/places outside Hong Kong (in chronological order)

Country	Date of incident	Summary
Macau	March 2000	A suicide pact of a Hong Kong man and a woman seems to be the first case of charcoal burning suicide in Macau. Another report estimates that there were totally 12 cases of burning charcoal suicides in 2000 [63].
Taiwan	June 2000	A female researcher killed herself by burning charcoal in the bathroom. Police investigation indicated she had learned the method from the Internet. This case was reported as the first charcoal burning suicide in Taipei [64].
United Kingdom	March 2001	An Asian chemical engineering student killed himself by using charcoal burning. Coroner inquest indicated that he had discovered this way of self-killing from websites [65].
Japan	February 2003	Charcoal burning suicide of three strangers, who met each other on the web, is known as the first "net suicide" in Japan [60].
Malaysia	April 2004	An unemployed man died by burning charcoal at home with the air-con turned on. The news report indicated the victim had learned about this from a Hong Kong soap opera [66].
USA (California)	September 2004	A Chinese native female immigrant attempted suicide with her son by using burning charcoal.
United Kingdom	September 2005	Two strangers who met online killed themselves by burning charcoal in a car. This incidence is known to be the first Internet suicide pact in UK [67].

The case in the United Kingdom, which happened in 2001, indicated evidence that the victim had collected information about charcoal burning from the websites. The subsequent case in 2005 was even known as the first UK "net suicide pact". Another case of charcoal burning in UK was also likely to be linked with the information available online [61].

Moreover, the cases of charcoal burning suicide in Macau and Malaysia are both found to have certain associations with Hong Kong, in which the male victim was from Hong Kong in the Macau case and that the victim had prior exposure to Hong Kong media in the Malaysia case.

It is interesting to observe that the suicides by gas poisoning in South Korea remained at a very low level between 1998 and 2005, despite the marked increases observed in her neighboring Asian countries (Figure 1). We speculate that the usage of non-Korean languages, like Chinese or English, in South Korea is not popular locally and therefore information about charcoal burning, mostly available in Chinese or English, cannot be easily propagated to South Korea through the mass media or the Internet.

In addition, substantial increase in suicides by gas poisoning does not seem to occur in Mainland China where the media and the Internet are often censored by the government and the proportion of population who has access to the Internet is still limited comparing to the developed countries. This may be part of the reason why the cross-border contagion of charcoal burning suicides originated from Hong Kong have yet to influence on her neighboring motherland, Mainland China. Also, the urban region which has higher Internet penetration has only about one third of the suicide rate comparing to the rural region. If there is any contagious effect of charcoal burning suicide in the urban region, the impact is still limited on the overall suicide rate [62].

Discussion

Theoretical Explanations

Several social theories have been suggested to account for the media influences on suicidal behaviors [68, 69].But very few have been empirically tested. The most frequently cited theoretical explanation comes from the social cognitive theory, which offers an explanation for human learning through observing others' behavior [70]. According to the theory, an individual who models or adopts another person's values or behaviors through observational learning is reinforced to perform the learned behavior or discouraged from performing, based on the perceived consequences, reward or punishment respectively [71]. Moreover, a person's self-efficacy belief, referring to a judgment of self capabilities to execute certain action, is suggested by the theory as the major source of motivation of human behavior [71]. Social cognitive theory has been empirically examined to account for the media influences on people's suicidal ideation, and as a result it is supported to postulate a theoretical framework of observational learning, which consists of successive processes governing the media influences, including attentional, retention, production, and motivational processes [72]. Following the core concept of the social cognitive theory, online exposure to a specific suicide method and learning the details of how to execute that method may become motivators to drive one's belief in his or her self-efficacy to manage the suicidal plan, and therefore lead to an increase in suicidal risk.

Another theoretical explanation to account for such Internet effect on the choice of suicide method comes from the theory of media priming, which is the media effect of preceding stimulus or event on how people react to some subsequent actions [73]. People in Hong Kong, Taiwan and Japan are so used to the novel ways of dying by suicide through their exposure to mass media reporting on suicide cases. For instance, 47% of the suicide deaths in Hong Kong were found to have newspaper coverage in 2000 [74]. The extensive and sensational coverage of suicide deaths in Hong Kong and Taiwan media is much more easily and commonly found than that of some non-Asian countries [75]. Some readers, especially those vulnerable in suicidal risk, may conceive that suicide by a rare method is a "normal" or a "common" response to someone's personal problems. These vulnerable people who have thought about suicide may intend to seek more information and learn the technical descriptions of some suicide methods. More than that, being exposed to web postings that encourage people to consider suicide may motivate those vulnerable people to turn suicidal thought into action. So the Internet itself becomes a catalyst, and it provides this group of people an interactive, privacy-protected and self-initiated medium to acquire the information they need, as well as to de-normalize their thought of suicide by using a rare method.

What Can we Do to Prevent the Contagion via Internet?

Many different approaches to control and regulate online suicide contents have been discussed elsewhere [76]. Self-regulation is suggested as a way to reduce the potential harm of Internet suicide. This approach complies more with the principle of freedom of speech, but its efficacy is questionable. In the Web 2.0 era, the user-initiated web applications like Wikipedia, Blog or Facebook have been growing rapidly every minute. These media are virtually impossible to be regulated by the traditional models, such as self-regulation by the code of practice, licensing or even filtering techniques.

Lawful enforcement is proposed in some countries. Apart from the first legislation on Internet regulation in Australia [76], Taiwanese lawmakers have passed a bill to protect teenagers against the suggestive suicide through the Internet [77]. Nevertheless, legislation may be effective but care should be taken to avoid sacrificing the freedom of expression enjoyed by the whole Internet world.

In view of the global nature of the Internet, it seems logical that a global effort, say through the collaborations in the World Health Organization (WHO), is needed to contain the negative effect of Internet on suicidal behaviors. Educating and raising the awareness on the harmful effect of online suicide related information in the community should be promoted. A revised version of the WHO media recommendations has included a session on the effects of Internet [78].

Call for Research

The review in this chapter suggests an association between people's exposure to Internet contents and their choice of suicide method, but it is far less enough to have sufficient understanding on their relationship. This research area is still at the very beginning state of knowledge. In the future, more research should be done to advance our understanding in this area, by testing the assertions we make above, as well as broadening the scope of research across disciplines. To end the chapter, the following recommendations are made to address some of the current research void.

Understanding the Epidemiology of Internet Effect on Suicide

Little is known about the overall phenomenon of Internet usage with respect to the effects on viewers' suicidality. What we do know is that there are some reported suicide cases which are allegedly associated with the victims' Internet usage (as summarized in this chapter), and thus we postulate that currently a sizable number of Internet users would search through the web similarly for suicide related information. Nonetheless, before we move forward and develop our knowledge based on the preliminary evidence, we need to answer the following questions: How large is the base of these Internet users? Where are they? What are the frequency and the prevalence rate of such Internet usage? What are the search engine keywords the suicidal individuals would probably use? What kind of websites they would likely browse? Without the basic and fundamental epidemiological information, the development of the body of research on this subject will hardly be advanced.

Operationalizing the Exposure to Internet Effect

Media influence on suicidality has been operationalized in many different ways, but there is still lack of a systematic approach to define the said construct, as well as a psychometrically valid and reliable operationalization [72]. An operationalization of media influences on suicidal ideation has been shown to have acceptable factorial, convergent, and discriminant validity [72]. Similar effort to develop an operationalization of Internet effect on suicidality is essentially important.

Methodological Issues

Researching on Internet effect on human behavior has its inherent methodological difficulties. Self-report media usage may not be reliable, especially when socially undesirable web contents, like suicide, are involved. Internet traffic diary and logging are the valuable and reliable sources to record a web user's online traffics and the websites he or she has browsed. Analyzing the loggings of an Internet user should require his or her prior consent but blind experiment is often essential. As a result of privacy concern, this ethical requirement may lead to higher refusal rate, as a result a threat to the external validity of the study. Resolving these methodological issues is one of the primary concerns in this research area.

Evaluating the Interventions

Many ways to contain the contagious effects of Internet, like law enforcement, filtering, self-regulation, censorship etc, have been suggested. But effectiveness studies are essentially required to establish the evidence-based practices for these interventions. Yet, evaluation studies on these interventions are currently not available. In future, any novel and innovative suggestions for this purpose should be embedded with a build-in evaluation component to examine the measure's efficacy of reducing suicides.

ACKNOWLEDGEMENT

We are grateful to Ms. Fiona Yau for her proofread and editorial effort on this manuscript.

REFERENCES

[1] Hawton K, Williams K. Media influences on suicidal behaviour: evidence and prevention. In: Hawton K, ed. *Prevention and Treatment of Suicidal Behaviour: From Science to Practice*. Oxford: Oxford University Press, 2005:293-306.

[2] Pirkis JE, Blood RW. Suicide and the media. Part I: Reportage in nonfictional media. *Crisis* 2001;22:146-54.

[3] Schmidtke A, Schaller S. The role of mass media in suicide prevention. In: Hawton K, Heeringen K, eds. *The international handbook of suicide and attempted suicide*. New York: Wiley, 2000:675-97.

[4] Stack S. Suicide in the media: a quantitative review of studies based on non-fictional stories. *Suicide Life Threat Behav* 2005;35:121-33.

[5] Cheng AT, Hawton K, Lee CT, et al. The influence of media reporting of the suicide of a celebrity on suicide rates: a population-based study. *Int J Epidemiol* 2007.

[6] Fu KW, Yip PS. Estimating the risk for suicide following the suicide deaths of three Asian entertainment celebrities: A meta-analysis approach. *J Clin Psychiatry;*accepted for publication, forthcoming.

[7] Yip PSF, Fu KW, Yang KCT, et al. The effects of a celebrity suicide on suicide rates in Hong Kong. *J Affect Disord* 2006;93:245-52.

[8] Marzuk PM, Tardiff K, Hirsch CS, et al. Increase in suicide by asphyxiation in New York City after the publication of Final Exit. *N Engl J Med* 1993;329:1508-10.

[9] Gilson T, Parks BO, Porterfield CM. Suicide with inert gases: addendum to Final Exit. *Am J Forensic Med Pathol* 2003;24:306-8.

[10] Byard RW, Simpson E, Gilbert JD. Temporal trends over the past two decades in asphyxial deaths in South Australia involving plastic bags or wrapping. *J Clin Forensic Med* 2006;13:9-14.

[11] Tam J, Tang WS, Fernando DJS. The internet and suicide: A double-edged tool. *European Journal of Internal Medicine* 2007;18:453-5.

[12] Chan KP, Lee DT, Yip PS. Media influence on suicide. Media's role is double edged. *BMJ* 2003;326:498.

[13] Hsiung RC. A suicide in an Online mental health support group: Reactions of the group members, administrative responses, and recommendations. *Cyberpsychology & Behavior* 2007;10:495-500.

[14] Murray CD, Fox J. *Do Internet self-harm discussion groups alleviate or exacerbate self-harming behaviour?*, 2006. (http://www.auseinet.com/journal/vol5iss3/murray.pdf).

[15] Stoney G. Suicide prevention on the Internet. Suicide Prevention: *The global context* 1998:237-44.

[16] Suresh K, Lynch S. Psychiatry and the WWW: Some implications. *Psychiatric Bulletin* 1998;22:256.

[17] Neimark G, Hurford MO, DiGiacomo J. The Internet as collateral informant. *Am J Psychiatry* 2006;163:1842-.

[18] Senior C, Phillips ML, David AS. Psychiatry and the WWW: Some implications. *Psychiatric Bulletin* 1997;21:775-8.

[19] Janson MP, Alessandrini ES, Strunjas SS, et al. Internet-observed suicide attempts. *J Clin Psychiatry* 2001;62:478.

[20] Mandrusiak M, Rudd MD, Joiner TE, et al. Warning signs for suicide on the Internet: A descriptive study. *Suicide Life Threat Behav* 2006;36:263-71.

[21] Thompson S. The Internet and its potential influence on suicide. *Psychiatric Bulletin* 1999;23:449-51.

[22] Sher L. The Internet, suicide, and human mental functions. *Canadian Journal of Psychiatry-Revue Canadienne De Psychiatrie* 2000;45:297.

[23] Gray C. Death on the Internet. *Can Med Assoc J* 1995;153:193-5.

[24] Baume P, Cantor CH, Rolfe A. Cybersuicide: The Role of Interactive Suicide Notes on the Internet. Crisis: *The Journal of Crisis Intervention and Suicide Prevention* 1997;18:73-9.

[25] Alao AO, Soderberg M, Pohl EL, et al. Cybersuicide: Review of the Role of the Internet on Suicide. *CyberPsychology & Behavior* 2006;9:489-93.

[26] Rajagopal S. Suicide pacts and the internet. *BMJ* 2004;329:1298-9.

[27] Naito A. Internet suicide in Japan: Implications for child and adolescent mental health. *Clinical Child Psychology and Psychiatry* 2007;12:583-97.

[28] McCurry J. Police warn against suicide gas that can kill neighbours. *Guardian* 1st May, 2008.

[29] Biddle L, Donovan J, Hawton K, et al. Suicide and the internet. *BMJ* 2008;336:800-2.

[30] Recupero PR, Harms SE, Noble JM. Googling Suicide: Surfing for Suicide Information on the Internet. *J Clin Psychiatry* 2008:878-88.

[31] Becker K, Schmidt MH. Internet chat rooms and suicide. *J Am Acad Child Adolesc Psychiatry* 2004;43:246.

[32] Becker K, Mayer M, Nagenborg M, et al. Parasuicide online: Can suicide websites trigger suicidal behaviour in predisposed adolescents? *Nord J Psychiatry* 2004;58:111-4.

[33] Lee DTS, Chan KPM, Yip PSF. Charcoal burning is also popular for suicide pacts made on the internet. *BMJ* 2005;330:602-b-.

[34] Chan KP, Yip PS, Au J, et al. Charcoal-burning suicide in post-transition Hong Kong. *Br J Psychiatry* 2005;186:67-73.

[35] Liu KY, Beautrais A, Caine E, et al. Charcoal burning suicides in Hong Kong and urban Taiwan: an illustration of the impact of a novel suicide method on overall regional rates. *J Epidemiol Community Health* 2007;61:248-53.

[36] Fallows D. *How Women and Men Use the Internet.* Washington, D.C.: Pew Internet & American Life Project, 2005.

[37] Pietsch J, Schulz K, Schmidt U, et al. A comparative study of five fatal cases of Taxus poisoning. *Int J Legal Med* 2007;121:417-22.

[38] Jones LS, Wyatt JP, Busuttil A. Plastic Bag Asphyxia in Southeast Scotland. *The American Journal of Forensic Medicine and Pathology* 2000;21:401-5.

[39] Grassberger M, Krauskopf A. Suicidal asphyxiation with helium: Report of three cases. *Wien Klin Wochenschr* 2007;119:323-5.

[40] Byard RW, Simpson E, Gilbert JD. Temporal trends over the past two decades in South Australia in asphyxial deaths involving plastic bags or wrapping. *J Clin Forensic Med* 2006;13:9-14.

[41] Schön CA, Ketterer T. Asphyxial Suicide by Inhalation of Helium Inside a Plastic Bag. *The American Journal of Forensic Medicine and Pathology* 2007;28:364.

[42] Haut F. The internet and the future of psychiatry. *Psychiatric Bulletin* 1998;22:641-2.

[43] Nordt SP, Kelly K, Williams SR, et al. "Black plaque" on the Internet. *J Emerg Med* 1998;16:223-4.

[44] Alao AO, Yolles JC, Armenta W. Cybersuicide: The Internet and suicide. *Am J Psychiatry* 1999;156:1836-7.

[45] Athanaselis S, Stefanidou M, Karakoukis N, et al. Asphyxial Death by Ether Inhalation and Plastic-bag Suffocation Instructed by the Press and the Internet. *J Med Internet Res* 2002;4:e18.

[46] Wehner F, Gawatz O. [Suicidal yew poisoning--from Caesar to today--or suicide instructions on the internet]. *Arch Kriminol* 2003;211:19-26.

[47] Gallagher KE, Smith DM, Mellen PF. Suicidal asphyxiation by using pure helium gas: case report, review, and discussion of the influence of the internet. *The American journal of forensic medicine and pathology: official publication of the National Association of Medical Examiners* 2003;24:361-3.

[48] Prior TI. Suicide methods from the Internet. *Am J Psychiatry* 2004;161:1500-1.

[49] Prahlow JA, Doyle BW. A Suicide Using a Homemade Carbon Monoxide "Death Machine". *The American Journal of Forensic Medicine and Pathology* 2005;26:177.

[50] Vennemann B, Pollak S. Death by hanging while watching violent pornographic videos on the Internet - suicide or accidental autoerotic death? *Int J Legal Med* 2006;120:110-4.

[51] Forsthoff A, Hummel B, Moller HJ, et al. Suicidality and the Internet - Danger from new media. *Nervenarzt* 2006;77:343-5.

[52] Louie JP, Peterson J. Not a Basic Case. *Pediatr Emerg Care* 2006;22:461-3.

[53] Arachchillage DRJ, Hewapathirana N, Fernando DJS. The role of the internet in facilitating yellow oleander poisoning and in providing effective treatment. *European Journal of Internal Medicine* 2007;18:167.

[54] Wang EE, Mahajan N, Wills B, et al. Successful treatment of potentially fatal heavy metal poisonings. *J Emerg Med* 2007;32:289-94.

[55] Lee DT, Chan KP, Lee S, et al. Burning charcoal: a novel and contagious method of suicide in Asia. *Arch Gen Psychiatry* 2002;59:293-4.

[56] Center for Suicide Research and Prevention. Research findings into suicide and its prevention. *The Hong Kong Jockey Club Center for Suicide Research and Prevention,* the University of Hong Kong, 2005.

[57] Yip PSF, Lee DTS. Charcoal-burning suicides and strategies for prevention. Crisis-the *Journal of Crisis Intervention and Suicide Prevention* 2007;28:21-7.

[58] Lin JJ, Lu TH. Suicide mortality trends by sex, age and method in Taiwan, 1971-2005. *BMC public health* 2008;8:6.

[59] Pan YJ, Lee MB. Charcoal burning and maternal filicide-suicide trends in taiwan: the impact of accessibility of lethal methods. *J Formos Med Assoc* 2008;107:811-5.

[60] Naito A. Internet suicide in Japan: implications for child and adolescent mental health. *Clinical child psychology and psychiatry* 2007;12:583-97.

[61] Patel F. Carbon copy deaths: Carbon monoxide gas chamber. *Journal of Forensic and Legal Medicine* 2008;15:398-401.

[62] Yip PSF, Liu KY. The ecological fallacy and the gender ratio of suicide in China. *Br J Psychiatry* 2006;189:465-6.

[63] [Charcoal burning suicide killed 12 people this year]. Macau Daily November 23, 2000.

[64] [Female Chemistry researcher died by burning charcoal]. Taiwan Daily 19th June, 2000.

[65] *Suicide student got idea on Internet.* Birmingham Post July 12, 2001, Thursday, 2001:6.

[66] Man found dead in room filled with poisonous fumes. *New Straits Times* (Malaysia) April 24, 2004, Saturday, 2004:9.

[67] Martin N. Strangers die after suicide pact on internet. *The Daily Telegraph September* 30, 2005, 2005:1.

[68] Blood RW, Pirkis J. Suicide and the media. Part III: Theoretical issues. *Crisis* 2001;22:163-9.

[69] Phillips DP. Suicide, Motor-Vehicle Fatalities, and the Mass-Media - Evidence toward a Theory of Suggestion. *Am J Sociol* 1979;84:1150-74.

[70] Bandura A. Social cognitive theory of mass communication. *Media Psychol* 2001;3:265-99.

[71] Bandura A. Social foundations of thought and action: a social cognitive theory. Englewood Cliffs, N.J: Prentice-Hall, 1986.

[72] Fu KW, Chan YY, Yip PSF. Testing a Theoretical Model based on Social Cognitive Theory for Media Influence on Suicidal Ideation: Results from a Panel Study. *Media Psychol*, 2009;12:26-49.

[73] Roskos-Ewoldsen DR, Roskos-Ewoldsen B, Carpentier FRD. Media Priming: A Synthesis. In: Jennings Bryant, Zillmann D, eds. *Media effects: advances in theory and research*. London: Lawrence Elbaum Associates, 2002:97-120.

[74] Au JS, Yip PS, Chan CL, et al. Newspaper reporting of suicide cases in Hong Kong. *Crisis* 2004;25:161-8.

[75] Fu KW, Yip PS. Changes in Reporting of Suicide News After the Promotion of the WHO Media Recommendations. *Suicide Life Threat Beha*v 2008;38:631-6.

[76] Mishara BL, Weisstub DN. Ethical, legal, and practical issues in the control and regulation of suicide promotion and assistance over the Internet. *Suicide Life Threat Behav* 2007;37:58-65.

[77] Ko YT. [300,000 penalty for encouraging suicide online]. *China Times* 23 April, 2008:A11.

[78] World Health Organization. Preventing Suicide: A Resource for Media Professionals. Department of Mental Health, *Social Change and Mental Health,* WHO, 2008.

In: Internet and Suicide
Editors: L. Sher and A. Vilens

ISBN 978-1-60741-077-5

Chapter 11

"I AM SO SICK OF THIS LIFE": A SEMIOTIC ANALYSIS OF SUICIDAL MESSAGES ON THE INTERNET

Itzhak Gilat[1,2] and Yishai Tobin[1]
[1]Ben-Gurion University of the Negev, Beer Sheva, Israel; [2]The Israeli Association for Emotional First Aid, Israel

ABSTRACT

The present study exploited the fully documented writings of suicidal individuals who sought help from an online emotional first aid service in order to better understand the suicidal mind. Three messages posted to an online support group and three personal chats conducted between suicidal individuals and trained volunteers were analyzed using methods derived from a semiotic approach to linguistic analysis [1, 2].The methods are based on the premise that there is a causal connection between the non-random distribution of the language in a spoken and written discourse/text and the extra-linguistic message of that discourse/text. Consistent with previous reports, our findings revealed that suicidal individuals who sought help experienced a conflict between an attraction to death and a perceived connection to life. The semiotic analysis made a unique contribution by illuminating the attitudes of the suicidal individuals towards life, and also showed that these individuals perceive life as an obligation that they are forced to fulfill against their will. This view of life produces severe emotional distress characterized by a complete loss of energy. These findings are interpreted in light of the existential view that depicts life as absurd, but also suggests solutions that enable individuals to lead happy lives. The applicability of these solutions to online interactions with suicidal individuals may be examined in a future study.

Introduction

The following message was sent to an online support group (forum) moderated by paraprofessional volunteers:

A man in this world
Is full of doubts and thoughts
What is my role? – I do not know
Why am I here?
Life is full of pitfalls
Difficulties, trials and failures
Why, then, was man created???
Man, man you should understand
To be part of this world you must be involved
You must relentlessly labor and struggle
Even when you have no strength left
In this world you will find no rest
In this world you will find no happiness or peace
In this world everything is so black
Perhaps a bit of gray
And even though sometimes it seems
Those things are getting rosier
Remember – this is only momentary
It will pass; surely it will not stay forever
This I know from my personal experience…
So enjoy this moment, for in the next one
You will feel bad
Why God – why?
Why aren't you willing to take me now?!
This is my last request
I will not ask for anything more…
Please, God, I have no more strength
Please do it fast!
I am tired of fighting my impulses,
Tired of the emotions, the pain that takes me over
I am tired of feeling depressed
I am tired of being obsessed
I am tired of the downs, the hardships
Even though I sometimes feel good
I am simply tired of it all, I've had enough
None of your honey none of your sting
I don't need what's good
Evil has taken me over
I do not desire joy
For I am overwhelmed by woe

The moderator who received this message was faced with a dilemma regarding the appropriate response strategy: should emergency measures involving police intervention be taken, or would a supportive response suffice to change the caller's suicidal attitude? To assess the degree of risk, the volunteer cannot rely on non-verbal cues such as facial expressions or paralinguistic cues such as prosody [and especially intonation] which are valuable sources of information in face-to-face interactions with suicidal individuals. There is no alternative but to rely on the language used by the suicidal individual, which reflects the thoughts and emotions and may help the volunteer understand the suicidal mind and assess the risk. Linguistic analysis of texts produced by individuals in suicidal crisis is useful in disclosing some of the mysteries of the suicidal mind. This chapter presents and illustrates an application of the semiotic approach to the linguistic analysis of online texts produced by suicidal individuals.

The semiotic approach is based on the premise that the primary unit of linguistic analysis is not limited to the word or the sentence but the linguistic sign. A sign is part of an abstract code containing a signal that is used to signify an invariant meaning that can be interpreted as conveying different messages in different linguistic and situational contexts. The methods of semiotic-linguistic analysis are based on the premise that there is a causal connection between the non-random distribution of the language in a spoken and written discourse/text and the extra-linguistic message of that discourse/text.

The semiotic-linguistic methods were applied to texts produced by individuals in suicidal crisis who opted for the online environment as an appropriate medium for receiving help. The help was offered by ERAN, an Israeli volunteer-based service for emotional first aid that offers online help through personal chats and an online support group. We exploited the naturally-occurring, fully documented texts in order to uncover some of the mysteries of the suicidal mind.

THEORETICAL BACKGROUND

The Quest for Understanding Suicide

Suicidal behavior, which is deemed one of the most mysterious human phenomena, has attracted a great deal of attention among diverse disciplines that attempt to uncover its hidden processes and suggest ways to cope with its devastating consequences. Professionals generally agree that suicide is a multidimensional phenomenon involving biological, psychological, sociological, cultural and existential factors. Psychologists' efforts to better understand this intra-psychic drama on an interpersonal stage" [3] are guided by both theoretical and practical motives. Theoretically, the effort is directed at understanding the reasons that drive individuals to kill themselves in spite of the powerful survival instinct. Practically, the effort is focused on developing strategies that may prevent suicidal individuals from carrying out this irreversible act.

The quest for understanding suicide by means of empirical investigation suffers from an inherent limitation due to the lack of accessibility to direct evidence. The methods employed by behavioral scientists to investigate suicidal behavior can be divided into two categories: (a) statistical data on rates of suicide among different socio-cultural populations and on the psychological correlates of suicide [4] (b) qualitative data on suicidal behavior based on interviews with relatives of suicide completers, narratives of suicide survivors, and texts produced by individuals in suicidal crisis. Personal documents written by suicidal individuals can constitute a uniquely valuable source of information for shedding light on the suicidal mind. The use of writing in the study of the psychological states of individuals is based on the premise that various aspects of people's personalities and emotional states are reflected in their writing, which is more revealing than speaking [5]. This claim was supported by empirical evidence showing that writing may reflect psychological disorders [6] and can be used for psychological treatment, also in an online environment [7].

With regard to the use of documents in the study of suicide, Shneidman, one of the major contributors to the study of suicide, has stated in his book, *The Voice of Death* [8], that such documents contain unique revelations of the human mind and that a great deal can be learned from them. Notes written by suicidal individuals were used as a research instrument in other studies, thereby promoting the understanding of the factors associated with suicidal behavior [6, 3].

Suicide and the Internet

The Internet has made a unique contribution to the investigation of suicide through written documents Its use as a valuable source for studying suicide can be explained by the massive "presence" of the topic on the web, as evidenced by the tremendous number of links to this topic. For instance, a search on Google (21.8.2008) produced 89,300,000 links to the keyword "suicide". The nature of the association between the Internet and suicide has been described as twofold. On the one hand, the Internet may trigger suicidal behavior by offering special websites that legitimate suicide and even encourage individuals to opt for it as a solution to their problems [9, 10, 11]. On the other hand, the Internet plays an important role in suicide prevention by offering emotional support to individuals in suicidal crisis through the various online channels, namely e-mails [12], personal chats [13] and support groups [14]. Empirical evidence reveals that the attractiveness of the Internet as a source of help for suicidal individuals is significantly higher than that of telephone hotlines, which shares some common characteristics with the Internet [15, 16]. The appeal of the Internet for individuals in suicidal crisis can be attributed to the characteristics of the online environment that exert specific effects on the nature of emotional expression.

Some psychological considerations may lead us to conclude that the medium of the Internet would be poor in its capacity for emotional expression in interpersonal communication. Emotional bonds originate and form in unmediated face-to- face interpersonal situations. Children learn to interpret emotional messages and express their emotions through spoken language. Although some people deliver emotional messages such as declarations of love by means of written language, the vast majority of emotional communication is spoken. In addition, the lack of non-verbal cues limits the richness and subtlety of emotional expression and may reduce the potential to project_rapport and warmth. Consequently, many Internet interactions may be misconstrued as cold, distant and antagonistic.

Interestingly enough, a growing body of knowledge reveals that interpersonal communication on the Internet abounds with emotional expression, and that intimate relationships develop easily. The most widely reported finding from research studies on the interpersonal aspect of communication in the online environment is the disinhibition that occurs. John Suler, a prominent researcher of behavior in cyberspace, states that "every day users on the Internet – as well as clinicians and researchers – have noted how people say and do things on the Internet that they wouldn't ordinarily do in the face to face world. They loosen up, feel less restrained, and express themselves more openly. So pervasive is the phenomenon that a term has surfaced for it: the *disinhibition effect*" [17, p. 321]. This elimination of the barriers to emotional expression is explained by the features of the online environment– particularly invisibility and anonymity. The lack of visual clues informing the other party of the sender's status and position enhance the opportunity to feel at ease with others. Anonymity diminishes the psychological threat that prevents many people from expressing their emotions in face-to-face situations. The use of writing may also help many individuals express their thoughts and emotions freely. Writing is known to be a channel whereby numerous people express their inner feelings and thoughts in a way that is more revealing than talking [5].

The disinhibition effect may explain the phenomenon of many individuals in suicidal crisis using the Internet as a channel to seek help through personal chats, support groups or e-mails. An analysis of the language they use in their messages and in the interactions with their responders may increase the understanding of both the internal processes of suicidal individuals and the interpersonal interactions between them and their environment. So far, few studies have applied a linguistic analysis to the naturally-occurring online interactions of suicidal individuals, which are fully documented as written texts. One study [18] investigated an interaction in an online support group moderated by paraprofessionals, following a suicidal message sent by an adolescent boy. They demonstrated how the moderators and the other participants, dubbed a "virtual rescue team" by the authors, succeeded in shifting the boy's perspective on life from a meaningless entity that he wanted to end to fruitful possibilities for a meaningful life. Another study [19] compared the writing characteristics of suicidal individuals to those of emotionally distressed, non-suicidal persons seeking help in online support groups. It was found that a significantly greater number of expressions of self-focus, unbearable mental pain and cognitive constriction in the writings of the suicidal group. The present study focused on the unique expressions in the writings of suicidal individuals but did not examine the holistic nature of the messages they sent in their cry for help.

The Current Study

When we study suicidal behavior or any other aspect of human behavior through written interactions retrieved from the Internet, we cannot avail ourselves of non-verbal cues such as facial expressions or prosody which are valuable sources of information in studying face-to-face interactions. Therefore, we focus on the written language as an exclusive source of data and apply text analysis methods in order to draw conclusions about the investigated phenomena. Two methodological advantages can be noted with regard to the Internet as a means of investigating suicidal behavior: (1) the writings of the suicidal individuals and their interactions with other users are fully documented and easily accessible; (2) texts that appear on the Internet are highly valid sources since they reflect natural occurrences of behavior without any interference on the part of researchers.

In the present study, we set out to examine the messages sent by individuals in suicidal crisis by applying methods of semiotic-linguistic analysis to written texts retrieved from the Internet. The interactions took place in the context of an Israeli mental health service called "ERAN" (the Hebrew acronym for "Emotional First Aid"). The service offers emotional first aid to a broad spectrum of psychological distress and is guided by the following professional and ethical guidelines: (a) The encounter between the two parties is technologically mediated – help is provided via telephone calls or online interactions; (b) Callers have the option of remaining anonymous in order to bolster their trust and enhance self-disclosure ; (c) Support is offered by trained volunteers who are not professionals in the field of mental health but receive special training for their task; (d) The volunteers remain anonymous to the callers in order to facilitate a process of projection whereby the callers shape the character of their responder in accordance with their psychological needs; (e) The availability of help is high owing to the use of the telephone or the Internet as channels of communication.

The present study focused on the messages of suicidal individuals who sought help through two online channels offered by ERAN: personal chats and support groups. Personal chats are synchronous (real-time) conversations between two participants who exchange written texts on the Internet using one of the available types of software such as ICQ. In the case of the online support groups, the Internet users post messages on a publicly accessible Internet page that can be read and responded to by anyone who enters the site. Communication in the support groups is asynchronous – messages can be sent 24 hours a day, but the responses are delayed and not always guaranteed. We selected interactions from personal chats and support groups in order to examine whether the linguistic analysis of the suicidal messages might be generalized into two different types of Internet situations representing different types of online language. The language of the chat is speech-like – it is characterized by spontaneity, brief messages and high-paced communication, whereas the language of the asynchronous group is similar to traditional writing – it can be well planned, messages may be long, and the pace of communication is slow.

Data and Analysis

The data comprised three messages retrieved from the online support groups and three transcripts of personal chats. Common to all six texts was the suicidal crisis that was clearly manifested by the individuals who sought help from ERAN. The support group messages were responded to by both volunteers and lay participants, and the personal chats were responded to by the volunteers. In the present study, we focused on the messages of the suicidal individuals.

The linguistic methods that we employed to analyze the suicidal messages are based on a semiotic approach to language [1, 2]. This approach is based on the premise that the primary unit of linguistic analysis is not the sentence or the word, but the linguistic sign. A sign is part of an abstract code containing a signal that is used to signify an invariant meaning that can be interpreted as conveying different messages in different linguistic and situational contexts, for example: "I read a BOOK in the library" vs. "BOOK me a table in the restaurant" vs. "He is a serious student – a veritable BOOK-worm" …

Signs may be manifested by a variety of linguistic units such as morphemes, parts of words, words, word order, prosodic units, zero, pauses, sentences, larger units of discourse and even an entire text [1]. The meaning of the sign is invariant, but it is used to express various messages in concrete contexts of communication. Thus, the semiotic view of language is a dichotomy between two systems: (a) an abstract system of linguistic signs with invariant meanings, and (b) a concrete system of contextual communication of specific messages. The goal of linguistic analysis is to bridge the gap between the two systems and reveal how the invariant meanings of the linguistic signs are exploited by individuals to communicate specific messages.

The methods for text analysis developed by the semiotic approach are based on the premise that there is a causal connection between the non-random distribution of the language in a spoken and written discourse/text and the extra-linguistic message of that discourse/text. The goal of this textual analysis is to uncover this non-random distribution of the language of the text and indicate its direct and indirect contribution to the extra-linguistic message of the discourse/text.

In the present study, two sign-oriented or semiotic methods were utilized to analyze the online texts produced by the suicidal individuals: "*from sign to text*" and "*word systems*". The "from sign to text" approach points out the connection between the non-random distribution of linguistic signs and the various themes or leitmotifs that occur in the text. In other words, it allows us to observe a favoring of one sign over another in a system that can be directly linked to the themes of a text [2]. We were keen to uncover the messages sent by suicidal individuals seeking help by looking for the non-random distribution of linguistic signs in their texts. The "word systems" and "strategies of communication" methods [20, 21] are ways of showing the coherence of a text by identifying recurrent words, verbal patterns or strategies with a common linguistic denominator that may be semantic, phonological, conceptual or associative. The recurrent use of these words or strategies in a text may be viewed as a mechanism that creates textual compactness and captures the essence of the text. The systems can be regarded as a nucleus of a text, which nurtures the theme and message of the text with a greater intensity than the sum total of the language employed throughout the discourse [22]

Results

Individuals in suicidal crisis are preoccupied with thoughts of life and death. Therefore, it is reasonable to expect that these themes will be prevalent in their discourse and written texts. Applying a semiotic approach to explore the messages sent by the suicidal individuals seeking help from ERAN, we examined the linguistic context in which direct and indirect expressions of life and death appeared in the written interactions. Based on the premise that the non-random distribution of the language in a text is causally connected to the extra-linguistic message, we determined whether these contexts shared common characteristics. The results are presented separately for the online support group and the personal chats.

Semiotic Analysis of Messages in an Online Support Group

The three messages below are presented as they were displayed on the page of the online support group. The title preceding each message was written by the individual who sent the message.

Message 1. I am sick of life

I am so sick of this life
I am so down
I simply do not understand the meaning of my existence
Just what am I doing in this world???
I feel I do not belong and I feel so
Down
I am just tired of being disappointed of suffering of crying of hurting
people and of being hurt by people
And I am just tired of doing things the things we
do every day I am just tired of doing
them...I am tired of getting up in the morning I am tired of brushing
teeth, eating, talking, breathing...simply everything
I simply do not understand the meaning of my existence
I do not understand anyone
and no one understands me
I live and breathe not because I want to but because I do not have a choice
Although I do not understand anyone and do not understand anything
about my life
There are still people who love me and I love
them...So I live for them...But what will happen
when they are not here anymore?! What will become of me?

An examination of the message reveals two distinct parts: In the first part (lines 1-15), the writer focuses on her emotional state, describing herself as alienated from other people and from the meaning of life, and portraying her life as unbearably painful. A word system related to "being sick of..." can be identified in this part of the text. The writer repeats seven times in 16 lines that she is tired of life itself and of various regular activities people do in their life. She also repeats four times in this short text the word "understand" in a context of negation, stating that she does not understand the meaning of her existence, does not understand other people, and feels that she is not understood. The message delivered in this part expresses a desire to terminate a meaningless existence. In the second part (lines 16-21), the writer shifts the focus of the message from expressing a negative attitude toward her existence to explaining why she goes on living. She explains that it is her sense of duty toward other people who love her that keeps her alive rather than her own will.

The two parts differ with regard not only to their content but also to their linguistic characteristics. The first part consists almost exclusively of words that express emotions, all of them negative in character, while the second part is constructed mainly of cognitive statements such as attributions and explanations. Moreover, the emotion mentioned in this part is love. In addition, the first part is composed of decisive and absolute statements whereas the second part ends with a question. Finally, the first part, which may be viewed as "death-focused", is twice as long as the second, "life-focused", part.

Message 2. I cannot bear my life

1 *I cannot suffer anymore*
2 *I do not love myself and the way I live or do not live*
3 *I have no direction I have no future I have no purposes or wishes*
4 *I have nowhere to go or to progress, for over and over again I fall down further*
6 *from the place where I fell last time*
7 *The falls hurt more and more so why and for what should I get up??*
8 *The meaning of life is the meaning that we give it so that we can bear it*
9 *So this meaning is practically our invention!!!*
10 *It is all invented so what is life???*

In the first part of this message (lines 1-7), the writer expresses repulsion for herself and her life. Viewing her present life as meaningless and anticipating a deterioration in her situation, she concludes this part with a rhetorical question about the reason to go on living. This view is consistent with the statement she made at the beginning of the message, namely, that life is unbearable. Thus a wish to die is conveyed although not explicitly expressed. In the second part of the message (lines 8-10), she shifts the focus from herself to a philosophical idea about life and offers an existential view of people's ability to shape the meaning of life. This idea may be viewed as her (possibly unconscious) explanation of the fact that she goes on living in spite of her unbearable pain and feeling of emptiness.

Linguistic differences between the two parts can be identified by several characteristics. First, the writing of the first part is self-focused – the writer refers to herself in almost all the statements she makes, whereas in the second part, she shifts the focus to life as a general entity. Second, a word system related to negation can be identified in the first part – the title and each one of the first four lines open with a negation, whereas no such expressions are found in the second part. Third, expressions of emotion are common in the first part, while the second part focuses on the abstract words "meaning" and "life". Fourth, the writer presents decisive statements about her acute emotional state in the first part but ends the message with a question about the meaning of life. Finally, the first part is much longer than the second.

Message 3. Noooooo, I feel it is coming up…

1 *The depression, the wish to die, the endless self-hatred, the thought that nothing goes...*
2 *I do not achieve anything that I want*
3 *I am tired of everything.*
4 *I have no strength to live. I have no will at all.*
5 *I will not commit suicide because I think about my family and friends, but nothing matters.*
6 *I am tired of everything...*
7 *Even to write I had to use all my inner strength.*
8 *What am I supposed to do? The obvious solution is to die but it is impossible, so what to do?????????*

This message is also constructed in two parts. In the first part (lines 1-4), the writer describes an acute emotional state of suffering and pain and directly expresses his wish to die. A dominant feature of his mental pain is a lack of energy and of the will to fight, as reflected in the expression, "I am tired of everything", which appears twice in this short message. In the second part (lines 5-8), he explains that his thoughts about his family and friends prevent him from fulfilling his death wish, although "nothing matters". Hence, the connection with the significant figures in his life is perceived not as a source of strength but rather as an obligation.

A linguistic analysis of this message reveals that words retrieved from the semantic field of negative emotions such as depression, self-hatred and apathy are much more prevalent in the first part. Moreover, in the second part, the writer mentions his inner strength thereby revealing that he is not totally in the clutches of depression. In addition, the expressions of negation that occur frequently in the first part are almost totally absent in the second. Finally, the writer of this message also uses very decisive statements in the first, "death-focused", part, whereas the second, "life-focused", part ends with a dilemma.

An analysis of the three messages shows that each of them consisted of two parts that differed with respect to both content and linguistic criteria. An examination of the messages from the content perspective reveals that one part focused on the personal meaning of death for the writer, and included direct and indirect expressions of a death wish as well as a detailed list of reasons for this wish. The writers describe their emotional distress as insurmountable and view their lives as meaningless and worthless. The other part focused on the personal meaning of life and included an explanation of why they kept on living. Moreover, a hint of an optimistic outlook, albeit indirect or disguised, can be detected in each of the messages.

From a linguistic perspective, the three messages share several common characteristics: (a) The "death-focused" part appears first in the message and is noticeably longer than the "life-focused" part; (b) The first part abounds with words and expressions that belong to the emotional domain. More specifically, these words can be associated with the semantic field of mental pain, a well-known concept in the domain of suicidal behavior, defined as " a wide range of subjective experiences characterized as an awareness of negative changes in the self and in its functions accompanied by negative feelings" [23]. A dominant component of the mental pain expressed in the three messages is the feeling of being tired of life. In the second part of the three messages, emotional expressions are scarce and the writers employ a more cognitive-oriented language that includes presenting ideas, making attributions and raising dilemmas; (c) The first part is almost totally self-focused, while in the second part, the writers refer to other persons (such as family) or entities (such as the meaning of life) as well; (d) The two parts of the messages exhibit different types of thinking: the ideas in the "death-focused" part are expressed as absolute statements without a trace of doubt, while the "life-focused" part reveals the doubts and dilemmas that exist in the writers' minds, as reflected in the question that closes each of the messages.

Semiotic Analysis of Messages in Personal Chats

For each of the three cases, we shall present a succinct description of the suicidal individual who sought help in ERAN's chat, followed by the semiotic-linguistic analysis. The titles of the chats were coined by the authors.

Chat 1: "I Want to Die but I Need to Be here for her"

The caller (D.) is a 20-year-old man who lives with his parents whom he describes as hostile and sometimes even violent toward him. He suffers from depression and from social anxiety, "does not function at all", cries a lot, is socially isolated and scarcely leaves his home. He has undergone psychological treatment, but now he only takes medication. The only ray of light in his dark world is an "amazing dog" [called Nanny] that lives with him and that he describes as his reason for staying alive.

At the beginning of the chat, D. raises the issues of death and life several times. While his attitude toward death is expressed directly, his thoughts about life are sometimes direct and can occasionally be inferred from his talk about the dog. The dog can be considered as a representation of life in his discourse.

The semiotic analysis reveals two linguistic patterns that appear throughout the text. First, words that signify "death" co-occur with words from the semantic field of "will", while words that signify "life" (or representations of life) co-occur with words from the semantic field of "obligation". Second, a word system related to a loss of energy can be identified in the text. These two patterns are presented below.

The co-occurrence of "death" with words from the semantic field of "will" is illustrated below.

"I have run out of strength and everything is bad... tears, memories all the time, I want to die all the time."

"There was violence at home, from my brother, my parents...for a very long time...since I was a little boy...I also have memories of a rape. Most of my memories are of violence, hatred and rape. But it doesn't matter...I simply feel like dying now."

"I am not actually doing anything [...] I don't brush my teeth, rarely wash myself...[...] tears in my room all day ...on the floor with no strength and say to myself that I feel like dying."

"I wish I could die, that everything would end."

An analysis of the text reveals that writing about the boy's life or about his dog (the representation of life) co-occurs with words from the semantic field of "obligation". This is illustrated in the following examples.

In his introductory sentences the boy writes: *"I have a dog I take care of and I need to be here for her."*

In response to the expressed death wish, the volunteers asked: "What will happen after you die?" The boy immediately replied: *"I don't care what will be/happen then, but it is impossible because of Nanny."*

D. explains at length the social anxiety that prevents him from going out *Nowadays I don't leave home at all except to take Nanny for a walk, which I have to do."*

"I hate the fact that I have to stay alive [...] because I need to be with her."

Twice in the conversation the boy reveals his attitude toward death and life in the same sentence: "*...tears, memories all the time I want to die, but I stay because I owe her."*

"I tell myself that I feel like dying but remind myself I am not allowed to feel this urge."

A word system related to the semantic field of "loss of strength" can be identified in the first part of the chat, when D. constructs his view of himself and his life.

In his opening sentence, he introduces himself by writing: *"Everything is bad, don't have any strength to do anything and there is no outlet anywhere."* In his reply to the volunteer's request to talk about himself, he writes: *"I don't do anything at all and I don't have the strength to do anything."*

After introducing his dog to the volunteer, D. uses "lack of strength" in the context of talking about the beloved dog, as illustrated in the following passage:

Volunteer: "Do you go outside – at least with the dog?"

D.: *"I don't have the strength to do anything" and everything is bad [....] I stay because I owe it to her."*

Volunteer: "It seems to me that you really love her."

D.: *"I can stay and cope with it but it takes all my strength."*

The two linguistic patterns described above suggest that the extra-linguistic message expressed by D. is "I want to die, but I am forced to live and as a result I have run out of strengths."

Chat 2: "This Struggle is too Hard for me"

The caller (R.) is a nursing student who feels extremely distressed because she has to submit a paper the next day and is unable to concentrate and complete the assignment. She tells the volunteer that the pressure she is experiencing triggers an urge to injure herself and that she recognizes this urge from similar situations in her history as a student.

The linguistic analysis reveals that the desire to inflict self-injury appears in a positive context:

"I would very much like to injure myself"

"It is not so critical to injure myself first and then relax"

"I cut myself [...] until the pain is too acute and then I relax."

In her text, the urge to injure herself is associated with a struggle, as illustrated in the following examples:

In her opening sentences, the student responds to the volunteer's comments that it is normal to feel pressure prior to submitting a paper as follows: *"...my problem is that I always feel a struggle not to injure myself! The two things always go together."*

In response to the volunteer's attempt to persuade her that the paper need not be perfect, the student adheres to the struggle by writing that *"sometimes I don't really have any control over the urge."*

The volunteer tries another strategy and reinforces the student's decision to seek help, calling it an indication of inner strength. The student protests and writes: *"I am very negative now! [...] This struggle is too hard for me."*

Chat 3: "The Obsession Fills my Life"

The caller is a 21-year-old man who suffers from depression and severe mental pain accompanied by suicidal ideations. He has undergone psychological treatment for a long time but feels that neither the treatment nor the medications has helped him so far. His reason for seeking help in the chat is the escalation of his pain, which caused him to consider stopping the medication and "letting the depression win". The only thing that keeps him alive is an attraction to a singer he saw on the Internet. He considers the singer to be perfect and describes his attitude toward her as an obsession: *"You see, I have this problem –I'm living in an extreme obsession for someone. She's a singer and I can't stop thinking about her and collecting information about her from the Internet"*.

An examination of the text reveals that the caller repeats the word "obsession" many times throughout the chat. In most cases, the obsession is presented in the context of explaining his attitude toward his life and the role played by the obsession in this attitude, as illustrated in the following examples:

In response to the volunteer's supportive comment that she understands his distress, the caller writes: *"You see, if you had suggested a way to stop this obsession, I would not have accepted it in spite of all the pain because this is the only thing that's worth something in my life [...] It is the only thing that gives me a reason to live [...] I am ready to pay any price for this obsession. In spite of all her negative things, she constitutes a significant part of my life, she fills me in a certain way and thanks to her I somehow feel alive."*

In response to the volunteer's wish that some magic potion would cure the obsession, the caller writes: *"The question is if this is the way I will always live. Do I need it? I don't have any other reason to live and what happens if my psychologist cures the obsession and I'm left with nothing?"*

CONCLUSION

Applying semiotic-linguistic analysis to suicidal messages retrieved from online support groups and interactions in personal chats revealed the attitude of individuals in suicidal crisis toward their death, the way they perceive their lives, and the process whereby their attitudes toward these two entities are integrated into an intra-personal dialogue that affects their psychological well-being.

Two characteristics of the attitude toward death emerge from the linguistic analysis of the texts. First, death constitutes a major component in the cognitive world of individuals in suicidal crisis, as can be inferred from the frequent use of linguistic signs that signify death in their texts. Second, thoughts about death occur in an emotional context of suffering and pain. The suicidal individuals express an explicit wish to end their lives and view death as a solution to the unbearable emotional pain. These two characteristics are consistent with the two aspects of the suicidal mind that are mentioned in the literature as being shared by all individuals in suicidal crisis, regardless of the specific personal and environmental context of the suicide: cognitive constriction and mental pain [3].

In the texts of the suicidal individuals, their approach to life differs from their approach to death with respect to both form and content. Unlike the thoughts about death, which occupy center stage in their discourse, ideas about life receive less attention. In some cases, life is not directly mentioned but can be inferred from other figures in the individuals' environment–figures that represent this part of their self-view (for instance, a beloved dog). Furthermore, the suicidal individuals' thoughts about their lives appear almost exclusively in a cognitive context, which may indicate that they are not emotionally connected to the aspects that constitute life. As for the meaning of life, the analysis revealed that suicidal individuals view their lives as forced upon them by external factors such as significant figures in their surroundings. Their experience of living lacks a sense of meaning, a desire, internal motivation or a feeling of joy. Life is perceived as a burden to be borne or an obligation to be fulfilled against their will. This view of life has direct implications for their psychological well-being, as reflected in the frequent use of words that imply a loss of energy. This sense of emotional and physical collapse can be explained by the fact that they expend their energies on fighting their wish to die rather than on productive activities that are rewarding and generate motivation.

An internal dialogue between life and death in the mental world of individuals in suicidal crisis has long been reported as a major characteristic of the suicidal mind. Based on the analysis of suicidal notes, Leenaars concluded that "there are complications, concomitant contradictory feelings, attitudes and thrusts toward a person and even toward life. Not only is it love and hate but it may be also a conflict between survival and unbearable pain" [3]. Another conceptualization of this conflict has been suggested by [23] who claim that suicidal behavior evolves around a conflict among four sets of attitudes: (a) attraction to life arising from the fulfillment of needs; (b) repulsion by life arising from pain and suffering; (c) attraction to death arising from the notion that some aspects of death might be preferable to life; and (d) repulsion by death arising from the fear of permanent cessation. Empirical evidence based on a scale for measuring this multi-attitude suicidal tendency revealed that suicide attempters received higher scores on repulsion by life and lower scores on attraction to life than suicide ideators, while no difference was found between the two groups with regard to attitudes toward death.

The conflict between life and death is also manifested in another area of suicide crisis: the assessment of suicide risk. A multifaceted model for the assessment of suicide risk among callers to the National Suicide Prevention Lifeline was suggested by [24]. This model is based on the premise that the level of risk depends on the interplay between the attraction to death and the connection to life. Three components of the model act as risk factors that motivate the person to commit suicide. These are (a) suicidal desire expressed by psychological pain, hopelessness, perceived burden to others, feeling trapped and feeling intolerably alone; (b) suicidal capability characterized by a sense of fearlessness and a sense of competence to make the attempt; and (c) suicidal intent characterized by a plan to hurt self and preparatory behavior. The fourth facet is a connection to life, which acts as a buffer against suicidality and includes aspects such as perceived support, ambivalence for core values (family or religious duties), a sense of purpose and planning the future. The authors claim that if the three components of risk are present, the risk is high, regardless of the presence of the fourth facet; however, if the suicidal desire is paired with either capability or intent, the connection to life may act as a buffer and decrease the risk.

We see that connection to life is deemed a major factor in the decision-making process of individuals in suicidal crisis. Our findings shed light on the nature of this facet by showing that suicidal individuals view this connection as a burden that they have to bear against their will. This personal view of the suicidal individuals can be associated with the philosophical view of life as absurd, as suggested by the existential approach. In his famous essay, "The Myth of Sisyphus", Albert Camus claimed that the philosophical absurdity results from the futile quest for meaning, unity and clarity in the face of an unintelligible world. Camus compared the absurdity of man's life with the situation of the mythological Sisyphus, who was condemned to accomplish a meaningless task of pushing a heavy rock up a mountain only to see it roll down again. However, unlike the participants in our study who expressed a wish to cope with the absurdity of life by committing suicide, Camus suggested an alternative solution that enables Sisyphus to be happy: the very struggle against the absurdity of life is enough to infuse life with meaning and fill a person's life.

Can the solution proposed by the existentialists be appropriate for suicidal individuals who feel that they are condemned to a meaningless life that generates unbearable pain? An analysis of their texts can lead to a positive answer: they present aspects of their life that can yield meaningful experiences and fulfill healthy needs of interpersonal relationships and self-actualization. They perceive these aspects, such as relationships with significant figures or completing professional training, as burdens that they are doomed to bear. If they could alter their perspectives and view these aspects as internal motivations rather than external forces, they might succeed in adopting a more optimistic attitude toward their own lives. Such a change may be achieved through interactions with skilled helpers.

The present study focused on the attitudes of the suicidal individuals toward their lives. Future research should examine whether such a change occurs following the interactions between the suicidal individuals and their responders.

REFERENCES

[1] Tobin Y: *Semiotics and Linguistics.* London/New York: Longman, 1991.

[2] Tobin, Y: Invariance, Markedness and Distinctive Feature Analysis: A Contrastive Study of Sign Systems in English and Hebrew. Amsterdam/Philadelpia: John Benjamins, 1994.

[3] Leenaars A: Suicide: A multidimensional malaise. *Suicide Life Threat Behav*1996; 26 221-236.

[4] Gould MS, Greenberg T, Velting DM, Shaffer D: Youth suicide risk and preventive interventions: A review of the past ten years. *J Am Acad Child* 2003; 42: 386-405.

[5] Pennebaker JW, Mehl MR, Niederhoffer KG: Psychological aspects of natural language use: Our words, our selves. *Annu Rev Psychol* 2003; 54: 547-577.

[6] Joiner TE, Pettit JW, Walker RL, Voelz ZR, Cruz J, Rudd MD, Lester D: Perceived burdensomeness and suicidality: Two studies on the suicide notes of those attempting and those completing suicide. *J Soc Clin Psychol* 2002; 21: 531-545.

[7] Wright J, Chung MC: Mastery or mystery? Therapeutic writing: A review of the literature. *Br J Guid Counc* 2001; 29: 277-291.

[8] Shneidman E: *The voice of death.* New York: Harper & Row, 1980.

[9] Baume P, Cantor CH, Rolfe A: Cybersuicide: The role of interactive suicide notes on the Internet. *Crisis* 1997; 18: 73-79.

[10] Becker K, Mayer M, Nagenborg M, El-Faddagh N, Schmidt MH: Parasuicide online: Can suicide websites trigger suicidal behavior in Predisposed adolescents? Nordic *Journal of Psychiatry* 2004; 58: 111-114.

[11] Mishara BL, Weisstub DN: Ethical, legal and practical issues in the control and regulation of suicide promotion and assistance over the Internet. *Suicide Life Threat Behav* 2007; 37: 58-65.

[12] Wilson G, Lester D: Suicide prevention by e-mail. Crisis Intervention 1998; 4: 81-87.

[13] Barak A: Emotional support and suicide prevention through the Internet: A field project study. *Comput Human Behav* 2007; 23: 971-984.
[14] Miller JK, Gergen JG: Life on the line: The therapeutic potentials of computer-mediated conversation. *Journal of Marital and Family Therapy* 1998; 24: 189-203.
[15] Gilat I, Shahar G: Emotional first aid for a suicide crisis: Comparison between telephonic hotline and Internet.*Psychiatry: Interpersonal and Biological Processes* 2007; 70: 12-18.
[16] Gould Ms, Munfka, JL, Lubell K, Kleinman M, Parker S: Seeking help from the Internet during adolescence. *Journal of the American Academy of Child and Adolescent Psychiatry* 2002; 41: 1182-1190.
[17] Suler J: The online disinhibition effect. *Cyber Psychology & Behavior* 2004; 7: 321-326.
[18] Kupferberg I, Green D: (2005). *Troubled Talk: Metaphorical Negotiation in Problem Discourse.* Berlin: Mouton de Gruyte, 2005.
[19] Barak A, Miron, O: Writing characteristics of suicidal people on the Internet: A psychological investigation of emerging social environments. *Suicide Life Threat Behav* 2005; 35: 507-524.
[20] Aphek E, Tobin Y: Word Systems in Modern Hebrew: Implications and Applications. Leiden, New York: Brill,1988.
[21] Aphek E, Tobin Y: *The Semiotics of Fortune-Telling*. Amsterdam/Philadelphia: John Benjamins, 1989.
[22] Aphek E: *Word Systems: Readings in the Style of S. Y.* Agnon. Tel Aviv: Dekel, 1979 (Hebrew).
[23] Orbach I, Mikulincer M, Sirota P,. Gilboa-Schechtman, E: Mental pain: A multidimensional operationalization and definition. *Suicide Life Threat Behav* 2003; 33: 219-230.
[24] Joiner T, Kalafat J, Draper J, Stokes H: Establishing standards for the assessment of suicide risk among callers to the National Suicide Prevention Lifeline. *Suicide Life Threat Behav* 2007;. 37: 353-364.

In: Internet and Suicide
Editors: L. Sher and A. Vilens

ISBN 978-1-60741-077-5

Chapter 12

THE INTERNET AND SUICIDE PACTS

Sundararajan Rajagopal
South London & Maudsley NHS Foundation Trust, Adamson Centre for Mental Health, St. Thomas' Hospital, London, United Kingdom

ABSTRACT

The phenomenon of suicide pacts influenced by the Internet (cybersuicide pacts) emerged a few years ago. Although cybersuicide pacts are very rare, in view of the enormous publicity that such pacts generate, it would be useful for psychiatrists and other health professionals to be aware of important issues relevant to this topic. This chapter aims to provide a summary of the current state of knowledge on cybersuicide pacts with information gathered from both the academic literature and the mainstream media. It covers traditional suicide pacts initially and then looks at cybersuicide pacts specifically, highlighting the key differences between the two types of suicide pacts. Examples of cybersuicide pacts from around the world are given to practically illustrate this worrying phenomenon. The potential ways in which the Internet may influence suicide pacts are discussed. In addition, related issues such as legislative attempts made by governments to tackle this problem, and the potential impact of the quality of media reporting of incidents of cybersuicide pacts are also touched upon.

INTRODUCTION

A suicide pact is an agreement between two or more people to commit suicide at the same time together. Suicide pacts in general (referred to in this chapter as 'traditional suicide pacts') have been a well recognized, global phenomenon for many years. Suicides that are influenced by the Internet are called cybersuicides, and similarly, suicide pacts that are influenced by the Internet are called cybersuicide pacts. As the Internet, a relatively modern technology, is implicated in some way in cybersuicide pacts, these pacts are much more recent than traditional suicide pacts. Cybersuicide pacts were first reported in the medical literature in December 2004 [1], with a handful of reports in the mainstream press preceding that [2,3]. Initially, cybersuicide pacts were mainly confined to Japan and other parts of East Asia. The first reported cybersuicide pact in Japan appears to have happened in 2000 [4,5]. Since then, isolated cases have been reported from different parts of the world, including Western countries. As they are extremely rare, when compared to suicides overall, the cybersuicide pacts naturally tend to attract an enormous amount of publicity in the lay media whenever they happen. Therefore, it would be useful for psychiatrists and other mental health professionals to be cognizant of the key aspects of this topic.

Traditional Suicide Pacts

According to the World Health Organization (WHO), there are almost a million suicides annually worldwide [6]. Traditional suicide pacts have been reported for several years, but they account for only a small proportion of overall suicides. In most countries, suicide pacts are responsible for less than 1% of all suicides.

There are clear differences between individual suicides and suicide pacts.

While individual suicides are about three times as common in men as in women, suicide pacts tend to have an approximately 1:1 sex ratio; this is because, a suicide pact is usually between a man and a woman, commonly between a husband and wife.

Those who kill themselves in a suicide pact tend to be older, are more likely to be married and childless, and to be of a higher socio-economic class than those who kill themselves on their own [7].

Suicide pact victims are more likely to leave suicide notes than those committing solitary suicide [7,8], indicating a greater degree of motivation and planning, and therefore, a possibly lesser likelihood of being prevented by psychiatric or other interventions.

While most solitary suicide victims have a psychiatric diagnosis, only about half of suicide pact victims have a history of psychiatric disorder [9].

Relatively less painful methods like poisoning by car exhaust fumes are more common in suicide pacts than in solitary suicides [9], but more violent methods may be used in suicide pacts depending on availability [8].

In a traditional pact, the number of victims is almost always two, and they characteristically employ the same method [9].

In a study comparing suicide pacts in four countries [10] (United States of America, United Kingdom, Japan and India), the frequency of suicide pacts was found to be highest in Japan. Suicide pacts between spouses predominated in the USA and UK, 'lover' pacts were commonest in Japan while pacts between friends occurred with the highest frequency in India. This study also reported that suicide pact victims, in general, opted for less violent methods to kill themselves.

Suicide pact victims tend to be in a typically exclusive relationship that is isolated from the rest of society [11], and the precipitant for the suicide pact is usually an impending threat to the continuation of the relationship. For example, a husband and wife, who have been married for many decades and are childless, may decide to kill themselves together when one of them is diagnosed with an untreatable physical disorder which is likely to lead to death soon. So, rather than the other member of the couple living on their own after the spouse's death, the two of them may decide to commit suicide together.

In some suicide pacts, the decision to die may not be mutual; one member may be coerced by the other to commit suicide. A study of survivors of suicide pacts showed that in such a non-mutual pact, the instigator is likely to be male, to have a history of depression / self-harm and the coerced is likely to be female, and not to have a history of depression / self-harm [12].

Non-mutual suicide pacts have some similarities to homicide-suicide [12]. A homicide-suicide or murder-suicide is an event in which an individual perpetrates a homicide, and then commits suicide soon after, usually within hours. Homicide-suicides are most likely committed by men [13]. Depression is an important risk factor for both suicide pacts and homicide-suicides [12,13]. Other risk factors for homicide-suicides include chronic chaotic relationships, verbal threats, physical violence, jealousy and alcoholism, and the triggering factor is frequently the withdrawal from the relationship by the female partner [13]. Chronic pain has also been reported as a potential risk factor for homicide-suicide [14]. Children and pets may also be victims in homicide-suicide, and analogous to mutual suicide pacts, the same method is mostly used for both the homicide and the suicide, but the methods used tend to be more violent than those used in mutual suicide pacts [13].

Suicide pacts have been reported in the context of a relatively uncommon delusional psychiatric disorder called folie a deux [15]. Folie a deux is a psychotic illness in which two people share the same or very similar delusion. Characteristically, it occurs in a couple who are in a close relationship (e.g. sisters who are spinsters and who are living together). The dominant member of that relationship develops the delusion first, and due to the imbalanced nature of the relationship, that person is then able to 'impose' their false beliefs on to the more passive, dependent member who then starts to share the delusion. The relationship between sufferers of folie a deux tends to be isolated from the rest of society, very similar to the relationship characteristics of suicide pact victims. A suicide pact between folie a deux sufferers is likely to be a non-mutual one in which the dominant member coerces the other person into committing suicide together.

Cybersuicide Pacts

The term 'Cybersuicide pact' encompasses any type of suicide pact that is, in some significant way, influenced by the Internet.

In a typical cybersuicide pact, strangers meet for the first time on the Internet, for example in an online chatroom. After deciding to commit suicide together, these people then meet in person in order to kill themselves together.

Thus the most important difference between traditional suicide pacts and cybersuicide pacts is that in the former, the pact is between people very well known to each other while in the latter it is between those who were complete strangers until contact was initiated on the internet.

The victims of cybersuicide pacts, especially from the data available from Japan where most of the cases have happened, are very young; mostly, young adults in their twenties and thirties, and even some teenagers. This contrasts with traditional suicide pacts in which the majority of the cases involve elderly victims.

In a traditional suicide pact, each pact almost always involves only two members. In a cybersuicide pact, many more people can kill themselves together at the same time; for example, seven young people (all in their teens or early twenties) killed themselves in a single cybersuicide pact in Japan in 2004 [2].

Most of the cybersuicide pacts have been reported in Japan. In 2004, there were 91 victims who killed themselves in 34 cybersuicide pacts in Japan. Out of these, 57 were males and 34 were females, and the majority were in their twenties and thirties [16].

There may be some reasons as to why cybersuicides and cybersuicide pacts are more common in Japan:

1. Japan has been known to have a very high rate of suicide among the developed nations [17]. Japan has a suicide rate of about 25 per 100,000 population, and about 30,000 people commit suicide in Japan every year.
2. Traditional suicide pacts are also commoner in Japan than in other countries [10].
3. As it is a highly technologically advanced country, the use of Internet is likely to be relatively higher than in most other nations
4. Suicide appears to have had a historical and cultural significance in Japan: for example, Samurai warriors reportedly chose suicide instead of surrender.

As in traditional suicide pacts, a range of methods may be employed in cybersuicide pacts, and similar to the traditional suicide pacts, in most of the cases, less violent suicide methods are used. As many people may be involved in a cybersuicide pact, a method that can be simultaneously shared is usually used. The most common method used in cybersuicide pacts appears to be carbon monoxide poisoning by burning barbecue charcoal in an enclosed space like a sealed car or apartment room. This procedure appears to have gained popularity over the Internet as a painless method that can be shared with several others [18].

More recently, another method has been used, again after being allegedly popularized over the Internet. This method involves mixing common household detergents to release hydrogen sulphide gas, which leads to death after inhalation. This process also carries with it the risk of potentially endangering the lives of people living nearby, and in one incident in Japan, the police had to evacuate hundreds of people from their homes after one of their neighbours used this method [19].

Some examples of probable cybersuicide pacts and related incidents are given below, with details of the year, country, ages of victims, and methods used:

1. In Japan, in October 2000, a 46 year old man (a dentist) and a 25 year old woman killed themselves by an overdose of sleeping pills [5]. This appears to have been the first reported cybersuicide pact. They had left suicide notes. They had originally met in a website that provided information on different ways to commit suicide and a bulletin board with messages from people wishing to kill themselves.
2. In October 2004, in Japan, two separate cybersuicide pacts were reported on the same day. In the first one, seven young people were found dead in a van. There were four men and three women in this group, and all seven were in their teens or early twenties [2]. They had died from carbon monoxide poisoning by burning charcoal. In

the second cybersuicide pact, two women, who had also used the same method, were found dead in a car. Police reported that all the victims were strangers who had first met via 'special suicide sites' on the Internet.

3. Five people committed suicide in South Korea in 2004 [20]. According to police, the three men and two women, aged between 19 and 29 were originally strangers who had first met over the Internet and then planned to commit suicide together. The method of death was cyanide poisoning. Suicide notes were left in the hotel room where the bodies were found, and also on the Internet.
4. In February 2005, again, two cybersuicide pacts occurred in Japan on the same day. The first group of four were all in their twenties or thirties, and the second group of three even included a 14 year old girl. Both pacts involved death by carbon monoxide poisoning by burning charcoal [21].
5. In February 2005, in the United States, a 26 year old man was arrested by the police on charges of solicitation of murder [22]. Using an Internet chat room, he had allegedly planned a mass suicide pact involving upto 32 people on Valentine's Day. The plan had reportedly involved using the Internet to coordinate the simultaneous suicides.
6. The first officially recorded cybersuicide pact in England took place in February 2005. A 25 year old man from Manchester and a 42 year old woman from London, were found dead in the woman's car in London. They had died of carbon monoxide poisoning after burning barbecue charcoal inside the car. It was reported that they were strangers who had made their first contact in an Internet 'suicide' chatroom, and both victims reportedly had histories of self-harm [23].
7. In August 2005, a 36 year old man was arrested in Japan on charge of 3 murders. The victims aged 25, 14 and 21 years were killed in February, May and June respectively. He had lured them individually via websites as if he was seeking someone to die with [24]. Instead, he suffocated his victims.

   Thus, those arranging to commit suicide with a stranger over the Internet are potentially placing themselves at risk of murder. Instead of the 'painless' shared suicide they expect, they may end up as victims of brutal homicides. This incident in Japan seems to be the first instance of a serial 'cyberhomicide'.
8. In June 2007, in Northern Ireland, two men, aged 20 and 24, committed suicide by drowning in a lake [25]. It was reported that they were also strangers who had first established contact over the Internet. They had sent letters to their families explaining what they had planned and where to find their bodies.
9. In May 2008, three young men, in their 20s and 30s, were found dead in a car in Japan [19,26]. According to reports, they had mixed detergents and other common household chemicals to release the toxic gas, hydrogen sulphide, the inhalation of which resulted in the deaths.

Role of the Internet in Suicide Pacts

By definition, the Internet has to play some role in cybersuicide pacts. But, its influence can be different in different cybersuicide pacts.

In the classical cybersuicide pact, the Internet in some form (e.g. chatrooms, bulletin boards, social networking sites, etc.) serves as the first meeting point for strangers, who then go on to kill themselves together after meeting in person.

The initial contact is generally made in pro-suicide chatrooms in which most participants mutually encourage suicide, discuss suicide methods, etc.

Contact can also be initiated in general discussion forums which can then be continued separately, say by e-mail, between selected individuals.

Applied more loosely, the term cybersuicide pact can also cover some suicide pacts which have many traditional suicide pact features (e.g. 2 people in a longstanding relationship), but the information to commit suicide is obtained from the internet.

A recent study reported that it was very easy to obtained detailed technical information about methods of suicide from both pro-suicide sites as well as general information websites [27]. In this UK study, they conducted searches using twelve search terms in the four most popular search engines; while they found that there were an almost equal number of pro-suicide sites as suicide prevention sites, the three most frequently occurring sites were all pro-suicide.

When patients are assessed after unusual suicidal attempts (either individually or in a pact), consideration should be given to whether they had obtained the information about the methods from the Internet [28,29].

In some rare cases, different people may decide to kill themselves separately but at the same time. This would also count as a cybersuicide pact if the individuals concerned are strangers, and the decision was made over the Internet.

The main question is: Is the Internet solely responsible for some of these deaths? In other words, will some of those victims not have committed suicide without the influence, in some way, of the Internet.

It is likely that most of those who kill themselves by cybersuicide pacts would have killed themselves anyway on their own. Those who enter into cybersuicide pacts, may have already made the decision to commit suicide even before viewing these websites. Their purpose of joining pro-suicide chatrooms may be to only find out if there are others who may want to die alongside them, or to obtain information about suicide methods.

In a very small proportion of cases, a person may go into such websites with perhaps fleeting suicidal ideation. But the subsequent discussion (e.g. encouraging suicide, discouraging seeking psychiatric treatment, recruiting persons to join a suicide pact, etc.) may crystallize these suicidal ideas and result in actual suicide either alone or in a pact. It has been suggested that suicide websites can trigger suicidal behaviour in predisposed adolescents [30].

More definitive assertions about the role of the Internet in cybersuicide pacts can only be made after detailed analysis of all the relevant factors: e.g. past psychiatric history of the victims, past history of self-harm, other risk factors for suicide, the nature of websites used by the victims, the reasons for suicides in the different victims (from suicide notes), etc.

Cybersuicide pacts form only a very small proportion of suicide pacts, which in turn form only a very small proportion of all suicides. So, even if a few of these cybersuicide pacts included some deaths that would not have happened without the influence of the Internet, they are unlikely to alter the overall suicide statistics.

PREVENTION OF CYBERSUICIDES AND CYBERSUICIDE PACTS

The same overall principles for prevention that apply to suicides in general should also pertain in relation to preventing cybersuicides and cybersuicide pacts: e.g. public education and awareness, early recognition and treatment of mental illnesses such as depression, reducing access to lethal means, responsible portrayal of incidents in the media, etc. In addition, extra measures would have to be considered specifically for cybersuicides and cybersuicide pacts, to try to address the added factor of the influence of the Internet.

Public education and awareness of mental illness plays an important role in combating stigma against mental illness. Such education and awareness can encourage people to seek help for mental illness from professionals rather than having to deal with it on their own. Also, if people do not have access to mental health services, it makes it more likely for them to share their distress with others who may not be well equipped to deal with these problems, or they may get inappropriate and counter-productive treatments from unqualified people.

As patients with depression tend not to socialize whilst being depressed, their only social contact with the outside world might then be with other depressed and suicidal people through pro-suicide websites, from the privacy of their homes.

Early recognition and effective treatment of mental illnesses associated with suicide (depression and other mood disorders, schizophrenia, personality disorders, co-morbid alcohol and substance abuse, etc.) can help reduce the risk of all types of suicide (individual suicides, suicide pacts, cybersuicides and cybersuicide pacts).

Reducing access to suicide methods has been shown to reduce the risk of suicide from those methods. For example, the detoxification of domestic gas led to a significant decrease in the overall number of suicides [31, 32]. Similarly, in those countries where access to firearms is made more difficult or if the ownership of firearms declines, the risk of suicide using firearms comes down [33,34]. With the introduction of catalytic converters in cars, suicides due to carbon monoxide poisoning from car exhaust fumes have shown a general decline [35,36].

However, new methods are being spread through the Internet, that use easily available products. As mentioned earlier, these include burning barbecue charcoal to release carbon monoxide, and mixing detergents and other household chemicals to release hydrogen sulphide. Obviously, it would be very difficult to prevent such methods, as there is little restriction that can be imposed regarding the availability of these common products.

The media has a potentially important role in being levelheaded in the portrayal of suicides (whether traditional or internet-influenced), in order to reduce the likelihood of copycat suicides.

A copycat suicide is a suicide that duplicates a previous suicide, which the person duplicating had become aware of either through a local incident or through a personal experience or through reports in the media or through depiction in books, films or television. A copycat suicide has also been termed the 'Werther effect' [37]. It is called the Werther effect after a character of that name in an 18th century novel by the German writer Goethe. In the novel, Werther commits suicide by shooting himself in the head. After publication of the novel, it was reported that several young men committed suicide by the same method.

This phenomenon was observed much more recently in the United States following the publication of a book in 1991 called 'Final Exit', in which suicide by poisoning and asphyxiation (using a plastic bag) were recommended as suicide methods for terminal illnesses. In the year of the publication of this book, there was an over 30% increase in asphyxiation suicides and about a 5% increase in poisoning suicides in the United States [38].

Copycat suicides may lead to a suicide cluster. A suicide cluster refers to a group of suicides that occur closer together in time and space than would normally be expected in a given community, with suicides occurring later in the cluster being motivated by earlier suicides which serve as the models for the later ones.

Copycat suicides are more likely following reports involving celebrities and females [39]. The Werther effect has been demonstrated following television movies [40]. Copycat suicides are most likely to occur in that sub-section of the population that shares the same age group and sex of the person whose suicide is depicted in the movie; copycat suicides also tend to use the same method as the depicted suicide [41]. Media reports that romanticize or dramatize the suicidal deaths are more likely to lead to copycat suicides [42].

A Japanese study reported that the number of newspaper articles about suicide is a predictor of suicides in both males and females, and Internet use was a predictor of suicide in males [43].

It has been shown that responsible reporting by the media can contribute to a reduction in suicides. In Austria, where guidelines were issued to the media in 1987 as a suicide-prevention measure, there has been a reduction in overall suicides, suggesting that due an improvement in the quality of reporting of suicides the guidelines have had a positive impact [44].

The World Health Organization has issued guidelines to the media on reporting suicides [45]. The guidelines suggest some 'do's' and 'don'ts'.

The do's include:

1. Working closely with health authorities
2. Referring to suicides as 'completed' and not as 'successful'
3. Reporting suicides on the inside pages
4. Providing information of helplines and other resources
5. Highlighting warning signs of suicide and alternatives to suicide

The don'ts include:

1. Not publishing photographs / suicide notes
2. Not sensationalizing or glorifying suicides
3. Not providing details of methods
4. Not offering simplistic reasons or stereotypes
5. Not apportioning blame

The media should be particularly mature while reporting cybersuicide pacts, especially considering the young age of the victims, which could potentially increase the risk of copycat imitation suicides.

In western, liberal societies, attempting or committing suicide is not a crime, but actively encouraging or abetting suicide is a crime. So, Internet sites that actively promote suicide may be committing a crime.

Some governments have initiated action to combat cybersuicides and cybersuicide pacts. For example, the Australian government, in its Criminal Code Amendment (Suicide Related Material Offences) Act 2005, introduced penalties for those counseling or inciting suicide through the Internet [46].

The laws of individual nation states can usually only bring to justice those citizens who fall within that country's jurisdiction. As the Internet is a pan-national medium, laws of individual countries will have their limitations, unless these measures are supported by an international consensus.

Governments have also started working with Internet Service Providers (ISPs) to try to tackle the issue of pro-suicide websites. Use of filtering softwares, to block websites with dangerous pro-suicide content, is an option that has been highlighted for preventing access to such sites, especially by vulnerable individuals like children.

In Japan, there was an increase in the number of cybersuicide pact deaths from 34 in 2003, through 55 in 2004 to 91 in 2005. However, more than half of the cybersuicide pacts in 2005 occurred in the first three months of that year, before joint measures were taken by the Japanese authorities and ISPs [16]. This seems to suggest that, with such cooperative efforts, the number of cybersuicide pacts can be reduced; but it is not clear whether this reduction would reflect an absolute reduction in suicide numbers or whether there would just be a shift of these numbers from cybersuicide pacts to individual suicides.

Conclusion

Cybersuicide pacts are most likely here to stay as a very infrequent but highly publicized recurring phenomenon. Given their rarity they are unlikely to cause a significant change in overall suicide numbers. The overwhelming majority of victims of cybersuicide pacts would likely have killed themselves on their own, even otherwise, as it is improbable for someone who is not suicidal to become suicidal purely due to the influence of the Internet.

Clinicians need to be aware of the very rare risk of cybersuicide or cybersuicide pacts in their depressed patients, especially in those who are reported (either by self-report or by their carers) to be spending increasingly more time on the Internet. By sensitive questioning, information can be gathered as to the nature of the websites being visited (whether the sites are positive self-help sites or neutral general information sites or negative pro-suicide sites). If appropriate, patients can be specifically asked whether they are looking for suicide methods on the Internet, and whether they are in contact with other people who are suicidal like them. Patients, relatives and professionals may need to be made aware of the existence of pro-suicide websites and the risks that they pose.

As the Internet is a medium that is not restricted by national borders, clinicians also need to realize their limitations in being able to prevent these incidents of cybersuicide pacts.

One should not lose sight of the fact that the Internet, overwhelmingly, is an invaluable source of useful knowledge, which, if used appropriately, can be of immense benefit to both patients and professionals.

From a psychiatric perspective, early identification and effective treatment of mental illness remains the single biggest protective factor against all types of suicide.

REFERENCES

[1] Rajagopal S: Suicide pacts and the internet. *BMJ* 2004; 329:1298-1299.

[2] *BBC News: Nine die in Japan 'suicide pacts'.* http://news.bbc.co.uk/1/hi/world/asia-pacific/3735372.stm

[3] *MSNBC: Japan's chilling Internet suicide pacts.* http://www.msnbc.msn.com/id/3340456/

[4] Ueno K: Suicide as Japan's major export? A note on Japanese Suicide Culture. http://www.espacoacademico.com.br/044/44eueno_ing.htm

[5] *BBC News: Japan couple in net suicide pact.* http://news.bbc.co.uk/1/hi/world/asia-pacific/998566.stm

[6] *World Health Organization: World Health Report 2003:* Shaping the Future. http://www.who.int/whr/2003/en/whr03_en.pdf

[7] Brown M, Barraclough B: *Epidemiology of suicide pacts in England and Wales,* 1988-92. BMJ 1997; 315:286-287.

[8] Fishbain DA, D'Achille L, Barsky S, Aldrich TE: A controlled study of suicide pacts. *J Clin Psychiatry* 1984; 45:154-157.

[9] Brown M, Barraclough B: Partners in life and death: the suicide pact in England and Wales 1988-1992. *Psychol Med* 1999; 29:1299-1306.

[10] Fishbain DA, Aldrich TE: Suicide pacts: international comparisons. *J Clin Psychiatry* 1985; 46:11-15.

[11] Rosen BK: Suicide pacts: a review. *Psychol Med* 1981; 11:525-533.

[12] Rosenbaum M: Crime and punishment - the suicide pact. *Arch Gen Psychiatry* 1983; 40:979-982.

[13] Lecomte D, Fornes P: Homicide followed by suicide: *Paris and its suburbs,* 1991-1996. J Forensic Sci 1998; 43:760-764.

[14] Fishbain DA, Goldberg M, Rosomoff RS, Rosomoff HL: Homicide-suicide and chronic pain. *Clin J Pain* 1989; 5:275-277.

[15] Salih MA: Suicide pact in a setting of Folie a Deux. *Br J Psychiatry* 1981; 139:62-67.

[16] BBC News: Web suicide pacts surge in Japan. http://news.bbc.co.uk/1/hi/world/asia-pacific/4695864.stm

[17] World Health Organisation: Mental Health. http://www.who.int/mental_health/prevention/suicide/suiciderates/en/

[18] Lee DT, Chan KP, Yip PS: Charcoal burning is also popular for suicide pacts made on the internet. *BMJ* 2005; 330:602.

[19] CNN.com: *3 dead in Japanese 'detergent suicide' pact.* http://edition.cnn.com/2008/WORLD/asiapcf/05/12/detergent.suicide/index.html

[20] *BBC News: S Koreans in 'net suicide pact'.* http://news.bbc.co.uk/1/hi/world/middle_east/3560103.stm

[21] *Guardian.co.uk: Seven die in online suicide pact in Japan.* http://www.guardian.co.uk/technology/2005/mar/02/japan.internationalnews

[22] *BBC News: Man 'set Valentine suicide pact'.* http://news.bbc.co.uk/1/hi/world/americas/4259079.stm
[23] Guardian.co.uk: Clampdown on chatrooms after two strangers die in first internet death pact. http://www.guardian.co.uk/uk/2005/oct/11/socialcare.technology
[24] *The Japan Times: Alleged killer linked to suicide site.* http://search.japantimes.co.jp/cgi-bin/nn20050807a2.html
[25] *BBC News: Men 'made internet suicide pact'.* http://news.bbc.co.uk/1/hi/northern_ireland/6751597.stm
[26] *ShortNews.com: Detergent Suicide Pact Claims 3 More.* http://www.shortnews.com/start.cfm?id=70662
[27] Biddle L, Donovan J, Hawton K, Kapur N, Gunnell D: Suicide and the internet. *BMJ* 2008; 336: 800-802.
[28] Haut F, Morrison A: The Internet and the future of psychiatry. *Psychiatric Bulletin* 1998; 22:641-642.
[29] Prior TI: Suicide Methods From The Internet. *Am J Psychiatry* 2004; 161:1500-1501.
[30] Becker K, Mayer M, Nagenborg M, El-Faddagh M, Schmidt MH: Parasuicide online: Can suicide websites trigger suicidal behaviour in predisposed adolescents? *Nord J Psychiatry* 2004; 58:111-114.
[31] Ashford JR, Lawrence PA: Aspects of the epidemiology of suicide in England and Wales. *Int J Epidemiol* 1976; 5:133-144.
[32] Lester D, Abe K: The effect of restricting access to lethal methods for suicide: a study of suicide by domestic gas in Japan. *Acta Psychiatr Scand* 1989; 80:180-182.
[33] Kapusta ND, Etzersdorfer E, Krall C, Sonneck G: Firearm legislation reform in the European Union: impact on firearm availability, firearm suicide and homicide rates in Austria. *Br J Psychiatry* 2007; 191:253-257.
[34] Miller M, Azrael D, Hepburn L, Hemenway D, Lippmann SJ: The association between changes in household firearm ownership and rates of suicide in the United States, 1981-2002. *Inj Prev* 2006; 12: 178-182.
[35] Thomsen AH, Gregersen M: Suicide by carbon monoxide from car exhaust-gas in Denmark 1995-1999. *Forensic Sci Int* 2006; 161:41-46.
[36] Amos T, Appleby L, Kiernan K: Changes in rates of suicide by car exhaust asphyxiation in England and Wales. *Psychol Med* 2001; 31:935-939.
[37] Phillips DP: The influence of suggestion on suicide: substantive and theoretical implications of the Werther effect. *Am Sociol Rev* 1974; 39:340-354.
[38] Marzuk PM, Tardiff K, Leon AC: Increase in fatal suicidal poisonings and suffocations in the year Final Exit was published: a national study. *Am J Psychiatry* 1994; 151:1813-1814.
[39] Stack S: Suicide in the media: a quantitative review of studies based on non-fictional stories. *Suicide Life Threat Behav* 2005; 35:121-133.
[40] Gould MS, Shaffer D: The impact of suicide in television movies. Evidence of imitation. *N Eng J Med* 1986; 315:690-694.
[41] Schmidtke A, Hafner H: The Werther effect after television films: new evidence for an old hypothesis. *Psychol Med* 1988; 18:665-676.
[42] Sudak HS, Sudak DM: The media and suicide. *Acad Psychiatry* 2005; 29:495-499.
[43] Hagihara A, Tarumi K, Abe T: Media suicide-reports, Internet use and the occurrence of suicides between 1987 and 2005 in Japan. *BMC Public Health* 2007; 7:321.

[44] Niederkrotenthaler T, Sonneck G: Assessing the impact of media guidelines for reporting on suicides in Austria: interrupted time series analysis. *Aust N Z J Psychiatry* 2007; 41:419-428.

[45] *World Health Organisation: Preventing suicide: a resource for media professionals.* Geneva, 2000. http://www.who.int/mental_health/media/en/426.pdf

[46] *Commonwealth of Australia Law: Criminal Code Amendment* (Suicide Related Material Offences) Act 2005. http://www.comlaw.gov.au/ComLaw/Legislation/Act1.nsf/framelodgmentattachments/E73F3E4D3B48C0A1CA2570380018EF3B

In: Internet and Suicide
Editors: L. Sher and A. Vilens

ISBN 978-1-60741-077-5

Chapter 13

INTERNET AS A HEALING OR KILLING TOOL IN YOUTH SUICIDE PHENOMENON

Milica Pejovic Milovancevic, Dusica Lecic Tosevski, Smiljka Popovic Deusic and Zagorka Bradic
Institute of Mental Health, Belgrade, Serbia

ABSTRACT

Children and adolescents are growing up in the world saturated with mass media. They spend an average of 3-5 hours per day with a variety of media, including television, radio, videos, videogames, and the internet. Media is offering to young people great opportunities for fun, learning and development. On the other hand, there must be concern of inappropriate information they are presenting to the youth, often lowering their threshold for and increasing the risk of suicidal behavior. Therefore the media should exercise restraint in describing concrete details especially when reporting on youth suicides. The association between media portrayal and suicidal behavior is probably the strongest in young people, with clear evidence that reporting on specific suicidal methods has significant impact to shape the behavior of vulnerable adolescent population. Wide acceptance of the internet, fortunately, makes it also a powerful tool for recognition of the at-risk individuals, for prevention of suicide and support to survivors.

Keywords: children, adolescents, internet, suicidal behavior, suicide, at-risk individuals

INTRODUCTION

Adolescence is life time with dramatic changes. The journey from childhood to adulthood is very complex and challenging. There is tremendous pressure on young people to be successful at school, home and in social groups. At the same time, they lack the life experience important in understanding and managing problems. Many researches of suicide are focused on adolescence, period when young people are expected to resolve the most difficult task – the identity creation. Unfortunately, for some adolescents the suicide is the choice for the identity. Mental health problems commonly seen in adults (such as depression) are also affecting young people; being a highly vulnerable population they often seek relief of different unresolved problems unfortunately even in suicide.

In the era when the incidence of mortality and morbidity among youth decline with medical technology progress, it is tragic irony that persistent high suicidal and suicidal behavior rate among youth stay stabile as a leading cause of death among this generally strong and healthy population. Suicide among youth is an indicator of mental health and mental well being. Youth suicide act has always deep impact on family, friends and wider society and provokes destabilization among them. It is the result of multidimensional conflict in young person. Among professionals faced with this phenomenon, there is general notion that the number of youth suicide is underestimated; they point out stigma as key factor that distracts early identification of risk factors.

Many factors can put a young person at risk for suicide. The most common are history of previous suicide attempts, family history of suicide, history of depression or other mental disorders, alcohol or drug abuse, stressful life events or loss, easy access to lethal methods, exposure to suicidal behavior of the others [1,2,3].

Youth suicide has been a major contributing factor to overall mortality and morbidity during last thirty to forty years [4]. It is a serious public health problem and for youth between the ages 10 to 24 it is the third leading cause of death. Boys are more likely to die because of suicide and girls are more likely to attempt suicide [1]. Of all the reported suicide cases in 10-24 age groups, 83% were males and 17% females [2]. A 21 year longitudinal study reports suicide ideation in 28.8% of youth and suicide attempts in 7.5% by the age of 21 years [5].

It is considered that the number of suicide attempts among youth is far greater than the estimations, due to the fact that many suicidal adolescents are not treated at hospitals and not recorded at all. Survey data from 1999 indicate that 19.3% of high school students had seriously considered attempting suicide, 14.5% had made plans to attempt suicide, and 8.3% had made a suicide attempt during the year preceding the survey [1].

Suicide can be an impulsive act. But more often, a person thinks about it for some time before taking action. It is estimated that 8 out of 10 people who attempt suicide or die by means of suicide had previously mentioned their plans. The use of internet is one way to send a suicidal note or to make suicidal plan. Those warning signs can be directed to a known or unknown friend. When she or he has desire for death there is always almost the same desire for life. Along with this ill desire, there is also fear of death which persists in the same time. This delicate balance creates a great opportunity for action and suicide prevention.

THE INTERNET

Children and adolescents spend an average of 3-5 hours per day in contact with a variety of media, including television, radio, videos, videogames, and the internet [6]. They are growing up in a world saturated with the mass media with presentation of a world where unhealthy behaviors (such as physical aggression, unprotected sex, smoking, drinking) are glamorous and risk-free [7]. Ownership of media-related technologies tends to be higher in households with children than in households without children. Children's bedrooms are increasingly becoming multi-media centres. Television set is the most commonly available device in children's bedrooms, but there is a wide variety of other media including games consoles and webcams. Infiltration of technologies in bedrooms is increasing with the age of children.

The most popular activity next to television for children aged 5-15 years is the internet. Differences in levels of access to the internet among children of various ages are driven by their needs and skill levels. Children 8-11 year olds are most likely to go online for game purposes; 12-15 year olds are using it as an educational tool as well as for downloading music/movies/videos and watching video clips; the oldest age group (16-17 year olds) are most likely to be sending e-mail, visiting social networking sites, uploading photos/videos and either maintaining their own or contributing to other people's blogs/sites [8]. Accessible networking information will continue to grow for at least next 20 years and the number of access points into the internet will expand in number, variety and mobility [9].

The internet, as a widespread source of communication, has a significant influence in medicine and psychiatry. Although the internet has a great potential in psychiatric education, clinical care, and research, its impact on social issues should not be underestimated [10]. It is playing an increasingly important role in relation to emotional crisis and suicidal behavior [11]. The internet can lower the threshold for and increase the risk of suicidal behavior. As a means of communication it may encourage suicidal behavior in terms of depicting ways by which suicide may be committed, or persuading someone to commit suicide [12, 13, 14].

Vulnerable young people see internet as a medium, new form of information sharing, and some of them are leaving interactive notes to share their suicidal ideation with others, followed by suicide fatalities [15]. Internet websites may discourage people with mental health problems from seeking psychiatric help, and forbid entry to anyone offering help to those who attempt to committed suicide. There are many new group and bulletin boards on the net that positively advocate suicide and some of them discourage individuals from seeking psychiatric help.

Some data indicate that young individuals who access net (especially suicidal promoting sites) are more psychologically vulnerable persons with high risk behaviors, substance use and depression [16]. To create the profile of person who will use the internet as a medium for suicidal behavior would be too ambitious, but certain case reports are discussing the presence of personality disorders and borderline intellectual functioning with rigid, concrete or maladaptive coping strategies [17].

In contrast to the above mentioned, the internet could be a resource for a potentially suicidal person to get help. It can help to identify those at risk for suicide, communicate with them, and potentially prevent a suicide. As a powerful communication tool the internet can be used to benefit suicidal patients. It can be used in internet-based mental health screening and treatment [18] as well as a collateral informant in the psychiatric encounter [19]. The use of internet is always ambiguous. On one hand it is easy, fast and cheap, but on the other at least controversial – the issues of ethics, privacy and legality should be always addressed. With the advent of the internet, and widespread publication of e-mail addresses on web pages, it is increasingly easy to correspond with members of the health professions. E-mails could be a genuine cry for help and their appropriate use should be encouraged, but there is also great potential for abuse, with the concomitant waste of time. It is recommended to establish tighter regulations of harmful sites including those giving graphic details of suicide methods and chat rooms dedicated to the promotion of suicide in order to control access of vulnerable young people to the pro-suicide sites [20].

There are several ways how internet and youth suicide might be connected which will be mentioned below. They can be divided into two main groups: "killing" and "healing" relationships.

"Killing" Relationship - Net Suicide, Net Suicide Pact

The number of websites concerning suicide is increasing. Younger people, especially teenagers (as highly vulnerable population) are easily influenced by these sites and can join the suicidal pacts [21]. *Net suicide* refers to the suicide pacts that are prearranged between strangers who meet over the internet [22]. *Suicide pact* is an agreement between two or more people to commit suicide at the same place and time; its account is less than 1% of the total number of suicides [23]. Adolescents visit suicide web forums, where they research reliable suicide methods and contact an anonymous user. This is in contrast to traditional suicide pacts, in which the victims are people with close relationships [23].

Internet, in addition to connecting otherwise isolated persons in forming suicide pacts, has played an important role in spreading new suicide methods across societies [24]. For example, charcoal burning is popular method for suicide pacts made on the internet (smoldering barbecue coal in a small and sealed environment with the aim of producing a carbon monoxide chamber in a short time) [23]. Some other rare suicidal method, such as asphyxiation by use of pure helium gas, or poisoning by the yew leaves were found on Internet by young people [25, 26].

In some countries of the world, such as a Japan, a growing number of suicide attempts are being made by people brought together via internet [27]. Usually, teenagers meet in electronic notice boards only by their nick names, plan suicide and then gather at the given place to commit suicide. According to the National Policy Agency in Japan, during 2003 two teenagers, and during 2004 seven teenagers died in suicide pacts made via internet. All of them had been strangers until they met via internet and gathered at agreed-upon place to commit suicide.

Suicide Contagion among Teens via Internet

Suicide contagion is a process by which exposure to the suicide or suicidal behavior of one or more persons influences others to commit or attempt suicide. Contagion may be transmitted by personal communication, through templates provided by teen icons and by media [28]. There is increasing evidence of suicide contagion among teenagers. This phenomenon is further exacerbated by the availability of long-range communication channels like the internet [29].

Contagion clusters suppose three or more cases of suicide. Internet helps that a story of someone's death (for example celebrity) spreads all over the world within minutes, initiating selfdestructive behavior and suicide activities among those who identify themselves with the suicide victim. The suicide of rock star Kurt Cobain in 1994 raised immediate and intensive professional and public concerns related to potential risk of his death to spark copycat suicides, especially among vulnerable youth. The data obtained from the Seattle King County area suggest that the expected "Werther effect" apparently did not occur, but there was a significant increase in suicide crisis calls following his death. [30]. A Werther effect, also known as copycat suicide, is defined as a duplication of another suicide that the person attempting suicide knows about, either from local knowledge or due to accounts or depictions of the original suicide on television or other media. The well-known suicide serves as a model, in the absence of protective factors, for the next suicide. This is referred to as suicide contagion and occasionally spreads through school systems, communities, or nationwide.

Relation between Suicide and Internet Abuse

Kim [31] made a survey in 2007 with correlation design in order to examine the relationship of internet addiction, depression and suicidal ideation. His results have shown that 1.6% of subjects were diagnosed as internet addicts, and 38.0% were classified as possible internet addicts. The prevalence of internet addiction did not vary with gender. The levels of depression and suicidal ideation were the highest in the group of internet-addicts. Future studies should investigate the direct relationship between mental health problems and internet dependency. As schools are often the first line for the identification of potential life-threatening behaviors, school professionals (especially school-based health professionals) need to be aware of measures and procedures for the assessment of internet addiction, depression, and suicidal ideation [32].

Suicide Forums and Youth

Suicide forums, or interactive forums on the Internet, are attractive to suicidal youth [33]. The question whether participation in these forums might be dangerous (because of imitation and contagion) or should it be considered as helpful (being a chance to talk openly with others) is still considered controversial. Case reports about online parasuicides reveal that vulnerable youths researched reliable suicide methods, contacted anonymous users and purchased substances for the implementation of suicide. Therefore the psychiatric exploration should include questions of manner and frequency of media use among youths [34], along with a focus for a nursing intervention in implications for suicide prevention [15].

The Role of Media

The media should exercise restraint in describing concrete details especially when reporting on youth suicides [35]. The association between media portrayal and suicidal behavior is probably the strongest in young people. There is clear evidence that the reporting or portrayal of specific suicidal methods of suicidal behavior has significant impact to shape behavior of vulnerable individuals [11, 36, 37]. Oversimplified pictures given by media and overemphasized relatively unimportant factors in order to shock or entertain publics may lead to the notion that suicidal behavior is “common and understandable way” of problem solving. Public suicide portrayal provides a model which can induce ambivalent individuals toward suicide.

The number of newspaper articles about suicide is a predicting factor of suicide among both male and female subjects. Internet use is also a predictor of suicide, but more among males, probably because they spend more time online than females [38]. The media reporting on suicides of entertainment celebrities may affect suicide rates due to an imitation effect. The celebrities, the idols of younger generations, popular singers or actors and their suicidal behavior, attempts or committed suicides can influence suicidal ideas among their followers. There was a marked increase in number of suicide rates four weeks after media reported suicide of the celebrity. The increase was stronger in men, especially in younger age group (using the same highly lethal method described and reported in media) [39].

Many studies have reported a significant degree of clustering of suicides following media coverage of a suicidal event or personal contact with a suicide victim. Many of these suicides mimic the methods (“copy-cat suicides”) which is especially popular among adolescents, particularly if the initial victim was famous or if the suicide provoked the great interest [40]

In 1999 WHO strated a worldwide initiative for the prevention of suicide and published several booklets addressed to suicide report and one of them covered media Media strongly influence human attitudes, beliefs and behavior, and plays a vital role in their lives. Some forms of media coverage of suicides are associated with statistically significant excess of suicide; the impact appears to be strongest among young people. On the other hand and due to strong influence that media has on community, it can also play an active role in the prevention of suicide [41].

Clinicians and researchers acknowledge that it is not news coverage of suicide *per se,* but certain types of news coverage, that increase suicidal behaviour in vulnerable populations. There is always the possibility that publicity about suicide might make the idea of suicide being “normal”. Repeated and continual coverage of suicide tends to induce and promote suicidal preoccupations, particularly among adolescents and young adults.

WHO suggested specific issues that need to be addressed when reporting on suicide and they include: careful and correct statistic interpretations, use of authentic and reliable sources, carefull use of impromptu comments, avoidance of generalizations based on small figures, etc [41].

“Healing” Relationship

Wide acceptance of the internet makes it a powerful tool for recognition of the at-risk individuals, for prevention of suicide and support to survivors, when chat rooms are taking role of telephone help lines. This is very important knowing that teenagers prefer to communicate via internet.

Many physicians are still unaware of the power of the internet. But in the age of technology and information, it is vital for mental health professionals to use all available means of informing and empowering the public and patients-including the internet. The internet has also a role in training, providing accessible self-help sites for potentially suicidal adolescents and web-based prevention services (all of which remain sadly under-utilized) [42,

43]. Telematic technologies offer innovative and creative resources to address needs of youth especially adolescent suicide survivors by means of web-based psychoeducational programmes [44]. In addition to survivors, potential program users include social supporters of suicide survivors, mental health professionals and survivor support groups.

Development of information technology has created new opportunities and challenges in suicide prevention, research, and clinical practice. Interventions using the internet, telephone, and videoconferencing (including crisis intervention, referral, and support, suicide risk assessment, psychotherapy for individuals at risk, and online-based suicide prevention training and education) are some of the procedures [45,46].

Mental health professionals should always ask adolescents about their internet use. Depressed, suicidal, or potentially suicidal youth who use the internet may especially be at risk because of the accessibility of potentially harmful resources, such as pro-suicide forums [47]. Clinicians may assist patients in locating helpful, supportive resources online so that patients internet use may be rather therapeutic than harmful.

The risk of internet use by vulnerable youth should be emphasized. That's why psychiatric exploration should also include questions on the manner and frequency of media use. Association between media portrayal and suicidal behavior may be the strongest in young people but modeling process can lead the ambivalent individual toward life rather than suicide and could give the constructive alternatives to suicidal behavior in order to reduce the effect of suicide stories [11]. The internet can be seen as a way to reach young people in need, and as a powerful healing tool in suicide prevention.

Research data on adolescent suicide are pointing out that there is almost always continuum in self-destructive behavior among adolescents. That's why every suicidal attempt, suicidal ideas and deliberate self harm should be taken in serious consideration, meaning that intervention procedures should be taken as early as possible.

The Institute of Mental Health, as a leading institution in this field in Serbia recognized the need for action on youth suicide prevention and has developed *Youth suicide prevention program* which would be supported by the Ministry of Health. One of the objectives of this program is to develop internet networking system where youth suicide will be addressed in informative way (informations regarding demographic data, causes, risk factors and treatment).

Internet as a Tool in Screening of Suicide

There are reports on the internet discussion groups and message boards members that completed a web questionnaire assessing measures of body satisfaction, eating disorders, and childhood trauma and suicide ideation. Self-harmers who reported a history of childhood sexual abuse scored higher on measures of body dissatisfaction, eating disorders, suicide ideation, physical abuse, physical neglect, emotional abuse and emotional neglect. Therefore, internet can be used as a handy tool for research in child and adolescent psychiatry [48, 49].

Internet Based Mental Health Services Programms for Youth

Telematic technologies offer innovative and creative resource to address patient needs by offering them web-based psychoeducational program. Through educational effort via novel technologies, people could be directed toward better understanding of the destructive effects that suicide has on survivors, family members and others. Programs that discuss suicide without moralizing are essential to address social stigma toward suicide survivors [44].

Psychoeducational programs promote health, prevent problems and reduce consequences. In the development of web-based psychoeducational programs the situation analysis indicated a clear need of adolescents, especially those with self-destructive behavior, suicidal ideation or adolescent suicide survivors, to receive effective social support and psychoeducational interventions [44].

On the other hand, a novel use of telemedicine is presented to professional awareness in which healthcare information is provided via internet-based information and communication technologies (ICTs) to an intermediary (a third-party observer) rather than directly to the patient to deliver suicide prevention e-healthcare [50,51].

The development of a comprehensive web-based program that deals with experiences of adolescent suicide survivors is available [44]. Potential program users include adolescent suicide survivors, social supporters of suicide survivors, mental health professionals and survivor support groups. Online training is a valuable option to meet suicide prevention training needs, in terms of employing flexible, easy-to-use, and inexpensive internet technology [4, 43]. Suicides in online mental health support groups are inevitable [52].

Online Support Chat

Deep, smooth conversations that yield positive responses and arouse clients' emotions in online support are more helpful than shallow, bumping conversations that leave clients emotionally indifferent. Longer writing, online support chat, both by helpers and clients, seems to be an important factor, as well [53].

Mutual social support through suicide interactive forums plays a significant role in suicide prevention. Social support in suicide forums is rated as high as the support obtained from friends and even higher than the family support. Social support is higher in suicide forums where discussions on suicide methods do not occur. Higher social support in suicide forums correlates with participants' ratings of suicidality reduction [33]. Forums are used as internet-based self-help groups and they offer some specific advantages such as 24-hour access to other sufferers [54]. The internet has a powerful effect on society and also on psychiatric patients. It offers suicide prevention services but also is a source of information and exchange of thoughts on how to commit suicide. The issue of suicide warning signs on the Internet should be seriously considered by clinicians [55].

Conclusion

The internet, as a widespread source of communication, has a significant influence on young people, especially those who prefer to communicate that way. The internet and video games offer a range of opportunities for fun, learning and development. Although the internet has a great potential in psychiatric education, clinical care, and research, its impact on social issues should not be underestimated. There are concerns over its potentially inappropriate informations, related to the content of the offered materials [56].

The internet can lower the threshold for and increase the risk of suicidal behavior. As a means of communication it may encourage suicidal behavior in terms of depicting ways by which suicide may be committed, or persuading someone to commit a suicide [57]. On the other hand, wide acceptance of the internet makes it a powerful tool for recognition of the at-risk individuals, for prevention of suicide and support to survivors, when chat rooms are taking role of telephone help lines. Therefore it is very important to share the responsibility with media, industry, governments, families, and professionals in order to reduce the availability of potentially harmful materials, and to offer help whenever needed.

References

[1] Calculated from data provided in: National Center for Health Statistics, *GMWK291 Death Rates for 72 Selected Causes by 5-Year Age Groups, Race, and Sex:* United States, 1979-98, p.485. Centers for Disease Control and Prevention.

[2] *Centers for Disease Control and Prevention.* WISQARS (Web-based Injury Statistics Query and Reporting System)

[3] U.S. Public Health Service (1999). *The Surgeon General's Call to Action to Prevent Suicide,* p. 3. Washington, D.C.

[4] Omar HA. A model program for youth suicide prevention. *Int J Adolesc Med Health* 2005; 17(3):275-8.

[5] Fergusson DM, Woodward LJ, Horwood LJ. Risk factors and life processes associated with the onset of suicidal behavior during adolescence and early adulthood. *Psychol Med* 2000; 30:23-39.

[6] Strasburger VC, Donnerstein E. Children, adolescents, and the media in the 21st century. *Adolesc Med* 2000; 11(1):51-68.

[7] Brown JD, Witherspoon EM. The mass media and American adolescents' health. *J Adolesc Health* 2002; 31(suppl 6):153-70.

[8] Dutton WH, Helsper E. *The Internet in Britain* 2007, http://www.oii.ox.ac.uk/microsites/oxis/

[9] Biocca F. New media technology and youth: trends in the evolution of new media. *J Adolesc Health.* 2000; 27(suppl2):22-29.

[10] Alao AO, Soderberg M, Pohl EL, Alao AL. Cybersuicide: review of the role of the internet on suicide. *Cyberpsychol Behav* 2006; 9(4):489-493.

[11] Sisask M, Värnik A, Wasserman D. Internet comments on media reporting of two adolescents' collective suicide attempt. *Arch Suicide Res* 2005; 9(1):87-98.

[12] Forsthoff A, Hummel B, Möller HJ, Grunze H. Suicidality and the Internet. Danger from new media. *Nervenarzt* 2006; 77(3):343-345.

[13] D'Hulster N, van Heeringen C. Cyber-suicide: the role of the internet in suicidal behavior. A case study. *Dutch Journal of Psychiatry* 2006; 48(10):803-807.

[14] Chodorowski Z, Sein Anand J. Internet as a means of persuading a patient to commit a suicide. *Przegl Lek* 2002; 59(4-5):375-376.

[15] Baume P, Cantor CH, Rolfe A. Cybersuicide: the role of interactive suicide notes on the Internet. *Crisis* 1997; 18(2):73-79.

[16] Thompson S. The internet and its potential influence on suicide. *Psychiatr Bull* 1999; 23:449-51.

[17] Prior T. Suicide Methods from the Internet. *Am J Psychiatry* 2004; 161(8):1500-1501.

[18] Farrell SP, Mahone IH, Guibaud P. Web technology for persons with serious mental illness. *Arch Psychiatr Nurs* 2004; 18:121-125.

[19] Neimark G, Hurford MO, DiGiacomo J. The Internet as a Collateral Informan. *Am J Psychiatry* 2006; 163:10.

[20] Coombes R. Safety nets. *BMJ* 2008, 12:336(7648):803.

[21] Hitosugi M, Nagai T, Tokudome S. A voluntary effort to save the youth suicide via the Internet in Japan. *Int J Nurs Stud* 2007; 44:157.

[22] Naito A. Internet suicide in Japan: implications for child and adolescent mental health. *Clin Child Psychol Psychiatry* 2007; 12(4):583-97.

[23] Rajagopal S. Suicide pacts and the internet. *BMJ* 2004; 329:1298-9.

[24] Lee DTS, Chan KPM, Yip PSF. Charcoal burning is also popular for suicide pacts made on the internet. *BMJ* 2005; 330:602.

[25] Gallagher KE, Smith DM, Mellen PF. Suicidal asphyxiation by using pure helium gas. Case report, review and discussion of the influence of the Internet. *Am J Forensic Med Pathol* 2003; 24:361–363.

[26] Wehner F, Gawatz O. Suicidal yew poisoning--from Caesar to today--or suicide instructions on the internet. *Arch Criminol* 2003; 211(1-2):19-26.

[27] Hitosugi M, Yokoyama T, Kido M, Nagai T, Tokudome S. *Trend in suicide pacts made via the Internet in Japan.* http://www.bmj.com/cgi/eletters/330/7491/602-b#101798

[28] Johansson L, Lindqvist P, Eriksson. Teenage suicide cluster formation and contagion: implications for primary care. *BMC Family Practice* 2006; 7:32.

[29] Nicolis H. Nonlinear dynamics and probabilistic behavior of adolescent suicidal outbreaks. *Nonlinear Dynamics Psychol Life Sci* 2007; 11(4):451-472.

[30] Jobes DA, Berman AL, O'Carroll PW, Eastgard S, Knickmeyer S. The Kurt Cobain suicide crisis: perspectives from research, public health, and the news media. *Suicide Life Threat Behav* 1996;26(3):260-269

[31] Kim K, Ryu E, Chon MY, Yeun EJ, Choi SY, Seo JS, Nam BW. Internet addiction in Korean adolescents and its relation to depression and suicidal ideation: a questionnaire survey. *Int J Nurs Stud* 2006; 43(2):185-192.

[32] Ryu EJ, Choi KS, Seo JS, Nam BW. The Relationships of Internet Addiction, Depression, and Suicidal ideation in Adolescents. *J Korean Acad Nurs* 2004; 34(1):102-110.

[33] Winkel S, Groen G, Petermann F. Social support in suicide forums. *Prax Kinderpsychol Kinderpsychiatr* 2005; 54(9):714-727.

[34] Becker K, Mayer M, Nagenborg M, El-Faddagh M, Schmidt MH. Parasuicide online: Can suicide websites trigger suicidal behavior in predisposed adolescents? *Nord J Psychiatry*. 2004; 58(2):111-114.

[35] Klostermann P, Ganswindt M, Schneider V. Suicide among adolescents and young adults. *Forensic Sci Int* 2005; 17; (suppl 147):41-42.

[36] Hawton K, Williams K. The connection between media and suicidal behavior warrants serious attention. *Crisis* 2001; 22:137-140.

[37] Schmidtke A, Schaller S. What do we know about media effects on imitation of suicidal behavior in sucide prevention: a holistic approach. Edited by Leo DD, Schmidtke A, Diekstra RWF.Dordrecht: Kluwer Academic, 1998, pp.121-137.

[38] Hagihara A, Tarumi K, Abe T. Media suicide-reports, Internet use and the occurrence of suicides between 1987 and 2005 in Japan. *BMC Public health* 2007:7:321.

[39] Cheng AT, Hawton K, Lee CT, Chen TH. The influence of media reporting of the suicide of a celebrity on suicide rates: a population-based study. *Int J Epidemiol* 2007; 36(6):1229-1234.

[40] Thompson S. The Internet and its potential influence on suicide. *Psychiatr Bull* 1999; 23:449-451.

[41] WHO, Department of Mental Health. *Mental and Behavioral Disorders.Preventing suicide a resource for media professionals.* Geneva, 2000

[42] Tam J, Tang WS, Fernando DJ. The internet and suicide: A double-edged tool. *Eur J Intern Med* 2007; 18(6):453-455.

[43] Stone DM, Barber CW, Potter L. Public health training online: the National Center for Suicide Prevention Training. *Am J Prev Med* 2005; 29(suppl 5):247-251.

[44] Hoffmann WA. Telematic technologies in mental health caring: a web-based psychoeducational program for adolescent suicide survivors. *Issues Ment Health Nurs* 2006; 27(5):461-474.

[45] Krysinska KE, De Leo D. Telecommunication and suicide prevention: hopes and challenges for the new century. *Omega* (Westport) 2007; 55(3):237-253.

[46] Gilat I, Shahar G. Emotional first aid for a suicide crisis: comparison between Telephonic hotline and internet. *Psychiatry* 2007; 70(1):12-18.

[47] Recupero PR, Harms SE, Noble JM. Googling Suicide: Surfing for Suicide Information on the Internet. *J Clin Psychiatry* 2008; 13:e1-e11.

[48] Hidaka Y, Operario D. Attempted suicide, psychological health and exposure to harassment among Japanese homosexual, bisexual or other men questioning their sexual orientation recruited via the internet. *J Epidemiol Community Health* 2006; 60(11):962-967.

[49] Murray CD, Macdonald S, Fox J. Body satisfaction, eating disorders and suicide ideation in an Internet sample of self-harmers reporting and not reporting childhood sexual abuse. *Psychol Health Med* 2008; 13(1):29-42.

[50] Wang YD, Phillips-Wren G, Forgionne G. E-delivery of personalized healthcare information to intermediaries for suicide prevention. *Int J Electron Health* 2005; 1(2):396-412.

[51] Swanton R, Collin P, Burns J, Sorensen I Engaging, understanding and including young people in the provision of mental health services. *Int J Adolesc Med Health* 2007; 19(3):325-332.

[52] .Hsiung RC. A suicide in an online mental health support group: reactions of the group members, administrative responses, and recommendations. *Cyberpsychol Behav* 2007; 10(4):495-500.

[53] Barak A, Bloch N. Factors related to perceived helpfulness in supporting highly distressed individuals through an online support chat. *Cyberpsychol Behav* 2006; 9(1):60-68.

[54] Pfeiffer-Gerschel T, Niedermeier N, Hegerl U. Modern discussion forum "depression, suicidality". *MMW Fortschr Med* 2006; 148(31-32):22-27.

[55] Mandrusiak M, Rudd MD, Joiner TE Jr, Berman AL, Van Orden KA, Witte T. Warning signs for suicide on the Internet: a descriptive study. *Suicide Life Threat Behav* 2006; 36(3):263-271.

[56] Mehlum L. The internet, suicide, and suicide prevention. *Crisis* 2000; 21(4):186-188.

[57] Becker K, Mayer M, Nagenborg M, El-Faddagh M, Schmidt MH. Parasuicide online: Can suicide websites trigger suicidal behavior in predisposed adolescents? *Nord J Psychiatry* 2004; 58(2):111-114.

In: Internet and Suicide
Editors: L. Sher and A. Vilens

ISBN 978-1-60741-077-5

Chapter 14

EXPLORING SELF-INJURY AND SUICIDE IN RELATION TO SELF-HARM DISCUSSION GROUPS ON THE INTERNET

Craig D. Murray and Jenny Shilton Osborne
Lancaster University, Lancaster, United Kingdom

ABSTRACT

In recent years concerns have been raised regarding the risk factors of on-line self-injury peer groups to exacerbate self-harming, suicidal behaviour by subscribed members. The current chapter considers these concerns with an illustrative, qualitative examination of the interactions of self-harming individuals on an Internet self-injury discussion group. Taken from a larger study, we present here an illustrative discourse analysis of the features and functions of posts to one Internet discussion group. This includes consideration of how individuals who self-injure represent themselves and their behaviour and how meanings and opinions are negotiated through on-line discussions. Here, discursive devices are highlighted which function to convey opinion as fact, externalise self-harming behaviour, remove blame from the individual and minimise agency, and construct significant others in particular ways. The possible implications of such discursive exchanges for the alleviation or exacerbation of self-injury are discussed. It is suggested that discourse analysis is appropriate and informative in the study of sensitive and controversial topics such as self-injury, in particular for improving knowledge of the meanings individuals assign to their behaviour, which in turn may inform and improve treatment interventions.

INTRODUCTION

Self-injurious behaviour is widely considered in the research literature to be a coping device used by individuals who have often suffered serious psychological trauma. [1-3] Individuals engaging in self-harming behaviour often report experiencing alienation, isolation, loneliness, chronic emptiness and extreme negative emotions. [4,5] While a variety of terms and definitions are in use, the present chapter focuses of injurious behaviours which involve deliberate self-inflicted damage to one's own body, such as cutting, banging, hitting, and scratching, [6,7] and the terms self-harm and self-injury are used interchangeably to refer to these behaviours.

Quantitative studies have been valuable in identifying risk factors associated with self-harm. Such research has found a clear increase in the behaviour in the teenage years, the highest rates being for those aged between 15-19 years old. [8] Females have also been found to have the highest incidence of self-injury. [9] It is often found in the context of psychiatric illnesses such as borderline personality disorder [10] and depression. [11]

A relatively smaller body of work has used qualitative methods to explore the points of view of those people who inflict harm on themselves. For example, interviews conducted with four young women self-harmers by Soloman and Farrand [1] highlighted deliberate self-harm as a form of coping. A similar qualitative approach was adopted by Harris, [12] who undertook a correspondence study with six women who engaged in self-harm. Self-injury was found to function as a communication of pain and distress, although not necessarily to a responsive or aware audience, and on occasions to express intense hatred and self-loathing. It was also reported to be a method of staying in control in an otherwise uncontrollable situation. The women reported experiencing an intense feeling of relief and calm after self-cutting, a release of tension and an emotional rush after a long period of depression, and expressed the importance to them of the sight of blood: "As the blood flows down the sink, so does the anger and anguish" (Harris [12], p.167).

The advent of the Internet provides new sources of social communication and support for collectives of people with common interests or concerns, such as self-harmers. Electronic discussion groups have the potential to provide readily accessible emotional support and social integration, from the comfort of home or the workplace, at any time of day and night. [13] The topic of self-harm is ubiquitous on the Internet, with hundreds of on-line discussion groups dedicated to the issue. The advantages of these groups over groups which meet face-to-face may help to explain the recent proliferation of self-harm Internet discussion groups as an attractive form of support. [8]

Although the Internet allows connectivity on a scale not previously possible between individuals who self-harm, it has been suggested that the Internet is a source of 'potentially destructive information' and as such may have a detrimental effect on some persons, making it 'difficult' for professionals working with self-harmers to recommend their 'surf[ing] the Internet' (p.400). [14] Health professionals who work with self-harmers may also be concerned that these groups do not usually involve trained counsellors, for example, but rely predominantly on peers who also self-injure.

In a study of help available over the Internet Prasad & Owens [15] found that this mainly took the form of information, advice and guidance, often with constructive and illustrative suggestions. They also found it very difficult to obtain information which could be used to commit further harm, and frequent warnings if a post was likely to 'trigger' self-harm, suggesting the most frequent function of Internet resources is alleviation. Murray & Fox [16] addressed the question of whether Internet discussion groups exacerbate or alleviate self-harming behaviour using questionnaires responded to by users of an on-line self-harm forum. Administering both open and closed questions, and applying content analysis on the answers to the open questions, Murray & Fox concluded that the self-harming discussion group either reduced or did not affect the self-harming behaviour of the users.

More recently Whitlock, Powers & Eckenrode [17] examined the messages posted on self-injury discussion groups. Using content analysis, they concluded that on-line interactions provide important social support for members who would otherwise be socially isolated. However, they expressed a concern that such messages might normalise and encourage self-injurious behaviour. The posts made to self-injury discussion groups may, for example, contain the type of detail which the media have been urged to avoid when reporting on suicides so as not to encourage the behaviour in others, such as 'how to' descriptions and the presentation of the behaviour as a means to solve problems. [18]

Although the above work provides inroads to understanding how self-harm discussion groups may impact upon the self-harming behaviour of discussants and 'lurkers' (those who read but do not post messages), to date there has not been an examination of the exchanges which take place on such forums using a data analytical approach with clearly elaborated theoretical underpinnings. The current chapter presents just such an examination. A qualitative research method, discourse analysis, is used to explore how self-harmers present themselves in an on-line forum, and how they explain their behaviour.

The discourse analysis (DA) paradigm was developed during the 1980s and 90s and represents a radical departure from the traditional cognitive approach in psychology. Discourse based work has made problematic the use of quantitative studies of attitudes and beliefs as it has been argued that there is variability in the expression of these by individuals across different contexts, and that the representation of participants' internal mental state by items within such work is questionable. [19] Within this view standard psychological topics are re-conceptualised as discourse practises [20] and there has been critique and reworking of a range of psychological concepts including attribution [21,22] and attitudes. [19,23] Moreover, this shift has been accompanied by a call to study naturally occurring data rather than that which is produced as part of an experiment, questionnaire or interview study. [20]

One of the main contentions from the discursive perspective is that whereas traditionally language has been conceived of as representing direct expressions of thought, discourse should more appropriately be studied as social action. [24] In this approach, rather than event descriptions being directly derived from how people perceive and understand the world, accounts are seen to be pragmatically constructed. [25,26] A common analytical theme is that people use language to do things [23] and events can be described in a range of different ways, depending upon the orientation of the speaker or writer. [19-26]

The data drawn upon in this chapter is naturally occurring data - written conversations which occurred on a self-injury Internet discussion group between distally-located participants - but conversations all the same. The data comprised 52 threads (conversations) over a three-month period. While claims about what has happened in these conversations can be made, it is not appropriate to argue for the extrapolation of any conclusions drawn from the analysis to any wider population of either self-harmers or world-wide-web users. However, this does not undermine the validity of using such a method. In-depth and detailed observations can be made as regards to such actions as apportioning blame and the justifications provided for self-harming behaviour within the context in which they appear.

The analytical procedure here involved the repeated reading and cyclical analysis of discussion 'threads', with the following questions in focus: How does the individual present him/herself? Does the individual present any justification for his/her behaviour? How does this shape the reader's possible interpretation of them? What devices have been used to present this reading? What and how are social actions being performed?

The qualitative approach adopted here contrasts with quantitative, statistically based approaches which aim to quantify and investigate the frequency of devices revealed through that analysis. Here, no attempt is made at quantification as the interest is in how and why accounts are presented in particular ways rather than how often. However, the discourse analytical approach also contrasts with other qualitative approaches which treat language as the medium or vehicle through which thoughts, beliefs, opinions, and experiences are passively transmitted from one person to another.

Discursive psychology treats the notion of *accounts as accurately and simply reflecting reality* as problematic, rejecting the notion of a world 'out there' which can be simply summarised, described and predicted. Therefore the aim here is not to make generalisations concerning particular interactional phenomena but to highlight the ways in which speakers manage factuality through the collaborative construction of self-harming behaviour and related experiences. Furthermore the analysis produced hinges upon the theoretical questions asked, and does not claim to be exhaustive. Indeed it has been suggested that any discourse analysis can only be provisional. [25]

Within our illustrative analysis here we highlight emergent discursive themes of how members of the discussion group represent other people in contrast with users of the site; how they construct self-harming behaviour as addictive; and how they present the physical and psychological effects of self-injury.

THE CONSTRUCTION OF 'US' AND 'THEM'

The people who communicate via the on-line group examined here are most likely to be people who self-injure, given that this is the topic of the board. Therefore there is an already assumed common ground between the members. Given that self-harm is a culturally unacceptable behaviour it is likely that members will also have had similar interactions with other people, and may have experienced similar stigma. References to people who did not engage in self-harm, be they friends, family members, or people who were unknown to the members, was common. This may function as a cohesive device for the group, as a way of dividing the world into 'us' and 'them', where accusations of ignorance can be made, and *this* can be interpreted as the source of any conflict rather than the behaviour of the people who self-injure. The below excerpts, sequential exchanges on the board between three members, are illustrative of this issue:

[Posted by Sally]

had a very rough day emotionally today. was having anxiety and was upset over something. pretty much to the point that i was freaking out. couldnt seem to think straight. couldnt deal with all the emotions/feelings so i cut myself. not bad, its never too bad. anyways i even tried talking to people but that only made it worse when one person was so unsympathetic. so i cried then i cut. what an exhausting day emotionally. maybe i would have gotten more/better support if i came here first

[First Response Posted by Pumpkin]

if u find the people around you unsupportive, try internet chat rooms or helplines...people who are used to these kinds of problem are usually more helpful in my experience

[Second Response Posted by Fairy]

I feel like that a lot too... and nobody seems to think that its a big deal and just shrug it off

Sally's message is presented as though she could have been writing in her diary, so she may have treated the exercise in part as a way to make concrete her interpretation of her experience. If nobody had replied, then she would not necessarily have been ignored as she did not explicitly direct her message to anyone, and she does not appear to have been rejected. She makes no mention of the site until the last line. She uses the passive tense "was having anxiety" and "was upset" rather than "I was anxious" which places the locus of the emotions externally, as if they were happening *to* her due to an outside force, rather than there being something *about her* which caused the emotions. She uses the term "freaking out" to express the severity of the situation, a phrase which has connotations of not being in control, and an extreme emotional state which provides a justification for why she might cut, minimising opportunities to attribute blame to herself. She is vague about what it was that caused her to feel anxious ("was upset over something"), which serves her emphasis on the reaction of her friends.

Her construction of friends is negative and provides further justification for her cutting; they were "so unsympathetic". She contrasts this with the ethos of the site and the empathy of the members who give "more/better support". Her attempt at using another method of support is constructed as failing due to the insensitivity of her friends, and is further identified as contributing significantly to the impetus for her to self-injure.

Pumpkin responds with the 'If...then' formulation described by Edwards [26] as portraying predictable and logical events ("if...try"). Sneijder & te Molder [27] suggest that by responding in this way, a respondent is claiming a certain expertise on the subject, first by choosing to respond, and second by suggesting a certain course of action which they imply has worked before or has predictable consequences. Pumpkin's claim that she has herself experienced this adds further supports to her authority.

In her reply, Pumpkin both implicitly accepts Sally's construction of her friends as unhelpful by not questioning it, and explicitly orients to her comment that the support given by resources such as the discussion group is better and more sympathetic than other sources. Fairy responds rather differently, although to similar effect. She orients instead to the construction of unhelpful friends, and supports Sally's claim about her friends by drawing on her own experience. Again, Fairy corroborates (and therefore implicitly validates) Sally's experience, but both use vague descriptions ("nobody seems to..." "…tried talking to people…") which are difficult to challenge. Both present themselves as the victims of unsympathetic, insensitive friends who reject their requests for support. This serves as another justification for cutting; not only was Sally feeling emotionally distraught but her friends' rejection served to push her to breaking point, so cutting seemed to be her only solution.

There is often an implicit construction of friends and relatives having different values to the members of the group. This is represented by comments in the analysed threads such as "they don't really understand, do they?...it upsets her [a friend she once confided in] and makes her uncomfortable…" and "Everyone looks down on it [the scars and cutting], but they don't realise how much it does for me…I'm tired of people thinking I'm a freak for doing it…" (Messed_Up). In these excerpts, the responsibility for understanding the self-harm is placed on other people. This in effect presents other people as 'the ones with the problem'. Goffman [28] found this was a common occurrence in groups of stigmatised individuals – in societies where such people spend a larger amount of time feeling isolated and alienated, these situations provide an opportunity to feel accepted and normal. Given that the community on this message board is one for which self-injury is a regular occurrence, it is important for members that in *this* community, *they* are the normal ones and others are abnormal.

Another way to make sense of the reactions of other people is to attribute it to certain personality characteristics. In this sense, again, the members are portrayed as normal, easy to understand, and others are 'cruel', hateful or uncompassionate: "the people at my school…are extremely cruel…" (Messed_Up); and "they're evidently rather stupid, spiteful fickle and feeble…[t]hey're rather cruelly fucking you about now, as they shall in the future if they're so whole-heartedly obsessed with popularity and such cynical creatures" (Johnno). The last excerpt was in response to a post by Messed_Up, although in a different conversation, in which she presented a catalogue of events leading to her general unhappiness and self-harm, some of which revolved around the reactions of her friends to her self-harm. The aggressive response by Johnno, using profanities to refer directly to the school friends and his strong, abusive language, make clear his feelings towards 'unsympathetic' friends. He locates blame for their reaction to Messed_Up internally to them, constructing the situation where she is a victim and has been mistreated. Furthermore, it is a *permanent* feature of their behaviour, thus nothing to do with how Messed_Up may have behaved. In fact, they're not even human, he declares, referring to them as "creatures" to further increase the gap between Messed_Up and her friends.

Construction of Cutting as an Addiction

It is a regular feature of discourse that blame is externalized in order to justify why some action is taken. For an action as serious, dangerous and culturally unacceptable as self-harm, the justification for this will have to be persuasive. Establishing self-injury in discourses as an addiction is one way of externalizing the blame for this behaviour. If a behaviour is addictive it is almost impossible to avoid; it is a physiological dependence, one which is necessary for the body to function. Addictions are also implied to be due to the nature of the thing that is addict*ive*, not due to the nature of the person who is addict*ed*, which again, localises the blame outside of the individual. This discursive theme is illustrated by the below exchange:

[Posted by Messed_Up]

i dont find self harm bad, just horrible bcoz of scars
i just dont understand exactly why im still thinking of self harm, im quite happy now-
but still all these ideas come into my head....

[Response Posted by James Bright]

The harm is, at least to my feeling, the chance for slipping and doing more damage than you intended, and the chance for side effects depending on method.
Sounds like the beginning of an addiction. It is an incredibly addictive behaviour--be careful of getting yourself further hooked on it.

Messed_Up purports to be happy, but still thinking about harming herself, which implies a certain level of it being beyond her control. James Bright picks up especially on this implication and orients directly to it: "sounds like the beginning of an addiction". He detaches responsibility for this diagnosis by using the passive tense and avoiding the use of "I". This implies it would be a diagnosis anyone could or would make, but it also implies some authority on the subject, which he then compounds by stating that it is in fact an "incredibly addictive behaviour". The hyperbole serves to emphasise the extent of the addictiveness of the behaviour, which also minimises the agency Messed_Up has and justifies her behaviour to some extent. His cautionary comment for her to be careful implies that it is not entirely beyond her control. The following extract illustrates how a discourse of 'cutting as an addictive behaviour' can be used in an attempt to persuade a user of the on-line group to find alternative methods of coping.

[Posted byAngel]

I don't know if I'll get shouted at for this being "bad taste" or whatever, so if I'm wrong I apologise and I won't come back. I just don't know where else to go for this.
I want to cut tonight as I haven't felt as depressed as I do tonight in my entire life, but I wanted to ask this before I can't hold back from doing it any longer; are there any guides or safety tips out there regarding cutting
Thanks for your time.
-me, UK

[Response Posted by Pandora]

i'd rather you find other ways to cope with feeling so bad, so that cutting isn't necessary.
cutting's amazingly addictive, and has lots of ramifications down the road.
how about talking to someone, instead? that's what your local crisis number is for, if you don't have any friends you can confide in.
good luck tonight. -pandora

Angel writes giving the impression that she has never cut before, but has considered it before now. The hyperbolic statement "I haven't felt as depressed as I do tonight in my entire life" provides a justification for why she wants to cut. Pandora replies within an hour, and signs off wishing Angel 'good luck', supporting a discourse of the behaviour not being within Angel's control.

Pandora orients to Angel's request for advice on how to cut, and tries to persuade her to find another way to cope. Here, she tries to negotiate a certain behaviour in the recipient by using the construction "I'd rather you...". She justifies her suggestion by highlighting the addictive nature of self-injury and the long-term implications it might have for her. Like James Bright she adds the hyperbole 'amazingly' to 'addictive' to emphasise how easy it might be to become addicted, justifying not only Angel's urge to cut, but also her own and anyone else on the site's behaviour. In order that she does not leave Angel without any help Pandora makes a suggestion about what else she could try – talking rather than cutting. There is a construction here of cutting stemming from a need to communicate feelings and doing this will relieve the urge to cut.

The Physical and Physiological Effects of Self-harming

The discursive theme of self-injury as addictive is further supported by interactions between members which constructed the physical effects of the behaviour as pleasurable or as easing psychological discomfort:

[Posted by Misunderstood]

I was just wondering, how would you lot describe the way cutting makes you feel?
Because i just cut myself, and i've just noted that i become cold and shiver a lot, and the cuts itch a lot if they're shallow ones.

[First Response Posted by Andy]

it makes me feel less aggressive and gets rid of pent up emotion inside of me. My temperature sensor thingy seems to go completely crazy, i go from feeling too hot to feeing too cold, but sometimes I just feel too hot and sweat

[Second Response Posted by Alone]

It felt good. It's like the feeling after masturbation, as/after the orgasm is ebbing away.

[Third Response Posted by Sd_Nd]

Hmm...I can't really describe it. It releases something, and mends some of the pain. Adds the (momentarily and temporarily) possibility to go on for a little while longer.

[Fourth Response Posted by James Bright]

It mostly just feels "right" when I do it, I don't really know how to express it

Misunderstood places herself outside the group momentarily using the term "you lot" to describe other members, but this also makes it clear that she is addressing the whole of the rest of the group. The colloquial term is how one might greet a group of friends and establishes an easy and friendly relationship between her and the other users. To increase the chances of some people answering her question, Misunderstood offers her own response, which also demonstrates the kind of answer she is looking for – she is referring to physical symptoms. Andy's response at first offers psychological reasons for cutting (decreasing aggression and providing a release), and then he addresses his physiological symptoms. The physiological symptoms seem to be reminiscent of how one might talk about how an addiction is felt, addressed earlier.

Alone describes the feeling as entirely pleasurable, and natural, as does James Bright. One interpretation here is that if it feels good, then it it is easier to understand as a logical act. Sd_Nd conveys that he is giving deep consideration to how to describe how it feels, thus assigning relative importance to the nature of the question. As well as describing the release it gives him, he also talks about it in terms of staying alive – 'if I didn't cut I wouldn't be here'. It is a potent, extreme argument to claim that the choice is either to cut or die, with the choice to cut being positioned as the preferable course of action. This justification is also used in another conversation about whether self-harmers always eventually commit suicide: "I SI to avoid suicide...if I didn't SI I think I would probably have been dead by now" (Pumpkin).

Another way of presenting self-injury is as a failure. While we may accept and try to understand that someone does something because it is pleasurable, a stronger emotional response is given in this circumstance. Sympathy is the appropriate response to someone who is trying very hard to do something, yet admits their failure. This is how Tabitha presents her situation.

[Posted by Tabitha]

hi guys
i hadn't cut since a year back in August and today i cut myself to shreds. I'm such a failure and I'll never be free of this. It was either cutting or doing something worse.
i can't believe I've not cut in such a long time and then today i go and flush all my good work down the toilet.
i've been feeling more depressed again lately and i'm now on the max dosage of lofepramine again. i don't think the're working.
i'm devastated at my failure. just want to go to bed and forget all about it. i get very tired as well after i cut.
The usual endorphins kick in when i was cutting and i love to see the blood flow down my body. it's so calming.
got docs on tuesday. he'll be so disappointed with me. not looking forward to that.
sorry.
xxx

[Response Posted by Laura]

Don't feel bad about it..it happened but theres nothing you can do about it now...don't feel ashamed..you did what you thought was best and what may have saved you from doing something even worse my heart goes out to you
laura

Tabitha's post is emotionally charged. She uses metaphors to describe how she is feeling and what she has just done, such as "cut myself to shreds", how she "flushed her good work down the toilet" and she'll "never be free". This rhetoric is descriptive and compelling; constructing the behaviour as an external force with a physical hold over her. Emotionally laden words like "devastated" and "failure" add to the texture of the message.

She lets the reader know that she has been able not to cut for almost a year and a half, which is a year and a half of success. Having now cut she is upset with herself, and it is not something which she felt she had control over at the time. Tabitha gives several justifications for her having cut – she has been feeling depressed recently; the medication she was taking has failed to work; and the cathartic effect of cutting, seeing the blood flow and the physical effect of the endorphins which take effect. This firstly places blame on external circumstances for the medication failing to relieve her depression, and secondly constructs self-injury as a pleasurable experience, which has been discussed above.

However, Tabitha also implies some sort of responsibility toward her support mechanisms, by saying of her doctor "he'll be so disappointed in me", and to the group, "sorry". This seems paradoxical given that other parts of her message imply she is not responsible, but it can be taken as an acknowledgment that perhaps she could have done more to avoid cutting, despite the elements of her life which she feels have been failing her recently.

Tabitha's message elicits a sympathetic response from Laura, who accepts Tabitha's construction of it being beyond her control. She uses the passive tense to describe the event ("it happened") minimising Tabitha's agency. She consoles Tabitha, and says that it was better to do that than something worse, implying that she was in a desperate situation and may have committed suicide had she not cut and so made a good choice.

CONCLUSION

Within this chapter we have focussed on providing an illustrative (rather than exhaustive) discourse analysis of the discursive interactions between members on an on-line Internet discussion group for self-harmers. This work is in part a response to recent concerns over the possible negative impact that such groups may have on the self-harming behaviour of those who read and respond to other members' posts. We do not claim to offer any definitive answer as to the net benefit of participation in such groups, nor can we claim that the group under consideration in our analysis presented here are typical of all self-harm discussion groups. However, our analysis does find, contrary to some of the concerns expressed to date, interactions which are designed by participants to be supportive, to contribute to positive self-esteem (for instance by constructing potentially negative personal attributes as separate to the person) and to aid in the normative goal (for the group in this study) of cessation from self-injury.

From the diversity of topics on the discussion group, a number of discursive themes emerged following the analysis. This included constructions and attributions regarding self-harmers and self-harming behaviour, as well as the construction and positioning of important others. Distinctions were made between the users of the site and others, including friends and relatives, and they were often constructed as insensitive and not trying to understand why people engaged in self-injury. The behaviour of the users was frequently justified and explained in terms of things outside of their own control. For example, cutting was reported to be an addiction, a pleasurable experience, and understandable in terms of the gravity of the life situations the individuals were experiencing. That cutting is an addiction was not contested, although functioned in one instance as a plea to avoid cutting and find other ways of coping. Thus cutting was not always presented in a positive light.

Propensity for agency was frequently minimised, by the posters themselves, and their responders, which also served to externalise blame for their actions. Group cohesion was attended to in many cases, by calling on the role the group played in mutual support, and by alluding to common ground or similar emotional experiences between users. The group seemed to function as a method of exploration and exchange of ideas, and conversation was frequently geared towards justifying behaviour, but not encouraging it. Members attempted to discourage others from engaging in self-injury. Justifications were provided both by posters and responders, demonstrating that this was an important function of the group. Justifications consisted of the addictive nature of cutting, the pleasurable nature of it, and unpleasant and difficult life circumstance. However, these justifications were not advanced as arguments for the indefinite continuation of self-injury, but more often as account of the difficulties involved in cessation and for lapses in attempts at cessation.

In summary, the present work provides an illustration of how discursive analyses of the communications between members of on-line self-injury discussion groups can begin to address the concerns which have been raised about them. We hope that the work presented here encourages further research in this important area.

REFERENCES

[1] Soloman Y, Farrand J: "Why don't you do it properly?" Young women who self-injure. *J Adolesc* 1996; 19: 111-119.

[2] Pembroke L: Only scratching the surface. *Nurs Times* 1998; 94: 38-39.

[3] Gratz KL: Risk factors for and functions of deliberate self-harm: An empirical and conceptual review. *Clin Psychol: Science and Practice* 2003; 10: 192-205.

[4] Favazza AR, Conterio K: The plight of chronic self-mutilators. *Community Ment Health J* 1998; 24: 252-269.

[5] Warm A, Murray C, Fox J: Why do people self-harm? *Psychology Health and Medicine* 2003; 8(1): 71-79.

[6] Favazza AR: The coming of age of self-mutilation. *Journal of Nervous and Mental Disease* 1998; 186: 259-268.

[7] Feldman MD: The challenge of self-mutilation: A review. *Compr Psychiatry* 1998; 29: 252-269.

[8] Warm A, Murray C, Fox J: Who helps? Supporting people who self-harm. *J Ment Health* 2002; 11(2): 121-130.

[9] Hawton K, Fagg J, Simkin S, Bale E, Bond A: Trends in deliberate self-harm in Oxford, 1985-1995. *Br J Psychiatry* 1997; 171: 556-560.

[10] Linehan MM: *Cognitive-Behavioral Treatment of Borderline Personality Disorder.* New York, Guildford Press. 1993.

[11] Hawton K, Kingsbury S, Steinhardt K: Repetition of deliberate self-harm by adolescents: the role of psychological factors. J Adolesc 1999; 22: 369-378.

[12] Harris J: Self-harm: Cutting the bad out of me. *Qualitative Health Research* 2000; 10(2): 164-173.

[13] Murray CD, Sixsmith J: Qualitative health research via the Internet: practical and methodological issues. *Health Informatics J* 2002; 8: 47-53.

[14] Thompson S: Suicide and the internet. *Psychiatr Bull R Coll Psychiatr* 2001; 25: 400.

[15] Prasad V, Owens D: Using the internet as a source of self-help for people who self-harm. *Psychiatr Bull R Coll Psychiatr* 2001; 25: 222-225.

[16] Murray CD, Fox J: Do internet self-harm discussion groups alleviate or exacerbate self-harming behaviour? *Australian e-Journal for the Advancement of Mental Health* (AeJAMH) 2006; 5(3): 1-9.

[17] Whitlock JL, Powers JL, Eckenrode J: The virtual cutting edge: The Internet and adolescent self-injury. *Dev Psychol* 2006; 42(3): 407-417.

[18] World Federation for Mental Health: Responsible media reporting guidelines. In Building Awareness - Reducing Risk: Mental Illness and Suicide. *World Mental Health Day Project,* 2006 [Global Education Packet]. Available from www.wfmh.org/wmhday 2006.htm

[19] Potter J, Wetherell M: *Discourse and social psychology: Beyond attitudes and behaviour*. London, Sage. 1987.

[20] Edwards D, Potter J: *Discursive psychology.* London, Sage. 1992.

[21] Edwards D, Potter J: The Chancellor's memory: Rhetoric and truth in discursive remembering. *Applied Cognitive Psychology* 1992, 6: 187-215.

[22] Edwards D: Script formulations: An analysis of event descriptions in conversation. *Journal of Language and Social Psychology* 1994; 13: 211-247.

[23] Gill R: Discourse analysis: Practical implementation. In Richardson, J.E.T. (ed) *Handbook of qualitative research methods for psychology and the social sciences. Leicester,* British Psychological Society. 1996.

[24] Potter J, Wetherell M, Gill R, Edwards D: Discourse: Noun, verb or social practise? *Philosophical Psychology* 1990; 3: 205-217.

[25] Billig M: Rhetorical and discursive analysis: How families talk about the Royal Family. In N. Hayes (Ed.) *Doing qualitative analysis in Psychology London,* Psychology Press. 1997 (pp.39-54).

[26] Edwards D: *Discourse and Cognition.* London, Sage. 1997.

[27] Sneijder P, Te Molder FM: Health should not have to be a problem': Talking health and accountability in an Internet forum on veganism. *J Health Psychol* 2004; 9(4): 599-616.

[28] Goffman E: Stigma: *Notes on the Management of Spoiled Identity.* New Jersey USA, Penguin Books. 1963.

In: Internet and Suicide
Editors: L. Sher and A. Vilens
ISBN 978-1-60741-077-5

Chapter 15

"ACROSS THE STREET – NOT DOWN THE ROAD" - STAYING ALIVE THROUGH DELIBERATE SELF-HARM

Inger Ekman and Stig Söderberg
Umeå University, Umeå, Sweden

ABSTRACT

While the psychiatric therapeutic community is focused on individual diagnostic tools to understand deliberate self harm, self-destructive acts among young persons in Western society is increasing to a level where it arguably must be regarded as a cultural rather than an individual problem. While psychiatry adheres to its expert role, trying to find explanations for the individual behaviour in past life experiences and subsequent personality formation, the world outside of the therapy room is changing. In this outside world, on the Internet deliberate self harm is not described as a pathological behaviour that needs to be corrected, but as a powerful tool to cope with present life stressors, a way to form an identity and even as a way of staying alive. Against a background of present trends in society and how these influence identity formation, these narratives give important clues for finding new approaches to the experiences and life strategies of young persons living in modern society. In encounters with young persons whose self-harming acts have become intimately woven into the fabric of life, the keys to opening up different perspectives and find other ways to cope probably can not be found without accrediting the strength and determination inherent in the self-harming acts and closely and attentively pay attention to their own understanding of the situation, their own strengths and their own abilities.

INTRODUCTION

- "We've got this new patient at the ward; a young woman with repeated self-destructiveness, now in inpatient care for the first time after a quite serious suicide attempt".
- "Probably a borderline case".
- "We need a thorough evaluation". (Morning conversation at the clinic)

This young woman had been cutting herself frequently the last few years. This time, the cut was a little too deep and the bloodshed too profuse for her to handle it on her own, so she had sought emergency care. After a few stitches she had been referred for psychiatric evaluation, had been regarded suicidal and was now involuntarily admitted to inpatient care. "It wasn't down the road, it was across the street, don't you understand", she said as we met – referring to the well known metaphor on the Internet "Down the road - not across the street" for wrist-cutting with suicide intent. We did not understand, at the time.

What else did we not understand? What other themes in her life did we not acknowledge? Was her narrative of her situation properly captured in the records? Sad to say, it was not. In retrospective, in the records we find diagnostic tests, diagnostic discussions and a focus on how she would fit into a certain diagnosis. After being dismissed from the ward this young woman had no further contact with the psychiatric clinic – but in an interview seven years later she declared "I fit the diagnosis, but the diagnosis didn't fit me" [1].

NUMBERS, LABELS AND ILLUSIONS

Self-destructive acts, especially among young women, are increasing in the Western world, as well as in urbanized parts of the developing countries. Since the self-destructive acts usually are not brought to medical attention, the frequency is hard to assess, but a large-scale self-report survey in England, including 6020 adolescents, reported acts of self-harm among 11.2 % of the girls and 3.2 % of the boys during the last year [2]. Among these, only 12.6 % had sought medical attention due to the act. Similar figures are found in other reports during the last few years. The magnitude of these figures indicates self-destructiveness to be a cultural rather than an individual phenomenon.

In psychiatry, the focus is still diagnostic, regarding self-destructiveness as an expression of a disorder of the individual. The diagnostic powers of psychiatry, and the ever-increasing number of intricate and detailed diagnoses in the manual, usually results in a match for a disorder of some kind [3]. As the self-destructive acts are often associated with impulsivity, instability of affect and vague identity formation in a maturing individual, criteria for a personality disorder are often met, especially borderline personality disorder, a diagnosis which includes self-destructiveness as one of the criteria [4]. Among persons seeking medical attention due to recent self-destructive acts, a borderline personality has been identified in up to 55% [5].

But, what is a borderline personality disorder? Peter Tyrer [6] has described the borderline concept as a motley diagnosis in need of reform, a prediagnosis with little intrinsic value because of its heterogeneity, and acknowledges that the concept was borrowed from horticulture, where it signifies the border between two crops – and in such a borderline area anything may grow. He argues that the concept may hold no core whatsoever. Andrew Skodol [7] has shown that a borderline personality disorder may appear in 151 different shapes, as there are that many different combinations of the nine criteria. In this way, two individuals, both diagnosed with a borderline personality disorder, may share only one common characteristic. There is also a lack of empirical support for a qualitative distinction between normal and abnormal personality functioning [7]. Furthermore, the borderline personality disorder diagnosis, although regarded to be related to personality traits, time and again has shown poor stability over time [8]. Due to observations like these, the diagnosis is at present strongly questioned, and a substantial revision is due [9].

Judith Butler [10] has described that every categorization of an individual means exclusion of important characteristics of this person, and that knowing what someone "is" only brings the uncertainty of what this categorization really signifies about the individual. So really, what is the rationale of the present diagnostic concept, still commonly used to try to conceptualize the characteristics and needs of a young person? What does the use of such a concept signify, what does it convey about the state of the psychiatric community? Does it amount to anything more than a label aimed at upholding an illusion of expert knowledge?

On the Internet

Quite a different focus is found outside of the therapy room, in real life encounters with young persons or on the Internet. On the Internet, search terms like "cut myself", "self harm" or "self injury" will result in literally millions of hits. Interspersed with sites trying to explain the behaviour and offer advice, and some quite nasty stuff aimed at triggering severe self-destructive acts, you will find narratives of people who engage in self-harming acts, describing their life experiences and their life situation without the filter of the diagnosing professional. In these narratives of young persons, another perspective than that of the diagnostic community is presented, a perspective with a different focus. In these narratives, the self-inflicted physical pain is described as a way to deal with quite common stressors in life, a way to handle frustration and cope with mental pain. Self harm is described as a way to get relief, to feel better. Watching the blood flow is described as a way to release the pain and stress bottled up inside, bringing a sense of calmness, even of beauty. Some also describe their self-harming acts as giving a sense of identity, an identity different from others.

Albeit, the acts are often associated with feelings of shame, and measures are taken to keep it secret from others. There are several descriptions of futile attempts to refrain from self-harming acts, but time and again resorting back to it, finding no equally powerful alternative. In such narratives, the help offered by psychiatry has often been tried and proven invalid.

The relief that the self-harming acts bring is often described as addictive, as an otherwise inarticulate and unbearable inner pain is focused to the wound. The inner pain is suddenly visible, tangible, measurable. This deep this time. These many wounds. This much pain. So deep and so wide is the pain that needs to be expressed that this time it is not only the arms, but also the legs, the thighs, the stomach… Sometimes the act may almost be ritualized, with measures to collect and sometimes save the blood. In these narratives, self-cutting is often described as a life-preserving and even life-affirmative activity – a way to endure, to go on, to stay alive yet a while. There are also narratives of the comfort brought by the visible proof of the bloodflow – that life must not go on, that it is possible to escape, to end the inner pain and frustration for good. "Down the road, not across the street". Across the street this time – maybe down the road later on…

To Understand or to Listen?

The narratives found on the Internet by people who engage in self-harming acts correspond well with the narratives of persons we meet in clinical practice, referred for psychiatric evaluation due to their behaviour and the fright this has awoken among relatives and/or professionals. The behaviour holds a tinge of strangeness to the world of established professionals, whose life experiences usually differ considerably from that of the young person. Within the clinical setting, the initial impulse is often to seek for reasons and to try to explain the behaviour. Measures are taken to find a background variable behind the self-destructiveness, such as an insurmountable life trauma; abuse, early abandonment or dysfunctional family relationships, and personality traits developed on this basis. Due to such preconceptions of the professional, the dialogue is diverted from the present pressures of life and the place of the self-destructiveness in the current life strategies of the person. Self-destructiveness is easily regarded as a symptom that must be taken care of and eliminated, the sooner the better. A genuine understanding based on the person's own narrative of the situation is seldom accomplished in this way.

In the attempts to understand and explain the behaviour, psychiatry often resorts to generalized categorizations, focusing common traits among persons with self-destructive behaviour, and classifies the behaviour as an expression of self-hate, difficulties in affect regulation and suchlike. But, as becomes obvious when listing the 151 variants of the Borderline personality disorder [7], what characterizes a group must not needs characterize the individual in question [11], and there are substantial dangers in approaching the experience of an individual with the help of generalized categories. Through the generalization the nuances of the narrative go unobserved, and individual experiences are transformed to "typical" behaviour of a category of persons, instead of being respected as a young person's own way to try to handle her situation. Such an approach may lead to severe neglect of current experiences and pressures on the individual, and may distort an adequate understanding of the situation, and hinder a process of mutual work in coming to terms with the actual stressors behind the present self-harming acts.

On the Internet, as well as in clinical practice, if you listen attentively you may find statements such as "I don't hurt myself because I hate myself, but I hate myself because I hurt myself". In narratives like this, self-destructiveness and self-hate are intertwined, without a clear-cut linear connection. Rather, there is a circular connection, without any obvious starting point or endpoint, without discernable cause and effect, intimately woven into the fabric of life. Possibly it is in this circular fabric we may find the keys to try other ways to deal with the stressors – and the only expert on this fabric is the young person herself.

TO STAY CLOSE

For a young person who has come to use self-harming acts as a way to cope with the life situation, the attempts of the grown-ups to understand and explain the behaviour in terms of a linear connection, cause and effect, is seldom helpful. Instead, on the Internet you will find descriptions of the help gained from someone who listened attentively because they did not understand, and did not try to explain. Someone gained their trust by being there to listen, ask questions, try to get a picture of the situation and respect and even stand by them in their way of coping with their situation. Time and time again, such a relationship is described to have been crucial for the ability to come to terms with the situation and find other ways to cope.

The descriptions in these narratives on the Internet are affirmed in research investigating the perspective of young women with a history of self-harm [12]. The descriptions are also supported by clinical research [1], where persons who formerly resorted to self-harming behaviour describe the process that enabled them to leave this behaviour behind. In these narratives, psychiatry and the focus offered in psychiatric care is often described as one of the things that had to be left behind to be able to come to terms with life. Instead, the support of someone who showed honest and sincere interest in them, and offered predictability in the relationship, pawed the way for change. In accord with these narratives, such elements of the relationship has been shown to be the basic prerequisite to gain and continue to deserve trust from a person who for different reasons have difficulties in trusting others [13;14].

IS THERE A PLACE FOR PSYCHIATRY?

The young woman referred to in the introduction was severely misunderstood in her first encounter with clinical psychiatry – and her story is not an exception. Psychiatry, with its focus on diagnosis and treatment, may distort or even pervert the identity formation of a maturing individual, who may accept the diagnostic concept applied on her situation, and start adapting to traits within the concept that until then was of no relevance to her. Diagnostics tend to bind a person to how the professional perceives the situation, and continue treatment based on such a (mis)conception, adhering to what Bateson calls a dormitive principle [11]. The diagnostic concept implies a process that is separate from the person, with its own course, regardless of the context of the patient [15]. Accordingly, traditional psychotherapeutic models of treatment often show to be unfruitful for persons with repeated self-harming behaviour [16], and the experience of not getting any help tends to accentuate the symptoms [1;16].

However, among those with self-harming acts there are persons whose self-destructive acts are related to having suffered severely dysfunctional relationships, abandonment, emotional neglect or emotional/sexual abuse in childhood [17], and due to these experiences have far-reaching needs of support. Their self-destructiveness is usually related to feelings of despair and a perceived unbearableness of the present situation or frame of mind, and a sense of lack of control over life circumstances [17;18;19]. For these persons, there is often need for well-structured long-term treatment with close and frequent interaction, such as treatment centres, which seems to be necessary to broaden the basis for understanding their life circumstances and ways of thinking [20]. A process of trust demands sincerity and predictability [21], and this standpoint is verified in the experience of the two therapeutic models that so far have shown positive results in working professionally with persons with repeated severe self-harming behaviour; the dialectical behavior therapy of Marsha Linehan [22] and the mentalization based programmes of Anthony Bateman and Peter Fonagy [23;24]. They are both characterized by reliable and easily accessible long-term relationships with predictable roles as a basis for therapeutic work. Such treatment methods are witnessed to be of crucial importance for recovery [1;25] and recent research shows that such methods can dramatically increase the rate of improvement [16].

For this reason, when meeting someone who has committed self-harming acts, it is important to keep an open mind for narratives of severe traumatic experiences, to be able to look for adequate support early in the process [20].

The Pace of Change

Psychiatry of today has developed methods for offering help to those whose self-harming acts are related to severe traumatic life experiences. But what about the others – those whose self-destructiveness is interwoven with their present life experiences, the pressures of the day, as an anxiety relief and a way to cope – those whose narratives correspond with those often found on the Internet?

As the increasing rates of deliberate self-harm among the young in Western society seems to be culturally mediated, and possibly related to changes in society during the last decades, the answer to the above question depends on our understanding of the present trends in this culture, and the associated exposures and experiences of young persons of today.

Within sociology, Anthony Giddens [26] denotes the accelerating pace of change and the increasing focus on individualism as a profound power, influencing our identity formation and the way we experience ourselves, especially when we are young. The demand on individual choices regarding everything from cellphones to sexual preferences is ever growing in modern Western society, and the practical and moral choices available are multiplying by the numbers. The pace of change is so fast that it is almost impossible to get an accurate overview of present available choices in any single area. Even such basics of human life as gender and sexual identity are no longer regarded genetically determined, but rather subject to individual choice.

On top of this, face to face interpersonal contacts are increasingly reduced in favour of virtual encounters through phone, e-mail, blog communities, message boards and web sites on the Internet. Physical distance no longer limits the ability to stay in contact, and relationships may be global in their nature. Modern life also offers constantly changing roles in ever varying different settings, where there is every possibility to present a partial or even fake image of oneself over the phone, through the e-mail or on the Internet. In such encounters, even such basics of identity as age and gender of the persons that interact may be ignored or distorted.

In this context of constantly shifting styles, increasingly questioned norms and increasing pace of social change, the individual in her identity formation is left without the support formerly offered by the confines of an established community of shared values. For young persons, contacts over the Internet have become a common way to share experiences and search for answers. Young persons, rather than asking for the advice of elders or professionals, increasingly look to their peers over the Internet to discuss their needs and exchange support to find self-acceptance and effective ways to cope with the life situation [27]. In this way, attitudes and behaviour radically different from that of the older generation may spread at a fast pace, and networks of persons with shared values may offer support and guidance on ways to cope with life.

ME AND I IN THE 21ST CENTURY

Another perspective that may shed light on the trends in modern society can be found in symbolic interactionism, a perspective developed in the fist decades of the 20th century. Symbolic interactionism is also known as "the Chicago School", and can be seen as an early cybernetic formulation of the circularity of human relationships. Symbolic interactionism states that man and society cannot be separated from each other, as they are two sides of the same coin [28].

In symbolic interactionism, the focus is on our interdependence of one another, and how our world views and attitudes are formed in interaction with others. Basically, in all our acting we are interacting with others, and these interactions will influence and eventually form our assumptions of mankind, our expectations for the future and our attitude towards others. As a consequence, our present assumptions about the world will form the way we act. For example, should our experiences in interactions with others have led to the assumption that others cannot be trusted, we will surely act according to this assumption in subsequent encounters – and it will take a substantial amount of experience of trustworthiness on the part of others to change such a basic assumption. This interactive process, where former experience guides future actions, has been eloquently formulated in what has become known as the theorem of Thomas; "if men define situations as real, they are real in their consequences" [29].

It goes without saying that life experiences that repeatedly or strongly contradict our present assumptions may lead to a re-evaluation of the former views, and symbolic interactionism strongly stresses the continuity of such changes throughout life. In this way, human interaction will continue to reshape the individual's views and attitudes in a never-ending dynamic process.

This interactionistic view on the way our views and attitudes are formed naturally has a bearing on our identity formation. In symbolic interactionism our identity is regarded to be closely related to the way others look at us, and identity is formed through our interaction with others. Persons who become especially important in this interactive identity process are called "significant others". The process of identity formation is not static, but active throughout life, and therefore subject to continuous change.

In an attempt to describe this process of identity formation, George Herbert Mead [30] used the constructs of "Me" and "I". These constructs signify two parts of the self that interact in forming identity. According to Mead, "Me" is the integrated views we presently have of ourselves and the world, our basic assumptions, attitudes, values and priorities that guide our actions. "I", on the other hand, is the part that is spontaneous and creative and willing to take risks, sometimes infringing on or even contradicting certain aspects of "Me", violating the present borders of this self concept. This spontaneous risk-taking of the "I" leads to new experiences, adjusting the former borders of "Me". Eventually, these experiences due to the activity of the "I" are integrated in a new understanding of "Me". In this way, the identity concept of the individual is constantly modified [31].

Let's adapt this perspective to a young woman who looks to the Internet for answers to her life stressors. She finds a website that describes self-cutting or other forms of self harm as a powerful tool for taking control over otherwise inarticulate anxiety. Her present view of herself, her "Me", may initially reject such an assumption – but as anxiety bottles up inside, her "I" may find it worth trying. Should she find the self-cutting a rewarding experience for relieving her anxiety, this experience will be built into her "Me". And should this strategy to control anxiety be established through repeated use, it may become part of her identity, her integrated "Me". The next time she joins a chat forum, she may share her experience of self-harm as a powerful tool to handle anxiety and despair. In this way self harming acts may be perpetuated over the Internet through shared experiences, and young persons may inadvertently empower each other to use self-harming acts as a tool worth trying when the stressors of life become unbearable.

In ways such as these, the present trends spread quickly and may radically influence the way young persons are thinking and acting. These changes put radically new demands on how to meet the needs of young persons of today.

Paths ahead, Bridging the Gap

As people move with the times, grown-ups increasingly find themselves to be like dinosaurs, derived from another time and another setting. Is it possible to find ways to offer support to someone like the young woman described above, who does not easily fit into a diagnostic category? Are there ways to meet her although her integrity rejects the expert stance of the psychiatrist, and her experience of personal choices in every other area makes her rebel against the elements of power inherent in present day psychiatry? Are there ways to bridge this gap, to offer support to a young person who has come to use self-harming acts as a way to cope with life? Is there a possibility that we as grown-ups, despite our limitations, might become "significant others" in her identity formation without being intrusive and without resorting to preconceived explanatory ideas about her behaviour? Are there any guidelines to be found on how to deserve and keep her trust?

Systemic Approaches

An important demarcation line from traditional psychotherapeutic methods is found in the latest developments in systemic therapy, such as the language systems therapy of Harlene Anderson [32], the solution focused therapies of Steve de Shazer and Insoo Kim Berg [33;34] and the narrative traditions of Michael White [35] and others. These approaches stem from a social constructionist methodological and philosophical standpoint that radically questions traditional professional expertise and interpretative therapeutic interventions. Harlene Anderson [32] argues an approach that focuses the dialogue; what is said, and how it is being said; what can be observed, not what may be inferred. The focus is on careful and attentive listening in a not-knowing position, arguing you can not know anything about another human being until you through dialogue have come to develop a mutual understanding of how she experiences her situation. Steve de Shazer and Insoo Kim Berg [33;34] argue a short-term therapy where interpretations and linear cause and effect explanations are discarded for a circular understanding of human relationships. The task of the therapist is to attentively and without reservation accept how the other person describes her situation and how she constructs her reality, and in the course of therapy bring into focus the times when she found a different way to cope, in this way enabling formerly overlooked abilities to form "a difference that makes a difference" [11]. Michael White [35] emphasizes the power of the personal narrative, and how a widening of the story may help someone acknowledge capacities forgotten or unrecognized, enabling a different view of the present and other ways to cope with the future. These approaches hold important implications for encounters with young persons trying to come to terms with life.

Empowerment Strategies

Another stance holding hopes for the future is the growing interest in empowering perspectives on both a practical and theoretical level. Empowerment perspectives, being rooted in social work with the impoverished, are focused on encouraging people to become subjects rather than objects in their lives. Empowerment strategies regard each human being as the expert of her own life, and seriously challenge the medical model of expert defined assessment, diagnostics and treatment, and redefines positions of power in health care settings [36;37]. Accordingly, empowerment practices focus the narratives of the individual; her own description, her own understanding of herself and her situation, her own language, her own strengths and her own abilities.

Basically, the empowerment approach argues confidence in a person's own capacity to find her own solutions and strategies – and a readiness to offer support in this quest. Applied to self-harming acts, an empowerment approach would focus the strengths revealed in the young persons choice of method to take charge of her anxiety – the determination and courage it takes to violate her own bodily integrity, the fearlessness it shows, the bravery inherent in her will to come to terms with the pressures of life – and explore her own description of this process, her own understanding of her situation, her own view of how this has come to be her very special way of taking responsibility for her life. In such a dialogue, dreams and visions of other ways to cope might reveal itself, which due to the strengths already revealed in her present acts might not be too far out of reach. But once again, such a process must be focused on her own understanding of herself and her situation, and the preconceived assumptions, policies and terminologies of the helper should be discarded, as such a language in an empowerment perspective is an expression of a power relation. A practical example of how empowerment strategies can be applied when working with persons who deliberately harm themselves can be found in the feminist therapy of Laura Brown and Tracy Bryan [38].

Implications

Empowerment strategies, as well as systemic oriented therapeutic models, demand a break-up from the present confines of the psychiatric therapeutic community, with its focus on preconceived explanations derived from theories on human behaviour, and expert knowledge derived from generalized conceptions, codified in diagnostic manuals. Such a process demands a return to the basics of human encounters with the aim to offer support and help – the open mind for the individual story, the personal narratives, the interest in the other as another human being, the willingness to be there, to take part, to develop thoughts, ideas and actions for the future together, and offer a place to reconsider when things do not work out the way it was planned, and other ideas has to be formed and tried. Needless to say, to achieve such a change in organization and ways of thinking is no piece of cake.

A process of empowerment, however, is not limited to the context of therapy, as the identity process of every individual according to symbolic interactionism will take place in everyday encounters with persons that for some reason become "significant others" to this individual. Even if psychiatry fails to offer adequate support, a friend, a relative, a partner, a spouse, a workmate, or someone on the Internet may be the one who in the interaction offers new perspectives that makes possible a different understanding, enabling the individual to form other coping strategies and a new integration of her abilities.

Conclusion

In narratives of young persons, on the Internet and elsewhere, we find quite another picture of self-harming acts than that presently predominant within psychiatry. We find self-harm within a context of determination, of strength and of courage in coping with life stressors. Therefore, what is often seen as a failure, a shortcoming and a weakness within the context of the present day therapeutic community may actually have quite different connotations for the young person herself. Not to recognize, acknowledge and accredit such characteristics of the self-harming strategies, and instead label a young person with a diagnosis that excludes important aspects of the personal narrative, would seem unprofessional and even unethical.

In the interactive interplay on the Internet between young persons with self-harming acts there are elements of empowerment strategies, of careful and attentive listening and acceptance of the life stories and coping strategies of the individual. Attention to these narratives enables a widening of the perspective on self-harm. In encounters with young persons who resort to self-harming acts, professionalism today would be not to take over responsibility for controlling the behaviour, not to adapt to an expert role, but to accept the not-knowing position, to be curious and interested in the personal narrative, the young person's own description of her situation, to accept her the way she is and endorse the strengths inherent in her struggle to cope with life and her efforts of staying alive.

REFERENCES

[1] Söderberg S: *To leave it all behind. Factors behind parasuicide – Roads towards stability.* Umeå, Umeå University Medical Dissertations, 2004. http://www.diva-portal.org/umu/abstract.xsql?dbid=362

[2] Hawton K, Rodham K, Evans E, Weatherall R: Deliberate self harm in adolescents: self report survey in schools in England. *BMJ* 2002; 325:1207-1211.

[3] Nock MK, Joiner TE Jr, Gordon KH, Lloyd-Richardson E, Prinstein MJ: Non-suicidal self-injury among adolescents: diagnostic correlates and relation to suicide attempts. *Psychiatry Res* 2006; 144:65-72.

[4] DSM-IV-TR. *American Psychiatric Association: Diagnostic and statistical manual of mental disorders,* 4th ed, Text Revision. Washington, DC, American Psychiatric Association, 2000.

[5] Söderberg S: Personality disorders in parasuicide. *Nord J Psychiatry* 2001; 55:163-167.

[6] Tyrer P: Borderline personality disorder: a motley diagnosis in need of reform. *Lancet* 1999; 354:2095-2096.

[7] Skodol AE, Gunderson JG, Pfohl B, Widiger TA, Livesley WJ, Siever LJ: The borderline diagnosis I: psychopathology, comorbidity, and personality structure. *Biol Psychiatry* 2002; 51:936-950.

[8] Skodol AE: Longitudinal course and outcome of personality disorders. *Psychiatr Clin North Am* 2008; 31:495-503.

[9] Livesley W J: A framework for integrating dimensional and categorical classifications of personality disorder. *J Personal Disord* 2007; 21:199-224.

[10] Butler J: Imitation and gender subordination, in *The Second Wave. A Reader in Feminist Theory.* Edited by Nicholson L. New York, Routledge, 1997, pp 300-315.

[11] Bateson G: *Steps to an ecology of mind.* New York, Random House, 1972.

[12] Ryan K, Heath MA, Fischer L, Young EL: Superficial self-harm: Perceptions of young women who hurt themselves. *Journal of Mental Health Counseling* 2008; 30:237-254.

[13] Livesley W J: Progress in the treatment of borderline personality disorder. *Can J Psychiatry* 2005; 50:433-434.

[14] Oldham JM: Borderline personality disorder and suicidality. *Am J Psychiatry* 2006; 163:20-26.

[15] Wilson HJ: The myth of objectivity: is medicine moving towards a social constructivist medical paradigm? *Fam Pract* 2000; 17:203-209.

[16] Fonagy P, Bateman A: Progress in the treatment of borderline personality disorder. *Br J Psychiatry* 2006; 188:1-3.

[17] Söderberg S, Kullgren G, Renberg ES: Life events, motives, and precipitating factors in parasuicide among borderline patients. *Arch Suicide Res.* 2004; 8:153-162.

[18] Paris J: *Personality Disorders Over Time. Precursors,* Course, and Outcome. Washington, DC, American Psychiatric Publishing, 2003.

[19] Holm AL, Severinsson E: The emotional pain and distress of borderline personality disorder: a review of the literature. *Int J Ment Health Nurs* 2008; 17:27-35.

[20] Söderberg S, Kullgren G, Salander Renberg E: Childhood sexual abuse predicts poor outcome seven years after parasuicide. *Soc Psychiatry Psychiatr Epidemiol* 2004; 39:916-920.

[21] Gunderson JG, Ridolfi ME: Borderline personality disorder. Suicidality and self-mutilation. *Ann N Y Acad Sci* 2001; 932:61-73.

[22] Lieb K, Zanarini MC, Schmahl C, Linehan MM, Bohus M: Borderline personality disorder. *Lancet* 2004; 364:453-61.

[23] Bateman A, Fonagy P. Treatment of borderline personality disorder with psychoanalytically oriented partial hospitalization: an 18-month follow-up. *Am J Psychiatry* 2001; 158:36-42.

[24] Bateman A, Fonagy P: *Psychotherapy for Borderline Personality Disorder: Mentalization-based treatment*. Oxford, Oxford University Press, 2004.

[25] Bateman A, Fonagy P: 8-year follow-up of patients treated for borderline personality disorder: mentalization-based treatment versus treatment as usual. *Am J Psychiatry* 2008; 165:631-638.

[26] Giddens A: Modernity and self-identity. Self and society in the late modern age. London, Polity Press, 1991.

[27] Whitlock J, Lader W, Conterio K: The internet and self-injury: what psychotherapists should know. *J Clin Psychol* 2007; 63:1135-1143.

[28] Cooley CH: *Social process*. New York, Scribner's, 1918.

[29] Thomas WI, Thomas DS: *The Child in America*. New York, Knopf, 1928.

[30] Mead GH: *Mind, self and society*. Chicago, University of Chicago Press, 1965 (1934).

[31] Charon JM: Symbolic interactionism. *An introduction, an interpretation, an integration,* 6th edition. New Jersey, Prentice Hall, 1998.

[32] Anderson H, Gehart DR: *Collaborative Therapy: Relationships and Conversations that make A Difference*. New York, Routledge, 2006.

[33] de Shazer S, Dolan Y: More than Miracles. *The State of the Art of Solution-Focused Brief Therapy*. NewYork, The Haworth Press, 2007.

[34] De Jong P, Berg I K: *Interviewing for solutions,* 3rd ed. Pacific Grove, CA, Brooks/Cole, 2008.

[35] White M: *Maps of Narrative Practice*. New York, Norton, 2007.

[36] Hewitt-Taylor J: Challenging the balance of power: patient empowerment. *Nurs Stand* 2004; 18:33-37.

[37] Laugharne R, Priebe S: Trust, choice and power in mental health: a literature review. *Soc Psychiatry Psychiatr Epidemiol* 2006; 41:843-852.

[38] Brown LS, Bryan TC: Feminist therapy with people who self-inflict violence. *J Clin Psychol* 2007; 63:1121-1133.

In: Internet and Suicide
Editors: L. Sher and A. Vilens
ISBN 978-1-60741-077-5

Chapter 16

BORDERLINE PERSONALITY, CONTAGION, AND THE INTERNET

***Randy A. Sansone*[1] *and Lori A. Sansone*[2]**
[1]Wright State University School of Medicine, Dayton, Ohio;
Kettering Medical Center, Kettering, Ohio;
[2]Primary Care Clinic, Wright-Patterson Air Force Base,
Dayton, Ohio, USA

ABSTRACT

Borderline personality is an Axis II disorder that is characterized by chronic self-harm behavior, which collectively includes self-mutilation, suicide attempts, and completed suicide. In this chapter, we address the question, "Are these individuals genuinely susceptible to internet material related to suicide?" Current evidence suggests a moderate degree of susceptibility. The following data and clinical observations support this impression: (1) individuals with borderline personality are, by definition, self-harming, so such risks are ever-present; (2) a variety of factors are empirically associated with the risk of suicide in individuals with borderline personality, and these include psychological as well as *environmental* factors; (3) suicide attempts in relationship to internet material has already been documented, including the case of a patient with borderline personality; (4) a relationship between borderline psychopathology and internet susceptibility seems probable given the propensity of these individuals to exhibit "emotional hyper-responsiveness" to external stimuli, particularly negative stimuli; and (5) based upon clinical observation, patients with borderline personality are prone to contagion phenomena, particularly with regard to self-harm behavior. In this chapter, we will review these various data and clinical observations, and conclude that there is a moderate risk of susceptibility.

Introduction

In the *Diagnostic and Statistical Manual of Mental Disorders, 4th Edition, Text Revision* (*DSM-IV-TR*) [1], borderline personality is designated as an Axis II disorder in the Cluster B grouping of personality disorders (i.e., dramatic, emotional, erratic features). Within this cluster, this particular personality disorder is characterized by chronic self-harm behavior, which may include repetitive self-mutilation, multiple suicide attempts, and completed suicide. According to longitudinal studies over 27 years [2], there is a meaningful risk of completed suicide among such patients—approximately 10% (i.e., a substantial minority). Many internal and external influences appear to temper this devastating outcome. With the advent of internet technology, there are now additional environmental influences that may negatively affect these vulnerable individuals. In this chapter, we discuss the possible relationships among borderline personality disorder (BPD), contagion phenomenon, and the internet.

Borderline Personality: A Brief Overview

The clinical features and characteristics of BPD are well described in the *DSM-IV-TR* [1]. According to this diagnostic manual, BPD is distinguished by (a) frantic efforts to avoid abandonment; (b) a history of unstable and intense relationships with others; (c) disturbances in identity; (d) impulsivity in at least two functional areas such as spending, sex, substance use, eating, or driving; (e) recurrent suicidal threats or behaviors including self-mutilation; (f) affective instability with marked reactivity of mood; (g) chronic feelings of emptiness; (h) inappropriate and intense anger or difficulty controlling anger; and (i) transient stress-induced paranoid ideation or severe dissociative symptoms. These clinical features are reportedly longstanding (i.e., since the time of adolescence) and must be accompanied by some type of impairment in functioning.

From a pragmatic perspective, individuals with BPD tend to have three core clinical features: [1] a superficially intact social façade; [2] longstanding difficulties with self-regulation (e.g., eating disorders, alcohol/substance abuse, promiscuity, chronic pain), and [3] chronic self-harm behavior (e.g., cutting, burning, hitting, and/or scratching oneself; masochistic relationships with others; suicide attempts). These core clinical features contribute to the individual's position on a functional continuum, with lower-functioning patients at one end of the continuum and higher-functioning patients at the other end. Individuals on the lower end of the functional continuum exhibit more psychological, occupational, and interpersonal impairment, and may be at the greatest risk for negative environmental influences and serious self-harm behavior.

Known Suicide Risk Factors in Borderline Personality

Given that 10% of patients with BPD eventually commit suicide, this Axis II phenomenon is notable for having one of the higher mortality rates in the field of psychiatry. These findings are supported by a study that entailed a meta-analysis of the existing literature;

the authors concluded that completed suicide among patients with BPD undoubtedly exceeds that of the general population [3].

Suicide is clearly a dynamically complex event, particularly in an Axis II context. As expected, according to the literature, there are a number of factors, both internal and external in nature, that contribute to the suicide risk and high frequency of attempts encountered in individuals with BPD.

Internal Risk Factors

General Psychological Features

In terms of general psychological organization, a number of traits and states have been associated with a greater risk of suicide attempts in individuals with BPD. These include high levels of impulsivity [4,5], a hallmark of the disorder; feelings of hopelessness [5-7]; and poor social problem-solving skills [6].

Past Suicide Attempts

In addition to the previously noted psychological features, a number of BPD studies indicate that a past history of multiple suicide attempts is a risk factor for future suicide attempts [6,8]. These data denote that frequent attempters are not to be overlooked in the clinical setting, but rather have a heightened risk of future suicide completion.

Axis I Comorbidity

Several studies have examined whether or not particular Axis I disorders are over-represented in suicide attempters with BPD. The evidence is most robust for Axis I diagnoses relating to substance abuse [9-11] and the diagnosis of major depression [6,9,11,12]. (Note that many of these risk variables cluster with each other, such as substance abuse and the preceding finding of heightened impulsivity.)

Axis II Comorbidity

In addition to the risk loadings of the preceding Axis I disorders, additional personality pathology appears to contribute to suicide attempts in individuals with BPD [13]. In the literature, the most commonly noted Axis II features or disorder that is associated with a heightened risk is antisocial personality [5,14].

In addition to the preceding Axis I and II disorders, investigators have found that greater levels of overall psychopathology appear to be predictive of suicide attempts [6]. In other words, more psychologically ill patients are more likely to attempt suicide.

External Risk Factors

While a number of internal or psychological risk factors mediate the risk for suicide attempts in individuals with BPD, a number of external risk factors appear to moderate the risk, as well.

Adverse Life Events

According to the available empirical data, adverse life events are associated with a greater likelihood of suicide attempts in individuals with BPD [9] as well as turbulent early life experiences [5].

Parental Dysfunction

In long-term outcome studies of patients with BPD, parental cruelty has been associated with a heightened risk of suicide attempts [15]. On a side note, the role of biparental failure has been broached in the literature as a meaningful contributory variable to the overall development of BPD in offspring [16].

Poor Social Adjustment in the Immediate Family

Kelly and colleagues [17] found that poor social adjustment within the immediate family was a predictor of suicide attempts. Indeed, in their analyses, those individuals with poor family social adjustments were 16 times more likely to have attempted suicide.

Childhood Abuse

As expected, abuse in childhood heralds a number of unfortunate legacies in adulthood, including suicide attempts. In this regard, Kolla and colleagues [9] confirmed that a history of childhood trauma heightens the risk for suicide attempts in those with BPD. Brodsky and colleagues [7] echoed these findings and found that a history of childhood abuse demonstrated significant correlations with the number of lifetime suicide attempts.

In examining the subtypes of abuse in childhood, Soloff and colleagues [18] found that sexual abuse, but not physical abuse, was a significant contributory factor to suicide attempts in adulthood. Likewise, Bierer and colleagues [19] found that emotional abuse in childhood, rather than sexual or physical abuse, was related to suicide attempts in adulthood—but only in women, not men.

Interpersonal Stressors in Adulthood

Finally, according to the findings of Brodsky and colleagues [12], acute interpersonal stressors in adulthood contribute to suicidal ideation and attempts in individuals with BPD.

General Conclusions

In patients with BPD, there appear to be a number of risk factors, both internal (i.e., psychological) and external (i.e., environmental), that temper or mediate the emergence of suicidal ideation, attempts, and completions. However, there is no available *empirical* data with regard to the impact of the internet on suicidal ideation/attempts/completions in patients with BPD.

SUICIDE ATTEMPTS/COMPLETIONS AND THE INTERNET

As discussed in the previous section, the role of various environmental influences is well-known in the mediation of suicide attempts in BPD. However, very little information is available regarding the role of the internet as a *specific* environmental factor. In a case report, Mehlum [20] described two Europeans who committed suicide after meeting on the internet and discusses the issue of suicide pacts being negotiated over the internet. Webb and colleagues [21] also discuss the role of the internet with regard to contagion phenomena and the organization of suicide pacts. However, we were only able to find one case report of an internet-related suicide attempt in an individual with bona fide BPD [22]. In this case report, the patient was a 34-year-old female who claimed to have gotten the idea for suicide directly from the internet. Is there any further reason to consider *cultural* environmental influences such as the internet as potential risk factors for suicide attempts in patients with BPD? Existing data suggest so.

BORDERLINE PERSONALITY AND HYPER-RESPONSIVENESS TO THE ENVIRONMENT

According to the *Diagnostic and Statistical Manual of Mental Disorders, 4th Edition* [23], patients with BPD are portrayed as having a "...marked reactivity of mood." This reactionary mode in individuals with BPD may be explained by fundamental deficits in emotional regulation, which are well described by Linehan [24]. Herpertz [25] also captures this dynamic by labeling the tendency of these individuals to over-react to environmental stimuli with the moniker "emotional hyper-responsiveness."

The presence of emotional over-responsiveness in patients with BPD is empirically supported by several studies. For example, Jennings [26] found that when viewing evocative color slides of pleasant, neutral, and unpleasant themes, compared with controls, undergraduate students with borderline personality characteristics showed significantly greater overall magnitudes of startle response regardless of the valence of the slide content. Korfine and Hooley [27] presented study participants with words of different emotional valences; participants were then asked to forget the words. Compared with controls who were recruited from the community, those with BPD, who were recruited from newspaper advertisements and a day hospital, recalled significantly more of the high-valent words from the "forget" condition. Herpertz, Gretzer, Muhlbauer, Steinmeyer, and Sab [28] presented participants with a short story and found that those with BPD evidenced greater affective hyper-reactivity, which was characterized by a lower threshold for affective responses as well as intense and rapidly changing affects. Conrad and Stevens Morrow [29] examined male participants' responses to viewing videos depicting abandonment themes. Compared with controls and participants with few borderline symptoms, those with high levels of borderline personality symptomatology reported a significantly greater willingness to use verbal and/or symbolic aggression, including threats of violence, against a partner as well as actual violence against inanimate objects to prevent loss (i.e., they reacted more dramatically to viewing the videos). Finally, Domes and colleagues [30] found that, compared with healthy controls, women with borderline personality symptomatology had more difficulties suppressing irrelevant information of an aversive nature (i.e., sensitivity to negative stimuli). These preceding studies clearly support the impression that individuals with BPD have an emotional hyper-reactivity to environmental stimuli, particularly to stimuli of a negative nature.

We must emphasize that not all studies support the hyper-reactivity theory proposed in BPD. For example, in examining this phenomenon, Renneberg, Heyn, Gebhard, and Silke [31] found that, when presented with videos depicting positive or negative emotions, participants with BPD demonstrated *reduced* facial expressiveness to both. In addition, Herpertz and colleagues [32,33] found that, upon viewing slides with strong emotional content, participants with BPD did *not* demonstrate emotional hyper-responsivity. However, these negative findings are few in number and may be accounted for by sample selection and methodological approach.

Given that much of the research in this area suggests that individuals with BPD are emotionally reactive to particular stimuli in the external environment, particularly to negative stimuli, one final area warrants discussion—the role of contagion phenomena.

Contagion Phenomena

Contagion phenomena, or the assimilation of the observed behaviors of others, certainly is real [34] and has been observed in a number of different contexts. In a sociocultural context, contagion mundanely manifests in the fashion world as imitation. For example, with the advent of blonde-haired sex symbols in the 1930s, women in the general population at that time began to bleach their hair blonde, as well. With the arrival of Twiggy in the mid-1960s, adolescent and young-adult women began dieting to imitate the stick-like appearance of this former British super-model. In more recent times, women have meticulously duplicated the signature hairstyles of their favorite media stars, such as Jennifer Aniston.

However, contagion can certainly take on more ominous tones, particularly with regard to psychopathological behaviors. For example, we have clinically observed that individuals with BPD may quickly assimilate the psychopathological behaviors that they observe in others, particularly self-harm behaviors (e.g., self cutting), eating pathology (e.g., bulimia), and suicide attempts. Indeed, we have previously described contagion phenomena as a genuine clinical risk factor when admitting patients with BPD to the hospital—an environment where they will be exposed to other patients with BPD and risk the assimilation of newly observed self-destructive behaviors [35].

In addition to the preceding clinical observations, the empirical literature supports the phenomenon of contagion. For example, Stevens and Prinstein [36] examined adolescent friendship pairs and found that a best friend's reported level of depressive symptomatology was prospectively associated with the proband's own development of depressive symptoms. The authors described the findings of this study as evidence of "peer contagion effects."

In addition to contagion with depressive symptoms, the literature documents the assimilation via contagion of eating pathology, as well. For example, in a study of over fifteen thousand high school students, Forman-Hoffman and Cunningham [37] found evidence of a clustering effect of symptoms by county and concluded that this was indicative of a social contagion effect with eating disorders. In addition, in a study of college women, Vanlone [38] found that participants tended to develop eating attitudes and behaviors that were similar to those of other women in their small friendship clusters.

In addition to depressive and eating disorder symptoms, exposure to suicide may result in a contagion effect. For example, Stone [39] examined suicide contagion among 13 and 14-year-old girls in a non-clinical (middle school) sample and confirmed a contagion effect for suicidal thoughts and self-harming behaviors.

At a more relevant level for this chapter, there also appears to be evidence of suicide contagion with regard to media reports of such events. In this regard, Romer, Jamieson, and Jamieson [40] examined the effects of suicide events announced on local television news shows and found a subsequent increase in the incidence of local deaths by suicide among persons younger than 25 years. In addition, these investigators found that newspaper reports of suicide were associated with an increase in suicide deaths for both young persons as well as those over the age of 44 years. They describe these phenomena as "media contagion." Finally, Sudak and Sudak [41] reviewed the literature on media-related suicide and firmly concluded that there are an increased number of suicides resulting from media accounts of suicide, particularly those that romanticize or dramatize the description of the deaths. So, clearly, with regard to suicide attempts and completions, the general population evidences a certain degree of susceptibility to contagion phenomenon. However, we do not know how many of these susceptible individuals suffer from BPD.

Putting the Pieces Together

While we are not aware of any empirical studies that have explored or confirmed suicide vulnerability to internet material among individuals with BPD, we suspect that this is a case of "absence of evidence," which does not equal "evidence of absence." It may merely be that these types of data have not yet been examined.

Certainly, there are a number of lines of evidence to suggest that individuals with BPD might be susceptible to internet influences relating to suicide. First, individuals with BPD are characterized by longstanding self-harm behavior. Second, a number of environmental factors have been empirically associated with suicide attempts in individuals with BPD (i.e., why not the internet?). Third, there is a case report of an individual with BPD attempting suicide because of contact with the internet. Fourth, BPD is characterized by hyper-responsivity to the environment, which indicates a heightened response to environmental stimuli, particularly negative stimuli. Finally, individuals with BPD clinically evidence contagion phenomena with regard to various psychopathological behaviors, particularly self-mutilation and eating pathology. Putting all of these data together, it appears likely that these chronically self-harming individuals might be excessively stimulated by the suicide content on the internet (e.g., chat rooms, how-to sites, news reports) and act out, as they do with the observation of other psychopathological behaviors.

Conclusions

In this chapter, we have attempted to present empirical data as well as our clinical observations and impressions on the relationship between borderline psychopathology and the potential susceptibility of these individuals to internet-phenomena relating to suicide. We believe that the available empirical data and our observations moderately suggest that individuals with BPD are at a heightened risk of contagion phenomena with regard to internet-related suicide content. Because of these individuals' seemingly innate susceptibility to numerous environmental stimuli as well as the frequency of suicide attempts associated with this type of psychopathology, empirically confirming such a relationship will be challenging (i.e., a high number of potential confounds). However, we suspect that such a relationship of risk exists.

References

[1] American Psychiatric Association. *The Diagnostic and Statistical Manual of Mental Disorders, 4th Edition, Text Revision*. Washington, DC, American Psychiatric Association, 2000.

[2] Paris J. Implications of long-term outcome research for the management of patients with borderline personality disorder. *Harv Rev Psychiatry* 2002;10:315-323.

[3] Pompili M, Girardi P, Ruberto A, Tatarelli R. Suicide in borderline personality disorder: a meta-analysis. *Nord J Psychiatry* 2005;59:319-324.

[4] Links PS, Heslegrave R, van Reekum R. Impulsivity: core aspect of borderline personality disorder. *J Personal Disord* 1999;13:1-9.

[5] Black DW, Blum N, Pfohl B, Hale N. Suicidal behavior in borderline personality disorder: prevalence, risk factors, prediction, and prevention. *J Personal Disord* 2004;18:226-239.

[6] Berk MS, Jeglic E, Brown GK, Henriques GR, Beck AT. Characteristics of recent suicide attempters with and without borderline personality disorder. *Arch Suicide Res* 2007;11:91-104.

[7] Brodsky BS, Malone KM, Ellis SP, Dulit RA, Mann JJ. Characteristics of borderline personality disorder associated with suicidal behavior. *Am J Psychiatry* 1997;154:1715-1719.

[8] Mehlum L, Friis S, Vaglum P, Karterud S. The longitudinal pattern of suicidal behaviour in borderline personality disorder: a prospective follow-up study. *Acta Psychiatr Scand* 1994; 90:124-130.

[9] Kolla NJ, Eisenberg H, Links PS. Epidemiology, risk factors, and psychopharmacological management of suicidal behavior in borderline personality disorder. *Arch Suicide Res* 2008;12:1-19.

[10] Zanarini MC, Frankenburg FR, Hennen J, Reich DB, Silk KR. Axis I comorbidity in patients with borderline personality disorder: 6-year follow-up and prediction of time to remission. *Am J Psychiatry* 2004;161:2108-2114.

[11] Yen S, Shea T, Pagano M, Sanislow CA, Grilo CM, McGlashan TH, Skodol AE, Bender DS, Zanarini MC, Gunderson JG, Morey LC. Axis I and Axis II disorders as

predictors of prospective suicide attempts: findings from the Collaborative Longitudinal Personality Disorders Study. *J Abnorm Psychol* 2003;112:375-381.

[12] Brodsky BS, Groves SA, Oquendo MA, Mann JJ, Stanley B. Interpersonal precipitants and suicide attempts in borderline personality disorder. *Suicide Life Threat Behav* 2006;36:313-322.

[13] Links PS, Heslegrave R, van Reekum R. Prospective follow-up study of borderline personality disorder: prognosis, prediction of outcome, and Axis II comorbidity. *Can J Psychiatry* 1998;43:265 270.

[14] Soloff PH, Lis JA, Kelly T, Cornelius JR, Ulrich R. Risk factors for suicidal behavior in borderline personality disorder. *Am J Psychiatry* 1994;151:1316-1323.

[15] Stone MH. Long-term outcome in personality disorders. *Br J Psychiatry* 1993;162:299-313.

[16] Zanarini MC, Frankenburg FR, Reich DB, Marino MF, Lewis RE, Williams AA, Khera GS. Biparental failure in the childhood experiences of borderline patients. *J Personal Disord* 2000;14:264-273.

[17] Kelly TM, Soloff PH, Lynch KG, Haas GL, Mann JJ. Recent life events, social adjustment, and suicide attempts in patients with major depression and borderline personality disorder. *J Personal Disord* 2000;14:316-326.

[18] Soloff PH, Lynch KG, Kelly TM. Childhood abuse as a risk factor for suicidal behavior in borderline personality disorder. *J Personal Disord* 2002;16:201-214.

[19] Bierer LM, Yehuda R, Schmeidler J, Mitropoulou V, New AS, Silverman JM, Siever LJ. Abuse and neglect in childhood: relationship to personality disorder diagnoses. *CNS Spectr* 2003;8:737-740.

[20] Mehlum L. The internet, suicide, and suicide prevention. *Crisis: J Crisis Interv Suicide Prev* 2000;21:186-188.

[21] Webb M, Burns J, Collin P. Providing online support for young people with mental health difficulties: challenges and opportunities explored. *Early Interv Psychiatry* 2008;2:108-113.

[22] Alao A, Yolles JC, Airmenta W. Cybersuicide: the internet and suicide. *Am J Psychiatry* 1999;156:1836-1837.

[23] American Psychiatric Association. *Diagnostic and Statistical Manual of Mental Disorders, 4th Edition*. Washington, DC, American Psychiatric Association, 1994.

[24] Linehan MM. *Cognitive-Behavioral Treatment of Borderline Personality Disorder*. New York, Guilford Press, 1993.

[25] Herpertz SC. Emotional processing in personality disorder. *Curr Psychiatry Rep* 2003;5:23-27.

[26] Jennings ME. Emotion regulation in borderline personality disorder: a psychophysiological examination of emotional responding and recovery. *Dissert Abstr Int* 2004;64:5219B.

[27] Korfine L, Hooley JM. Directed forgetting of emotional stimuli in borderline personality disorder. *J Abnorm Psychol* 2000;109:214-221.

[28] Herpertz S, Gretzer A, Muhlbauer V, Steinmeyer EM, Sab H. Experimental detection of inadequate affect dysregulation in patients with self-destructive behavior. *Nervenarzt* 1998;69:410-418.

[29] Conrad SD, Stevens Morrow RS. Borderline personality organization, dissociation, and willingness to use force in intimate relationships. *Psychol Men Masculinity* 2000;1:37-48.

[30] Domes G, Winter B, Schnell K, Vohs K, Fast K, Herpertz SC. The influence of emotions on inhibitory functioning in borderline personality disorder. *Psychol Med* 2006;36:1163-1172.

[31] Renneberg B, Heyn K, Gebhard R, Bachmann S. Facial expression of emotions in borderline personality disorder and depression. *J Behav Ther Exp Psychiatry* 2005;36:183-196.

[32] Herpertz SC, Kunert HJ, Schwenger UB, Sass H. Affective responsivness in borderline personality disorder: a psychophysiological approach. *Am J Psychiatry* 1999;156:1550-1556.

[33] Herpertz SC, Schwenger UB, Kunert HJ, Lukas G, Gretzer U, Nutzmann J, Schuerkens A, Sass H. Emotional response in patients with borderline as compared with avoidant personality disorder. *J Personal Disord* 2000;14:339-351.

[34] Author. Reporting on suicide: recommendations for the media. *Suicide Life Threat Beh* 2002;32:viii-xiii.

[35] Sansone RA, Sansone LA. The psychological and behavioral management of patients with borderline personality disorder in the medical setting, in *Borderline Personality Disorder in the Medical Setting: Unmasking and Managing the Difficult Patient.* Sansone RA, Sansone LA. New York, Nova Science Publishers, 2007, pp.98-99.

[36] Stevens EA, Prinstein MJ. Peer contagion of depressogenic attributional styles among adolescents: a longitudinal study. *J Abnorm Child Psychol* 2005;33:25-37.

[37] Forman-Hoffman VL, Cunningham CL. Geographical clustering of eating disordered behaviors in U.S. high school students. *Int J Eat Disord* 2008;41:209-214.

[38] Vanlone JS. Social contagion of eating attitudes and behaviors among first year college women living in residence hall communities. *Diss Abstr Int* 2003;63:4390B.

[39] Stone JN. Containing the contagion: a case history of suicidal gestures and self-harming behaviors among 13 and 14 year old middle school girls. *Dissert Abstr Int* 1998;59:2438B.

[40] Romer D, Jamieson PE, Jamieson KH. Are news reports of suicide contagious? A stringent test in six U.S. cities. *J Commun* 2006;56:253-270.

[41] Sudak HS, Sudak DM. The media and suicide. *Acad Psychiatry* 2005;29:495-499.

In: Internet and Suicide
Editors: L. Sher and A. Vilens
ISBN 978-1-60741-077-5

Chapter 17

INFORMATION FOR CRISIS INTERVENTION AND SUICIDE PREVENTION RESOURCES FOR INDIVIDUALS WITH SUBSTANCE USE DISORDERS ON THE INTERNET

Barbara Schneider and Kristin Grebner
Johann Wolfgang Goethe-University, Frankfurt am Main, Germany

ABSTRACT

Substance use disorders like alcoholism are major risk factors for suicide. During the last decade, new media including the Internet were getting more and more important in delivering information. Using suicide-related terms, the few studies about internet search provided ambiguous results regarding help and support. A recent internet search in English and in German language with suicide- and addiction-related search terms revealed that the majority of websites was not associated with suicide at all. There are several challenges for future developments: Using different terms associated with suicidality and/or addiction, search engines should immediately tell web addresses of help services and advice centres and should not produce possibly dangerous suicide forums or pages not related to suicide; furthermore, search engines should more frequently deliver helpful information, e. g. present addresses of help services, and help services should be able to target various help-seeking groups adequately. In view of the scarce knowledge about substance abusers' opportunities to get information about crisis intervention and suicide prevention via the Internet, further research on this topic is necessary.

INTRODUCTION

Suicidal and addictive behaviours are major public health issues. In the US, lifetime prevalence of alcohol dependence was estimated to be about 20% in men and 8% in women, the prevalence of alcohol abuse was about 12% in men and 6% in women [1]. Data from a 1997 national survey showed Germany-wide prevalences of 12% for hazardous alcohol consumption (more than 20 g of pure alcohol for women and 40 g of pure alcohol for men daily, 14% for men and 7% for women), 5% for alcohol misuse and 3% for alcohol dependence [2]. About 9% and 5% of all men had lifetime prevalence of drug abuse or dependence (women: 6% and 3%; [3]). Worldwide, there are about 1.1 billion smokers [4]. In Germany, 36% of men and 28% of women aged 18 to 64 years reported that they currently smoked (during the last 30 days) in 2006 [5].

Worldwide, every year about one million people die from suicide (Germany: about 10,000). Suicide is estimated to represent 1.8% of the total global burden of disease in 1998 [6]. In Germany, lifetime risk of suicide in those with alcohol dependence is about 7% [7], stable throughout the lifetime course of the disorder. Furthermore, a huge proportion of all suicide victims had suffered from alcohol use disorders [8].

THE ASSOCIATION BETWEEN ADDICTIVE AND SUICIDAL BEHAVIOUR

The association between addiction and suicidal behaviour is well known. Evidence for an association of suicide with alcohol use disorders, smoking, and substance use disorders other than alcohol is largely based upon cohort studies and controlled postmortem psychological autopsy studies.

Alcohol use disorders (alcohol dependence and alcohol abuse) were associated with an highly increased suicide risk as shown by metaanalyses of follow-up studies [9, 10, 11] and the large Danish Psychiatric Case Register study with a follow-up up to 20 years [12]. Psychological autopsy studies have shown that a large proportion of suicides had suffered from alcohol use disorders; controlled psychological autopsies have identified alcohol-related disorders as risk factors for suicide in spite of differences in diagnostic methodology, age groups, and proportion of males [13 – 19].

There are several risk factors for suicide in alcoholism including being older than 50 years of age, poor social support, interpersonal losses, a major depressive episode, serious medical illness, suicidal communication, and prior suicidal behaviour [20, 21]. Protective factors include effective clinical care for psychiatric (including alcoholism and drug abuse) and physical disorders, easy access to a variety of clinical interventions and support for seeking help (see 22).

The acute effects of alcohol intake have been implicated in suicidal behaviour as much as the chronic effects of alcohol misuse. Post-mortem studies have shown detectable blood alcohol in up to 45% of all suicides, even in absence of organic signs of alcohol abuse at autopsy [23]. The relationship between alcohol consumption and alcohol use disorders with completed and attempted suicide is stronger for episodic heavy drinking than for overall consumption [24], as alcohol acutely decreases inhibition and increases impulsivity and the likelihood of unplanned suicidal behaviour [25, 26].

A link between cigarette smoking and suicide has been reported in epidemiological studies since the 1970s. More recent prospective studies have also reported a significant relationship between smoking and suicide [27 – 29], especially in young men [30], a dose-dependent relationship between smoking and suicide [31 – 37], and no elevated suicide risks in former smokers in contrast to current smokers [32 – 36]. Smoking was also associated with increased risk for suicide in our own case-control study using psychological autopsy method [38, 39] and in working female nurses [39]. Furthermore, an association between suicide ideas [41, 42] and suicide attempts [43 – 45] and smoking was found. Opiate use is associated with a particularly highly increased suicide risk [9]. Although a causal relationship between cannabis consumption and suicide is unclear, cannabis use was associated with an increased suicide risk [46].

Because of the highly increased suicide risk in addictive disorders, suicide prevention is a challenging task. During the last twenty years, new communication opportunities like the Internet were developed. Although the known negative impact of the Internet on suicidal behaviour by providing online suicide manuals and detailed descriptions of lethal methods [47 – 49], the risk of copycat cybersuicides [50], and suicide pacts initiated over the Internet [51], the Internet also provides information and support for individuals in crisis. In the following report we want to present information and help available on the Internet for people who suffer from addictive disorders. First, we searched bibliographic databases, seeking published material about the Internet and addiction. Studies of internet search behaviour suggest that most people use search engines. Furthermore, we searched the Internet using four different search engines. We visited English and German speaking sites and followed up links.

The Internet as a Source for Help and Support

Psychiatric patients who use the Internet reported that they found insight and support they needed in order to seek treatment for their substance use disorder. Additionally, patients often told that they have looked for institutional help using the Internet. Ybarra et al. [52] found that medical care seekers appear to be using the Internet to enhance their medical knowledge; they reported using the information online to diagnose a problem and feel more comfortable about their health provider's advice given the information found on the Internet [52]. Support seekers tend to be of slightly lower income compared to non-support seekers [52]. They are also significantly more likely to have searched for information about a loved one's medical or health condition, signalling that many of these consumers may be caretakers [52]. Most of the medical professionals regularly use the Internet for updating their medical knowledge [52].

The Internet is an increasingly popular source of information, especially for people confronting embarrassing issues such as addictive disorders and suicidality. It has been widely used as a tool for suicide prevention, intervention, and postvention. However, there are only a few reports about the Internet as source for support and help. Online suicide risk screening programs have been developed and implemented [53]. Barak [54] developed a suicide prevention project that uses the Internet to deliver crisis intervention services, including rescues of individuals in the process of attempting suicide. Email communication has been used for crisis intervention [55]; the Samaritans reported having got approximately

228,600 emails in 2007 compared to 184,000 emails in 2006; this means a plus of 25% [56]. Additionally, email communication is getting more and more significant in counselling and psychotherapy of suicidal patients (e. g. 57). Furthermore, the Internet provides online suicide prevention education and training [58 – 60].

Internet search using suicide-related terms provided ambiguous results with respect to support. Recupero et al. [61] found in a web-research using five popular engines and four suicide-related search terms in August and September 2006 that suicide-neutral and anti-suicide pages occurred most frequently, whereas pro-suicide pages were less frequent. Biddle et al. [62] analysed the first 10 sites from four search engines. The three most frequently occurring sites were pro-suicide and half of all these sites were judged to be encouraging, promoting, or facilitating suicide. Sites focusing on suicide prevention or offering support and sites forbidding or discouraging suicide accounted for 62 (13%) and 59 (12%) hits respectively [62]. MSN had the highest number of prevention or support sites, academic or policy sites [62]. However, it was discussed that these results were strongly influenced by their keywords and research phrases chosen [63].

Internet Pages for Help and Support for Addicts in English and in German Language

Similar to Recupero et al.'s [61] procedure, we used four frequently used search engines (Google, Yahoo, Ask.com, and Lycos), five suicide-related ('help and suicide', 'suicide', 'suicide forum', 'suicide prevention', 'suicide prophylaxis'), three addiction-related ('addiction', 'addicted', 'addiction help'), and one combined ('addiction and suicide') search terms. The Internet search was conducted in August 2008. Search results were classified as being pro-suicide, anti-suicide, suicide-neutral, not a suicide site, anti-addiction, addiction-neutral, pro-addiction, not an addiction site, or error (page could not be loaded). For the combined 'addiction and suicide' search term results were classified as 'anti-suicide', 'pro-suicide', or 'neutral'. Applying these search terms, we found 1,200 websites in English language.

Table 1. Numbers of 'anti-addiction' sites and 'no addiction' sites

Search term	Search result	Search engine				Total
		Google	Yahoo	Ask com	Lycos	
Addiction	ANTI	18	16	24	21	79
	NAS	12	14	6	9	41
Addicted	ANTI	2	1	8	2	13
	NAS	28	29	22	28	107
Addiction help	ANTI	28	28	29	27	112
	NAS	2	2	1	3	8

ANTI = 'anti-addiction' site, NAS = 'no addiction' site.

Table 2. Numbers of pro-suicide sites, anti-suicide sites, neutral sites, not a suicide site, or error

Search term	Search result	Search engine				Total
		Google	Yahoo	Ask com	Lycos	
Help + Suicide	ANTI	19	23	21	24	87
	NEU			1		1
	NSS	10	7	8	6	31
	ERR	1				1
Suicide	ANTI	15	22	19	24	80
	NEU	1				1
	NSS	14	8	11	6	39
Suicide Forum	ANTI	8	15	9	14	46
	NEU	2	3	3	4	12
	NSS	20	12	17	12	61
	PRO			1		1
Suicide prevention	ANTI	28	25	28	27	108
	NSS	2	5	2	3	12
Suicide prophylaxis	ANTI	2	0	4	4	10
	NSS	28	30	26	26	110

ANTI = 'anti-suicide' site, PRO = 'pro-suicide' site, NEU = 'neutral' site, NSS = 'no suicide' site, ERR = error;

The search term 'addiction help' provided the highest number of results and most of the found pages included help and support for addicts. Interestingly, we did not identify one single website which was 'pro-addiction' (Table 1).

Table 2 shows the results of the Web search for the 'suicide' search terms. More than half of all found pages were 'anti-suicide' sites; they frequently provided information about crisis intervention services including contact to help-lines. Most websites providing help were connected by links. Interestingly, many web pages did not contain any information about suicide ('NSS', Table 2). These 'no suicide' pages included often headlines of newspapers, titles of books or songs, or were other, mostly art-related, homepages. Only one webpage was judged to be promoting or facilitating suicide (Table 2).

Using the search term 'addiction and suicide', we identified 30 (25%) 'anti-suicide' and 90 (75%) pages that were not related to suicide ('NSS'). 'Pro-suicide' websites were not found.

Applying the above mentioned criteria with the German terms for 'addiction', 'addicted', and 'addiction help', we found – contrary to the findings on websites in English – less anti-addiction' pages than pages which were not relevant for addiction. In contrast to pages in English language, using suicide-related search terms more websites in German language which were not related to suicide at all than websites providing help and support were found. Most of the German 'support' pages were websites run by voluntary organizations and private persons. About 60% of the pages found for the search combination 'addiction and suicide' in German language were not associated with suicide.

CONCLUSION

Unfortunately, websites of professional help services for suicidal individuals or for substance abusers (see 64) – of which professionals would think immediately – were less frequently called up on the Net than websites which do not deliver help and support. Furthermore, it was difficult to get to ‚professional' sites and to find email addresses and telephone numbers for suicidal individuals, much less for suicidal substance abusers, on the spot. Instead of that, searching for 'suicide' and similar search terms often resulted in finding websites not related to suicide at all; these pages frequently showed advertisements or – even worse – news of suicides and suicide bombing. These results are in line with Baker and Fortune's [65] findings; their participants, who had been recruited directly from self-harm and suicide websites, described mental health services as inaccessible, unavailable, and unable to respond appropriately. In contrast, the participants described writing about their self-harming behaviours and interacting with fellow users as a 'coping strategy', as a way of managing severe social and psychological distress, and contributing to their recovery [65]. Sometimes, suicide fora in the Internet give the space to convey own suicidal feelings and thoughts [57], often by the communication with people by whom the fora users feel understood [66]. To feel someone understands one is particularly important when talking about topics that are largely under taboo – like addictive behaviour and suicidality.

Considering the difficulties for individuals with substance-related disorders to find adequate and immediate help and support by searching the Internet, there are challenges for future developments and future research. First, using different terms associated with suicidality and/or addiction, search engines should immediately tell web addresses of help services and advice centres and should not produce possibly dangerous suicide forums or pages not related to suicide. Second, professional help services should more frequently be present in the Internet and should be able to target various help-seeking groups adequately. Third, addiction help-group sites and qualified treatment for suicidal people and in particular suicidal addicts and their relatives should be better promoted. Fourth, taking up contact should be possible by email as well as by telephone; contact by email is easy and can be less terrifying than other kinds of contact. Furthermore, emails should be answered within a short time. Fifth, 'professional' help sites ought to provide adequate information and counselling. They should inform about the background of suicidal tendencies, warning signals, and risk factors, possibilities of immediate support, and about help services [67]. Sixth, webmasters should be trained to lead discussions and to recognize persons at risk and support their taking contact to professional services. Seventh, approaches should include post-inpatient treatment giving a suitable Internet environment for a confidential communication, which is user-friendly and effective [68]. Finally, psychiatrists, psychotherapists, self-help groups, and other services for substance abusers should take interest in their clients' Internet consumption and discuss the content with them. Information and improved communication on the Internet might diminish prejudices against professionals.

Challenges for Future Research

In view of the scarce knowledge about substance abusers' opportunities to get information about crisis intervention and suicide prevention via the Internet, further research on this topic is necessary. At least, it should be assessed, if internet-based information is tailored for specific types of users, not only professionals [69], but also for different patient groups, e. g. with addictive disorders, in order to guide users fast and directly to the information they seek. Additionally, future research should also target studies on (cost-)effectiveness and efficacy for crisis intervention, postvention, and prevention [70]. This research should include several demographic factors, cultural differences, and different psychiatric disorders like addiction. Future research could determine, if suicide prevention and effective interventions exclusively via the Internet are possible and as effective as 'conservative' face-to-face treatments. Furthermore, methods for research on suicide prevention and intervention on the Internet should be improved.

References

[1] Kessler R, Crum R, Warner L, Nelson C, Schulenberg J, Anthony J: Lifetime co-occurrence of DSM-III-R alcohol abuse and dependence with other psychiatric disorders in the National Comorbidity Survey. *Arch Gen Psychiatry.* 1997; 54(4): 313-321.

[2] Kraus L, Bauernfeind R: Repräsentativerhebung zum Konsum psychoaktiver Substanzen bei Erwachsenen in Deutschland 1997 [Representative survey of the consumption of psychotropic drugs in adults in Germany 1997]. *Sucht.* 1998; 44 (Suppl 1): 7-82.

[3] Kessler RC, Nelson CB, McGonagle KA, Edlund MJ, Frank RG, Leaf PJ: The epidemiology of co-occuring addictive and mental disorders. Implications for prevention and service utilisation. *Am J Orthopsychiatry.* 1996; 66(1): 17-31.

[4] Jha P, Chaloupka FJ: *Curbing the epidemic: governments and the economics of tobacco control.* Washington, DC: World Bank, 1999. Available from: http://www.globalink.org/tobacco/wb/ wb04.shtml, accessed 2007 December 6.

[5] Baumeister SE, Kraus L, Stonner TK, Metz K: Tabakkonsum, Nikotinabhängigkeit und Trends. Ergebnisse des Epidemiologischen Suchtsurveys 2006 [Tobacco use, nicotine dependence and trends. Results of the 2006 *Epidemiological Survey of Substance Abuse. Sucht.* 2008; 54 (Suppl 1): 26-35.

[6] *World Health Organization* [homepage on the Internet]. Available from: http://www.who.int/mental_health/prevention/suicide/suicideprevent/en/, accessed 2008 July 20.

[7] Inskip HM, Harris C, Barraclough B: Lifetime risk of suicide for affective disorder, alcoholism and schizophrenia. *Br J Psychiatry.* 1998; 172: 35-37.

[8] Schneider B: *Risikofaktoren für Suizid* [Risk factors for suicide]. Regensburg, Roderer Verlag; 2003, p.37.

[9] Harris EC, Barraclough B: Suicide as an outcome for mental disorders: a meta-analysis. *Br J Psychiatry.* 1997; 170: 205-228.

[10] Harris EC, Barraclough B: Excess mortality of mental disorder. *Br J Psychiatry.* 1998; 173: 11-53.

[11] Wilcox HC, Conner KR, Caine ED: Association of alcohol and drug use disorders and completed suicide: an empirical review of cohort studies. *Drug Alcohol Depend.* 2004; 76 (Suppl): S11-S19.

[12] Hiroeh U, Appleby L, Mortensen PB, Dunn G: Death by homicide, suicide, and other unnatural causes in people with mental illness: a population-based study. *Lancet.* 2001; 358(9299): 2110-2112.

[13] Lesage AD, Boyer R, Grunberg F, Vanier C, Morissette R, Menard-Buteau C, Loyer M: Suicide and mental disorders: a case-control study of young men. *Am J Psychiatry.* 1994; 151(7): 1063-1068.

[14] Cheng AT: Mental illness and suicide. A case-control study in East Taiwan. *Arch Gen Psychiatry.* 1995; 52(7): 594-603.

[15] Foster T, Gillespie K, McClelland R, Patterson C: Risk factors for suicide independent of DSM-III-R Axis I disorder. Case-control psychological autopsy study in Northern Ireland. *Br J Psychiatry.* 1999; 175: 175-179.

[16] Waern M: Alcohol dependence and misuse in elderly suicides. *Alcohol Alcohol.* 2003; 38(3): 249-254.

[17] Gururaj G, Isaac MK, Subbakrishna DK, Ranjani R: Risk factors for completed suicides: a case-control study from Bangalore, India. *Inj Control Saf Promot.* 2004; 11(3): 183-191.

[18] Kõlves K, Värnik A, Tooding LM, Wasserman D: The role of alcohol in suicide: a case-control psychological autopsy study. *Psychol Med.* 2006; 36(7): 923-930.

[19] Schneider B, Kõlves K, Blettner M, Wetterling T, Schnabel A, Värnik A: Substance use disorders as risk factors for suicide in an Eastern and a Central European city (Tallinn and Frankfurt/Main). *Psychiatry Res.*, in press.

[20] Murphy GE, Wetzel RD, Robins E, McEvoy L: Multiple risk factors predict suicide in alcoholism. *Arch Gen Psychiatry.* 1992; 49(6): 459-463.

[21] Conner KR, Beautrais AL, Conwell Y: Risk factors for suicide and medically serious suicide attempts among alcoholics: analyses of Canterbury Suicide Project data. *J Stud Alcohol.* 2003; 64(4): 551-554.

[22] Sher L: Risk and protective factors for suicide in patients with alcoholism. *ScientificWorldJournal.* 2006; 6: 1405-1411.

[23] Ferrada-Noli M, Ormstad K, Asberg M: Pathoanatomic findings and blood alcohol analysis at autopsy (BAC) in forensic diagnoses of undetermined suicide. A cross-cultural study. *Forensic Sci Int.* 1996; 78(2): 157-163.

[24] Brady J: The association between alcohol misuse and suicidal behaviour. *Alcohol Alcohol.* 2006; 41(5): 473-478.

[25] Borges G, Walters EE, Kessler RC: Associations of substance use, abuse, and dependence with subsequent suicidal behavior. *Am J Epidemiol.* 2000; 151(8): 781-789.

[26] Swahn M, Bossarte R, Sullivent E: Age of alcohol use initiation, suicidal behaviour, and peer and dating violence victimization and perpetration among high-risk, seventh-grade adolescents. *Pediatrics.* 2008; 121(2): 297-305.

[27] Angst J, Clayton PJ: Personality, smoking and suicide: a prospective study. *J Affect Disord.* 1998; 51(1):55-62.

[28] Tanskanen A, Tuomilehto J, Viinamäki H, Vartiainen E, Lehtonen J, Puska P: Smoking and the risk of suicide. *Acta Psychiatr Scand.* 2000; 101(3): 243-245.

[29] Hemmingsson T, Kriebel D: Smoking at age 18-20 and suicide during 26 years of follow-up – how can the association be explained? *Int J Epidemiol.* 2003; 32(6): 1000-1004.

[30] Riala K, Alaräisänen A, Taanila A, Hakko H, Timonen M, Räsänen P: Regular daily smoking among 14-year-old adolescents increases the subsequent risk for suicide: the Northern Finland 1966 Birth Cohort Study. *J Clin Psychiatry.* 2007; 68(5): 775-780.

[31] Davey Smith G, Phillips AN, Neaton JD: Smoking as "independent" risk factor for suicide: illustration of an artifact from observational epidemiology? *Lancet.* 1992; 340(8821): 709-712.

[32] Hemenway D, Solnick SJ, Colditz GA: Smoking and suicide among nurses. *Am J Public Health.* 1993; 83(2): 249-251.

[33] Tverdal A, Thelle D, Stensvold I, Leren P, Bjartveit K: Mortality in relation to smoking history: 13 years' follow-up of 68,000 Norwegian men and women 35-49 years. *J Clin Epidemiol.* 1993; 46(5): 475-487.

[34] Miller M, Hemenway D, Bell NS, Yore MM, Amoroso PJ: Cigarette smoking and suicide: a prospective study of 300,000 male active-duty army soldiers. *Am J Epidemiol.* 2000a; 151(11): 1060-1063.

[35] Miller M, Hemenway D, Rimm E. Cigarettes and suicide: a prospective study of 50,000 men. *Am J Public Health.* 2000b; 90(5): 768-773.

[36] Leistikow BN, Martin DC, Samuels SJ: Injury death excesses in smokers: a 1990-95 United States national cohort study. *Inj Prev.* 2000; 6(4): 277-280.

[37] Iwasaki M, Akechi T, Uchitomi Y, Tsugane S: Japan Public Health Center-based Prospective Study on Cancer and Cardiovascular Disease (JPHC study) Group. Cigarette smoking and completed suicide among middle-aged men: a population-based cohort study in Japan. *Ann Epidemiol.* 2005; 15(4): 286-292.

[38] Schneider B, Schnabel A, Weber B, Frölich L, Maurer, K, Wetterling T: Nicotine use in suicides: a case-control study. *Eur Psychiatry.* 2005; 20(2): 129-136.

[39] Schneider B, Wetterling T, Georgi K, Bartusch B, Schnabel A, Blettner M: Smoking differently modifies suicide risk of affective disorders, substance use disorders, and social factors. *J Affect Disord.* 2008 Jun 14. [Epub ahead of print].

[40] Hawton K, Simkin S, Rue J, Haw C, Barbour F, Clements A, Sakarovitch C, Deeks J: Suicide in female nurses in England and Wales. *Psychol Med.* 2002; 32(2): 239-250.

[41] Fergusson DM, Woodward LJ, Horwood LJ: Risk factors and life processes associated with the onset of suicidal behavior during adolescence and early adulthood. *Psychol Med* 2000; 30(1): 23-39.

[42] McGee R, Williams S, Nada-Raja S: Is cigarette smoking associated with suicidal ideation in young people? *Am J Psychiatry.* 2005; 162(3): 619-620.

[43] Hintikka J, Pesonen T, Saarinen P, Tanskanen A, Lehtonen J, Viinamäki H: Suicidal ideation in the Finnish general population. A 12-month follow-up study. *Soc Psychiatry Psychiatr Epidemiol.* 2001; 36(12): 590-594.

[44] Zhang J, McKeown RE, Hussey JR, Thompson SJ, Woods JR: Gender differences in risk factors for attempted suicide among young adults: findings from the Third National Health and Nutrition Survey. *Ann Epidemiol.* 2005; 15(2): 167-173.

[45] Ringbäck Weitoft G, Rosén M: Is perceived nervousness and anxiety a predictor of premature mortality and severe morbidity? A longitudinal follow-up the Swedish survey of living conditions. *J Epidemiol Community Health.* 2005; 59(9):794-798.

[46] Andréasson S, Allebeck P: Cannabis and mortality among young men: A longitudinal study of Swedish conscripts. *Scand J Soc Med.* 1990; 18(1): 9-15.

[47] Mehlum L: The Internet, suicide, and suicide prevention. Crisis. 2000; 21(4): 186-188.

[48] Thompson S. Suicide and the Internet. *Psychiatric Bulletin* 2001; 25: 400.

[49] Forsthoff A, Hummel B, Möller H, Grunze H: Suizidalität und Internet. Gefahren durch neue Medien [Suicidality and the Internet. Danger from new media]. *Nervenarzt* 2006; 77(3): 343-345.

[50] Becker K, Mayer M, Nagenborg M, El-Faddagh M, Schmidt MU: Parasuicide online: Can suicide Websites trigger suicidal behaviour in predisposed adolescents. *Nord J Psychiatry* 2004; 58(2): 111-114.

[51] Rajagopal S: Suicide pacts and the Internet. *BMJ.* 2004; 329(7478): 1298-1299.

[52] Ybarra M, Suman M: Help seeking behaviour and the internet: A national survey. *Int J Med Inform.* 2006; 75(1): 29-41.

[53] Ellen EF: Identifying and treating suicidal college students. *Psychiatric Times* 2002; 19: 8.

[54] Barak A: Emotional support and suicide prevention through the Internet: A field project report. *Comput Human Behav.* 2007; 23(4): 971-984.

[55] Bale C: Befriending in Cyberspace – challenges and opportunities. *Crisis.* 2001; 22(1): 10-11.

[56] *The Samaritans: Samaritans Annual Report & Accounts 2007/08*. Available at: http:// /www.samaritans.org/about_samaritans.aspx. Accessed September 05, 2008.

[57] Lindner R, Fiedler G: Neue Beziehungsformen im Internet - Virtuelle Objektbeziehungen in der Psychotherapie [New kinds of relationships on the internet. Virtual object relations in psychotherapy]. *Nervenarzt.* 2002; 73(1): 78-84.

[58] Penn D, Simpson L, Edie G, Leggett S, Wood L, Hawgood J, Krysinska K, Yellowlees P, De Leo D: Development of ACROSSnet: An online support system for rural and remote community suicide prevention workers in Queensland, Australia. *Health Informatics J* 2005; 11(4): 275-293.

[59] Stone DM, Barber CW, Potter L: Public health training online: The National Centre for Suicide Prevention Training. *Am J Prev Med.* 2005; 29(5 Suppl 2): 247-251.

[60] Howgood J, Irving R, Guo E, Gilmour M, De Leo D: Online education: The electronic suicide prevention skills training. *Paper presented at the Queensland Suicide and Self-Harm Prevention Conference,* Brisbane, Australia: 2006.

[61] Recupero P, Harms S, Noble J: Googling Suicide: Surfing for Suicide Information on the internet. *J Clin Psychiatry.* 2008; 69(6): 878-888.

[62] Biddle L, Donovan J, Hawton K, Kapur N, Gunnell D: Suicide and the Internet. *BMJ.* 2008; 336(7648): 800-802.

[63] Grohol JM: Study misses internet's greater collection of support websites. *BMJ.* 2008; 336(7650): 905-906.

[64] Althaus E: Suchthilfe im Internet [Addiction help in the Internet]. *Psychotherapeut* 2001; 46: 342.

[65] Baker D, Fortune S: Understanding self-harm and suicide websites: a qualitative interview study of young adult website users. *Crisis.* 2008; 29(3):118-122.

[66] Eichenberg C: Internet message boards for suicidal people: A typology of users. *Cyberpsychol Behav.* 2008; 11(1): 107-113.

[67] *Nationales Suizidpräventionsprogramm für Deutschland: Empfehlungen für die Berichterstattung in den Medien* [Recommendations for media reporting]. Available at: http:// http://www.suizidpraevention-deutschland.de/downloads.html. Accessed September 05, 2008.

[68] Kordy H, Golkaramnay V, Wolf M, Haug S, Bauer S: Internetchatgruppen in Psychotherapie und Psychosomatik. Akzeptanz und Wirksamkeit einer Internet-Brücke zwischen Fachklinik und Alltag [Internet chatgroups in psychotherapy and psychosomatics. Acceptance and effectivenesss of an internet-bridge between hospital and everyday-life]. *Psychotherapeut.* 2005; 51: 144-153.

[69] Wang YD, Phillips-Wren G, Forgionne G: E-delivery of personalised healthcare information to intermediaries for suicide prevention. *Int J Electronic Healthc.* 2005; 1(4): 396-412.

[70] Krysinska K, De Leo D: Telecommunication and suicide prevention: Hopes and challenges for the new century. *Omega* (Westport). 2007; 55(3):237-253.

In: Internet and Suicide
Editors: L. Sher and A. Vilens
ISBN 978-1-60741-077-5

Chapter 18

Effect of Mass Media on Suicidal Behavior in Patients with Psychotic Disorders

Eduardo J. Aguilar, Soledad Jorge, Ana Rubio and Samuel G. Siris
Clinical University Hospital, Valencia, Spain; Zucker-Hillside Hospital, North Shore - Long Island Jewish Health System. Glen Oaks, New York, USA

Abstract

Mass media have the capacity of influencing behavior, including suicidal behavior in vulnerable individuals. An imitation effect has been demonstrated although some questions and some controversies persist concerning what makes certain people more vulnerable, what the exact mechanisms of the effect are, and what constitute the best protective steps. Moreover, much of the evidence which has been gathered lacks clear specifications in regard with psychiatric diagnoses, making it difficult to ascertain what role is played by psychosis in the process. In particular, the Internet has a huge potential for communication and recent reports suggest it may both benefit and hamper preventive strategies against suicide. Additionally, telepsychiatry, a model of care with clear connections with Internet is now being used with fairly good evidence of success. Suicidal behaviors may be approached by this modality but a number of difficulties have yet to be overcome. Controversial findings, frequent and rapid changes in the mass media and a lack of research studies on these issues preclude definitive conclusions.

Unfortunately, data are particularly scarce on the potential effects of mass media on suicidal behavior in patients with psychotic disorders. This is especially true for the Internet. To our knowledge, no research study has specifically addressed the effects of this medium on the suicidal behavior of psychotic patients. Available data and reflections by the authors are presented in this chapter which is also aimed at helping mental health professionals to orientate their patients on how to take advantage of mass media while not being damaged from them.

INTRODUCTION

Suicide is a devastating outcome for several psychiatric conditions including schizophrenia, bipolar disorder and other psychotic disorders. While suicide rates for schizophrenia seem to be between 10% [1, 2] and 5% [3], an estimated 6%-15% of people with bipolar disorder commit suicide [4, 5]. Standardized mortality ratios (SMRs) allow for comparisons with the general population. Patients with schizophrenia have been reported to have between an 8- and a 13-fold increased risk of completing suicide than the general population [6, 7]. Bipolar disorder seems to even have a greater suicide risk. The SMR for suicide has been estimated to be 20 to 30 for patients with bipolar disorder [8] but data are not completely concordant and it could be as low as 10 [9].

The topic of the mass media, psychosis, and suicide, of course, occurs in the context of the relationship between psychiatry and the mass media – a relationship which has never been an easy one. Data from UK seem to indicate that psychiatry gets a particular bad press compared with medicine [10] and this no doubt extends to other countries as well. Cancer, for example, has some commonalities with schizophrenia and may be a good comparison element. Duckworth et al. (2003) compared schizophrenia and cancer coverage by newspapers from 1996 or 1997. Schizophrenia was mentioned in a metaphorical way in 28 percent of the articles while only 1 percent of articles referred to cancer in that manner [11]. What seems particularly regrettable is that while negative medical contents are centered on professionals, the focus changes to patients in the case of psychiatry [12].

Some authors have emphasized cultural differences regarding newspaper headlines about suicide [13, 14]. More recently, Huang & Priebe (2003) investigated articles on mental health care in the print media from an international perspective, including UK, USA and Australia. The tone of the articles, overall, was negative but there were slightly more positive articles in the USA and Australian media [15]. This perspective necessarily puts pressure on our patients with diverse negative consequences related to stigmatisation. At this point, stigma is a major concern since it has several troublesome correlates such as provoking despair in patients and keeping them away from seeking treatment, while also prompting some of them into suicidal thoughts or behaviors. This is particularly relevant for the purpose of this chapter since schizophrenia and related chronic psychotic disorders are especially vulnerable to stigmatization processes. It has even been suggested that a relationship exists between stigma and suicide [16]. Eagles et al. (2003) investigated a group of outpatients with severe and persistent mental illness to see what could help patients when they felt suicidal. Not surprisingly, negative influences for these patients included the media and the stigma of psychiatric illness [17].

Mental illnesses are usually depicted in a negative way in mass media including newspapers, television and films which contribute to enhanced mental illness stigma. Negative media (newspaper and, particularly, television) reports have been shown to potentiate the desire for social distance towards people with schizophrenia [18]. However, only a very small percentage of the variance of social distance was explained in this study by media consumption [18]. In particular, people with schizophrenia are seen by citizens as unpredictable and dangerous [19]. Films also sometimes depict a degrading image of schizophrenia [20]. As Byrne has further pointed out (2003), the Internet is a combination of the best and the worst of print media (rapid, accessible, worldwide and uncontrolled), including images and sounds in addition to text [12]. The potentiality of this medium is therefore obviously enormous and it will certainly be important to investigate it scientifically.

The media influence not only public attitudes towards mental illness but also policy development. Hallam (2002) studied how English newspapers impact on the development of mental health policy. The author based her work in two famous cases; one of them, a case of suicide that occurred in London, in December 1992. Ben Silcock, a person with schizophrenia, climbed into the lions' den at London Zoo and was mauled by the animal. She analyzed the press coverage this suicide received for a period of 8 years and the published material's effects on policy decisions. Policy measures taken under the shadow of public preoccupations after these rare events resulted in additional constraints on people with mental health problems, have further stigmatized people with these illnesses and have put more exigencies on service professionals [21].

Considering the importance of media depictions of mental illness, exploring whether a change is taking place seems a relevant question. A recent study assessing a possible change in the quality of reporting of schizophrenia in UK national daily newspapers, between 1996 with 2005, found little evidence for this hypothesis, particularly in regard with the use of stigmatizing descriptors [22].

We have enough indications to suspect that media can influence the suicidal tendencies of patients with psychotic disorders; probably both in positive and negative ways. Some data also suggest that potential negative influences are not under control. This review documents the present level of knowledge regarding these issues with a special attention to generating hypotheses and improving our capacity to deal with these phenomena.

Classical Mass Media and Suicidal Behavior

The influence of mass media on suicidal behavior has been a controversial issue for years although it has been extensively studied. The hypothesis suggesting that a suicide contagion may be transmitted through traditional mass media has repeatedly been reported. This so-called "Werther effect" refers to the wave of suicides that occurred after Goethe's publication of 'The Sorrows of Young Werther' [23]. Schmidtke & Häfner (1989) reviewed the influence of mass media on suicide and found evidence for imitation processes in proportion to the amount of detail of suicide methods and the degree of celebrity of the suicides [24]. On the contrary, an investigation of all US network television suicide news stories broadcast between 1973 and 1984 could not demonstrate a reliable association with the incidence of suicides during that period [25].

Several methodological problems may appear when investigating the effect of mass media on suicidal phenomena. For example, exposure to models may be age- and sex-specific and depend on size of coverage and audience or readership [13]. They and other authors have especially remarked the 'ecological fallacy' (interpretation of chance fluctuations as a media effect) as a frequent flaw in these type of studies [26, 27].

Several papers have explored the characteristics of both the model and the observer. According to Hawton & Williams (2002), younger people are most vulnerable to the influence of the media. Moreover, the impact of the media on suicidal behavior seems to be most likely when a method of suicide is specified or detailed, when it is portrayed dramatically or it is about a celebrity, and when the media stimulus or model and the observer are similar in terms of age, sex, and nationality [28]. Stack (2005) reported interesting information on nonfictional media. The presence of either an entertainment or political celebrity, and the focus on female suicide were more likely to be associated to a copycat effect. On the other hand, studies focusing on stories that stressed negative definitions of suicide or based on television stories (which receive less coverage than print stories) were less likely to find a copycat effect [29]. Pirkis et al. (2006) also investigated the characteristics of media items in Australian newspapers and on radio and television news and current affairs shows between March 2000 and February 2001. Stronger effects were found for a context of multiple reports on suicide (versus occurring in isolation), television versus other media, and if they were about completed suicide. Finally, an increase in male suicides was associated with items about an individual's experience of suicide and opinion pieces, and an increase in female suicides was associated with items about mass- or murder-suicide [30]. Blood et al. (2007) recently presented data on the reporting of suicide in Australia which suggests that the media present an image of suicide skewed towards violent and unusual methods, and that newsworthiness of the stories is given priority over accuracy and ethics [31].

Recent reviews have given further support to the notion of a relationship between mass media and suicide. A causal association has been demonstrated between nonfictional media reporting of suicide (newspapers, television, and books) and actual suicide. This might also be the case of fictional media portrayal (films, television, music, and plays) but the evidence for this is more equivocal [32, 33]. Sudak & Sudak (2005) have also reviewed the literature on media-related suicide to conclude that there are an increased number of suicides as consequence of media portrayals of suicide that romanticize or dramatize the description of suicidal deaths [34]. A recent well designed study by Cheng et al. (2007) also showed that the extensive media reporting of the suicide of a celebrity was followed by an increase in suicide attempts [35]. Regrettably, as with most of the studies on this issue, the authors did not report on the psychiatric diagnoses of attempters. Due to the nature of the subject matter, of course, there have been (and will be) no randomized controlled trials of the subject and we must settle for the less reliable fruits of observational data.

The presence of positive impacts of mass media on suicidality may be even more difficult to investigate and the level of evidence is even more limited in this case [13]. Changes in the style of reporting might have a preventive effect. Although not without controversy, potentially beneficial effects of the media portrayal of suicidal behavior were demonstrated by O'Connor et al. (1999)[36]. Moreover, some reports have suggested an educational role for reports explaining the lethality of methods in the case for drugs whose potential lethality is not well-known such as, for example, paracetamol [26, 37].

The Internet and Suicidal Behavior

A decade ago, some case reports suggested the potential for some 'suicide sites' to provoke or facilitate suicidal behaviors [38-40]. Baume et al. (1997) remarked on the ambivalence of some people and how vulnerable individuals were compelled by others to act on their suicidal plans [38]. Several papers have shown the presence of web forums on the Net which are clearly pro-suicide [41, 42] but, probably because of methodological difficulties, this phenomenon is still understudied and definitive conclusions about its dimensions cannot be reached at this point. This is especially true regarding psychotic patients. Disappointingly, data are not available about the incidence of cybersuicides (attempted or completed suicide influenced by the internet). This lack of data is particularly unfortunate when we consider the overall potential of the Internet. A Google search with the word 'Suicide' in September 2008 retrieved 90.100.000 entries. Interestingly, 1.510.000 entries appeared with the words 'Suicide & Psychosis', and 1.970.000 with the words 'Suicide' & 'Schizophrenia'.

A recent study has been the first one to demonstrate that Internet use was a predictor of (the incidence of) suicide among males, probably because males spent more time online than females [43]. Their findings suggest that Internet use and newspaper articles on suicide have a differential effect on suicide incidence in males and females. The authors covered a period of 218 months, from January 1987 to March 2005 in Japan, and were able to use information on Internet use available in Japan since 2001 (prevalence of household Internet use).

Mehlum (2000) explained several ways for a suicide contagion to happen through the Internet. First, many web sites present suicide as a solution to life's problems. Second, they may present details of methods for committing suicide. There exist really very few legal, technical, or financial obstacles to those who wish to provide the millions of internet users with detailed information on how to commit suicide. Third, discussion groups, which are increasingly interactive and sometimes created with a good purpose, are now frequently used as meeting places for people with severe depressive or other mental illness, particularly young people. These sites may work in both directions, as a place to share despair and suicidal thoughts that may be overcome with the help of others and as sites where these emotions may be fostered with the consequent suicide risk. These effects can occur, of course, over vast distances, complicating jurisdictional issues, and, in some cases, they may prompt Internet users into suicide pacts [44].

As Prior et al. (2004) remarked, there is not enough information detailing how frequently patients use the Internet, and whether there is actually a profile associated with individuals that use Internet to foster their suicide plans [45]. It could be that individuals who access the Net are qualitatively different to other individuals [46]. Regrettably, we do not have data on whether psychotic patients access to the Net and what type of sites they visit. Perhaps some psychotic patients who find it difficult to express themselves or to feel understood in other domains, find the structure of the Internet a better fit to their communication needs, especially when it comes to expressing strong feelings.

A particular mode of cybersuicide is suicide pact. Suicide pacts have been known for years as a rare phenomenon [47] but now they seem to be occurring among people that do not know each other. Remarkably, they are able to attract extensive media attention. Fishbain & Aldrich (1985) studied suicide pacts, prior to the advent of the Internet, from an international perspective. Twenty suicide pacts (double suicides) from the Florida Dade County Medical Examiner's Office were identified. These data were compared using a standardized instrument to published suicide pact data from England, Japan, and Bangalore City, India. In this study, the frequency of suicide pacts was found to be greatest for Japan; lover pacts were found to be typical for Japan; spouse pacts were typical for Dade County and England; and friend pact frequency was greatest for Bangalore City. In addition, interestingly, it was found that suicide pact victims, in general, choose nonviolent suicide methods [48]. Whether these tendencies continue to hold true for people relating on the Internet remains to be determined.

A recent review by Recupero et al. (2008) classified sites as pro-, anti-, or neutral suicide sites. Suicide-neutral and anti-suicide sites occurred most frequently. However, 41 web pages were pro-suicide and were easily accessible. Detailed how-to instructions for unusual and lethal suicide methods were easily located through the searches [49]. According to Biddle et al. (2008), potential effects include [42]:

1. Negative effects
   - Web forums in which people are being encouraged to commit suicide as a problem solving strategy.
   - Sites or forums with information on lethal methods.
   - Chat rooms where people pressure to each other to commit suicide, idolize those who have completed suicide, and facilitate suicide pacts.
2. Positive effects
   - Sites advising people to seek help and providing support links. These sites may also allow people to express, share, and work through their despair.
   - Sites that provide scientific information opening the possibility to get advice or encouraging potentially suicidal people to seek treatment.
   - Internet based interventions to treat depression.
   - Supportive message boards and web rings where people share a positive way of approaching suicidal thoughts.

Although very little information is available about a possible net effect of these influences, a net positive effect on suicide seems to be the case since, in England, rates of suicide among young (15-34 year old) men and women, the age groups that mostly use the internet, have been declining since the mid-1990s, a time when use of the internet has expanded rapidly [50].

Psychotic Suicide and Mass Media

Data are particularly scarce on the potential effects of mass media on suicidal behavior in patients with psychotic disorders. To our knowledge, no study has specifically addressed this point.

One of the few papers indirectly assessing this issue was published by Fakhoury (2000). The author audited a British mental health helpline SANELINE (1996-1998) and, remarkably, showed data about users' diagnoses (55% depression and 31% for people with psychosis). The distribution by gender showed that for psychosis, more calls involved males than females while the opposite was true for depression [51]. However, validating information on the results of these calls was limited and, in any case, these data may not be applicable to other settings.

Although very little information is available, several characteristics of psychotic suicide suggest that this group of patients may be especially vulnerable to Internet effects. The majority of suicides in cases of schizophrenia occur in young patients, early in the course of the illness [3]. This is also true for bipolar disorders [52]. An increased risk has also been associated with higher IQ and good premorbid function as well as with developing schizophrenia after having achieved academically [53]. Moreover, according to these authors, the availability of a method may be crucial in suicidal thoughts progressing into suicidal behaviors. The presence of depressive symptoms, and particularly hopelessness, together with fewer negative symptoms seem to be contributors to this risk [54-57]. Finally, cluster suicidal behaviors have been described in psychiatric patients including patients with schizophrenia [58].

These data bring us a picture of a vulnerable individual, somewhat similar to those that have been shown to be prone to cybersuicides. Family difficulties and perceived stigmatization have additionally been reported as possible contributing factors to suicide in patients with schizophrenia [16]. Stigma fostered by mass media including Internet and a higher accessibility of lethal methods are probably also contributing factors. Some authors have already pointed that restricting access to lethal methods and media reporting guidelines are important strategies to prevent suicide in patients with schizophrenia [59].

Imitative behavior has already been demonstrated for psychotic suicide. O'Donnell et al. (1996) interviewed 20 individuals, mostly patients with schizophrenia, who had attempted suicide by jumping in front of a railway train in London. In most cases the act had been impulsive and was characterized by an extremely high level of suicidal intent. For some of them, the idea of the underground as method of suicide came from knowing another inpatient who had used this method [60].

On the other hand, psychotic patients may have unique characteristics in regard to suicide. A striking resemblance between suicide pacts, which have already been mentioned as a particular issue in regard with Internet influences, and folie à deux is probably one of them. Greenberg (1956) published a very interesting review on the relationship between Folie à deux and crime. He reported several examples, some of them classical examples from the 19th century, of the tendency of such psychotic states to spread beyond the original (usually familial) group. Interestingly, suicide is closely related to murder in this setting. According to his review, a paranoid patient, particularly someone diagnosed as delusional disorder, may be particularly prone to induce somebody else's suicide. The schizophrenic contagion is limited to those closest to him but the paranoid fear coming from the patient with delusional disorder spreads beyond and the patient finds his defenders in the press and public [61]. We could question whether similar phenomena might be fostered by the Internet.

A more recent case report and a review of the literature have been published by Salih (1981). A case of folie à deux affecting two women friends who presented as a suicide pact (successfully treated) is described. Again, his review of the relevant literature revealed consistent theoretical similarities between folie à deux and suicidal pacts suggesting that the psychotic condition would precipitate the suicidal pact [62].

The phenomenon of suicide pacts and the Internet has been reviewed by Rajagopal (2004) after 9 deaths in Japan, in October 2004, apparently in two suicide pacts (seven suicides in one pact and two in the other). Instead of the usual close relationships held by the victims, here, the pacts had been planned by suicide websites [63].

Suicide pacts are a rare phenomenon, constituting less than 1% of the total number of suicides [47]. Just as in some suicide pacts where one person instigates the plan, in folie à deux the delusion is characteristically imposed by the dominant member of the relationship on to the other person. Scientific literature on cybersuicide mainly pertains to solitary suicides, and little information exists about the internet and suicide pacts. A referential study by Brown & Barraclough (1999) showed that mental disorder was present in half, and medical illness in one-third of suicide pacts Most interestingly, they gave data on diagnoses and showed that schizophrenia and manic depression were, by far (50 times), less frequent than depression. However, folie à deux could be of particular relevance in this setting. Although not fully meeting criteria for this disorder, five pacts were provoked by delusions, or over-valued ideas, of disease or financial ruin in one partner, and apparently shared by the other [64].

Internet Therapeutical Potential for Suicide Prevention in Psychotic Patients

There are reasons to believe that the Internet can be a useful resource to aid a psychotic patient in getting help. A major effect of the Internet on psychiatry was already anticipated a decade ago [65]. These authors remarked on its great potential in psychiatric education, clinical care, research, and administration, but also pointed out that major adjustments in individual and organizational expectations and responses would be needed.

Some authors have reported cases in which threats of suicide were made somewhat indirectly and discovered over the Internet [66]. It could even be the case that Internet characteristics such as anonymity could help some people to communicate their suicidal plans. Along this line, and without entering on obvious ethical and legal implications, an anecdotal report by Neimark et al. (2006) showed the possibility of obtaining relevant information on suicide risk assessment through the Internet although patients may be trying to hide it [67]. Prasad et al. (2001) looked for the information and support available for people with suicidal tendencies. They found information, and less often, sites that offered e-mail support and online discussions [68].

We have already mentioned the woeful lack of careful scientific information on this issue. One of the few related studies was done by Timms et al. (2005) that assessed people's online responses (> 4000) towards public education materials launched by the Royal College of Psychiatrists ('Help is at Hand' leaflets), and the acceptability and usefulness of information about mental health on the College website. Responses were globally positive but some negative responses (such as an augmentation of feelings of despair) were also found [69].

There are several guidelines for the media that should help to prevent 'copycat' suicide. A recent review of these guidelines showed noticeable similarities in approach, and noted that, without exception, all guidelines suggest avoiding specific and explicit detail about the suicide method (and location) [70]. Although these guidelines have not yet been scientifically evaluated, they have enough face validity to support their use. Several agencies have recently worked together in consensus guidelines that are now available. These agencies are the American Foundation for Suicide Prevention, the American Association of Suicidology, the Annenberg Public Policy Center, the Office of the Surgeon General, the Centers for Disease Control, the National Institute of Mental Health (NIMH), the Substance Abuse Mental Health Services Administration (SAMHSA), the World Health Organization (W.H.O.), the National Swedish Center for Suicide Research and the New Zealand Youth Suicide Prevention Strategy groups (available at several sites such as www.afsp.org or http://www.nimh.nih.gov/health/topics/suicide-prevention/reporting-on-suicide-recommendations-for-the-media.shtml). However, to our knowledge, no specific guidelines have been developed for specific illnesses such as schizophrenia, bipolar disorder or related psychoses.

We still do not know whether an adequate media portrayal of suicide events could help to reduce suicidal behavior. In fact, contagion effects are probably impossible to eradicate, but this should not prevent professionals from implementing efforts in this direction.

Restricting access to lethal methods reduces suicide rates [71]. However, we probably need to design specific interventions for psychotic patients. During a 4-year period, Hunt et al (2006) studied a consecutive series of suicides by people in contact with mental health services in England and Wales and showed how suicide methods and patients' characteristics vary according to diagnosis [72]. Stigma is a crucial issue. Destigmatisation to mental illness as well as suicide should be addressed. However, approaching suicide stigma may be a very difficult task since stigma associated to suicide may somewhat prevent some people from committing it [73]. Interventions among families, mental health professionals and church activists aimed at decreasing the stigma associated with mental illness and suicide may contribute to the reduction of deaths of psychotic patients by suicide [59].

Although, to our knowledge, no study has demonstrated that blacking out certain pro-suicide sites could have a preventive effect, this line of endeavor should also be pursued in the future. Meanwhile, mental health workers and researchers cannot ignore the potentiality of such a powerful instrument and several actions can already be implemented (Table 1).

Telemental health has now been present for decades and seems to be equivalent to face-to-face treatment. A recent paper by O'Reilly et al. (2007) has shown that psychiatric consultation and short-term follow-up can be as effective when delivered by telepsychiatry as when provided face to face [74]. A pioneer study showed that telepsychiatry (videoconsultation in this case) can be an acceptable and reliable method to assess patients with schizophrenia through well-known scales such as BPRS, SANS and SAPS [75].

Remote video care has been extensively studied in The Department of Veterans Affairs, with applications on multiple mental health diagnoses including schizophrenia [76]. This agency has recently considered suicide prevention a major priority and is trying to develop interventions through different telehealth modalities [76]. These authors have published a comprehensive review on the legal issues involved in remote assessment and interventions on suicidality. Major concerns are licensing requirements for remote delivery of care, legal procedures for involuntary detainment and commitment of potentially harmful patients, and liability questions (particularly abandonment and negligence issues). They conclude their review with a compilation of best practices which may well help orient future lines of both clinical and research endeavors [76]. Other agencies are also applying telepsychiatry to schizophrenia and other psychotic disorders. This is the case of the Schizophrenia Research Foundation (SCARF), at Chennai (India). It is remarkable that these initiatives are not without difficulties including an initial reluctance on the part of patients to use this facility [77]. Finally, a recent study used an Internet-delivered questionnaire to obtain information about suicide risk from parents of children and adolescents with a diagnosis of bipolar disorder [78]. Initiatives like these are now opening this field with promising results.

INTERNET RESOURCES

Psychotic patients may benefit from online crisis interventions, counseling opportunities, or help with concrete services that are now widely available. Clinicians should be aware of these resources in order to work with them effectively and be helpful to patients who stand to benefit from these services

Assistance may be found through several web-pages:

17. Specific for suicide prevention (crisis centres for suicide prevention) (Table 2):
    a. http://www.hopeline.com/. The Kristin Brooks Hope Center (KBHC) runs a national 1-800-SUICIDE hotline. This institution is working on a Program Psychiatric Emergency Response Network (PERN) that will connect the crisis center to community resources called Public Safety Answering Points (PSAPS) which include specific emergency psychiatric rescue teams. To our knowledge, no specific programs have been developed for psychotic patients.
    b. http://www.suicideinfo.ca/csp/go.aspx?tabid=77 and http://www.casp-acps.ca/crisiscentres.asp. The location of Canadian crisis centres is provided for all provinces.
    c. http://www.befrienders.org/. It is a 24-hour worldwide e-mail service delivered by the Samaritans. They mainly provide emotional support. Users can choose between centers with an email service or a full list of helplines in their own country.
    d. http://www.metanoia.org/suicide. It contains texts for suicidal persons to read.
    e. http://www.livingisforeveryone.com.au/. LIFE (Living is For Everyone). It provides evidences and resources for preventing suicide in Australia, addressed to people in the community who are involved in suicide prevention activities.
18. Mental health, non-specific for suicide (Table 3)
    a. http://psychcentral.com/. They give information on suicide and recommend contacting the National Suicide Prevention Lifeline toll-free at 800-273-8255. Additional crisis and suicide hotlines can be found in this web page.
    b. http://www.nami.org/. National Alliance on Mental Illness. Connection to discussion groups, information, a blog etc…
    c. http://www.nimh.nih.gov/health/publications/schizophrenia/complete-publication.shtml. Website of the National Institute of Mental Health. It offers information for patients and families about schizophrenia, its symptoms, treatment and prognosis.
    d. http://www.who.int/mental_health/management/schizophrenia/en/. Brief information about schizophrenia. Data are presented in an optimistic tone.
    e. http://www.mentalhelp.net/poc/center_index.php?id=7&cn=7. Broad information on schizophrenia, easily understandable with a quite neutral focus.
19. Psychosis sites (Table 4)
    a. http://www.reachoutpsychosis.com/psychosishelp/. A highly recommendable program of the British Columbia Schizophrenia Society. They look for educating young people and their parents about psychosis and reducing the stigma associated to these illnesses. This type of initiative may be useful for suicide

prevention. They also refer to the corresponding Crisis Intervention & Suicide Prevention Centre of British Columbia, a volunteer driven organization. Interestingly, it has a link to the corresponding Early Psychosis Intervention Program websites.

b. http://www.schizophrenia.com/. This site provides for information, support and education. They also include blogs and discussion forums. It has a Preventing Suicide resource (http://www.schizophrenia.com/suicide.html) that is very recommendable with clear and understandable information including, among others, a very interesting NAMI video (Coping with Suicidal Behavior) (http://video.google.com/videoplay?docid=-1676754491725405608&hl=es).
c. HealthyPlace.com - Schizophrenia and Suicide. High-quality information with links into specific topics on suicidal risk of patients with schizophrenia.
d. Suicide for Mental Healthcare Service Users. Irish program with a link to a handbook in pdf format with a chapter on suicide risk factors for patients with schizophrenia.
e. http://www.nimh.nih.gov/health/publications/bipolar-disorder/complete-publication.shtml. General information about bipolar disorder for patients and families with a small part devoted to the detection of suicide risk in patients with bipolar disorders.
f. http://www.mentalhelp.net/poc/center_index.php?id=4&cn=4. Broad document with very comprehensive information about diverse topics such as etiology, symptomatology, treatment and prognosis of bipolar disorders that also offers a specific area on suicide risk.

20. Worldwide organizations providing professional information (Table 5)
    - http://www.suicidology.org/. Website of the American Association of Suicidology (AAS). Website focused on the prevention strategies, orientated to health professionals with high quality bibliography references.
    - http://www.iasp.info/. Website of the International Association for Suicide Prevention (IASP). It has extensive contents with general information about suicide and mental health and it also offers a repertory of help resources such as telephone numbers in different countries of the world for people with suicidal intentions.
    - http://www.afsp.org/. Website of the American Foundation for Suicide Prevention. It has the double purpose of supporting for education and spread out its prevention campaigns.
    - http://www.sprc.org/suicide_prev_basics/glossary.asp. Website of the Suicide Prevention Resource Center. It includes training programs on suicide prevention for professionals.
21. List Serves that can be interesting to people who work in suicide prevention (Table 6)
    - 1-800-SUICIDE-subscribe@yahoogroups.com

      This group is exclusively for those crisis centers included in the National Hopeline Network to alert them of media events, problems, solutions and funding opportunities.
    - Crisis-intervention-subscribe@yahoogroups.com

The main purpose of this group is to facilitate the exchange of information and ideas among staff and volunteers of hotlines, crisis intervention centers, suicide prevention services, etc.

- FF0FSuicides-subscribe@yahoogroups.com

  The Friends of Families of Suicides (FFOS) runs this e-mail support group for those whose lives have been affected by suicide. They offer information and support to people (just adults) from different English-speaking countries.
- Suicidology-subscribe@yahoogroups.com

  The Suicidology group is a research information network. It is especially dedicated to mental health professionals but is also available to all the medical community and other people interested in suicide research and prevention.
- Suicidology2-subscribe@yahoogroups.com

  Suicidology 2 is a discussion group which provides a forum for professionals and others to discuss suicide research and issues. It is a partner group of Suicidology, a restricted research group.

22. Pro-suicide sites
    - Pro- suicide and how- to suicide web pages are very few when compared with those helpful sites available in the Net for those people with suicidal ideation that may seek for support. However, they are highly accessible and may be determinant on ambivalent patients' final decisions. Two of the most significant sites are 'The Church of euthanasia' (http://www.churcho feuthanasia.org/) and 'A practical guide to suicide' (http://www. francesfarmersrevenge.com/ stuff/suicideguide.htm). The recent review by Recupero et al. (2008) found up to 41 pro-suicide sites [49].

      Web Forums gather suicidal people that communicate to each other with endless potential interactions. Pro- and anti- suicide attitudes come together and sometimes yield a more than anecdotal suicide pact or different types of cluster suicides.

Table 1. Recommendations to improve mass media-psychiatry interaction

1.	A closer collaboration between the psychiatric profession and the mass media is required.
2.	Training courses for careers in the media should include adequate training regarding suicidality and suicide. Post-graduate training should also include information delivered by expert mental health professionals involved in suicide prevention, including that with psychotic patients.
3.	Psychiatric training must include advanced education on this topic.
4.	Inappropriate media reports of suicidal behavior should be highlighted and addressed.
5.	Specific internet sites should be created to reach out to psychotic and other patients with suicide risk.
6.	Mental health professionals should ask their psychotic patients about Internet use and facilitate their reaching helpful sites.
7.	Research studies on the use of the Internet by psychotic patients and specific interventions aimed at reducing suicide risk are needed.
8.	Internet potential for psychiatric education addressed to general public and mental health workers should be developed by public agencies.

Table 2. Specific sites for suicide prevention and support

- http://www.hopeline.com/
- http://www.casp-acps.ca/crisiscentres.asp
- http://www.befrienders.org/
- http://www.metanoia.org/suicide.
- http://www.livingisforeveryone.com.au/

Table 3. Mental health sites

- http://psychcentral.com/
- http://www.nami.org/
- http://www.nimh.nih.gov/health/publications/schizophrenia/complete-publication.shtml
- http://www.who.int/mental_health/management/schizophrenia/en/ http://www.mentalhelp.net/poc/center_index.php?id=7&cn=7

Table 4. Psychosis sites

- http://www.reachoutpsychosis.com/psychosishelp/
- http://www.schizophrenia.com/
- HealthyPlace.com - Schizophrenia and Suicide
- Suicide for Mental Healthcare Service Users
- http://www.nimh.nih.gov/health/publications/bipolar-disorder/complete-publication.shtml
- http://www.mentalhelp.net/poc/center_index.php?id=4&cn=4.

Table 5. Worldwide organizations providing professional information

- http://www.suicidology.org/
- http://www.iasp.info/
- http://www.afsp.org/
- http://www.sprc.org/suicide_prev_basics/glossary.asp

Table 6. List Serves for people who work in suicide prevention

- 1-800-SUICIDE-subscribe@yahoogroups.com
- Crisis-intervention-subscribe@yahoogroups.com
- FF0FSuicides-subscribe@yahoogroups.com
- Suicidology-subscribe@yahoogroups.com
- Suicidology2-subscribe@yahoogroups.com

Conclusion

Sensationalized descriptions or mass media reports of suicide deaths by famous people probably contribute meaningfully to suicide contagion (copycat suicides). On the other hand, appropriate coverage of suicide acts may help to educate the public, and help prevent potentially suicidal patients from attempting or committing suicide. In particular, the Internet, with its increasingly high level of availability and burgeoning repository of information and opinion, probably has the greatest paradoxical potentiality of helping patients in a suicidal crisis or prompting vulnerable patients into suicide.

Very little specific information is available on the potentiality of mass media, and particularly Internet, to promote or prevent suicidal behaviors in patients with psychotic disorders. Available data are promising but clinicians should be aware of the potential interactions between mass media and their patients, and researchers should make an effort to overcome methodological difficulties in order to explore this field.

References

[1] Caldwell CB, Gottesman II: Schizophrenics kill themselves too: a review of risk factors for suicide. *Schizophr Bull* 1990; 16: 571-589.

[2] Siris SG: Suicide and schizophrenia. *J Psychopharmacol* 2001; 15: 127-135.

[3] Palmer BA, Pankratz S, Bostwick JM: The lifetime risk of suicide in schizophrenia: a re-examination. *Arch Gen Psychiatry* 2005; 62: 247-253.

[4] Goodwin FK, Jamison KR: *Manic-depressive illness.* New York, Oxford University Press, 1990.

[5] Inskip HM, Harris EC, Barraclough B: Lifetime risk of suicide for affective disorder, alcoholism and schizophrenia. *Br J Psychiatry* 1998; 172: 35–37.

[6] Harris EC, Barraclough B: Suicide as an outcome for mental disorders. A meta-analysis. *Br J Psychiatry* 1997; 170: 205-228.

[7] Saha S, Chant D, McGrath J: A systematic review of mortality in schizophrenia: is the differential mortality gap worsening over time?. *Arch Gen Psychiatry* 2007; 64: 1123-1131.

[8] McIntyre RS, Muzina DJ, Kemp DE, Blank D, Woldeyohannes HO, Lofchy J, Soczynska JK, Banik S, Konarski JZ: Bipolar disorder and suicide: research synthesis and clinical translation. *Curr Psychiatry Rep* 2008; 10: 66-72.

[9] Dutta R, Boydell J, Kennedy N, Van Os J, Fearon P, Murray RM: Suicide and other causes of mortality in bipolar disorder: a longitudinal study. *Psychol Med* 2007; 37: 839-847.

[10] Lawrie SM: Newspaper coverage of psychiatric and physical illness. *Psychiatr Bull* 2000; 24: 104–106.

[11] Duckworth K, Halpern JH, Schutt RK, Gillespie C: Use of schizophrenia as a metaphor in US newspapers. *Psychiatr Serv* 2003; 54: 1402-1404.

[12] Byrne P: Psychiatry and the media. *Advances in Psychiatric Treatment* 2003; 9: 135-143.

[13] Schimdtke A, Schaller S: The role of mass media in suicide prevention, in The international handbook of suicide and attempted suicide. Edited by Hawton K, Van Heeringen K. Chichester, *John Wiley and Sons,* 2000; pp 676-697.

[14] Fekete S, Schmidtke A, Takahashi Y, Etzersdorfer E, Upanne M, Osvath P: Mass media, cultural attitudes, and suicide. Results of an international comparative study. *Crisis* 2001; 22: 170-172.

[15] Huang B, Priebe S: Media coverage of mental health care in the UK, USA and Australia. *Psychiatr Bull* 2003; 27: 331-333.

[16] Pompili M, Mancinelli I, Tatarelli R: Stigma as a cause of suicide. *Br J Psychiatry* 2003; 183: 173-174.

[17] Eagles JM, Carson DP, Begg A, Naji SA: Suicide prevention: a study of patients' views. *Br J Psychiatry* 2003; 182: 261-265.

[18] Angermeyer MC, Dietrich S, Pott D, Matschinger H: Media consumption and desire for social distance towards people with schizophrenia. *Eur Psychiatry* 2005; 20: 246-250.

[19] Crisp AH, Gelder MG, Rix S, Meltzer HI, Rowlands OJ: Stigmatisation of people with mental illnesses. *Br J Psychiatry* 2000; 177: 4-7.

[20] Byrne P: Stigma of mental illness and ways of diminishing it. *Advances in Psychiatric Treatment* 2000; 6: 65-72.

[21] Hallam A. Media influences on mental health policy: long-term effects of the Clunis and Silcock cases. *Int Rev Psychiatry* 2002; 14: 26–33.

[22] Clement S, Foster N: Newspaper reporting on schizophrenia: a content analysis of five national newspapers at two time points. *Schizophr Res* 2008; 98: 178-183.

[23] Phillips DP: The influence of suggestion on suicide: substantive and theroretical implications of the Werther effect. *Am Sociol Rev* 1974; 39: 340-354.

[24] Schmidtke A, Häfner H: Public attitudes towards and effects of the mass media on suicidal and deliberate self-harm behaviour, in Suicide and its Prevention: The Role of Attitude and Imitation. Edited by Diekstra R, Maris R, Platt S, Schmidtke A, Sonneck G). Leiden, World Health Organization/E. *J. Brill,* 1989, pp 313–330.

[25] Kessler RC, Downey G, Stipp H, Milavsky JR: Network television news stories about suicide and short-term changes in total US suicides. *J Nerv Ment Dis* 1989; 177: 551–555.

[26] Simkin S, Hawton K, Whitehead L, Fagg J, Eagle M: Media influence on parasuicide. A study of the effects of a television drama portrayal of paracetamol self-poisoning. *Br J Psychiatry* 1995; 167: 754-759.

[27] Hawton K, Simkin S, Deeks JJ, O'Connor S, Keen A, Altman DG, Philo G, Bulstrode C: Effects of a drug overdose in a television drama on presentations to hospital for self poisoning: time series and questionnaire study. *BMJ* 1999; 318: 972-977.

[28] Hawton K, Williams K: Influences of the media on suicide. *BMJ* 2002; 325: 1374-1375.

[29] Stack S: Suicide in the media: a quantitative review of suicides based on non-fictional stories. *Suicide Life Threat Behav* 2005; 35: 121-133.

[30] Pirkis JE, Burgess PM, Francis C, Blood RW, Jolley DJ: The relationship between media reporting of suicide and actual suicide in Australia. *Soc Sci Med* 2006; 62: 2874-2886.

[31] Blood RW, Pirkis J, Holland K: Media reporting of suicide methods. An Australian perspective. *Crisis* 2007; 28 (suppl 1): 64–69.

[32] Pirkis J, Blood RW: Suicide and the media, I: reportage in nonfictional media. *Crisis* 2001; 22: 146-154.
[33] Pirkis J, Blood RW: Suicide and the media, II: portrayal in fictional media. *Crisis* 2001; 22: 155-162.
[34] Sudak HS, Sudak DM: The media and suicide. *Acad Psychiatry* 2005; 29: 495-499.
[35] Cheng AT, Hawton K, Chen TH, Yen AM, Chen CY, Chen LC, Teng PR: The influence of media coverage of a celebrity suicide on subsequent suicide attempts. *J Clin Psychiatry* 2007; 68: 862-866.
[36] O'Connor S, Deeks JJ, Hawton K, Simkin S, Keen A, Altman DG, Philo G, Bulstrode C: Effects of a drug overdose in a television drama on knowledge of specific dangers of self poisoning: population based surveys. *BMJ* 1999; 318: 978-979.
[37] Stinson JC, O'Connell T, Chan R, Feely J: Medical messages on television. Grapevine effect. *BMJ* 1993; 306: 1415-1416.
[38] Baume P, Cantor CH, Rolfe A: Cybersuicide: the role of interactive suicide notes on the Internet. *Crisis* 1997; 18: 73–79.
[39] Haut F, Morrison A: The Internet and the future of psychiatry. *Psychiatr Bull* 1998; 22: 641–642.
[40] Alao AO, Yolles JC, Armenta W: Cybersuicide: the Internet and suicide. *Am J Psychiatry* 1999; 156: 1836–1837.
[41] Becker K, Schmidt MH: Internet chat rooms and suicide. *J Am Acad Child Adolesc Psychiatry* 2004; 43: 246-247.
[42] Biddle L, Donovan J, Hawton K, Kapur N, Gunnell D: Suicide and the internet. *BMJ* 2008; 336: 800-802.
[43] Hagihara A, Tarumi K, Abe T: Media suicide-reports, Internet use and the occurrence of suicides between 1987 and 2005 in Japan. *BMC Public Health* 2007; 7: 321.
[44] Mehlum L: The internet, suicide, and suicide prevention. *Crisis* 2000; 21: 186-188.
[45] Prior TI: Suicide methods from the internet. *Am J Psychiatry* 2004; 161: 1500-1501.
[46] Dobson R: Internet sites may encourage suicide. *BMJ* 1999; 319: 337.
[47] Brown M, Barraclough B: Epidemiology of suicide pacts in England and Wales, 1988-92. *BMJ* 1997; 315: 286-287.
[48] Fishbain DA, Aldrich TE. Suicide pacts: international comparisons. *J Clin Psychiatry* 1985; 46: 11-15.
[49] Recupero PR, Harms SE, Noble JM: Googling suicide: surfing for suicide information on the Internet. *J Clin Psychiatry* 2008; 69: 878-888.
[50] Biddle L, Brock A, Brookes S, Gunnell D. Suicides rates in young men in England and Wales in the 21st century: time trend study. *BMJ* 2008; 336: 539-542.
[51] Fakhoury WKH: Suicide: a call-sheet audit – Data from Saneline. *Psychiatr Bull* 2000; 24: 98-101.
[52] Osby U, Brandt L, Correia N, Ekbom A, Sparén P: Excess mortality in bipolar and unipolar disorder in Sweden. *Arch Gen Psychiatry* 2001; 58: 844-850.
[53] Hawton K, Sutton L, Haw C, Sinclair J, Deeks JJ: Schizophrenia and suicide: systematic review of risk factors. *Br J Psychiatry* 2005; 187: 9-20.
[54] Siris S: Depression in schizophrenia: perspective in the era of “atypical” antipsychotic agents. *Am J Psychiatry* 2000; 157: 1379–1389.

[55] Aguilar EJ, Leal C, Acosta FJ, Cejas MR, Fernández L, Gracia R: A psychopathological study of a group of schizophrenic patients after attempting suicide. Are there two different clinical subtypes? *Eur Psychiatr* 2003; 18: 190-192.

[56] Acosta FJ, Aguilar EJ, Cejas MR, Gracia R, Caballero-Hidalgo A, Siris SG: Are there subtypes of suicidal schizophrenia? A prospective study. *Schizophr Res* 2006; 86: 215-220.

[57] McGirr A, Tousignant M, Routhier D, Pouliot L, Chawky N, Margolese HC, Turecki G: Risk factors for completed suicide in schizophrenia and other chronic psychotic disorders: a case-control study. *Schizophr Res* 2006; 84: 132-143.

[58] Schimdtke A, Schaller S, Wasserman D: *Suicide clusters and media coverage of suicide, in Suicide, an unnecessary death.* Edited by Wasserman D. London, Martin Dunitz, 2001, pp 265-268.

[59] Pompili M, Amador XF, Girardi P, Harkavy-Friedman J, Harrow M, Kaplan K, Krausz M, Lester D, Meltzer HY, Modestin J, Montross LP, Mortensen PB, Munk-Jørgensen P, Nielsen J, Nordentoft M, Saarinen PI, Zisook S, Wilson ST, Tatarelli R: Suicide risk in schizophrenia: learning from the past to change the future. *Ann Gen Psychiatry* 2007; 6: 10.

[60] O'Donnell I, Farmer R, Catalán J: Explaining suicide: the views of survivors of serious suicide attempts. *Br J Psychiatry* 1996; 168: 780-786.

[61] Greenberg HP: Crime and folie a deux: review and case history. *J Ment Sci* 1956; 102: 772-779.

[62] Salih MA: Suicide pact in a setting of Folie à Deux. *Br J Psychiatry* 1981; 139: 62-67.

[63] Rajagopal S: Suicide pacts and the internet. *BMJ* 2004; 329: 1298-1299.

[64] Brown M, Barraclough B: Partners in life and in death: the suicide pact in England and Wales 1988-1992. *Psychol Med* 1999; 29: 1299-1306.

[65] Huang MP, Alessi NE: The Internet and the future of psychiatry. *Am J Psychiatry* 1996; 153: 861-869.

[66] Janson MP, Alessandrini ES, Strunjas SS, Shahab H, El-Mallakh R, Lippmann SB: Internet-observed suicide attempts. *J Clin Psychiatry* 2001; 62: 478.

[67] Neimark G, Hurford MO, DiGiacomo J: The internet as collateral informant. *Am J Psychiatry* 2006; 163: 1842.

[68] Prasad V. Owens D: Using the internet as a source of self-help for people who self-harm. *Psychiatr Bull* 2001; 25: 222-225.

[69] Timms P, Hart D, Cohen A. Briscoe M, McClure M: 'Help is at Hand' on the web – what do our readers think?. *Psychiatr Bull* 2005; 29: 24-27.

[70] Pirkis J, Blood RW, Beautrais A, Burgess P, Skehan J: Media guidelines on the reporting of suicide. *Crisis* 2006; 27: 82–87.

[71] Mann JJ, Apter A, Bertolote J, Beautrais A, Currier D, Haas A, Hegerl U, Lonnqvist J, Malone K, Marusic A, Mehlum L, Patton G, Phillips M, Rutz W, Rihmer Z, Schmidtke A, Shaffer D, Silverman M, Takahashi Y, Varnik A, Wasserman D, Yip P, Hendin H: Suicide prevention strategies: a systematic review. *JAMA* 2005; 294: 2064-2074.

[72] Hunt IM, Kapur N, Robinson J, Shaw J, Flynn S, Bailey H, Meehan J, Bickley H, Burns J, Appleby L, Parsons R: Suicide within 12 months of mental health service contact in different age and diagnostic groups: National clinical survey. *Br J Psychiatry* 2006; 188: 135-142.

[73] Shaffer D, Garland A, Gould M, Fisher P, Trautman P: Preventing teenage suicide: a critical review. *J Am Acad Child Adolesc Psychiatry* 1988; 27: 675-687.

[74] O'Reilly R, Bishop J, Maddox K, Hutchinson L, Fisman M, Takhar J: Is telepsychiatry equivalent to face-to-face psychiatry? Results from a randomized controlled equivalence trial. *Psychiatr Serv* 2007; 58: 836-843.

[75] Zarate CA Jr, Weinstock L, Cukor P, Morabito C, Leahy L, Burns C, Baer L: Applicability of telemedicine for assessing patients with schizophrenia: acceptance and reliability. *Clin Psychiatry* 1997; 58: 22-25.

[76] Godleski L, Nieves JE, Darkins A, Lehmann L: VA telemental health: suicide assessment. *Behav Sci Law* 2008; 26: 271-286.

[77] Thara R, John S, Rao K: Telepsychiatry in Chennai, India: the SCARF experience. *Behav Sci Law* 2008; 26: 315-322.

[78] Papolos, D., Hennen, J., Cockerham, M.S: Factors associated with parent-reported suicide threats by children and adolescents with community-diagnosed bipolar disorder. *J Affect Disord* 2005; 86: 267-275.

In: Internet and Suicide
Editors: L. Sher and A. Vilens

ISBN 978-1-60741-077-5

Chapter 19

THE USE OF THE INTERNET FOR RESEARCH ON SUICIDES IN THE ELDERLY

Ajit Shah
University of Central Lancashire, Preston, United Kingdom

ABSTRACT

Suicide rates traditionally increased with ageing and are among the highest in the elderly. The internet can be an invaluable source of information whilst conducting research on elderly suicides: (i) the use of literature search through traditional data-bases and of the "grey literature" (for example, reports produced by influential organisations) in the generation of research hypotheses, planning and design of research studies; (ii) comparison of cross-national variations in elderly suicide rates; (iii) cross-national and national studies examining trends over time for elderly suicide rates; (iv) cross-national and national studies examining age-associated trends in suicide rates; (v) cross-national studies and longitudinal studies over time within individual countries with an ecological design to examine potential risk and protective factors; and (vi) publishing the findings from research studies. The effective use of the internet in these different research areas is described using recent examples.

INTRODUCTION

In developing and developed countries the proportion of the elderly is increasing due to prolonged life expectancy and falling birth rates [1]. Suicide rates generally increase with age [2]. A recent cross-national study of 62 developing and developed countries reported an increase in suicide rates with ageing in males and females in 25 and 27 countries respectively [3]. Moreover, suicides are of considerable social and medical significance [2], are emotive, cause distress to relatives and professionals [4], may lead to litigation [5] and rank in the top ten causes of death in the elderly [6]. Thus, suicides in the elderly are an important public health concern. Comprehensive understanding of the substantial worldwide variation in population patterns of suicide may be critical for developing prevention programmes [7]. Thus, there is strong case for conducting research on various aspects of suicides in the elderly. Any facility, including the internet, that facilitates research on elderly suicides will help acheive this ambition.

Literature Search in the Planning Of Research

A number of research data-bases (for example, Medline, Embase, Psychinfo and Proquest) are readily available on the internet and allow searching for literature published in scientific journals. Through the university system and the National Health Service in the United Kingdom, a wide range of such data-bases are accessible from the Athens internet system for registered users. Many journals (e.g. Psychological Reports) also allow an internet based search of publications in their journal. Many scientific journals are publishing accepted scientific papers electronically through the internet well ahead of formal publication in the traditional paper format. Recently, a plethora of "open access" journals publishing only on the internet have emerged and more are likely to emerge, and usually access is free. A search through google and other search engines also allows identification of unpublished thesis pertaining to higher degrees and the "grey literature" published by influential organisations (for example, reports published by the National Confidential Enquiry into Homicides and Suicides in the United Kingdom). A systematic literature search, pertaining to elderly suicides, of scientific papers published in scientific journals, unpublished higher degree thesis, the "grey" literature and other reports published on the internet is now readily possible via the internet. Although such information can be ascertained for virtually any topic, it is of particular importance for elderly suicides because traditionally they have been poorly studied and neglected in the scientific literature. Thus, any of the above sources may produce invaluable information. A good literature search on elderly suicides would normally be a prelude to generating potentially testable research hypothesis and planning and designing research studies with appropriate methodology.

Cross-National Variations in Elderly Suicide Rates

Cross-national elderly suicide rates have been compared [2, 8-10]. For example, elderly suicide rates for 1992 were low in Malta, Greece, Albania, Armenia, Tajikistan, Uzbekistan, Mexico and Columbia and high in Austria, Belarus, Denmark, Estonia, Finland, France, Hungary, Kazakhstan, Latvia, Lithuania, Russia, Slovenia, Switzerland and rural China [2]. Studies demonstrating regional and cross-national variations in elderly suicide rates allow generation of potentially testable aetiological hypothesis including cross-national differences in genetic factors, prevalence of mental illness in the elderly, life expectancy, socio-economic deprivation, social fragmentation, cultural factors, the availability of appropriate healthcare services, and public health initiatives to improve the detection and treatment of mental illness, mental health and suicide prevention [11].

These earlier studies were based on suicide rates available in paper format from the World Health Organisation (WHO) in their publications on national mortality data. The WHO now formally publishes data on mortality rates and the cause of mortality, including those due to suicide, for almost 200 countries on their website (www.who.int/whosis/database/mort/table1.cfm). These data are available for both sexes for the ten age-bands of less than 1 year, 1-4 years, 4-15 years, 16-24 years, 25-34 years, 35-44 years, 45-54 years, 55-64 years, 65-74 years and 75+ years. However data on elderly suicide rates are only available for half of the listed countries [11].

The above data allows comparison of elderly suicide rates between males and females across countries, between elderly age-bands of 65-74 years and 75+ years across countries, and identification of regional patterns of elderly suicide rates [11]. A recent study using data on elderly suicide rates from the WHO website listed above demonstrated that: suicide rates were higher in males than females in the age-bands 65-74 years and 75+ years; suicide rates were higher in the age-band 75+ years compared to age-band 65-74 years in both sexes; and there was wide cross-national and regional variation in elderly suicide rates with rates being the lowest in Caribbean, central American and Arabic countries, and the highest in central and eastern European, some oriental and some west European countries [11].

Cross-National and National Studies Examining Trends in Elderly Suicide Rates over Time

Trends over time in elderly suicide rates have been examined in cross-national studies and studies from individual countries. Elderly suicide rates in both sexes declined in many countries between 1989/1990 and 1992/1993 [8]. However, there were exceptions: an increase in elderly suicide rates in both sexes in Denmark, in men in Israel and in women in France, Bulgaria, Iceland and Malta; and, there was no change in elderly suicide rates in Norway, Poland and Sweden [8]. Moreover, elderly suicide rates in selected western and eastern European countries between 1987 and 1991/1992 showed an increase in males in Denmark, Sweden and Latvia and in females in Norway, Belarus and Hungary [10]. Similarly, between 1974 and 1987, elderly suicide rates in men increased in 13 of 21 western countries, and in women an increase was observed in 10 western countries [12]. Furthermore, in a study of 13 European countries elderly suicide rates increased in Austria and Umea in Sweden and declined in the United Kingdom (UK) and Stockholm in Sweden between 1989-1993 [13].

Studies from individual countries reported that elderly suicide rates declined in Japan [14], Singapore [15,16], urban China [17], in some east European countries [10] and in men in the United States [6, 18]. Between 1985 and 1996, in England and Wales, elderly suicide rates declined in both sexes [19,20]; similar observations were evident between 1979 and 2002 for the whole of the UK [21]. Elderly suicide rates in Australia have declined over a 100 year period between 1891 and 1995 in both sexes [22].

Studies demonstrating regional and cross-national variations in trends over time for elderly suicide rates allow generation of potentially testable aetiological hypothesis including cross-national differences in genetic factors, prevalence of mental illness in the elderly, life expectancy, socio-economic deprivation, social fragmentation, cultural factors, the availability of appropriate healthcare services, and public health initiatives to improve the detection and treatment of mental illness, mental health and suicide prevention [11]. Additionally, comparisons between countries with an increase, with a decline and without a change in elderly suicide rates over time may allow identification of potentially testable aetiological factors [23].

These earlier studies were based on suicide rates available in paper format from the World Health Organisation (WHO) in their publications on national mortality data. The WHO now formally publishes data on mortality rates and the cause of mortality, including those due to suicide, for almost 200 countries on their website (www.who.int/whosis/database/mort/table1.cfm). More recent studies of trends in elderly suicide rates over time have been able to access data for up to 24 years from national and WHO websites [3,21]. However data on elderly suicide rates are only available for half of the listed countries [11] and for a variable period of time [24]. Nevertheless, recent studies have successfully used this data source [24].

Age-Associated Trends in Suicide Rates

Traditionally, suicide rates increased with ageing in many countries [2]. However, exceptions to this observation are emerging. Data from the WHO data bank in 1995 revealed that female suicide rates did not increase with age in Mauritius, Colombia, Albania and Finland [2]. Suicide rates for both sexes increased with age in Switzerland [25] and Brazil [26], but there were smaller peaks in the younger age-bands. Although, the female suicide rate increased with age in China, there was an additional peak in the younger the age-bands [27-29]. Male suicide rates were the highest in the age-band 25-29 years in Thailand [30]. In England and Wales the male suicide rate was the highest in the age-band 25-34 years [31,32]. Suicide rates for Australian, New Zealand and white American males increased with age, but suicide rates for females initially increased with age, peaking at menopause, and declined thereafter [33-35]. Suicide rates among non-white Americans [34,36], Indians [37,38], Jordanians [39], Indian immigrants to the United Kingdom [32,40] and some east European countries [10] declined with increasing age.

Cross-national and regional variations in trends in age-associated suicide rates can allow generation of potentially testable aetiological hypothesis including cross-national differences in genetic factors, prevalence of mental illness in the elderly, life expectancy, socio-economic deprivation, social fragmentation, cultural factors, the availability of appropriate healthcare services, and public health initiatives to improve the detection and treatment of mental illness, mental health and suicide prevention [3].

These earlier studies were based on suicide rates available in paper format from the World Health Organisation (WHO) in their publications on national mortality data. The WHO now formally publishes data on mortality rates and the cause of mortality, including those due to suicide, for almost 200 countries on their website (www.who.int/whosis/database/mort/table1.cfm). These data are available for both sexes for the ten age-bands of less than 1 year, 1-4 years, 4-15 years, 16-24 years, 25-34 years, 35-44 years, 45-54 years, 55-64 years, 65-74 years and 75+ years. However data on elderly suicide rates are only available for half of the listed countries [11]. Many national websites provide similar data for individual countries such as the National Statistics Office website in the UK. Nevertheless, recent studies of age-associated trends in suicide rates have used data from national and WHO websites [3,41].

Protective and Risk Factors

A range of potential risk factors for elderly suicides at an individual-level have been reported in the literature [2], although the literature on protective factors is sparse. These include age, sex, social isolation, marital status, life events, adversity early in life, physical illness, pain, personality characteristics and psychiatric morbidity [2]. Currently, the internet is less useful in research studies of individual-level risk or protective factors for elderly suicides because data on these factors need to be ascertained for individual suicide vicitims, and such data for individuals cannot be made available on the internet because of confidentiality issues.

A range of potential risk factors for elderly suicides at an aggregate-level have been reported in the literature [2], although the literature on protective factors is sparse. Earlier studies in this area have used data from paper-based data sources from the WHO, the United Nations and national data sets from individual countries. Data from the internet across different countries or over time in single countries can allow examination of risk and protective factors at an aggregate-level using an ecological design. Recent studies, using this approach, have successfully examined the relationship between elderly suicide rates and: socio-economic status [42], income inequality [42], life expectancy and child mortality rates [42], elderly population size and the proportion of elderly in the general population [24, 42], elderly dependency ratios [43], availability of healthcare services [42,44], availability of mental health services [45,46], funding for mental health services [44,45], national mental health policies [44,45], societal unemployment rates [47], societal crime rates [48], degree of urbanisation [49], fertility rates [50], gender inequality [51] and smoking [52].

Data on socio-economic status measured by gross national domestic product (GDP), income inequality measure by the Gini coefficient, life expectancy and child mortality rates, the elderly population size and general population size, healthcare funding, mental health care funding, mental health service provision, mental health national policies, unemployment rates, crime rates, gender inequality, educational attainment, degree of urbanisation and fertility rates for individual countries on the United Nations Development Programme (UNDP) website (www.hdr.undp.org/reports/global/2005/pdf/hdr05_HDI.pdf), the WHO website (www.who.int/countries/en/) and the WHO's Mental Health Atlas 2005 (http://globalatlas.who.int/globalatlas/default.asp).

Pitfalls in Using Data on Elderly Suicide Rates from the Internet

However, researchers need to be aware of a number of potential methodological pitfall. First, data are not always available from all countries. In a recent study data on elderly suicide rates were only available for 87 countries (under 50%) [11, 42] and this may influence the findings of any correlational analysis [53]. Second, for some countries only the raw numbers of suicide are available rather than suicide rates [11]. Third, there is a wide range from 1985 to 2003 for the latest available year for data on suicide rates [11]. Fourth, some countries provide data on suicides using the International Classification of Diseases version 9 (ICD-9) coding and other countries provide this using the ICD-10 coding. Although these data are likely to be comparable, the validity of comparing suicide rates across countries using two different methods of coding has not be formally examined. Fifth, in countries like England and Wales, the coroner can only return a verdict of suicide if it can be proved beyond a reasonable doubt. Therefore, some genuine suicides may be misclassified under an open verdict when suicide cannot be proved conclusively. Thus, researchers have used a wider definition of probable suicide by combining deaths due to suicides (ICD-10 codes X60-X84) and open verdicts (ICD-10 codes Y10-Y34) [19,20,55], and the different definitions of suicide may influence the findings of any correlational analysis [56]. Data on open verdicts are only available on the WHO website for countries reporting deaths using the ICD-10 codes; this broad category is not given on the WHO website for countries using the ICD-9 codes. Moreover, the WHO provides mortality data by the ICD-10 codes X60 to X84 amalgamated and ICD-10 codes Y10-Y36, Y87 and Y89 amalgamated. Therefore, it is not possible to exclude deaths due to ICD-10 codes Y33.9, Y35, Y36, Y87 and Y89, all of which are not related to suicide.

Although not directly related to the internet, researchers need to be aware of other pitfalls in using cross-national data on elderly suicide rates including: the validity of this data is unclear [9, 57]; the legal criteria for the proof of suicide vary between countries and in different regions within a country [8, 57]; some countries, particularly low-income countries, may have poor death registration facilities [8]; and, cultural and religious factors and stigma attached to suicide may lead to under-reporting of suicides [57,58].

Data on potential risk and protective factors from the WHO, the United Nations and the Mental Health Atlas 2008 should also be viewed cautiously because: data are not available for all countries; the validity of the data is unclear; and some countries, particularly low income countries, have a poor infrastructure for collecting data on the potential risk and protectvice factors at an aggregate level [45, 56].

Nevertheless, in the main, data from the internet both for elderly suicide rates and potential risk and protective factors, allow conduct of within-country or cross-national ecological studies. However, any identified relationships need to be viewed cautiously because of the above methodological issues and because they may be subject to ecological fallacy. Thus, clear and unequivocal conclusions about an aetiological relationship and the direction of this relationship cannot be reached, but such aggregate-level studies allow generation of aetiological hypothesis that can be further tested in case-control or cohort studies at an individual-level.

Miscellaneous Use of the Internet in Research of Elderly Suicides

A recent study of resources a suicidal person may find through search engines on the internet classified the website pages as: suicide neutral, 31%; anti-suicide, 29%; and, pro-suicide, 11% [59]. Internet websites and chat rooms can actively promote suicide, provide detailed information on methods of suicide, provide detailed information on online pharmacies and tips for bypassing governmental regulations and customs in the use of these overseas pharmacies, allow posting of suicide notes, facilitate suicide pacts, discourage mentally ill individuals from seeking help, and some sites deny access to individuals discouraging others from committing suicide [60-63]. Internet websites and chat rooms may also have positive benefits for individuals with suicidal ideation: be a resource to help suicidal individuals to seek help; identify individuals at risk of suicide; provide a method of communication with suicidal individuals, and this has been successfully used by the Samaritans; support survivors of suicide attempts; and chat rooms may act in a manner akin to telephone helplines [60, 62,63]. The impact of these different aspects of the internet on elderly suicide rates has not been formally examined and requires formal study. A study of an "on line" questionnaire on a German internet message board for suicidal people identified the profile of individuals using this site [64]. A time series analysis reported a positive correlation between general population male suicide rates and the prevalence of households using the internet in Japan [65]. Such studies could be conducted for the elderly. Other studies examining the impact of the internet on elderly suicide rates include: indepth case studies of elderly suicide attempters addressing their use of the internet using qualitative methodology; examination of suicidal intent in elderly individuals who use "pro-suicide" [59] websites and chat rooms; and psychological postmortem studies carefully examining the use of the internet by suicide victims, and technological advances now allow investigation of the websites and chat rooms that may have been used by accessing the relevant computers. Findings of such studies may have implications for clinical practice, prevention of suicides and legislation regulating websites and chat rooms.

Publication of the Findings of Research on Elderly Suicides

Traditionally research findings on elderly suicides have been published in peer-reviewed scientific journal and they were originally only published in a paper format. However, increasing number of journals publishing research on elderly suicides are additionally publsihing on the internet. Some new "open access" journals are exclusively publishing on the internet and access to these journals is usually free. Additionally, researchers now also have the facility to also publish their findings on their institutional websites. Essentially, publication of research studies on elderly suicide on the internet is likely to lead to increased dissemination of results and enhance and raise the profile of research and clinical issues surrounding elderly suicides. This has substantial implications for provision of clinical care, public health measures and policy development.

Conclusion

The internet is an invaluable resource supoorting research on elderly suicides: (i) it allows extensive systematic literature search of the scientific literature and the "grey literature" for generation of testable hypothesis and design and planning of research studies;

(ii) it provides data for comparison of cross-national variations in elderly suicide rates, examination of cross-national and national trends over time in elderly suicide rates, examination of cross-national and national trends in age-associated suicide rates; (iii) it provides data for cross-national studies and longitudinal studies over time within individual countries with an ecological design to examine potential risk and protective factors; and (iv) publishing the findings of research studies pertaining to elderly suicides.

REFERENCES

[1] Shah AK, MacKenzie S: Disorders of ageing across cultures, in *Textbook of Cultural Psychiatry.* Edited by Bhugra D, Bhui K. Cambridge, Cambridge University Press, 2007, pp 323-344.

[2] Shah AK, De T: Suicide and the elderly. *Int Journal Psychiatry Clin Prac* 1998; 2: 3-17.

[3] Shah AK: The relationship between suicide rates and age: an analysis of multinational data from the World Health Organisation. *Int Psychogeriatr* 2007; 19: 1141-1152.

[4] Little JD: Staff response to inpatient and outpatient suicide: what happened and what do we do? *ANZ J Psychiatry* 1992; 4: 162-167.

[5] Cheung P: Suicide preventions for psychiatric inpatients: a review. *ANZ J Psychiatry* 1992; 26: 592-597.

[6] Blazer DG, Bachar JR, Manton KG: Suicide in late life – review and commentary. *J Am Geriatr Soc* 1986: 13: 743-749.

[7] Knox KL, Conwell Y, Caine ED: If suicide is a public health problem, what are we doing to prevent it? *Am J Pub Health* 2004; 94: 37-45.

[8] Shah AK, Ganesvaran T: *Suicide in the elderly, in Functional Psychiatric Disorders of the Elderly.* Edited by Chiu E, Ames D. Cambridge, Cambridge University Press. 1994, pp 221-244.

[9] Diekstra RFW: Suicide and attemptede suicide: an international perspective. *Acta Psychiatr Scand* 1989; 80 (Suppl 354): 1-24.

[10] Sartorius N: Recent changes in suicide rates in selected eatern European and other European countries. *Int Psychogeriatr* 1995; 7; 301-308.

[11] Shah AK, Bhat R, MacKenzie S, Koen C: Elderly suicide rates: cross-national comparisons and association with sex and elderly age-bands. *Med Sci Law* 2007; 47: 244-252.

[12] Pritchard C: Changes in elderly suicides in the USA and the developed world 1974-1987: comparison with current homocide. *Int J Geriatr Psychiatry* 1992; 7: 125-134.

[13] De Leo D, Padoani W, Scocco P. et al: Attempted and completed suicide in older subjects: results from the WHO/EURO multicentre study of suicidal behaviour. *Int J Geriatr Psychiatry* 2001; 16; 300-310.

[14] Watanabe N, Hasegawa K, Yoshinaga Y: Suicide in later life in Japan: urban and rural differences. *Int Psychogeriatr* 1995; 7: 253-261.

[15] Ko SM, Kua EH: Ethnicity and elderly suicide rates in Singapore. *Int Psychogeriatr* 1995; 7: 309-317.

[16] Kua EH, Ko SM: A cross cultural study of suicide in the elderly in Singapore. *Br J Psychiatry* 1992; 160: 558-559.

[17] Yip PSF, Liu KY, Ku J and Song XM: Suicide rates in China during a decade of rapid social change. *Soc Psychiat Psychiatr Epidemiol* 2005; 40: 792-798.

[18] McIntosh JL; Components of the decline in elderly suicides: suicide in young old and old old by race and sex. *Death Education* 1984; 8; 113-124.

[19] Hoxey K, Shah AK: Recent trends in elderly suicide rates and methods in England and Wales. *Int J Gertiatr Psychiatry* 2000; 15: 274-279.

[20] Shah AK, Elanchenny N, Collinge T: Trends in age band-specific suicide rates in the elderly. *Med Sci Law* 2001; 41: 102-106.

[21] Shah AK;) Elderly suicide rates in the United Kingdom: trends from 1979 to 2002. *Med Sci Law* 2007; 47: 56-60.

[22] Goldney RD, Harrison J: Suicide in the elderly: some good news. *Australasian J Ageing* 1998; 17: 54-55.

[23] Shah AK: Are age-related trends in suicide rates associated with life expectancy and socio-economic factors? *Int J of Psychiat Clin Prac* 2008. In Press.

[24] Shah AK, Bhat R, MacKenzie S, Koen C: Elderly suicide rates: cross-national comparisons of trends over a 10-year period. *Int Psychogeriatr* 2008; 20: 673-686.

[25] Ajdacic-Gross V, Bopp M, Gostynski M, Lauber C, Gutzwiller F, Rossler W: Age-period-cohort analysis of Swiss suicide data, 1881-2000. *Eur Arch Psychiatry Clin Neurosciences* 2002; 256: 207-214.

[26] Mello-Santos C, Bertolote JM, Wang YP: Epidemiology of suicide in Brazil (1980-2000): characterisation of age and gender rates of suicide. *Rev Bras Psiquiatr* 2005; 27: 131-134.

[27] Pritchard C: Suicide in the People's Republic of China categorised by age and gender: evidence of the influence of culture on suicide. *Acta Psychiatr Scand* 1996; 93: 362-367.

[28] Yip PSF, Callanan C, Yuen HP: Urban/rural and gender differences in suicide rates: East and West. *J Affect Dis* 2000; 57: 99-106.

[29] Qin P, Mortensen PB: Specific characteristics of suicide in China. *Acta Psychiat Scand* 2002; 103: 117-121.

[30] Lotrakul M: Suicide in Thailand during the period 1998-2003. *Psychiatry & Neurosciences* 2006; 60: 90-95.

[31] McClure GMG: Changes in suicide in England and Wales 1960-1997. *Br J Psychiatry* 2000; 176; 64-67.

[32] Neeleman J, Mak V, Wessely S: Suicide by age, ethnic group, coroner's verdict and country of birth. A three-year survey in inner London. *Br J Psychiatry* 1997; 181: 463-467.

[33] Skeeg K, Cox B: Suicide in New Zealand 1957- 1986: influence of age, period and birth cohort. *ANZ J Psychiatry* 1991; 25: 181-190.

[34] Woodbury MA, Manton KG, Blazer D: Trends in US suicide mortality rates 1968-1982: race and sex differences in age, period and cohort components. *Int J Epidemiol* 1987; 17: 356-352.

[35] Snowdon J, Snowdon D: Suicide in Australia. *Paper presented at the 8th Congress of the International Psychogeriatric Association,* Sydney, Australia. 1995.

[36] Seiden RH: Mellowing with age: factors affecting the non-white suicide rate. *Int J Age Hum Develop* 1981; 13; 265-284.
[37] Adityanjee DR: Suicide attempts and suicide in India: cross-cultural aspects. *Int J Soc Psychiatry* 1986; 32: 64-73.
[38] Bhatia SC, Kahn MH, Medirrata RP. High risk suicide factors across cultures. *Int J Soc Psychiatry* 1987; 33: 226-236.
[39] Daradekh TK: Suicide in Jordan 1980-1985. *Acta Psychiat Scand* 1989; 79: 241-244.
[40] Raleigh VS, Bulusu L, Balarajan R: Suicides among immigrants from the Indian subcontinent. *Br J Psychiatry* 1990; 156: 46-50.
[41] Shah AK: The influence of exclusion criteria on the relationship between suicide rates and age in cross-national studies. *Int Psychogeriatr* 2007; 19: 989-992.
[42] Shah AK, Bhat R, MacKenzie S, Koen C: A cross-national study of the relationship between elderly suicide rates and life expectancy and markers of socio-economic status and healthcare status. *Int Psychogeriatr* 2008; 20; 347-360.
[43] Shah AK, Padayatchi M, Das K: The relationship between elderly suicide rates and elderly dependency ratios: a cross-national study using data from the WHO data bank. *Int Psychogeriat* 2008; 20: 594-604.
[44] Shah AK, Bhat R: Relationship between elderly suicide rates and markers of healthcare. *J Chinese Clin Med* 2008; 3: 52-55.
[45] Shah AK, Bhat R: The relationship between elderly suicide rates and mental health funding, service provision and national policy: a cross-national study. *Int Psychogeriat* 2008; 20: 605-615.
[46] Shah AK, Bhat R: Are elderly suicide rates improved by increased provision of mental health service resources? *Int Psychogeriat.* In Press.
[47] Shah AK: Possible relation of elderly suicide rates with unemployment in society: a cross-national study. *Psychol Rep 2008;* 102: 398-400.
[48] Shah AK:. Possible realtion between suicide rates of elderly with societal crime: a cross-national study. *Psychol Rep 2008;* 102: 95-98.
[49] Shah AK: A cross-national study of the relationship between elderly suicide rates and urbanization. *Sui Life Threat Beh.* In Press.
[50] Shah AK: Association of suicide rates in elderly persons with fertility rates. *Psychol Rep 2008;* 102: 369-376.
[51] Shah AK: Association of suicide rates for elderly age bands with gender equality. *Psychol Rep.* In Press.
[52] Shah AK: Is there a relationship between elderly suicides and smoking? *Int J Geriatr Psychiatry 2008;* 23; 308-313.
[53] Shah AK: The effect of missing data in cross-national studies of elderly suicide rates. *J Chinese Clin Med 2008;* 3:153-155.
[54] O'Donnell I, Farmer R: The limitations of official suicide statistics. *Bri J Psychiatry 1995;* 166: 458-461.
[55] Hoxey K, Shah AK: Recent trends in elderly suicide rates and methods in England and Wales. *Int J Gertiat Psychiatry 2000;* 15: 274-279.
[56] Shah AK: Pure elderly suicide rates versus combined pure elderly suicide, accidental and undetermined death rates: methodological issues in crossnational studies. *J Chinese Clin Med 2007*; 2: 504-506.

[57] Wasserman D, Cheng Q, Jiang GX: Global suicide rates among young people aged 15-19. *World Psychiatry 2005;* 4: 114-120.

[58] Abrahams VJ, Abrahams S, Jacob KS: Suicide in the elderly in Kanyambadi block, Tamil Nadu, South India. *Int J Geriat Psychiatry 2005;* 20: 953-955.

[59] Recupero PR, Harms SE and Noble JM: Googling suicide: surfing for suicide information on the internet. *J Clin Psychiatry*. In Press.

[60] Thompson S: The internet and its potential influence on suicide. *Psychiatric Bulletin 1999;* 23: 449-451.

[61] Rajagopal S: Suicide pacts and the internet: complete strangers may make cyberspace pacts. *Bri Med J 2004;* 329: 1298-1299.

[62] Alao AK, Soderberg M, Pohl EL, Alao AL. Cyberspace: review of the role of internet on suicide. *Cyberpsychol & Beh 2006;* 9: 489-493.

[63] Tam J, Tang WS, Fernando DJS: The internet and suicide: a double-edged tool. *Eur J Int Med 2007*; 18: 453-455.

[64] Eichenberg C: Internet message boards for suicidal people: a typology of users. *Cyberpsychol & Beh 2008;* 11: 107-113.

[65] Hagihara A, Tarumi K and Abe T: Media suicide-reports, internet use and the occurance of suicides between 1987 and 2005 in Japan. *BMC Pub Health 2007;* 7: 231-238.

In: Internet and Suicide
Editors: L. Sher and A. Vilens
ISBN 978-1-60741-077-5

Chapter 20

For Better or for Worse? Suicide and the Internet in the World Today

Wally Barr and Maria Leitner
University of Liverpool, Liverpool, United Kingdom

Abstract

In this chapter we firstly discuss the international evidence for a direct association between the suicide rate and the way in which suicide is reported in written or televised media accounts. We consider comparisons made between the internet and these other media and the frequent claim that it poses an even greater risk in terms of suicide-contagion. We examine the evidence for this and aim to provide a balanced discussion on the basis of published research findings. Our conclusion is that although the internet is as capable as any other medium of facilitating so-called copycat suicides, some groups of people appear to be considerably more susceptible to this than others. Whilst it may very well be true that young people use the internet more frequently than their older counterparts, this does not automatically mean they are most at risk. At least the evidence for this remains far from conclusive. What's more, we should remember that the internet can have a decidedly positive influence: it can enable the delivery of treatment and training and can allow vulnerable people an anonymous venue in which they can vent their feelings to those whom they believe can empathise. It is well known that the release of pent-up emotions can lead to a sense of relief, and perhaps this might forestall an act that would put their lives in danger? In any event, control of the internet is hugely problematic and the usual governmental response of regulation and control simply will not work. The fact is, we may have to learn to live with an unfettered internet. We should direct our efforts into conducting research that will provide sound evidence from which we can learn to harness the potential of the internet to the benefit of those at greatest risk.

Introduction

The Media and Suicide

A substantial body of research evidence now clearly shows the powerful influence the media can have on suicide rates (e.g. 1-5). These studies have all shown how news media depictions of suicide are capable of directly increasing the risk of suicide in those viewing or reading media content. The seminal work in the field of suicide-related media contagion was published in 1974, when Phillips coined the term 'Werther-effect' for the phenomenon whereby suicide rates increase following the publication of suicide stories in the media (6). The term is based on a 'suicide epidemic' among young men following the publication of Goethe's novel *The Sorrows of Young Werther* in 1774 (7). Evidence for the Werther-effect has been found in a number of countries over the years since Phillips' early work (8-13). These suicides often mimic the methods employed in the index suicide and it has now become clear that non-fictional portrayals of suicide have an even stronger influence than fictional stories (5). These 'copycat suicides' are especially prevalent among young people and are most apparent when the individual whose death triggered the news story was famous (4) or when the suicide provoked particularly widespread media interest. Despite differences in presentation and pattern, the essence of the various models proposed to describe the effect is much the same, namely that media accounts of suicide are potentially harmful and that the way in which suicide is described in the news can contribute to a contagious or copycat effect in vulnerable persons. The aspects of news stories that are most powerful in this respect are reports that present simplistic reasons for suicide, that repeatedly or excessively report specific suicides, that provide sensationalist coverage, report suicide methods in excessive detail, portray suicide as a means to a specific end, glorify the act of suicide and/or the deceased individual, or focus solely on the character of the deceased person (cited from 14). The internet is a very significant component of modern media coverage and, by its nature, provides an environment in which the contagion-effect might be expected to flourish. Unsurprisingly, there has therefore been considerable speculation about the impact of internet accounts of suicide on subsequent suicides and on suicide rates - a level of speculation sometimes approaching tabloid frenzy. In contrast, hard evidence confirming or disconfirming the role of the internet has not so far been forthcoming.

The Internet and Suicide

Concern about the possible influence of the internet on suicide has been expressed in a number of academic publications (e.g. 15-18) and there is little reason, *a priori*, to doubt that its contribution to the contagion-effect is any different from that of other media. If anything, the capacity of the internet to circulate news stories and hence to rapidly transmit content that may romanticise and glorify the act of suicide must be regarded as greater than that of other media. Alao et al (2006)(19) have echoed this view in suggesting that the internet can provide an even more 'stream-lined service' for potential suicides than other media, and others have pointed out that the medium may have a particular capacity to facilitate the disclosure of suicidal ideas among vulnerable people (20). It is not surprising, therefore, that the internet should have been linked to a number of suicide deaths. In the UK, for example, the national charity *Papyrus* has made the claim that "at least 34" deaths can be attributed to the influence of the internet (21). Despite this and other reports of deaths following internet contact, however, there are as yet no reliable empirical data on the risk of suicide that can unequivocally be related to contact with internet sites (22). This is not to say there is no association, of course. It simply means that convincing evidence of the 'internet effect' is so far lacking. Given the rapid expansion of the web, it might be expected that evidence confirming or disconfirming an association between suicides and internet material must soon emerge. It is certainly true that suicide-related websites have proliferated in recent years. Biddle et al (2008) (23) applied twelve simple search terms (including 'suicide', 'suicide methods' and 'how to kill yourself') in the four most popular search engines, *Google*, *Yahoo*, *MSN* and *Ask*, and found 480 sites. Of these, 90 (19%) were dedicated to suicide, 45 (9%) were in favour of suicide, 59 (12%) were against, and 43 (9%) described methods of suicide. Whilst these outcomes may be regarded as disturbing, it should be noted that this study has been criticised for over-stating the problem. For example, it has been claimed that a simple search using the term 'suicide' reveals no pro-suicide 'hits' in the top ten sites (24), the same author going on to observe that support websites "greatly outnumber" pro-suicide sites. Others have reported similar findings. For example, Recupero et al (2008) (25) used five popular search engines (*Google*, *Yahoo!*, *Ask*, *Lycos* and *Dogpile*) to search the terms 'suicide', 'how to commit suicide', 'suicide methods' and 'how to kill yourself'. Of their 373 hits, they found 115 were suicide-neutral and 109 were anti-suicide, whereas only 41 were considered to be pro-suicide. Nevertheless, they found these to be easily accessible, along with detailed instructions on unusual and lethal methods of suicide (25). But even given this, in the absence of solid research evidence, we have no reason to conclude that pro-suicide sites are necessarily more likely to be causally linked to promoting suicide than are neutral sites. It may be, for example, that raising the issue of suicide allows vulnerable people to experience a sense of sharing and empathy, a feeling that they are not 'alone', which could have the effect of reducing their risk of suicide.

So, what are we to make of the real influence of the internet? It is acknowledged that the medium certainly has the potential to bring its own specific dangers. While some have reported findings suggesting that it may *not* be easy to source explicit information on how to complete suicide (e.g. 26) there is wider agreement that, as noted earlier, the internet is as capable as any other medium of facilitating the contagion-effect. An additional risk stems from the fact that the international nature of the web appears to be particularly effective in offering to vulnerable people the possibility of accessing prescription drugs and other poisons that would otherwise be tightly controlled by government regulation and custom controls. The internet is also peculiarly well-placed to enable the establishment of suicide pacts between people who were hitherto strangers but who have met on the net (27). This phenomenon seems to be most prevalent in Japan, where at least 60 people have died in suicide pacts with like-minded contacts made on the internet (28). In view of these issues, it is perhaps reasonable to surmise that certain groups of people may be more susceptible than others to any potential dangers posed by the internet.

Who Is most Vulnerable?

It has been suggested that socially isolated and alienated individuals may find it easier to make influential relationships with anonymous internet contacts they have not met face-to-face (16). The demographic group that may be considered at greatest risk in this context is adolescents, where clusters of suicides have suggested the contagion effect may be a particularly potent risk (29). Subsequent evidence ruled out the likelihood of an assumed internet connection between 20 recent young suicides in the Welsh town of Bridgend (30). Nevertheless, the WHO/EURO Multicentre Study on Parasuicide has clearly shown that in most of the participating countries 'attempted suicide' rates are highest in adolescents and young adults (31). Several reports have indicated a widespread view that this is also the demographic group that most uses the internet and, furthermore, there is evidence that young people who engage in self-harm are significantly more likely than other young people to have a close relationship with someone they met online (32). Others have concluded that particular types of website may be prone to triggering suicidal behaviour in predisposed adolescents (14). These websites - known as newsgroups, chat rooms or message boards - allow users to post or respond to other users' messages, and have become a very popular form of internet communication. They offer the opportunity to seek peer support, to vent and receive validation for feelings, and to share views about life and personal problems. Sites facilitating discussion of the option of suicide enable open and anonymous communication which, as Baume et al (1997) (16) observed over ten years ago, can make it "all too easy for self-destructive individuals to incite others to kill themselves". These researchers went on to suggest that vulnerable people may be compelled so strongly by other influential site-users that to back out or seek help would entail 'losing face'. Similar findings have been reported by others in relation to individuals who non-fatally self-harm, where negative harmful behaviours may be legitimized and normalised by those responding to these messages (33). When this is followed by completed suicide, the question of whether such behaviour can be construed as assisting suicide is inevitably raised. However, this remains very debateable. Under UK legislation, the *Suicide Act 1961* (34) decriminalised suicide, but section 2:1 makes it clear that to "aid or abet" another person in taking their own life remains illegal (with a maximum 14-year imprisonment for transgression). To what extent internet discussion can be considered to be aiding or abetting remains a highly problematic issue.

Notwithstanding any evidence there may be to link increased internet use with an increased risk of suicide in young people, Biddle et al (2008) (23) have observed that in England the rate of suicide in all young people aged 15-34 has been declining in recent years (35). They conclude that cases of internet-induced suicide may be offset by the beneficial effects of the net or by other prevention approaches (23). However, our own recent research - a systematic review of interventions to prevent suicide - indicates this latter claim at least, is unlikely to be true. We reviewed 200 primary studies and 37 previous systematic reviews and were unable to identify even one single intervention that could be considered to have unequivocal supporting evidence in reducing the risk of suicide (36).

On the other hand there is considerable evidence that the internet itself *can* have a beneficial influence. For example, websites can offer support to depressed and suicidal people (37-39). They can offer opportunities for self-help (26), for professional intervention (40) and for research (e.g. 41). The question is, how best can we maximise the beneficial aspects of the internet whilst minimising any harmful aspects?

For Better or for Worse? Making the Best of it

Given the potentially damaging nature of a minority of websites, we would be justified in asking why legislation has not been enacted to regulate some internet activities. One important consideration here, is the difficulty in demonstrating that activity on a specific site can be causally related to aiding and abetting a death by suicide, notably given the frequently substantive temporal and geographical distances between participants. Another factor inhibiting legislative control is the conflict that would arise with the cherished value placed in many countries on the freedom of expression if access to websites were to be curtailed. Several countries have made attempts to block access to specific sites, but Australia is the only country that has so far passed legislation outlawing sites that promote suicide or provide information on suicide methods. Practical difficulties, such as cross-border jurisdiction differences, make water-tight control unfeasible in any case. Despite these serious obstacles to legal control over the internet, in the UK it is claimed that there is "overwhelming support" from the general public for the introduction of a law to outlaw sites that publish material that has the sole purpose of encouraging and aiding suicide (42). The British government is currently reviewing legislation and the *House of Commons Culture, Media and Sport Committee* recently advised the government to pursue discussions with the relevant agencies on whether the law on assisted suicide is worded clearly enough to include websites which encourage suicide and, if necessary, to block access to these sites (43). The outcome of these deliberations remains to be seen.

Rather than direct governmental intervention, a more frequently used 'damage limitation' approach is the regulation of websites by Internet Service Providers (ISPs). The European Union Safer Internet Plan (44) called upon ISPs to act responsibly to control, limit or deny access to sites that are illegal or dangerous. In the UK, ISPs are also urged to provide automatic links to supportive sites, such as the *Samaritans* or *Childline*, when users attempt to locate online information relating to suicide. Further, the Internet Watch Foundation (http://www.iwf.org.uk/), an independent charity, works in partnership with the British government and other agencies to minimise the availability of illegal content online, although this is not specifically focused on suicide sites. An alternative approach to website regulation, commonly used in other contexts, is for parents or others responsible for children or vulnerable persons to install filtering and monitoring software as well as a firewall in their family PC (45). One difficulty here is that filters will not necessarily discriminate between desirable and undesirable sites, so they may block access that could be helpful to suicidal individuals. A further difficulty is the lack of technical skills in parents who might otherwise wish to install filters, although advice on these matters is available from a number of sites (e.g. Papyrus: http://www.papyrus-uk.org/pdf/ACTion.pdf; Internet Watch Foundation: http://www.iwf.org.uk/). One imaginative approach that could potentially undercut many of the problems presented by too-easy access to pro-suicide websites has been suggested by Biddle et al (2008) (23). They offer the relatively simple advice that sites providing support to vulnerable people could be assisted in having an enhanced likelihood of listing when a search is carried out. That is, they advocate the use of website optimisation methods to improve the presence of supportive sites in the results of a search.

Many countries have introduced media guidelines for reporting suicides (46) and there is limited evidence that these can be a promising approach to reducing copycat suicides (47). The media can also inform users of the causes of suicide, warning signs, treatment and so on.

However, whilst responsible reporting relates fairly clearly to newspapers and television, it is far less clear how it could be applied to an essentially unregulated service like the internet.

Although website control, restriction and regulation are superficially attractive approaches to the problems generated by unfettered access to worldwide internet suicide sites, these are largely unachievable - and no doubt many people will continue to applaud the contribution an uncontrolled internet makes to personal freedom. But perhaps the most important message to take from this discussion is that there is an alternative to control and censorship: to harness the internet for positive use in assisting suicidal people. It is in this that health professionals can play a central role.

How Can Clinicians Help?

It has been suggested that, at a minimum, health professionals who are involved in the care of people who self-harm or who are vulnerable to suicidal behaviour, would benefit from a basic knowledge of the range of material available on the internet (26, 48). Becker and colleagues (2004) (14) advise those conducting psychiatric examination to ask patients about their use of computers and the internet, as well as their recreational activities and television viewing times. They are particularly keen that professional helpers are able to form some opinion of the patient's frequency and duration of internet access and their preferred websites and chat platforms. Recupero and colleagues (2008) (25) echo this view, suggesting that clinicians could assist patients in locating helpful and supportive online resources. Mishara and Weisstub (2007) (22) advise that those involved in suicide prevention should themselves enter chat discussions to dissuade the vulnerable from their suicidal path and to encourage help-seeking. This view is taken further by Mehlum (2000) (17), who advises that suicidologists should create their own internet sites to reach out to vulnerable groups that are otherwise difficult to contact. He reaffirms the aim of the International Association for Suicide Prevention (IASP: http://www.iasp.info/index.php) to use the internet to strengthen public awareness of the issues around suicide and to provide information about resources and possibilities for suicide prevention. One example of this would be to exploit the internet as a vehicle for the delivery of suicide prevention strategies and for training health professionals (49).

At the level of the individual in need, the internet provides opportunities for identifying those who are most vulnerable (20, 50), for preventive work (51) and intervention or support (32, 40, 52). However, to balance this optimism it is worth noting that our systematic review of interventions to prevent suicide was unable to identify even one high-quality study where the internet had been shown to have a measurable preventive capacity in relation to suicide risk (36). This was not because studies had failed to demonstrate a successful outcome, but rather that there were simply no high quality studies available in the published literature, which in itself is a clear indication that further research in this area is urgently needed.

CONCLUSION

Clearly much of the content described in this chapter relies on speculation and conjecture. Does the internet have an overall positive or an overall negative influence on suicide? In many ways the jury is still out. Perhaps what we *can* say with some confidence, however, is that he evidence against the internet, that it in some way 'creates' suicides that would not otherwise occur, remains circumstantial; the evidence that, in related contexts like depression at least, the internet can be a force for good is quite firm. It is nevertheless not firm enough. We still need sound, evidence-based data on the influence the internet currently has in encouraging *or* in preventing suicide. We must also make an effort to determine which groups may be most vulnerable to any risks presented by the internet and to identify those who are most susceptible to its benefits. There is much work to do, but do it we must. It is over ten years since Baume and colleagues pointed out the reality of cybersuicide (16) and we should ask ourselves if we have really taken this message to heart. Whether for better or for worse, it is clear that the internet and suicide is one relationship that is here to stay.

REFERENCES

[1] Hawton K, Williams K: The connection between media and suicidal behaviour warrants serious attention. *Crisis* 2001; 22: 137-140.

[2] Pirkis J, Blood RW: Suicide and the media. *Crisis* 2001; 22: 146-154.

[3] Stack S: Media impacts on suicide: A quantitative review of 293 findings. *Social science Quarterly* 2000; 81: 957-971.

[4] Stack S: Media coverage as a risk factor in suicide. *Journal of Epidemiology and Community Health* 2003; 57: 238-240.

[5] Stack S: Suicide in the media: A quantitative review of studies based on nonfictional stories. *Suicide and Life-Threatening Behavior* 2005; 35: 121-133.

[6] Phillips DP: The influence of suggestion on suicide: Substantive and theoretical implications of the Werther effect. *Am Sociol Rev* 1974; 39: 340-354.

[7] Goethe JW: The sorrows of the young Werther, Sawtry: Dedalus, 1988.

[8] Schmidtke A, Häfner H: The Werther effect after television films: New evidence for an old hypothesis. *Psychol Med* 1988; 18: 665-676.

[9] Jonas K: Modelling and suicide: A test of the Werther effect. *Br J Soc Psychol* 1992; 31: 295-306.

[10] Lee DTS, Chan KPM, Lee S, Yip PSF: Burning charcoal: A novel and contagious method of suicide in Asia. *Arch Gen Psychiatry* 2002; 59:293-294.

[11] Frei A, Schenker T, Finzen A, Dittmann V, Kraeuchi K: The Werther effect and assisted suicide. *Suicide Life Threat Behav* 2003; 33: 192-200.

[12] Etzersdorfer E, Voracek M, Sonneck G: A dose-response relationship between imitational suicides and newspaper distribution. *Arch Suicide Res* 2004; 8: 137-145.

[13] Lee DT, Chan KP, Yip PS: Charcoal burning is also popular for suicide pacts made on the internet. *BMJ* 2005; 12 (7491): 602.

[14] Becker K, Mayer M, Nagenborg M, El-Faddagh M, Schmidt MH: Parasuicide online: Can suicide websites trigger suicidal behaviour in predisposed adolescents? *Nord J Psychiatry* 2004; 58: 111-114.

[15] Alao AO, Yolles JC, Armenta W: Cybersuicide: The internet and suicide. *American Journal of Psychiatry* 1999; 156: 1836-1837.

[16] Baume P, Cantor CH, Rolfe A: Cybersuicide: The role of interactive suicide notes on the internet. *Crisis* 1997; 18: 73-79.

[17] Mehlum L. The internet, suicide and suicide prevention. *Crisis* 2000; 21(4): 186-188.

[18] Richard J, Werth JL, Rogers JR: Rational and assisted suicidal communication on the internet: A case example and discussion of ethical and practice issues. *Ethics and Behavior* 2000; 10: 215-238.

[19] Alao AO, Soderberg M, Pohl EL, Alao AL: Cybersuicide: Review of the role of the internet on suicide. *Cyberpsychol Behav* 2006; 9: 489-493.

[20] Thompson S: The internet and its potential influence on suicide. *Psychiatric Bulletin* 1999; 23: 449-451.

[21] Papyrus Press Office: Suicide prevention charity calls on Ministry of Justice to support law amendment 31st July 2008; http://www.papyrus-uk.org/Press/internet.html. Accessed 26.8.08.

[22] Mishara BL, Weisstub DN: Ethical, legal, and practical issues in the control and regulation of suicide promotion and assistance over the internet. *Suicide and Life-Threatening Behavior* 2007; 37(1): 58-65.

[23] Biddle L, Donovan J, Hawton K, Kapur N, Gunnell D: Suicide and the internet. *BMJ* 2008; 336: 800-802.

[24] Grohol JM: Study misses internet's greater collection of support websites. *BMJ* 2008; 336: 905-906.

[25] Recupero PR, Harms SE, Noble JM: Googling suicide: Surfing for information on the internet. *J Clin Psychiatry* 2008; 69(6): 878-88.

[26] Prasad V, Owens D: Using the internet as a source of self-help for people who self-harm. *Psychiatric Bulletin* 2001; 25: 222-225.

[27] Rajajopal S: Suicide pacts and the internet. *Am J Psychiatry* 2004; 329: 1298-1299.

[28] Naito A: Internet suicide in Japan: Implications for child and adolescent mental health. *Clin Child Psychol Psychiatry* 2007; 12(4): 583-597.

[29] Jobes DA, Berman AL, O'Carroll PW, Eastgard S, Knickmeyer S: The Kurt Cobain suicide crisis: Perspectives from research, public health, and the news media. *Suicid Life Threat Behav* 1996; 26: 260-271.

[30] The Independent: Ministers seek curbs on internet suicide sites for teenagers. *The Independent online news,* http://www.independent.co.uk/news/uk/politics/ministers-seek-curbs-on-internet-suicide-sites-for-teenagers-882604.html. Accessed 26.8.08.

[31] Schmidtke A, Bille-Brahe U, De Leo D, Kerkhof A, Bjerke T, Crepet P et al: Attempted suicide in Europe: Rates, trends and sociodemographic characteristics of suicide attempters during the period 1989-1992. Results of the WHO/EURO Multicentre Study on Parasuicide. *Acta Psychiatr Scand* 1996; 93: 327-338.

[32] Mitchell KJ, Ybarra ML: Online behavior of youth who engage in self-harm provides clues for preventive intervention. *Prev Med* 2007 Nov; 45(5):392-6.

[33] Rodham K, Gavin J, Miles M: I hear, I listen and I care: A qualitative investigation into the function of a self-harm message board. *Suicide Life Threat Behav* 2007; 37(4): 422-430.

[34] HMSO, 1961. *Suicide Act 1961* (c.60 9_and_10_Eliz_2), London: HMSO. http://www.statutelaw.gov.uk/content.aspx?activeTextDocId=1132509. Accessed 26.8.08.

[35] Biddle L, Brock A, Brookes S, Gunnell D: Suicide rates in young men in England and Wales in the 21st century: time trend study. *BMJ* 2008; 336: 539-542.

[36] Leitner M, Barr W, Hobby L: Effectiveness of interventions to prevent suicide and suicidal behaviour: A systematic review. *Scottish Government Social Research,* Edinburgh, 2008. ISBN 978- 0- 7559- 6904- 3 (http://www.scotland.gov.uk/Resource/Doc/208329/0055247.pdf).

[37] Becker K, Schmidt MH: When kids seek help on-line: Internet chat rooms and suicide. *Reclaim Child Youth* 2005; 13(4): 229-230.

[38] Cohen D, Putney R: Suicide website resources for professionals and consumers. *J Ment Health Aging* 2003; 9(2): 67-72.

[39] Murray CD, Fox J: Do internet self-harm discussion groups alleviate or exacerbate self-harming behaviour? *Aust e-J Adv Ment Health* 2006; 5(3): 1-9.

[40] Hoffman WA: Telematic technologies in mental health caring: A web-based psychoeducational program for adolescent suicide survivors. *Issues Ment Health Nurs* 2006; 27: 461-474.

[41] Murray CD, Macdonald S, Fox J: Body satisfaction, eating disorders and suicide ideation in an internet sample of self-harmers reporting and not reporting childhood sexual abuse. *Psychology, Health and Medicine* 2008; 13(1): 29-42.

[42] Papyrus Press Office: Overwhelming support for change in suicide law 2008, http://www.papyrus-uk.org/Press/YouGov.html. Accessed 26.8.08.

[43] House of Commons Culture, Media and Sport Committee: Harmful content on the internet and in video games: *Tenth report of session 2007-08.* HC 353-1. http://www.publications.parliament.uk/pa/cm200708/cmselect/cmcumeds/353/353.pdf. Accessed 26.8.08.

[44] *European Union: The European Union safer internet plan.* Brussels, EU Decision number 276-1999.

[45] Coombes R. Safety nets: How can parents protect vulnerable children and young people from pro-suicide sites? *BMJ* 2008; 336: 803.

[46] Pirkis J, Blood RW, Beautrais A et al: Media guidelines on the reporting of suicide. *Crisis* 2006; 27: 82-87.

[47] Niederkrotenthaler T, Sonneck G: Assessing the impact of media guidelines for reporting on suicides in Austria: Interrupted time series analysis. *Australia and New Zealand Journal of Psychiatry* 2007; 41: 419-428.

[48] Baume P, Rolfe A, Clinton M: Suicide on the internet: A focus for nursing intervention? *Aust NZ J Ment Health Nurs* 1998; 7(4): 134-141.

[49] Tam J, Tang WS, Fernando DJS: The internet and suicide: A double-edged tool. *European Journal of Internal Medicine* 2007; 18: 453-455.

[50] Barak A, Miron O: Writing characteristics of suicidal people on the internet: A psychological investigation of emerging social environments. *Suicide Life Threat Behav* 2005; 35: 507-524.

[51] Omar HA: A model program for youth suicide prevention. *Int J Adolesc Med Health* 2005; 17: 275-278.

[52] Barak A, Bloch N: Factors related to perceived helpfulness in supporting highly distressed individuals through an online support chat. *Cyberpsychol Behav* 2006; 9(1): 60-68.

In: Internet and Suicide
Editors: L. Sher and A. Vilens ISBN 978-1-60741-077-5

Chapter 21

MEDIA SUICIDE-REPORTS, INTERNET USE AND THE INCIDENCE OF SUICIDES IN JAPAN

Akihito Hagihara and Takeru Abe
Kyushu University Graduate School of Medicine, Fukuoka, Japan

ABSTRACT

Although Internet use has greatly increased, its influence on suicide is completely unknown. In addition, previous investigations regarding the effects of suicide reports in the media on suicide incidence in Japan have been limited and inconclusive. Thus, the relationship between newspaper articles about suicide, Internet use, and the incidence of suicide in Japan was examined. A linear model was fitted to time series data from January 1987 to March 2005 (218 months). Consistent with previous findings, the number of newspaper articles about suicide was a predictor of suicide among both male and female subjects. Internet use was also a predictor of suicide among males, probably because males spent more time online than females. Since this is the first, preliminary study examining the association between Internet use and suicide, further research is required to verify the present findings.

BACKGROUND

Numerous studies into the effect of suicide reporting on the incidence of suicide have been conducted in the United States and Europe [1–4]. According to Stack [5], there were 293 investigations concerning suicide news reports and suicide as of 1999. Although the findings have been mixed, the overall trend indicates that the media does have an impact on suicide [6–10]. Therefore, it is widely believed that suicide reports in the Japanese media lead to an increased number of suicides. In April 1986, an 18-year-old female singer committed suicide in Japan. The singer was very popular among the younger generation, especially teenagers, and news of her suicide came as a great shock. However, the coverage of this event was considered by many to be excessive. This prompted the Japanese Suicide Prevention Association, who were aware of the danger of suicide reporting, to send letters to media companies requesting that they cease their coverage [11].

The existing information on the effects of suicide reporting on suicide in Japan are very limited and inconclusive. As of July 2005, only eight studies had been conducted, and four of these compared the incidence of juvenile suicide before and after the suicide of the aforementioned female singer on 8 April 1986 [5, 11–17]. Yoshida *et al.* compared the observed and expected numbers of suicides in the under-20 age group after April 8, 1986. The expected number of suicides was calculated using a Poisson distribution and the observed number of suicides in the under-20 age group prior to 8 April 1986. Because the observed number of suicides was significantly higher than the expected number, the authors concluded that suicide reporting did have an effect on suicide incidence [11, 17]. Kurusu reported the daily number of suicides after April 8, 1986 among four age groups (i.e., 10–14, 15–19, 20–24, and 25–29 years) according to gender. After 8 April 1986, an increase in the number of suicide cases was observed for four days among 10–14-year-old females [15]. Using a multiplicative model of annual and monthly expected suicides, Fukutomi *et al.* determined the months in which the observed suicide rate was significantly greater than the expected rate. However, the effect of suicide reports in the media was not included in this study [13]. In summary, these studies suggested that media reports influence suicide.

Two subsequent studies concluded that the media does have an effect on suicide [5, 14]. These studies used time series data and economic models, such as the Yule–Walker and Granger causality models. In particular, the Granger causality model was able to evaluate the causal relationship between suicide reports and suicide [14]. However, these studies were limited by several methodological problems. In the study by Stack, articles concerning suicide from the *New York Times* and the *Japan Times* were used as a measure of media coverage [5], even though these two newspapers have a very limited circulation in Japan. In the study by Ishii, the length of the articles on suicide in the *Mainichi* and *Asahi* newspapers was used as a measure of suicide reporting; however, suicide articles from the *Yomiuri* newspaper, which has the largest circulation in Japan, were not used [14].

Although two studies demonstrated that the media does affect suicide, we can safely say that these findings were limited and inconclusive. The study periods analyzed in these eight studies ranged from 1954 to 1986 [5, 11–17]. No study has used more recent data to analyze the effect of mass media on suicide. However, several major factors that could potentially influence suicide have arisen in Japan since 1986. These include the publication of a book entitled "Suicide Manual" [18], increased Internet use, and the proliferation of web sites about suicide [19]. "Suicide Manual" was published on 4 July 1993, and shocked Japanese society [16]. As of 1 August 2005, there were more than 17,000 Japanese web sites that offered information on suicide and its methods [19].

On 11 February 2003, a 17-year-old high school senior committed suicide by carbon monoxide poisoning using a briquette. Since 2003, there have been frequent reports of young people meeting together for the first time via the Internet and committing group suicide. Carbon monoxide poisoning using a briquette has often been used as a method of group suicide, and information on this method seems to have been acquired via online suicide sites. Access to suicide information has become easier in Japan due to increased Internet availability since the 1990s. Therefore, we used recent data from 1987 to 2005 to examine whether newspaper articles about suicide and Internet use are related to the incidence of suicide in Japan.

METHODS

Study Period

The study period was from January 1987 to March 2005 (218 months).

Data Collection

Male and female monthly suicide statistics for 1987– 2005 were obtained from the Vital and Health Statistics summary published by the Statistics and Information Department of the Japanese Ministry of Health, Labor, and Welfare.

Five of the most widely circulated Japanese newspapers were examined (2004 circulation figures in parentheses): *Yomiuri* (10,120,000), *Asahi* (8,250,000), *Mainichi* (3,940,000), *Nikkei* (3,020,000), and *Sankei* (2,140,000) [20]. The Nikkei Telecom 21 database covers newspaper articles from 1980 to the present. This database includes articles from the *Nikkei* and *Asahi* from as early as 1980 and articles from the *Yomiuri*, *Mainichi*, and *Sankei* from as early as September 1986, January 1987, and September 1992, respectively [21]. The *Sankei* entered the database much later and has the smallest circulation among the five papers; therefore, the *Sankei* was excluded from the analysis. Data from January 1987 to March 2005 were analyzed for the remaining four papers (*Nikkei*, *Asahi*, *Yomiuri*, and *Mainichi*). We counted the monthly number of articles with headlines that contained the keyword "suicide". The effect of newspaper articles is assumed to depend on the type of newspaper as well as on circulation. However, these four major Japanese newspapers are very similar in terms of content and reader profile; thus, only circulation was used as a factor to assess the overall impact of suicide news [14]. Specifically, the total amount of suicide news was calculated as follows: (number of articles in *Yomiuri*) × (circulation of *Yomiuri*) + (number of articles in *Asahi*) × (circulation of *Asahi*) + (number of articles in *Mainichi*) × (circulation of *Mainichi*) + (number of articles in *Nikkei*) × (circulation of *Nikkei*).

Internet use on a commercial basis began in December 1992, and the Japanese Ministry of Internal Affairs and Communications has conducted a survey on the prevalence of Internet use among households since 1996 [22]. Using these data, we calculated the monthly household Internet use in Japan between 1987 and 2005.

Data Analysis

A linear model was fitted to the data with the number of suicides in a month as a dependent variable. The independent variables were the number of newspaper articles reporting suicide in the previous month, the prevalence of household Internet use in the previous month, the national jobless rate in the previous month, and dummy variables for 12 months. To eliminate problems with multicollinearity, outliers (or influential observations), and autocorrelation, the model was fitted using the ordinary least squares (OLS) method. Variance inflation factors (VIFs) and Cook's *D*-statistics showed that there were no problems with multicollinearity or outliers (or influential observations) in either male or female subjects. However, the Darbin–Watson *d*-statistics were 0.53 in males and 0.54 in females, and the first-order autocorrelation coefficients were 0.71 in males and 0.72 in females, indicating that the OLS estimation was highly problematic [23]. To purge the data of the effects of autocorrelation, alternative autocorrelation correction methods were considered. These were the Yule–Walker (YW) estimation, iterated YW, unconditional least squares (ULS), and unconditional maximum likelihood (ML). According to Spitzer's Monte Carlo study, the YW method did as well, or better, in estimating the structural parameter when the autoregressive parameter was not too large. However, when the autoregressive parameter was large, Spitzer recommended using ML methods [24]. In view of the autoregressive parameters of our data (i.e., autocorrelation coefficients of 0.71 in male subjects and 0.72 in females), ML methods were used to fit linear models. The analysis of a time series requires that the series is stationary and that the variance or volatility of the series is constant over time. Thus, dependent variables, rather than raw data, were log transformed, and the analysis was performed [25]. As only the dependent variable was log transformed, the coefficient value shows a change in rate when there is a change of 1 unit in an independent variable. The analysis was performed using the SAS/ETS AUTOREG procedure [26].

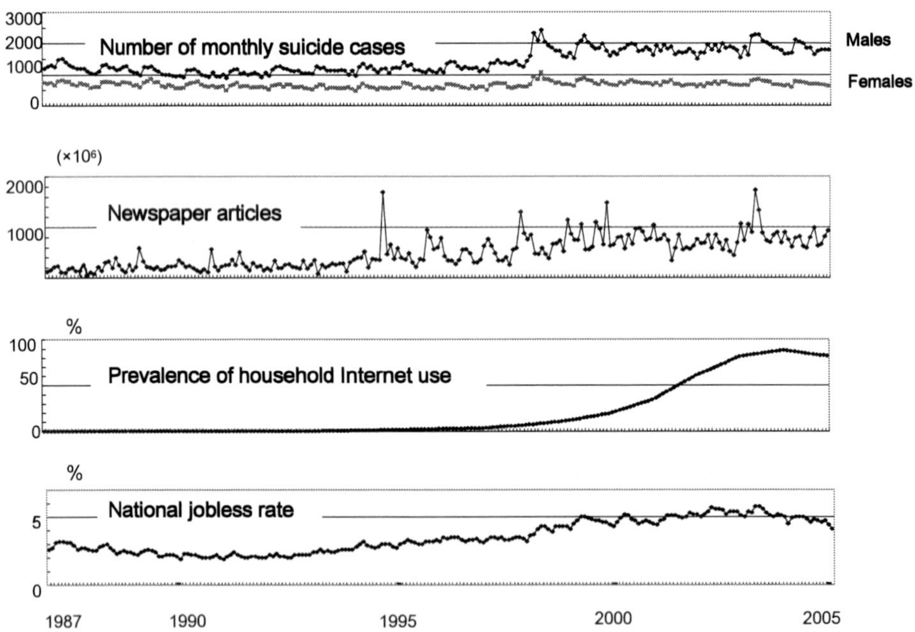

Figure 1. Monthly change in study variables between January 1987 and March 2005. Newspaper articles, prevalence of household internet use, and national jobless rate are the values in the previous month.

Table 1. Study variables in Japan, 1987–2005

Variables	Mean ± SD	Range
Number of monthly suicide cases		
Males	1415.71 ± 352.38	888–2423
Females	672.74 ± 90.88	479–1062
Number of monthly suicide cases in the previous month		
Malcs	1415.71 ± 352.38	888–2423
Females	672.74 ± 90.88	479–1062
Newspaper articles about suicide in the previous month ($\times 10^6$)	480.33 ± 300.3	56.9–1685.23
Prevalence of household Internet use in the previous month (%)	17.65 ± 29.12	0–88.1
National jobless rate in the previous month (%)	3.43 ± 1.14	1.90-5.80

RESULTS

The study variables are presented in Table 1. Changes in the study variables during the study period are also shown in Figure 1. During the study period (January 1987–March 2005), the monthly number of suicides for males showed an upward trend, and ranged between 888 and 2434. The monthly number of suicides for females remained at the same level during the same level, and ranged between 479 and 1062. The mean monthly number of suicides was 1415.71 (± 352.38) for males and 672.74 (± 90.88) for females; the number of suicides among male subjects was more than double that of females. The number of newspaper reports about suicide is expressed in units of 10^6. During the study period, the number of articles showed an upward trend, and ranged from 56.9 to 1685.23 ($\times 10^6$).

Since the launch of commercial Internet services in December 1992, the prevalence of household Internet use has increased rapidly, from 0% in December 1992 to 88.1% in March 2005. During the study period, the mean national jobless rate was 3.43% (± 1.14).

Table 2 shows the results of the unconditional ML corrections of autocorrelation according to gender. To test whether the coefficients were biased due to unequal variance in the error term between values of the independent variables (heteroscedasticity), the *Q*-statistics test for changes in variance across time was performed [26]. This test showed no possibility of heteroscedasticity in the equations for male or female subjects. With respect to males, newspaper articles on suicide ($p< 0.001$), the prevalence of Internet use ($p< 0.05$), and the national jobless rate in the previous month ($p< 0.0001$) were significant predictors of suicide ($P < 0.001$, 0.5, and 0.0001, respectively). This suggests that, after controlling for other factors, an increase in newspaper articles by 1 unit (10^6 distributed articles), an increase in household internet use by 1%, or an increase in the national jobless rate in the previous month by 1% will lead to increases of 0.01%, 0.16%, and 12.7%, respectively, in male suicides. The months from February to June, October and December, had significantly more suicides, respectively, than the referent month, January. Because a dummy variable was introduced for 12 months, the regression coefficient in this case refers to the difference between the mean change rate in a dependent variable in subgroups with or without the attribute shown by the dummy variable [27]. Thus, with regard to March, April, May, June, and October, the β-values were 0.1127 ($P < 0.0001$), 0.1169 ($P < 0.0001$), 0.1461 ($P < 0.0001$), 0.0853 ($P < 0.000$), and 0.0484 ($P < 0.01$), suggesting that, after controlling for other variables, March, April, May, June and October showed 11.27%, 11.69%, 14.61%, 8.53%, and 4.84% increases in suicide incidence, respectively, compared to January. With regard to February and December, the β-values were –0.0712 ($P < 0.0001$) and –0.0480 ($P < 0.01$), suggesting that, after controlling for other variables, February and December showed 7.12% and 4.80% decreases in the incidence of suicide, respectively, compared to January.

Table 2. Effects of publicized suicide stories and Internet use on the monthly suicide rate, 1987–2005 ($n = 218$)

	Males			Females		
	Coefficient	Standard Error	*t*-statistics	Coefficient	Standard Error	*t*-statistics
Intercept	6.6852****	0.0650	102.82	6.3286****	0.0744	85.10
Newspaper suicide reports in the previous month	0.0001***	0.0000	3.44	0.0001***	0.0000	3.97
Prevalence of Internet use in the previous month	0.0016*	0.0008	1.98	0.0001	0.0009	0.09
National jobless rate in the previous month	0.1270****	0.0208	6.09	0.0172	0.0238	0.72
February	–0.0712****	0.0149	–4.78	–0.0722****	0.0165	–4.38
March	0.1127****	0.0174	6.49	0.1434****	0.0193	7.44
April	0.1169****	0.0188	6.21	0.1703****	0.0209	8.16
May	0.1461****	0.0196	7.45	0.1975****	0.0217	9.09
June	0.0853***	0.0202	4.22	0.1211****	0.0224	5.41
July	0.0715	0.0206	3.47	0.1068****	0.0228	4.68
August	0.0159	0.0201	0.79	0.0516*	0.0223	2.31
September	0.0207	0.0195	1.06	0.0243	0.0216	1.13
October	0.0484**	0.0184	2.62	0.0518*	0.0204	2.53
November	–0.0056	0.0167	–0.33	0.0245	0.0185	1.32
December	–0.0480**	0.0163	–2.95	–0.0117	0.0181	–0.64
	$R^2 = 0.96$, DW = 1.81			$R^2 = 0.80$, DW = 2.02		

*$P < 0.05$, **$P < 0.01$, ***$P < 0.001$, ****$P < 0.0001$

With respect to female subjects, the number of newspaper articles about suicide in the previous month was a significant predictor of suicide ($P < 0.001$). These results suggest that, after controlling for other factors, an increase in the number of newspaper articles by 1 unit ($\times 10^6$ distributed articles) will lead to an increase of 0.01% in the incidence of suicide among females. The months from March to August, and October, had significantly more suicides, respectively, than the referent month, January. In March, April, May, June, July, August, and October, the β-values were 0.1434 ($P < 0.0001$), 0.1703 ($P < 0.0001$), 0.1975 ($P < 0.0001$), 0.1211 ($P < 0.0001$), 0.1068 ($P < 0.0001$), 0.0516 ($P < 0.05$) and 0.0518 ($P < 0.05$), suggesting that after controlling for other variables, these months showed 14.34%, 17.03%, 19.75%, 12.11%, 10.68%, 5.16% and 5.18% increases in suicide cases, respectively, compared to January. With regard to February, the β-value was –0.0722 ($P < 0.0001$), suggesting that after controlling for other variables, February showed a 7.22% decrease in suicide incidence compared to January.

To determine whether the association between suicides and media reports (previous month) for males and females (Table 2) was a spurious relationship between suicide deaths in one month and suicide deaths in the previous month (autocorrelation), we preformed additional multiple regression analyses. We used (1) the same model as in Table 2 except the media reports were from the same month instead of the previous month and (2) a model including suicides in the previous month as an independent variable in addition to those in Table 2. In the first analysis, the number of newspaper articles on suicide (same month) was a significant predictor of suicide among males (B = 0.0001, $t = 3.46$, $p < 0.0001$) and females (B = 0.0001, $t = 4.05$, $p < 0.0001$). In the second analysis, the number of suicides (previous month) was a significant predictor of suicide among males (B = 0.0001, $t = 4.29$, $p < 0.0001$) and females (B = 0.0001, $t = 3.49$, $p = 0.0006$). Furthermore, the other significant variables were exactly the same as those shown in Table 2 [*i.e.*, prevalence of internet use (previous month), national jobless rate (previous month), month dummies for males, and month dummies for females]. Thus, there should be no problems related to autocorrelation in Table 2.

DISCUSSION

Based on data from 1987 to 2005 in Japan, we evaluated the effect of newspaper articles about suicide and Internet use on the occurrence of suicide, according to gender. Several conclusions can be drawn from our findings. Because the β-values for newspaper articles about suicide were positive and significant in males ($\beta = 0.0001$, $P < 0.001$) and females ($\beta = 0.0001$, $P < 0.001$), it is likely that newspapers articles affect the occurrence of suicide in both genders. These results are consistent with two previous studies based on time series data [5,14]. With respect to the association between Internet use and suicide, our results differed for males and females. The β-values for the prevalence of Internet use were positive and significant for males ($\beta = 0.0016$, $P < 0.05$), but not for females (Table 2). These results may be the result of gender-based differences in Internet use. According to the Japan Policy Agency, the numbers of suicide cases and victims among people meeting for the first time via the Internet were, respectively, 19 and 55 in 2004 and 34 and 91 in 2005, showing an upward trend [28]. A survey on Internet use in the city of Yamato, which is near the Tokyo metropolitan area, revealed several differences between males and females with respect to their attitudes toward the Internet and Internet use [29]. At the time of the study in 2000, 47.52% of males had access to the Internet compared to only 36.1% of females. Furthermore, female respondents were less willing to express their opinions on the Internet, and indicated that they found computers difficult to use. According to a study in 2003 conducted by the National Institute of Communications Technology (NICT), Internet use was higher among 12–74-year-old males (55.7%) than females (49.9%) [30]. These findings suggest that Internet use and newspaper articles on suicide have a differential effect on suicide incidence in males and females.

This is the first study to examine the association between Internet use and the number of suicides in Japan. The NICT survey reported that the mean time spent online was longer than the mean time spent reading newspapers in 2004 (37 versus 31 min per day, respectively) [31]. The time spent online is expected to increase in Japan until Internet use becomes as saturated as it is in the United States, meaning that the Internet will continue to be a potential predictor of the suicide rate in Japan [31].

The β-coefficient for the national jobless rate was only positive and significant in males ($\beta = 0.1270$, $P < 0.0001$; Table 2). Several previous studies have reported the association between economic strain and suicide [14, 32]. Our results show that the unemployment rate was a significant predictor of suicide among males, but not females. Inoue *et al.* recently reported that the annual suicide rate among Japanese males was significantly correlated with the annual unemployment rate, whereas the suicide rate for Japanese females was not associated with unemployment [33]. Although our results are consistent with these previous findings, further investigation is required to determine why unemployment is not a predictor of suicide in females.

Certain months of the year were also significant predictors of suicide (Table 2). The β-coefficients for the months of March to June were significant and positive for both males and females, and July was also significant and positive for females (Table 2). Based on combined data for males and females, Stack reported that the months from March to June were positive predictors of suicide in Japan [5]. Similarly, Fukutomi *et al.* reported that the number of suicides was high in April and low in December [13]. Our findings are consistent with these previous studies.

We attempted to improve upon the methodological issues and limitations of previous studies. First, of the eight studies investigating the effect of media reports on suicide in Japan [5, 11–17], only two analyzed the time series data using the appropriate models [5, 14]. To produce a more reliable assessment of this issue, we analyzed time series data using a linear model. We also used suicide reports and the national jobless rate during the previous month to establish a temporal relationship between stimuli (suicide news) and response (suicide). With respect to suicide data, Phillip and Bollen pointed out the importance of daily data. Given that those who are influenced by news media will commit suicidal acts on a daily basis, it might be difficult to accurately evaluate stimuli (suicide news) and response (suicide) relationships on the basis of monthly data. Thus, Bollen and Phillips used daily data instead of monthly data in their analyses [34, 35]. However, we were required to rely on monthly data because daily data on newspaper articles related to suicide and Internet use were not available. Furthermore, the model used in our study does not consider other possible or known risk factors for suicide, such as the rise in alcohol use, drug use, domestic violence, and the poor provision of mental health care. More sophisticated models based upon daily data including these variables need to be tested in future studies.

Previous studies used articles from English language newspapers circulated in Japan or from a limited number of the larger domestic Japanese papers [5, 14]. To improve the accuracy of our measure, we used articles on suicide from the four largest domestic newspapers. However, articles were selected based on the keyword "suicide" in the headline. This approach may have excluded articles that discussed suicide but were not specifically suicide reports, such as editorials, commentaries, and fictional stories. Likewise, this approach may have included non-relevant articles that used "suicide" in another context. In addition, it is possible that some relevant articles were excluded because the headlines may have cited the method of suicide rather than the keyword "suicide". In this connection, we need to refer to news articles related to "9-11" in 2001. Owing to the worldwide reporting of suicide bombing attacks in recent years, one might think that this approach has led to biased results. However, suicide and suicide bombing attacks are pronounced and expressed quite differently in Japanese. Thus, in reality, there was no overlap between articles on "suicide" versus "suicide bombing (attacks)". Finally, other potentially important factors, such as front-page coverage or photos or illustrations of the deceased, were not considered when searching for newspaper articles about suicide. Future studies will require a more refined measure of the impact of newspaper articles.

Detailed information on Internet use has been available since 2001 [30], allowing us to include the prevalence of household Internet use in our study. However, the extent of exposure to Internet news was not determined, and thus our results concerning Internet use should be interpreted cautiously. The Internet may be used for leisure or communication purposes rather than reading the news. Perhaps only a small percentage of Internet users were exposed to suicide reports, and an even smaller proportion of these were influenced by the news. In addition, help organizations now offer help via the Internet and, thus, Internet use may have had a preventive impact on the number of suicides that was not evaluated in this study. Although worldwide Internet use has increased in the observed time period, suicide incidence has decreased in many countries. Therefore, it is important to determine if Japanese web sites devoted to suicide or suicide prevention differ from web sites in other countries, and whether a decrease in suicide incidence is accompanied by an increase in Internet use. Further studies will be required to thoroughly evaluate the positive and negative effects of online suicide reports.

We examined whether suicide incidence increased more rapidly before or after 1992 and the advent of the Internet; however, no difference in the increase of suicide incidence was observed. Future studies will require a more precise measure of exposure to suicide reports and related topics via the Internet.

It can be expected that the Internet and newspaper articles have different effects on people, according to age and gender. An article from *Internet Watch* reported that the time spent online per month increased by 58% in the 2–12-year-old age group, 44% in the 50–59-year-old age group, and 3% in the 16–19-year-old age group between March 2001 and 2002 [31]. Although the mean time spent online has increased more than that spent reading newspapers in 2004, people in their 60s or older spend more time reading newspapers than going online [30]. Our study design was not able to evaluate the differential influence of news articles and Internet use on suicide incidence in terms of gender and age. This is an area for future study.

In conclusion, we examined the relationship between newspaper articles about suicide and Internet usage and the number of suicides in Japan from 1987 to 2005. We found the following: (1) newspaper articles about suicide are a predictor of suicide for both male and female subjects, which is consistent with previous findings, and (2) Internet use was a predictor of suicide among males, who spent longer hours online, as compared to females. More research is required to verify our findings regarding Internet use and suicide incidence.

REFERENCES

[1] Blumental S, Bergner L: Suicide and newspaper: a replicated study. *Am J Psychiat* 1973; 130:468–477.

[2] Gould MS, Saffer D: The impact of suicide in television movies: evidence of imitation. *New Engl J Med* 1986; 315:690–694.

[3] Motto JA: Newspaper influences on suicide. *Arch Gen Psychiat* 1970; 23: 143–148.

[4] Phillips DP: Motor vehicle fatalities increase just after publicized suicide stories. *Science* 1977; 196:1464–1465.

[5] Stack S: The effect of the media on suicide: evidence from Japan, 1955–1985. *Suicide Life Threatening Behavior* 1996; 26:132–142.

[6] Phillips DP: The influence of suggestion on suicide. *American Sociological Review* 1974; 39:340–354.

[7] Stack S: Celebrities and suicide: a taxonomy and analysis, 1948–1983. *American Sociological Review* 1987; 52:401–412.

[8] Wasserman I: Imitation and suicide: a replication of the Werther effect. *American Sociological Review* 1984; 49:427–436.

[9] Stack S: Suicide in the media: a quantitative review of suicides based on non-fictional stories. *Suicide Life Threatening Behavior* 2005; 35:121-133.

[10] Niederkrotenthaler T, Sonneck G: Assessing the impact of media guidelines for reporting on suicides in Austria: interrupted time series analysis. *Australian N Z J of Psychiatry* 2007; 41:419-428.

[11] Yoshida K, Mochizuki Y, Fukuyama Y: The effects of media reporting on teenagers' suicide in Hokkaido, Japan. *Nippon Koshu Eisei Zasshi* 1989; 36:370–374. [in Japanese]

[12] Fujii K, Kurusu E: Teenagers' suicide death and newspaper reports. *Syakai-Seishin-Igaku* 1990; 13:133–144. [in Japanese]

[13] Fukutomi K., Hashimoto S, Nishida S, Hayashi K, Fujita T, Minowa M: Teenagers' suicide death. *Kusei-no-Sihyo* 1988; 35:3–8. [in Japanese]

[14] Ishii K: Measuring mutual causation: effects of suicide news on suicides in Japan. *Social Science Research* 1991; 20:188–195.

[15] Kurusu E: The effects of mass media upon teenagers' suicides. *Syakai-Seishin-Igaku* 1992; 15:169–177. [in Japanese]

[16] Yoshida K: Suicides and mass media. *Kikan-Seishinka-Shindan-Gaku* 1993; 4:185–193. [in Japanese]

[17] Yoshida K, Mochizuki Y, Fukuyama Y: Clustering of suicides under age 20. Seasonal trends and the influence of newspaper reports. *Nippon Koshu Eisei Zasshi* 1991; 38:324–332. [in Japanese]

[18] Dokyumento: "Kanzen Jisatsu Manyuaru" Kisei Soudou (Document: "Suicide manual" and controversy concerning regulation of the book). (n.d.) Retrieved August 1, 2005, from [http://hp1.cyberstation.ne.jp/straycat/watch/manual.htm] [in Japanese]

[19] Jisatsu-houhou (Methods to commit a suicide) [http://search.yahoo.co.jp/bin/query?p=%bc%ab%bb%a6%ca%fd%cb%a1&fr=top] [in Japanese]

[20] Japan Audit Bureau Circulations: *Hanki Hanbai-busuu Jikeiretsu Hyou* (Table of the numbers for newspaper circulation on a half-year basis). Tokyo: Japan Audit Bureau Circulations; 2005. [in Japanese]

[21] Nikkei Media Marketing Co. Ltd: *Nikkei Telecon 21*. Tokyo: Nikkei Media Marketing Co. Ltd; 2005. [in Japanese]

[22] Economic Research Office, General Policy Division, Information and Communications Policy Bureau, Ministry of Public Management, Home Affairs, Posts and Telecommunications: *2004 White Paper. Information and Communications in Japan. Building a ubiquitous network society that spreads throughout the world.* Tokyo, Ministry of Public Management, Home Affairs, Posts and Telecommunications; 2005. [in Japanese]

[23] Johnston J: *Econometric methods.* New York, MacGraw–Hill, 1984.

[24] Spitzer JJ: Small-sample properties of nonlinear least squares and maximum likelihood estimations in the context of autocorrelated errors. *J Am Stat Assoc* 1979; 74:41–47.

[25] Vandaele W: *Applied time series and Box-Jenkins models.* New York, NY, Academic Press, 1983, pp. 11-30.

[26] SAS Institute, Inc: SAS/ETS user's guide. Cary, NC, SAS Institute Inc., 1993.

[27] Pedhazur FJ: *Multiple regression in behavioral research.* Fort Worth, TX, Harcourt Brace College Publishers, 1997.

[28] Japan Police Agency. *Inta-netto jyo no jisatsu yokoku jian eno taiou-jyokyo ni tuite* (Counteract to the notification of suicide on Internet). Japan Police Agency, February 9, 2006. [in Japanese]

[29] The City of Yamato, Department of Planning and External Affairs: *Survey on the network and its use in the City of Yamato.* Yamato, Japan, The City of Yamato, 2000. [in Japanese]

[30] National Institute of Communications Technology: *Report on the Internet use in Japan.* Tokyo, National Institute of Communications Technology, 2004. [in Japanese]

[31] Internet watch. Kodomo (2–12sai) no Internt Riyou-jikan ga Kyuuzou: Kounai Chousa (Rapid increase in hours for the Internet use among children between 2 and 12: a survey in Japan) [http://www.watch.impress.co.jp/internet/www/article/2002/0422/netr.htm] [in Japanese]

[32] Stack S, Wasserman I: Economic strain and suicide risk: a qualitative analysis *Suicide Life Threatening Behavior* 2007; 37:103-112.

[33] Inoue K, Tanii H, Kaiya H, Abe S, Nishimura Y, Masaki M, Okazaki Y, Nata M, Fukunaga T: The correlation between unemployment and suicide rates in Japan between 1978 and 2004. *Legal Medicine* 2007; 9:139-142.

[34] Phillip DP: The incidence of suggestion on suicide. *American Sociological Review* 1974; 39:340-354.

[35] Phillip DP, Bollen K: Same time last year: selective data dredging for negative findings. *American Sociological Review* 1985; 50:101-116.

In: Internet and Suicide
Editors: L. Sher and A. Vilens
ISBN 978-1-60741-077-5

Chapter 22

INTERNET-ASSOCIATED SUICIDE IN JAPAN

Masahito Hitosugi
Dokkyo Medical University School of Medicine, Tochigi, Japan

ABSTRACT

The internet is a frequently used source of information and a rapid method of communication. To lessen the suicide rate in developed countries, recent trends in internet-related suicides should be examined and effective preventive measures should be considered. People express their negative feelings and share them with like-minded people on the internet. Recently, the internet has also become a tool used by suicidal individuals to find death companions—suicide-related websites are claimed to have facilitated suicide pacts among strangers who have met and then planned their suicides on the internet. Charcoal burning is commonly used in suicide pacts, and information on this method seems to have spread via suicide-related websites. In addition, there are concerns about drugs and illegal substances that can be bought obtained via the internet. Regulation of websites that promote suicide is perhaps the most effective means of suicide prevention. In addition to the restriction of suicide-related websites, restricting access to sedative and other toxic substances is also important. In Japan, following the establishment of a voluntary internet guideline, 43 persons with suicidal intentions were saved in 2006. Although the regulation was effective, psychological health problems of individuals with suicidal thoughts, as well as internet dependency in young people, should be investigated. Then, comprehensive preventive measures should be promoted in the future.

INTRODUCTION

The internet is a frequently used source of information and a rapid method of communication. Internet use has dramatically increased in Japan and other developed countries. According to a 2003 study conducted by the National Institute of Communications Technology in Japan, people spend 37 min/day on the internet, longer than the average time spent reading newspapers, 31 min/day [1]. Individuals also use the internet to find solutions for health problems; a nationally representative sample of adults in the United States estimated in 2004 that eight out of 10 internet users searched for health information [2]. Along with the significant advances being made in communication technology, there are potential hazards—the internet is being used by young people to facilitate group suicides. Although psychological studies, involving psychological autopsy and suicide note analyses, have previously investigated the causes of suicide, the relationship between suicide and internet use has recently received wider attention. To lessen the suicide rate in developed countries, recent trends in internet-related suicides should be investigated and effective preventive measures should be considered. This chapter uses the case of suicide in Japan to introduce the characteristics of internet-related suicides, especially involving suicide pacts, emphasizing the importance of suicide prevention.

Overview of Suicide in Japan

Suicide claims over 1 million lives per year worldwide, and attempted suicide is estimated to occur up to 40 times more frequently [3]. Although suicide is often related to psychiatric disorders, it may be more preventable than other diseases and unintentional injuries. Therefore, the prevention of suicide is an important global health care issue.

Here, I discuss recent suicide trends in Japan. Usually, mortality data based on death certificates are used in suicide studies; however, death certificates issued when information about the cause of death is limited might contain inaccuracies. In Japan, when a death occurs that may be a suicide, the police first investigate the body and the surroundings to determine whether the death is truly a suicide. For this reason, we used data collected from the National Police Agency, owing to its higher reliability. In Japan, the number of suicides has increased in recent years; since 1998, the number of suicides has continued to be in excess of 30,000 (Figure 1). In 2003, 34,425 persons (24,963 males and 9,464 females) committed suicide, the highest number ever recorded in Japan. In 2007, the total number suicides was 33,093 (23,478 males and 9,615 females), and suicide was the 6th most common cause of death in Japan. For young and middle-aged persons, however, suicide is the most common cause of death: 43.9% of all deaths of persons aged 20 - 24 were suicides; 45.1% for those aged 25 - 29; 35.9% for those aged 30 - 34; and 29.2% for those aged 35 - 39.

The age-adjusted mortality rate due to suicide in Japan is 25.9 (per 100,000 population) overall, 37.7 in males and 14.7 in females. Rates were almost twice as high for males and three times higher for females compared with those from the United States. The overall mortality rates due to suicide of various age groups are shown in Figure 2. With increasing age, the mortality rate gradually increases, reaching the highest rate (38.1) in persons between 50 and 59 years old. Some possible reasons for this result are as follows. First, later in life, depression and disruption often occur [4]. Second, unemployed persons or those who have failed to succeed in spite of their best efforts are found in large numbers in the middle to old age groups [5]. Third, middle to older aged persons often have difficulties adjusting to new social phenomena [6]. Fourth, in traditional Japanese culture, suicide was considered an honorable way of escaping failure when confronted with the social stigma of mental illness or failure in professional and private life [7]. In ancient Japanese myths, a warrior (*samurai*) would cut his stomach to show his spirit to his enemy.

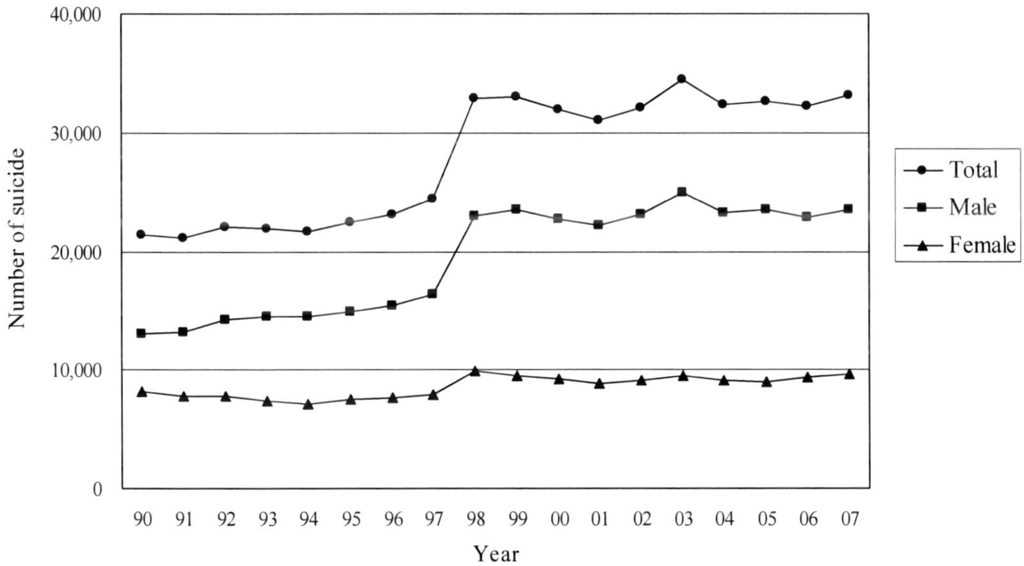

Figure 1. Trend in number of suicides in Japan.

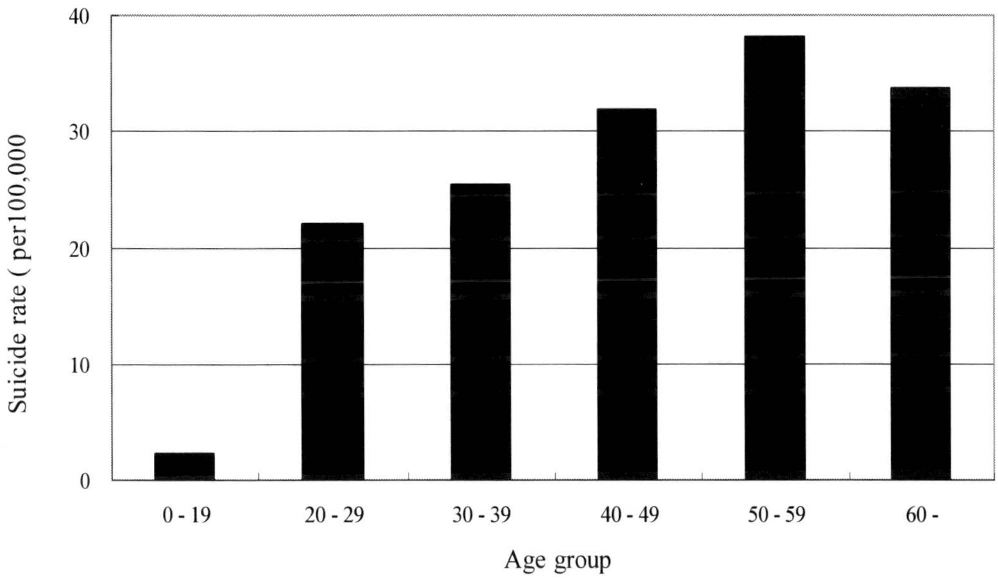

Figure 2. Suicide rates by age group in Japan (2007).

Figure 3 shows the distribution of antecedents (causes) of suicide in 2007. The two biggest causes were identified as health and financial worries. Regarding the distribution of occupations in suicide victims, more than half of victims (57.4%) were unemployed (Figure 4). In agreement with previous reports suggesting that the annual suicide rate among Japanese males is significantly correlated with the annual unemployment rate, unemployment is a predictor of suicide, especially for males [8]. Clearly, a poor economy seems to have contributed to the growing number of suicides in Japan. Other data also suggest that, of those who committed suicide, three-fourths had suffered from mental health problems such as depression, schizophrenia, or emotional or behavioral problems caused by drug use [9]. Concerning the method of suicide, hanging represented the majority (70% for males and 60% for females), followed by jumping from a height. In the United States, however, the most common method of suicide is firearms for both genders. The differences in suicide method between the United States and Japan are partially due to religious and cultural differences.

INTERNET DEPENDENCE IN YOUTH

Internet is an indispensable tool for young persons in Japan. According to a communication use survey carried out by the Ministry of Internal Affairs and Communications in 2003, the internet population in Japan was 69.4 million, the second largest figure in the world after the United States. Considering the internet utilization rate by age, the highest was 89.8% in the 20 - 29 age group, followed by 88.1 % in the 13 - 19 age group, and 85.0% in the 30 - 39 age group [10]. In addition, 42.9% of the persons surveyed used the internet at least once a day. Similar trends were also observed in Korea; the prevalence of internet usage of Korean adolescents between 6 and 19 years old was 90.6% in 2002 [11]. This dramatic increase in internet use has led to various psychological changes, especially in adolescents. Young people who become dependent on internet use tend to isolate themselves from real-life experiences and eventually from life itself. Extensive internet use may create a heightened level of arousal, resulting in little sleep, failure to eat for long periods, and limited physical activity, possibly resulting in the physical and mental health problems such as depression, loneliness, low self-esteem, and anxiety [11]. This state is known as internet addiction. Internet addiction increases when the individual is able to satisfy his or her desires. According to Kim et al., 1.6% of high-school students in Korea were diagnosed as internet addicts with a high level of suicide ideation and 38.0% were classified as possible internet addicts [11].

In the internet age, people are able to express their negative feelings and share them with like-minded people on the internet. Although the internet can be a way of making friends for life, it can also be used as a tool to find companions in death.

THE INTERNET AND SUICIDE

Media reporting about suicide on television are known to influence suicidal behavior, particularly of the public's understanding of suicide methods [12]. News media reports of suicides have a risk of increasing the rate of suicide among those who watch the reports. Generally, the more publicity suicides receive, the higher the suicide rate among the target demographic [13]. It has been scientifically confirmed that newspaper articles and media reports about suicide are predictors of suicide for both genders [14, 15].

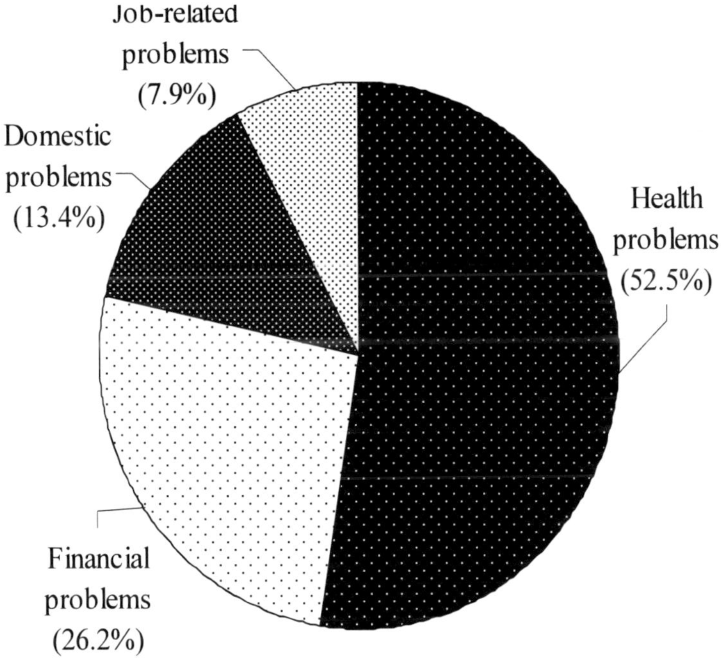

Figure 3. Causes of suicide in Japan (2007).

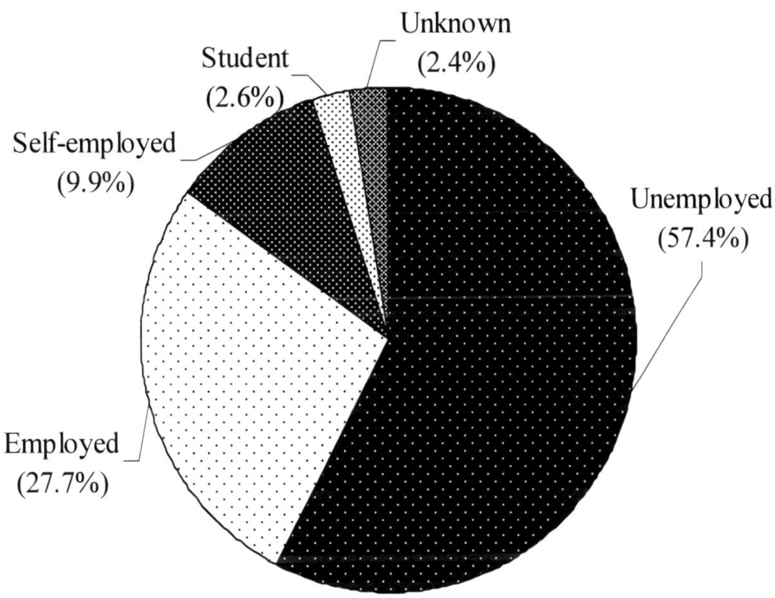

Figure 4. Occupations of suicide victims in Japan (2007).

Large amounts of information relating to suicide are also available via the internet. Some websites provide details of particular suicide methods, advocate specific techniques, or describe particular individual and group suicides.

Although the internet has become a popular source of information, the internet's influence on suicidal behavior is not well understood [16]. Some suicide-related websites encourage troubled individuals to commit suicide as a way of solving their problems. In a study of internet use by vulnerable youth, Becker et al. suggested that 30% of all adolescents have suicidal thoughts and approximately half of them visit suicide-related websites [17].

A suicide pact is an agreement between two or more people to commit suicide together at a given place and time. Suicide-related websites are claimed to have facilitated suicide pacts among strangers who have met and then planned their suicides through the internet. Young people in particular who have suicidal desires tend to use the internet to look for companions with the same interest in suicide. After finding suicide companions, these individuals plan their deaths via specialized suicide-related websites or chat rooms.

SUICIDE WEBSITES

There are currently more than 100,000 websites that provide detailed information on suicide methods; for example, what medications to mix to create a lethal poison or how to successfully hang oneself [18]. In Japan, more than 17,000 Japanese web sites offering information on suicide and suicide methods were investigated in August 2005 [14]. Recupero et al. searched the websites with five popular search engines (Google, Yahoo, ASK, Lycos, and Dogpile) using four suicide-related terms (suicide; how to commit suicide; suicide methods; how to kill yourself) in August and September 2006 [19]. Of 373 unique websites, enhancement of suicide was shown in 41 pages (11.0%). In May 2007, Biddle et al. searched for websites providing instructions and information about suicide methods with four popular search engines (Google, Yahoo, MSN, and ASK) using 12 simple search terms (suicide; suicide methods; suicide sure methods; most effective methods of suicide; methods of suicide; ways to commit suicide; how to kill yourself; how to commit suicide; easy suicide methods; best suicide methods; pain-free suicide; quick suicide) [12]. Of the 240 different websites subsequently analyzed, 45 (18.8%) were judged to encourage, promote, or facilitate suicide. The authors also suggested that it is easy to obtain detailed technical information about suicide methods from general information websites such as Wikipedia, not just from specialized suicide-related websites, and that suicide information is also readily available in chat rooms. Chat room contributors may exert peer pressure on others to commit suicide, idolize those who have committed suicide, or facilitate suicide pacts [20]. Such discussion may lessen any doubts or fears suicidal individuals may be feeling.

Some suicides in Japan were performed based on information about drugs and illegal substances obtained from websites. The internet provides services and information ranging from general information to online orders of prescription drugs and other substances that bypass government regulations and custom controls. Online pharmacies located in other countries can supply prescription drugs over the internet without valid prescriptions [21]. In addition, some websites offer a list of overseas pharmacies and provide tips on how to avoid legal implications when dealing with these systems. Suicides due to drug overdoses or illegal substances connected to information obtained from the internet are often reported.

Clearly, the internet is a powerful information resource that can easily influence vulnerable young people into taking their own lives.

Internet Suicide Pacts

According to a recent report, young people are more likely to be influenced by the internet to commit suicide than by other people [18]. This is because young people have a high incidence of high-risk behaviors, comorbid substance abuse, and depressive disorders. Adolescents without social support may be particularly vulnerable. Gender differences regarding internet suicide pacts have also been investigated in Japan—a survey on internet use in an urban Japanese city revealed that males used the internet more often than females [22]. Hagihara et al. suggested that internet use is a predictor of suicide among males who spend more time online, as compared to females [14]. Possible reasons for this difference could be that females are less willing to express their opinions on the internet, and some find computers difficult to use. The rate of pact-related suicides among all suicide deaths has not been published in Japan; however, in England, suicide pacts accounted for less than 1% of the total number of suicides [23].

It is believed that the first "wave" of internet suicide pacts occurred in 2000 in Korea. In Japan, the first internet-linked suicide pact occurred in 2003. From February to early June, at least 20 Japanese people died in suicide pacts. On October 2004, nine people died in one night; seven in one pact and two in another. They met on an online message board, knowing each other only by their internet screen names, and planned their deaths; they then gathered at a given place to commit suicide. According to the National Police Agency in Japan, 34 persons including two teenagers in 2003; 55 persons including seven teenagers in 2004; and 91 persons including eight teenagers in 2005 died as a result of internet suicide pacts [24]. Carbon monoxide poisoning achieved by burning barbecue charcoal in a small, sealed-off environment is the most common suicide method used in these pacts, and information about this method seems to have been acquired via suicide-related websites. In other Asian countries as well, the number of suicide pact-related deaths by charcoal burning are rapidly increasing [25]. However, the precise number of suicides due to charcoal burning is not well understood throughout the world because of the absence of a specific code for suicide by charcoal burning in the latest version of the International Classification of Diseases. The charcoal burning method is frequently chosen by members of suicide pacts because charcoal is easily obtained in shops and because the method is simple, easy, and painless.

I also suggest the concern about any drugs and illegal substances. As burnt charcoal produces carbon monoxide, individuals must remain in a sealed-off space for a short period to inhale a significant amount of carbon monoxide. Therefore, individuals aiming to commit suicide often take other substances in order to sedate themselves. In Japan, as psychotropic drugs cannot be obtained without a prescription, persons with suicidal ideations obtain drugs or illegal substances by private means, mainly via the internet. One suicide pact case in which illegal substances were used in Japan is presented as follows [26]. Three Japanese persons were found dead in a car with burning charcoal. They had met via the internet and agreed to commit suicide together. Forensic autopsy revealed high levels of carboxy-hemoglobin (77.0% to 86.4%) and 1.5 to 3.1 ng/ml of melatonin in the blood. Cause of death was carbon monoxide poisoning following the administration of melatonin. Melatonin, a neurohormone synthesized mainly by the pineal grand, is used as a dietary supplement for insomnia or jet lag. Although melatonin is not sold in Japan, it can be easily obtained by private importation via the internet. For this reason, it is extremely important to regulate the circulation of sleep aids via the internet.

Recently, another suicide method has been popularized by the internet—inhalation of deadly hydrogen sulphide gas, which can be produced by mixing shop-bought household detergents. In 2007, almost 300 persons, most of them in their 20s and 30s, died from hydrogen sulphide inhalation after learning how to make the gas on the internet [27].

In summary, reported cases of internet suicide pacts have the following characteristics: a suicide group consisting of two to four people who are strangers and often from different parts of Japan; pact members meet on the internet, often using only their online screen names, and plan their deaths on the internet; and pact members gather at a designated spot and commit suicide in a room or sealed-off car.

Suicide Prevention

In order to decrease the suicide rate in Japan, the Japanese government enacted a suicide prevention law in October 2006. Under the consideration that suicide is a social —rather than an individual—problem, anti-suicide measures are performed at the social level. The Japanese government aimed to reduce the country's suicide rate by one-fifth by 2016.

As mentioned above, mental health problems are a risk factor for suicide. Early identification and treatment of mental disorders are therefore of considerable importance in suicide prevention. According to the World Health Organization, early identification and treatment of persons with suicidal ideation are important tasks in preventive medicine. The Japanese organization "Inochi-no-denwa" provides a community mental health telephone service. The organization provides telephone counseling support to individuals who call the hotline and reveal suicidal ideation. However, this system is not effective enough—young people (teenagers) prefer to communicate via the internet, as mentioned above.

Regulation of suicide-promoting websites is perhaps the most effective means of suicide prevention. In addition to the restriction of suicide-related websites, restricting access to sedative and other toxic substances is also important. One of the major issues in internet control is the protection of minors and other vulnerable persons, such as elementary, junior high-school, or high-school students, or persons with psychiatric disorders.

In most countries, there is little or no control of internet content because of constitutional guarantees of freedom of expression. To my knowledge, Australia is the only country that currently has laws restricting internet content—in 2006, Australia passed a law targeting websites that promote suicide or provide information on suicide methods [28]. However, in other countries, the main approaches to reducing potential harm from suicide sites include self-regulation by internet service providers and the use of filtering software to block sites from being viewed by susceptible young people. "The European Union Safer Internet Plan" (EU, 1999) essentially proposes that internet organizations and internet service providers act responsibly to control what is available and limit or deny access to sites that are illegal or dangerous [28]. In Japan, a voluntary guideline was established on October 2005 by four associations managing internet provider service. This guideline stipulates that police should be alerted when individuals express their plan to commit suicide on the internet or seek suicide companions on suicide-related websites [29].

The internet may also have beneficial effects on suicide by providing sources of help for potentially suicidal people. In addition, it can aid in the evaluation, treatment, and prevention of suicidal individuals. With the advent of the internet, more patients have been participating in support groups on the internet. Many forms of mental health interventions are available to the public on the internet, including online symptom screening tools, online support groups, online individual therapy, and online group therapy [30]. Such websites also allow people to express and share their distress, get advice, and encourage others to seek help and treatment. Thus, interactions on the internet may also have a positive function for individuals with psychiatric symptoms. Indeed, in England, the suicide rates for young populations who use the internet most have decreased since the mid-90s, when internet use rates began rapidly expanding [31].

The extent to which internet sites contribute to suicide risk must be elucidated. As many physicians are unaware of the power of the internet, they should ask patients about their internet use. Depressed, suicidal, or potentially suicidal patients who use the internet may be especially at risk. Physicians may wish to assist patients in locating helpful, supportive online resources so that internet use may be more therapeutic than harmful [19].

PREVENTION OF SUICIDE PACTS IN JAPAN

In Japan, following the establishment of the voluntary internet guideline in October 2005, the lives of 14 individuals were saved by police from October to December 2005 [29]. According to Japan's National Police Agency, 75 cases involving 79 persons with suicidal intentions were reported to the police by internet providers under the voluntary guideline in 2006. The outcomes of these cases are shown in Table 1. One person had already committed suicide and was dead when the police arrived; four persons had initiated suicide but were saved by immediate aid; 39 persons were convinced not to attempt suicide through counseling; and 20 persons were found not to be in danger of committing suicide. Due to the self-regulation of internet services in Japan, a total of 43 lives (54.4%) were saved in 2006. Although the regulation was effective, psychological health problems that increase the risk of suicide and internet dependency in young people should be investigated in Japan. Comprehensive preventive measures should then be promoted in the future.

Table 1. Outcomes of persons with suicidal intentions in 2006

Outcome	Number	(%)
Death (committed suicide)	1	(1.3)
Alive (attempted suicide)	4	(5.1)
Avoided suicide attempt	39	(49.4)
Not in danger of suicide attempt	20	(25.3)
Unknown	15	(19.0)
Total	79	100

Conclusions

This article has described the trends in internet-related suicides in Japan. As suicide pacts have dramatically increased in recent years—owing largely to the development of information technology—young people with internet dependencies often suffer from crimes or accidents, not only thoughts of suicide. Although more than 73,000 persons have died of external causes—i.e., accidents, homicides, and suicides—comprehensive preventive measures have yet to be established in Japan. To lessen these external causes of death, including suicide, persons with health or mental problems who frequently use the internet must be closely monitored. The present article might be useful for the primary prevention of suicide and other external causes of death.

References

[1] National Institute of Communications Technology: *Report on the internet use in Japan.* Tokyo, National Institute of Communications Technology, 2004. In Japanese.

[2] Mandrusiak M, Rudd D, Joiner TE, Jr, Berman AL, Van Orden KA, Witte T: Warning signs for suicide on the internet: a descriptive study. *Suicide Life Threatening Behavior* 2006; 36: 263-271.

[3] World Health Organization, department of mental health: *Preventing suicide, a resource for general physicians,* Geneva, 2000.

[4] Conwell Y, Duberstein PR, Caine ED: Risk factors for suicide in later life. *Biol Pshiciat* 2002; 52: 193-204.

[5] Boor M, Relationship between unemployment rates and suicide rates in eight countries. *Psychol Rep* 1980; 47: 1095-1101.

[6] Crump A: Suicide in Japan. *Lancet* 2006; 367: 1143.

[7] Domino G, Takahashi Y. Attitudes toward suicide in Japanese and American medical students. *Suicide Life Threatening Behavior* 1991; 21: 345-359.

[8] Inoue K, Tanii H, Kaiya H, Abe S, Nishimura Y, Masaki M, Okazaki Y, Nata M, Fukunaga T: The correlation between unemployment and suicide rates in Japan between 1978 and 2004. *Leg Med* 2007; 9: 139-142.

[9] Naito A: Internet suicide in Japan: implication for child and adolescent mental health. *Clin Child Psychology Psychiat* 2007; 12: 583-597.

[10] Ministry of Internal Affairs and Communications: *Communication usage trend survey in 2002.* http://www.johotsushintokei.soumu.go.jp/statistics/statistics05a.html, 2003. In Japanese.

[11] 11.Kim K, Ryu E, Chon MY, Yeun EJ, Choi SY, Seo JS, Nam BW: Internet addiction in Korean adolescents and its relation to depression and suicidal ideation: a questionnaire survey. *Int J Nurs Stud* 2006; 43: 185-192.

[12] Biddle L, Donovan J, Hawton K, Kapur N, Gunnell D: suicide and the internet. *Brit Med J* 2008; 336: 800-803.

[13] Phillips DP: The influence of suggestion on suicide: substantive and theoretical implications of the Werther effect. *Am Sociological Rev* 1974; 39: 340-354.

[14] Hagihara A, Tarumi K, Abe T: Media suicide-reports, internet use and the occurrence of suicides between 1987 and 2005 in Japan. *BMC Public Health* 2007; 7: 321.

[15] Stack S: The effect of the media on suicide: evidence from Japan, 1955-1985. *Suicide Life Threatening Behavior* 1996; 26: 132-142.

[16] Becker K, Schmidt MH, Internet chat rooms and suicide. *J Am Acad Child Adolesc Psychiat* 2004; 43: 246-247.

[17] Becker K, Mayer M, Nagenborg M, El-Faddagh M, Schmidt MH: Parasuicide online: can suicide websites trigger suicidal behaviour in predisposed adolescents? *Nordic J Psychiat* 2004; 58: 111-114.

[18] Dobson R: Internet sites may encourage suicide. *Brit Med J* 1999; 319: 337.

[19] Recupero PR, Harms SE, Noble JM: Googling suicide: surfing for suicide information on the internet. *J Clin Psychiatry* 2008; 69: 878-888.

[20] Baume P, Cantor CH, Rolfe A: Cybersuicide: the role of interactive suicide notes on the internet. *Crisis* 1997; 18: 73-79.

[21] Beatson S, Hosty GS, Smith S: Suicide and the internet. *Psychiatric Bull* 2000; 24: 434.

[22] The city of Yamato, Department of Planning and External Affairs: Survey on the network and its use in the City of Yamato, Japan. T*he City of Yamato,* 2000. In Japanese.

[23] Brown M, Barraclough B: Epidemiology of suicide pacts in England and Wales, 1988-1992. *Brit Med* J 1997; 315: 286-287.

[24] Hitosugi M, Yokoyama T, Kido M, Nagai T, Tokudome S: Trends in suicide pacts made via the internet in Japan. *Brit Med* J 2005; e-letter, 29 March.

[25] Chan KPM, Yip PSF, Au J, Lee DTS: Charcoal burning suicide in post-transition Hong Kong. *Brit J Pshichat* 2005; 186: 67-73.

[26] Hitosugi M, Matsushima K, Omura K, Kido M, Kurosu A, Nagai T, Tokudome S: Group suicide with melatonin. *Jpn J Toxicol* 2006; 19: 55-56. In Japanese.

[27] McCurry J: Japan to rethink suicide-prevention policies. *Lancet* 2008; 371: 2071.

[28] Mishara BL, Weisstub DN: Ethical, legal, and practical issues in the control and regulation of suicide promotion and assistance over the internet. *Suicide Life Threatening Behavior* 2007; 37: 58-65.

[29] Hitosugi M, Nagai T, Tokudome S: A voluntary effort to save the youth suicide via the internet in Japan. I*nt J Nurs Stud* 2007; 44: 157.

[30] Ybarra ML, Eaton WW: Internet-based mental health interventions. *Mental health Service Res* 2005; 7: 75-87.

[31] Biddle L, Brock A, Brookes S, Gunnell D. Suicides rates in young men in England and Wales in the 21st century: time trend study. *Brit Med J* 2008; 336: 539-542.

In: Internet and Suicide
Editors: L. Sher and A. Vilens
ISBN 978-1-60741-077-5

Chapter 23

HARD-TO-REACH POPULATIONS AND STIGMATIZED TOPICS: INTERNET-BASED MENTAL HEALTH RESEARCH FOR JAPANESE MEN WHO ARE GAY, BISEXUAL, OR QUESTIONING THEIR SEXUAL ORIENTATION

Yasuharu Hidaka and Don Operario
Kansai University of Nursing and Health Sciences, Awaji, Japan;
Brown University, Providence, Rhode Island, USA

ABSTRACT

This chapter explores the utility of the Internet for conducting research with hard-to-reach populations and on topics that are socially stigmatized. We present findings from a series of studies of mental health, suicide, and sexuality among Japanese men who are gay, bisexual or questioning their sexual orientation. Due in part to social biases and cultural stigmas, very little previous research has examined these issues and this population. Use of the Internet has facilitated access to members of this group, offered an economic modality for recruiting participants and collecting data, maximized respondents' feelings of comfort and privacy, and produced new insights into developmental milestones and mental health outcomes such as suicidality for these men. Internet-based approaches are also a promising strategy for delivering interventions, counseling, education, and referrals to these men who are at high risk for mental health problems and sexual risk including HIV.

INTRODUCTION

Although numerous studies of male populations that are gay, bisexual, or questioning their sexual orientation (GBQ) have been conducted in the United States (U.S.) and the West, it has been extremely difficult to conduct research focused on non-heterosexuals in more traditional or conservative cultures, such as Japan. Despite a growing presence of a gay, lesbian, and bisexual community in Japan, scientific research understandings and social service capacities regarding the psychological and health needs of this community are highly limited. There are several reasons for this paucity of research in Japan.[1-3] First, there is a general lack of social consciousness and acceptance in Japanese culture of diverse sexual orientations outside of heterosexuality. Thus, discrimination, prejudice, and stigmas against other sexual orientations remain deeply rooted, and GBQ men may experience severe discomfort in openly acknowledging their sexuality to researchers. Second, within academia, investigations and evaluation studies of sexual minority populations have not been widely supported or funded; very few researchers have attempted scientific investigations in this area and those that do face challenges and resource constraints in reaching the population. Although few in number, some past academic studies have reinforced Japanese societal discrimination and bias against homosexual populations. As a result, some gay men harbor preconceived negative notions about researchers and feel afraid or uneasy about being turned into "research material."

Owing to the structural and social challenges in conducting research with Japanese GBQ men, innovative approaches have been deemed necessary to overcome community members' anxiety associated with participation in sexuality research, enhance confidentiality and privacy for participants, and reach large numbers of GBQ men with relatively low infrastructural costs. The Internet permits this type of research, and is a promising frontier in conducting mental health investigations and interventions with hard-to-reach populations, such as Japanese GBQ men.[4,5] Specifically, the Internet allows for outreach and data collection from GBQ men who might otherwise feel uncomfortable engaging in research. The Internet maximizes privacy for GBQ men, who can complete surveys and qualitative questionnaires at home or in private locations, with minimal disclosure of identifying information. Additionally, Internet technology facilitates cost-effective targeted outreach and recruitment, which otherwise would be difficult in working with this hard-to-reach and often hidden population.[6]

In this chapter, we describe findings from a program of Internet-based research on mental health and individual milestones experienced by Japanese GBQ. We will also consider the potential usefulness of the Internet in providing interventions to address the health needs of these men. Throughout, this chapter underscores the promise of the Internet for accessing hard-to-reach populations and addressing health and social inequalities associated with marginalized groups. This chapter is organized into three sections. First, we briefly present the general social challenges for Japanese GBQ men. Second, we review findings from recent Internet-based studies on mental health, suicide, and stigma among Japanese GBQ men. Third, we discuss how the Internet may play a role in efforts to address psychological and health problems – particularly risk for suicidality and HIV – for Japanese GBQ men.

DIFFICULT SOCIAL CONDITIONS FOR JAPANESE GBQ MEN

Although Japan is a global leader in many domains of international and economic development, social conditions for GBQ men show challenges.[1] The challenges facing these men may be due to cultural traditions that encourage harmony, social congruency (or "fitting in"), and avoiding shame or dishonor.[7] Japanese GBQ breach normative standards of heterosexuality, masculinity, and family responsibility regarding marriage and reproduction that are each heavily emphasized in the culture, and so these men are prone to bias and discrimination in the community as well as within families. In order to minimize the propensity of bias and stigma, GBQ men often choose to conceal their same-sex desires, behaviors, and relationships. Consequently, GBQ men have largely been an invisible population in society, with the exception of a few gay enclaves in urban centers.

Japanese GBQ men are vulnerable to daily forms of indirect stigma. Most people in Japanese society assume that those around them are heterosexual; this assumption is probably apparent in casual questions exchanged in conversations such as, "Do you have a girlfriend?" or "What type of women do you like?" as well as questions about family and children. These questions, which are premised on the assumption of romantic relations between men and women, also show how the heterosexual majority unconsciously excludes non-heterosexuals.[8] Gay and bisexual men feel pressure to get married and fulfill their parents' expectations of having grandchildren. Violation of this expectation, as manifested in minor daily interactions such as being asked whether one has a girlfriend or wife, may contribute to their psychological distress.[1,9]

Men who are openly gay may also be at risk for blatant forms of prejudice and discrimination.[1,10] However, this has been difficult to document in the Japanese context, compared with the U.S. According to data from the U.S. government, the number of hate crimes—crimes motivated by race, religion, sexual orientation, ethnicity, or disability—committed was 7,489 in 2003, and 7,649 in 2004. Of those, hate crimes based on sexual orientation accounted for 1,239 in 2003 and 1,197 in 2004, comprising roughly 16% of total hate crimes committed in the U.S for each year.[11,12] In Japan, however, there has been no definition of hate crimes, and no law concerning hate crimes has been enacted. As a result, there currently is no way of documenting the incidence of hate crimes at the national level. Voluntary reporting of homosexuality-related hate crimes among victims might be minimized due to stigma associated with GBQ status, as well as stigma associated with victimization in general. It is possible that the lack of any statistics on damage due to hate crimes could be misconstrued to mean that there are no such crimes—even though hate crimes are probably quite frequent.

The likelihood for experiencing some form of discriminatory treatment among GBQ may be reflected in general public opinion data. In a national poll conducted in Japan, 70% of men and 60% of women responded that they "cannot understand homosexuality as one form of love."[13] Furthermore, on contemporary television variety shows and comedies, gays are stereotyped, caricatured, and made objects of ridicule; in many cases, gay men are presented as excessively feminine characters, such as cross-dressers.[9] Many male celebrities who are themselves gay make wearing women's clothing or speaking in an effeminate manner one of the selling points of their image and career, perhaps as a way to commodify their sexuality and align themselves with popular notions of homosexuality – i.e., as comedic jokes. The mass media, therefore, presents a damaging view of gay men.

One of the scientific paradigms that has facilitated research on Japanese GBQ men is the field of HIV prevention.[14] Currently, there is a growing awareness that HIV/AIDS is a health concern of gay men in Japan. According to current reports by the Japanese Ministry of Health, Labor and Welfare (MHLW), 60% of new HIV cases each year are attributed to male same-sex behavior.[15] Given these circumstances, some behavior surveys aimed at gay men have been conducted for use as preventative measures, but these surveys have been few in number. Furthermore, because of the relatively low national HIV prevalence in Japan, it is unlikely that sexual health research of GBQ men will reach priority status and, consequently, studies of these men may remain under-supported.

Additional research is vital to documenting, characterizing, and, ultimately, addressing the problems experienced by Japanese GBQ due to social stigma and bias. An ideal research design would involve the national government adding questions about sexual orientation to one of its large-scale surveys conducted through random sampling, which would make it possible to estimate the prevalence of social problems and the health and psychological conditions of sexual minorities in Japan. However, the national census and public opinion polls have yet to include any questions on sexual orientation and, consequently, the present status of sexual minorities at the national level in Japan is completely unknown. Alternative methodologies can fill the information gap. Internet-based surveys targeting sexual minorities are one potential route for improving the state on knowledge of GBQ men's psychological, social, and health needs.

Internet Studies of Milestone Events among Japanese GBQ Men

Internet technologies provide a feasible, culturally acceptable, and relatively inexpensive approach to collecting information about the life experiences, needs, and psychological and health problems of Japanese GBQ men. The strong technological capacity among Japan adults supports the use of Internet-based surveys.

Since 1999, Hidaka and colleagues have conducted a series of Internet-based studies targeting GBQ men. Internet-administered questionnaires included comprehensive assessments on the respondent's lifestyle, including early developmental history, mental health, and experiences of stigma and bullying, as well as measures of HIV risk behavior. Internet survey methodology for these studies of Japanese GBQ are described elsewhere.[10] Briefly, informational announcements were posted at on-line websites or in print magazines that cater to GBQ men in Japan, provided information about the research projects and eligibility criteria, and directed interested individuals to the Internet URL website which contained study information. Respondents entered the secure website and completed informed consent procedures and items to screen out individuals who were not eligible for participation. In these studies which focused on GBQ men, "screener" items asked participants to identify the correct slang terminology for homosexual men and for heterosexual men; respondents who could not correctly identify the terminology were excluded from analysis. To minimize the likelihood that individuals completed the survey multiple times, we checked internet protocol addresses associated with each completed on-line survey and deleted any duplicates.

Here we summarize some findings about personal development milestones and psychological challenges in the lives of Japanese GBQ men (n=1,025) who completed Internet-administered surveys in 1999.[16] Respondents completed both closed-ended and open-ended questions describing their realization of having same-sex desires. Milestones are important to understand for GBQ men, whose sexual development trajectories might contribute to risk outcomes. Internet technology permitted collection of this data, which represents the first known study of these issues.

Table 1. Milestone events among gay, bisexual or other men questioning their sexual orientation in Japan (N=1,025)

Event	Mean years of age	Median years of age	Standard Deviation (SD)	Number of respondents having the experience	Experience rate (% of 1,025 total respondents)
Age at which respondents first sensed they were gay	13.1	13.0	3.8	984	96.0%
Age at which respondents first learned the word "homosexual"	13.8	14.0	3.0	985	96.1%
Age at which respondents thought they might not be heterosexual	15.4	15.0	4.1	786	76.7%
Age at which respondents first thought of suicide	16.4	15.0	5.0	656	64.0%
Age at which respondents were clearly conscious they were gay	17.0	17.0	4.4	970	94.6%
Age at first suicide attempt	17.7	17.0	4.8	155	15.1%
Age at which respondents first met another gay man	20.0	20.0	4.6	899	87.7%
Age at which respondents first had sex with a man	20.0	20.0	4.8	828	80.8%
Age at first suicide attempt due mainly to sexual orientation	20.2	20.0	6.0	65	6.4%
Age at which respondents first were friends with a gay male	21.6	21.0	4.8	847	82.6%
Age at which respondents first got a gay lover	22.0	21.0	4.8	679	66.2%

Milestone Events During Early Teenage Years: Coming to Terms with Sexuality

Data on GBQ men's developmental milestones are presented in Table 1. On average, respondents first "somehow realized they were gay" at 13.1 years of age (standard deviation [SD]=3.8), and first learned the word "homosexual" when they were 13.8 years old (SD=3.0). This was followed by respondents' thoughts that they might not be heterosexual, at age 15.4 (SD=4.1).

We found from respondents' open-ended answers that many GBQ men had begun to feel anxiety, confusion, or discomfort about their sexual preference around the time that their friends started to talk about the opposite sex or the type of girls/women they liked. Some gay men in our study described consulting dictionaries to find out what the word "homosexuality" meant, because they lacked basic language to describe their feelings. However, until the 1990s, many Japanese books conspicuously defined homosexuality as "abnormal" or a "sexual perversion," contributing to the likelihood that some gay or bisexual men internalized negative ideas about themselves before they had reached 14 years of age.

Milestone Events during Late Teenage Years: Suicidal Thoughts

Respondents described experiencing their first thoughts of suicide at 16.4 years of age on average (SD=5). Overall, 64.0% of respondents (n=646) experienced suicidal thoughts. Suicidal thoughts generally preceded respondents having a full recognition that they were gay, which they generally experienced by age 17 (SD=4.4). Fifteen percent of respondents (n=155) reported having ever attempted suicide, and their first actual suicide attempt occurred on average at 17.7 years of age (SD=4.8).

Thus, the milestone events occurring in the late teens of the population surveyed were intimately tied to psychological conflicts and the establishment of sexual orientation and gay identity.

Milestone Events during Early Adulthood: Sexual Behavior

The average age at which respondents first encountered another gay man was at 20.0 years of age (SD=4.6), the same age as respondents had sex with a man for the first time (SD=4.8). Six percent of participants (n=65) described ever having attempted suicide primarily because of their sexuality; this occurred on average at 20.2 years of age (SD=6.0).

Respondents described developing their first friendship with a gay male at an average age of 21.6 years (SD=4.8), and had their first gay lover at an average age of 22.0 years (SD=4.8). However, whereas 88.3% of respondents (n=847) affirmed having at least one gay male friend, only 66% (n=679) had ever had a gay lover.

Thus, from age of 13 until the beginning of adulthood, gay and bisexual men experienced numerous related milestone events, culminating in men's first sexual experiences and the establishment of gay friendship networks and intimate relationships. Many respondents had their first sexual experience before they had a gay friend or lover. One gay man remarked that, "From around the time I was in junior high school, I struggled and agonized over my sexual orientation and the fact that I was attracted to the same sex. But in the end, the only way to really confirm whether I was gay or not was to experience sex with a man." Although the significance of one's first sexual experience probably means different things to different people, for gay and bisexual men, their first sexual experience may also have been a way to confirm one's own identity and sexual orientation.

MENTAL HEALTH, SUICIDAL IDEATION AND SUICIDE ATTEMPTS

This Internet study allowed for the collection of data on mental health indicators, including suicidal ideation and attempts. Mental health and suicide in particular have been shown to be major issues for sexual minorities.[17-19] According to a survey conducted by the U.S. government in 1989, the percentage of sexual minorities who attempted suicide was 2 to 3 times higher than that of heterosexuals, 30% of suicides among teenagers were related to their sexual orientation, and roughly 30% of sexual minorities attempted suicide by the time they were 15.5 years of age.[20] In a series of studies, it was reported that 20% to 50% of gay men attempted suicide once or made repeated suicide attempts.

With 30,000 suicides occurring per year, Japan is regarded as the suicide capital of the world.[21] Despite national recognition of the suicide crisis, the social conditions contributing to suicide attempts are not known at the national level. Furthermore, when the motives and background factors of people who commit suicide are recorded, sexual orientation is not taken into account. Thus, the connection between suicide and sexual orientation in Japan is not clear.

In our Internet study of Japanese GBQ men (n=1,025) , 17% had ever been bullied at school and 59% had been verbally harassed for being gay, and 71% were classified as showing high levels of anxiety and 13% as clinically depressed, based on validated psychological measures. Moreover, 64% of all respondents said that they had considered suicide, and 15.1% actually had attempted suicide.[10] In a separate study of 5,731 GBQ respondents conducted in 2005 using similar Internet-based methodology, prevalence of suicidal ideation and suicide attempts were nearly identical (65.9%, 14%) , suggesting that these results were reproducible.[22] Factors related to suicide attempts were analyzed through multivariate analysis using logistic regression methods. Findings revealed that history of attempted suicide in this sample was significantly associated with history of verbal harassment and with psychological distress. Attempted suicide was also independently associated with ever having had sex with a woman, disclosure of sexual orientation to parents, disclosure of sexual orientation to 2 or more friends, and meeting a man through the Internet.

These studies provide several interesting suggestions. Findings suggest that a history of heterosexual activity might predispose GBQ men to suicide risk. This may perhaps be due to a conflict with their sexual identity, as men who reported having sex with men exclusively were significantly less likely to have attempted suicide. In addition, disclosure appears to be a significant predictor of attempted suicide – which might be indicative of the mental health consequences of stigma and discrimination following disclosure. In fact, our survey showed that only about 50% of all gay men in Japan had "come out" (i.e., revealed their homosexuality) to their heterosexual friends. Moreover, our survey demonstrated that most "non-closeted" gay men had come out to no more than 2 or 3 friends. According to our survey, only 10% of gay men had come out to their parents. Our finding which shows the mental health risks associated with "coming out" might explain why relatively few GBQ men in this society disclosure their sexual orientation to others – i.e., men recognize that coming can be a risk to their psychological health and well-being.

The elevated risk for attempted suicide among sexual minorities was corroborated in a non-Internet administered survey, which used street intercept recruitment in a busy downtown area of Osaka, Japan, to recruit 2,095 young men and women ranging from 15 to 24 years of age. The survey found that 9% of respondents (6% of men and 11% of women surveyed) had attempted suicide.[23] Among men, a significant association was found between attempted suicide and sexual orientation, even when the data was adjusted for the influence of other factors. Non-heterosexuals were six times more likely to attempt suicide than were heterosexuals (adjusted odds ratio [AOR]=5.98; 95% confidence interval [C.I.]=2.65-13.48). This finding indicates that in Japan, just as in the U.S., sexual orientation is very influential among the background factors of people who attempt suicide.

Heterosexual Role Conflict and Pressures to Remain Invisible

Our Internet study of 1,025 GBQ men revealed pressures for these men to be heterosexual, which we refer to as heterosexual role conflict.[8] In open-ended response, men described specific occasions where they experience heterosexual role conflict:

> "When the subject of marriage comes up."
> "When parents say they want to see their grandchildren soon."
> "When I am asked why I don't have a girlfriend and I have to say something."
> "When a woman tells me she likes me, and I lie or change the subject."
> "When I go with other men to visit establishments where female hostesses entertain male clients."

We conducted an exploratory factor analysis of items reflecting heterosexual role conflict, and found 6 independent factors: marriage, accommodation to heterosexuality, friendships, male lovers, traditional gender roles, and female lovers (Table 2).In addition, when the respondents were divided into three groups based on the degree of heterosexual role conflict experienced (low, medium, and high), it was clear that the higher the degree of heterosexual role conflict that men reported, the greater the depression, anxiety, sense of loneliness, and characteristics of self-restraining behavior they experienced. Higher degrees of heterosexual role conflict were also associated with significantly lower self-esteem (Table 3).

Table 2. Heterosexual role conflict scale

1) When I feel pressure to get married
2) When my parents say they want to see their grandchildren soon
3) When I am asked why I don't have a girlfriend and I have to say something
4) When my heterosexual friends laugh at negative caricatures of gays on television and I join in
5) When I have a boyfriend, but refer to him as a girlfriend when talking about him to my heterosexual friends
6) When I see an attractive man but cannot make comments about him in front of my heterosexual friends
7) When I cannot speak casually to my heterosexual friends about my gay friends
8) When I go to a restaurant with my boyfriend and feel like people are staring at us
9) When I cannot buy gay magazines openly
10) When I hear that men should be emotionally strong
11) When I lower my voice to sound more masculine
12) When I am around girls and people comment that I have "flowers in both hands" (slang for being popular with girls)
13) When a woman tells me she likes me and I lie or change the subject
14) When I am not interested in women but say things to make it sound like I am
15) When I go with other men to visit establishments where female hostesses entertain male clients

Table 3. Relationships between Heterosexual Role Conflict and Mental Health (M, SD)

Psychological scale	Range	Heterosexual role conflict t			Sig
		Low	Medium	High	
Depression (SDS)	20 ~ 80	37.29(8.13)	39.66(8.16)	42.90(8.64)	**
Anxiety (STAI)	20 ~ 80	44.47(11.22)	49.22(10.09)	53.84(9.70)	**
Self-esttem (Rosenberg)	10 ~ 50	34.34(6.59)	32.12(6.30)	31.20(6.51)	**
Loneliness (Revised UCLA)	20 ~ 80	40.04(11.01)	43.58(11.37)	47.98(10.90)	**
Self-restraining behavior (Munakata)	10 ~ 20	9.63(3.54)	11.24(3.65)	12.33(3.77)	*

Group differences tested using one-way analysis of variance.
* p<.05, ** p<.01

Open-ended responses collected from this Internet survey allowed men to explain in more detail their experiences of heterosexual role conflict[h]:

> "I actually want to love women, and I feel guilty about being gay."
>
> "The movements attempting to affirm gay identity are strong, but I am different. I am attracted to men, but I want to love women. In fact, I want to stop being a gay. I think it is OK to live life denying that I'm gay."
>
> "While there's a growing trend toward accepting life as a gay man, this is more of a burden for me. I cannot understand why I have to vociferously come out about my sexuality."

> "I feel terrible when I sense a glacial glare from others for not producing offspring in a society with a declining birthrate."

However, not all men described themselves as currently experiencing this internalized conflict. Instead, they reported feelings of comfort and acceptance with regard to their sexuality:

> "I am glad I was born gay, because I have become more open-minded than the majority of people in society, and I believe it is easier for me to understand the feelings of people who face discrimination."
>
> "I was able to protect myself from stress, once I distanced myself from social constraints and created a lifestyle and environment that allows me to live freely."
>
> "When I realized that I might be gay or bisexual, I was shocked and upset. After I became a full member of society, I learned about the gay community and that it is not such an extreme minority. I came to think that this might just be another way of life."
>
> "Although I am not particularly outstandingly happy, I also do not believe that I am unhappy simply because I am gay. I have accepted the fact that I am gay, and people around me also accept this, so I am not particularly worried about being gay. However, I feel anxious when I think about my future. I understand how hard it is to live as a gay person, but I also feel that even if I was reincarnated, I would want to be gay again in the next life, too."

These findings demonstrate that in a society where heterosexuality is presumed to be universal, gay men may experience psychological tension and adverse mental health consequences due to heterosexual role conflicts. In light of these results, improving mental health and formulating measures to prevent suicide attempts are urgent matters of health concern for gay men.

In summary, we observed from these qualitative responses diversity in how GBQ men were coming to terms with their sexual orientation. Although some participants positively accepted their sexual orientation, other participants felt guilt or discomfort. After having experienced past distress about their sexual orientation, some participants finally had come to think of their sexual orientation positively. Conversely, some participants thought that their current positive feelings about their sexuality might be transitory, fostered by a good environment and relationships with other people. However, if these social conditions were to change, their positive feelings and comfort with sexual orientation might be lost.

HIV Prevention in Japan

Although GBQ men's mental health issues have been understudied, HIV and AIDS among gay men in Japan are currently receiving attention by researchers and public health professionals. In Japan and other countries, several countermeasures for preventing HIV infection have been planned and funded.[14] Due to the understudied and relatively inconspicuous nature of health problems other than HIV/AIDS that affect GBQ men in Japan, countermeasures for preventing other health problems have not been taken. Furthermore, medical practitioners and human services professionals may lack awareness of the existence of other health problems in the gay male population.

The dissemination of accurate knowledge is crucial for HIV prevention. However, as several studies have pointed out, some people at risk who have sufficient knowledge fail to take action to prevent infection, and men who have not disclosed their sexuality may be unlikely to access HIV prevention education.[24] In short, education aimed at transmitting knowledge alone is not sufficient, and efforts to target HIV prevention at openly gay community settings may not reach many men who remain secretive about sexuality. What is needed is the implementation of specific, individualized measures for identifying factors that are barriers to HIV preventative behavior, as well as innovative strategies for reaching Japanese men who do not openly acknowledge their sexuality or who do not affiliate at gay venues.

In a 2003 Internet-administered survey of Japanese gay men (N=2,062)[25] which focused on psychological problems as some of the factors inhibiting action to prevent HIV, it was clear that men who showed psychological issues related to homosexuality, such as the need to feel affirmed by men or fear of turning away potential partners, also reported higher unprotected sexual activity. For example, some of the gay male respondents prioritized connectedness to their partners over personal safety and condom use, saying, "Disease prevention is important, but it is more important to me to feel connected to my partner" or, "If someone is willing to have sex with me, it is not necessary to use a condom." Gay male respondents who felt that using a condom might be an obstacle to intimacy with their partner were also unlikely to use condoms, as reflected by one participant who stated, "I'm worried that if I use a condom, it might feel awkward."

Indeed, some reports have found that poor mental health and low self-esteem can be obstacles to behavior aimed at HIV prevention.[26] Low self-worth or a lack of self-confidence can give rise to repondents' feelings such as, "What can I do if my partner refuses to use a condom?," or "They might hate me if I tell them to wear a condom."[27] Internet findings have shown that stress and the sense of feeling out of place, which are both conditions that arise from living in a predominantly heterosexual society, have a major negative and reciprocal impact on sexual behavior between homosexual men.

CONCLUSIONS

Within a society dominated by heterosexuality and negative attitudes toward homosexuality, many GBQ men in Japan men feel chronic stress and suffer from poor mental health. Moreover, the difficulties GBQ men experience in their early development, including bullying by others and suicide attempts, can lead to a decline in self-esteem, which is a factor that contributes to high risk for suicide and risk for HIV. Despite this phenomenon, Japan still does not have any effective countermeasures in place to address the health concerns of the gay male population.

In light of the influence of education and medicine and their power to yield effective results in preventative health, an increase in knowledge and understanding among human services professionals in the fields of education and psychological counseling about the psychological challenges for Japanese GBQ men, as well as an improvement in available support systems, are measures that require urgent attention. Although education regarding homosexuality and sexual orientation is not included in the official school curriculum in

Japan, we believe that it would be possible to deal with the existence of sexual minorities as a part of education on human rights. Alternatively, if it is difficult to publicly address the issue of sexual minority mental and physical health, it is important to at least pay attention to whether sexual orientations other than heterosexuality are being discriminated against in health services. This is an issue that needs to be addressed, not only in education, but also in the field of medicine and general societal interactions. Through the accumulation of evidence in detailed surveys, it will become increasingly important to discover ways to solve health problems in the GBQ population in Japan.

We have argued that, due to stigma against homosexuality, it is extremely difficult to collect accurate data from GBQ populations, and challenging to recruit GBQ men into health and psychological service interventions. The Internet can substantially facilitate research and services targeting GBQ men in Japan. Currently, it is technologically possible to offer web-based support and information for the improvement of mental health, as well as HIV prevention. Our own experience has shown that GBQ men are responsive to Internet research, feel comfortable completing online psychological and health needs assessments, and can be extremely descriptive in narratives about their personal lives and sexuality issues. It is possible for educational and counseling interventions to be delivered via electronic media, and chat-room sessions can offer small groups of GBQ men the opportunity to converse in a safe space about their experiences, without compromising their sense of privacy. Internet-administered assessments can also immediately provide referrals to health and psychological professional services to GBQ men, which our research shows are highly needed in this population. In the future, we will look forward to the development of Internet-based health support programs that GBQ men can use while maintaining their anonymity and comfort.

References

[1] DiSetfano, D. S. (2008). Suicidality and self-harm among sexual minorities in Japan. *Qualitative Health Research, 18,* 1429-1441.

[2] Harada, M. (2001). Japanese male gay and bisexual identity. *Journal of Homosexuality, 42,* 77-100.

[3] McLelland, M. (2002). Is there a Japanese ‘gay identity’? *Culture Health Sexuality 2,* 459–472.

[4] Birnbaum, M. H. (2004) Human research and data collection via the Internet *Annual Review of Psychology, 55,* 803–32.

[5] Rhodes, S. D., Bowie, D. A., & Hergenrather, K. C. (2003) Collecting behavioural data using the world wide web: considerations for researchers. *Journal of Epidemiology Community Health, 57,* 68–73.

[6] Gosling, S. D., Vazire, S., Srivastava, S., & John, O. P. (2004). Should we trust Web-based studies? A comparative analysis of six preconceptions about Internet questionnaires. *American Psychologist, 59,* 93–104.

[7] Markus, H. R., & Kitayama, S. (1991). Culture and the self: implications for cognition, emotion, and motivation. *Psychological Review, 98,* 224–53.

[8] Hidaka Y. (2000). Heterosexual role conflict and psychological health among gay and bisexual men. *Shishunkigaku* (*Adolescentology*), *18*: 264-272 (in Japanese).

[9] Valentine, J. (1997). Skirting and suiting stereotypes: Representations of marginalized sexualities in Japan. *Theory, Culture, and Society*, *14*, 57–85.

[10] Hidaka, Y, & Operario, D. (2006). Attempted suicide, psychological health and exposure to harassment among Japanese homosexual, bisexual or other men questioning their sexual orientation recruited via the internet. *Journal of Epidemiology and Community Health, 60,* 962-967.

[11] U.S. Department of Justice and Federal Bureau of Investigation: HATE CRIME Statistics 2003, 2004.

[12] U.S. Department of Justice and Federal Bureau of Investigation: HATE CRIME Statistics 2004, 2005.

[13] Adachi, K. (1998). Detailed Report of National Opinion Survey (Periodic Survey of National Awareness: Men and women). *Asahi Soken Report, 130,* 117-142 (in Japanese).

[14] Nemoto T. (2004). HIV/AIDS surveillance and prevention studies in Japan: Summary and recommendations. *AIDS Education and Prevention, 16,* 27-42.

[15] AIDS surveillance committee MHLW: Annual surveillance report of HIV/AIDS in Japan, 2006 . Ministry of Health, Labour and Welfare, 2007.

[16] Hidaka, Y. Report of results of survey regarding the mental health of gay and bisexual men (website) (in Japanese). http://www.joinac.com/tsukuba-survey/ (in Japanese).

[17] King, M., McKeown, E., Warner, J., Ramsay, A., Johnson, K., Cort, C., Wright, L., Blizard, R., & Davidson, O. (2003). Mental health and quality of life of gay men and lesbians in English and Wales. *British Journal of Psychiatry, 183,* 552–8.

[18] Paul, J. P., Catania, J., Pollack L, Moskowitz, J., Canchola, J., Mills, T., Binson, D., & Stall, R. (2002). Suicide attempts among gay and bisexual men: lifetime prevalence and antecedents. *American Journal of Public Health, 92,* 1338–45.

[19] Warner, J., McKeown, E., Griffin, M., Johnson, K., Ramsay, A., Cort, C., & King, M. (2004). Rates and predictors of mental illness in gay men, lesbians and bisexual men and women. *British Journal of Psychiatry,185,* 479–85.

[20] Gibson, P. (1989). Gay male and lesbian youth suicide. In M. Feinleib (Eds.), Prevention and intervention in youth suicide (Report to the Secretary's Task Force on Youth Suicide, Vol.3). U.S. Department of Health and Human Services.

[21] Desapriya, E. B., & Iwase, N. (2003). New trends in suicide in Japan. *Injury Prevention, 9,* 284

[22] Hidaka Y, Kimura H, & Ichikawa S. (2007). Gay and Bisexual men's health report 2. http://www.gay-report.jp/2005/ (in Japanese).

[23] Hidaka, Y., Operario, D.,Takenaka, M., Omori, S., Ichikawa, S., Shirasaka, T. (2008). Attempted suicide and associated risk factors among youth in urban Japan. *Social Psychiatry and Psychiatric Epidemiology, 43,* 752-757.

[24] Goldbaum, G., Perdue, T. R., & Higgins, D. (1996). Non-gay-identifying men who have sex with men: Formative research results from Seattle, Washington. *Public Health Reports, 111,* 36-40.

[25] Hidaka Y. (2005). Gay and Bisexual Men's Health Report. http://www.j-msm.com/report/report01/ (in Japanese).

[26] Stokes, J. P., & Peterson, J. L. (1998). Homophobia, self-esteem and risk for HIV among African American men who have sex with men. *AIDS Education and Prevention, 10,* 278-292.

[27] Hidaka, Y., Ichikawa, S., & Kihara, M. (2004). HIV risk behavior, mental health and milestone life events among gay and bisexual men. *Journal of the Japanese Society for AIDS Research, 6*, 165-173 (in Japanese).

In: Internet and Suicide
Editors: L. Sher and A. Vilens
ISBN 978-1-60741-077-5

Chapter 24

SUICIDE IN CHINA IN THE ERA OF THE INTERNET

Samuel Law, XueZhu Huang and Pozi Liu
University of Toronto, Canada; Tsinghua University, Beijing, People's Republic of China

ABSTRACT

China's economic reform in the last three decades has produced the world's current biggest, continuous economic growth; with that, also a growth rate in technology and Internet use that outpaces the developed world. Clinical issues such as Internet related suicide has caught attention of all concerned. This Chapter reviews the unique epidemiological characteristics of suicide in China, socio-cultural factors and explanations related to suicide, and some recent findings on suicide issues related to the Internet. Particular attention will be paid to suicide of urban youth, the population that is behind the sharp increase in Internet use in China.

INTRODUCTION

Within the last three decades, China has rapidly transformed itself from an agrarian, developing country, to a market economy that is the third largest in the world [1]. With 1.3 billion in population, and increasing pace of modernization, a recent scholarly survey ranked China first in the world in numbers of both cellular phones and fixed-line telephones [2]; and with more than 140 million users on the Internet, China ranked only second to the United States but poised to surpass that in the near future [3]. Among the Internet users in China, 53.5% are those under 24 years of age (40% of them spend more than three hours per day on-line), and 88.2% are those under 35 years of age [4,5]. With the scale and rapidity of growth in telecommunication technology, related clinical concerns such as Internet related suicide, like those in the west [e.g., 6], are also growing. This Chapter will first review the research and unique characteristics of suicide in China; then provide an overview of the mental health system to put these suicide findings in sociological, economic, and cultural contexts; and finally, review specifically key urban youth suicide issues and survey the current media reports and literature on Internet-related suicide in China.

EPIDEMIOLOGY OF SUICIDE IN CHINA

Compared to World Health Organization's published global average suicide rate of 10.7 per 100,000, China's suicide rate is two to three times higher, with more than 300,000 suicides per year, and roughly 3 million attempts per year by estimation; in percentages, with 21% of world's population, China has 44% of the world's total suicides and 56% of world's female suicides [7, 8, 9]. In a more recent analysis, the rise of suicide rates may be slightly slowing down or decreasing, but the rates remain overall high [10]. Behind these alarming numbers, there are a number of notable characteristics.

I. Youth and Elder Suicides Rates Are High

Studies in China show that there are two peaks in the age demographics of suicide: one in the youth group, and one in the elderly. The leading cause of death in those aged 15 to 34 years is suicide, with a rate of 26 per 100,000, accounting for 18.9% of all deaths in this age group; in the over-65 age group, suicide rates reach 50 to 200 per 100,000, which is four to five times that of the national average, with male rates higher than female and rural rates about five times those of urban rates [8, 11]. Suicide rates in China, like most countries, increase with age, but the youth peak is relatively unique, and the high elderly rate is more pronounced than the global average [12].

II. Higher Female Suicide Rates than Males

Unlike the international pattern of suicide demographics, where male suicide rates typically surpass that of female rates, the Chinese female suicide rates, in the under-60 age group, exceed male rates by an average of 26%; this is even more pronounced along the rural-urban divide, where rural female rates exceed rural male rates by 66% [8, 11].

III. Suicide Rates are Higher in Rural Areas than Urban Areas

Also a reversal pattern to that of typical global trend, China's rural suicides rates are three to five higher than urban rates. This applies to both male and female rates, and across all age groups. Given that 70% of Chinese population is rural, and 93% of all suicides in China are rural, rural suicides largely account for the high Chinese national suicide rates and high female rates [8, 13].

IV. The Level of Mental Illness, Particularly Depression, in Suicide Victims Are Relatively Low

Amongst suicide victims in China, the prevalence of Axis I mental illness is relatively low, at approximately 30-70%, with depression at around 40% [14-17]. In contrast, in the West, 90% of suicides are associated with some form of mental illnesses, with a large majority suffering from depression (60%), schizophrenia (10% to 15%), or substance related problems (15% to 25%) [18-19].

SUMMARY OF SOCIO-CULTURAL UNDERSTANDINGS OF UNIQUE CHINESE SUICIDE EPIDEMIOLOGY

In the backdrop of these remarkable Chinese suicide figures is the rapid economic reform that has been taking place in the last 30 years and its attendant sociological and psychological changes. While much of the reform is generally positively received, many suicide researchers see strong association between social factors - such as the immense shift from a near-total state controlled economy to that of market economy with loss of job security, massive urbanization, related destabilization of rural families and socio-relational networks, loss of universal health care, and increasing gap between the rich and poor etc. – and the deteriorating state of mental health, and likely in turn, escalating suicide rates [11, 20-23]. Well known social determinants of mental health, such as rates of marital breakdown, family violence, substance abuses, sexually transmitted diseases, and pathological gambling, etc., have also increased in recent years [24-26]. For example, one study found a twenty-fold increase in alcohol related problems during a ten-year period of the economic reform [27].

More specifically, the high level of elder suicide in China is remarkable and counterintuitive. Given the Chinese traditional values that stress respect and filial obligations towards the elderly, one would expect relatively low rates of elder suicide. However, the high elder suicide rates, particularly high rural elder suicide rates that are four to five times that of the urban rates, are possible reflections of the negative social changes in the era of economic reform. These negative changes may have affected the rural communities particularly strongly. Some research evidence show continued rural poverty, changed family composition due to rural able-bodies leaving to work in cities, and loss of health care insurance so the elderly see themselves as a financial and physical burden to their families, etc., may all have contributed to these alarming rates [20, 28-29].

The understanding behind the high female rates of suicide in China is intimately connected to the high rural suicide rates. Similar to international reports on gender differences in suicide attempts, Chinese females attempt suicide more often than males by about 3:1 [14, 20, 30-31]. However, unlike the rest of the world - where the overall female rates of death by suicide is lower than males - Chinese females have a higher suicide rates than males. The most likely explanation is that Chinese rural females more fatally complete their suicide attempts by means of highly lethal suicide methods found in poison or pesticide, frequently in settings where medical rescue is unavailable [15]. Poison and pesticide are highly accessible in rural China as they are typically stored at home [32]. Suicide methods studies in China indeed show pesticide or rat poison being the most commonly used means (30% to 67%), followed by hanging (8% to 44%), drowning (3% to 14%), and jumping from a high place (3% to 7%); almost no firearm suicide is reported [11]. In contrast, firearm is the most common means of completed suicides in the United States, and drug ingestion (mostly among women) accounts for 70% of failed suicide attempts [18]. Moreover, the Chinese female suicides are concentrated in the young, 15 - 34 age group. Thus, China's high rates of suicide, high youth and young adult rates, high rural vs. urban, and high female vs. male suicide epidemiological characteristics are highly related to the high rates of rural, young females dying from their highly frequent and highly lethal suicide behavior [14].

Sociologically, researchers point to the tradition of low social status of women, systemic oppression of women, and lack of education of women as the primary reasons for their high suicide rates [21, 23, 33-35]. The evidence for such claims are rooted in the practice, particularly in rural China, of selective abortion of females [33]; selective termination of schooling of girls by families (again more prevalent in rural China; national female illiteracy is 13.6%, vs. 4% in males [21, 36]); and rural land title dispossession of females due to traditionally male-dominated family decision making (despite national legislation on gender equality) [21, 34, 37]. Educational and economic deprivations appear to be linked to current and historical gender discrimination in China, and perhaps, in turn, to female suicide rates.

The phenomenon of high rural vs. urban suicide rates in China is becoming less unique, as reports are surfacing to show a similar international trend, possibly as a result of significant social changes in terms of weakening social integration and worsening economic deprivation that are occurring in rural regions globally [9, 38-39]. The influential nineteen century French sociologist Durkheim's theory [40] described that western rural communities had lower suicide rates than their urban counterparts because there was a more cohesive, mutually supportive, and interdependent social network in rural cultures. In the current economic changes in China, this kind of protection has likely been eroded [16, 20]. At a cultural and historical level, some scholars have also point to the effect of "moral-emotional sequelae of disastrous political conditions"—referring to political turmoil in recent Chinese history – on suicide [23, 41].

On the issue of lower mental health problems found in Chinese suicide victims, researchers found the reasons behind many of the young, rural females who attempt and complete suicide with lethal pesticides are not necessarily related to major mental illnesses such as depression, but rather reactions to interpersonal, social, and financial crises [14, 17] - crises such as relationship breakups, losing face, feeling "no way out," social experience of intense shame, and loss of honor. These individuals are not typically clinically depressed, but socially powerless and marginalized [11]. These suicides are impulsive, or "low-planned", highly associated with acute stresses, and the time period between these crises and suicide are typically hours to days [15, 42-44]. On the other hand, researchers have advocated the need to conceptualize depression as a dimensional, incremental illness rather than a categorical diagnosis. They found that many Chinese suicide victims have depressive symptoms but were sub-threshold for a full diagnosis, and suicide risk may increase with exposure to multiple risk factors in a "dose-dependent" fashion [14, 17]. Furthermore, it is likely also that the overall rate of depression may indeed be lower in China as a whole, when compared to international rates [45-47] – for example: one large epidemiological study found the point prevalence of depression disorder in Chinese general population was 2.2% [48], as compared to contemporaneous American figure of approximately 5.9% [49].

On an anthropological level, some researchers contend that suicide in China may not carry as much cultural or religious prohibition as it does in the western world. Suicide acts have been portrayed in literature and history in various positive lights, often associated with notions of romance, loyalty, courage, preservation of personal dignity and integrity, redeeming one from disgrace, or as an act of extreme social criticism to induce shame in others [11, 20, 23]. Thus, the social environment is arguably more permissive for suicide in China than in the west. On the other hand, some strong contemporary views on suicide are that suicide is not typically equated with mental illness, but associated with personal weakness, social failings, and silent suffering, all factors that render the act of suicide highly stigmatized [8]. In addition, many people associate suicide strongly as an act that leads to failure of filial piety – the duty to care for the elderly and family, and the inability to transmigrate the sole to some form of afterlife or other world – therefore one is eternally trapped in the present world [50]. Furthermore, there are diverse cultural and local contexts even within different Chinese communities - societies like Taiwan, Singapore, and Hong Kong do not have suicide rates as high as those in mainland China [20].

Alcohol and substance abuse, a typical co-morbid condition or risk factor for suicide in the west, remains much lower in China. For example, in North America, approximately 24% of those who die of suicide have an alcohol problem [18], compared with about 7% in China [14]. Further theories about the high suicide rates point to a general lack of mental health awareness, and the lack of resources in terms of mental health services [24].

STATE OF CHINA'S MENTAL HEALTH SERVICES

As the pace of socio-economic reform accelerates and significant social changes take place, China is experiencing increased rates of mental health problems. However, China's current overall health care spending is relatively low - about 5% of its Gross Domestic Product, about a third of that of the United States; furthermore, spending in mental health is even less [24, 51]. Eighty percent of Chinese health spending goes to the cities, where medical facilities and much supportive resources are concentrated, while 70% of the nation's population lives in rural areas [22]. Regional differences are that coastal regions, along with regional centers such as Beijing, Shanghai, Chengdu, and Guangzhou, are typically more developed than the in-land regions, while remote places like the territory of Tibet does not have any psychiatric hospital [52-53].

The formal Chinese mental health system is currently concentrated in forms of specialized psychiatric hospitals, with little community-based delivery of services. The informal system of support through family, kinship and work place plays a significant part in mental health care [23, 54]. Overall, the delivery of mental health services is limited. In terms of professional training, psychiatry still occupies a historical low status within the medical profession; there are very few allied professionals such as counselors, psychologist, psychiatric social workers; level of stigma about psychiatric issues is high [20, 24, 54]. A 1999 baseline report found 13,000 physicians working in psychiatric hospitals in China as a whole, with only 2000 of them fully qualified psychiatric specialists or consultants; and most mental health workers had only high-school education [55]. Improvements have been made since but psychiatric or mental health service penetration is generally low – one study in a economically vibrant coastal city found at least 40% of mentally ill patients in general, and 23.5% patients with affective disorders or schizophrenia specifically, have not received any treatment [54]. Other studies found much lower rates still: one reported 5% of individuals with depression received treatment [7]; another, using psychological autopsy approach, found that only 7% of the suicide victims had seen any mental health professional before their deaths [14]; and another study on suicide attempters found about 30% had sought help for psychological problems [37]. The rate of care is even lower in rural areas [56].

China's push towards privatization and marketization of the health care system in the last three decades has resulted in a near-complete abandoning of its former state-funded universal medical insurance that covered all its citizens. This loss has also resulted in worsened system-wide service coordination, a shift from a public health and illness prevention orientation to that of treatment focused, high-tech savvy medical culture, and the attendant sharp increase in medical costs [25] - a recent conservative estimate showed that less than half of the people have adequate medical insurance [57]. Many people simply do not seek formal medical help [58]. Medical related opportunistic exploitation and profiteering have drastically increased in a climate of prohibitive costs and poor medical professional regulation [24].

Parallel to the lack of resources in mental health is the low level, and delayed help seeking for mental health problems [59]. Often, explanatory models of mental health problems are based on bad fortune, bad 'fate', not having worked hard enough to get better, having a lack of discipline, or being demon possessed. The high level of negative views and stigmatization of mental illness in China have led to extensive discrimination against the mentally ill in education settings, at work, and in the community at large [20, 24]. As a result, faced with mental health problems, many fear stigma and do not seek help from families or friends or professionals. Families also typically try to manage their family members who are ill at home for as long as possible, in order to protect the families' reputation and avoid the shame and stigma of mental illness [60-61].

At the time of writing of this chapter, China's media is reporting a national level debate on the future of health care reform, including ideas of a return to a universal health insurance, or at least to insure the poor and needy for critical illnesses [62]. There are also encouraging recent developments in the state's prioritizing mental health at a national level, recognition of mental illness as a legitimate form of disability, and the emerging "third sector" - non-governmental organizations that champion for the welfare of the mentally ill [63-65].

Overview of Suicide Epidemiology for Chinese Urban Youth

In 2004, there were reportedly 19 suicide deaths at Beijing University - China's top university, and many more university student suicides across the city, stirring national attention in a country that reveres higher education [66-67]. Other studies also found high level of suicidal thoughts, and depressive symptoms among university students, youth and young adults in general [68-70]. These reports highlight the fact that suicide is the number one cause of death in the 15-34 age group, (26 per 100,000, accounting for 18.9% of all deaths in this age group), and is affecting both urban and rural youth.

There is a sizable literature that focuses on suicide issues of youth in urban areas of China, particularly on prevalence of suicidal behaviors and associated risk factors. In an research area that often lacks precise data, and comparisons cross-culturally are often difficult, these studies generally show that the prevalence of suicidal behavior and associated risk factors do have more in common with those in western countries than not; with a few exceptions and unique features. A recent large study of the general population in urban settings in China used 5201 interviews to specifically examine prevalence of suicidal behaviors and their relationship with mental disorders found the overall lifetime prevalence of suicidal ideation, plans, and attempts were 3.1%, 0.9%, and 1.0% respectively, with young people (age 18-34) having consistently the highest odds of having these suicidal behaviors in all three categories [59]. The study also found risk factors for suicide were young adulthood, prior suicide attempts, being unmarried, recent onset of ideation and plan, female sex, low education and the presence of mental disorders, especially mood disorder. These general figures and risk factors are similar to those reported in western countries [71-73].

Other suicide risk factor studies of youth in China show aspects which may be somewhat more specific to the Chinese setting. These include: "loss of face" (shame), social embarrassment, ultra-high expectations from parents, perceived and real academic failures, economic difficulties, being beaten by parents, and conflict with parents [74-75]. In particular, Chinese adolescent, especially urban populations tend to report parental expectations and pressure to do well academically as major sources of stress, significantly more so than their counterparts in the US [76]. Many parents judge how "good" or "bad" their children are by their school achievements; adolescents spend larger proportion of their time attending school, doing homework, and extra-curricular activities geared towards academic success [77].

With regard to conflict with parents, inter-parental conflicts, and inadequate parenting practices as risk factors for suicide, studies found more specifically that authoritarian parenting style, low verbal communication, heavy physical discipline, and frequent arguments between parents to be highly associated with increased youth suicide behavior [78]. Adding to the complexity, these parent related phenomena and practices are also observed to be quite common, and are largely perceived to be culturally tolerated. On the other hand, these phenomena do support the approach of family intervention as a potentially highly effective suicide prevention strategy for youth in China.

In terms of other differences between China and the west, researchers have found the overall rates of suicidal behavior being related to 'any' mental illness in Chinese youth are still lower than their western counterparts (about 40-50% vs. 90%); and completed female youth suicide rates are moderately higher than males in China [59, 72, 74, 79]. Furthermore, research show history of sexual or physical abuse, and substance abuse are much less commonly linked to youth suicide in China as they do in the west [74]. Some of the above conclusions are not without controversy, as a recent large survey in a coastal region of China found 2 to 3 times higher suicidal behavior rates than comparable US data - with close to 50% of urban adolescents having anxiety symptoms that interfere with normal life, 30% having a history of depression, 16% had at times felt life was not worth living, and 9% reported a history of suicide attempts; only 1% had sought professional help [80].

On another front, special attention has been paid to the effect of china's one-child policy and its impact on the mental health of the children. It is argued that children who grew up in a single-child environment get overly protected by the "six-parent family" (i.e. parents and two sets of grandparents), and miss having adequate exposure to adversity and opportunities to develop self-reliance and resilience [69]. However, empirical evidence is mixed, with some refuting this hypothesis [e.g. 80], while others supporting it [e.g. 59, 81]. One supporting study found children from urban one-child only families experienced significantly lower "love awareness" from family, higher "neurotic and social depression, trait anxiety, perceived stressors, and interpersonal dependency" than those from multi-sibling families – these were associated with negative mental health conditions [81]; and another found the cohort born in the era of one-child policy having much higher (relative odds of 4.7) incidence of developing a mental disorder in their life time when compared to the control cohort (age >65) [59]. The debate seems to continue on whether growing up as a single child has a disadvantage on mental health.

Finally, to social scientists, the high numbers of youth and young adult suicide remains a challenge to explain. Stress from having to cope with a changing society can possibly affect the young more selectively, as they have less mature coping skills and less formed self identity [16, 20, 82]. Related to this, some researchers remark on the fact that elevated youth suicide is paradoxical, given how China has enjoyed increased material wealth and socio-political stability in recent decades, measured against the era in recent Chinese history that contained decades of brutal wars, natural disasters, and political turmoil [16, 69]. On the other hand, research is emerging on how massive social economic changes can impact negatively on mental health of families, and in turn render the children/youth more vulnerable [20].

Overall, despite the challenges of meaningful, cross-cultural comparisons and the limited reliability of some of the study data that were cross-sectional in designs and relied heavily on self report, the literature does provide a remarkable picture of the wide range of concerning issues related to urban youth suicide in China.

Overviews of Popular Psychosocial Explanations on Urban Youth Suicide

In addition to academic studies, popular opinions and discussions on urban youth suicide provide a worthwhile contribution to the subject of. They are reviewed from the Internet and summarized below:

1. *Life and situational crises* such as failure of romance or experience of rejection leading to impulsive suicide. One Crisis Intervention Center's survey in a large northern Chinese city found 44.2% of the college students cited failure in relationship as the reason for their suicidal ideation.
2. *Academic pressure* in the Chinese education system is well known to be enormously high. Intense competition generates tremendous pressure on the students. Education success is seen as the predominant path of social acceptance and economical improvement. The above-cited Crisis Intervention Center survey showed 29.8 % of college students reported academic pressure as causes of suicide ideation. The need to gain admission to top tier high schools and then reputable universities and then Graduate Schools is deeply embedded in a culture that reveres and values education and brand name of the schools. Such pressure is incessant from an early age on, and

affects almost all students at some stage of their lives, perhaps particularly pronounced in post-secondary school age. Some surveys show that college students generally have higher suicide rates than non-students in the same age group; top-ranked university students have higher rates than lower ranked universities; and graduate students more than undergraduates.

3. *Parental factors* such as over protection, over intrusiveness on the lives of their children, severe punishment are commonly cited.
4. *One-child-only policy* enforced since the early 1980s are responsible for the current cohorts of the young generation, who grew up without siblings, often coddled by their parents, and burdened by high expectations from parents and grandparents alike.
5. *Social pressure* in the era of massive economic reform, the mixture of a highly competitive job market, rapidly rising costs of living, and an increasingly individualistic and profit-oriented social setting is unprecedented in Chinese history. Many youth are reported to be chronically anxious about job prospects and job security, unlike a mere 20 years ago when the state planned and controlled the entire job and commodity markets.
6. *New media's* focus on the phenomenon of suicide may have unwittingly promoted the general awareness of suicide as an outlet to solve personal and social problems. The high level of exposure, especially the Internet, is strongly perceived to have negative effects on the population at large, and the youth in particular.
7. *Lack of support and services* for those in suicide crises or depression is increasingly seen as a significant factor. At present, only the major, economically well-off cities are known to have psychological crisis intervention hotlines, for example. The level of training of the currently available counselors is also limited.
8. *The stigma of mental health problems* and the related reluctance to seek help and to disclose private concerns remains also a parallel problem to the lack of services.
9. *Generation gap* in the age of rapid social changes magnify age group differences, and the collision of old and new concepts can create overwhelming conflicts in family, school, and work place settings.
10. *Low level of general awareness of mental health issues* may contribute to youth suicide. The combination of the youth's lack of coping skills, self knowledge, and resilience, and a low societal "fund" of knowledge or recognition of psychological needs can leave this age group particularly vulnerable.
11. *Relatively low level of youth protection policies or their implementation* is perceived by some social observers to also contribute to youth suicide problems. Families, not the state, remain the almost exclusive caretaker of children and youth in China; the concept of state intervention in situations of domestic abuse, mal-treatment, or neglect, is relatively rare and a foreign concept. Youth at risk are not easily detected at an early stage through child protections networks or services.

INTERNET RELATED SUICIDE IN CHINA

The above background information highlights the rapid growth of the economy and Internet usage, the state of the mental health system, and the unique social-cultural understanding of suicide in China. These considerations help to contextually place the relatively new and dynamically changing phenomena of Internet related suicides in China. According to media documents, Internet related suicide was first reported in China in 2001, and "suicide sites" and Internet-based "suicide manual" first appeared in 2002 [83]. To date, there are wide ranging suicide related topics and entries on-line, including many suicide prevention information portals, discussions on the legal and moral responsibilities of those who use the Internet to broadcast ideas of suicide, reports on dramatic suicides, suicide related chat room reviews and critiques, warnings about suicide pacts abroad, and outing of suicide promoters and profiteers, to name a few [e.g. 84-87]. However, in general, there is a noticeable absence of sites directly promoting or instructing suicide.

One recent highly covered on-line story involved a self-proclaimed physician promoting non-painful method of suicide and medications on the Internet to those who wish to commit suicide. Linked to this website had been a site for a suicide group that had 147 members, who discussed and exchanged their ideas, fears, and methods of suicide in details. Jumping, drowning, car crashing, and using medicines were popular topics in this group. This site was later blocked by the state run media control; no report is known about the fate of these members [84]. Samples of the postings still available from this group are informative of the kind of content: they showed: "I am a failure, and I have no work, no love, no self-confidence, only loneliness and despair. I would like to leave this world, because I cannot see my future. Even though suicide is despicable and very selfish, but I want to do it. I do not know if people will not have the soul after death, but I hope I will no longer struggle…"; and "Suicide is a choice from the position of strength, I decide on my own fate and life, I am not avoiding problems nor am I weak – I am making a rational choice at a very peaceful time with a peaceful mind. Choosing what method to die is ultimately my choice, and it is the ultimate freedom of being human" [84]. There were many entries condemning these postings as well.

Of the most dramatic form of Internet related suicide, Chinese on-line media has reacted very actively to the large scale Internet suicide pact phenomenon in Japan, where up to 9 people died together on one occasion, and at least a total of 45 died from Internet suicide pacts during the period between January 2003 and June 2004, and more than 60 die each year in this fashion [85, 88]. In another part of Asia, at least 10 people committed suicide in similar fashion in Korea during roughly the same period [89]. At the time of writing of this Chapter, a thorough search on China's top commercial search engine (www.Baidu.com), top academic literature archive search engine (www.ckni.net), and Google (www.Google.com), in both Chinese and English, on the subject of suicide pact found no report of Internet related suicide pact occurring in mainland China. Also, there has been no notable empirical study on Internet related suicides; most academic articles on the subject are reviews and commentaries on the subject.

Therefore, it is difficult to establish the extent, if any, to which Internet suicide or suicide pact is happening in mainland China. The reasons for this relative absence could be related to China's much tighter media control and strong prohibition of any Internet site that promote or disseminate messages of suicide. However, the fact that the Internet is ultimately global and virtually unrestrictable does suggest that this relatively new suicide phenomenon has not occurred in mainland China to any degree close to that of Japan which leads the world in this phenomenon [90].

There are, however, reports of suicide pacts made on-line in Hong Kong, China's most modern, self-administrative city. Researchers reported suicide pacts very similar to that of Japan, and highlighted that 20 of the 22 suicide pacts in Hong Kong from 2002-2003 used a suicide method identical to that used by all the Japanese suicide pacts – using carbon monoxide poisoning from charcoal burning in a air tight setting [88, 91-93]. This method is considered desirable by those who chose it for its high lethality, putative painlessness, and non-disfiguring of the body [88, 92]. Researchers found suicides by charcoal burning increased rapidly in the last five years in both Hong Kong (and urban Taiwan), without any sign of corresponding decreases in suicide rates by other methods, resulting in more than 20% increase in the overall suicide rates in these regions [92-94]. This phenomenon further highlighted the fact that contagion, or Werther effect of suicide can be magnified by the power of the Internet [95-96]. In Asian context, the Werther effect is well known, as exemplified by one recent suicide death of a mega celebrity in Hong Kong that was followed by a surge of similar method suicides in Hong Kong and beyond [97].

Prominent Chinese Views on and Reactions to Internet Related Suicide

China's academic and media reaction to Japan and Korea's Internet suicide pacts is a representative example of its reaction to Internet related suicide at large. It has first and foremost highlighted the power of social groups in the Asian context. In Asian cultures where the stigma against mental health problems is strong, expressions of private and negative feelings are often perceived as a sign of weakness - sharing them on the Internet with like-minded people in a largely anonymous way can be very attractive to the lonely and disenfranchised people [98]. One exemplifying study in Taiwan found strong evidence showing that those who spent the most time on line had the least amount of socially adaptive skills [99]. Research in the west also show these individuals may be specifically drawn to the Internet [100] – a study in northern Europe found 30% of adolescents studied had suicidal thoughts, and half of them use the Internet to express feelings, worries, and fears on line, instead of talking to their family or friends [101]; another study in Germany found the greatest percentage of users (48%) on suicide chat-line or forum tend to be people who look for sympathetic help from those who can understand them [102].

To further understand Internet related suicide, researchers in China favor the hypothesis that the universal, natural tendency to need to feel a sense of belonging and being understood, plus the Chinese cultural tendency to follow and act according to the ethos of the collective, may render the Chinese netizens particularly vulnerable to development of suicide pacts [89]. This fact may help to explain the puzzling question on why such presumably unhappy and lonely sounding individuals go to the length of finding partners to carry out what is typically a very private and hidden act, or historically an act between very familiar people if done in pacts [88, 103]. The immediacy in availability and convenience to form social group/units on the Internet is unprecedented in history, and fast growing in China, causing many concerns about potential copycats of "net suicides" in China [89].

Further analyses of the group dynamics by Chinese researchers emphasize that, while it is accepted that suicide activities are generally precipitated by both internal (e.g. depression, personality, substance abuse) and external (e.g. abuse, life failures) risk factors, Internet suicide pacts form because of the strong potential power of persuasion, facilitation (e.g. methods teaching), and peer pressure from a kindred spirited social group. Beyond the name of "pact", the psychological significance of a group is stressed, and such suicides need to be viewed as "group suicide". The fact that Asian history and culture is rich with passionately pursued ideology, high prevalence of cult and personality worship, and highly socially approved sense of personal honor attached to loyalty to a group or a cause may contribute to the prevalence and potential growth of Internet suicide pacts. In addition, given that the typical users of Internet in China are the young, psychologically immature youth and young adults, they may be particularly vulnerable [104].

Japanese researchers on suicide pacts in Japan found a prominent theme from the exchanges amongst participants of the pact: the concept of freedom to choose to die, as part of human rights [88]. Chinese researchers have debated at length the significance of this. The freedom to choose to die, like in most parts of the world, is not permitted in China. Popular arguments against Internet suicide, and suicide in general, stress the views that families, mental health experts, and society at large do not share the view that one has the right to commit suicide, and the potential for abuse and victimization of the vulnerable, particularly the young and clinically depressed, is tremendous. At a moral ethical level, Chinese commentators focus on how Internet suicide pacts will lead to devaluing the sanctity of human lives, failure in their responsibility to society, and debasing the moral environment of the Internet at large [89].

Unlike the west, where debates are alive in literature about whether the Internet help to prevent or promote suicide, or whether exposure to suicide topics will trigger more suicide [101, 105-107], or whether the initially ambivalent contemplators of suicide will become more or less resolved to commit suicide after exposure to suicide [95, 108] - the (available, more state-controlled) views in China's media and academic discussions are more unequivocally decisive about the deleterious effects of suicide discussions on the Internet, and asserts that control must be enforced [84]. In general, China has a very prominent and explicit emphasis on teachings of morality in its media and its education system.

The fact that the Internet as a media is conducive to anonymity, false identity taking, plagiarism, pornography, violence, and other asocial and antisocial behaviors, etc is a great concern to the state and social leaders alike on its potential negative impact on the character and moral development of China's youth [104, 109]. Some are particularly concerned about the Internet's overtly western dominated political persuasions, value systems, and world views [109]. The notion that those who commit suicide have abandoned their responsibility to the larger society is particular highlighted in Chinese discussions, where traditional Confucius values still assert strong influences. In this tradition, family is valued as the fundamental unit of the society, and the foundation of the family is the children – also made more poignant in the era of one-child only policy- who have the paramount filial duty to respect and support their parents and elders. A nation's harmonious, stable, and prosperous existence depends on the success of each family. Thus, the volitional destruction of self cuts off this historical and cultural connection, and is therefore an egregious failure in familial and social obligations

[110-111]. With these understandings, the general views found in Chinese publications tend to strongly favor state regulation and intervention targeting Internet sites that promote or discuss suicide.

In terms of legal and societal strategies against Internet related suicide, efforts in Korea, Denmark, and Australia, etc., to enact anti-suicide legislations to specifically address Internet related suicide - making it unlawful and a chargeable offence to disseminate suicide knowledge and promote suicide - are very positively regarded in China [89, 95, 106]. Proposed strategies to curtail Internet related suicide in China reflect such societal values and philosophy. These include: tighter state control on subjects of suicide on the Internet by working directly with internet service providers (ISPs) to block and prosecute site operators if found hosting sites that encourage suicide; restricting discussion forums, chat rooms, and general postings on subjects other than suicide prevention; and wider participation of operators and owners of Internet cafes, webmasters, and Internet users for reporting such content. In general, there is an implicit acknowledgement in Chinese media that the Internet is too important to be seriously curtailed, but tighter monitoring and control is advocated; balanced also, in culturally appropriate ways, with the need to take advantage of the constructive aspects of Internet based suicide prevention strategies such as on-line counseling, psycho-education, risk screening, support referrals, etc [89, 105-106, 109, 112].

It is of note that, generally, involvement of the state in blocking and prosecuting specific Internet sites is not typically considered in countries like the US, Canada, or Great Britain, where the importance of civil liberty and guaranteeing of freedom of speech will typically outweigh the potential pitfall of increased suicide rates. Self-regulation by the ISPs is usually the only protection available [106]. This is perceived by the Chinese as generally inadequate. In Japan, where the political and individual rights culture is very similar to that of North America and western Europe, a voluntary guideline to gather information and report internet suicide pact to the police, set up by a coalition of ISPs in Japan, has been credited with saving 14 lives in a 3 months period in 2005 [113]. How many more lives it could have saved if more media/state control is available, and the pros and cons contrasting the self regulations by ISPs approach vs. that of state's active intervention in China are all thought provoking questions. From a societal perspective, social commentators and researchers in China believe that the ability to prevent Internet related suicide is a hallmark of civil society. Systematic education about the risk and nature of suicide at the levels of family, school, work place, and youth organizations can help to detect early signs of problematic Internet use behavior, depression, and suicide ideation. They also advocate enhanced and meaningful engagement of the youth in order to promote positive life perspectives, hopefulness about the future, and life-embracing attitudes [114].

Finally, another prevention strategy emphasized in China to prevent Internet related suicide is to target support for the "Internet addicted" individuals. Chinese researchers have found as much as 36% of college students having Internet addiction problems using an established instrument in the field [98, 115]. Suicides of problematic Internet users have caused concerns. For example, one website collected and posted numerous youth suicide notes and letters from families – all the suicides were related to "addictive" Internet gaming. The documents suggested evidence of disintegrated family relationships and friendships, losing touch with social connections, and higher crime rates in these addicted gamers who had committed suicide. (e.g. one suicide note totaled four pages, full of names of the spirits and characters and plots of an Internet game, but not one word mentioning the family) [116].

International research show there are high levels of mental health problems, including depression and suicidal ideation, high levels of feeling alienated, and compulsivity in those who are Internet addicted [117-119]. An interesting research in Japan on primary and secondary school children (8-14 year olds) found 15.4% of them believe that "a dead person could return to life", and 29.2% of these children attributed this view to what they have learned on media such as TV, movies or video games [88].

Though strong empirical evidence is still lacking and it may be that these Internet addicted individuals have little or no elevated risk of suicide when compared to others, the intuitive sense is that these "addicted" individual may be very isolated from the real world, ill equipped to face the challenges of the daily realities, and prone to develop sense of disappointment, emptiness, and world weariness, therefore increasing the risk of depression and be at risk for suicide [120]. A further argument to focus on this group is to have a healthier relationship with the Internet in general. A recent report of a young person dying out of exhaustion after spending three straight days in an Internet game room has reinforced this argument [121].

CONCLUSION

China has high rates of suicide and several unique findings. Understandings of these phenomena can be enhanced by knowing the specific cultural, economic, and social contexts. Suicide risk factors found in China are complex, interdependent, and likely intimately related to its recent rapid economic growth and attendant social changes. The research on impulsive suicide by young, disenfranchised, rural females using lethal pesticides is an example of the multifaceted, interconnected nature of suicide in China.

Current research also highlights the unique characteristics of suicide in the urban youth, and the challenges they face. These are examples of how suicide behaviors are deeply affected by biological vulnerabilities, and the social-cultural context within which they take place.

Suicide, as a universally present condition of tragic personal and societal loss, serves as a powerful reflector of the society at large. Internet related suicide tells us much about the rapidly modernizing China, where the fast pace of technological change is unprecedented in human history and Internet usage is approaching the level of western industrialized countries. Although the current available literature is limited on this subject, there appears to be a healthy discussion on the intensely personal and societal matter of suicide and how it interfaces with the Internet. There are culturally and politically unique aspects. For example, China is faced with the same dilemma as others in terms of balancing between deriving benefits from the informational power and ease of access and expression of the Internet, and the duty to protect the citizens from the growth of suicide phenomenon on-line. The current survey suggests China is approaching it with a higher level of control through the state, and the impact and outcome of such efforts will be very interesting to study over time when compared to those of the rest of the world.

REFERENCES

[1] Zakaria F: Does the future belong to China? *Newsweek,* May 9, 2005. http:/www.cis.gsu.edu~dtruex/courses/IB8710/Articles/China/DoestheFutureBelong2China.pdf

[2] Harwit E: Spreading telecommunications to developing areas in China: telephones, the internet and the digital divide. *The China Quarterly* 2004; 180:1010-1030.

[3] Pan PP: The click that broke a government's grip. *Washington Post,* Feb. 19, 2006: http://msl1.mit.educ/furdlong/docs/washpost/2006-02-19 washpostchina fe 1.pdf

[4] Lei J: Influence of harmful net information on youth and children and countermeasures. *Journal of Hunan First Normal College* 2006; 6(1):39-41. [In Chinese]

[5] Xiang W: The harmful effects to the teenagers' psychological health of the network and the countermeasures. *Humanities & Social Sciences Journal of Hainan University 2007;* 25(2): 234-237. [In Chinese]

[6] Alao AO, Yolles JC, Armenta WR: Cybersuicide; the Internet and suicide. *American Journal of Psychiatry* 1999; 156:1836-1837.

[7] Murray CJ, Lopez AD: The global burden of disease: a comprehensive assessment of mortality and disability from diseases, injuries, and risk factors in 1990 and projected to 2020. Cambridge, MA, Harvard University Press, 1996.

[8] Phillips MR, Li X, Zhang Y: Suicide rates in China, 1995-99. *Lancet* 2002; 359:835-840.

[9] *World Health Organization: Mental health: suicide prevention.* World Health Organization website. http://www.who.int/mental_health/prevention/suicide/suicideprevent/en/index.html. Accessed 2008, September

[10] Yip PS, Liu KY, Hu J, Song XM: Suicide rates in China during a decade of rapid social changes. *Soc. Psychiatry Psychiatri Epidemiol* 2005; 40(10):792-798.

[11] Ji J, Kleinman A, Becker AE: Suicide in contemporary China: a review of China's distinctive suicide demographics in their sociocultural context. *Harv Rev Psychiatry* 2001; 9:1–12.

[12] Cantor CH: Suicide in the Western world. In *International Handbook of Suicide and Attempted Suicide.* Edited by Hawton K, van Heringen K. Chichester, England: John Wiley and Sons, 2000: pp9–28.

[13] Yang GH, Zhou LN, Huang ZJ.: The trend and geographic distribution of suicide in Chinese population. *Chinese Journal of Epidemiology 2004;* 25:280–284. [In Chinese]

[14] Phillips MR, Yang G, Zhang Y, Wang LJ, Ji HY, Zhou MG.: Risk factors for suicide in China: a national case-control psychological autopsy study. *Lancet* 2002; 360:1728–1736.

[15] Conner KR, Phillips MR, Meldrum S, Knox KL, Zhang YP, Yang GH.: Low-planned suicides in China. *Psychol Med 2005;* 35:1197–1204.

[16] Xiao SY, Wang XP, Xu HN: Current issues in China's suicide research and prevention. *Chin J Psychiatry 2003*; 36:129–131. [In Chinese]

[17] Phillips MR, Shen Q, Liu XH, Pritzker S, Streiner D, Conner K, Yang GH.: Assessing depressive symptoms in persons who die of suicide in mainland China. *J Affect Disord 2007;* 98:73–82.

[18] Sadock BJ, Sadock VA: Kaplan and Sadock's synopsis of psychiatry: Behavioral Sciences/Clinical Psychiatry, Edn. 10. Baltimore: Lippincott Williams & Wilkins; 2007.

[19] American Psychiatric Association: Practice guideline for the assessment and treatment of suicidal behaviors. *Am J Psychiatry 2003*; 160(11 Suppl):1–60.

[20] Phillips MR, Lui HQ, Zhang YP: Suicide and social change in China. *Cult Med Psychiatry 1999;* 23:25–50.

[21] Liu B: On reasons of high suicide rate of rural women in China. *Journal of Chinese Agricultural University 2004;* 4:63–67. [In Chinese]

[22] Phillips MR: The transformation of China's mental health services. *China J 1998;* 39:1–36.

[23] Kleinman A, Kleinman J: The transformation of everyday social experience: what a mental and social health perspective reveals about Chinese communities under global and local change. *Cult Med Psychiatry 1999;* 23:7–24.

[24] Chang DF, Kleinman A: Growing pains: mental health care in a developing China. *Yale-China Health Study Journal 2002;* 1:85–89.

[25] Blumenthal, D., Hsiao, W: Privatization and its discontent-the evolving Chinese health care system. *The New England Journal of Medicine 2005;* 353(11): 1165-1170.

[26] Hao W, Xiao S, Liu T, Young D, Chen S, Zhang D, Li C, Shi J, Chen G, Yang K: The second National Epidemiological Survey on illicit drug use at six high-prevalence areas in China: prevalence use and use patterns. *Addiction 2002;* 97:1305–1315.

[27] Hao W, Young DS, Xiao SY, Li LJ, Zhang YL: Alcohol consumption and alcohol-related problems: Chinese experience from six area samples. *Addiction 1994;* (10):1467-1476.

[28] He ZX, Lester D: Elderly suicide in China. *Psychol Rep 2001;* 89:675–676.

[29] Silverstein M, Cong Z, Li S: Intergenerational transfers and living arrangements of older people in rural China: consequences for psychological well-being. *J Gerontol 2006;* 61(B):S256–S266.

[30] Pearson V, Phil D, Phillips MR, He F, Ji H: Attempted suicide among young rural women in the People's Republic of China: possibilities for prevention. *Suicide Life Threat Behav 2002;* 32:359–369.

[31] Hawton K: Gender differences in suicidal behavior. *Br J Psychiatry 2000;* 177:484–485.

[32] Zhang J, Conwell Y, Zhou L, Jiang C: Culture, risk factors and suicide in rural China: a psychological autopsy case control study. *Acta Psychiatr Scand 2004;* 110: 430–437.

[33] Zeng Y, Tu P, Gu BC: Causes and implications of the recent increase in the reported sex ratio at birth in China. *Popul Dev Rev 1993;* 19:283–302.

[34] Pearson V: Goods on which one loses: women and mental health in China. *Soc Sci Med 1995;* 41:1159–1173.

[35] Liu M: Rebellion and revenge: the meaning of suicide of women in rural China. *Int J Soc Welf 2002;* 11:300–309.

[36] Qin P, Mortensen PB: Specific characteristics of suicide in China. *Acta Psychiatr Scand 2001;* 103:117–121.

[37] Li XY, Xu YC, Wang YP: Characteristics of serious suicide attempts treated in rural general hospital. *Chin Ment Health J 2002;* 16:681–683. [In Chinese]

[38] Hill SA, Pritchard C, Laugharne R: Changing patterns of suicide in a poor, rural county over the 20th century. *Soc Psychiatry Psychiatr Epidemiol 2005;* 40:601–604.
[39] Hirsch JK: A review of the literature on rural suicide. *Crisis 2006;* 27:189–199.
[40] Durkheim E: *Suicide.* New York: New York Free Press; 1951.
[41] Lester D: Suicide and the Chinese Cultural Revolution. *Arch Suicide Res 2005;* 9:99–104.
[42] Simon TR, Swann AC, Powell KE: Characteristics of impulsive suicide attempts and attempters. *Suicide Life Threat Behav 2001;* 32(Suppl):49–59.
[43] Li XY, Phillips MR, Wang Y: The comparison of impulsive and non-impulsive attempted suicide. *Chin J Neurol Psychiatry 2003;* 29:27–30. [In Chinese]
[44] Ran MS, Xiang MZ, Li J, Huang J, Chen EYH: Correlates of lifetime suicide attempts among individuals with affective disorders in a Chinese rural community. *Arch Suicide Res 2007;* 11:119–127.
[45] Parker G, Gladstone G, Chee KT: Depression in the planet's largest ethnic group: the Chinese. *Am J Psychiatry 2001;* 158:857–864.
[46] Law S, Liu PZ: Suicide in China: unique demographic patterns and relationship to depressive disorder *Current Psychiatric Reports 2008;* 10(1):80-86.
[47] Shen YC, Zhang MY, Huang YQ, He YL, Liu ZR, Cheng H, Tsang A, Lee S, Kessler RC: Twelve-month prevalence, severity, and unmet need for treatment of mental disorders in metropolitan China. *Psychological Medicine 2006;* 36:257-67.
[48] Cooper JE, Sartorius N: Mental Disorders in China: Results of the National Epidemiological Survey in 12 Areas. Glasgow, Scotland: Gaskell; 1996.
[49] Robins LN, Regier DA, eds: *Psychiatric Disorders in America: The Epidemiological Catchment Area Study.* New York: New York Free Press; 1991.
[50] Tzeng WC, Lipson JG: The cultural context of suicide stigma in Taiwan. *Qualitative Health Research 2004;* 14:345-358.
[51] Kauman M, Stein R: Record share of economy spent on health care. *The Washington Post*, January 10, 2006: A01
[52] Zhu ZQ, Zhang MY, He YL: The disposition of mental health professional institutions in China. *Shanghai Archives of Psychiatry 2002;* 14(suppl):5-6. [In Chinese]
[53] Zhu ZQ, He YL, Zhang MY: The staff serving for mental health in China. *Shanghai Archives of Psychiatry 2002;* 14(suppl):10-12. [In Chinese]
[54] Chen HL, Zhou PL: The treatment rate of patients with mental disorders and the utilization status of health resources in Jiangsu province. *Chinese Journal of Clinical Rehabilitation 2005;* 9:187–188. [In Chinese]
[55] Chung KF, Wong MC: Experience of stigma among Chinese mental healthy patients in Hong Kong. *Psychiatric Bulletin 2004;* 24:451-454.
[56] Lee S: Diagnosis postponed: Shenjing shuairuo and the transformation of psychiatry in Ran MS, Xiang MZ, Li SX, Shan, YH, Huang MS, Li SG, Chen YH, Chan CLW: Prevalence and course of schizophrenia in a Chinese rural area. *Australian and New Zealand Journal of Psychiatry 2003;* 37:452-457.
[57] Yip W, Hsiao WC: The Chinese health system at a crossroads. *Health Affairs 2008;* 27(2):460-468.
[58] Gao J, Tang S, Tolhurst R, Rao K: Changing access to health services in urban China: implications for equity. *Health Policy and Planning 2001;* 12(4):302-312.

[59] Lee S. Fung Sc. Tsang A, Liu ZR, Huang YQ, He YL, Zhang MY, Shen YC, Nock MK, Kessler RC: Lifetime prevalence of suicide ideation, plan, and attempt in metropolitan China. *Acta Psychiatrica Scandinavica 2007;* 116(6):429-37.

[60] Ip GSH, Mackenzie AE: Caring for relatives with serious mental illness at home: the experiences of family careers in Hong Kong. *Archives of Psychiatric Nursing 1998;* 12(5):288-294.

[61] Tsang HWH, Tam PKC, Chan F: Sources of family burden of individuals with mental illness. *International Journal of Rehabilitation Research 2003;* 26:123-130.

[62] Anon: China Medical Reform Report. Sohu Health Online 2008: http://health.sohu.com/20070514/n250001546.shtm [In Chinese]

[63] Yip KS: An historical review of the mental health services in the people's republic of China. *International Journal of Social Psychiatry 2005;* 51(2):106-118.

[64] Hampton NZ: An evolving rehabilitation service delivery system in the People's Republic of China. *The Journal of Rehabilitation 2001;* 67:20-25.

[65] Yin DK: The current situation, problems and strategy of Chinese mental health work: report on China / WHO awareness raising symposium. *Chinese Mental Health Journal* 2000; 14(1):4-5. [In Chinese]

[66] Poonam: *Depression playing havoc with students at Beijing University.* Sept 6, 2006: http://www.depressionblog.org/entry/depression-targeted-quarter-students-at-beijing-university/

[67] Jiang MJ, Hu ZQ, Cao Y: Suicide deaths concentrated in Beijing universities. *Am J Psychiatry 2007;* 164:1758.

[68] Liu B, Chen JH, Wu YP, Li YZ, He JF, Li N, Xie X: Analysis of character of college students on psychological crisis condition. *Chinese Journal of Behavioral Medical Sciences 2006;* 15(10): 919-921. [In Chinese]

[69] Tang XN: Current suicide trend in university students—a sign of decline in humanism in university life. *J Educ Res 2006;* 10:125–126. [In Chinese]

[70] Wang P, Feng WD: Analysis on idea of suicide and its influence factors among 4066 adolescents in Liuzhou city. *Practical Preventive Medicine 2007;* 14(2):390-392. [In Chinese]

[71] Shaffer D, Gould MS, Fisher P, Trautman P, Moreau D, Kleinman M, and Flory M: Psychiatric diagnosis in child and adolescent suicide. *Arch. Gen. Psychiatry 1996;* 53:339–348.

[72] Gould MS, Greenberg T, Velting DM, Shaffer D: Youth suicide risk and preventive interventions: a review of the past 10 years. *Journal of the American Academy of Child and Adolescent Psychiatry 2003;* 42:386–405.

[73] Borowsky IW, Ireland M, Resnick MD: Adolescent suicide attempts: risks and protectors. *Pediatrics 2001;* 107:485-493.

[74] Li XY, Phillips MR, Zhang YP, Xu D, Yang GH: Risk factors for suicide in China's youth" a case-control study. *Psychological Medicine 2008;* 38:397-406.

[75] Liu X, Tein JY, Zhao Z, Sandler IN: Suicidality and correlates among rural adolescents of China. *J Adolesc Health* 2005; 37:443–451.

[76] Crystal DS, Chen CS, Fuligni AJ: Psychological maladjustment and academic achievement: a cross-cultural study of Japanese, Chinese, and American high school students. *Child Development 1994;* 65: 738-753.

[77] Liu XC, Kurita H, Uchiyama M, Okawa M, Liu LQ, Ma DD: Life events, locus of control in behavioral problems among Chinese adolescents. *J Clin Psychol 2000;* 56:1565-1577.

[78] Zhou Q, Eisenberg N, Wang Y, Reiser M: Chinese children's effortful control and dispositional anger/frustration: relations to parenting styles and children's functioning. *Dev. Psychology 2004;* 40: 352-366.

[79] Yip PS: An epidemiological profile of suicides in Beijing, China. *Suicide & Life-Threatening Behavior. 2001;* 31(1):62-70.

[80] Hesketh T. Ding Qu Jian: Anxiety and depression in adolescents in urban and rural China. *Psychological Reports April 2005,* 96(2): 435-44.

[81] Liu C, Munakata T, Onuoha FN: Mental health condition of the only-child: study of urban and rural high school students in China. *Adolescence 2005;* 40(160): 831-45.

[82] Hesketh T. Ding Q, Jenkins R: Suicide ideation in Chinese adolescents. *Social Psychiatry and Psychiatric Epidemiology 2002;* 37(5):230-235.

[83] Anon: ChungQing Evening News: *Online suicide manual legally liable;* 2005 April l: http://tech.sina.com.cn/i/2005-04-01/1104568517.shtml [In Chinese]

[84] Anon: Communications Times: *Legal drug sales to suicide groups on-line;* 2006 April 13: http://news.qq.com/a/20060413/000066.htm [In Chinese]

[85] Anon: Jiangsu, *Culture.com: Japan's Internet Suicide growth; 2005 July 29:* http://www.jschina.com.cn/gb/jschina/culture/node6457/node6481/userobjectlai881394.htm [In Chinese]

[86] Anon: *Focusing on Suicide: Various Suicide Topics;* accessed Oct 2008: http://www.jktimes.net/zisha/ [In Chinese]

[87] Anon: Medical Student Information: *Suicide websites and Internet suicides; 2003* Nov 2: http://www.cmm.zju.educ.cn/student/main/love/abc/200322/02001220.htm [In Chinese]

[88] Naito A: Internet Suicide in Japan: Implications for child and adolescent mental health. *Clinical Child Psychology and Psychiatry 2007;* 12(4):583-597.

[89] Zan YL, Xu WX: Examination of youth suicide pact on the Internet - a preliminary review of the societal impact and prevention strategies. *Journal of Youth Criminology* 2005; 4:36-38. [In Chinese]

[90] Fishbain DA, Aldrich TE: Suicide pacts: international comparisons. *Journal of Clinical Psychiatry 1985;* 46: 11-15.

[91] Chan KPM, Yip PSF, Au J, Lee DTS: Charcoal burning suicide in post-transition Hong Kong. *Br J Psychiatry 2005,* 186:67-73.

[92] Lee TS, Chan KPM, Yip PS: Charcoal burning is also popular for suicide pacts made on the internet. *BMJ 2005;* 330:602.

[93] Lee TS, Yip PS: Burning charcoal: a novel and contagious method of suicide in Asia. *Arch Gen Psychiatry 2002;* 59:293-294.

[94] Liu, KY, Beautrais A, Caine E: Charcoal burning suicides in Hong Kong and urban Taiwan; an illustration of the impact of a novel suicide method on overall regional rates. *Journal of Epidemiology and Community Health 2007;* 61:243-253.

[95] Biddle L, Donovan J, Hawton K, Kapur N, Gunne D: Suicide and the Internet. *BMJ 2008;* 336:800-802.

[96] Hagihara A, Tarumi K, Abe T: Media suicide-reports, internet use and the occurrence of suicides between 1987 and 2005 in Japan. *BMC Public Health 2007;* 7:321-329.

[97] Yip P, Fu K, Yang K, Ip B, Chan C, Chen E, Lee D, Law F, Hawton K: The effects of a celebrity suicide on suicide rates in Hong Kong. *Journal of Affective Disorders 2003;* 93:245-252.

[98] Peng Y, Zou SJ: Review on internet addictions in youth. *Journal of Hunan University of Science and Engineering 2006;* 27(12):151-153. [In Chinese]

[99] Lo SK, Wang CC, Fang W: Physical interpersonal relationships and social anxiety among online game players. *CyberPsychology & Behavior 2005;* 8(1):15-20.

[100] Morahan-Martin J, Schumacher P: Loneliness and social uses in the Internet. *Computers in Human Behavior 2003;* 19:659-671.

[101] Becker K, Mayer M, Nagenborg M, El-Faddagh M, Schmidt MH: Parasuicide online: can suicide websites trigger suicidal behavior in predisposed adolescents? *Nordic Journal of Psychiatry 2004;* 58:111-114.

[102] Eichenberg C: Internet message boards for suicide people: a typology of users. *CyberPsychology & Behavior 2007;* 11:107-113.

[103] Rajagopal S: Suicide pacts and the internet. *British Medical Journal 2004;* 32:1298-1299.

[104] Fan Q: Deleterious influences of the Internet on the youth – an overview and strategies of prevention, *Journal of Liaoning Administrative College 2007;* 9(2):160-161. [In Chinese]

[105] Alao AO, Soderberg M, Pohl EL, Alao AL: Cybersuicide: review of the role of the Internet on suicide. *CyberPsychology & Behavior 2006;* 9(4): 489-493.

[106] Mishara BL, Weisstub DN: Ethical, legal, and practical issues in the control and regulation of suicide promotion and assistance over the Internet. *Suicide & Life-Threatening Behavior 2007;* 37(1):58-66.

[107] Grohol JM: Suicide and the Internet: study misses internet's greater collection of support websites. *BMJ 2008;* 336:905-906.

[108] Baume P, Cantor CH, Rolfe A: Cybersuicide: the role of interactive suicide notes on the Internet. *Crisis 1997;* 18:73-79.

[109] Song ZL: Negative impact of the Internet on healthy development of the youth and proposed responses. *Journal of Youth Criminology 2003;* 6: 20-22. [In Chinese]

[110] Yu TL: The revival of Confucianism in Chinese schools; a historical-political review. *Asia Pacific Journal of Education 2008;* 28(2):113-129.

[111] Hwang KK: Filial piety and loyalty: two types of social identification in Confucianism. *Asian Journal of Social Psychology 1999;* 2:163-183.

[112] Krysinska KE, De Leo D: Telecommunication and suicide prevention: hopes and challenges for the new century. *Omega 2007;* 55(3): 237-253.

[113] Hitosugi M, Nagai T, Tokudome S: A voluntary effort to save the youth suicide via the Internet in Japan. *International Journal of Nursing Studies 2007;* 44:157.

[114] *Chinese Youth League: Understanding China's youth suicide.* Accessed Sept, 2008: http://www.ccyl.org.cn/bulletin/qvb_scyqv/

[115] Anon: Liberation Evenings News; *Internet addition a factor in University student suicide;* 2006 January 18: http://health.sohu.com/20060118/n241498979.shtml [In Chinese]

[116] *Anon: Internet youth suicide documented;* accessed Sept 2008: http://blog.voc.com.cn/upload/1133245164.doc [In Chinese]

[117] Kim KH, Ryu EJ, Chu MY, Yeun EJ, Choi SY, Seo JS, Nam BW: Internet addiction in Korean adolescent and suicidal ideation: a questionnaire survey. *International Journal o Nursing Studies* 2006; 43: 185-192.

[118] Ryu EJ, Choi KS, Seo JS, Nam BW: The relationships of Internet addiction, depression, and suicidal ideation in adolescents. *CyberPsychology & Behavior* 2004; 7(4):379-383.

[119] Whang LS, Lee S, Chang G: Internet over-users' psychological profiles: a behavior sampling on Internet addiction. *CyberPsychology & Behavior* 2003; 6(2):143-150.

[120] Li WB: The influence of being addicted to internet on interpersonal association of youngsters. *Journal of Educational Science of Hunan Normal University* 2006; 5(1): 99-102. [In Chinese]

[121] *Associated Press: Man dies after 3-day gaming, binge* :http://www.cnn.com/2007/TECH/09/17/internet.death.ap/inex.html

In: Internet and Suicide
Editors: L. Sher and A. Vilens

ISBN 978-1-60741-077-5

Chapter 25

INTERNET COMMUNICATION ABOUT ASSISTED OR "RATIONAL" SUICIDE: LEGAL AND ETHICAL CONSIDERATIONS FOR PRACTICE

Thomas J. Rankin[1], Elena S. Yakunina[1], Jessica Richmond Moeller[1] and James L. Werth, Jr.[2]

[1]The University of Akron, Akron, Ohio, USA and [2]Radford University, Radford, Virginia, USA

ABSTRACT

Assisted suicide and "rational" suicide are each divisive issues that cause legal and ethical quandaries for physicians and mental health professionals in their practices. This chapter uses a case example of a person with amyotrophic lateral sclerosis (ALS; i.e., Lou Gehrig's disease) to explore the benefits and risks that the Internet and related electronic communication technology have brought to professionals' consideration of how to appropriately engage with people who are thinking about assisted or rational suicide. ALS is a progressive, neurological disease that slowly destroys nerves and atrophies muscles. Most people with ALS eventually become paralyzed, unable to breathe or swallow on their own, and require the use of a ventilator to survive. The case example of a person with ALS considering assisted or rational suicide by writing about it online is utilized to elucidate legal responsibilities that physicians or psychotherapists owe to non-patients and patients. Medical, psychological, and counseling ethical codes are examined for suggestions regarding best practices toward non-patients and patients considering assisted or rational suicide. Those codes are also examined for their views about the proper role of the Internet in mental health care. The benefits of Internet communication with medical or psychotherapeutic patients are elaborated, dangers to patient confidentiality posed by electronic communication are detailed and potential solutions explored. Finally, the Internet as a source of unprecedented information and misinformation for patients is described, and thoughts are offered about how to encourage professionals and patients to make the most of the medium while minimizing its inherent risks.

INTRODUCTION

Terminology is important when discussing end-of-life issues and decisions because the topics are value-loaded and emotionally charged. In order to minimize confusion, we begin with definitions of "rational" suicide and assisted suicide and then move into a case illustrating these concepts and how they may become a reality for professionals who spend time online. Before proceeding, it is important to note that regardless of whether a particular death by suicide is deemed to be rational or irrational, the act of suicide itself is not prosecuted as a crime in the United States [1]. We also wish to note that many object to using the term suicide in the types of situations we will be describing. Several organizations specifically state that "value-neutral" language should be used to differentiate the typical case of suicide – which ordinarily results from impulsivity or is influenced by a psychological condition such as severe clinical depression [2] – from the situations discussed in the rational or assisted suicide literature [3]. However, because of the focus of this book, we will retain the phrasing rational suicide and assisted suicide.

Defining rational suicide is a difficult endeavor. Some believe that suicide can never be rational. However, for those who are not irresolutely skeptical, depending on how the term is defined and which group is surveyed, studies have found that between 57% and 84% of American legislators, physicians, nurses, psychologists, and counselors believe that suicide can sometimes be rational [4,5,6]. For a suicide to be considered rational, many professionals consider the following criteria to be necessary: first, the person has a severe condition that is terrible to endure and extremely unlikely to improve; second, the person engages in a sound decision-making process; and third, the person is not under duress from others but rather makes a free choice of his or her own will [5]. The first criterion may seem the most objective but it is actually very difficult to reach agreement upon, because for some only terminal illness or unremitting physical pain is sufficient, while others would include psychological pain, mental debilitation, or unsatisfying quality of life as well.

Assisted suicide is a subset of rational suicide: physicians or others generally consider assisting someone to die only when it seems a rational response to the patient's difficult situation. Assisted suicide occurs when an individual intentionally provides the means through which another person can end his or her life, with the knowledge that that person intends to use those means to kill himself or herself. When physicians engage in assisted suicide with a patient (often by providing the patient with large quantities of barbiturates) it is called physician-assisted suicide (PAS). Euthanasia is different from assisted suicide, in that the physician not only provides the means of death, but also actually administers the lethal means, such as through a lethal injection [7]. Although debates regarding the legalization of euthanasia often revolve around the involvement of medical professionals, non-physicians can also find themselves the in position of performing euthanasia.

Assisted suicide has been explicitly legalized only in the state of Oregon [8]. Internationally, assisted suicide is also usually a criminal offense, with some notable exceptions. Australia had a brief brush with allowing physician-assisted suicide in its

Northern Territories during nine months in 1996-1997, but after a political furor the Australian Federal government overrode the law and to this day PAS is a crime in Australia [9]. In 2002 The Netherlands codified its 20-year practice of not prosecuting physicians who perform euthanasia or PAS if certain conditions were met, and Belgium enacted similar legislation that same year [10]. A history of non-criminal PAS in Switzerland is longstanding, resting on Swiss Penal Code Article 115, enacted in 1942, which provides for imprisonment only if the person who assists the suicide acts from selfish motives (e.g., for financial gain through inheritance); since the 1980s this has been consistently interpreted to allow PAS [11,12]. Despite these examples from Oregon, Switzerland, Belgium, The Netherlands, and Australia, however, the vast majority of countries and U.S. states impose criminal sanctions for those who assist someone's suicide.

Although assisted suicide is usually unlawful, surveys of physicians have found that there are situations in which at least a substantial minority of physicians believes that helping someone else take her or his own life should be ethically permissible, or even that assisting suicide would be the right thing to do [13]. Interviews and questionnaires with physicians in the Netherlands and Oregon who had euthanized a patient or assisted a suicide revealed that most such physicians felt comfort after helping the person die and most would do so again for another patient; however, most physicians' experience also was that assisting a suicide was emotionally difficult for them [14]. Given the diversity of opinion and intensity of emotion surrounding assisted and rational suicide, it might be helpful to examine a concrete case example rather than discuss the issues at a merely abstract level.

Case Example of A Person With ALS who is Considering Suicide

For purposes of discussion, let us assume that a hypothetical person with ALS, whom we will call Alice, visits a chat room. Although there are chat rooms specifically for persons with ALS, Alice wishes to expand her social world and thus begins chatting in a free chat room that is open to the public. Coincidentally, a mental health professional named Ed is also engaging in light conversation in the chat room, trying to unwind after a stressful day on the job. With an upcoming presidential election, the discussion naturally turns to politics, which leads to talk about abortion, and ultimately ends up on the appropriateness of assisted or rational suicide. The chat grows rather heated, and it is clear to Ed that this is a very personal issue for Alice, perhaps one that she struggles with herself. Ed is familiar with suicide assessment and considers writing a direct, specific question of Alice such as, "Are you thinking about ending your own life?" [15]. However, although he thinks that he probably ought to use his expertise to try to help someone in need of psychological help, he isn't sure whether doing so will put him at legal risk [16]. On the other hand, he also fears *not* helping, because he doesn't really know if he is ethically or legally required to help Alice.

While Ed is considering the implications of the situation, Alice begins writing about the reasons she has for living and the reasons she has for dying. Ed may decide that he cannot sit idle as she expresses her suffering. He makes several empathic statements reflecting her feelings of emptiness, frustration about loss of physical control, and hopelessness about the future – all the while becoming more convinced that Alice is in need of professional mental health assistance. He has not disclosed his professional status at this point. Soon, however, the exchange moves to the following:

Alice: What I really want is help getting me what I need to kill myself.

Ed: You want to kill yourself but you don't know how to do it given your physical limitations?

Alice: The doctors have said that I have only a short time until I will need to go on a ventilator and be fed by tubes. I am already paralyzed from the waist down and I want to do something while I still have the use of my hands.

At this point a third person – let's call him John – becomes involved in the exchange. He begins to offer specific information and advice about how Alice can kill herself:

John: Actually there's a great forum that can help you find ways to kill yourself: [gives web link]

Alice: Really? But I'm afraid of guns, I'm thinking pills will be an easier way to go.

John: Well you could always order [names a lethal substance] through an online pharmacy.

Alice: Right but I would have to do it fast before I begin to lose the ability to swallow…

Ed has a strong reaction to this exchange and freezes, not knowing what to do. Should he disclose that he is a mental health professional and direct Alice to seek professional help immediately? Should he try to figure out Alice's location and summon police or a mobile psychiatric evaluation unit to that location? Should he "go along" with the tone of this conversation in order to gain Alice's trust, hoping to use that trust to gather identifying information that he can then pass along to emergency personnel? Should he point out the terrible guilt that any friend or family member would likely feel if that person unknowingly assisted in Alice's suicide?

Civil Liability for Physicians and Psychotherapists

In order to resolve the dilemma described in the case example presented above, Ed will need to consider the potential civil liabilities that exist for physicians and psychotherapists working with individuals who are actively considering self-harm. In the United States and England, the general background rule of law is that if a therapeutic or helping relationship has not been established, one does not have a duty to help others in peril [17,18]. Unless a special relationship exists between the professional and the person communicating suicidal thoughts or attempting suicide, no civil liability will attach for failure to help a suicidal individual [19]. Thus, if we assume that Alice is not Ed's patient, he has no legal duty to help her. This does not imply that Ed does not have an ethical duty as a professional to help Alice – rather, the presence or absence of an ethical duty will be analyzed in a later section. Further, even though he may not have a legal duty, Ed may have a natural desire to reach out to a person who is suffering; we do not want to minimize this possibility, but in this section and the next we are differentiating professional legal and ethical obligations from personal choices.

Special relationships such physician/patient or psychotherapist/patient change this background rule to one in which the treating professional owes a duty of due care to the patient (for the rest of this article, we will use the term "professional relationship" to facilitate ease of reading). Although it is less likely to be the case that Ed will encounter a current client than a stranger in an online chat room, for the purposes of illustrating the obligations that professionals have, let's change the circumstances presented above. Now imagine that Alice was Ed's pre-existing patient, and he had happened to go into a public chat room and engage her in conversation, then it could be argued that he would owe Alice a duty to act with the knowledge or skill of an average similar professional in like circumstances [20,21]. It would be up to a jury, after hearing expert testimony on the issue, to decide whether he did have a duty to act and, if so, exactly what an average similar professional ought to have done. The jury would also need to decide whether the breach of this duty directly caused the damage suffered by Alice (or her family). This is the "but for" causation test [22]: but for the breach, would Alice not have suffered damage? If the jury decides that by not inquiring further Ed breached his duty to Alice, and this breach directly contributed to her death or injury, he could end up owing Alice (or her family) money to compensate for the damage caused by Ed's negligence.

Notice that this is a fact-based inquiry, dependent upon exactly what Alice wrote and whether the expert witnesses believe the statements constituted warning signs of suicide and whether Ed's actions/inactions directly contributed to Alice's death or injury. Because it is a written medium, the records of the chat room could be subpoenaed and the jury and experts could have access to the precise statements written by both Ed and Alice. Even if there were a pre-existing professional relationship between Ed and Alice, those statements would not be covered by confidentiality because they were made in a public forum (the chat room) and thus are not confidential communications. Furthermore, if Ed is sued by Alice's family for his actions as Alice's physician/psychotherapist, confidential communications would be admissible, assuming they were relevant to the substance of the negligence allegations.

With this legal background established, now let us assume again that Alice is *not* a pre-existing patient of Ed. If Ed does decide to offer assistance to Alice, he should be careful that he does not inadvertently thereby create a professional relationship that might give rise to potential liability. The absence of a written contract or even an oral promise to pay for services rendered does not preclude the creation of a professional relationship; rather, acts such as giving specific medical or psychological advice to an individual, diagnosis, prescription, or treatment each can create a professional relationship by themselves [23]. In contrast, speaking in generalizations, hypothetical terms, or urging the person to seek treatment from another (thereby implying that the professional speaking is not providing such care) can each make it less likely that a court would find a professional relationship to exist. The length of the chat room exchange could also factor into this equation, just as a long phone conversation with a potential patient could be seen as evidence of the creation of a professional relationship [24]. Explicit disclaimers of a professional relationship can be made, but if actual medical care is provided, the physician or psychotherapist will nonetheless be obligated under the law to provide competent care.

In conclusion, whether Ed is legally responsible to protect Alice in this situation depends on whether a special treatment relationship is established between them. If Alice is not Ed's patient then he would have no legal obligation to protect her from self-harm. If, on the other hand, Alice is Ed's patient or a therapeutic relationship is established between them over the Internet, Ed may be considered legally obligated to prevent Alice's self-harm attempt. In addition to these legal considerations, however, some important ethical and logistical dilemmas remain to be addressed. The next section reviews several professional ethics codes and the way these codes handle the issues of Internet communication and assisted or rational suicide.

ETHICAL CODES, GUIDANCE STATEMENTS, AND THE INTERNET

The fact that Alice and Ed are communicating via the Internet instead of face-to-face makes ethical and legal analysis more complex. They are not in the same location, so different state laws may apply, which is an issue that will be discussed below. Neither Alice's nor Ed's identity can be as easily verified as if Ed's diplomas and licensure were hanging on the wall of his office, or as if Alice's physical appearance made it clear she was not a minor. Body language and facial expression can be directly observed in face-to-face interaction, whereas in online situations such observation requires cameras and microphones and depends on the quality and perspective of such equipment. Different professional organizations handle the challenge that the Internet poses to responsible practice in varying ways. In this section we address only the issue of Internet service provision; in the next section we review issues associated with providing services to non-patients.

If Ed were a psychologist, he would be bound by the ethical code of the American Psychological Association (APA). APA's code of ethics does not specifically address delivery of services over the Internet except to say in the "Introduction and Applicability" section that the code applies to a psychologists' professional use of the Internet and their electronic communications [25]. Rather, Ed would be encouraged to analyze provision of Internet services to Alice on a case-by-case basis, paying special attention to issues of boundaries of competence (Standard 1.04c), structuring the therapy relationship (Standard 4.01), informed consent to therapy (Standard 4.02), and confidentiality (Standards 5.01-5.11) [26].

If Ed were a member of the American Counseling Association (ACA), on the other hand, he would receive more guidance from his professional organization. ACA spends a portion of its ethical code – section A.12 – directly addressing the Internet as it relates to counseling [27]. ACA's position is that a growing body of evidence shows that cybercounseling can be effective, but that a counselor who engages with technology to provide services ought to become thoroughly conversant with the ethical and legal issues involved. For example, members of the ACA Ethics Revision Task Force (which updated the ACA Ethics code in 2005 from its prior 1995 version to directly address technology in counseling) cite crossing jurisdictional lines as one of the most significant legal challenges to ethical cybercounseling [21]; specifically, they note that most legal authorities believe that the state in which the client resides is the state in which cybercounseling occurs (regardless of the counselor's location). Therefore, it is wise to check with that state's licensing board to see whether the counselor needs to be licensed to practice in the client's state [28]. Conversely, one ought to verify whether one's own state of licensure/residence/practice has rules regarding out-of-state counseling.

If Ed were a physician, the American Medical Association (AMA), through its ethics code and policy statements, would also provide clear guidance on the use of the Internet in medical care. The AMA, in the Council on Ethical and Judicial Affairs (CEJA) opinion 5.026 (The Use of Electronic Mail) explicitly encourages e-mail communication between physicians and patients but cautions that the physician-patient relationship should not initially be created by e-mail but rather through more personal interactions [29, p. 131]. In tension with this rule, though, the very next opinion – 5.027, Use of Health-Related Online Sites – permits physicians to use interactive online websites to provide health information to people a physician does not already know, including individual advice, diagnosis, or therapeutic services; to do so requires that the website provide informed consent on the limitations of the electronic medium, as well as secure or encrypted technology if private patient information is to be transmitted [28, pp. 131-132].

In summary, statements by professional organizations may provide some assistance regarding issues to consider when making decisions regarding providing services online. We can also assume that any obligations that would hold for a patient seen in person would also apply for cyber-clients. The next issue to consider is what a professional who is online and encounters a non-patient who may be considering ending her or his own life (with or without assistance) must, or may, do. The situation becomes even more complicated when the person who is suffering may be making a well-reasoned decision that death is her or his best option. Because of the ambiguities present in these types of situations, it behooves the prudent practitioner to delve further in the literature for direction.

ETHICAL CODES, ORGANIZATIONAL STATEMENTS, AND ASSISTED OR RATIONAL SUICIDE

The Internet is ultimately just the medium through which the major ethical issue – whether and how Ed should help Alice with her struggle around suicide – will be played out. Alice and Ed each have to decide for themselves whether suicide is rational in Alice's situation and, if so, whether assistance (by someone other than Ed) is appropriate or necessary. Ed may hope to resolve his ethical dilemma by consulting the relevant professional ethics codes and examining his organization's stance on the issues of rational and assisted suicide as well as whether he has a duty to do anything if Alice is not his patient.

If Ed is a psychologist, the APA's ethical code [25] will not provide a precise answer to his question: the APA does not address suicide – assisted, rational, or irrational suicide -- directly in its ethical code [21,25]. Many psychologists believe that standard 4.05, on limitations to confidentiality, mandates breaking confidentiality if a client is suicidal but a close reading shows that this is a misunderstanding: "Psychologists disclose confidential information without the consent of the individual only as mandated by law, or where permitted by law for a valid purpose such as… [to] protect the client/patient, psychologist, or others from harm…." [25, p. 1066]. Notice that the passage does not say that psychologists *shall* disclose confidential information in all such circumstances, but rather that disclosing confidential information without the consent of the client/patient is permitted *only if* mandated or permitted by law. Thus, the APA ethics code *allows* but does not require intervention if the psychologist is concerned about someone's suicidal thoughts or behaviors.

Thoughts about rational or assisted suicide are a relatively unique type of suicidal ideation. To help the public understand the issues involved, the APA created a task force that issued a public statement on mental health considerations relevant to assisted suicide. The APA intentionally timed the release of the document to anticipate the U.S. Supreme Court's well-publicized rulings on the constitutionality of assisted suicide [30]. Subsequently, the APA established a Working Group on Assisted Suicide and End-of-Life Decisions ("Working Group"). In 2000, the Working Group submitted its Report to the Board of Directors of APA, which noted that motives for requesting assisted suicide are often psychological. Rather than primarily stemming from uncontrollable physical pain, such requests are often impacted by clinical depression, feelings of loss of control, issues with dependency or burdensomeness, or other nonphysical feelings of discomfort [31]. After considering the arguments for and against assisted suicide, the APA Resolution on Assisted Suicide took a position that was neither for nor against the issue, instead stating that assisted suicide is a complex issue on which reasonable people can differ [32].

The APA ethical code [25] is virtually silent on the issue of whether Ed has an ethical obligation to provide aid to a non-patient – either by offering professionally informed information, by giving aid in an emergency, or by taking Alice on as a patient. Standard 2.02 allows psychologists to provide services outside the boundaries of their competence if other mental health services are not available. However, the language used is permissive, not mandatory. Likewise, Ed could look to the five general principles of the code for guidance, though they also are aspirational rather than enforceable standards. Principle E, "Respect for People's Rights and Dignity," seems the most relevant, stating that all people have the right to self-determination, which might suggest that Alice's considered judgment about rational suicide should be respected by Ed. However, the following sentence specifically cautions Ed to employ "special safeguards" when people have "vulnerabilities [that] impair autonomous decision-making." [25, p. 1063]. Suicidal people often suffer from depression, which may impair their cognitive judgments, and Alice could also be considered by some to be vulnerable because of her physical condition. This suggests that if Ed engages with Alice online, he might pay particular attention to discovering whether she is receiving mental health care and whether she feels pressured by others to end her life. Still, the ethics code and associated documents do not address the specific situation being discussed herein, leaving it to Ed himself in the moment and through any subsequent consultation to identify and resolve the technology-related and assisted/rational suicide-related ethical and legal dilemmas involved in establishing a professional relationship with Alice online.

If Ed belongs to the ACA instead of the APA, his organization similarly does not take a position for or against assisted or rational suicide. However, it does address end-of-life care for terminally ill clients directly in section A.9 of its ethical code [27]; the 2005 revision of the ACA code of ethics added section A.9 to deal with the issue head-on [33]. If appropriate given the particular situation and the applicable state's laws, the code allows counselors to break a client's confidentiality, or not, if that client is considering hastening his or her own death. This would apply in a true emergency situation, for example if Ed found out through e-mail that Alice were imminently in danger of dying by suicide. In non-emergency situations, the code expressly allows counselors to either choose not to work with potential clients or to refer out current clients who struggle with terminal illness; appropriate reasons are varied and include a lack of competence in end-of-life issues or even personal or moral issues working with such clients. Essentially, this gives Ed permission to engage or not engage with Alice however he chooses, though of course if she were his patient and he did not believe he could provide appropriate services any more, he would need to terminate therapy in an appropriate fashion and give referrals to other mental health professionals. The ACA code, however, fails to address how the above concerns should be addressed with a non-patient encountered on the Internet, leaving Ed with little guidance in such a situation.

Like the ACA, if Ed were a medical doctor, his professional organization is crystal clear that unless it is an emergency, physicians "shall... be free to choose whom to serve." [29, p. xv]. Therefore the AMA allows Ed to take Alice on as a patient, or not, entirely within his own personal discretion, which could mean that Ed has no obligations to provide any assistance to Alice. Furthermore, the AMA is quite directive on the issue of assisted suicide. In contrast to the ethical codes of counselors or psychologists, the AMA takes a firm stance in CEJA opinion 2.211 ("Physician-Assisted Suicide") against physician assisted suicide (PAS) [29, p. 96]. The AMA views assisted suicide as inconsistent with the physician's role as a healer and suggests that requests for PAS should be viewed as signals that the patient's needs are not adequately being met. Instead of PAS, opinion 2.211 advocates for more effective education on pain management techniques, increased reliance on hospice care, and multidisciplinary interventions by pastoral counselors, family counselors, or specialty consultants. The American Nurses Association, the American Psychiatric Association, and the National Hospice and Palliative Care Organization each followed the lead of the AMA and took similarly clear anti-assisted suicide positions; however, the National Association of Social Workers, similar to the ACA, took an approach that maximizes the self-determination of the patient and therefore would allow a client to end her or his life through rational or assisted suicide [34].

Based on this review, it appears as if Ed probably does not have a professional, ethical obligation to try to help Alice. This could end the matter. However, if he were to get involved he would want to take the perspective of his professional organization in to account, even if he were to try to interact not as a professional but as another human being. Neither the APA nor ACA documents would direct him to try to talk her out of her suicidal thoughts but following the AMA guidance would lead him to try to prevent her from taking any action. Assuming, for the sake of continuing the discussion, that Ed decides he wants to try to be of assistance to Alice, we next discuss some of the issues he may want to consider when interacting with Alice.

Empirical Literature, Consultation, and Self-Examination

Laws and ethical codes are not the only places that modern professionals can look for guidance. Ed can also search the empirical literature to see what research suggests are appropriate factors to take into consideration given Alice's situation. Several authors have suggested practical guidelines, checklists, and flow charts that professionals can use when confronted with a patient considering rational or assisted suicide [16,35,36]. Recent reviews provide a bibliography of psychiatric, palliative care, and terminal illness research within the last decade [37] as well as an overview of terminally ill patients' self-perceived burdensomeness to others and its impact on treatment decisions by family caregivers and physicians [38]. Ed would also want to familiarize himself with the medical realities of Alice's situation by reading current literature regarding ALS as well as any available case studies in which a patient with ALS wanted to die [39].

We also recommend that, time permitting, Ed consult with people knowledgeable about ALS, online communication, and rational/assisted suicide [16]. This will be especially important because it is likely that Ed's values will have an impact on how he feels, thinks, and responds [40]. He will need to examine his own values regarding rational and assisted suicide, therapeutic relationships, and on-line communication. As noted earlier, although no legal or ethical obligation exists for Ed in the case in which Alice is not his patient, he may still decide to establish a helping relationship based on his personal ethics and moral values. Thus, an extensive process of self-questioning and self-examination is recommended regardless of the nature of the relationship between Alice and Ed.

Initiating Mental Health Treatment Online

Without focusing on the issues associated with rational or assisted suicide, for the moment, in the case that Ed decides to establish and maintain a treatment relationship with Alice online, he would need to consider a number of relevant issues. If Ed decides to enter into a treatment relationship with Alice, he must first determine whether he is licensed to practice in the state in which Alice resides – otherwise he risks practicing outside the scope of his license [41]. This requires that Ed inquire about Alice's current state of residence. He would also need to obtain information regarding Alice's age, real name, telephone number, and address for record-keeping purposes (although asking for this information in the context of a discussion about rational/assisted suicide could lead Alice to be suspicious of Ed's motives).

Assuming that Ed is licensed in her state of residence it may be ethically defensible for him to treat her in an online modality. If Ed decides to treat Alice through the Internet, he can take solace from the fact that electronic communication is gaining credence in treatment of a variety of serious disorders. Daily thought records e-mailed to the treating psychiatrist have shown promise in case study reports for recovering addicts [42], and daily e-mail contact has allowed anorexic patients to share their mood and calorie intake without unduly impinging on the psychiatrist's time [43]. In order to keep e-mail interactions manageable, Ed should establish clear expectations with Alice so that most daily e-mails she sends will not require a response between online therapy sessions.

Utilizing different subject headings, such as "daily journal" for ordinary e-mails and "urgent" for those requiring a response, can also help Ed manage his inbox. Given her issues, he would need to be clear about what she should do in an emergency and what his response may be if he is concerned about her safety [21]. Ed also ought to remind Alice of the limitations of e-mail as a secure medium and give her a good sense of the ordinary times when he checks his e-mail each day. Finally, as an electronic communication about protected health information (PHI), e-mail falls under the auspices of the Health Insurance Portability and Accountability Act (HIPAA), so it is required that Ed give Alice a notice of privacy practices detailing how her PHI will be handled [44].

E-mail is not the only medium that Ed could use to treat Alice. Other electronic media that have been used in similar ways by psychiatrists and psychotherapists include Internet relay chat ("instant messaging" through use of ICQ, AOL, Facebook, or other providers), text messaging (through cell phones), video conferencing, and sharing media such as video, pictures, or graphics [45]. The Internet also can serve an important role in providing consultation and support for the mental health professional through the use of listservs. Assuming that Alice's identifying information is not provided, using listservs could allow Ed to consult with knowledgeable peers throughout the country or the world [46]. Finally, if at some point in treatment it should become important for Ed to be able to see and hear Alice, inexpensive webcams are now widely available and adequate bandwidth to transmit video and audio through the Internet has become affordable for the average practitioner, although he would have to take into account Alice's financial situation before attempting to integrate such technology into the professional relationship.

Although electronic therapy undoubtedly provides benefits in terms of convenience, record-keeping, and access to specialists who are geographically distant, it also imposes costs by making potentially sensitive medical information more available to third parties. When Alice sends an e-mail to Ed, a copy of the information is stored on Alice's Internet service provider's (ISP) server, as well as on the Ed's ISP's server. If the e-mail is not encrypted, ISP employees could access and read confidential communications between Alice and Ed. Usually this does not violate the terms of commercial ISP's contracts with consumers; and even if Ed were to contract for additional confidentiality with his ISP, the fact that Ed might have a breach of contract claim against his ISP is of little consolation to Alice when her confidential medical information has been exposed.

In addition, both Ed and Alice need to be aware that e-mails from dominant market providers of e-mail are not encrypted; neither are university-provided e-mail accounts unless VPN technology is provided and utilized. Although not apparently the case here, it is worth noting that a further complication is added when patients e-mail about their mental health from a computer at their workplace. Most employers have policies that prohibit or severely limit the use of workplace computers for personal use, and virtually all retain the right to inspect their employees' communications from a workplace computer. Courts have found that sending e-mail from a workplace computer destroys the sender's expectation of privacy and have even abrogated the attorney-client privilege when a hospital printed copies of e-mails from a physician to his lawyer about a lawsuit against that very hospital-employer [47]. Often, therefore, it is incumbent upon the mental health professional to educate relatively naïve patients about the limitations to confidentiality dependent upon the e-mail account and origin of their electronic communication.

In addition to using e-mail and other online communication as the medium through which to establish a professional relationship with Alice, Ed could also make use of the educational potential offered by the Internet. Nine out of ten physicians use the Internet for clinical purposes and nearly a third of physicians have their own online website [48]. More than a third of Americans look for health care information online at least three times a month, over 90% found the health care information they obtained online to be useful, and that information influenced their health care treatment decisions almost half the time [49]. There are at least 100,000 health-related websites available, with 1500 more being added each month; about six million Americans look for health advice online each day [50].

Although much of the information online can be beneficial, some of it is dangerous. What might be needed to make the Internet a helpful rather than a harmful source of mental health information is some guidance for the user. For example, peer moderation of discussion boards at universities has shown promise in guiding users toward quality health information [51]. Likewise, online mentoring for mentally, emotionally, or physically challenged youth seemed to help teenagers learn to use the Internet more effectively as well as promote psychosocial development and online friendships [52]. To return to our case of Ed and Alice, if Ed is able to point Alice toward reliable, quality Internet sites that could deepen Alice's understanding of her mental, physical, and emotional health possibilities, he would thereby reduce the dangers of the Internet and increase the likelihood that the Internet would help Alice find meaningfulness in her life. This would require an investment of time on Ed's part, as he would need to become familiar with both helpful and harmful Internet sites, and he would need to ask Alice what sites she regularly connects with.

The above issues related to effective and ethical use of the Internet and online counseling need to be extended in the case of working with a person who may be considering rational or assisted suicide. Of course, the primary issue is that the person may decide to go ahead with a decision to end her or his life at any point during the course of the counseling. Although this may happen during in-person therapy, the dangers are heightened in online situations for all the reasons outlined earlier (e.g., lack of nonverbal cues). Non-chronically/non-terminally ill individuals have been encouraged to kill themselves via e-mail and other forms of online communication [53] and there are case examples detailing the support that such individuals have been given by others who view such a situation as one of rational suicide [16]. Given those facts, a therapist who knows that his or her patient has suicidal thoughts and that the patient is discussing them with others online must be very careful to follow risk management suggestions throughout treatment [20,21]. The fact that everything leaves a written record can be a source of solace or doom for the professional. On one hand there is thorough documentation of what actually happened but, on the other hand, without contemporaneous documentation by the professional about what was intended and thought of but not tried, anyone sitting in judgment will be left with a potentially stark dialogue that leaves much room for inferring other things the professional could or should have done if the client is injured or dies as a result of a suicidal action. As noted earlier, consultation (and documentation of the consultation) is crucial to establish that the professional lived up to the standard of care.

If a professional decides to engage in an online discussion about rational or assisted suicide as a legitimate option for the patient, ideally the professional would enter into an explicit written agreement with the patient regarding the purposes of treatment. That contract would outline the type of discussion/evaluation that will take place, the responsibilities of the patient and professional, and the potential responses of the professional given the circumstances (e.g., calling the police, or not) [35]. This would be different than "no-suicide contracts" utilized by many professionals despite the absence of evidence for their efficacy [54]. Rather, the purpose of the agreement would be to achieve maximum clarity about the intentions and limits of the risky endeavor in which the professional and the patient are agreeing to be engaged. The professional could then engage in a thorough review of the issues experienced by the ill person; he or she would want to independently verify the person's factual claims to the utmost degree possible. Strategies for independent confirmation would include requesting medical records and obtaining signed releases to confer with others in the person's life, including loved ones and professional care providers. A thorough set of issues to consider when discussing end-of-life decisions was developed by the APA Working Group [55] and others have published additional categorizations of psychosocial issues relevant to end-of-life decision-making [56]. We wish to note that the professional should only engage in this discussion if she or he can genuinely allow the person to consider all options and, after a thorough evaluation, perhaps even select death as the best option. If the professional's values would never permit the client to make such a choice, the professional owes it to the client to be clear about that up front, rather than after pretending to consider an alternative that the professional would never permit the client to choose.

CONCLUSION

The Internet as a source of unparalleled breadth and ease of access to mental health information is not going away. Although formal ethical codes offer some guidance to mental health professionals engaged in adjunctive or primary online therapy, an ethical professional still needs to invest time and energy in familiarizing himself or herself with the variety of high- and low-quality websites that patients are likely to encounter. Assisted and rational suicide remain ethically uncertain terrain for professionals, with the AMA taking a firm stance against assisted suicide but APA and ACA allowing members to engage in discussions about options with clients. Legally, the situation is more clear, because assisted suicide is only explicitly legal in one U.S. state, and deliberately encouraging another person to die by suicide is a crime in some states [57] and possibly a breach of federal conspiracy, fraud, or computer access laws [58,59]. However, courts have given no indication that participating in a discussion with a patient about suicide as an option would be likely to trigger the application of any such laws, regardless of whether the person is engaged in face-to-face or online therapy.

Mental health professionals may feel ethically obligated to provide helpful information to non-patients online considering suicide, but they should be careful to limit the extent and specificity of their online interactions so that they do not inadvertently create a professional relationship. If there is such a relationship, care must be taken to adhere to the standard of professional care in the community, and confidentiality should be ensured through the use of encrypted e-mail or communication through a secure website. Finally, an ethical professional engaging in online mental health treatment should become familiar with common suicide-related websites that patients are likely to access [60,61], in order to help the patient access high-quality online health educational materials instead of naïve blanket support for an expressed wish to die.

REFERENCES

[1] Simon RI, Levenson JL, Shuman DW: On sound and unsound mind: the role of suicide in tort and insurance litigation. *J Am Acad Psychiatry Law* 2005; 33:176-182.

[2] Hendin H, Foley K: Physician-assisted suicide in Oregon: a medical perspective. *Mich Law Rev* 2008; 106:1613-1639.

[3] Tucker KL, Steele FB: Patient choice at the end of life: getting the language right. *J Leg Med* 2007; 28:305-325.

[4] Westefeld JS, Sikes C, Ansley T, Yi H-S: Attitudes toward rational suicide. *J Loss & Trauma* 2004; 9:359-370.

[5] Werth JL, Holdwick DJ: A primer on rational suicide and other forms of hastened death. *The Counseling Psychologist* 2000; 28:511-539.

[6] Rogers JR, Guelette CM, Abbey-Hines J, Carney JV, Werth JL: Rational suicide: an empirical investigation of counselor attitudes. *J Counseling & Development* 2001; 79:365-372.

[7] Quill TE, Lo B, Brock DW: Palliative options of last resort: a comparison of voluntarily stopping eating and drinking, terminal sedation, physician-assisted suicide, and voluntary active euthanasia, in *Giving Death a Helping Hand: Physician Assisted Death and Public Policy.* Edited by Birnbacher D, Dahl E. Berlin, Springer, 2008, pp 49-64.

[8] Ganzini L, Dahl E: Physician-assisted suicide in Oregon, in *Giving Death a Helping Hand: Physician Assisted Death and Public Policy*. Edited by Birnbacher D, Dahl E. Berlin, Springer, 2008, pp 67-75.

[9] Rothschild A: Physician-assisted death: an Australian perspective, in *Giving Death a Helping Hand: Physician Assisted Death and Public Policy.* Edited by Birnbacher D, Dahl E. Berlin, Springer, 2008, pp 97-112.

[10] Griffiths J: Physician-assisted suicide in the Netherlands and Belgium, in *Giving Death a Helping Hand: Physician Assisted Death and Public Policy.* Edited by Birnbacher D, Dahl E. Berlin, Springer, 2008, pp 77-86.

[11] Guillod O, Schmidt A: Assisted suicide under Swiss law. *Eur J Health Law* 2005; 12:25-38.

[12] Baezner-Sailer EM: Physician-assisted suicide in Switzerland: a personal report, in *Giving Death a Helping Hand: Physician Assisted Death and Public Policy.* Edited by Birnbacher D, Dahl E. Berlin, Springer, 2008, pp 141-148.

[13] Kaldjian LC, Jekel JF, Bernene JL, Rosenthal GE, Vaughan-Sarrazin M, Duffy TP: Should disagreement about physician-assisted suicide discourage professional societies from engaging in public debate? A survey of 677 Connecticut internists. *Connecticut Medicine* 2002; 66:603-609.

[14] Stevens KR: Emotional and psychological effects of physician-assisted suicide and euthanasia on participating physicians. Issues in Law & Medicine 2006; 21:187-200.

[15] Barber ME, Marzuk PM, Leon AC, Portera L: Gate questions in psychiatric interviewing: the case of suicide assessment. *J Psychiatr Res* 2001; 35:67-69.

[16] Richard J, Werth JL, Rogers JR: Rational and assisted suicidal communication on the Internet: a case example and discussion of ethical and practice issues. *Ethics & Behavior* 2000; 10:215-238.

[17] Slovenko R: "Special relationships." *J Psychiatry & Law* 2006; 34:109-118.

[18] Williams K: Physicians as good Samaritans: some empirical evidence concerning emergency medical treatment in Britain. *J Law & Society* 2003; 30:258-282.

[19] Dyer SG: Is there a duty?: limiting college and university liability for student suicide. *Mich Law Rev* 2008; 106:1379-1403.

[20] Slovenko R: Malpractice, non-medical negligence, or breach of contract. *J Psychiatry & Law* 2005; 33:445-467.

[21] Werth JL Jr, Welfel ER, Benjamin GAH (Eds.): *The Duty to Protect: Ethical, legal, and Professional Considerations for Mental Health Professionals*. Washington, D.C.: American Psychological Association, 2009.

[22] Dute J: Medical malpractice liability: no easy solutions. *Eur J Health Law* 2003; 10:85-90.
[23] Baker KD: A doctor's legal duty – erosion of the curbside consult. *FDCC Quarterly* 2002; 52:393-408.
[24] Bongar B: *The Suicidal Patient: Clinical and Legal Standards of Care.* Washington, D.C.: American Psychological Association, 2002.
[25] American Psychological Association: Ethical principles of psychologists and code of conduct. *American Psychologist* 2002; 57:1060-1073.
[26] American Psychological Association (APA) *Ethics Committee: APA statement on services by telephone, teleconferencing, and Internet.* 1997; Available at: http://www.apa.org/ethics/stmnt01.html. Accessed June 26, 2008.
[27] American Counseling Association (ACA): *ACA code of ethics.* 2005; Available at: http://www.counseling.org/Resources/CodeOfEthics/TP/Home/CT2.aspx. Accessed August 14, 2008.
[28] Kaplan D: Ethical use of technology in counseling. *Counseling Today* 2006: 49:11,43.
[29] American Medical Association, Council on Ethical and Judicial Affairs: Code of Medical Ethics of the American Medical Association: *Current Opinions with Annotations*. Chicago, IL: American Medical Association, 2006.
[30] APA Working Group on Assisted Suicide and End-of-Life Decisions: *Introduction to the report from APA working group on assisted suicide and end-of-life decisions.* 2000; Available at: http://www.apa.org/pi/aseol/introduction.html. Accessed August 14, 2008.
[31] APA Working Group on Assisted Suicide and End-of-Life Decisions: *Section 3 of the report from APA working group on assisted suicide and end-of-life decisions.* 2000; Available at: http://www.apa.org/pi/aseol/section3.html. Accessed August 14, 2008.
[32] American Psychological Association: APA Council resolution on assisted suicide. 2001; Available at: http://www.apa.org/ppo/issues/asresolu.html. Accessed August 14, 2008.
[33] Kocet, MM: Ethical challenges in a complex world: highlights of the 2005 ACA code of ethics. *J Counseling & Developmen*t 2006; 84:228-234.
[34] Werth JL: The appropriateness of organizational positions on assisted suicide. *Ethics & Behavior* 2000; 10:239-255.
[35] Werth JL: Mental health professionals and assisted death: perceived ethical obligations and proposed guidelines for practice. *Ethics & Behavior* 1999; 9:159-183.
[36] Emanuel LL: Facing requests for physician-assisted suicide: toward a practical and principled clinical skill set. *JAMA* 1998; 280:643-647.
[37] Chochinov HM: Dying, dignity, and new horizons in palliative end-of-life care. CA: A *Cancer Journal for Clinicians* 2006; 56:84-103.
[38] McPherson CJ, Wilson KG, Murray MA: Feeling like a burden to others: a systematic review focusing on the end of life. *Palliative Medicine* 2007; 21:115-128.
[39] Appel SH: Euthanasia and physician-assisted suicide in ALS: a commentary. *Am J Hospice & Palliative Medicine* 2004; 21:405-406.
[40] Corey G, Corey M, Callanan P: *Issues and Ethics in the Helping Professions.* Belmont, CA: Thomson Brooks Cole, 2007.
[41] Mallen MJ, Vogel DL, Rochlen AB: The practical aspects of online counseling: ethics, training, technology, and competency. *The Counseling Psychologist* 2005; 33:776-818.

[42] Collins B, McAllister MS, Ford DB: Patient-provider e-mail communication as an adjunctive tool in addiction medicine. *J Addict Dis* 2007; 26:45-52.

[43] Yager, J: E-mail therapy for anorexia nervosa: prospects and limitations. *European Eating Disorders Review* 2003; 11:198-209.

[44] Mermelstein HT, Wallack JJ: Confidentiality in the age of HIPAA: a challenge for psychosomatic medicine. *Psychosomatics* 2008; 49:97-103.

[45] Coyle D, Doherty G, Matthews M, Sharry J: Computers in talk-based mental health interventions. *Interacting with Computers* 2007; 19:545-572.

[46] Collins LH: Practicing safer listserv use: ethical use of an invaluable resource. *Professional Psychology: Research & Practice* 2007; 38:690-698.

[47] Journal of Internet Law: Workplace e-mail destroyed attorney-client privilege. *J Internet Law* 2008; February:21.

[48] Bovi AM: Use of health-related online sites. *Am J Bioethics* 2003; 3:W48-W52. Available at: http://www.bioethics.net/journal/j_article.php?aid=86. Accessed August 17, 2008.

[49] Blumenthal D: Doctors in a wired world: can professionalism survive connectivity? *Milbank Quarterly* 2002; 80:525-546.

[50] Lewis CE: My computer, my doctor: a constitutional call for federal regulation of cybermedicine. *Am J Law & Medicine* 2006; 32:585-609.

[51] Richards D, Tangney B: An informal online learning community for student mental health at university: a preliminary investigation. *British J Guidance & Counselling* 2008; 36:81-97.

[52] Shpigelman CN, Reiter S, Weiss PLT: E-mentoring for youth with special needs: preliminary results. *CyberPsychology & Behavior* 2008; 11:196-200.

[53] Mishara BL, Weisstub DN: Ethical, legal, and practical issues in the control and regulation of suicide promotion and assistance over the internet. *Suicide & Life-Threatening Behavior* 2007; 37:58-65.

[54] Rudd MD, Mandrusiak M, Joiner TE: The case against no-suicide contracts: the commitment to treatment statement as a practice alternative. *Journal of Clinical Psychology: In Session* 2006; 62:243-251.

[55] APA Working Group on Assisted Suicide and End-of-Life Decisions: *Appendix F of the report from APA working group on assisted suicide and end-of-life decisions.* 2000; Available at: http://www.apa.org/pi/aseol/appendixf.html. Accessed September 16, 2008.

[56] Werth JL, Gordon JR, Johnson RR: Psychosocial issues near the end of life. *Aging & Mental Health* 2002; 6:402-412.

[57] Mazzarella WP: When a client makes a threat: lawyers face a confidentiality dilemma when they know of a client's ongoing or threatened criminal conduct. *California Bar Journal* 2008; August:10-11.

[58] Weiss DC: Legal theory used in MySpace suicide criminalizes website lies [news release]. *American Bar Journal;* May 19, 2008. http://abajournal.com/news/legal_theory_used_in_ myspace_suicide_criminalizes_website_lies/. Accessed August 20, 2008.

[59] Neil M: Friend's mom charged with fraud over MySpace cyberbullying suicide [news release]. *American Bar Journal;* May 15, 2008. http://abajournal.com/news/friends_

mom_charged_with_ fraud_over_myspace_cyberbullying_suicide/. Accessed August 20, 2008.

[60] Recupero P, Harms S, Noble J: Surfing for suicide information on the internet. *J Clin Psychiatry* 2008; 69:878-888.

[61] Biddle L, Donovan J, Hawton K, Kapur H, Gunnell D: Suicide and the internet. *BMJ* 2008; 336:800-802.

In: Internet and Suicide
Editors: L. Sher and A. Vilens

ISBN 978-1-60741-077-5

Chapter 26

CAN SUICIDE BE QUANTIFIED AND CATEGORIZED?

Said Shahtahmasebi
The Good Life Research Centre Trust, Rangiora. North Canterbury, New Zealand

ABSTRACT

There has been some concern about the influence of the media (including the internet, the reporting of and the portrayal of suicide in the entertainment industry) on suicidal behaviour. The internet is hailed as the information super highway, which provides an uncontrolled media environment. With its ever increasing popularity, it is not surprising that the spotlight is on the internet as a medium with particular reference to suicidal behaviour. However, the evidence suggests that despite the huge amount of literature on suicide we still know very little about suicide. And as frustrated researchers we tend to interpret any red herring as a new lead. For too long studies of human behaviour have been viewed as cause and effect thus researchers have been examining the probability of an effect from an identified cause. Studies of this kind have no doubt influenced policy. But, there is evidence that poor methodology and a lack of attention to substantive and statistical issues behind such studies may have inadvertently made researchers, policy makers and the public part of the problem. Whilst western societies advocate "freedom", our solutions often involve the opposite. We lock up patients and force treatment (often a cocktail of medications) onto them, and encourage health practitioners to prescribe anti-depressants for symptoms resembling depression, when often what is required is to simply listen. We treat suicide as depression. In this chapter I discuss some of the relevant issues in studying human behaviour which will also include researchers, practitioners and the media. For example, because the processes of belonging to a society is often ignored the internet is yet another red herring pursued by researchers. Thus, if suicide is viewed as a process of decision making then the internet is merely another information tool which is developed and managed, facilitated and utilised by the society.

INTRODUCTION

Like most studies of this type, the research is divided over the relationship between suicide and the internet. Some authors recommend the utilization of the internet to prevent/intervene suicide[1,2], some claim insufficient evidence to warrant a causal association[3] whilst others appear to presume an indirect causality as the reason to investigate the internet[4,5]. Recently the BMJ published an article on suicide and the internet[4] supposedly to demonstrate the ease with which methods of suicide can be accessed. It appears that this publication has helped raise issues of methodology, ethical, substance (see Rapid Responses to Biddle et al. http://www.bmj.com/cgi/eletters/336/7648/800). It further appears that the BMJ, a well respected source in the public mindset, was being quoted by the popular media with sensationalised headlines on suicide and the internet. Rather ironic behaviour from researchers and publishers at a time when they themselves have been scrutinising the media and calling for responsible reporting[6-9]. Therefore, in attempting for a wider dissemination the researchers have unleashed the full force of the popular media to publicise the internet as a source to verify and search for new methods of terminating one's own life. As a result of such publications and the ensuing publicity a proportion of the public will be exposed to the web for suicide information purely to satisfy their curiosity. This is very similar to the smoking prevention policies of various governments where the actions of the antismoking camp (mainly based on uncritical use of the 'evidence') draw undue attention to tobacco smoking – reducing the need for advertising by the grateful tobacco manufacturers[10].

There is much talk about the influences of media on suicidal behaviour and that the media should be regulated for responsible reporting and portrayal of suicide. The common perception is that the discussion of suicide in the public domain will lead to more suicide (e.g see [4,11]; Also see Rapid Responses to Biddle et al. [4] http://www.bmj.com/cgi/eletters/336/7648/800). The gravity of concern about public discussion of suicide by the authorities and government departments is better demonstrated by the coverage of suicide by a broadsheet newspaper in New Zealand in 2005[12]. To generate a debate and discussion, the newspaper published names and a summary of a coroner's report for ten suicide cases which had been before the coroner's court at that time. From the ensuing letters and report from suicide survivors and practitioners there were no clear conclusions about the role of the media but the messages that were emphasized included depression and mental illness, and that men should seek help. The newspaper omitted methods of suicide from the case histories and coroner's report. One would assume the newspaper's action as courageous and noble, albeit, a one off act. But, it is the media itself that, by playing politics and the rating game, fuel the creation of sub-cultures and in doing so publicise suicide and provide free airtime and a platform to pro-suicide groups e.g. see [http://www.scoop.co.nz/multimedia/tv/national/10243.html]. Now, the concern appears to be over the utilisation of the methods of suicide which is reported in the news media or portrayed fictionally. So much so that suicide has become taboo. It has become "that thing that should not be mentioned". Interestingly, the guidelines from the New Zealand Suicide Prevention Strategy published in the same edition of the newspaper advised the public if they are worried about someone to call a mental health care team or a psychiatric unit. This is all very well. However, the two main issues often ignored are: what do individuals' look for in a treatment; and what do the practitioners offer as treatment if an individual were to seek help?

We seem to make a lot of assumptions about what the suicide survivors need in order to deal with their loss, especially not knowing the reason why their loved one committed suicide. In response, researchers and practitioners assume cause, which is impossible to know as the only person who can provide the answers is deceased. Some may argue that various study methods and populations such as psychological autopsy and study of attempters has provided evidence of a cause and effect e.g. mental illness and suicide[13]. However, as discussed elsewhere [14,12,15] such studies have often relied on the views of others (friends and family) who to all intent and purposes had no idea about the case's intentions until after the event. Furthermore, their views and perceptions are often attenuated and influenced by the general assumptions promoted by the medical model. That is, the immediate assumption by association that suicide is caused by depression and mental illness. Critically, it is not the information gathered in this way that is faulty, but the use of it and failure to account for various observed and unobserved relationships that causes faulty research and thus make the wrong conclusion.

On the other hand, our ignorance of the dynamics of human behaviour has led researchers, practitioners and policy makers down a slippery track that seeks to impose limitations and restrictions on the public. We can not with any certainty assume that the suicides following a broadcast were specifically related to the media. There is evidence to suggest that those with an intention to die may switch between methods of suicide. Therefore, if a case was exposed to a broadcast of suicide prior to completing suicide this maybe coincidental and that the inevitable would have happened anyway. The flipside of the coin is that we are unable to ascertain what proportion of suicide cases may have planned their intentions prior to the television broadcast, what proportion changed their plans and switched methods due to the broadcast, and what proportion planned their intentions after the broadcast? And the fact that research appears to look for the usage of a suicide method broadcasted in the media may in itself explain the higher incidence of suicide using the reported method. This is similar to the conclusion reported by the Doncaster Public Health Intelligence Unit on limiting access to co-proxamol e.g. see [15]. Despite the data showing a decrease in usage before the policy implementation with an increase after the policy was implemented, the report bases its conclusion on the final time point, which was down only to the pre policy implementation level anyway, to suggest that their policy of limiting access had affected a decrease in suicides using co-proxamol.

Studies e.g.[4,5] and policies that attempt to cut off public access to information on the methods/tools of suicide, or treat suicide for depression e.g.[13,21,23] do not properly address suicide. These are mere attempts to cut off access to the methods/tools of suicide, and, are reminiscent of a comedy sketch by the Two Ronnies (a very popular BBC programme in the 70s and 80s):-

> "...since most accidents occur at home, the Royal Society for the Prevention of Accidents advise you to move!"

By the same token, the media's restricted and restrained reporting of suicide coupled with authoritative preventional policies applying control may have the same effect as prohibition such as those observed with adolescent smoking [10,16]. It appears that the proponent of a medical model often locked in a self righteous bubble advocating control continue to miss the point: Biddle et al's [4] concern appears to stem from an assumption that people who are intent on suicide will easily search the internet for methods. This is a very ill-considered assumption by experienced and leading researchers. We do not really know how those intent on suicide think or behave. We may guess, but our guesses are based on the recall of others e.g. family, friends and relatives. On the other hand, the main issue is not for individuals specifically searching the internet for suicide but the accidental exposure by an unsuspecting public of all ages. One of the points raised by the commentaries:

[http://www.bmj.com/cgi/eletters/336/7648/800] was that opponents of suicide should optimize their web pages with search engines. But, optimization of web pages is not exclusive to opponents, by the same token proponents of suicide may have already achieved it to get their message across, e.g. euthanasia groups and assisted-suicide supporters. Of similar concern is the increasing likelihood of exposure of children (and others) to undesirable web pages purely by accident using an innocent search term. It is high time to think of suicide prevention in societal terms as opposed to controlling its individual members. In this chapter I discuss suicide in the context of human behaviour and the process of decision making in relation to the Internet.

The Internet, Media and Suicide

I am not an avid user of the internet but I am aware that it is unregulated and that under the notion of freedom of expression and information any textual or graphic expression of any quality can be found. The trick is obviously knowing where or how to search. Indeed, the internet is commonly being promoted and established in the public mindset as the source of information. At schools, pupils of all ages are taught to search the internet for answers to research questions. From an academic point of view, this poor practice has diminished the skills of query about the quality of information. As a result few people double check their findings through the use of the library and its resources (e.g. journals & books). The biggest problem is, of course, the absence of a critical judgement by users. The lack of, or difficulty to regulate the quality of information has made it possible for text of any quality to be searched and absorbed.

Therefore, whilst the media may appear to exercise self regulation and rely on the guidelines set by the relevant authorities, the fictional portrayal of suicide (through the entertainment industry) and information reported on the internet are much more individual specific i.e. based on the personal belief of the person who created the webpage. Bearing this in mind, a Google search of the internet using the keyword "suicide" yielded 99,600,000 hits. Using Yahoo and the same keyword yielded 281,000,000 hits for suicide. In comparison, using the same keyword, a search of peer reviewed and scholarly articles such as Medline (PubMed) and Google Scholar yielded 45,890 and 1,190,000 hits respectively. Are we to assume, as the researchers before us [4,5] have, that a distressed suicidal individual would be sifting through such a huge volume of 'information' seeking out their intended results?

The first few pages of search results from Google and Yahoo were quite similar but not the same. My intention of the internet search was not to examine and evaluate the search results however, the first few pages appeared to be on suicide prevention with one for suicide with the word "euthanasia" plainly visible in the search result. The first and only page on method was the 49th on page 5 graphically describing the top ten methods, how to carry out a suicide, their effectiveness and the consequences of failure. The page carried a warning that the list contained adult content and images! Such warnings often used in the entertainment industry are ridiculous; they seem to suggest that it is all right for adults to behave antisocially. There is a very strong feedback effect from such mentality. Trawling through results from a search performed by the researchers e.g. see [4,5] appear laborious and disconcerting at the best of times let alone for a specific reason as suicide. Authors who pursue studies involving searching the internet[4,5] render their research useless by ignoring practice (behaviour) and placing themselves above the public i.e. practicing a top-down approach. Due to the optimisation adopted by most web pages a logical and well thought out search strategy may result in a huge number of hits whilst an accidental or less logical but more commonsense search terms may result in more successful hits first time. For example, as suggested above if using the search strategy suggested by the authors e.g. [4,5] such as variations of 'suicide methods', persons experiencing suicidal behaviour would have to logically choose a search strategy and then would have to patiently analyse the results to find what they were looking for. On the contrary, assuming the suicidal individuals do consult the internet for advice, a stressed suicidal person may perform an internet search using the media's contribution e.g. "Dr death" and "New Zealand" and "euthanasia". A google search using these terms in combination yielded 1650 hits, and when further restricting the search by adding "video" it produced 603 very relevant hits with the highly relevant material on the first page of the search results. Note that the term "New Zealand" was added because the search was done outside of New Zealand, however, at the time of writing/producing this chapter the New Zealand media had made a big issue of "Dr Death" – see later.

Within the suicide literature, despite the large volume of work, criticisms have been aired that our knowledge of suicide is based on scant scientific evidence[17-19]. The study design and the quality of data have been cited as being responsible for the ambiguities in the evidence. One of the consequences of accepting this relationship to explain suicide is to concentrate on building a case that would associate the suicide case with mental illness. And given the public mindset it would be only too easy to suggest a link to mental illness after the event. For example, in suicide research Beautrais[13,20,21] claims that depression and mental illness are the cause of suicide, Khan et al[22] claim that antidepressants do not reduce suicide and may increase the risk of suicide while Hall et al[23] claim that antidepressants reduce suicide rates. The latter study compared the first point in the time series with the last point which happened to be lower than the first point and did not make much of the upward trend of suicide rates in between. Suicide data, in particular those based on psychological autopsy type investigations such as Beautrais[13,20,21], are often plagued with a high degree of bias and the confounding and compounding of random effects with the structural error such as error-in-variables. Given the current public mindset, helped by the medical model and the media, that depression causes suicide, the collection of data on suicide cases after the event from friends and relatives will be highly biased towards mental ill-health as in the Canterbury Suicide Project[13,20,21]. These studies have failed to address the methodological issues related to design, data collection and analysis thus resulting in misleading conclusions. *Uncritical* use of this type of information as evidence to inform practice will lead to a disparity in service development and delivery. While, some practitioners will adopt, only a few may exercise caution. For example, the NZ Medical Journal claims depression is a common, serious and significant illness and links it to suicide and recommends medication [http://www.nzma.org.nz/journal/117-1206/1200/]. It is not surprising to hear that young people have been prescribed antidepressants including preschool children. But more alarming is the prescribing of antidepressants to some children under a year old [http://www.nzherald.co.nz/section/1/story.cfm?c_id=1&objectid=10462684]. It seems to me that, as a result, if discovered early enough, suicide is commonly treated as depression regardless of the circumstances (also see Shahtahmasebi 2008 [15]).

It is this ambiguity in the literature, possibly due to poor study design, inappropriate methodology and inadequate statistical and analytical methods[24,10], that encourages an elective approach to decision making where decisions are made subjectively and the evidence to support them is sought after policy implementation (also see Short[25]). There is also ample anecdotal evidence to suggest that such an elective modelling approach encourages policies that artificially tackle an outcome i.e. in effect manipulating outcome(s) rather than attending to the associated parameters.

Putting aside the BMJ's (the British Medical Journal) motives for publication, the study [4] suffers from the same ambiguity. The assumption behind the study lacks an in-depth understanding of suicide. Those intent on suicide may achieve their goal [14]: even of those who receive treatment some pursue their goal whilst in care; some suicide within hours of discharge; and some within six months. Furthermore, in order for the authors to justify and carry out their study Biddle et al[4] make assumptions about the behaviour of suicidal cases. In other words, suicidal individuals would turn to the internet to seek out the information. The relationship between suicide and internet is not due to the "internet" but due to society and human behaviour; the publicity about suicide, about the internet, about methods of suicide, and about right to choose and so on. For example, the media thwarts its own attempts for responsible reporting of suicide by reporting on other forms of suicide e.g. euthanasia, assisted suicide. It is no longer uncommon for the media's coverage of assisted suicide and euthanasia to include references to books or proponents of euthanasia. This example is from the BBC news service:-

> * Ex-minister backs assisted death *
> Former health minister, Lord Warner, backs calls for assisted death for terminally-ill patients to be legalised. Full story: http://news.bbc.co.uk/go/em/-/1/hi/health/7465920.stm

A recent euthanasia case in New Zealand attracted the media's interest (the following links provide a hint of the type of report that was broadcasted in the news media [http://www.thestar.com.my/metro/story.asp?file=/2008/6/13/central/21498803&sec=central], [http://www.stuff.co..nz/4559993a10.html] and in the process details of the method of suicide were repeatedly (in many different versions) reported. Notably, the reports appeared to emphasise how help was sought and by whom. Detailed and graphic references were made to a book on "how to" and proponents of euthanasia self-help tool kits. The media reporting of this case included references to the internet. The reports provided details of how the internet was used and implied it as the culprit in bringing such a tragic end to someone's life; how the whole deal had been arranged via the internet using email correspondence between the case and the alleged helper from the USA, and that such information is readily available on the internet. In reporting this case the media unashamedly publicised the "no go" areas of the internet and how to get there! In their attempt to be conscientious and raise issues of negative social behaviour, the media's reporting of this case and generally of suicide easily translate into no more than a practical guide to suicide, assisted suicide and euthanasia. It is not surprising that a proportion of the population whether they are contemplating suicide or simply are curious researchers may wish to validate the reported information sources for themselves. Another example of the New Zealand media is related to the euthanasia advocate referred to as Dr Death. Advocates of the assisted suicide philosophy and their willingness to help, have much to be grateful to the media, and are well set in the public mindset. Therefore, why should a distressed suicidal individual waste time searching the internet for "suicide methods" when they can easily type "dr death" and restrict it with the term "video" to get what they need. This particular video is available courtesy of the media [http://www.scoop.co..nz/multimedia/tv/national/10243.html]. The media in attempting to condemn a euthanasia workshop organised in New Zealand also reported pro-suicide activities including a video demonstration of a suicide method (see the above link). The report included extracts from the video which left little to the imagination! The news item was screened before the watershed at 6 pm and provided free exposure for the public who had not subscribed to the workshop. What better publicity could Dr Death have wish for?

On the other hand, we live in the era of information technology. The continuous advancement in technology has made the transition from a human/social culture to a technological culture almost seamless. This, at a time when the access to information is only limited by the technology itself, the public has been conditioned into thinking that their need to have access to information has never been greater. This feedback is heavily used to roll over the next generation of smaller and faster communication devices even more desirable. For example, we are no longer restricted to wires/cables and fixed coordinates to be able to access information. Limited access to the internet is possible from cell phones, with full access to the internet being available through notebooks and palmtops from anywhere using mobile technology.

The risks with an information superhighway such as the internet are, of course, related to the quality of information [26] and the intended audience. However, as mentioned earlier, given the nature of the internet, the intended audience may be any member of the public searching for information through accidental hits or through news reports or by word of mouth (email and text messages). Perhaps a pressing question to ask is why do some encourage others to terminate their lives whilst they themselves live? Are these individuals or groups exposed to a higher risk of suicide? Are these individuals or groups in more need of help? Do they have problems coping in society? And so on.

QUANTIFYING SUICIDE

Viewed as an illness of the mind, suicidal behaviour when it is diagnosed e.g. failed attempts, is met with formal and authoritarian medical attention; by law all self-harm cases coming into contact with the health services must be assessed by a psychiatrist. However, suicide research has, over and above depression, followed many directions such as a link with fatty acids[27,28], eating disorders and anorexia nervosa[29,30], persons with an intellectual disability[31,32], cannabis and alcohol misuse[33-36], allergy symptoms[37] and clinical settings[35,38], suicide in dermatological patients[39], suicide in pregnancy (pre- and post natal)[40], suicide in Huntington disease patients[41]. Pharmacological treatment of mental illness, depression and suicidal behaviour on its own may be controversial[42] others suggest holistic medicine as a more effective treatment[43-46].

The literature seems to suggest that suicide prevention policies ought to address and tackle methods of suicide. If access to sources of information and methods of suicide is censored and restricted somehow suicide will not occur. Such assumptions by the researchers and decision makers, if true, provide the clearest and strongest evidence yet that we have lost sight of the main issue "suicide". Anecdotal evidence to support "a lost cause" may be found in practice. So some health authorities seek to identify methods of suicide and selectively attempt to restrict access to that method. For example, Doncaster Public Health Intelligence Unit reported [47] a policy of restricting access to co-proxamol, because it was thought that this method of overdose was becoming more frequent. However, the data presented in this report[47, Page 8] suggest no change in the pattern of suicide before and after the policy implementation. If this trend of restricting access continues, it would mean the end of social freedom as people may be locked up, restrained, medicated etc, if they exhibit signs of depression, bereavement, and other factors that have been listed as risk factors, e.g. see the New Zealand Suicide Prevention Strategy[48], to stop them from self harm or suicide. Will we need authorisation and permission to visit a DIY (hardware) store? What about access to high rise buildings, and natural features/landscapes (e.g. sea, river, cliffs) that have often been used for suicide

Generally, prevention appears to take the form of prohibition through restricting access. This approach is quite clear in smoking and suicide and is evidence of a frustrated society that can not understand these outcomes (smoking & suicide) in order to help prevent them. Some indications about the latter was given earlier, also see [12,14,15]. The former may be viewed through government antismoking policies and public health campaigns[10,16,49]. In some countries, smoking bans are operational in public areas and in the workplace. Furthermore, there are policies on access to tobacco by young people, and, some countries have or are in the process of operating a complete ban on public tobacco displays by retailers. Such wisdom to remove or restrict public access to the means of smoking may not be as laughable if human behaviour was static; for example a ban on tobacco advertising has not stopped the public exposure to tobacco smoking. In the age of information technology, exposure to tobacco smoking can easily be achieved through continuous controversy[10], through the entertainment industry, the internet and so on. Even the antismoking lobby appears to lend a hand and increase exposure to smoking through their anti-smoking messages carried through images of people smoking [10]. Given that various stakeholders and lobbyists are pushing for legislation on retail cigarette displays and on euthanasia and assisted suicide, the issues are likely to remain in the public domain for some time to come in the future. Through these exposures we are repeatedly reminded by the entertainment industry, media and researchers where to look, what to look for, how to search and the most popular and frequently used methods!

The greatest common factor between suicide and smoking prevention policies are the unwitting exposure they provide to these issues by those who argue public safety to prevent public exposure in the first place!

Certainly, the suicide literature appears to suggest a large number of variables with the emphasis on mental illness and depression to be associated with suicide. For example, the New Zealand Suicide Prevention Strategy [48] lists a whole host of reasons for suicide including mental illness, drug and alcohol, bereavement, education, etc. The author of the report goes on to claim that 90% of suicides are caused by depression! [http://www.beehive.govt.nz/ViewDocument.aspx?DocumentID=27352]. The consequence of associating a high proportion of suicides with mental illness is the inevitable bias in the allocation of budgets and resources.

On the other hand, Goldstein et al[50] claimed that their statistical model failed to select any of the reported contributory factors as predictors of suicide. This may indicate that we have been forcing a causal link with suicide where there possibly is not one. One possible explanation could be due to the nature of suicide research. For example, studies such as the Canterbury Suicide Project [13,20,21] are based on seeking information about the suicide case from family and friends who on the whole had no idea of the case's mental health let alone their decision to terminate their life. Therefore, the responses are biased due to an association with the event "suicide". Most studies of this type fail to account for bias through design and analysis.

However, there is anecdotal evidence that the current treatment of suicide may be a contributory factor in a suicidal case's unwillingness to seek help. The following are narratives sent to the author by community members with some alteration to maintain anonymity:-

Case 4J – late teens - suffered emotional sever trauma when very young. Rejected by mother after death of first brother and second brother. Brought up by father when mother suffered further breakdowns. She was sexually abused in her early teens by older boys around and by mother's boyfriend. He mother continued to reject her. She moved to city to finish her schooling. Moving away from an isolated community to a busy metropolitan area meant the additional stress from a culture shock, a feel of not being socially accepted, and social isolation. She became severely depressed and was admitted to mental health unit where she was seen by mental health psychiatrists. She was medicated but this did not help and she was advised to have electro-convulsive therapy (also being told that if she did not agree she would be committed). Her father did his best to prevent this but was told he had no say as she was over the age of consent. She was later discharged with medication via GP and no counseling. She was lonely and withdrawn and uncomfortable staying with mother who continued to reject her. She moved into a flat and despite support from her father and brother, committed suicide. In her diary she listed the drugs she would take, when she would do so and apologised to people closest to her and to her doctor. Her comment – "this is the only way I can find to stop the pain."

Case 5J – Female 35 – history of depression with prescriptions from GP with no further follow-up by mental health system after 2 years. Previously admitted to MH institution after overworking and almost suiciding. Recently felt she was not coping so went to private (as opposed through the heath service system) psychiatrist who assessed her and began seeing her on a weekly basis. She planned and almost executed her suicide plan but decided against it for the sake of her children. In her mind, she said the *planning was clear and precise.* She sees a private psychiatrist weekly and he has told her he is available at any time day or night. He monitors her medication and is not prepared to make instant diagnoses.

Case 2V – male – a long history unstable youth and adulthood. A series of failed relationships, gender confusion, and a career … experimenting with drugs – in and out of mental health service due to addiction and attempted suicide – not satisfied with the treatment – he complained that they (the professionals) don't listen – they never listen – they always medicate you. With his mother as his support and confidant he has decided to live. He regularly confide in his mother and has made plans for the future including writing a book. He has not made any attempts in terminating his life since falling back on to his mother as his confidant.

Case 3M [comments received soon after the event] : –apparently had quite a history of mental problems of what ever degree I am not totally sure… caused his family great anxiety over the years and his health worsened latterly. His last attempt was remembered very clearly at the hospital by the orderlies... Hospital staff said that nobody quite knew how he managed to survive - Skilful Doctors and nurses probably. Made a right proper mess of himself. Really horrific. Nobody who saw him has forgotten. Well this time he had it sussed - even more gruesome … And so he died of blood loss [and probably shock] and what a bloody unpleasant and painful way to exit this world. The irony is that every time they save a life … then leave them to their own devices… back to square one!

Ventegodt & Merrick[46] present the treatment of a 22 year old patient presenting a long history of childhood sexual abuse, incest and rape. In this case the authors adopted their "holistic" approach to developing treatments and applied it to this case. After 100 hours of intensive therapy the case, through this holistic approach was supported and taught to confront her life issues, understand them and deal with them in such a way to help her make an informed and "free" choice about "life" or "death", as opposed to a "command" choice based on drug therapy. The authors, quite rightly argue against the current medical model of treating suicide; the use of medication and drugs may only treat the symptoms and the real issues that the patient should be made aware of and given the skills to deal with them are masked.

None of these cases fit a medical model; those who completed suicide medication and medical treatment did not seem to help them, and those that are still alive did so by their own decision to find help that suits them.

The main point of concern that all of us (not just the practitioners and researchers) must remember, is that at the centre of this decision making process there is a person. In the case of the young adolescent, the individual had already gone through their own process of decision making by which time it is too late for any external influence/intervention as these would have been interpreted as interference. In the case presented by Ventegodt & Merrick[46], even though a holistic approach was used the person had shown a degree of willingness to agree to a treatment. Regardless of whether the person had suicide intentions, it was her decision processes that led her to receiving treatment. The apparent success of the treatment rests solely with the "holistic" approach of placing the patients in the driving seat and providing them with a useful map and the skills to navigate through past life events and to prepare for the future (e.g. also see Cassidy et al[51]). For cases 5J and 2V (above) the individuals' process of decision making had placed them in the driving seat.

Omar [52] suggests a holistic suicide prevention approach going beyond the individuals. Whilst Ventegodt & Merrick's holistic approach[46] was mainly treatment i.e. intervention,

Omar's approach is more preventional. Although, still in its eighth year initial results suggest positive outcomes:-

> Youth suicide in the area covered by the programme has been stable or declining since the project started. That is holding up 7 years in a row.
>
> Hospitalizations for suicide attempts in the area have dropped by 30%.
>
> The rest of the state: completed suicide and suicide attempts have increased by 20% for the same period.

This approach, too, is subject to influence from other social processes such as central and local government policies, the media and entertainment industry e.g. see [15]. However, a collective effort by all the stakeholders involved will increase the likelihood of a sustainable success. Thus, providing some evidence for the need for higher social involvement in developing heath promotion policies[26].

To use the current knowledge in the literature to describe suicide (risk factors) would mean that the *whole* population becomes the *at risk* population. Just because this description does not fit the current practice in making a policy decision does not mean that it can not be true. It does make sense: we all have to deal with death and dying directly or indirectly throughout our lives be it bereavement, accidents, war etc, which put our own impending demise in perspective. The issue with suicide is that although we are exposed to the 'risk factors' only a small proportion of the public will make a decision to intervene to bring forward their own demise. Because the way suicide research has been conducted and hampered by politics at all levels and poor methodology (see introduction) it is difficult, at least in New Zealand, to access some basic linked event history data, such as:-

- the proportion of repeat hospitalisations and new cases due to suicide attempt,
- the proportion of repeat attempters not going through the hospital system,
- the proportion who have received psychiatric care, for how long and the outcome,
- the proportion who have received any medical care in the community, for how long and the outcome,
- the proportion of those going through the system who have completed suicide,
- the proportion of those who go through the system who never attempt again i.e the duration between treatments and the next attempt, and so on.

Our understanding of suicide varies depending on whichever angle or slant we study it. For example medical models view suicide as an illness of the mind; social models view it as resulting socio-economic circumstances, individual personality or the social environment; philosophical and religious/spiritual models explain a lack of belonging or belief leading to hopelessness and despair in times of great need and so on. Other models are loosely based on individual characteristics and advocate resilience.

Each model on its own may therefore appear flawed outside of the context it was developed e.g. roughly over two-third of suicide cases do not come into contact with the psychiatric services and nothing is known about them but with the application of the medical model these cases would have suffered mental illness and depression! By the same token other cases with similar characteristics may not be explained by a social or religious model. Over the years this lack of fit has frustrated health professionals and researchers and policy makers, because, every short term benefit from preventional strategies based on what may appear to be a new link to explaining suicide has been thwarted in the medium to long-term. This may have actually compounded and confounded the issue as a result of the feedback effect through policies thus making professionals and researchers part of the problem and not the solution[15,10,16,24,49]. As a result, the parameters that appear to be linked to suicide, in particular those that have not been studied before (e.g. the current fashion to push for restricting access to the internet), are quickly promoted into preventional strategies – therefore maintaining the feedback effect.

Can we teach resilience, or, self-confidence, or, spiritualism? By the same token, can we stop the internet being used, or, stop people jumping off tall buildings/bridges/cliffs, or, can we place everyone under surveillance? These are individual characteristics intertwined with human behaviour (social behaviour, beliefs, culture etc), some individuals have them and some acquire them but only some learn to use them. Given the decades of feedback from suicide research and policy implementation and decades of social dealignment, individuals still choose death over life for whatever reason. And after decades of research all we have to go with is a very broad model of suicide that at best suggests the whole population is at risk and at worst treats suicide for depression and recommends antidepressants for all.

Clearly, suicide is the outcome of a decision making process. Processes are by nature dynamic and are governed by (and also influence) other processes. Therefore suicide research must adopt a dynamic and holistic approach[26]. One such idea is based on the above understanding that *death* has been researched and has not provided us sufficient insight to understand suicide – perhaps we need to confirm our understanding of life first in order to gain insight into death.

It is clear that the suicide population is extremely heterogeneous and not all can be described by a single model such as medical, religion or social models. It seems to me that society as a whole will have a better chance of describing and preventing suicide. Social behaviour (to include economic policy, social policy, health policy, food and nutrition policy, culture and beliefs etc) can describe a society and how that society behaves towards its public. However, within any society, tribal or grouping behaviour and conditioning is possible and occurs naturally. Various social studies are indicative that individuals may be classified in a group according to some personal characteristics and behaviour e.g. see [53]. There is evidence to suggest that an individuals' health and social needs may be predicted by their social outlook and allegiances - this has already been applied to the elderly successfully [53]. Rather than subscribing to a single model such as a medical model where based on a selection of individuals a cause and its risk factor may be probabilistically identified, a study of suicide based on society may lead to groups with descriptive parameters. One of the outcomes of a holistic approach may be the development of preventional schemes based on the above (dynamic) grouping, if one can be found. Such a model will have implications for informing the policy development *process*. This is the subject of a proposal currently being developed.

CONCLUSION

Whilst the media appears to follow a self-regulatory restraint in the reporting of suicide and in particular methods of suicide, no restrain is exercised when reporting the proponents of euthanasia. As mentioned earlier, the media coverage of euthanasia supporters often provide substantial air time to their activities and recommendations including the graphic broadcasting of the methods to end one's life and sources to find information about the methods such as the internet, books and videos!

The current philosophy that knowledge of methods of suicide will increase the suicide rate is not well developed and should not be used to inform policy. A discussion of the wisdom of such a philosophy to base practice on is not the subject of this chapter, however, adopting such an approach will require a complete sheltering of the public from suicides and how they were achieved and the removal of access to every equipment deemed as possible instruments for suicide. An impossibility! Despite a high level of security and round the clock surveillance suicide still occurs in prisons and in secure psychiatric units. The point is that there are other processes that influence human behaviour leading to feedback effects and finally an individual's process of decision making.

It seems as though as long as suicide reporting is not related to a case, then various aspects including methods can be discussed by the media. If the link between exposure to suicide and methods is so strong then how does society allow suicide to be regularly featured in media as news items, as concern for public safety, and in the entertainment industry? For example, a search of the internet reveals a Rock band called "Suicide"; the theme music of one of the longest running sitcoms "MASH" describes suicide as painless and was in the singles chart; a recent article in the New York Times http://www.nytimes.com/ discusses suicide; and so forth. Moreover, news media treatment of suicide is no different: the concerned TV news editors and reporters through a news item at peak hours, in effect, publicised the arrival of a leading proponent of euthanasia in New Zealand and the release of a video demonstrating how to end it all (TV3 Tuesday 8/7/2008, 6 pm o'clock news – for an extract see http://www.scoop.co..nz/multimedia/tv/national/10243.html). As if the mentioning of the video was not enough the news programme dedicated air time to broadcasting extracts from the video! The media's behaviour is much more interesting to note: the media provides free air time and space to someone whom they themselves categorised as a social outcast and a public enemy who presumably has no access to mass media to promote his ideals, and tools including an infamous book that is banned in New Zealand! On the other hand it may be that "Dr Death" is making a clever use of the relationship between controversy and the media.

As discussed in the introduction, in the age of information the boundaries between the public and professionals have become blurred; anyone with access to the internet appears to be knowledgeable about every conceivable subject: what is it about the help and services from psychiatric units that drive people away?

Out of desperation researchers target anything that is fashionable in the literature in this case the internet, but never the pathways leading to the use of internet as a suicide information resource. It is therefore society (e.g. researchers, media and policy makers) who may also be influencing the pathways of suicide. Quite apart from a critical analysis of published work on suicide, a critical analysis of suicide in the media as a *social behaviour* is essential.

Finally, if it took a holistic approach including 100 hours of intensive counseling to help a 22 year old to choose life over death, and furthermore, if, 90% of completed suicides are caused by depression and given that (a) on average, two third of the cases do not come into contact with mental health services and that we knew very little about them; (b) that depression is treatable; and (c) if suicide occurs during and post treatment, then suicide should not be categorized as depression or mental illness for the general population. By the same token suicide can not be categorised as a social or religious outcome such as drug addiction, lack of confidence, bereavement, resilience or a lack of faith and belief. For that reason, the answer to the question posed in this chapter's title ought to be no – however, with a change in approach [26,46,52] it does not have to be "no".

REFERENCES

[1] Tam, J., Tang, WS. & Fernando, DJS. (2007). The internet and suicide: a double-edged tool. *European Journal of Internal Medicine*, 18(6):453-455.

[2] Hitosugi, M., Nagai, T. & Tokudome, S. (2007). A voluntary effort to save the youth suicide via the internet in Japan. *Internation Journal of Nursing Studies*, 44(1):157-157.

[3] Mishara, BL. & Weisstub, DN. (2007). Ethical, legal, and practical issues in the control and regulation of suicide promotion and assistance over the internet. *Suicide and Life Threatening Behaviour*, 37(1):58-65.

[4] Biddle, L., Donovan, J., Hawton, K., Kapur, N. &Gunnell, D. (2008). Suicide and the Internet. *BMJ*, 336(7648):800-802.

[5] Recupero, PR., Harms, SE. & Noble, JM. (2008). Googling suicide: surfing for suicide information on the internet. *Journal of Clinical Psychiatry* 69(6):878-888.

[6] Etzersdorfer, Elmar. and Sonneck, Gernot. (1998) Preventing suicide by influencing mass-media reporting. The Viennese experience 1980–1996. *Archives of Suicide Research*, 4:67-74.

[7] Gould, MS. (2001). Suicide and the Media. *Annals of the New York Academy of Sciences*, 932:200 – 224.

[8] Mann, JJ., Apter, Alan., Bertolote, Jose., Beautrais, Annette. et al. (2005). Suicide Prevention Strategies: A Systematic Review. *JAMA*, 294(16):2064-74

[9] Hawton, Keith., Williams, Kathryn. (2002). Influences of the media on suicide Researchers, policy makers, and media personnel need to collaborate on guidelines. *BMJ*, 325(7377): 1374–1375.

[10] Shahtahmasebi, S. (2007a) "Teenage smoking: researching behaviour" Int. J. of Psychology Research; *forthcoming.*

[11] Hagihara, A., Tarumi, K., Abe, T. (2007). Media suicid-reporting, Internet use and occurrence of suicides between 1987 and 2005 in Japan. BMC Public Health, 7:Art. No. 321.

[12] Shahtahmasebi, S. (2005) "Suicide in New Zealand." *TheScientificWorldJOURNAL, 5, 527-534.*

[13] Beautrais, AL. (2001). Suicides and serious suicide attempts: two populations or one? *Psychological Med.* 31, 837-845.

[14] Shahtahmasebi, S. (2003) "Suicides by Mentally Ill People." *TheScientificWorldJOURNAL,* 3, 684-693.

[15] Shahtahmasebi, S. (2008) "Suicide Research and Adolescent Suicide Trends in New Zealand." TheScientificWorldJOURNAL; *forthcoming.*

[16] Shahtahmasebi, S. (2007b) "Teenage smoking: what are the main issues?" In Martin M. Lapointe (Ed) *Adolescent Smoking and Health Research.* Nova Science Publishers, Inc. *Forthcoming.*

[17] De Leo, D. (2002). Why are we not getting any closer to preventing suicide? *Br J Psychiatry* 181, 372-4.

[18] Institute of Medicine. (2002). *Reducing Suicide: A National Imperative.* National Academic Press, Washington DC.

[19] Cutcliffe, JR. (2003). Research endeavours into suicide: a need to shift the emphasis. *Br J Nurs* 12(2):92-9.

[20] Beautrais, AL., Joyce, PR., Mulder, RT. (1994). The Canterbury suicide project: Aims, overview and progress. *Community Mental Health in New Zealand* 8(2), 32-39.

[21] Beautrais, AL. (1996). *Serious suicide attempts in young people: a case control study.* [PhD]. Christchurch: Christchurch School of Medicine.

[22] Khan, A., Warner, HA., Brown, WA. (2000). Symptom Reduction and Suicide Risk in Patients Treated With Placebo in Antidepressant Clinical Trials: An Analysis of the Food and Drug Administration Database. *Arch Gen Psychiatry* 57, 311-317.

[23] Hall, WD., Mant, A., Mitchell, PB., Rendle, VA., Hickie, IB., McManus, P. (2003). Association between antidepressant prescribing and suicide in Australia, 1991-2000: trend analysis. *BMJ* 326(7397), 1008.

[24] Shahtahmasebi, S. (2006) "The Good life: A holistic approach to the health of the population" *TSWJ-Holistic Health and Medicine*, 1, 153-168.

[25] Short, Stephanie. (1996). *Elective Affinities: Research and Health Policy Development.* Heather Gardner (Ed.) Health Policy in Australia. Oxford University Press. Melbourne. 1996.

[26] Shahtahmasebi, S. (2008) "Researching health service information systems development." In Ashish Dwivedi (Ed.) *Handbook of Research on IT Management and Clinical Data Administration in Healthcare.* IGI Publishing. *In press.*

[27] Brunner, J., Parhofer, KG., Schwandt, P., Bronisch, T. (2002). Cholesterol, essential fatty acids, and suicide. *Pharmacopsychiatry* 35(1), 1-5.

[28] Ainiyet, J., Rybakowski, J. (1996). Low concentration level of total serum cholesterol as a risk factor for suicidal and aggressive behavior. *Psychiatria Polska* 30(3), 499-509.

[29] Dancyger, Ida F., and Fornari, Victor M. (2005). A review of eating disorders and suicide risk in adolescence. *TheScientificWorldJOURNAL* 5, 803-811.

[30] Latzer, Yael., and Hochdorf, Zipora. (2005). A review of suicidal behaviour in anorexia nervosa. *TheScientificWorldJOURNAL* 5, 820-827.

[31] Merrick, Joav., Merrick, Efrat., Lunski, Yona., and Kendel, Isack. (2005). Suicide behaviour in persons with intellectual disability. *TheScientificWorldJOURNAL* 5, 729-735.

[32] Merrick, Joav., Merrick, Efrat., Morad, Mohammed., and Kendel, Isack. (2005). Adolescents with intellectual disability and suicidal behaviour. *TheScientificWorld JOURNAL* 5, 724-728.

[33] Maharajh, Hari D., and Konings, Monique. (2005). Cannabis and suicidal behaviour among adolescents: a pilot study from Trinidad. *TheScientificWorldJOURNAL* 5, 576-585.

[34] Sher, Leo. (2006). Risk and protective Factors for suicide in patients with alcholism. *TheScientificWorldJOURNAL* 6, 1405-1411.

[35] Sher, Leo. (2006). Alcohol and suicide: neurobiological and clinical aspects. *TheScientificWorldJOURNAL* 6, 700-706.

[36] Sher, Leo. (2006). Relation between rates of geriatric suicide and consumption of alcohol beverages in European countries. *TheScientificWorldJOURNAL* 6, 383-387.

[37] Postolache, Teodor T., Lapidus, Manana., Sander, Evan R., Langenberg, P.Hamilton, Robert G., et al. (2007). Changes in allergy symptoms and depression scores are positively correlated in patients with recurrent mood disorders exposed to seasonal peaks in aeroallergens. *TheScientificWorldJOURNAL* 7, 1968-1977.

[38] Pompili, Maurizio., Girardi, Paolo. Lester, David., and Tatarelli, Roberto. (2006). Suicide soon after generalized tonic-clonic seizure. A possible Peri-Ictal Phenomenon? *TheScientificWorldJOURNAL* 6, 356-360.

[39] Cotterill, JA., & Cunliff, WJ. (1997). Suicide in dermatological patients. *British Journal of Dermatology*, 137(2):246-250.

[40] Dell, D. & O'Brien, BW. (2003). Suicide in pregnancy. Obstetrics & Gynecology, 102(6):1306-1309.

[41] Di Maio, L., Squitieri, F., Napolitano, G., Campanella, G., et al. (1993). *BMJ*, 30:293-295.

[42] Farley, Rachel L. (2005). Pharmacological treatment of major depressive disorder in adolescents. *TheScientificWorldJOURNAL* 5, 420-426.

[43] Ventegodt, Soren., Kandel, Isack., Neikrug, Shimshon., and Merrick, Joav. (2005). Clinical holistic medicine: the existential crisis- life crisis, stress, and burnout. *TheScientificWorldJOURNAL* 5, 300-312.

[44] Ventegodt, S., Andersen, N.J., Neikrug, S., Kandel, I., and Merrick, J. (2005). Clinical holistic medicine: holistc treatment of mental disorders. *TheScientificWorldJOURNAL* 5, 427-445.

[45] Ventegodt, S., and Merrick, J. (2005). Suicide from a holistic point of view. *TheScientificWorldJOURNAL* 5:958-766.

[46] Ventegodt, S., Clausen, B., and Merrick, J. (2006). Clinical Holistic Medicine: The Case Story of Anna. III. Rehabilitation of Philosophy of Life During Holistic Existential Therapy for Childhood Sexual Abuse. *TheScientificWorldJOURNAL* 6, 2080-2091.

[47] Doncaster PHUI (2003) *Suicide*. Doncaster Public Health Intelligence Unit, White Rose House, Ten Pound Walk, DONCASTER, DN4 5DJ, UK. www.doncasterhealth.co.uk/phiu.

[48] Associate Minister of Health. (2006). *The New Zealand Suicide Prevention Strategy 2006-2016*. Ministry of Health 2006. Wellington. http://www.moh.govt.nz/suicideprevention.

[49] Shahtahmasebi, S. (2007c) "Teenage smoking: longitudinal vs. cross-sectional modeling". In Rene S. Grenell (Ed) Adolescent Behaviour Research Studies. Nova Science Publishers, Inc. *Forthcoming.*

[50] Goldstein, RB., Black, DW., Nasrallah, A., Winokur, G. (1991). The prediction of suicide. Sensitivity, specificity, and predictive value of a multivariate model applied to suicide among 1906 patients with affective disorders. *Archives of General Psychiatry*, 48(5): 418-422.

[51] Cassidy, B., Clarke, A., & Shahtahmasebi, S. (2004). Quality of life: Information and Learning Resources in Supporting People with Severe Life-Changing Injuries to Return to Independence. *TheScientificWorldJOURNAL,* 4:536-543.

[52] Omar, Hatim. (2005). A model program for youth suicide prevention. Int J Adolesc Med Health 17(3):275-8.

[53] Wenger, C., Shahtahmasebi, S. (1990). "Variations in support networks: implications for social policy", in *Aiding and Ageing: The coming crisis.,* John Mogey (eds.). Westport, CT:Greenwood Press.

In: Internet and Suicide
Editors: L. Sher and A. Vilens
ISBN 978-1-60741-077-5

Chapter 27

MENTAL ILLNESS AND SUICIDE

Jiunn Yew Thong
Institute of Mental Health, Singapore

ABSTRACT

Studies have demonstrated that most individuals who attempted suicide have a mental illness, the most common being depression and substance abuse or dependence. Individuals suffering from schizophrenia also have high mortality from suicide. Certain factors increase the suicide risk of this already at-risk population with mental illness. Having a comorbid mental illness increases suicide risk significantly, especially in combinations such as depression with comorbid alcohol abuse or dependence, and schizophrenia with comorbid depression. For those mentally-ill individuals who are unfortunate enough to be diagnosed with a serious and debilitating medical illness, their suicide risk is also increased. Anyone who attempted suicide, especially those who used a highly lethal method to try to kill themselves, should be assessed thoroughly and followed-up adequately. Besides depression being a risk for suicide, a psychotic state of mind (such as delusions) is also associated with suicidal behaviour. Clinicians should pay attention to the period following discharge from inpatient treatment, as this period of one month or so is a time of highest risk for suicide. This is the time when the depressed regain enough drive to carry out suicidal acts, and when individuals with schizophrenia regain insight to appreciate the devastating effects of the illness on their lives. Closer monitoring is vital during this period.

INTRODUCTION

Prospective studies have shown that in populations with mental illness (both inpatient and outpatient), 5.4 % died by suicide [1], and the excess mortality by suicide in such individuals was variously estimated at 5 to 9.8 times the number expected in the general population. Presence of mental illness is a strong risk factor for completed suicide, and psychological autopsies have found that over 90% of all completed suicides in Eastern and Western societies are associated with mental illness, most commonly depressive disorders and alcohol abuse and dependence [2,3,4]. Harris and Barraclough [5] did a comprehensive meta-analysis of studies of suicide risk in all psychiatric disorders and wrote that virtually all mental disorders have an increased risk of suicide except mental retardation and dementia. The suicide risk is highest for functional and lowest for organic disorders, with substance misuse disorders lying in between.

In addition, comorbidity makes suicidal acts more likely, and the 2 most frequent comorbid disorders linked to suicide are depression and substance abuse or dependence. Beautrais [6] calculated that the odds for serious suicidal attempts escalated from 17 for those with one disorder to 89 for those with two or more DSM-III-R mental disorder diagnoses. Similarly, Cornelius [7] reported a synergistic effect.

Studies have shown that there are many risk factors associated with suicide in the mentally ill. One example is a case-control study of 234 recently discharged psychiatric patient suicides in Wessex [8], which revealed the following risk factors: living alone, suicidal ideation precipitating admission, hopelessness, admission under different consultant, relationship difficulties, loss of job, inpatient deliberate self-harm, unplanned discharge and significant care professional leaving/on leave. Another study [9] looking at suicide in Hong Kong ethnic Chinese patients after discharge from inpatient psychiatric treatment showed that suicide was associated with unemployment, past suicide attempts, maternal mental illness and suicidal ideation or attempt before the last admission.

However, not all studies reported identifiable risk factors distinguishing suicide cases from living controls. A case-control study done in Victoria, Australia, showed that cases and controls could not be distinguished on the majority of patient- or treatment-based characteristics [10].

Depression and Suicide

Suicide risk is elevated in depressive disorders. It was reported that the lifetime risk of suicide for patients with depression is as high as 15% [11], although lower figures were often used [12]. Inskip quoted a lifetime risk of 6% for affective disorders [13]. Suicidal ideation is a common symptom in depressed individuals. Very importantly, a feeling of hopelessness as measured by the Beck Hopelessness Scale was significantly related to eventual suicide [14]. Henriksson [2] found that depressive disorders (including major depression, bipolar disorders and dysthymia) were present in 59% of suicides. Comorbidity of mental disorders was also common: among the suicides with major depression, 28% had alcohol dependence or abuse, 31% had personality disorders, 49% suffered from physical illness and only 15% were without any comorbidity.

In another psychological autopsy study, Cheng [4] found that major depression was diagnosed in 87% of his East Taiwan sample. 56% of the suicides had a comorbid mental disorder, and major depression with comorbid substance use disorders was most common (43%), followed by double depression with substance use disorders (26%). Hence, it can be seen that substance abuse and depression is an especially lethal combination. Those with dual diagnoses of mood disorder and substance misuse may self-medicate the mania or depression using drugs and alcohol, thereby impairing judgement, worsening depression and hopelessness, and thus increasing the risk of impulsively killing themselves. A clinician therefore needs to be aware of the patient's current substance use status. Obtaining a clear picture of the role of substance dependence in depressed individuals is greatly enhanced by observing these patients while drug-free. Like many other psychiatric disorders, a past history of suicide attempt increases subsequent suicide risk. Sinclair [15] showed that a history of deliberate self-harm is a significant risk factor for suicide in depressed patients.

Another issue was under-detection and under-treatment of depression in the general population. In a study by Barraclough [3] on 64 depressed cases who committed suicide, only one-third of depressed patients had been prescribed antidepressants, mostly in doses below recommended, and over half displayed warnings of suicidal thinking, but modern psychiatric treatment was not always effectively deployed.

Bipolar Disorder and Suicide

Bipolar disorder is also associated with high suicide risk, and it was estimated that up to 18.9% of deaths among bipolar patients were due to suicide [16]. A meta-analysis gave a suicide risk of 15 times the expected, but with variation between studies of 0-133 times, probably because some studies had small sample sizes [5]. Increased risk was related to time since discharge, both recent [17] and up to five years before [18] and alcohol abuse [19]. Suicide in bipolar patients is associated with having a first-degree family history of suicide, having more suicide attempts, and onset with mood-congruent psychotic features [20]. A Finnish psychological autopsy study reported that most suicides of persons with bipolar disorder occurred during a major depressive episode (79%), but in some cases it occurred during a mixed state (11%) or even during or immediately after remission of psychotic mania (11%) [21].

Lithium prophylaxis is thought to reduce suicide risk [22]. The lower relative mortality of lithium-treated patients from the 1960s when compared with those of earlier this century suggested [23] that lithium prophylaxis prevented suicide in the manic-depressive. The higher suicide risk found in those who stopped their lithium compared with those who continued led Muller-Oerlinghausen [22] to the same conclusion. Long-term lithium treatment has been associated with a nearly 6-fold reduction of the crude average rate for completed suicide and a nearly 9-fold lower risk in a meta-analysis of 22 studies [24]. There are some explanations for lithium's effect of reducing suicide: one is that it reduces the risk or severity of recurrences of depression or mixed states. Others have suggested that lithium may have specific effects against suicide independent of its mood-stabilising actions. Müller-Oerlinghausen [25] suggested that lithium reduces suicidal behavior in patients who do not benefit from the lithium treatment in terms of episode reduction, and concluded that caution is required when lithium is discontinued because such a patient might have been protected against suicidal impulses in spite of an incomplete response as to the number and quality of depressive or manic episodes. Such an additional specific value of lithium treatment may include reduction of impulsivity or aggressive and hostile behaviour, possibly mediated through the central serotonin system.

SCHIZOPHRENIA AND SUICIDE

Schizophrenia, being a less common psychiatric illness than depression, is less well represented in completed suicides. However, the population with schizophrenia is actually at high risk of suicide. It was estimated that the lifetime risk of suicide for individuals with schizophrenia ranges from 4% [13] to 10% [26].

Many studies have shown that schizophrenic patients who commit suicide do so at a younger age, mostly within 10 years of the onset of their illness [5]. The older the patient, the smaller is the risk. It was thought that this was related with the stabilization of the illness after the first 10 years, as well as to the fact that most loss situations resulting from the disorder occur in the early period of the illness.

Like individuals with primary diagnoses of depression, patients with primary diagnoses of schizophrenia are at higher risk of suicide if they have comorbid mental illness. The Finnish National Suicide Prevention Project [27] reported that a depressive syndrome, present during a residual phase of the illness or present during the active phase, was found in nearly two-thirds of schizophrenic suicide victims. Alcohol abuse or dependence was found among one-fifth of suicide victims with schizophrenia. In a case-control study in Taiwan [28], it was found that suicide completers were more likely than living controls to have a history of comorbid mental disorders, especially depressive syndrome in residual phase. However, the rates of comorbid alcoholism and/or substance use disorders were low in this study, possibly reflecting the lower general prevalence of disorders in this Chinese society. In another case-control study, it was found that significantly more suicides than controls had in the past both been diagnosed as suffering from a comorbid depressive episode and treated in the past for depression with either antidepressants or electroconvulsive therapy [29]. Depression is actually common in schizophrenia. Each psychotic episode severely disrupts the life of the sufferer, and irreparable damage is done to his or her relationships, occupation, education and self-esteem. For previously high-functioning young patients with schizophrenia, risk of suicide is triggered when, in remission, insight is regained and the losses to one's life are apparent. The acknowledgement that one is suffering from a severe mental illness with a chronic disabling course often leads to depression, despair and even suicidal behaviour. Hence the clinician must be alert to such symptoms and not be distracted by numerous other matters the patient usually has, such as behaviorial problems, social difficulties and discharge problems. Comorbid depression should be distinguished from negative symptoms and side-effects, and can be treated adequately with antidepressants [30]. Feelings of hopelessness, despair and suicidal ideation should be addressed.

Various studies have shown that psychotic disorders, mostly schizophrenia, are associated with increased risk of suicide. In particular, those with paranoid disorders and paranoid schizophrenia are highlighted as being at increased risk. These disorders are characterized by significant positive symptoms, including delusions and hallucinations. Fenton [31] found that two positive symptoms (suspiciousness and delusions) were more severe among completed suicides. The paranoid schizophrenia subtype was associated with an elevated risk (12%) and the deficit subtype was associated with a reduced risk (1.5%) of suicide. Fenton suggested that the progressive loss of social drive, the diminished capacity to experience affect, and the indifference toward the future associated with deficit symptoms may preclude the painful self-awareness associated with suicide. In contrast, the good premorbid functioning, late illness onset, preservation of affect and cognitive capacities, and intermittent course associated with nondeficit and paranoid subtypes of schizophrenia lead to dysphoric and hopeless states. Also, pronounced cognitive deficits impair the mental processes needed to plan and execute suicide attempt. Heilä [27] found that suicides occurred throughout the course of schizophrenia, but both active illness (78%) and depressive symptoms (51%) were highly prevalent immediately before suicide. In a Singaporean study [32], significantly more mentally ill patients who committed suicide had delusions and suicide-commanding auditory hallucinations in the 6 months before death. However, only 8.8% of cases with schizophrenia had suicide-commanding hallucinations, similar to the 9% figure in Heilä's study [27] - this suggested the lesser likelihood that psychotic patients killed themselves in response to voices telling them to do so. It is probable that in some cases, psychotic individuals killed themselves to escape from certain distressing symptoms such as delusions of being persecuted or pursued by others.

The use of second-generation antipsychotics, with their reduced likelihood to cause side-effects, may be used for patients who are non-compliant to medication because of troublesome side-effects. Clozapine has been shown to have a positive effect on suicide risk in schizophrenia patients as compared with patients treated with older neuroleptics. This decrease in suicidality with clozapine treatment patients was associated with improvement in depression and hopelessness [33].

In summary, Hawton [34] in a systematic review showed that risk of suicide in individuals with schizophrenia is strongly associated with depression, previous suicide attempts, drug misuse, agitation or motor restlessness, fear of mental disintegration, poor adherence to treatment and recent loss. Prevention of suicide in schizophrenia may be directed at treating depression, improving compliance to treatment and closer monitoring in patients with risk factors.

History of Suicide Attempts

Individuals who repeat suicidal behaviours are widely diverse, with differing degrees of suicide intent. At one extreme are those who utilized highly lethal methods such as jumping and hanging to try to end their lives. These are the ones that are of great concern for the clinician. Many others engage in deliberate self-harm such as self-cutting, and had little or no real suicide intent. However, many self-multilators also make serious attempts at some time and many serious attempters do not eventually kill themselves. Generally suicide attempters are a high-risk group and clinicians should target them as part of a suicide prevention strategy.

A history of self-harm is a risk factor for eventual completed suicide in most studies. Such self-harm acts occurred in around 50% of cases of psychiatric patients who committed suicide [35, 36]. In addition, Flood and Seagar [37] found that the last admissions of suicides were twice as likely to have followed a parasuicide.. The Wessex Recent In-Patient Suicide Study [8] found that a history of deliberate self-harm increased the risk of suicide 4-fold, and another study in Hong Kong [9] showed that past suicidal attempts increased risk of suicide by 3.4 times. Other studies investigated the lethality of past suicide attempts. Suicide cases that had a history of deliberate self harm or suicide attempts using non-lethal method (such as self-cutting and minor drug overdoses) had the risk of eventual suicide doubled, whereas cases that used lethal means (such as hanging or jumping) during previous suicide attempts had a 28-fold increase in risk of suicide [32]. Yip [9] found that patients who had used a violent method in the last suicide attempt prior to completed suicide had an increased suicide risk of 4.5 times.

In view of the high prevalence of prior attempts among the mentally ill patients who committed suicide, it would be logical to focus treatment and closely monitor suicide attempters, in hope of reducing rates of completed suicides. The clinician should be alerted if there is a history of suicide attempts using lethal methods, and he or she must diligently search for other risk factors, treat depression or psychosis if present, and involve multidisciplinary teams such as social workers to look into financial, accommodation and other social aspects.

Comorbid Physical Illness and Suicide

Severe, stressful life events, in background of an underlying mental disorder, can precipitate suicide in vulnerable individuals. The three most common groups of life stressors that have been identified in completed suicides are conflict-separation-rejection, economic problems, and medical illness [38], and these vary in importance according to the victim's age and gender. Economic difficulties such as job losses or financial strain are important stressors in midlife, particularly in men. Medical illness is the dominant stressor in older adult suicides: the majority of the stressors among subjects 80 years old or older were medical illnesses. Stressors most commonly associated with completed suicides in youth and young adults include interpersonal conflict, separation or rejection, and legal problems such as arrest and incarceration [39].

Most patients with acute or chronic physical diseases do not commit suicide, but for some who do, certain risk factors predispose to suicide. These factors include the presence of preexisting mental illness, the inability to manage stress, and the unavailability of social, financial and psychological support. An altered mental state due to delirium, depression, anxiety or psychosis are also risk factors. Harris and Barraclough [40] reported increased suicide risk patients with HIV/AIDS, malignant neoplasms as a group, head and neck cancers, Huntington disease, multiple sclerosis, peptic ulcer, renal disease, spinal cord injury, and systemic lupus erythematosus. These illnesses are generally chronic, debilitating, painful and dependency causing.

Similarly Thong [32] reported that having a comorbid physical illness that inflicted significant suffering and disability increased suicide risk by 7.5 times, and half of these suicides with physical ailments had definitive medical diagnoses. The other half of suicide cases had no definite medical diagnoses and suffered from ill-defined but nonetheless significant "pain" and "discomfort" of the body and limbs. Henriksson also reported that at least one comorbid Axis III diagnosis was made for about half of suicides with mental illness [2].

Hence mental health care providers need to be aware of their psychiatric patients' perception of their chronic or debilitating physical illnesses, because of the likelihood of increased risk for suicide and other suicidal behaviours. The studies showed that one should not merely dismiss the mentally ill patients' complaints of bodily pain, or just perceive it as a somatic expression of psychological distress, which can sometimes be the case when the symptoms are ill-defined. Also, these studies highlighted the need for physicians working with chronically physically ill (such as in a hospice) to be able to effectively assess suicidality and intervene early.

Post Discharge Clustering of Suicides

It is well known that suicide risk remains high soon after discharge. Many suicides had recently received psychiatric care before their deaths. For example, an audit of suicides by psychiatric patients in Victoria, Australia found that half of these patients had received care (as inpatient and community patients) in the month before death [41]. A similar study in the United Kingdom showed that 50% received care in the week before death [42]. Such patterns of close contact are unsettling for the clinician, who is in a unique position to identify and intervene to prevent suicide.

Flood and Seager [37] found that more than half of their suicides were committed within 3 months of in-patient discharge, despite outpatient follow-up in many cases. Roy [35] reported 18% of suicides dying within only 1 week of entering outpatient care, 44% within a month, and 89% within 1 year. Yim's [9] sample of Chinese patients who completed suicide showed that 19.3% died within first 2 weeks of discharge, 27.4% died within 1 month, 46.6% within 3 months, 67.1% within first 6 months of discharge, and nearly 80% killed themselves within 1 year of discharge from psychiatric inpatient care. Thong [32] reported that 15.1% of cases had died by suicide within 1 week post-discharge, 20.8% within 2 weeks, and by 4 weeks, 26.4% were dead. He also compared suicide cases who suicided within 30 days of discharge from hospital and cases who suicided after 30 days. It was found that early suicides were significantly more likely to be stressed by relationship problems, more likely to have expressed suicidal ideation, had more frequent hospitalizations (average of 6 compared to 3.5 in later suicides), had more frequent visits to the psychiatric emergency room and had greater rates of default of outpatient treatment. Hence these results showed that in the course of an episode, maximum risk occured after in-patient discharge (presumably during and after illness resolution), especially in the first 1-3 months. These results have a significant impact on how the clinician plan outpatient follow-up after discharge. It appears that an outpatient review 2 weeks after discharge may not be soon enough to prevent suicide in those who kill themselves very early after discharge. In a busy hospital where appointment slots are often fully booked, seeing patients within a few days of discharge may be difficult, but worth considering for certain patients at high risk of suicide. These results also highlight the importance of community care (community psychiatric nurses are very useful in this respect) on suicide reduction, since it is during these times that patients are managed without inpatient supervision.

For individuals with schizophrenia in resolution of their psychotic symptoms, the depression and despair caused when they are able to perceive the loss inflicted by the illness predisopose them to suicide. The figures of these early suicides might also suggest, perhaps, that discharge might be premature. One possibility could be due to the patients giving a false impression of wellness so as to gain discharge from hospital. Another possibility could be that the symptoms were not picked up due to lack of time or clinical acumen of the treating team in the ward.

Post Visit Suicide

By arranging an early outpatient follow-up after discharge, clinicians assume that seeing a doctor will help reduce the risks of suicide, especially at the time just after consultation. Unfortunately, studies have shown that this does not apply to all patients, with 5% of cases dead by suicide the very next day and 27.7% dead within 1 week of consultation with a mental health professional [32]. Myers and Neal's study [36] reported that 36% of their sample killed themselves within a week of seeing a doctor, and 63% within 1 month. Another study reported that in 18% of the cases, the last contact with a health care professional occurred on the day of suicide itself, and 47% occurred 1-7 days before suicide, and 19% occurred 8-14 days before suicide. However, in only 22% of cases was the issue of suicide discussed during the final visit [43]. This failure to communicate suicidal thoughts may be due to a few reasons: failure of health professional to recognize depression and warning signs of suicidality, as well as failure of patient to express suicidal ideation due to hopelessness, avolition and affective blunting. On the other hand, another study showed that subjects with schizophrenia communicated their suicide intent more frequently than those with other psychiatric illnesses [44].

Suicidal ideation is not uncommon, even in the non-psychiatric population: it has been estimated that 31% of the clinical population and 24% of the general population considered suicide at some time of their lives [45]. Having suicidal ideation voiced out to mental health-care providers 3 months before suicide is associated with higher risk of suicide [32]. King [8] also found higher risk of suicide associated with having suicidal ideas at the last admission before suicide. From this, one can learn that one should always take communication of suicidal ideas seriously. When a suicidal patient is seen by the clinician at the clinic, the clinician is in a unique position to change the suicidal path that the patient is taking, even if that meant an involuntary admission

Conclusion

Suicide prevention strategies that aim to reduce risk in the general population as a whole often appear difficult to implement and achieve. High-risk preventive strategies, on the other hand, seem more realistic and easier to implement, since smaller and more specific groups with high risk are more easily identified and treated. Suicide prevention for psychiatric patients starts with *identification* of high risk subgroups. Factors such as certain psychiatric diagnoses, presence of comorbidities, particular features of the mental state, suicidal career and course of illness interact dynamically to affect suicidal risk. Knowing these risk factors allow us to focus on these high risk groups. By knowing that suicide risk is highest after discharge from hospital, clinicians can intensify followup and increase vigilance at *high-risk periods,* such as the first months following hospital discharge. The community psychiatric team is also invaluable in augmenting efforts to monitor these high-risk patients, especially in countries where inpatient stays are short.

References

[1] Tanney BL (1992) Mental disorders, psychiatric patients, and suicide. In R.W. Maris, A.L. Berman, J.T. Maltsberger, & R.I. Yufit (Eds.), *Assessment and Prediction of Suicide*. New York: Guilford Press.

[2] Henriksson MM, Aro HM, Marttunen MJ, Heikkinen ME , Isometsä ET , Kuoppasalmi KI and Lonnqvist JK: Mental disorders and comorbidity in suicide. *Am J Psychiatry* 1993; 150: 935-940 .

[3] Barraclough BM, Bunch B, Nelson B, Sainsbury P: A hundred cases of suicide: clinical aspects. *Br J Psychiatry* 1974, 125:355-373.

[4] Cheng ATA : Mental Illness and suicide, a case control study in East Taiwan. *Arch Gen Psychiatry* 1995; Vol 52: 594-603.

[5] Harris EC, Barraclough B: Suicide as an outcome for mental disorders. *Br J Psychiatry* 1997; 170: 205-228.

[6] Beautrais AL, Joyce PR, Mulder RT: Prevalence and comorbidity of mental disorders in persons making serious suicide attempts: a case-control study. *Am J Psychiatry* 1996; 153: 1009-1014.

[7] Cornelius JR, Salloum IM, Mezzich J, Cornelius Jr, Fabrega H, Ehler JG, Ulrich RF, Thase ME, Mann JJ: Disproportionate suicidality in patients with comorbid major depression and alcoholism. *Am J Psychiatry* 1995; 152: 358-364.

[8] King EA, Baldwin DS, Sinclair JMA, Baker NG, Campbell MJ, Thompson C: The Wessex recent in-patient suicide study, 1 *Br J Psychiatry*; 2001,178:531-536.

[9] Yim PHW, Yip PSF, Li RHY, Dunn EL.W, Yeung WS. Miao YK: Suicide after discharge from psychiatric inpatient care: a case-control study in Hong Kong. *Aust N Z J Psychiatry* 2004; 38:65-72.

[10] Pirkis J, Burgess P, Jolley D: Suicide among psychiatric patients: a case-control study. *Aust N Z J Psychiatry* 2002; 36:86-91.

[11] Guze SB, Robins E: Suicide and primary affective disorders. *Br J Psychiatry* 1970; 117:437-438.

[12] Bostwick JM, Pankratz VS: Affective disorders and suicide risk: a reexamination. *Am J Psychiatry* 2000; 157(12):1925-1932.

[13] Inskip HM., Harris EC, Barraclough B: Lifetime risk of suicide for affective disorder, alcoholism and schizophrenia. *Br J Psychiatry* 1998; 172: 35-37.

[14] Beck AT, Brown G, Berchick RJ, Stewart BL, Steer RA: Relationship between hopelessness and ultimate suicide: a replication with psychiatric outpatients. *Am J Psychiatry* 1990; 147: 190-195.

[15] Sinclair JM, Hariss L, Baldwin DS, King EA: Suicide in depressive disorders: a restrospective case-control study of 127 suicides. *J Affect Disord* 2005; Jul; 87(1):107-13.

[16] Goodwin FK, Jamison KR. Manic depressive illness. New York, NY: Oxford University Press; 1990.

[17] Perris C, d'Elia G: A study of bipolar (manic depressive) and unipolar recurrent depressive psychoses. X: Mortality, suicide and life-cycles. *Acta Psychiatr Scand* 1966; suppl. 194: 172-183.

[18] Newman, SC, Bland, RC: Suicide risk varies by subtype of affective disorder. *Acta Psychiatr Scand* 1991 (a); 83: 420-426.

[19] Noreik K: Attempted suicide and suicide in functional psychoses. *Acta Psychiatr Scand* 1975; 52: 81-106.

[20] Tsai SY, Kuo CJ, Chen CC, Lee HC: Risk factors for completed suicide in bipolar disorder. *J Clin Psychiatry* 2002; 63:6: 469-476.

[21] Isometsä ET, Henriksson MM, Aro HM, Lönnqvist JK: Suicide in bipolar disorder in Finland. *Am J Psychiatry.* 1994 Jul;151(7):1020-4.

[22] Muller-Oerlinghausen B, Muser-Causemann B, Volk J: Suicides and parasuicides in a high-risk population group on and off lithium long-term medication. *J Affect Disord*; 1992; 25: 261-270.

[23] Kay DWK, Petterson U: Manic-depressive illness: a clinical, social and genetic study. VI: Mortality. *Acta Psychiatr Scand* 1977, suppl. 269: 55-60.

[24] Tondo L, Hennen J, Baldessarini RJ: Reduced suicide risk with long-term lithium treatment in major affective illness: a meta-analysis. *Acta Psychiatr Scand* 2001; 104: 163-72.

[25] Müller-Oerlinghausen B: Arguments for the specificity of the antisuicidal effect of lithium. *Eur Arch Psychiatry Clin Neurosci* 2001; 251 Suppl. 2: 72-5.

[26] Miles CP: Conditions predisposing to suicide: a review. *J Nerv Mental Dis*; 1977, 164: 231-246.

[27] Heilä H, Isometsä ET, Henriksson MM: Suicide and schizophrenia: a nationwide psychological autopsy study on age- and sex-specific clinical characteristics of 92 suicide victims with schizophrenia. *Am J Psychiatry* 1997; 154:1235–1242.

[28] Kuo CJ, Tsai SY, Lo CH, Wang YP, Chen CC: Risk factors for completed suicide in schizophrenia. *J Clin Psychiatry.* 2005 May; 66(5):579-85.

[29] Roy A: Suicide in chronic schizophrenia. *Br J Psychiatry.*1982; Aug;141:171-7.

[30] Peuskens J: The management of depressive symptoms in schizophrenia. *New Therapeutic Indications of Antidepressants*, pp. 84-95. Basel:Karger.

[31] Fenton WS, McGlashan TH, Victor BJ, Blyler CR: Symptoms, subtype, and suicidality in patients with schizophrenia spectrum disorders. *Am J Psychiatry* 1997; Feb;154(2):199-204.

[32] Thong JY, Su AH, Chan YH, Chia BH: Suicide in psychiatric patients: case-control study in Singapore. *Aust N Z J Psychiatry.* 2008 Jun; 42(6):509-19.

[33] Meltzer HY, Okayli G: Reduction of suicidality during clozapine treatment of neuroleptic-resistant schizophrenia: impact on risk-benefit assessment. *Am J Psychiatry* 1995; 152:183-190.

[34] Hawton K, Sutton L, Camilla, Sinclair J, Deeks JJ: Schizophrenia and suicide: systemic review of risk factors. *Br J Psychiatry* 2005; Vol 187; July 2005: pp 9-20.

[35] Roy A: Risk factors for suicide in psychiatric patients. *Arch Gen Psychiatry* 1982; 39: 1089-1095.

[36] Myers DH, Neal CD: Suicide in psychiatric patients. *Br J Psychiatry* 1978; 133: 38-44.

[37] Flood RA. Seager CP: A retrospective examination of psychiatric case records of patients who subsequently committed suicide. *Br J Psychiatry* 1968; 114: 443-450.

[38] Rich CL, Warsradt GM, Nemiroff RA: Suicide, stressors and the life cycle. *Am J Psychiatry* 1991; 148:524-527.

[39] Brent DA, Perper JA, Moritz GM, Baugher M, Roth C, Balach L, Schweers J : Stressful life events, psychopathology, and adolescent suicide: A case-control study. *Suicide Life Threat Behav* 1993 (b): 23:179-187.

[40] Harris EC & Barraclough B: Suicide as an outcome for medical disorders. *Medicine* 1994 73: 281-296.

[41] Burgess P, Pirkis J, Morton J, Croke E: Lessons from a comprehensive clinical audit of users of psychiatric services who committed suicide. *Psychiatric Services* 2000; 51:1555-1560.

[42] Appleby L, Dennehy JA, Thomas CS, Faragher EB, Lewis G: Aftercare and clinical characteristics of people with mental illness who commit suicide: a case-control study. *Lancet* 1999, 353: 1397-1400.

[43] Isometsä ET, Heikkinen ME.; Marttunen MJ, Henriksson MM, Hillevi MA, Lonnqvist, JK: The Last Appointment Before Suicide: Is Suicide Intent Communicated? *Am J Psychiatry* 1995; 152(6):919-922.

[44] De Leo D, Klieve H: Communication of suicide intent by schizophrenic subjects: data from the Queensland Suicide Register. *Int J Ment Health* Syst 2007, 1:6.

[45] Linehan MM, Laffaw JA: Suicidal behaviours among clients of an outpatient clinic versus the general population. *Suicide Life Threat Behav*, 1982; 12: 234-239.

In: Internet and Suicide
Editors: L. Sher and A. Vilens

ISBN 978-1-60741-077-5

Chapter 28

THE CONCEPT OF POST-TRAUMATIC MOOD DISORDER, SUICIDAL BEHAVIOR IN WAR VETERANS AND POSSIBLE USE OF INTERNET-BASED THERAPIES IN THE TREATMENT OF WAR VETERANS WITH POSTTRAUMATIC MOOD DISORDER

Leo Sher
Columbia University and New York State Psychiatric Institute,
New York, New York, USA

ABSTRACT

Post-traumatic stress disorder (PTSD) is a common psychiatric disorder. PTSD is frequently comorbid with major depressive disorder (MDD). I have previously proposed that some or all individuals diagnosed with comorbid PTSD and MDD have a separate psychobiological condition that can be termed "post-traumatic mood disorder" (PTMD). The suggestion was based on the fact that a significant number of studies suggested that patients suffering from comorbid PTSD and MDD differed clinically and biologically from individuals with PTSD alone or MDD alone. Individuals with comorbid PTSD and MDD are characterized by greater severity of symptoms and the higher level of impairment in social and occupational functioning compared to individuals with PTSD alone or MDD alone. Neurobiological evidence supporting the concept of PTMD includes the findings from neuroendocrine challenge, cerebrospinal fluid, neuroimaging, sleep and other studies. The wars in Iraq and Afghanistan have presented Soldiers and Marines with a unique set of stressors that are chronic in nature, including civilian threats such as guerilla warfare tactics and terrorist actions. Many returning war veterans suffer from comorbid PTSD and depression, i.e., they have PTMD. PTMD is associated with suicidal behavior. It is important to develop interventions to prevent PTMD in war veterans, measures to prevent suicidal behavior war veterans with PTMD, and to study psychobiology of PTMD in order to develop treatments for PTMD. Priorities for intervening to reduce suicidal behavior in war veterans lie with interventions focused upon the improved recognition, treatment and management of veterans with psychiatric disorders including PTMD. Possibly, Internet based self-management programs may help to treat mental health problems in war veterans.

POST-TRAUMATIC STRESS DISORDER

Post-traumatic stress disorder (PTSD) is a common psychiatric disorder precipitated by exposure to a psychologically distressing event. PTSD first appeared in the Diagnostic and Statistical Manual of Psychiatric Disorders (DSM-III) in 1980 [1,2], arising from studies of the Vietnam war, and of civilian victims of natural and man-made disasters [3,4]. However, the study of PTSD dates back more than 100 years. Before 1980, post-traumatic syndromes were recognized by different names, including railway spine, shell shock, traumatic (war) neurosis, concentration-camp syndrome, and rape-trauma syndrome [2,3]. The symptoms described in these syndromes overlap considerably with what we now recognize as PTSD. According to the most recent edition of the Diagnostic and Statistical Manual of Psychiatric Disorders (DSM-IV-TR) [5], the essential feature of PTSD is the development of characteristic symptoms following exposure to an extreme traumatic stressor characterized by: direct personal experience of an event that involves actual or threatened death or serious injury, or other threat to one's physical integrity; or witnessing an event that involves death, injury, or a threat to the physical integrity of another person; or learning about unexpected or violent death, serious harm, or threat of death or injury experienced by a family member or other close associate. The person reacts to this event with fear and helplessness, and tries to avoid being reminded of it.

PTSD holds an important place in psychiatric thinking for several reasons. First it is one of the few disorders (besides disorders induced by substances or general medical conditions) in which an etiology is specified, despite the effort of DSM-IV to be atheoretical. As a consequence it has become a paradigm for understanding the role of the environment in psychopathology. Throughout the history of the concept of PTSD there has been a tension between an emphasis on factors relating to the host and factors relating to the nature of the trauma in the understanding of the etiology of this disorder.

PTSD is characterized by the presence of three distinct, but co-occurring, symptom clusters [2,5]. *Reexperiencing symptoms* describe spontaneous, often insuppressible intrusions of the traumatic memory in the form of images or nightmares that are accompanied by intense physiological distress. *Avoidance symptoms* involve restricting thoughts and distancing oneself from reminders of the event, as well as more generalized emotional and social withdrawal. *Hyperarousal symptoms* reflect more overt physiological manifestations, such as insomnia, irritability, impaired concentration, hypervigilance, and increased startle responses. These symptoms must be severe enough to impair social, occupational, or interpersonal function and co-occur for at least 1 month. The impairment from PTSD is amplified by poor coping strategies, substance abuse, co-occurring mood and anxiety disorders, lack of social support, and the accelerated development of stress-related medical conditions. A large body of research indicates that there is a correlation between PTSD and suicide [2,5]. There is evidence that traumatic events such as sexual abuse, combat trauma, rape, and domestic violence generally increase a person's suicide risk.

PTSD is a disorder of forgetting perhaps even more than of remembering [6,7]. It is the inability to forget the trauma that leads to the pathology and suffering in PTSD. Forgetting is a critical component of recovery. Of course, if we could not forget, our brains would rapidly be cluttered with information and observations and perhaps more limited in cognitive control functions for other activities.

War, terrorism, and natural disasters create large populations in distress [6]. Not all distress amounts to mental disorder, but fear, worry, insomnia, and changes in health-risk behaviors all contribute to the health burden of mass violence and are targets for early public health intervention. Substantial evidence supports essential principles of immediate and midterm mass trauma interventions that are now described as psychological first aid. [8]

About 30 armed conflicts are occurring now around the globe involving more than 25 countries [9,10]. For those in the United States and the United Kingdom, Iraq and Afghanistan are the present teachers of lessons long known and too often forgotten. Epidemiological surveys conducted during the current conflicts in Iraq and Afghanistan suggest that as many as 13% to 17% of service members screen positive for PTSD [11].

In 1996 The Task Force on Adolescent Assault Victim Needs reported that the onset of PTSD in childhood or adolescence can cause life-long impairment because it can interfere with normal adolescent development and prevent children from acquiring the basic life skills needed to become independent and self-sufficient adults [12]. Middle adolescence is an age at which major structural change occurs in the brain [13]. Trauma during this period of rapid brain development may arrest neurological development or produce a regression to an earlier stage of neural structure.

It is important to note that the most serious consequence of PTSD during adolescence is its association with the heavy use of alcohol and/or other drugs. Substance abuse has immediate consequences in the form of increased accidents, injuries, and long-term effects in terms of occupational and familial instability and early mortality. Furthermore, substance abuse, in itself, is often a risk factor for additional traumatic exposures either through accidents or interpersonal violence. The use of alcohol and/or other drugs is associated with suicidal behavior.

THE CONCEPT OF POST-TRAUMATIC MOOD DISORDER

PTSD and major depression are frequently comorbid. For example, Brown and colleagues [14] assessed lifetime anxiety and mood disorders comorbidity in a community sample of outpatients and found that PTSD was the anxiety disorder most likely to be associated with MDD, with 69% of individuals with PTSD also meeting criteria for MDD. Findings from the National Comorbidity Survey indicated that 78% of individuals meeting criteria for both disorders reported that their PTSD preceded the MDD [15].

Many research groups reported that individuals with comorbid PTSD and MDD were characterized by greater severity of symptoms and the higher level of impairment in social and occupational functioning compared to individuals with PTSD alone [16-23]. One study found that comorbidity of PTSD and MDD was associated with more severe symptoms as well as higher levels of disability on all indices (global dysfunction, distress, social impairment, and occupational disability) [23]. Another research group observed that a severity of overall symptoms was three- to fivefold greater in subjects with comorbid PTSD and MDD compared to those with PTSD alone [18]. A large-scale epidemiological survey found that the comorbid group was five times more likely to manifest functional impairment compared to those diagnosed with PTSD alone [16]. A recent study reported that patients with comorbid PTSD and MDD had higher objective MDD, impulsivity, and hostility scores and were significantly more likely to have made a suicide attempt compared to subjects with MDD alone [24]. We found that depressed subjects with comorbid PTSD tended towards earlier age of first hospitalization and a higher number of hospitalizations compared to depressed individuals without comorbid PTSD [25].

Maes et al. [26] reported that there is an association between PTSD with concurrent major MDD and lower affinity of alpha-2 adrenoreceptors, as well as higher plasma tyrosine availability to the brain, not found in patients suffering from PTSD alone. This indicates that monoaminergic mechanisms may play a role in the pathophysiology of comorbid PTSD and MDD.

Woodward et al. [27] found that patients with comorbid PTSD and MDD exhibited less slow wave sleep and less facial (mentalis) electromyographic activity, compared with PTSD patients without comorbid MDD. Patients with comorbid PTSD and MDD did not exhibit the classic rapid eye movement sleep architectural modifications associated with unipolar depression, despite the fact that several other psychophysiological indices of dysphoria were detectable in their sleep.

Cortisol response to placebo or fenfluramine was examined in depressed patients with or without comorbid PTSD and in a control group of healthy volunteers [28]. Depressed patients with comorbid PTSD had the lowest plasma cortisol; depressed patients without comorbid PTSD had the highest plasma cortisol; and healthy volunteers had intermediate levels.

We compared the effect of age on cortisol levels in depressed patients with or without comorbid PTSD and in healthy volunteers [29,30]. We found that cortisol levels increased with age in depressed patients with PTSD alone; they did not increase in depressed patients with comorbid PTSD or in healthy volunteers. We also observed that the number of previous major depressive episodes was a predictor of the cortisol response to fenfluramine administration in depressed patients without PTSD, but not in depressed patients with comorbid PTSD.

We also reported that depressed subjects with comorbid PTSD had higher cerebrospinal fluid (CSF) homovanillic acid (HVA) levels compared with depressed subjects without comorbid PTSD or healthy volunteers [25]. Higher CSF HVA was present after adjustment for sex, lifetime aggression severity and depression scores, alcoholism, tobacco smoking, comorbid cluster B personality disorder, reported childhood abuse, and psychosis.

Davidson et al. [31] investigated the relationship between chronic PTSD and family psychiatric morbidity. A shared liability for PTSD and MDD, with familial loading for MDD predicting chronic PTSD in trauma survivors was found.

Koenen et al. [32] analyzed data from about 7,000 members of the Vietnam Era Twin Registry. They found substantial genetic overlap between PTSD and MDD and suggested that genes implicated in the etiology of MDD are strong candidates for PTSD and vice versa.

Subjects with PTSD without comorbid MDD and patients with PTSD with comorbid MDD were examined using the script-driven symptom-provocation paradigm adapted to functional magnetic resonance imaging [33]. This study found different patterns of brain activation in subjects with PTSD without comorbid MDD compared to patients with PTSD with comorbid MDD.

PTSD patients with comorbid MDD relative to both healthy controls and trauma-exposed control subject showed reduced norepinephrine transporter expression in the left thalamus [34]. PTSD patients without comorbid MDD did not show differences in norepinephrine transporter expression relative to healthy controls and trauma-exposed control subject, i.e., PTSD patients showed reduced left thalamic norepinephrine transporter expression only when having comorbid MDD.

The dexamethasone suppression-corticotrophin releasing hormone (DEX-CRH) test has shown to be a more sensitive test to assess HPA-axis dysregulation in MDD and therefore may provide a useful test tool to probe HPA-axis regulation in MDD and PTSD [35,36]. To evaluate the effect of PTSD on HPA-axis regulation, the response to a DEX-CRH test between male veterans with PTSD and male veterans, who had been exposed to similar traumatic events during their deployment, without PTSD was compared [37]. Patients and controls were matched on age, year and region of deployment. The DEX-CRH test did not reveal HPA-axis abnormalities in PTSD patients as compared to trauma controls. PTSD patients with a co-morbid MDD showed an attenuated ACTH response compared to PTSD patients without co-morbid MDD, suggesting the presence of subgroups with different HPA-axis regulation within the PTSD group. Altered sensitivity of the CRH receptors at the pituitary or differences in AVP secretion might explain these differences in response.

In summary, clinical and neurobiological evidence strongly suggests that patients suffering from comorbid PTSD and MDD differ clinically and biologically from individuals with PTSD alone or MDD alone. I have previously suggested that some or all individuals diagnosed with comorbid PTSD and MDD have a separate psychobiological condition that can be termed "post-traumatic mood disorder" (PTMD) [38,39].

The Concept of PTMD and Suicidal Behavior in War Veterans

Since October 2001, approximately 1.64 million U.S. troops have been deployed for Operations Enduring Freedom and Iraqi Freedom (OEF/OIF) in Afghanistan and Iraq [40]. The war in Iraq has presented Soldiers and Marines with a unique set of stressors that are chronic in nature, including civilian threats such as guerilla warfare tactics and terrorist actions [11,40,41]. Soldiers and Marines need to maintain constant vigilance to deal with unpredictable threats like roadside bombs, and to discern safe civilians from potential enemy combatants [42]. Military personnel involved in the OEF face similar problems in Afghanistan.

Early evidence suggests that the psychological toll of these deployments—many involving prolonged exposure to combat-related stress over multiple rotations—may be disproportionately high compared with the physical injuries of combat. In the face of mounting public concern over post-deployment health care issues confronting OEF/ OIF veterans, several task forces, independent review groups, and a President's Commission have been convened to examine the care of the war wounded and make recommendations. The challenge of identifying veterans or active duty military who are suffering from PTSD, MDD, and/or those at risk for suicide has been receiving high-profile attention within the military and the Department of Veterans Affairs, as well as on Capitol Hill. Concerns have been most recently centered on two combat-related injuries in particular: posttraumatic stress disorder and traumatic brain injury [43-45]. Many recent reports have referred to these as the signature wounds of the Afghanistan and Iraq conflicts. With the increasing incidence of suicide and suicide attempts among returning veterans, concern about depression is also on the rise. It has been estimated that nearly 20% of members of the military service (about 300,000 individuals) who have returned from Iraq and Afghanistan report symptoms of PTSD or MDD.

The risk of suicide attempts among the PTSD population is six times greater than in the general population [46,47] and even higher among treatment seeking war veterans with PTSD [48]. In fact, war veterans are two times more likely to die of suicide than are nonveterans [49]. Considering these statistics, it is possible that many soldiers returning from Iraq and Afghanistan may at some time experience suicidal ideation or make a suicide attempt.

The comorbidity of one or more disorders with PTSD significantly impacts the likelihood that veterans may choose suicidal behavior as an avenue for relief [50]. Comorbidity of PTSD and mood disorders is high, compounding symptom severity and social dysfunction. Some 40% of PTSD patients acutely, and up to 95% lifetime, also meet MDD criteria [51]; and up to 34% meet criteria for dysthymic disorder [52]. Persons with PTSD and comorbid MDD are at a high risk for suicidal behavior [38,39,53-55]. Comorbidity of PTSD and MDD is associated with increased illness burden, poorer prognosis, and delayed response to depression treatment [38]. In one study, veterans were assessed for suicidal thinking and behaviors, and symptoms of PTSD and depression [51]. Thoughts of ending one's life and a previous suicide attempt were significantly correlated with a diagnosis of PTSD. Veterans with a diagnosis of PTSD and MDD or dysthymia were also more likely to report suicidal thinking and behaviors than veterans with only one of the diagnoses.

Possible Use of Internet-based Therapies

Among veterans, stigma is an important barrier to care for many mental health problems, including PTSD and depression. Internet-based mental health interventions may be a promising vehicle to overcome many barriers to care.

Recently, a randomized, controlled trial of an Internet-based, therapist-assisted self-management treatment for posttraumatic stress disorder has been conducted [56]. Service members with PTSD from the attack on the Pentagon on September 11th or the Iraq War were randomly assigned to self-management cognitive behavior therapy or supportive counseling. The self-management cognitive behavior therapy was designed to teach patients strategies to help them cope and manage their reactions to situations that triggered recall of traumatic experiences (and negative affect and arousal). The self-management cognitive-behavior therapy consisted of the following: 1. Self-monitoring of situations that triggered trauma-related distress; 2. The generation of a serial ordering (hierarchy) of these trigger contexts in terms of their degree of threat or avoidance; 3. Didactics on stress management strategies that, once practiced, were used for 4. Graduated, self-guided, in vivo exposure to items from the personalized hierarchy (starting with the least threatening or least avoided item); 5. Seven online trauma writing sessions; 6. A review of progress (charts of daily symptom reports were presented), a series of didactics on relapse prevention, and the generation of a personalized plan for future challenges. The majority of the supportive counseling intervention entailed participants being asked to self-monitor daily nontrauma-related concerns and hassles and online writing about these experiences. Psychoeducation materials were available about the psychological, emotional, and cognitive effects of trauma, but there was no skills training or prescriptions for proactive action. Through e-mail and the telephone, supportive counseling therapists were instructed to be empathic and validating, nondirective and supportive, and to focus on non-trauma-related present-day concerns. The authors observed that participants who received self-management cognitive behavior therapy reported greater gains than those who received supportive counseling. The results of this study suggest the need for future research into Internet-based therapies to assist patients with PTSD. Possibly, Internet based self-management programs may help to treat mental health problems in war veterans, including PTMD.

Conclusion

Combat-related mental health pathology is a critical medical and social problem. It is important to develop interventions to prevent PTMD in war veterans, measures to prevent suicidal behavior in war veterans with PTMD, and to study psychobiology of PTMD in order to develop treatments for PTMD. Priorities for intervening to reduce suicidal behavior in war veterans lie with interventions focused upon the improved recognition, treatment and management of veterans with psychiatric disorders including PTMD.

References

[1] American Psychiatric Association. Diagnostic and Statistical Manual of Mental Disorders. Third Edition. Washington, DC, *American Psychiatric Association,* 1980: 236–238.

[2] Schnurr PP, Friedman MJ, Bernardy NC. Research on posttraumatic stress disorder: epidemiology, pathophysiology, and assessment. *J Clin Psychol* 2002; 58: 877–889.

[3] Saigh PA, Bremner J. The history of posttraumatic stress disorder. In: Saigh PA, Bremner J, eds. *Posttraumatic Stress Disorder. A Comprehensive Text.* Boston: Allyn & Bacon, 1999: 1–17.

[4] Hageman I, Andersen HS, Jorgensen MB. Post-traumatic stress disorder: a review of psychobiology and pharmacotherapy. *Acta Psychiatr Scand 2001;* 104: 411–422.

[5] American Psychiatric Association. Diagnostic and Statistical Manual of Mental Disorders, Fourth Edition, Text Revision. Washington DC, *American Psychiatric Association, 2000:* 463–468.

[6] Ursano RJ, Benedek DM, Fullerton CS. Posttraumatic Stress Disorder: Neurobiology, Psychology, and Public Health. *Psychiatric Times, 2008;* 25(3). http://www.

consultantlive.com/pathologic-processes/article/10168/1147506?page Number =2 Accessed August 7, 2008
[7] Kuhl BA, Dudukovic NM, Kahn I, Wagner AD. Decreased demands on cognitive control reveal the neural processing benefits of forgetting. *Nat Neurosci 2007;*10:908-914.
[8] Hobfoll SE, Watson P, Bell CC, et al. Five essential elements of immediate and mid-term mass trauma intervention: empirical evidence. *Psychiatry 2007;*70: 283-315.
[9] *Project Plowshares Armed Conflicts Report 2007 Summary.* Available at: http://www.ploughshares.ca/ libraries/ACRText/Summary2006.pdf. Accessed August 5, 2008.
[10] http://www.globalsecurity.org/military/world/war/index.html Accessed August 8, 2008.
[11] Hoge CW, Castro CA, Messer SC, et al. Combat duty in Iraq and Afghanistan, mental health problems and barriers to care. *N Engl J Med* 2004;351:13-22.
[12] The Task Force on Adolescent Victim Needs. A review of the issues and a model protocol. *Pediatrics 1996;*98:991-1001.
[13] Pynoos RS, Steinberg AM, Ornitz EM, Goenjian AK. Issues in the developmental neurobiology of traumatic stress. *Ann NY Acad Science 1997;*821:176-193.
[14] Brown TA, Campbell LA, Lehman CL, Grisham JR, Mancill RB. Current and lifetime comorbidity of the DSM-IV anxiety and mood disorders in a large clinical sample. *J Abnorm Psychol 2001;* 110: 585-599.
[15] Kessler RC, Sonnega A, Bromet E, Hughes M, Nelson CB. Posttraumatic stress disorder in the National Comorbidity Survey. *Arch Gen Psychiatry 1995;* 52: 1048-1060.
[16] Mollica RF, McInnes K, Sarajlic N, Lavelle J, Sarajlic I, Massagli MP. Disability associated with psychiatric comorbidity and health status in Bosnian refugees living in Croatia. *J Am Med Assoc 1999;* 282: 433-439.
[17] Shalev AY, Freedman S, Peri T, Brandes D, Sahar T, Orr SP, Pitman RK. Prospective study of posttraumatic stress disorder and depression following trauma. *Am J Psychiatry. 1998;* 155: 630-637.
[18] Karam EG. Comorbidity of posttraumatic stress disorder and depression. In: Fullerton C, Ursano RJ (editors). Posttraumatic Stress Disorder: Acute and Long-Term Responses to Traumas and Disaster. *Progress in Psychiatry Series, No. 51.* American Psychiatric Press, Washington, DC, 1997; pp. 77-90.
[19] Moore LJ, Boehnlein JK. Posttraumatic stress disorder, depression, and somatic symptoms in U.S. Mien patients. *J Nerv Ment Dis 1991;* 179: 728-733.
[20] Skodol AE, Schwartz S, Dohrenwend BP, Levav I, Shrout PE, Reiff M. PTSD symptoms and comorbid mental disorders in Israeli war veterans. *Br J Psychiatry. 1996;* 169: 717-725.
[21] Koren D, Arnon I, Klein E. Acute stress response and posttraumatic stress disorder in traffic accident victims: a one-year prospective, follow-up study. *Am J Psychiatry. 1999;* 156: 367-373.
[22] Mintz J, Mintz LI, Arruda MJ, Hwang SS. Treatments of depression and the functional capacity to work. *Arch Gen Psychiatry 1992;* 49:761-768.
[23] Momartin S, Silove D, Manicavasagar V, Steel Z. Comorbidity of PTSD and depression: association with trauma exposure, symptom severity and functional impairment in Bosnian refugees resettled in Australia. *J Affect Disord 2004;* 80: 231–248.

[24] Oquendo M, Brent DA, Birmaher B, Greenhill L, Kolko D, Stanley B, Zelazny J, Burke AK, Firinciogullari S, Ellis SP, Mann JJ. Posttraumatic stress disorder comorbid with major depression: factors mediating the association with suicidal behavior. *Am J Psychiatry 2005;* 62: 560-566.

[25] Sher L, Oquendo MA, Li S, Burke AK, Grunebaum MF, Zalsman G, Huang YY, Mann JJ. Higher cerebrospinal fluid homovanillic acid levels in depressed patients with comorbid post-traumatic stress disorder. *Eur Neuropsychopharmacol 2005;* 15: 203-209.

[26] Maes M, Lin AH, Verkerk R, Delmeire L, Van Gastel A, Van der Planken M, Scharpe S. Serotonergic and noradrenergic markers of post-traumatic stress disorder with and without major depression. *Neuropsychopharmacology 1999;* 20: 188–197.

[27] Woodward SH, Friedman MJ, Bliwise DL. Sleep and depression in combat-related PTSD inpatients. *Biol Psychiatry 1996;* 39: 182–192.

[28] Oquendo MA, Echavarria G, Galfalvy HC, Grunebaum MF, Burke A, Barrera A, and others. Lower cortisol levels in depressed patients with comorbid post-traumatic stress disorder. *Neuropsychopharmacology 2003;* 28: 591– 598.

[29] Sher L, Oquendo MA, Galfalvy HC, Cooper TB, Mann JJ. Age effects on cortisol levels in depressed patients with and without a history of post-traumatic stress disorder, and healthy volunteers. *J Affect Disord 2004;* 82: 53-59.

[30] Sher L, Oquendo MA, Galfalvy HC, Cooper TB, Mann JJ. The number of previous depressive episodes is positively associated with cortisol response to fenfluramine administration. In: Yehuda R, McEwen B (editors). Biobehavioral Stress Response: Protective and Damaging Effects. *Ann N Y Acad Sci 2004;* 1032: 283-286.

[31] Davidson JR, Tupler LA, Wilson WH, Connor KM. A family study of chronic post-traumatic stress disorder following rape trauma. *J Psychiatr Res 1998;* 32: 301–309.

[32] Koenen KC, Fu QJ, Ertel K, Lyons MJ, Eisen SA, True WR, Goldberg J, Tsuang MT. Common genetic liability to major depression and posttraumatic stress disorder in men. *J Affect Disord 2008;*105(1-3):109-15.

[33] Lanius RA, Frewen PA, Girotti M, Neufeld RW, Stevens TK, Densmore M Neural correlates of trauma script-imagery in posttraumatic stress disorder with and without comorbid major depression: a functional MRI investigation. *Psychiatry Res.* 2007;155(1):45-56.

[34] Czermak C, Ding Y, Henry S, B.Planeta-Wilson B, S.Kasserman S, J.Frost J, W.Williams W, J.Krystal J, R.Carson R, A.Neumeister A. Norepinephrine transporter imaging in posttraumatic stress disorder. In: *46th Annual Meeting of the American College of Neuropsychopharmacology,* Boca Raton, Florida, December 9-13, 2007. Abstracts. Program No. 133.

[35] Sher L, Cooper TB, Mann JJ, Oquendo MA. Modified dexamethasone suppression – corticotropin-releasing hormone stimulation test: a pilot study of young healthy volunteers and implications for alcoholism research in adolescents and young adults. *Int J Adolesc Med Health* 2006;18(1):133-137.

[36] Ising M, Kunzel HE, Binder EB, Nickel T, Modell S, Holsboer F. The combined dexamethasone/CRH test as a potential surrogate marker in depression. *Prog Neuropsychopharmacol Biol Psychiatry. 2005;*29(6):1085-93.

[37] de Kloet C, Vermetten E, Lentjes E, Geuze E, van Pelt J, Manuel R, Heijnen C, Westenberg H. Differences in the response to the combined DEX-CRH test between

PTSD patients with and without co-morbid depressive disorder. *Psychoneuro-endocrinology 2008;*33(3):313-20.

[38] Sher L. The concept of post-traumatic mood disorder. *Med Hypotheses* 2005;65(2):205-10.

[39] Sher L. Posttraumatic mood disorder: a new concept. *Can J Psychiatry 2005;*50(2):127-8.

[40] Tanielian T, Jaycox LH, et al. Invisible Wounds of War. *Psychological and Cognitive Injuries, Their Consequences, and Services to Assist Recovery.* Santa Monica, CA.: RAND Corporation, 2008.

[41] Hoge CH, Castro CA, Messer SC, McGurk D, Cotting DI, Koffman RL. Combat duty in Iraq and Afghanistan, Mental Health problems, and barriers to care. *N Engl J Med 2004;*351(1):13-22.

[42] Litz BT. *A brief primer on the mental health impact of the war in Irak and Afganistan.* A National Center for PTSD fact sheet. Boston.: National Center for PTSD; 2005.

[43] Friedman MJ. Acknowledging the psychiatric cost of war. *N Engl J Med 2004;*351(1):75-7.

[44] Hebert B. Wounds You Can't See. *The New York Times.* 2008, Jun 24.

[45] Asnis GM, Kohn SR, Henderson M, Brown NL. SSRIs versus non-SSRI's in posttraumatic stress disorder: an update with recommendations. *Drugs 2004;*64(4):383-404.

[46] Kessler RC. Posttraumatic stress disorder: the burden to the individual and to society. *J Clin Psychiatry 2000*;61(Suppl 5):4-12.

[47] Zivin K, Kim HM, McCarthy JF et al. Suicide mortality among individuals receiving treatment for depression in the Veterans Affairs health system: associations with patient and treatment setting characteristics. *Am J Public Health 2007;*97(12):2193-8.

[48] Tarrier N, Gregg L. Suicide risk in civilian PTSD patients. Predictors of suicidal ideation, planning and attempts. *Soc Psychiatry Psychiatr Epidemiol 2004;*39:655-661.

[49] Shaley AY, Freeman S, Peri T, et al. Prospective study of posttraumatic stress disorder and depression following trauma. *Am J Psychiatry 1998;*155:630-7.

[50] Keane TM, Wolfe J. Comorbidity in post-traumatic stress disorder: an analysis of community and clinical studies. *J Applied Social Psychology 1990;*20:1776-88.

[51] Kramer TL, Lindy JD, Green BL, Grace MC, Leonard AC. The comorbidity of post-traumatic stress disorder and suicidality in Vietnam veterans. *Suicide Life Threat Behav 1994;*24(1):58-67.

[52] Oquendo M, Brent DA, Birmaher B et al. Posttraumatic stress disorder comorbid with major depression: factors mediating the association with suicidal behavior. *Am J Psychiatry 2005;*162(3):560-6.

[53] Oquendo MA, Friend JM, Halberstan B et al. Association of comorbid posttraumatic stress disorder and major depression with greater risk for suicidal behavior. *Am J Psychiatry 2003;*160:580-582.

[54] Sher L. The concept of post-traumatic mood disorder and its implications for adolescent suicidal behavior. Minerva Pediatr, in press.

[55] Campbell DG, Felker BL, Chuan-Fen L et al. Prevalence of PTSD-Depression comorbidity: Implications for clinical practice guidelines and primary care interventions. *J Gen Intern Med 2007;*22:711-8.

[56] Litz BT, Engel CC, Bryant RA, Papa A. A randomized, controlled proof-of-concept trial of an Internet-based, therapist-assisted self-management treatment for posttraumatic stress disorder. *Am J Psychiatry 2007;*164(11):1676-83.

In: Internet and Suicide
Editors: L. Sher and A. Vilens
ISBN 978-1-60741-077-5

Chapter 29

INTERNET SUICIDE PHENOMENON IN JAPAN

Masahito Fushimi
Akita Prefectural Mental Health and Welfare Center, Akita city, Japan

ABSTRACT

Internet suicide is a type of suicide pact; however, it is different in nature from the traditional suicide pacts in that it is prearranged between strangers who meet over the Internet. Internet suicide, also known as "net suicide," is a phrase that has become one of the most notorious terms for the Japanese in recent times. In 1998, the number of suicides in Japan increased sharply, and the annual number of suicides exceeded 30,000. Since then, the figure has remained above 30,000. Presently, Japan has one of the highest suicide rates in the world. In recent times, a critical situation that is deteriorating in Japan is that net suicides are increasing. To prevent net suicides, the Japanese government has formulated a policy as a measure for suicide prevention by both regulating detrimental content related to suicide behavior on the Internet and offering useful information related to suicide prevention adversely. Conventionally, in Japan, suicide prevention measures have been adopted mainly by implementing prevention measures for depressive disorder; however, the number of suicides did not decrease as expected. In view of this situation, the suicide prevention law, which was enacted in 2006, has clarified as a basic policy that suicide is a social problem rather than an individual problem and that it should be tackled at the societal level. It is of vital importance that net suicide prevention be specifically tackled at the societal level, although this can be said to be applicable to suicide prevention on the whole.

INTRODUCTION

In net suicide, a suicidal individual recruits others who meet via the Internet and then commit suicide. It is believed that the case in which three people died in early 2003, for which the cause of death was deemed as carbon monoxide poisoning, was the first reported case of net suicide in the Japanese media. Since then, many similar cases have been reported frequently by the Japanese media. Therefore, in recent years, net suicide has gained notoriety in Japan. According to an announcement made by the National Police Agency (NPA), 34 people committed net suicides in 2003. Thereafter, the figure increased to 91 in 2005. The characteristics of these reported cases were as follows: suicidal individuals, who met via the Internet, planned and committed suicide; a net suicide group usually comprised two or three people who were from different areas and were strangers to each other; the cause of death was mostly via carbon monoxide poisoning by burning charcoal (Japanese '*rentan*'); and the places selected for committing suicide were usually either in a sealed room or car [1-3].

The main factor that contributed to the surge of suicides in 1998 was the high suicide rate among middle-aged men [4]. Therefore, it was considered to be related to the drastic social changes occurring around that time, such as the national economic crisis (Japan's deep recession) and the termination of the lifetime employment practice at many major companies [5-9]. However, many victims in net suicides were younger people [10, 11]. In Japan as well as other countries, it is common that relatively young people are more likely to be influenced by the "suicide contagion" or the "chain reaction of suicide." Net suicide is a problem not only in Japan but also in the other Asian countries (such as China or Korea), Europe, and the USA [1, 3, 12, 13]. Although net suicide has never been peculiar to Japan, it appears to be peculiar to Japan as a result of the repeated publicity provided by the Japanese media. There is a clear difference between traditional suicide pacts and net suicide. In other words, traditional suicide pacts were made by people with close relationships such as spouses, lovers, or friends; however, net suicides are committed by strangers who have known each other only through websites or chat rooms on the Internet [1, 2]. Although many reports have already been published regarding traditional suicide pacts [14-23], studies related to net suicides are still limited [24-26]. Therefore, more detailed studies on net suicides are required. Suicide is not a crime in itself (but assisting a suicide is a criminal act); therefore, it seems that the police was not active in suicide prevention until recently. However, in view of the increase in posts on websites that called for people to commit group suicides since 2003, which subsequently increased in 2004, business organizations of Internet service providers have released a guideline in 2005 for providing useful information on preventing net suicides to the police. It can be said that these organizations have clearly shown their resolve to collaborate with the police through this guideline. Moreover, in 2006, the suicide prevention law was enacted [3, 9]. As per this law, suicide prevention measures, which were conventionally inclined toward medical measures (mainly, anti-depression measures), have been positioned as a general social measure. In addition, suicide prevention has now become a national duty. As a result, the police began to play an active role in suicide prevention. One of the roles was to check for suicide notices on various websites.

In this chapter, first, the trends of suicides in Japan, wherein the suicide rate is one of the highest in the world, are discussed with a special focus on the data related to the year 2003, in which the problem of net suicides was highlighted. Thereafter, the trends of the penetration of the Internet and Internet-related suicides in Japan are described. Furthermore, prevention measures for Internet suicides—particularly those advocated by the Japanese government—are introduced and discussed. Incidentally, it is a fact that there are cases wherein the media has promoted suicide contagion [3, 10, 25, 27], and the notion of suicide contagion is indispensable to understand the notion of net suicides. However, a generalized or theoretical commentary on suicide contagion is briefly provided in this chapter.

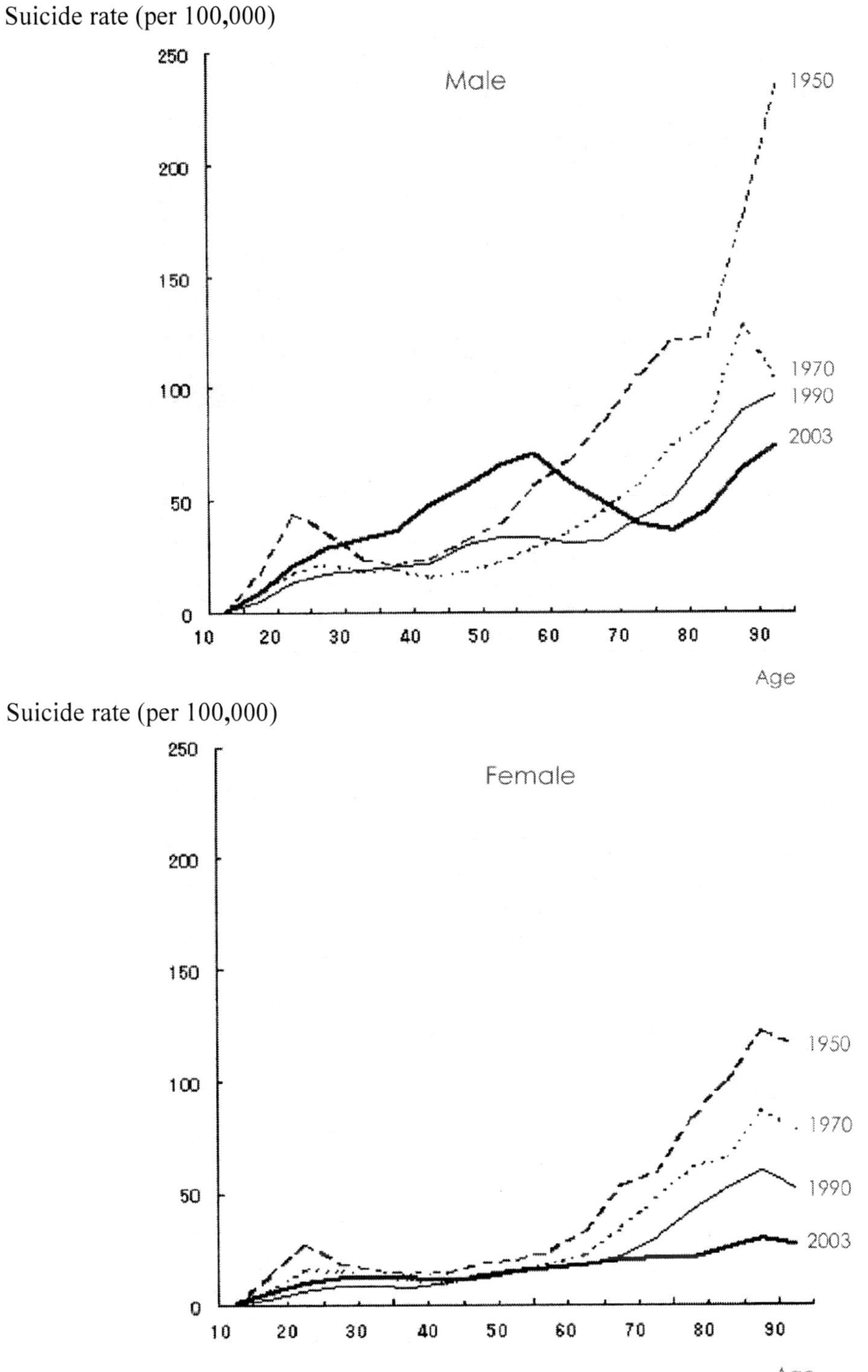

Source: Japanese Ministry of Health, Labour and Welfare.

Figure 1. Comparison of the annual suicide rate (per 100,000) for the selected years (1950, 1970, 1990, 2003) by gender and age.

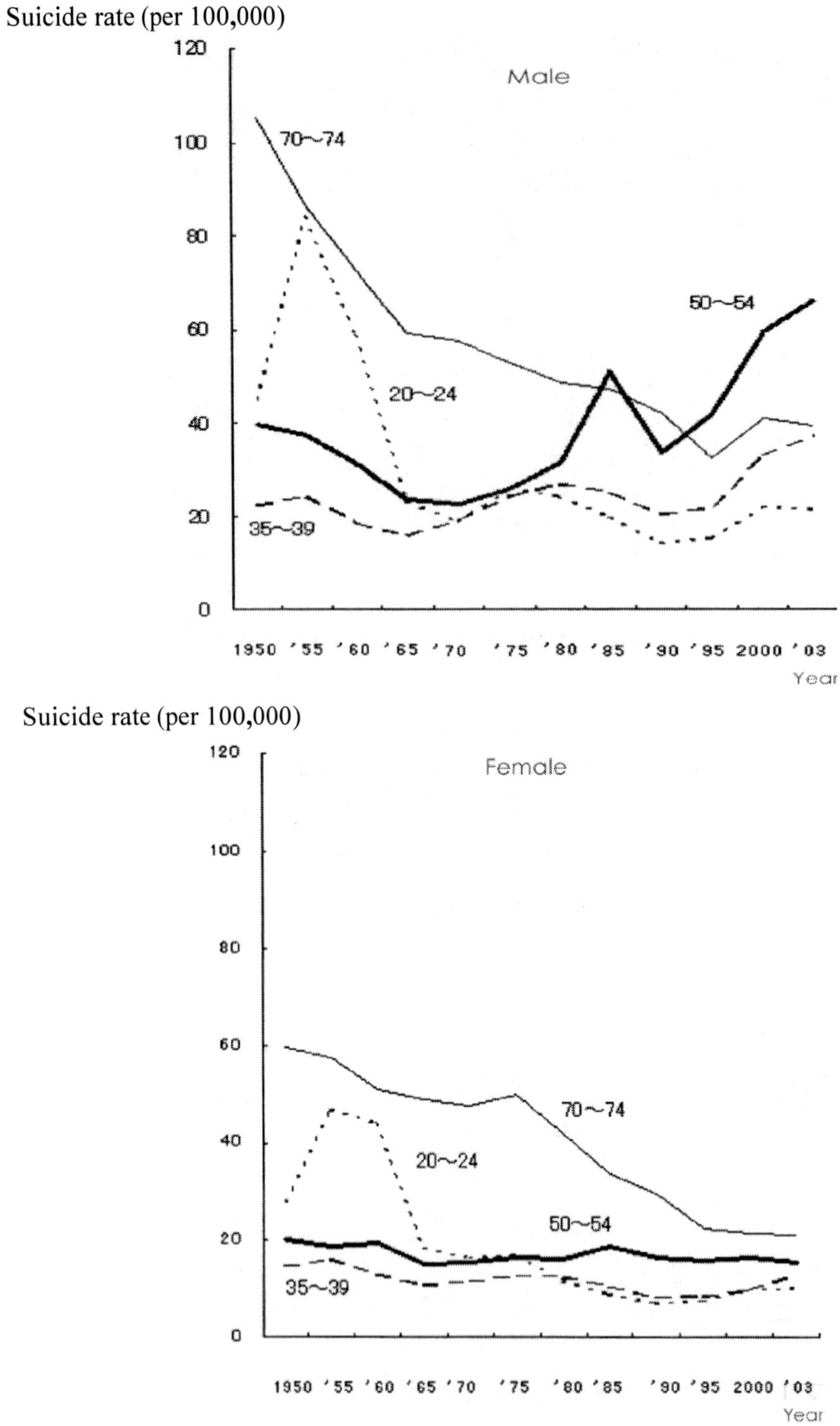

Source: Japanese Ministry of Health, Labour and Welfare.

Figure 2. Progression of the annual suicide rate (per 100,000) by gender and selected age groups (20–24, 35–39, 50–54, 70–74).

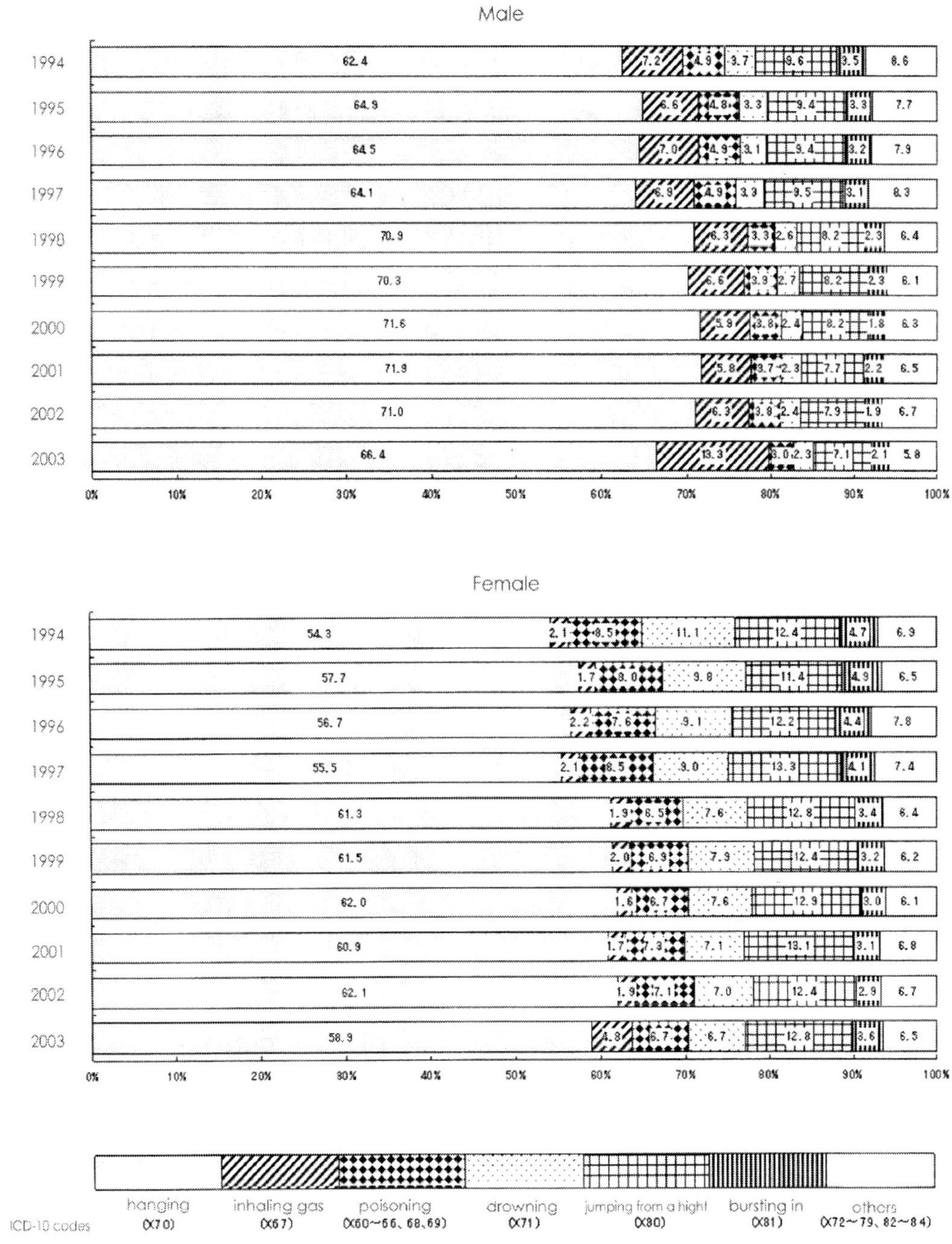

Source: Japanese Ministry of Health, Labour and Welfare.

Figure 3. The percentage of the use of each suicide method from 1994 to 2003.

SUICIDE TRENDS IN JAPAN

According to NPA records, the annual number of suicides in Japan was mostly under 25,000 until 1997; however, this number surged to over 30,000 in 1998. Since then, the figure has remained above 30,000 [4-9]. In addition, this figure illustrates that death by suicide amounted to more than 80 victims (about 90 victims) per day on average. Incidentally, in 1998, the increase in the number of suicides from the previous year was 8,472 (up 34.7%), and about 75% (6,382 victims) of these comprised people in their 40s, 50s and over 60s. Thereafter, in 2003, when 34,427 suicides were classified according to motives, health-related problems (15,416 victims) represented the leading cause of suicides, followed by economic and life-related problems (8,897 victims); moreover, these two motives accounted for about 70% of all suicides [4]. In the increased number in 1998, the proportion of economic and life-related problems had increased substantially, although health-related problems were conventionally the primary problem in Japan. Therefore, it was often stated that these findings suggested a potential relationship between the surge of suicides and economic struggles [5-9]. According to the vital statistics of the Ministry of Health, Labour and Welfare, in 2003, suicide was the sixth leading cause of death, and it was the first leading cause of death for people in their 20s and 30s [28, 29]. Suicide mortality trends by gender and age in the long term show that the peak suicide rate of males is in their 50s in 2003 and that there are no obvious facts that suicides are particularly increasing among the youth (Figure 1 and Figure 2). Moreover, vital statistics in 2003 show that the most common method of suicide was hanging (66.4% of males, 58.9% of females). And the method of suicide by inhaling gas, including carbon monoxide poisoning, accounted for 13.3% of males and 4.8% of females (6.3% and 1.9% in the previous year, respectively). In addition, from the previous year, the increase in the incidence of suicides by inhaling gas was very high in comparison to the other methods of suicide in 2003 (Figure 3). Incidentally, the reports prepared both by the National Police Agency and by the Ministry of Health, Labour and Welfare provide data on suicides in Japan; however, the corresponding figures in these data do not match. According to the World Health Organization, the suicide rate in Japan in the year 2004 was 24.0 per 100,000, which was the 10th highest in the world (9th highest by more recent data), and this was the highest in any G7 nation [9, 30].

INTERNET PENETRATION TRENDS IN JAPAN

The Internet is an indispensable tool in this information-oriented age. According to the "Communication Usage Trend Survey in 2002" conducted by the Ministry of Internal Affairs and Communications (data at the end of 2002), the number of Internet users in Japan was 69.42 million, and this figure was the second largest in the world, after that of the USA. The penetration rate was 54.5% (a 10.5 point year-on-year increase), surpassing 50% for the first time. Moreover, the Internet penetration rate of households increased rapidly to 81.4% (up 20.9 points from the previous year). In terms of Internet usage rates by age, the highest was 89.8% among 20–29-year olds, followed by 88.1% (13–19-year olds) and 85.0% (30-39-year olds). The Internet usage rate was high even among 6–12-year olds (52.6%). Furthermore, among Internet users, a large number of them (42.9%) accessed the Internet at least once per day [31]. These Internet penetration trends have progressed such that at the end of 2007, the number of Internet users reached 88.11 million people and the diffusion rate reached 69.0%. In addition, Internet usage rates among 13–49-year olds was over 90% [32]. The amount of information related to suicides available on the Internet is enormous and varied. On bulletin boards or chat rooms, some people describe the details of particular suicide methods or advocate specific methods, some describe particular individual or group suicides, some demonstrate the graphic images of the deceased or the articles left by them such as suicide notes, and some discuss about suicides along with visitors. Considering the background of this phenomenon, it is perceived that anonymity appears to have contributed to the popularity of the Internet, and making friends without actually physically meeting people appears to be one of the principal attractions of Internet communication.

Internet Suicide Trends in Japan

The case of three people who died in early 2003 by charcoal burning, for which the cause of death was deemed as carbon monoxide poisoning, was believed to be the first reported case of net suicide in Japan. Judging from the circumstantial evidence, it was concluded that this was an ordinary suicide pact. However, in due course, it emerged that this was a prearranged suicide pact formed over the Internet. As a result of repeated publicity of this unusual incident (namely, group suicide via the Internet) by the media, an increasing number of people began accessing suicide related websites for obtaining information. This is believed to have lead to the secondary social phenomenon of chain suicides, whereby vulnerable individuals, especially youngsters, triggered a "chain reaction" by imitating earlier cases reported by the media. According to media reports based on announcement by the NPA, group suicides via the Internet, i.e., the so called net suicides, in Japan involved as many as 91 people in 34 cases in 2005; this represented an increase of 36 people and 15 cases from the previous year. With regard to gender, 54 of them were males and 37 were females. In terms of age, the highest figure for the number of suicides was 38 for people in their 20s, followed by 33 for people in their 30s, 9 for people in their 40s, 8 for people in their 10s, and 1 each for people in their 50s and 60s; therefore, approximately 40% of these people were in their 20s. The 2005 data represented an approximately twofold increase from the previous year (55 people, 19 cases). Moreover, this data represented an approximately threefold increase from 2003 (34 people, 12 cases), the year in which the NPA began maintaining this record. The enterprises that provide Internet access services began disclosing relevant information, such as suicide notices posted on websites, to the police from October 2005. Subsequently, 11 people died of net suicide from October to December in 2005, indicating a decrease of 25 people from the same period of the previous year. These figures related to the progression of net suicide appear to be increasing in the number of suicides by youth; however, statistics from the NPA indicate that from among the total number of suicides in 2005 (32,552), the number among 40–59 year olds was 12,794 and the number for those under 29 was 4,017, which was about one-third of the former [4]. As mentioned above, the most common method of suicide was not inhaling gas including carbon monoxide poisoning, but hanging, which accounted for approximately 60% of all the methods (Figure 3). Moreover, considering the long-term progression of suicide rates in Japan, there are no obvious facts to support the notion that suicides are particularly increasing among the youth (Figure 1 and Figure 2); however, the fact that net suicide has become one of the most notorious phrases may give an impression of an increase in the number of suicides among the youth. Thus, carbon monoxide poisoning by charcoal burning is becoming the most popular method of net suicide in Japan. Of course, one of the reasons for charcoal burning being adopted as the most popular method of suicide was its repeated publicity by the media. It is believed that the popularity of charcoal burning as a method of suicide has grown due to a number of reasons. One reason is that charcoal burning is a method that can be easily shared with others, unlike other methods of suicide such as jumping from a height or hanging oneself. It would therefore be considered as a desirable method for those who feel more secure about dying in groups. Another factor is that similar to other means of carbon monoxide poisoning, it is often portrayed as non-disfiguring and painless. Finally, it can be said that charcoal is easily available, since having a barbecue is a common leisure activity, making charcoal widely available in supermarkets and convenience stores [12, 13, 33]. Ironically, as a result of its use by net suicide victims, charcoal burning is now associated more with net suicide than with barbecue. Moreover, a worrying new trend of net suicides has emerged in recent times; there is a sharp increase in the number of suicides adopting "inhaling hydrogen sulfide gas" as a new method of suicide, which was introduced on the Internet as an alternative to charcoal burning, and this led to a further increase in the number of suicides. This worrying trend is believed to have been influenced by a certain bulletin board that was uploaded on the Internet in 2007. On this board, at first, only suicide incidents were reported; however, the sentence implying "a new suicide method instead of charcoal burning has been developed" was added in early 2008. Thereafter, the written notes increased. Some of the suicide prevention specialists were concerned about this bulletin board and insisted on the need for the Japanese government to adopt corrective measures. People all over Japan began to successively commit suicides by adopting the method of inhaling hydrogen sulfide gas, which was introduced on the Internet in early 2008, and the number of suicides increased remarkably in April 2008. Furthermore, these trends continued nationwide even in May with every passing day. The publicity received by this method of suicide may have contributed to its popularity.

INTERNET SUICIDE PREVENTION STRATEGIES

In 1998, the number of suicides in Japan had increased significantly, and a chief factor for this was an increase in the number of victims with financial problems. With regard to this factor, it is likely that the number of suicides may decrease with the recovery of the economy or improvement of the job situation in Japan; however, suicides related to the Internet, especially by youngsters, are considered to be another problem. Therefore, other novel strategies are required to tackle this worrying trend of suicide. As mentioned earlier, the organizations of some enterprises that provide Internet access services have begun to disclose relevant information (e.g., name and address of the individuals who write suicide notices or messages to call for suicidal companions) to the police from October 2005. Moreover, these organizations have also released guidelines for this disclosure of information. It can be said that these organizations have clearly shown their resolve to collaborate with the police by releasing these guidelines. Thereafter, the NPA announced that, in three months until the end of 2005, they had been offered the information of 12 cases and had saved more than 10 people from suicide deaths. Furthermore, the NPA announced that in 2007, they had intervened in the information regarding 121 suicidal applicants who had announced their suicidal intentions on the Internet, and the resulting action has led to persuasion to refrain from committing suicide, saving the lives of approximately 70 individuals. Although it is certain that admonition is effective to a certain degree, it is yet to be identified as to what type of communication or collaboration was adopted in terms of psychiatric practice or social welfare after such persuasion and relief efforts following the disclosure to the police. In addition, we must not forget that suicide attempters tend to repeat their actions. Moreover, in view of the state of emergency that occurred due to the rapid increase in the use of hydrogen sulfide for committing suicides, the NPA designated a note, which was uploaded on the Internet and explained the method of the hydrogen sulfide outbreak, as detrimental information at the end of April 2008. Further, the NPA proposed a policy to direct Internet service providers to delete detrimental information whenever the police informed them of the existence of such information. There is a problem in the request for the deletion of information in that it is opposed to "freedom of expression"; however, in view of the present situation (that is, the number of suicide victims is increasing), the opinion in the mainstream is that such information should be deleted. As mentioned earlier, the introduction of the suicide prevention law, which was enacted in 2006 in view of the continued high level of suicide rate in Japan, presents the background of these actions for suicide prevention by the police. This law has clarified that suicide is a social problem rather than an individual problem and that it should be tackled at the societal level. Furthermore, in view of an increase in the amount of illegal or detrimental information being posted on the Internet, the Japanese government has been conducting meetings attended by the specialists thus far. The Japanese government has advocated a basic policy for prevention measures against the posting of illegal or detrimental information on the Internet on the basis of the results of these meetings. This can also be referred to as the basic policy adopted by the government to prevent net suicides. The summary of the policy is as follows:

- Spreading filtering software
    - Promoting the spread of filtering software
        - Planning the introduction of filtering software in public institutions
        - Providing enlightenment on the use of filtering software in homes
        - Requesting enterprises providing Internet services to notify illegal or detrimental sites to enable their filtration
    - Development of new filtering technology
        - Promotion of development of filtering software used by mobile devices (mobile phones, etc.) as well as personal computers
        - Promotion of development of filtering technology to support not only still images but also animations or game software
- Supporting self-imposed restraint by Internet service providers
    - Introducing restraining measures for websites that induce suicidal behavior
    - Consideration of the self-imposed restraint by Internet service providers
    - Development of a system through which content can be judged beforehand as being appropriate or inappropriate for use on a website

- Consideration of the self-imposed restraint by website content providers
- Substantiality of moral education against illegal or detrimental information
    - Publicity through the Internet homepages for educating people
    - Reinforcement of the education process (e.g., using an educating opportunity for the prevention of misdeeds among the youth)
    - Promotion of measures to address the detrimental environment surrounding the youth
- Preparation for an increase in the number of opportunities for access to counseling services
    - Reinforcement of the access function for providing consultation to people
    - Substantiality of websites for suicide prevention

CONCLUSION

The abovementioned policies advocated by the Japanese government to prevent the occurrence of net suicides can be categorized into two types: one is restriction of information, and the other is supply of information. This shows that the Internet can prove to be useful as well as detrimental for its users. The fact that information on suicides is easily available on websites leads vulnerable people to commit suicides. In other words, information that is easily available from websites has the potential of lowering the threshold for suicides. On the other hand, it is obvious that it is impossible to intercept information in real time. Therefore, it is important that we should utilize the advantage of an information-oriented society and adopt a positive attitude by providing useful information to discourage people from committing suicides. In general, a person with a suicidal desire has ambivalent feelings of both wanting to die and wanting to be detained, and the person is believed to be alternating between these two feelings. Therefore, providing useful information on suicide prevention can prove to be important particularly for such vulnerable persons. The Japanese media frequently associated the sharp increase in the number of suicides in Japan in 1998 with dismissal from service or economic instability due to the deep recession. Since the surge of suicides in 1998, the Japanese government began focusing on suicide prevention measures [9, 34-37]. Moreover, among these suicide prevention measures, the chief measure was against depressive disorder. The suicide prevention law, which was enacted in 2006, has clarified that suicide is a social problem rather than an individual problem and that it should be tackled at the societal level. With regard to the recent trend of an increasing number of net suicides, it would certainly be impossible to tackle it by considering net suicide only as a personal problem. Therefore, it is essential for this problem to be tackled at the societal level. In Japan, the ratio of net suicides with respect to the total number of suicides is not high as yet. Presently, it is a matter of vital importance to adopt measures to tackle the problem of net suicides at an early stage.

REFERENCES

[1] Rajagopal S: Suicide pacts and the internet. *BMJ* 2004; 329:1298-1299.

[2] BBC News Online. *Nine die in Japan "suicide pacts."* http://news.bbc.co.uk/2/hi/asia-pacific/3735372.stm

[3] Naito A: Internet suicide in Japan: implications for child and adolescent mental health. *Clin Child Psychol Psychiatry* 2007;12:583-597.

[4] National Police Agency. *Brief Report on Suicides in 2006.* Tokyo, Japan, 2007. (in Japanese)

[5] Kishi Y, Kathol RG: Assessment of patients who attempt Suicide. *Prim Care Companion J Clin Psychiatry* 2002; 4: 132–136.

[6] Fushimi M, Sugawara J, Shimizu T: Suicide patterns and characteristics in Akita, Japan. *Psychiatry Clin Neurosci* 2005; 59:296–302.

[7] Fushimi M, Sugawara J, Saito S: Comparison of completed and attempted suicide in Akita, Japan. *Psychiatry Clin Neurosci* 2006; 60:289-295.

[8] Fushimi M, Sugawara J, Shimizu T: Suicide in Akita Prefecture, Japan. *International Psychiatry* 2006; 3:3.

[9] Fushimi M: Suicide Trends and Prevention in Akita Prefecture, Japan. *Quarterly Journal of Mental Health* 2007; 1:51-55.

[10] Patrick W, O'Carroll MD: The Kurt Cobain suicide crisis: perspectives from research, public health, and the news media. *Suicide Life Threat Behav* 1996; 26:260-271.

[11] Becker K, Mayer M, Nagenborg M, El-Faddagh MH: Parasuicide online: Can suicide websites trigger suicidal behaviour in predisposed adolescents? *Nord J Psychiatry* 2004; 58:111-114.

[12] Lee DT, Chan KP, Lee S, Yip PS: Burning charcoal: a novel and contagious method of suicide in Asia. *Arch Gen Psychiatry* 2002;59: 293-294.

[13] Chan KP, Yip PS, Au J, Lee DT: Charcoal burning suicide in post-transition Hong Kong. *Br J Psychiatry* 2005; 186:67-73.

[14] Cohen J: A study of suicide pacts. *Medico-legal J* 1961;29: 144-151.

[15] Rosen BK: Suicide pacts: a review. *Psychol Med* 1981;11: 525-533.

[16] Salih MA: Suicide pact in a setting of Folie a Deux. *Br J Psychiatry* 1981;139: 62-67.

[17] Rosenbaum M: Crime and punishment—the suicide pact. *Arch Gen Psychiatry* 1983;40: 979-982.

[18] Fishbain DA, D'Achille L, Barsky S, Aldrich TE: A controlled study of suicide pacts. *J Clin Psychiatry* 1984;45: 154-157.

[19] Fishbain DA, Aldrich TE: Suicide pacts: international comparisons. *J Clin Psychiatry* 1985;46: 11-15.

[20] Berman AL: Dyadic death: a typology. *Suicide Life Threat Behav* 1996;26: 342-350.

[21] Brown M, Barraclough B: Epidemiology of suicide pacts in England and Wales, 1988-92. *BMJ* 1997;315: 286-287.

[22] Lasczkowski G, Rohrich J, Bratzke H: Suicidal excess--presentation of an unusual case. *Arch Kriminol* 1998;202: 100-108.

[23] Brown M, Barraclough B: Partners in life and in death: the suicide pact in England and Wales 1988-1992. *Psychol Med* 1999;29: 1299-1306.

[24] Thompson S: The internet and its potential influence on suicide. *Psychiatr Bull* 1999;23: 449-451.

[25] Prior TI: Suicide methods from the internet. *Am J Psychiatry* 2004;161: 1500-1501.

[26] Biddle L, Donovan J, Hawton K, Kapur N, Gunnell D: Suicide and the internet. *BMJ* 2008;336: 800-802.

[27] World Health Organization. *Preventing suicide: a resource for media professionals,* 2000. http://www.who.int/mental_health/media/en/426.pdf

[28] Ministry of Health, Labour and Welfare. *Vital statistics of Japan*. Tokyo, Japan: Statistics and Information Department, Minister's Secretariat, Ministry of Health, Labour and Welfare, 2004. (in Japanese)

[29] Ministry of Health, Labour and Welfare. *Statistics of suicide: special report of vital statistics*. Tokyo, Japan: Statistics and Information Department, Minister's Secretariat, Ministry of Health, Labour and Welfare, 2005. (in Japanese)

[30] OECD. *OECD Health Data 2002.* Paris: CREDES, 2002.

[31] Ministry of Internal Affairs and Communications. *Communications Usage Trend Survey in 2002.* Tokyo, Japan, 2003. http://www.johotsusintokei.soumu.go.jp/tsusin_riyou/data/eng_tsusin_riyou02_2002.pdf

[32] Ministry of Internal Affairs and Communications. *Communications Usage Trend Survey in 2007*. Tokyo, Japan, 2008. http://www.johotsusintokei.soumu.go.jp/tsusin_riyou/data/eng_tsusin_riyou02_2007.pdf

[33] Lee DT, Chan KP, Yip PS: Charcoal burning is also popular for suicide pacts made on the internet. *BMJ* 2005; 330:602.

[34] The Planning Committee for the Health Japan 21. *The Health Japan 21* (National Health Care Campaign in the Twenty-first Century). Tokyo: Japan Health Promotion and Fitness Foundation, 2000. (in Japanese)

[35] Ueda K, Matsumoto Y: National strategy for suicide prevention in Japan. *Lancet* 2003; 361:882.

[36] McCurry J: Japan promises to curb number of suicides. *Lancet* 2006; 367: 383.

[37] Crump A: Suicide in Japan. *Lancet* 2006; 367:1143.

INDEX

A

B

C

D

E

F

G

H

I

J

K

L

M

N

O

Q

R

S

U

V

W

Y